TEST PREP 2018

Study & Prepare

Pass your test and know what is essential to become a safe,
competent pilot—from the most trusted source in aviation training

Private Pilot

READER TIP:
The FAA Knowledge Exam Questions can change
throughout the year. Stay current with test changes;
sign up for ASA's free email update service at
www.asa2fly.com/testupdate

Aviation Supplies & Academics, Inc.
Newcastle, Washington

Private Pilot Test Prep
2018 Edition

Aviation Supplies & Academics, Inc.
7005 132nd Place SE
Newcastle, Washington 98059-3153
425.235.1500
www.asa2fly.com

FAA Questions herein are from United States government sources and contain current information as of:
June 2017

None of the material in this publication supersedes
any documents, procedures or regulations issued by the
Federal Aviation Administration.

ASA assumes no responsibility for any errors or
omissions. Neither is any liability assumed for dam-
ages resulting from the use of the information contained
herein.

Important: This Test Prep should be sold with and used
in conjunction with *Airman Knowledge Testing Supplement for Sport Pilot, Recreational Pilot, and Private Pilot*
(FAA-CT-8080-2G).

ASA reprints the FAA test figures and legends contained within this government document, and it is also
sold separately and available from aviation retailers
nationwide. Order #ASA-CT-8080-2G.

ASA-TP-P-18
ISBN   978-1-61954-520-5

Printed in the United States of America

2018   2017   5   4   3   2   1

Stay informed of aviation industry happenings

Website www.asa2fly.com
Updates www.asa2fly.com/testupdate
Twitter www.twitter.com/asa2fly
Facebook www.facebook.com/asa2fly
Blog www.learntoflyblog.com

About the Contributors

Charles L. Robertson
Assistant Professor, UND Aerospace
University of North Dakota

Charles Robertson as ground and flight instructor, ATP, assistant professor and manager of training at UND Aerospace,
contributes a vital and substantial combination of pilot and
educator to ASA's reviewing team. After graduating with education degrees from Florida State University in 1967, and Ball
State University in 1975, he began his twenty-year career
in the United States Air Force as Chief of avionics branch,
58th Military Airlift Squadron, and went on to flight instruction, training for aircraft systems, and airport managing,
while gaining many thousands of hours flying international
passenger and cargo, aerial refueling and airlift missions.
As Division Chief in 1988, Robertson directed the USAF
Strategic Air Command's "Alpha Alert Force" and coordinated
its daily flight training operations.

Jackie Spanitz
Director of Curriculum Development
Aviation Supplies & Academics, Inc.

As Director of Curriculum Development for Aviation Supplies
& Academics, Jackie Spanitz oversees maintenance and
development of more than 750 titles and pilot supplies in
the ASA product line and integration of these products into
new and existing curricula. Ms. Spanitz has worked with airman training and testing for more than 20 years, including
participation in the ACS development committees. Jackie
holds a Bachelor of Science degree in aviation technology
from Western Michigan University, a Masters degree from
Embry Riddle Aeronautical University, and Instructor and
Commercial Pilot certificates. She is the author of *Guide to
the Flight Review*, and the technical editor for ASA's *Test
Prep* and *FAR/AIM* series.

Paul Hamilton
Sport Pilot and Light-Sport Aircraft Expert
Adventure Productions

Flight instructor, FAA Designated Examiner, and Sport/
Ultralight Pilot for more than 30 years, Paul contributed
sport pilot, light-sport aircraft information, and incorporation
of weight-shift control and powered parachute requirements.

About ASA: Aviation Supplies & Academics, Inc. (ASA)
has been providing trusted aviation training products for
more than 75 years to flight instructors, aviation maintenance
technicians, air traffic controllers, career aviators, students,
remote pilots and drone operators. ASA's pilot supplies,
software, and publications are supported with integrity, con-
sistency, superior quality, and the best customer service in
the industry. Aviators are invited to visit **www.asa2fly.com**
for a free copy of our catalog.

Contents

Continued

Chapter 5 **Procedures and Airport Operations**

Chapter 6 **Weather**

Chapter 7 **Weather Services**

Chapter 8 **Aircraft Performance**

Chapter 9 **Enroute Flight**

Chapter 10 **Navigation**

Chapter 11 **Communication Procedures**

Cross References

Preface

Welcome to ASA's Test Prep Series. ASA's test books have been helping pilots prepare for the FAA Knowledge Tests for more than 60 years with great success. We are confident that with proper use of this book, you will score very well on any of the private, sport, and recreational pilot certificate tests.

Begin your studies with a classroom or home-study ground school course, which will involve reading a comprehensive Private Pilot textbook. Conclude your studies with this Test Prep or comparable software. Read the question, select your choice for the correct answer, then read the explanation. Use the Learning Statement Codes and references that conclude each explanation to identify additional resources if you need further study of a subject. Upon completion of your studies, take practice tests at www.prepware.com (see inside front cover for your free account).

The FAA Private, Sport, and Recreational Pilot questions have been arranged into chapters based on subject matter. Topical study, in which similar material is covered under a common subject heading, promotes better understanding, aids recall, and thus provides a more efficient study guide. Study and place emphasis on those questions most likely to be included in your test (identified by the aircraft category above each question). For example, a pilot preparing for the Private Airplane test would focus on the questions marked "ALL" and "AIR," and a pilot preparing for the Private Helicopter test would focus on the questions marked "ALL" and "RTC."

It is important to answer every question assigned on your FAA Knowledge Test. If in their ongoing review, the FAA authors decide a question has no correct answer, is no longer applicable, or is otherwise defective, your answer will be marked correct no matter which one you chose. However, you will not be given the automatic credit unless you have marked an answer. Unlike some other exams you may have taken, there is no penalty for "guessing" in this instance.

The FAA exams are "closed tests" which means the exact database of questions is not available to the public. The question and answer choices in this book are based on our extensive history and experience with the FAA testing process. You might see similar although not exactly the same questions on your official FAA exam. Answer stems may be rearranged from the A, B, C order you see in this book. Therefore, be careful to fully understand the intent of each question and corresponding answer while studying, rather than memorize the A, B, C answer. You may be asked a question that has unfamiliar wording; studying and understanding the information in this book and the associated references will give you the tools to answer question variations with confidence.

If your study leads you to question an answer choice, we recommend you seek the assistance of a local instructor. We welcome your questions, recommendations or concerns:

Aviation Supplies & Academics, Inc.
7005 132nd Place SE
Newcastle, WA 98059-3153
Voice: 425.235.1500   Fax: 425.235.0128
Email: cfi@asa2fly.com   Website: www.asa2fly.com

The FAA appreciates testing experience feedback. You can contact the branch responsible for the FAA Knowledge Exams at:

Federal Aviation Administration
AFS-630, Airman Testing Standards Branch
PO Box 25082
Oklahoma City, OK 73125
Email: afs630comments@faa.gov

Updates and Practice Tests

Free Test Updates for the One-Year Life Cycle of Test Prep Books

The FAA rolls out new tests as needed throughout the year; this typically happens in June, October, and February. The FAA exams are "closed tests" which means the exact database of questions is not available to the public. ASA combines more than 60 years of experience with expertise in airman training and certification tests to prepare the most effective test preparation materials available in the industry.

You can feel confident you will be prepared for your FAA Knowledge Exam by using the ASA Test Preps. ASA publishes test books each June and keeps abreast of changes to the tests. These changes are then posted on the ASA website as a Test Update.

Visit the ASA website before taking your test to be certain you have the most current information. While there, sign up for ASA's free email Update service. We will then send you an email notification if there is a change to the test you are preparing for so you can review the Update for revised and/or new test information.

www.asa2fly.com/testupdate

We invite your feedback. After you take your official FAA exam, let us know how you did. Were you prepared? Did the ASA products meet your needs and exceed your expectations? We want to continue to improve these products to ensure applicants are prepared, and become safe aviators. Send feedback to: **cfi@asa2fly.com**

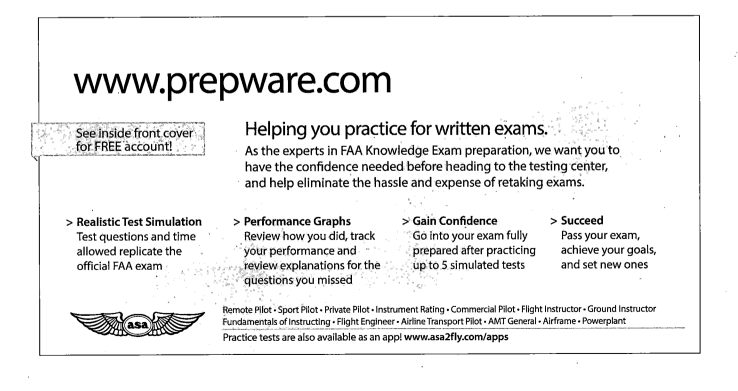

Description of the Tests

All test questions are the objective, multiple-choice type, with three choices of answers. Each question can be answered by the selection of a single response. Each test question is independent of other questions, that is, a correct response to one does not depend upon or influence the correct response to another.

As stated in 14 CFR §61.63, an applicant need not take an additional knowledge test provided the applicant holds an airplane, rotorcraft, powered-lift, or airship rating at that pilot certificate level. For example, an applicant transitioning from gliders to airplanes or helicopters **will** need to take the test. A person transitioning from weight-shift or powered parachute to airplane **will** need to take the test. An applicant transitioning from airplanes to gliders, or airplanes to helicopters, or airplanes to weight-shift or powered parachute, **will not** be required to take the test.

For the most efficient and effective study program, refer to the following table, placing emphasis on those questions most likely to be included on your test (identified by the aircraft category above each question number). Use the Prepware software or **www.prepware.com** to practice the test as if you were at the testing facility. These programs can also be used to obtain the endorsement you need to take the official exam.

Test Code	Test Name	Test Prep Study	Number of Questions	Min. Age	Allotted Time (hrs)
RPA	Recreational Pilot — Airplane	ALL, AIR, REC	50	15	2.0
RPH	Recreational Pilot — Helicopter	ALL, RTC, REC	50	15	2.0
RPG	Recreational Pilot — Gyroplane	ALL, RTC, REC	50	15	2.0
PAR	Private Pilot — Airplane	ALL, AIR	60	15	2.5
PRH	Private Pilot — Helicopter	ALL, RTC	60	15	2.5
PRG	Private Pilot — Gyroplane	ALL, RTC	60	15	2.5
PGL	Private Pilot — Glider	ALL, GLI	60	14	2.5
PBH	Private Pilot — Balloon–Hot Air	ALL, LTA	60	14	2.5
PBG	Private Pilot — Balloon–Gas	ALL, LTA	60	14	2.5
PLA	Private Pilot — Airship	ALL, LTA	60	15	2.5
PPP	Private Pilot Powered Parachute	ALL, PPC	60	15	2.5
PWS	Private Pilot Weight-Shift Control	ALL, WSC	60	15	2.5
PAT	Private Pilot Airplane/ Recreational Pilot — Transition	ALL, AIR	30	15	1.5
PGT	Private Pilot Gyroplane/ Recreational Pilot — Transition	ALL, RTC	30	15	1.5
PHT	Private Pilot Helicopter/ Recreational Pilot — Transition	ALL, RTC	30	15	1.5
PCP	Private Pilot Airplane Canadian Conversion*	ALL, AIR	40	16	2.0
PCH	Private Pilot Helicopter Canadian Conversion*	ALL, RTC	40	16	2.0

SPA	Sport Pilot Airplane	SPO, LSA	40	15	2.0
SPB	Sport Pilot Lighter-Than-Air (Balloon)	SPO, LSL	40	15	2.0
SPI	Sport Pilot Glider	SPO, LSG	40	15	2.0
SPL	Sport Pilot Lighter-Than-Air (Airship)	SPO, LSL	40	15	2.0
SPP	Sport Pilot Powered Parachute	SPO, LSP	40	15	2.0
SPW	Sport Pilot Weight-Shift Control	SPO, LSW	40	15	2.0
SPY	Sport Pilot Gyroplane	SPO, LSR	40	15	2.0

*This test focuses on U.S. regulations, procedures and operations, not airplane or helicopter know-how.

A score of 70 percent must be attained to successfully pass each test.

Knowledge Test Eligibility Requirements

If you are pursuing a recreational pilot or private pilot certificate, you should review Title 14 of the Code of Federal Regulations (14 CFR) Part 61, §61.23 "Medical Certificates: Requirement and Duration" and 14 CFR §61.35 "Knowledge Test: Prerequisites and Passing Grades."

If you are pursuing a **student pilot** certificate, you should review 14 CFR §61.83 "Applicability and Eligibility Requirements: General," for additional detailed information pertaining to eligibility.

If you are pursuing a **sport pilot** certificate, you should review 14 CFR Part 61 Subpart J for eligibility and operating limitation information.

If you are pursuing a **recreational pilot** certificate, you should review 14 CFR §61.96 "Applicability and Eligibility Requirements: General," for additional detailed information pertaining to eligibility.

If you are pursuing a **private pilot** certificate, you should review 14 CFR §61.103 "Applicability and Eligibility Requirements: General," for additional detailed information pertaining to eligibility.

Recreational pilot and private pilot tests are comprehensive because they must test your knowledge in many subject areas. If you are pursuing a recreational pilot certificate or added rating, you should closely examine and understand 14 CFR Part 61, §61.97 "Aeronautical Knowledge" for the applicable knowledge areas. If you are pursuing a private pilot certificate or added rating, you should closely examine and understand 14 CFR §61.105 "Aeronautical Knowledge" for the applicable knowledge areas.

Process for Taking a Knowledge Test

The FAA has designated holders of airman knowledge testing (AKT) organization designation authorization (ODA). These AKT-ODAs sponsor hundreds of knowledge testing center locations. The testing centers offer a full range of airman knowledge tests including: Aircraft Dispatcher, Airline Transport Pilot, Aviation Maintenance Technician, Commercial Pilot, Flight Engineer, Flight Instructor, Flight Navigator, Ground Instructor, Inspection Authorization, Instrument Rating, Parachute Rigger, Private Pilot, Recreational Pilot, Sport Pilot, Remote Pilot, and Military Competence. Contact information for the AKT-ODA holders is provided at the end of this section.

The first step in taking a knowledge test is the registration process. You may either call the testing centers' 1-800 numbers or simply take the test on a walk-in basis. If you choose to use the 1-800 number to register, you will need to select a testing center, schedule a test date, and make financial arrangements for test payment. You may register for tests several weeks in advance, and you may cancel your appointment according to the AKT-ODA holder's cancellation policy. If you do not follow the AKT-ODA holder's cancellation policies, you could be subject to a cancellation fee.

The next step in taking a knowledge test is providing proper identification. You should determine what knowledge test prerequisites are necessary before going to the computer testing center. Your instructor or local Flight Standards District Office (FSDO) can assist you with what documentation to take to the testing facility. Testing center personnel will not begin the test until your identification is verified.

Acceptable Forms of Authorization

When you go to take your FAA Knowledge Test, you will be required to show proper identification and have certification of your preparation for the examination, signed by an authorized Flight or Ground Instructor. Ground Schools will have issued the endorsements as you complete the course.If you choose a home-study for your Knowledge Test, you can either get an endorsement from your instructor or submit your home-study materials to an FAA Office for review and approval prior to taking the test.

1. Certificate of graduation or a statement of accomplishment certifying the satisfactory completion of the ground school portion of a course for the certificate or rating sought. The certificate or statement may be issued by a Federal Aviation Administration certified pilot school or an agency such as a high school, college, adult education program, Civil Air Patrol or Reserve Officers Training Corp (ROTC) flight training school.

2. Written statement or logbook endorsement from an authorized ground or flight instructor certifying that the applicant completed an applicable ground training or home study course and is prepared for the knowledge test.

3. Failed, passing or expired Airman Knowledge Test Report, provided the applicant still has the *original* test report in his/her possession. (*See* Retesting explanation.)

Private and Recreational Endorsement

I certify that *(First name, MI, Last name)* _____

has received the required training in accordance with [Private §61.105] [Recreational §61.97]. I have determined he/she is prepared for the *(Test name/Aircraft category; e.g., Private–Airplane)* _____

_____ knowledge test.

Signed _____ Date _____

CFI Number _____ Expires _____

Sport Pilot Endorsement

I certify that (First name, MI, Last name) _____

has received the required aeronautical knowledge training of 14 CFR §61.309. I have determined he/she is prepared for the Sport Pilot (category) _____ knowledge test.

Signed _____ Date _____

CFI Number _____ Expires _____

The Prepware software or **www.prepware.com** can be used to get your test authorization directly from ASA.

Test-Taking Tips

Prior to launching the actual test, the AKT-ODA holder's testing software will provide you with an opportunity to practice navigating through the test. This practice (or tutorial) session may include a "sample" question(s). These sample questions have no relation to the content of the test, but are meant to familiarize you with the look and feel of the system screens, including selecting an answer, marking a question for later review, time remaining for the test, and other features of the testing software.

Follow these time-proven tips, which will help you develop a skillful, smooth approach to test-taking:

1. Be careful to fully understand the intent of each question and corresponding answer while studying, rather than memorize the A, B, C answer choice — answer stems may appear in a different order than you studied.

2. Take with you to the testing center a sign-off from an instructor, photo I.D., the testing fee, calculator, flight computer (ASA's E6-B or CX-2 Pathfinder), plotter, magnifying glass, and a sharp pointer, such as a safety pin.

3. Your first action when you sit down should be to write on the scratch paper the weight and balance and any other formulas and information you can remember from your study. Remember, some of the formulas may be on your E6-B.

4. Answer each question in accordance with the latest regulations and guidance publications.

5. Read each question carefully before looking at the possible answers. You should clearly understand the problem before attempting to solve it.

6. After formulating an answer, determine which answer choice corresponds the closest with your answer. The answer chosen should completely resolve the problem.

7. From the answer choices given, it may appear that there is more than one possible answer. However, there is only one answer that is correct and complete. The other answers are either incomplete, erroneous, or represent popular misconceptions.

8. If a certain question is difficult for you, it is best to mark it for REVIEW and proceed to the other questions. After you answer the less difficult questions, return to those which you marked for review and answer them. Be sure to untag these questions once you have answered them. The review marking procedure will be explained to you prior to starting the test. Although the computer should alert you to unanswered questions, make sure every question has an answer recorded. This procedure will enable you to use the available time to the maximum advantage.

9. Perform each math calculation twice to confirm your answer. If adding or subtracting a column of numbers, reverse your direction the second time to reduce the possibility of error.

10. When solving a calculation problem, select the answer nearest to your solution. The problem has been checked with various types of calculators; therefore, if you have solved it correctly, your answer will be closer to the correct answer than any of the other choices.

11. Remember that information is provided in the FAA Legends and FAA Figures.

12. Remember to answer every question, even the ones with no completely correct answer, to ensure the FAA gives you credit for a bad question.

13. Take your time and be thorough but relaxed. Take a minute off every half-hour or so to relax the brain and the body. Get a drink of water halfway through the test.

14. Your test will be graded immediately upon completion. You will be allowed 10 minutes to review any questions you missed. You will see the question only; you will not see the answer choices or your selected response. This allows you to review the missed areas with an instructor prior to taking the Practical exam.

Test Reports

Your test will be graded immediately upon completion and your score will display on the computer screen. You will be allowed 10 minutes to review any questions you missed. You will see the question only; you will not see the answer choices or your selected response. This allows you to review the missed areas with an instructor prior to taking the Practical exam. After this review period you will receive your Airman Test Report, with the testing center's embossed seal, which reflects your score.

Validity of Airman Test Reports

Airman Test Reports are valid for the 24-calendar month period preceding the month you complete the practical test. If the Airman Test Report expires before completion of the practical test, you must retake the knowledge test.

Test Reports and Learning Statement Codes

The Airman Test Report lists the learning statement codes for questions answered incorrectly. The total number of learning statement codes shown on the Airman Test Report is not necessarily an indication of the total number of questions answered incorrectly. Study these knowledge areas to improve your understanding of the subject matter. *See* the *Learning Statement Code/Question Number Cross-Reference* in the back of this book for a list of which questions apply to each learning statement code.

Your instructor is required to provide instruction on each of the knowledge areas listed on your Airman Test Report and to complete an endorsement of this instruction. The Airman Test Report must be presented to the examiner prior to taking the practical test. During the oral portion of the practical test, the examiner is required to evaluate the noted areas of deficiency.

If you wish to have your test hand-scored (if you believe a question or your score are in error), you must submit a request, in the form of a signed letter, to the Airman Testing Standards Branch, AFS-630. The request must be accompanied by a copy of your Airman Knowledge Test Report and a legible photocopy of a government issued identification with your photograph and signature. Mail or fax this information to (e-mail requests are not accepted due to security issues): FAA, AFS-630, PO Box 25082, Oklahoma City, OK 73125 or fax to 405-954-4748.

Should you require a duplicate Airman Test Report due to loss or destruction of the original, send a signed request accompanied by a check or money order for $12 payable to the FAA. Your request should be sent to the Federal Aviation Administration, Airmen Certification Branch, AFS-760, P.O. Box 25082, Oklahoma City, OK 73125.

Airman Knowledge Testing Sites

The following airman knowledge testing (AKT) organization designation authorization (ODA) holders are authorized to give FAA knowledge tests. This list should be helpful in case you choose to register for a test or simply want more information. The latest listing of computer testing center locations is available on the FAA website at http://www.faa.gov/pilots/testing, under "Knowledge Testing" select "Commercial Testing Center List" and a PDF will download automatically.

Computer Assisted Testing Service (CATS)
Applicant inquiry and test registration: 800-947-4228 or 650-259-8550
www.catstest.com

PSI Computer Testing
Applicant inquiry and test registration: 800-211-2753 or 360-896-9111
www.psiexams.com

Use of Test Aids and Materials

Airman knowledge tests require applicants to analyze the relationship between variables needed to solve aviation problems, in addition to testing for accuracy of a mathematical calculation. The intent is that all applicants are tested on concepts rather than rote calculation ability. It is permissible to use certain calculating devices when taking airman knowledge tests, provided they are used within the following guidelines. The term "calculating devices" is interchangeable with such items as calculators, computers, or any similar devices designed for aviation-related activities.

Guidelines for Use of Test Aids and Materials

The applicant may use test aids and materials within the guidelines listed below, if actual test questions or answers are not revealed.

1. Applicants may use test aids, such as scales, straightedges, protractors, plotters, navigation computers, log sheets, and all models of aviation-oriented calculating devices that are directly related to the test. In addition, applicants may use any test materials provided with the test. -

2. Manufacturer's permanently inscribed instructions on the front and back of such aids listed in 1(a), e.g., formulas, conversions, regulations, signals, weather data, holding pattern diagrams, frequencies, weight and balance formulas, and air traffic control procedures are permissible.

3. The test proctor may provide calculating devices to applicants and deny them use of their personal calculating devices if the applicant's device does not have a screen that indicates all memory has been erased. The test proctor must be able to determine the calculating device's erasure capability. The use of calculating devices incorporating permanent or continuous type memory circuits without erasure capability is prohibited.

4. The use of magnetic cards, magnetic tapes, modules, computer chips, or any other device upon which prewritten programs or information related to the test can be stored and retrieved is prohibited. Printouts of data will be surrendered at the completion of the test if the calculating device used incorporates this design feature.

5. The use of any booklet or manual containing instructions related to the use of the applicant's calculating device is not permitted.

6. Dictionaries are not allowed in the testing area.

7. The test proctor makes the final determination relating to test materials and personal possessions that the applicant may take into the testing area.

Testing Procedures For Applicants Requesting Special Accommodations

If you are an applicant with a learning or reading disability, you may request approval from the local FSDO or FAA International Field Office (IFO) to take an airman knowledge test, using the special accommodations procedures outlined in the most current version of FAA Order 8080.6 "Conduct of Airman Knowledge Tests."

Prior to approval of any option, the FSDO or IFO Aviation Safety Inspector must advise you of the regulatory certification requirement of being able to read, write, speak, and understand the English language.

Retesting Procedures

Applicants retesting **after failure** are required to submit the applicable score report indicating failure, along with an endorsement (on the test report) from an authorized instructor who gave the applicant the additional training, and certifying the applicant is competent to pass the test. The original failed test report (with retest endorsement) presented as authorization shall be retained by the proctor and attached to the applicable sign-in/out log. The latest test taken will reflect the official score.

Applicants retesting **in an attempt to achieve a higher passing score** may retake the same test for a better grade after 30 days. The latest test taken will reflect the official score. Applicants are required to submit the **original** applicable score report indicating previous passing score to the testing center prior to testing. Testing center personnel must collect and destroy this report prior to issuing the new test report.

Note: The testing centers require a wait period of 24 hours before any applicant may retest.

Cheating or Other Unauthorized Conduct

Computer testing centers must follow strict security procedures to avoid test compromise. These procedures are established by the FAA and are covered in FAA Order 8080.6 Conduct of Airman Knowledge Tests. The FAA has directed testing centers to terminate a test at any time a test proctor suspects a cheating incident has occurred. An FAA investigation will then be conducted. If the investigation determines that cheating or unauthorized conduct has occurred, then any airman certificate or rating that you hold may be revoked, and you will be prohibited for 1 year from applying for or taking any test for a certificate or rating under 14 CFR Part 61.

Eligibility Requirements

Eligibility for the Private Pilot Certificate

Always check the current 14 CFR Part 61 for pilot certificate requirements. To be eligible for a private pilot certificate with an airplane, helicopter, or glider rating a person must:

1. Be at least 17 years old (16 for a glider or balloon rating).

2. Be able to read, speak, write, and understand English or have a limitation placed on the certificate.

3. Have at least a current third-class medical certificate or a driver's license and compliance with 14 CFR Parts 68 and 61.23.

4. Hold a U.S. student pilot certificate, sport pilot certificate, or recreational pilot certificate.

5. Score at least 70 percent on the required FAA Knowledge Test on the appropriate subjects.

6. Pass an oral exam and flight check on the subjects and maneuvers outlined in the Private Pilot Airman Certification or Practical Test Standards (#ASA-ACS-6, 8081-15, or 8081-3).

7. For an airplane or helicopter rating, have a total of 40 hours of instruction (for Part 61 programs) and solo flight time which must include the following:

   a. 20 hours of flight instruction including at least—

      i. 3 hours cross-country,

      ii. 3 hours at night including 10 takeoffs and landings and one cross-country flight of over 100 NM total distance for airplanes (50 NM for helicopters),

      iii. 3 hours of instrument flight training in a single-engine airplane for the airplane rating, and

      iv. 3 hours in an airplane or helicopter within the last 60 days in preparation for the flight test.

   b. 10 hours of solo flight time including at least —

      i. 10 hours in airplanes or helicopters

      ii. 5 hours cross-country for airplanes, each flight with a landing more than 50 NM from the point of departure and one flight of at least 150 NM with 3 landings, one of which must be least 50 NM from the departure point. In helicopters, 3 hours of cross-country with landings at three points at least 25 miles from each other and one cross-country flight of at least 75 NM total distance, with landings at a minimum of three points, and one segment of the flight being a straight-line distance of at least 25 NM between the takeoff and landing locations; and

      iii. 3 takeoffs and landings to a full stop at an airport with an operating control tower, each landing separated by an enroute phase of flight and involving a flight in the traffic pattern in a helicopter.

8. For a glider rating, have at least one of the following:

   a. If the applicant has not logged at least 40 hours of flight time as a pilot in a heavier-than-air aircraft, at least 10 hours of flight training in a glider, and 20 training flights performed on the appropriate areas, including —

    i. 2 hours of solo flight in gliders in the areas of operation that apply to gliders, with not less than 10 launches and landings being performed; and

    ii. Three training flights in a glider in preparation for the practical test within the 60-day period preceding the practical test.

  b. If the applicant has logged at least 40 hours of flight time in heavier-than-air aircraft, at least 3 hours of flight training in a glider, and 10 training flights performed on the appropriate areas, including —

    i. 10 solo flights in gliders on the areas of operation that apply to gliders, and

    ii. Three training flights in preparation for the practical test within the 60-day waiting period preceding the test.

9. For a lighter-than-air rating, have at least one of the following:

  a. For an airship rating:

    i. 25 hours of flight training in airships, which consists of at least:

      • 3 hours of cross-country flight training in an airship;

      • 3 hours of night flight training in an airship that includes:

        — A cross-country flight of over 25 NM total distance; and

        — 5 takeoffs and 5 landings to a full stop (with each landing involving a flight in the traffic pattern) at an airport.

    ii. 3 hours of instrument flight training in an airship;

    iii. 3 hours of flight training in an airship in preparation for the practical test within the 60 days preceding the date of the test; and

    iv. 5 hours performing the duties of PIC in an airship with an authorized instructor.

  b. For a balloon rating. At least 10 hours of flight training that includes at least 6 training flights with an authorized instructor, that includes —

    i. If the training is in a gas balloon, at least 2 flights of 2 hours each that consists of —

      • At least one training flight with an authorized instructor within 60 days prior to application for the rating on the areas of operation for a gas balloon;

      • At least one flight performing the duties of pilot in command in a gas balloon with an authorized instructor; and

      • At least one flight involving a controlled ascent to 3,000 feet above the launch site.

    ii. If the training is in a balloon with an airborne heater, at least —

      • Two 1-hour flights within 60 days prior to application for the rating on the areas of operation appropriate to a balloon with an airborne heater;

      • One solo flight in a balloon with an airborne heater; and

      • At least one flight involving a controlled ascent to 2,000 feet above the launch site.

10. For a powered parachute rating, have at least 25 hours of flight time in a powered parachute that includes at least 10 hours of flight training with an authorized instructor, including 30 takeoffs and landings, and 10 hours of solo flight training, that includes —

  a. 1 hour of cross-country flight with a landing at an airport at least 25 nautical miles from the airport of departure;

  b. 3 hours of night flight training in a powered parachute that includes 10 takeoffs and landings (with each landing involving a flight in the traffic pattern) at an airport;

c. 3 hours of flight training within the last 60 days in preparation for the practical test in a powered parachute; and

d. 3 hours of solo flight time in a powered parachute, consisting of at least —

    i. One solo cross-country flight with a landing at an airport at least 25 nautical miles from the departure airport; and

    ii. 20 solo takeoffs and landings to a full stop (with each landing involving a flight in a traffic pattern) at an airport, with at least 3 takeoffs and landings at an airport with an operating control tower.

11. For a weight-shift control aircraft rating, have at least 40 hours of flight time that includes at least 20 hours of flight training with an authorized instructor and 10 hours of solo flight training that includes —

a. 3 hours of cross-country flight training in a weight-shift control aircraft;

b. 3 hours of night flight training in a weight-shift control aircraft that includes —

    i. One cross-country flight over 75 nautical miles total distance; and

    ii. 10 takeoffs and landings (with each landing involving a flight in the traffic pattern) at an airport;

c. 3 hours of flight training within the last 60 days in preparation for the practical test in a weight-shift control aircraft, and

d. 10 hours of solo flight time in a weight-shift control aircraft, consisting of at least —

    i. 5 hours of solo cross-country time;

    ii. 1 solo cross-country flight over 100 nautical miles total distance, with landings at a minimum of three points, and one segment of the flight being a straight line distance of at least 50 nautical miles between takeoff and landing locations; and

    iii. 3 takeoffs and landings (with each landing involving a flight in the traffic pattern) at an airport with an operating control tower.

Eligibility for the Sport Pilot Certificate

Always check the current 14 CFR Part 61 for pilot certificate requirements. To be eligible for a Sport Pilot Certificate a person must:

1. Be at least 17 years old (16 if you are applying to operate a glider or balloon).

2. Be able to read, speak, write, and understand English or have a limitation placed on the certificate.

3. Score at least 70 percent on the required FAA Knowledge Test.

4. Pass a practical test on the subjects and maneuvers outlined in the Sport Pilot Practical Test Standards (ASA-8081-SPORT *Sport Pilot for Airplane, Weight-Shift Control, Powered Parachute, and Flight Instructor*).

5. See 14 CFR §61.329 for the special provisions for obtaining a Sport Pilot certificate as a registered ultralight pilot with an FAA-recognized ultralight organization.

6. The table on the next page explains the aeronautical experience you must have to apply for a Sport Pilot Certificate.

Aeronautical Experience for the Sport Pilot Certificate

If you are applying for a sport pilot certificate with...	Then you must log at least...	Which must include at least...
(a) Airplane category and single-engine land or sea class privileges,	(1) 20 hours of flight time, including at least 15 hours of flight training from an authorized instructor in a single-engine airplane and at least 5 hours of solo flight training in the areas of operation listed in §61.311,	(i) 2 hours of cross-country flight training, (ii) 10 takeoffs and landings to a full stop (with each landing involving a flight in the traffic pattern) at an airport; (iii) One solo cross-country flight of at least 75 nautical miles total distance, with a full-stop landing at a minimum of two points and one segment of the flight consisting of a straight-line distance of at least 25 nautical miles between the takeoff and landing locations, and (iv) 2 hours of flight training with an authorized instructor on those areas of operation specified in §61.311 in preparation for the practical test within the preceding 2 calendar months from the month of the test.
(b) Glider category privileges, and you have not logged at least 20 hours of flight time in a heavier-than-air aircraft,	(1) 10 hours of flight time in a glider, including 10 flights in a glider receiving flight training from an authorized instructor and at least 2 hours of solo flight training in the areas of operation listed in §61.311,	(i) Five solo launches and landings, and (ii) at least 3 training flights with an authorized instructor on those areas of operation specified in §61.311 in preparation for the practical test within the preceding 2 calendar months from the month of the test.
(c) Glider category privileges, and you have logged 20 hours flight time in a heavier-than-air aircraft,	(1) 3 hours of flight time in a glider, including five flights in a glider while receiving flight training from an authorized instructor and at least 1 hour of solo flight training in the areas of operation listed in §61.311,	(i) Three solo launches and landings, and (ii) at least 3 training flights with an authorized instructor on those areas of operation specified in §61.311 in preparation for the practical test within the preceding 2 calendar months from the month of the test.
(d) Rotorcraft category and gyroplane class privileges,	(1) 20 hours of flight time, including 15 hours of flight training from an authorized instructor in a gyroplane and at least 5 hours of solo flight training in the areas of operation listed in §61.311,	(i) 2 hours of cross-country flight training, (ii) 10 takeoffs and landings to a full stop (with each landing involving a flight in the traffic pattern) at an airport, (iii) One solo cross-country flight of at least 50 nautical miles total distance, with a full-stop landing at a minimum of two points, and one segment of the flight consisting of a straight-line distance of at least 25 nautical miles between the takeoff and landing locations, and (iv) 2 hours of flight training with an authorized instructor on those areas of operation specified in §61.311 in preparation for the practical test within the preceding 2 calendar months from the month of the test.
(e) Lighter-than-air category and airship class privileges,	(1) 20 hours of flight time, including 15 hours of flight training from an authorized instructor in an airship and at least 3 hours performing the duties of pilot in command in an airship with an authorized instructor in the areas of operation listed in §61.311,	(i) 2 hours of cross-country flight training, (ii) Three takeoffs and landings to a full stop (with each landing involving a flight in the traffic pattern) at an airport, (iii) One cross-country flight of at least 25 nautical miles between the takeoff and landing locations, and (iv) 2 hours of flight training with an authorized instructor on those areas of operation specified in §61.311 in preparation for the practical test within the preceding 2 calendar months from the month of the test.
(f) Lighter-than-air category and balloon class privileges,	(1) 7 hours of flight time in a balloon, including three flights with an authorized instructor and one flight performing the duties of pilot in command in a balloon with an authorized instructor in the areas of operation listed in §61.311,	(i) 2 hours of cross-country flight training and (ii) 1 hour of flight training with an authorized instructor on those areas of operation specified in §61.311 in preparation for the practical test within the preceding 2 calendar months from the month of the test.
(g) Powered parachute category land or sea class privileges,	(1) 12 hours of flight time in a powered parachute, including 10 hours of flight training from an authorized instructor in a powered parachute, and at least 2 hours of solo flight training in the areas of operation listed in §61.311,	(i) 1 hour of cross-country flight training, (ii) 20 takeoffs and landings to a full stop in a powered parachute with each landing involving flight in the traffic pattern at an airport; (iii) 10 solo takeoffs and landings to a full stop (with each landing involving a flight in the traffic pattern) at an airport, (iv) One solo flight with a landing at a different airport and one segment of the flight consisting of a straight-line distance of at least 10 nautical miles between takeoff and landing locations, and (v) 1 hour of flight training with an authorized instructor on those areas of operation specified in §61.311 in preparation for the practical test within the preceding 2 calendar months from the month of the test.
(h) Weight-shift-control aircraft category land or sea class privileges,	(1) 20 hours of flight time, including 15 hours of flight training from an authorized instructor in a weight-shift-control aircraft and at least 5 hours of solo flight training in the areas of operation listed in §61.311,	(i) 2 hours of cross-country flight training; (ii) 10 takeoffs and landings to a full stop (with each landing involving a flight in the traffic pattern) at an airport, (iii) One solo cross-country flight of at least 50 nautical miles total distance, with a full-stop landing at a minimum of two points, and one segment of the flight consisting of a straight-line distance of at least 25 nautical miles between takeoff and landing locations, and (iv) 2 hours of flight training with an authorized instructor on those areas of operation specified in §61.311 in preparation for the practical test within the preceding 2 calendar months from the month of the test.

Knowledge Exam References

The FAA references the following documents to write the FAA Knowledge Exam questions. You should be familiar with all of these as part of your ground school studies, which you should complete before starting test preparation:

FAA-H-8083-25 *Pilot's Handbook of Aeronautical Knowledge*

Sectional Aeronautical Chart (SAC)

FAA-H-8083-3 *Airplane Flying Handbook*
FAA-H-8083-13 *Glider Flying Handbook*
FAA-H-8083-21 *Helicopter Flying Handbook*

FAA-H-8083-29 *Powered Parachute Flying Handbook*
FAA-H-8083-5 *Weight-Shift Control Aircraft Flying Handbook*

FAA-H-8083-1 Aircraft Weight and Balance Handbook
FAA-H-8083-2 *Risk Management Handbook*

FAA-H-8083-11 *Balloon Flying Handbook*

FAA-S-ACS-6 Private Pilot Airplane Airman Certification Standards
FAA-S-8081-3 Recreational Pilot Practical Test Standards
FAA-S-8081-15 Private Pilot Helicopter Practical Test Standards
FAA-S-8081-29, FAA-S-8081-31 Sport Pilot Practical Test Standards

Chart Supplements U.S. (formerly Airport/Facility Directory or A/FD)

AC 00-6 *Aviation Weather*

AC 00-45 *Aviation Weather Services*

Aeronautical Information Manual (AIM)

14 CFR Parts 1, 43, 61, 68, 71, 91

49 CFR Part 830 (NTSB)

Visit the ASA website for these and many more titles and pilot supplies for your aviation endeavors: **www.asa2fly.com**

ASA Test Prep Layout

The sample FAA questions have been sorted into chapters according to subject matter. Within each chapter, the questions have been further classified and all similar questions grouped together with a concise discussion of the material covered in each group. This discussion material of "Chapter text" is printed in a larger font and spans the entire width of the page. Immediately following the sample FAA Question is ASA's Explanation in *italics*. The last line of the Explanation contains the Learning Statement Code and further reference (if applicable). *See* the EXAMPLE below.

Figures referenced by the Chapter text only are numbered with the appropriate chapter number, i.e., "Figure 1-1" is Chapter 1's first chapter-text figure.

Some Questions refer to Figures or Legends immediately following the question number, i.e., "3201. (Refer to Figure 14.)." These are FAA Figures and Legends which can be found in the separate booklet: *Airman Knowledge Testing Supplement* (CT-8080-XX). This supplement is bundled with the Test Prep and is the exact material you will have access to when you take your computerized test. We provide it separately, so you will become accustomed to referring to the FAA Figures and Legends as you would during the test.

Figures referenced by the Explanation and pertinent to the understanding of that particular question are labeled by their corresponding Question number. For example: the caption "Questions 3245 and 3248" means the figure accompanies the Explanations for both Question 3245 and Question 3248.

Answers to each question are found at the bottom of each page.

EXAMPLE:

| Chapter text |

Four aerodynamic forces are considered to be basic because they act upon an aircraft during all flight maneuvers. There is the downward-acting force called WEIGHT which must be overcome by the upward-acting force called LIFT, and there is the rearward-acting force called DRAG, which must be overcome by the forward-acting force called THRUST.

| **Category rating. This question may be found on tests for these ratings.*** |

ALL, SPO ◄——————————

3201. (Refer to Figure 14.) The four forces acting on an airplane in flight are

| **See separate book: *Airman Knowledge Testing Supplement* (CT-8080-XX)** |

A— lift, weight, thrust, and drag.
B— lift, weight, gravity, and thrust. ◄————
C— lift, gravity, power, and friction.

| **Question and answer choices** |

Lift, weight, thrust, and drag are the four basic ◄——— | **Explanation** |
aerodynamic forces acting on an aircraft in flight.
(PLT235) — FAA-H-8083-25 ◄————————

| **Code line. FAA Learning Statement Code in parentheses, followed by references for further study.** |

Answer (B) is incorrect because the force of gravity is always the same number and reacts with the airplane's mass to produce a different weight for almost every airplane. Answer (C) is incorrect because weight is the final product of gravity, thrust is the final product of power, and drag is the final product of friction. Power, gravity, and friction are only parts of the aerodynamic forces of flight.

| **Incorrect answer explanation. Reasons why answer choices are *incorrect* explained here.** |

* **Note:** The FAA does *not* identify which questions are on the different ratings' tests. Unless the wording of a question is pertinent to only one rating category, it may be found on *any* of the tests.

ALL = All aircraft
AIR = Airplane
GLI = Glider
LTA = Lighter-Than-Air (applies to hot air balloon, gas balloon and airship)
REC = Recreational
RTC = Rotorcraft (applies to both helicopter and gyroplane)
PPC = Powered Parachute
WSC = Weight-Shift Control

SPO = Sport Pilot (all aircraft categories)
LSA = Sport Pilot Airplane
LSG = Sport Pilot Glider
LSL = Sport Pilot Lighter-Than-Air
LSP = Sport Pilot Powered Parachute
LSR = Sport Pilot Rotorcraft
LSW = Sport Pilot Weight-Shift-control

Opportunity Knocking: Become a Flight Instructor!

by Greg Brown, 2000 FAA/Industry Flight Instructor of the Year

"Wanted—enthusiastic, knowledgeable pilots for part-time, full-time, or freelance professional flying. Fun and adventure, respected position, great learning experience! Age no factor. Get paid to fly!"

Where do Flight Instructors Come From?

The most visible certified flight instructors (CFIs) are often the aspiring airline pilots who populate flight schools on their way to a jet cockpit. Despite occasional concerns about "time-building," the vast majority of those folks do a super job.

But the current airline hiring boom is soaking up flight instructors faster than they can be replaced, and there's no end in sight. That means fewer CFIs to provide the quality instruction we need in both general and professional aviation.

Where can we find flight instructors with the commitment and long-term interest to meet the needs of general aviation? The answer is that more CFIs must sprout from the enthusiastic general aviation pilots we meet every day at the airport. You know, people like us, who find flying a 172, a Kitfox, or a Baron to be a blast. Pilots who delight in doing a professional job of piloting even while sustaining other full-time careers. Aviators who'd love a professional flying career, but who aren't interested in flying the "heavy iron."

Me? An Instructor?

Many student and private pilots wonder about the feasibility of one day becoming a CFI. Well, with the CFI shortage upon us and deepening rapidly, that ad up above has your name on it! Let's consider why becoming a flight instructor is a worthy mission for you to pursue right now.

We've already touched upon some reasons for becoming a CFI; demand is high, and your experience and dedication can benefit the industry. But there are other great reasons to become a flight instructor.

First, the old adage, "the best way to master a subject is to teach it," is most definitely true. As an active CFI your knowledge and flight proficiency will rapidly exceed your greatest expectations as a private pilot. By teaching others you will truly learn to fly as a pro.

Next comes the reward of setting goals and achieving them. Many of us find ourselves sitting at home on a given day, thinking, "Gee, I wish there was a reason to go flying today." Well, there is! Start working toward that CFI and you've got a meaningful personal and professional objective to justify the time, effort, and investment in continuing regular flying.

Then there's the contribution to be made to the aviation community. Not only can you as a CFI personally impact the safety and proficiency of pilots you train, but there's also the critically important role CFIs serve in recruiting new blood to aviation. The vast majority of new pilots sign up through the direct or indirect efforts of active CFIs, and we need your help carrying the flag.

Best of all, here's your big chance to become an honest-to-goodness pro. Almost every active pilot harbors the dream of flying professionally. But for many reasons—age, family and lifestyle considerations, success in another occupation—only a certain percentage of pilots are in position to pursue, say, the captain's seat in a Boeing or a LearJet. Well here's your opportunity to fly professionally under schedule and conditions more or less of your own choosing, all while having someone pay you to do it.

Continued

What Does It Take to Qualify?

"But hold on a minute," you say, "becoming a CFI takes years of full-time study, and many thousands of flight hours, right?"

Not at all! With dedication and concentrated effort one can become a CFI relatively quickly. After earning your private pilot certificate, it takes only three more steps to become a primary flight instructor: an instrument rating, the commercial pilot certificate, and then the flight instructor certificate itself. That's certainly not a long path.

Regulations allow new private pilots to begin training for the instrument rating as soon as they like. (All CFI applicants must be instrument rated, even if they never plan to fly IFR.) The instrument rating is roughly comparable in flight training hours to earning one's private certificate, and is something many of us go on to earn anyway. As with the private, FAA Knowledge (written) and Practical (oral and flight) Exams are required. But once earning your instrument rating the route to flight instructor status can be a quick one.

You'll need some flight experience to be eligible for your commercial pilot certificate—190 to 250 hours total flight time are required by the time you complete your training. But earning the rating itself requires only a fraction of the effort required to earn a private, it's entirely feasible to earn your commercial in fifteen hours or less, if you set your mind to it. Again there are Knowledge and Practical Exams to pass, and then you're ready to pursue your flight instructor certificate.

There is no minimum training requirement for the flight instructor certificate itself, but it will probably take you some fifteen to twenty flight hours to earn, plus a good deal of ground instruction. Along with Knowledge and Practical, there is an additional FAA exam addressing "Fundamentals of Instruction."

The oral portion of the CFI practical test is notoriously challenging, but what's covered there is largely material you've seen before, so keep sharp on the private and commercial pilot material you've learned, and you'll have little trouble mastering the CFI tests. Of course teaching technique is an important element of the test, too. If there's one certificate where you should seek out a truly outstanding instructor, the CFI is it.

As for flight physicals, CFIs fall into the most favorable regulatory status of almost any professional pilot. Regulations allow you to instruct with a third-class medical certificate, so if you qualify medically for a student pilot certificate you can instruct. What's more, some instruction can even be conducted without a medical.

And other than the fact that you must be eighteen to earn your commercial and therefore CFI certificates, there are no age limits on instructing. This is one case where the experience and maturity of older pilots is desirable and unrestricted. You're a sixty-year-old student pilot? Cool! Move right along and earn your CFI.

How Soon Can I Become an Instructor?

Before we get on with more privileges and benefits of instructing, here are a few tips to speed you along the path. First, many people don't realize that they can become certificated as Ground Instructors— teaching ground school and signing off applicants for their FAA Knowledge Exams—simply by passing several FAA written tests. That means you can start your instructing career almost immediately! Not only will ground instructing help pay for your flight training, but it's great preparation for flight instructing.

And for those who plan to knock off their commercial and CFI certificates in short order, here's a little trick to accelerate your progress. Arrange with your CFI and pilot examiner to train for and take your Commercial Pilot Practical Test from the right seat. That way your right-seat flying skills will already be nailed when you dive into CFI training—doing it this way could save you five or even ten hours of training. Ask at your flight school about the details for your situation.

What Are the Privileges and Benefits of Being a CFI?

Your initial flight instructor certificate will allow you to train private and commercial pilot applicants through to their certificates, and also authorize you to perform flight reviews. (Imagine, you giving the flight review!) Additional instructor ratings, such as instrument, multiengine, and those for other aircraft categories such as glider and helicopter, are relatively easy to add if you have journeyman skills in the ratings sought.

The really great news is that given today's demand for flight instructors, you can be assured of employability in most locations the moment you earn your temporary CFI certificate, and you'll likely have your choice of whether to do it full-time or part-time, or in some cases, as a freelancer.

Okay, now the part about "getting paid to fly": In the past, earnings have often been pretty limited for full-time flight instructors, depending on location, employer, number of students and other factors. But with the developing CFI shortage, instructor pay and benefits are rapidly going up. If you want to pursue a full-time instructing career, excellent positions are now to be had around the country.

However, a great many CFIs choose to join the part-timers and freelancers around the country who ply their trade in a professional manner, and contribute beyond their numbers to the well-being of general aviation. Many of those folks work other jobs, flying and non-flying, and instruct strictly for the fun and personal reward of it. When you look at instructing as a part-time activity that supports your flying and that of others, it's a pretty darned good deal.

First, instructing gets you up in the air on a regular basis at a price anyone can afford—free. Many part-time CFIs reinvest their instructing income into a fund for personal flying, yielding a good return in both professional and pleasure flying. Other not-so-obvious instructor benefits include discounts on aircraft rental, lower insurance premiums for aircraft owners, and broader insurability in the planes you fly.

Did you realize that as a CFI you get to log all the time flown by your students as PIC time? And as an instrument instructor the approaches flown by your students are often loggable for your own currency, too. And each of those ratings you earn in the process of becoming a flight instructor—the IFR, the commercial, and your CFI—count as flight reviews. That's the money-saving bureaucratic stuff. The important part is that you'll be sharp far beyond what flight reviews could do for you in themselves, and it all comes in the course of business without the need for lots of currency flights.

Instruct well and charge appropriately for your services, and you can generate some pretty good part-time income at this business. That also raises the possibility of deducting many flying expenses from your income taxes, including charts, headsets, recurrent training, your flight physical, and some or all flight training expenses. (Talk to your accountant for the official word on your situation.)

Now for the most important and rewarding reason to become a flight instructor—people. As a CFI you're going to meet many, many fine individuals from all walks of life who share your dream of flying. It will be you who introduces them to the special fraternity of aviators, you who delivers them the key to flight on their own, and you who conveys the skills and knowledge to help them fly safely and enjoyably with their thousands of future passengers. Your words will be riding with them many years in the future at times when they need you most.

Join the illustrious ranks of flight instructors. Whether you're eighteen, or beginning a new life after retirement; whether you're a schoolteacher with summers available, or looking to change careers altogether, we need you! No one cares whether you wear glasses or not, and the skies are yours to own in everything from light-sport aircraft to jets.

Just bring along your passion, your life experience, and some dedication. Here's your big chance to experience the ultimate thrill of flying, all from the seat with the world's greatest view—the spectacular high of opening doors of flight to yet another generation of pilots. Carpe diem! Become a CFI!

Portions of this material first appeared in *Flight Training* magazine. Greg Brown is the author of *The Savvy Flight Instructor: Secrets of the Successful CFI*, published by ASA.

Chapter 1
Basic Aerodynamics

Aerodynamic Terms

An **airfoil** is a structure or body which produces a useful reaction to air movement. Airplane wings, helicopter rotor blades, and propellers are airfoils. *See* Figure 1-1.

The **chord line** is an imaginary straight line from the leading edge to the trailing edge of an airfoil. *See* Figure 1-2. Changing the shape of an airfoil (by lowering flaps, for example) will change the chord line. *See* Figure 1-3.

In aerodynamics, **relative wind** is the wind felt by an airfoil. It is created by the movement of air past an airfoil, by the motion of an airfoil through the air, or by a combination of the two. Relative wind is parallel and in the opposite direction to the flight path of the airfoil. *See* Figure 1-4.

Continued

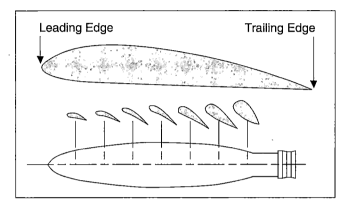

Figure 1-1. A typical airfoil cross-section

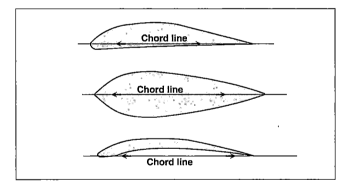

Figure 1-2. Chord line

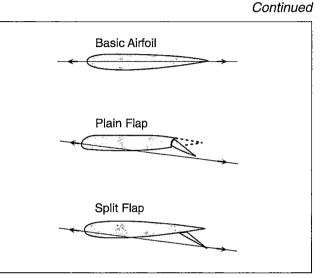

Figure 1-3. Changing shape of wing changes the chord line

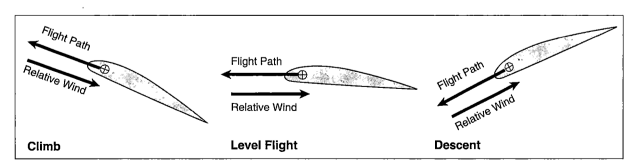

Figure 1-4. Relative wind

The **angle of attack** is the angle between the chord line of the airfoil and the relative wind. By manipulating the aircraft controls, the pilot can vary the angle of attack. *See* Figure 1-5.

The **angle of incidence** is the angle at which a wing is attached to the aircraft fuselage. The airplane pilot has no control over the angle of incidence. *See* Figure 1-6. The angle of incidence changes for a powered parachute based on the design, and is controlled by the pilot on a weight-shift control aircraft.

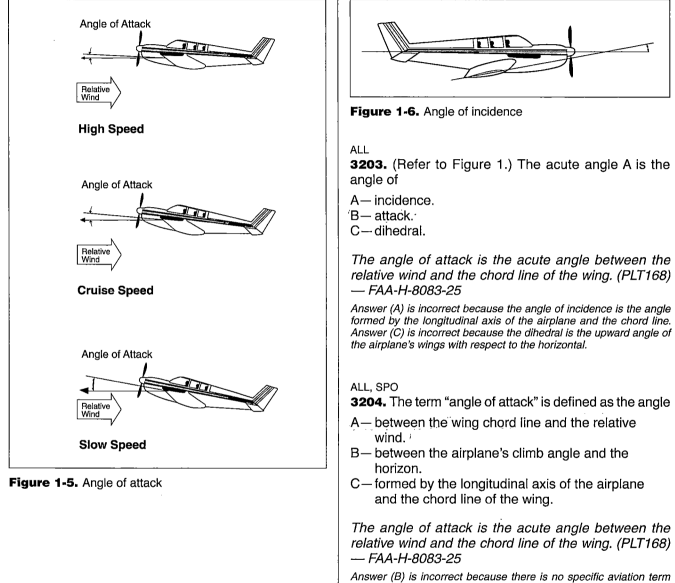

Figure 1-5. Angle of attack

Figure 1-6. Angle of incidence

ALL
3203. (Refer to Figure 1.) The acute angle A is the angle of

A— incidence.
B— attack.
C— dihedral.

The angle of attack is the acute angle between the relative wind and the chord line of the wing. (PLT168) — FAA-H-8083-25

Answer (A) is incorrect because the angle of incidence is the angle formed by the longitudinal axis of the airplane and the chord line. Answer (C) is incorrect because the dihedral is the upward angle of the airplane's wings with respect to the horizontal.

ALL, SPO
3204. The term "angle of attack" is defined as the angle

A— between the wing chord line and the relative wind.
B— between the airplane's climb angle and the horizon.
C— formed by the longitudinal axis of the airplane and the chord line of the wing.

The angle of attack is the acute angle between the relative wind and the chord line of the wing. (PLT168) — FAA-H-8083-25

Answer (B) is incorrect because there is no specific aviation term for this. Answer (C) is incorrect because this is the definition of the angle of incidence.

ALL

3204-1. The angle between the chord line of an airfoil and the relative wind is known as the angle of

A— lift.
B— attack.
C— incidence.

The angle of attack is the acute angle between the chord line of the wing and the direction of the relative wind. (PLT168) — FAA-H-8083-25

Answer (A) is incorrect because the angle of lift is not an aerodynamic term used in aviation. Answer (C) is incorrect because the angle between the chordline of an airfoil and the longitudinal axis of an aircraft is known as the angle of incidence.

ALL

3317. Angle of attack is defined as the angle between the chord line of an airfoil and the

A— direction of the relative wind.
B— pitch angle of an airfoil.
C— rotor plane of rotation.

The angle of attack is the angle between the chord line of the airfoil and the direction of the relative wind. (PLT168) — FAA-H-8083-25

SPO

2225. The angle of attack at which an airfoil stalls will

A— increase if the CG is moved forward.
B— remain the same regardless of gross weight.
C— change with an increase in gross weight.

When the angle of attack is increased to between 18° and 20° (critical angle of attack) on most airfoils, the airstream can no longer follow the upper curvature of the wing because of the excessive change in direction. The airfoil will stall if the critical angle of attack is exceeded. The indicated airspeed at which stall occurs will be determined by weight and load factor, but the stall angle of attack is the same. (PLT477) — FAA-H-8083-25

Answers (A) and (C) are incorrect because an airfoil will always stall at the same angle of attack, regardless of the CG position or gross weight.

SPO

2225-1. What is the effect of advancing the throttle in flight?

A— Both aircraft groundspeed and angle of attack will increase.
B— Airspeed will remain relatively constant but the aircraft will climb.
C— The aircraft will accelerate, which will cause a turn to the right.

During straight-and-level flight, if the angle of attack is not coordinated (decreased) with an increase of thrust, the aircraft will climb. (PLT132) — FAA-H-8083-25

Answers

| 3204-1 | [B] | 3317 | [A] | 2225 | [B] | 2225-1 | [B] |

Axes of Rotation and the Four Forces Acting in Flight

Aircraft have three axes of rotation: the lateral axis, longitudinal axis, and the vertical axis. *See* Figure 1-7.

The **lateral axis** is an imaginary line from wing tip to wing tip for an airplane. The rotation around this axis is called **pitch**. Pitch is controlled by the elevators, and this rotation is referred to as **longitudinal control** or **longitudinal stability**. *See* Figure 1-8.

The **longitudinal axis** is an imaginary line from the nose to the tail. Rotation around the longitudinal axis is called **roll**. Roll is controlled by the ailerons, and this rotation is referred to as **lateral control** or **lateral stability**. *See* Figure 1-9.

The **vertical axis** is an imaginary line extending vertically through the intersection of the lateral and longitudinal axes. Rotation about the vertical axis is called **yaw**. Yaw is controlled by the rudder, and this rotation is referred to as **directional control** or **directional stability**. *See* Figure 1-10.

The **center of gravity** (the imaginary point where all the weight is concentrated) is the point at which an airplane would balance if it were suspended at that point. The three axes intersect at the center of gravity. Weight-shift control and powered parachutes rotate around this center of gravity.

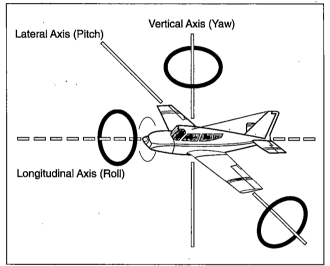

Figure 1-7. Axes of rotation

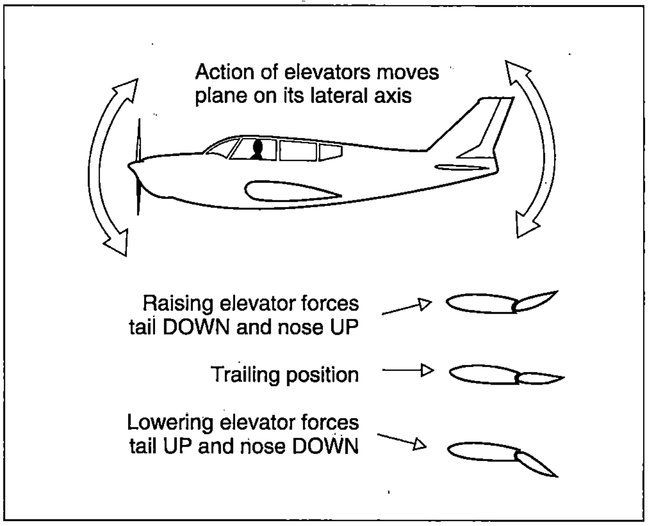

Figure 1-8. Effect of elevators

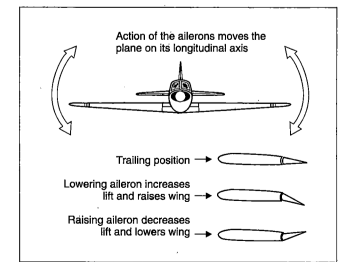

Figure 1-9. Effect of ailerons

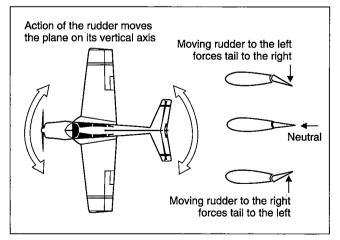

Figure 1-10. Effect of rudder

Four aerodynamic forces are considered to be basic because they act upon an aircraft during all flight maneuvers: there is the downward-acting force called **weight** which must be overcome by the upward-acting force called **lift**; and there is the rearward-acting force called **drag**, which must be overcome by the forward-acting force called **thrust**. *See* Figure 1-11.

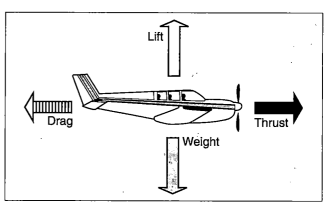

Figure 1-11. Relationship of forces in flight

Lift

Air is a gas which can be compressed or expanded. When compressed, more air can occupy a given volume and air density is increased. When allowed to expand, air occupies a greater space and density is decreased. Temperature, atmospheric pressure, and humidity all affect air density. Air density has significant effects on an aircraft's performance.

As the velocity of a fluid (gas or liquid) increases, its pressure decreases. This is known as **Bernoulli's Principle**. *See* Figure 1-12.

Lift is the result of a pressure difference between the top and the bottom of the wing. A wing is designed to accelerate air over the top camber of the wing, thereby decreasing the pressure on the top and producing lift. *See* Figure 1-13.

Several factors are involved in the creation of lift: angle of attack, wing area and shape (planform), air velocity, and air density. All of these factors have an effect on the amount of lift produced at any given moment. The pilot can actively control the angle of attack and the airspeed, and increasing either of these will result in an increase in lift.

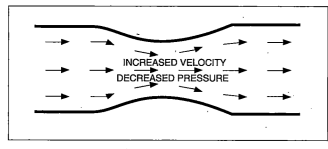

Figure 1-12. Flow of air through a constriction

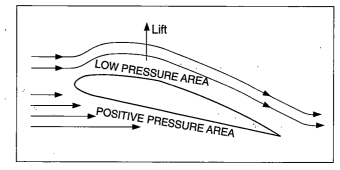

Figure 1-13. Development of lift

Weight

Weight is the force with which gravity attracts all bodies vertically toward the center of the earth.

Thrust

Thrust is the forward force which is produced by the propeller acting as an airfoil to displace a large mass of air to the rear.

Drag

Drag is a rearward-acting force which resists the forward movement of an airplane through the air. Drag may be classified into two main types: parasite drag and induced drag.

Parasite drag is the resistance of the air produced by any part of an airplane that does not produce lift (antennae, landing gear, etc.). Parasite drag will increase as airspeed increases.

Induced drag is a by-product of lift. In other words, drag is induced as the wing develops lift. The high-pressure air beneath the wing, which is trying to flow around and over the wing tips into the area of low pressure, causes a vortex behind the wing tip. This vortex induces a spanwise flow and creates vortices all along the trailing edge of the wing. As the angle of attack is increased (up to the critical angle), lift will increase and so will the vortices and downwash. This downwash redirects the lift vector rearward, causing a rearward component of lift (induced drag). Induced drag will increase as airspeed decreases. *See* Figure 1-14.

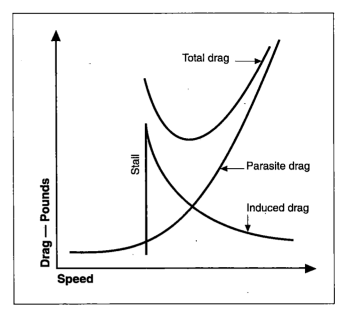

Figure 1-14. Drag curve diagram

During unaccelerated (straight-and-level) flight, the four aerodynamic forces which act on an airplane are said to be in equilibrium, or:

Lift = Weight and Thrust = Drag

3201-1. Which statement relates to Bernoulli's principle?

A— For every action there is an equal and opposite reaction.
B— An additional upward force is generated as the lower surface of the wing deflects air downward.
C—Air traveling faster over the curved upper surface of an airfoil causes lower pressure on the top surface.

Bernoulli's principle states in part that the pressure of a fluid (liquid or gas) decreases at points where the speed of the fluid increases. In other words, high-speed flow is associated with low pressure, and low-speed flow with high pressure. Air traveling faster over the curved upper surface of an airfoil causes lower pressure on the top surface. (PLT025) — FAA-H-8083-25

Answers (A) and (B) are incorrect because these refer to Newton's Third Law of Motion.

3201. The four forces acting on an airplane in flight are

A— lift, weight, thrust, and drag.
B— lift, weight, gravity, and thrust.
C— lift, gravity, power, and friction.

Lift, weight, thrust, and drag are the four basic aerodynamic forces acting on an aircraft in flight. (PLT242) — FAA-H-8083-25

3213. What is the purpose of the rudder on an airplane?

A— To control yaw.
B— To control overbanking tendency.
C— To control roll.

The purpose of the rudder is to control yaw. (PLT234) — FAA-H-8083-25

Answer (B) is incorrect because the ailerons control overbanking. Answer (C) is incorrect because roll is controlled by the ailerons.

Answers

3201-1 [C]   3201 [A]   3213 [A]

AIR, WSC, PPC, LSA, LSR, LSW, LSP
3205. What is the relationship of lift, drag, thrust, and weight when the airplane is in straight-and-level flight?

A— Lift equals weight and thrust equals drag.
B— Lift, drag, and weight equal thrust.
C— Lift and weight equal thrust and drag.

Lift and thrust are considered positive forces, while weight and drag are considered negative forces and the sum of the opposing forces is zero. That is, lift = weight and thrust = drag. (PLT241) — FAA-H-8083-25

AIR, GLI, WSC, PPC
3202. When are the four forces that act on an airplane in equilibrium?

A— During unaccelerated flight.
B— When the aircraft is accelerating.
C— When the aircraft is at rest on the ground.

In unaccelerated (steady state) flight the opposing forces are in equilibrium. (PLT242) — FAA-H-8083-25

Answer (B) is incorrect because thrust must exceed drag in order for the airplane to accelerate. Answer (C) is incorrect because when the airplane is at rest on the ground, the only aerodynamic force acting on it is weight.

LSA, LSG, LSW
2239. The best speed to use for a glide is one that will result in the greatest glide distance for a given amount of

A— altitude.
B— fuel.
C— drag.

The best speed for the glide is one at which the airplane will travel the greatest forward distance for a given loss of altitude in still air. This best glide speed corresponds to an angle of attack resulting in the least drag on the airplane and giving the best lift-to-drag ratio (L/D$_{MAX}$). (PLT257) — FAA-H-8083-3

LSA, LSR, LSW, LSP
2229. Climb performance depends upon the

A— reserve power or thrust.
B— maximum L/D ratio.
C— cruise power setting.

Climb depends upon the reserve power or thrust. Reserve power is the available power over and above that required to maintain horizontal flight at a given speed. (PLT125) — FAA-H-8083-25

LSA, LSG, LSW
2215. (Refer to Figure 72.) The horizontal dashed line from point C to point E represents the

A— ultimate load factor.
B— positive limit load factor.
C— airspeed range for normal operations.

C to E is the maximum positive load limit. In this case it is 3.8 Gs, which is appropriate for normal category airplanes. (PLT074) — FAA-H-8083-25

Answer (A) is incorrect because "ultimate load factor" is not a real term; it is not depicted in the figure. Answer (C) is incorrect because this is depicted by the vertical line from point A to point J, to the vertical line from point D to point G.

LSA, LSG, LSW
2216. (Refer to Figure 72.) The vertical dashed line from point E to point F is represented on the airspeed indicator by the

A— upper limit of the yellow arc.
B— upper limit of the green arc.
C— blue radial line.

V$_{NE}$ (never exceed airspeed), the vertical line from point E to F, is marked on airspeed indicators with a red radial line, the upper limit of the yellow arc. (PLT074) — FAA-H-8083-25

Answers

3205 [A]   3202 [A]   2239 [A]   2229 [A]   2215 [B]   2216 [A]

Stability

Stability is the inherent ability of an airplane to return, or not return, to its original flight condition after being disturbed by an outside force, such as rough air.

Positive static stability is the initial tendency of an aircraft to return or not return to its original position. *See* Figure 1-15.

Positive dynamic stability is the tendency of an oscillating airplane (with positive static stability) to return to its original position relative to time. *See* Figure 1-16.

Aircraft design normally ensures that the aircraft will be stable in pitch. The pilot can adversely affect this longitudinal stability by allowing the center of gravity (CG) to move forward or aft of specified CG limits through improper loading procedures. One undesirable flight characteristic a pilot might experience in an airplane loaded with the CG located aft of the aft CG limit would be the inability to recover from a stalled condition.

The location of the CG with respect to the center of lift (CL) will determine the longitudinal stability of an airplane. *See* Figure 1-17.

An airplane will be less stable at all airspeeds if it is loaded to the most aft CG. An advantage of an airplane said to be inherently stable is that it will require less effort to control.

Changes in pitch can also be experienced with changes in power settings (except in T-tail airplanes). When power is reduced, there is a corresponding reduction in downwash on the tail, which results in the nose "pitching" down.

A properly designed weight-shift control is stable because the center of lift is above the CG. Slower than trim, the center of lift moves aft. Faster than trim, the center of lift moves forward to make the aircraft stable.

Powered parachutes are stable because the center of gravity is well below the wing, creating pendulum stability.

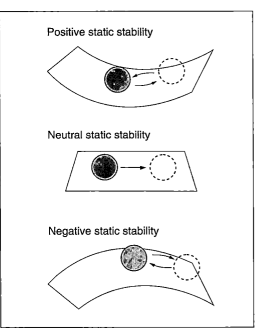

Figure 1-15. Static stability

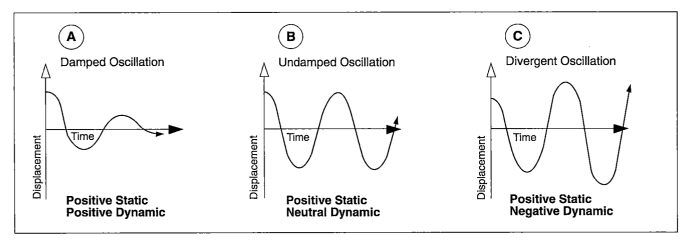

Figure 1-16. Positive static stability relative to dynamic stability

Effects of Forward CG
1. Increased longitudinal stability.
2. Lower cruise speed. The wing flies at a higher angle of attack to create more lift to counter the added downward forces produced by the tail, therefore the wing also produces more induced drag.
3. Higher stall speed. The wing flies at a higher angle of attack to create more lift to counter the added downward forces produced by the tail, therefore the wing also produces more induced drag.

Effects of Aft CG
1. Decreased longitudinal stability.
2. Higher cruise speed (for just the opposite reason listed above).
3. Lower stall speed.
4. Poor stall/spin recovery.

Figure 1-17. Effect of CG on airplane stability

AIR, GLI, LSA, LSR, LSG, LSW, LSP
3210. An airplane said to be inherently stable will

A— be difficult to stall.
B— require less effort to control.
C— not spin.

A stable airplane will tend to return to the original condition of flight if disturbed by a force such as turbulent air. This means that a stable airplane is easy to fly. (PLT213) — FAA-H-8083-25

Answer (A) is incorrect because stability of an airplane has an effect on its stall recovery, not the difficulty of stall entry. Answer (C) is incorrect because an inherently stable aircraft can still spin.

AIR, GLI
3211. What determines the longitudinal stability of an airplane?

A— The location of the CG with respect to the center of lift.
B— The effectiveness of the horizontal stabilizer, rudder, and rudder trim tab.
C— The relationship of thrust and lift to weight and drag.

The location of the center of gravity with respect to the center of lift determines to a great extent the longitudinal stability of an airplane. Center of gravity aft of the center of lift will result in an undesirable pitch-up moment during flight. An airplane with the center of gravity forward of the center of lift will pitch down when power is reduced. This will increase the airspeed and the downward force on the elevators. This increased downward force on the elevators will bring the nose up, providing positive

stability. The farther forward the CG is, the more stable the airplane. (PLT213) — FAA-H-8083-25

Answer (B) is incorrect because the rudder and rudder trim tab control the yaw. Answer (C) is incorrect because the relationship of thrust and lift to weight and drag affects speed and altitude.

AIR, GLI
3212. What causes an airplane (except a T-tail) to pitch nosedown when power is reduced and controls are not adjusted?

A— The CG shifts forward when thrust and drag are reduced.
B— The downwash on the elevators from the propeller slipstream is reduced and elevator effectiveness is reduced.
C— When thrust is reduced to less than weight, lift is also reduced and the wings can no longer support the weight.

The location of the center of gravity with respect to the center of lift determines to a great extent the longitudinal stability of an airplane. Center of gravity aft of the center of lift will result in an undesirable pitch-up moment during flight. An airplane with the center of gravity forward of the center of lift will pitch down when power is reduced. This will increase the airspeed and the downward force on the elevators. This increased downward force on the elevators will bring the nose up, providing positive stability. The farther forward the CG is, the more stable the airplane. (PLT351) — FAA-H-8083-25

Answer (A) is incorrect because the CG is not affected by changes in thrust or drag. Answer (C) is incorrect because thrust and weight have a small relationship to each other, unless thrust is opposite weight, as in the case of jet fighters and space shuttles.

AIR, GLI, WSC
3287. An airplane has been loaded in such a manner that the CG is located aft of the aft CG limit. One undesirable flight characteristic a pilot might experience with this airplane would be

A— a longer takeoff run.
B— difficulty in recovering from a stalled condition.
C— stalling at higher-than-normal airspeed.

Loading in a tail-heavy condition can reduce the airplane's ability to recover from stalls and spins. Tail-heavy loading also produces very light stick forces, making it easy for the pilot to inadvertently overstress the airplane. (PLT003) — FAA-H-8083-25

Answer (A) is incorrect because an airplane with an aft CG has less drag from a reduction in horizontal stabilizer lift, resulting in a short takeoff run. Answer (C) is incorrect because an airplane with an aft CG flies at a lower angle of attack, resulting in a lower stall speed.

Answers

3210 [B]   3211 [A]   3212 [B]   3287 [B]

AIR, GLI

3288. Loading an airplane to the most aft CG will cause the airplane to be

A— less stable at all speeds.
B— less stable at slow speeds, but more stable at high speeds.
C— less stable at high speeds, but more stable at low speeds.

Loading in a tail-heavy condition can reduce the airplane's ability to recover from stalls and spins. Tail-heavy loading also produces very light stick forces at all speeds, making it easy for the pilot to inadvertently overstress the airplane. (PLT328) — FAA-H-8083-25

Answers (B) and (C) are incorrect because an aft CG location causes an aircraft to be less stable at all airspeeds, due to less elevator effectiveness.

AIR, GLI, WSC

3211-1. Changes in the center of pressure of a wing affect the aircraft's

A— lift/drag ratio.
B— lifting capacity.
C— aerodynamic balance and controllability.

The center of pressure of an asymmetrical airfoil moves forward as the angle of attack is increased, and backward as the angle of attack is decreased. This backward and forward movement of the point at which lift acts, affects the aerodynamic balance and the controllability of the aircraft. (PLT214) — FAA-H-8083-25

Answer (A) is incorrect because the lift/drag ratio is determined by the angle of attack. Answer (B) is incorrect because lifting capacity is determined by angle of attack and airspeed.

Turns, Loads, and Load Factors

When an airplane is banked into a turn, a portion of the vertical lift being developed is diverted into a **horizontal lift component**. It is this horizontal (sideward) force that forces the airplane from straight-and-level flight and causes it to turn. The reduced **vertical lift component** results in a loss of altitude unless total lift is increased by increasing angle of attack, increasing airspeed, or increasing both. *See* Figure 1-18.

In aerodynamics, **load** is the force (imposed stress) that must be supported by an airplane structure in flight. The loads imposed on the wings in flight are stated in terms of load factor.

In straight-and-level flight, the wings of an airplane support a load equal to the sum of the weight of the airplane plus its contents. This particular load factor is equal to "One G," where "**G**" refers to the pull of gravity.

However, a force called **centrifugal force** is generated which acts toward the outside of the curve any time an airplane is flying a curved path (turns, climbs, or descents).

Whenever the airplane is flying in a curved flight path with a positive load, the load that the wings must support will be equal to the weight of the airplane plus the load imposed by centrifugal force; therefore, it can be said that turns increase the load factor on an airplane.

As the angle of bank of a turn increases, the load factor increases, as is shown in Figure 1-19.

The amount of excess load that can be imposed on the wing of an airplane depends on the speed of the airplane. An example of this would be a change in direction made at high speed with forceful control movement, which results in a high load factor being imposed.

An increased **load factor** (weight) will cause an airplane to stall at a higher airspeed, as shown in Figure 1-20.

Some conditions that increase the weight (load) of an aircraft are: overloading the airplane, too steep an angle of bank, turbulence and abrupt movement of the controls.

Because different types of operations require different maneuvers (and therefore varying bank angles and load factors), aircraft are separated into categories determined by the loads that their wing structures can support:

Answers

3288 [A]   3211-1 [C]

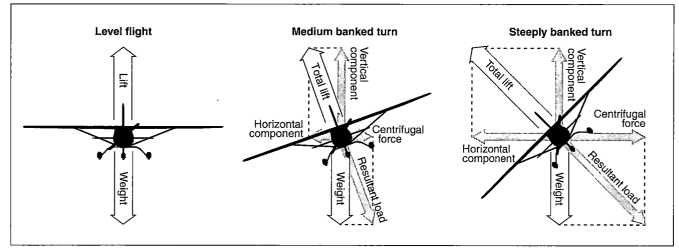

Figure 1-18. Forces during normal coordinated turn

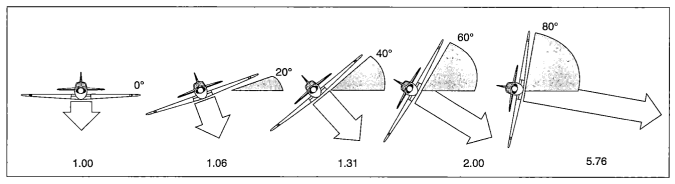

Figure 1-19. Increase in load on wings as angle of bank increases

Category	Positive Limit Load
Normal......................................(nonacrobatic) (N)	3.8 times gross wt.
Utility ....(normal operations and limited acrobatic maneuvers)	4.4 times gross wt.
Acrobatic.................................(A)	6.0 times gross wt.

The limit loads should not be exceeded in actual operation, even though a safety factor of 50% above limit loads is incorporated in the strength of the airplane.

ASTM consensus standards determine similar load limits for light-sport aircraft.

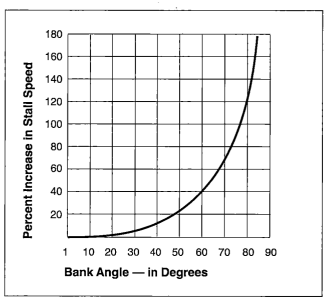

Figure 1-20. Effect of angle of bank on stall speed

AIR, WSC, PPC

3214. (Refer to Figure 2.) If an airplane weighs 2,300 pounds, what approximate weight would the airplane structure be required to support during a 60° banked turn while maintaining altitude?

A— 2,300 pounds.
B— 3,400 pounds.
C— 4,600 pounds.

Referencing FAA Figure 2, use the following steps:

1. *Enter the chart at a 60° angle of bank and proceed upward to the curved reference line. From the point of intersection, move to the left side of the chart and read a load factor of 2 Gs.*

2. *Multiply the aircraft weight by the load factor:*

   2,300 x 2 = 4,600 lbs

Or, working from the table:

   2,300 x 2.0 (load factor) = 4,600 lbs

(PLT309) — FAA-H-8083-25

AIR, WSC, PPC

3215. (Refer to Figure 2.) If an airplane weighs 3,300 pounds, what approximate weight would the airplane structure be required to support during a 30° banked turn while maintaining altitude?

A— 1,200 pounds.
B— 3,100 pounds.
C— 3,960 pounds.

Referencing FAA Figure 2, use the following steps:

1. *Enter the chart at a 30° angle of bank and proceed upward to the curved reference line. From the point of intersection, move to the left side of the chart and read an approximate load factor of 1.2 Gs.*

2. *Multiply the aircraft weight by the load factor:*

   3,300 x 1.2 = 3,960 lbs

Or, working from the table:

   3,300 x 1.154 (load factor) = 3,808 lbs

Answer C is the closest.

(PLT309) — FAA-H-8083-25

Answers (A) and (B) are incorrect because they are less than 3,300 pounds; load factor increases with bank for level flight.

AIR, WSC, PPC

3216. (Refer to Figure 2.) If an airplane weighs 4,500 pounds, what approximate weight would the airplane structure be required to support during a 45° banked turn while maintaining altitude?

A— 4,500 pounds.
B— 6,750 pounds.
C— 7,200 pounds.

Referencing FAA Figure 2, use the following steps:

1. *Enter the chart at a 45° angle of bank and proceed upward to the curved reference line. From the point of intersection, move to the left side of the chart and read a load factor of 1.5 Gs.*

2. *Multiply the aircraft weight by the load factor:*

   4,500 x 1.5 = 6,750 lbs

Or, working from the table:

   4,500 x 1.414 (load factor) = 6,363 lbs

Answer B is the closest.

(PLT309) — FAA-H-8083-25

AIR, WSC

3217. The amount of excess load that can be imposed on the wing of an airplane depends upon the

A— position of the CG.
B— speed of the airplane.
C— abruptness at which the load is applied.

At slow speeds, the maximum available lifting force of the wing is only slightly greater than the amount necessary to support the weight of the airplane. However, at high speeds, the capacity of the elevator controls, or a strong gust, may increase the load factor beyond safe limits. (PLT311) — FAA-H-8083-25

Answer (A) is incorrect because the position of the CG affects the stability of the airplane, but not the total load the wings can support. Answer (C) is incorrect because abrupt control inputs do not limit load.

Answers

| 3214 | [C] | 3215 | [C] | 3216 | [B] | 3217 | [B] |

AIR, WSC, PPC

3218. Which basic flight maneuver increases the load factor on an airplane as compared to straight-and-level flight?

A— Climbs.
B— Turns.
C— Stalls.

A change in speed during straight flight will not produce any appreciable change in load, but when a change is made in the airplane's flight path, an additional load is imposed upon the airplane structure. This is particularly true if a change in direction is made at high speeds with rapid, forceful control movements. (PLT309) — FAA-H-8083-25

Answer (A) is incorrect because the load increases only as the angle of attack is changed, momentarily. Once the climb attitude has been set, the wings only carry the load produced by the weight of the aircraft. Answer (C) is incorrect because in a stall, the wings are not producing lift.

AIR, GLI, WSC, PPC

3301. What force makes an airplane turn?

A— The horizontal component of lift.
B— The vertical component of lift.
C— Centrifugal force.

As the airplane is banked, lift acts horizontally as well as vertically and the airplane is pulled around the turn. (PLT242) — FAA-H-8083-3

Answer (B) is incorrect because the vertical component of lift has no horizontal force to make the airplane turn. Answer (C) is incorrect because the centrifugal force acts against the horizontal component of lift.

AIR, GLI, WSC

3316. During an approach to a stall, an increased load factor will cause the airplane to

A— stall at a higher airspeed.
B— have a tendency to spin.
C— be more difficult to control.

Stall speed increases in proportion to the square root of the load factor. Thus, with a load factor of 4, an aircraft will stall at a speed which is double the normal stall speed. (PLT312) — FAA-H-8083-25

Answer (B) is incorrect because an airplane's tendency to spin does not relate to an increase in load factors. Answer (C) is incorrect because an airplane's stability determines its controllability.

Answers

3218 [B]   3301 [A]   3316 [A]

Maneuvers

Rectangular Course

For best results when planning a **rectangular course**, the flight path should be positioned outside the field boundaries just far enough that they may be easily observed from either pilot seat by looking out the side of the airplane. The closer the track of the airplane is to the field boundaries, the steeper the bank necessary at the turning points. *See* Figure 1-21.

Turns Around a Point

When flying **turns around a point**, the wings will be in alignment with the pylon only during the time the airplane is flying directly upwind or directly downwind. At all other points, a **wind correction angle** will keep the wings from pointing directly at the pylon.

If the student is instructed to not exceed a 45° bank in a turn around a point maneuver, the best place to start is the point where the bank angle will be steepest, which is when flying downwind. Throughout the remainder of the maneuver, the bank will be shallowing out.

The ground speed will be equal where the airplane is flying with the same headwind component. The angle of bank will be the same only where the airplane is flying directly crosswind. *See* Figure 1-22.

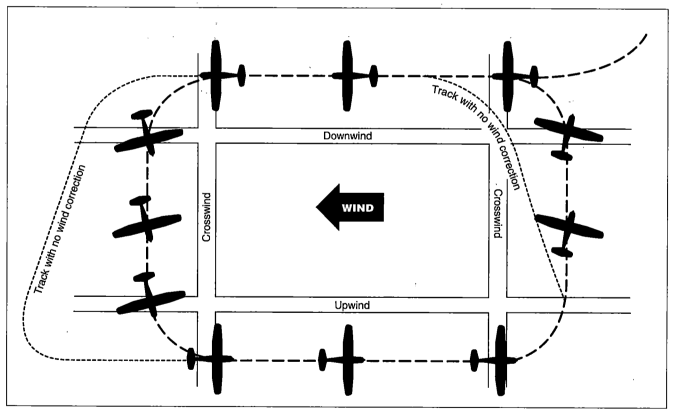

Figure 1-21. Rectangular Course

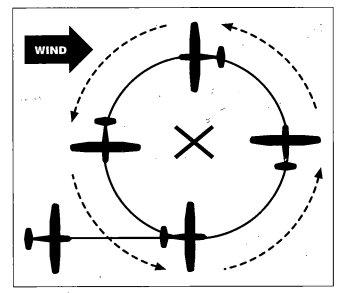

Figure 1-22. Turns around a point

S-Turns

In a steep turn, the ground speed will be the same when the airplane has the same headwind component. The steepest angle of bank is required at the points where the airplane is flying downwind. The airplane will have to be crabbed into the wind the greatest amount where it is flying crosswind.

In the first half of an **S-turn**, the bank should begin shallow and increase in steepness as the airplane turns crosswind, and become steepest where the turn is downwind. If the turn is started with too steep a bank angle, the bank will increase too rapidly and the upwind half of the "S" will be smaller than the downwind half. The turn will not be completed by the time the airplane is over the reference line. *See* Figure 1-23.

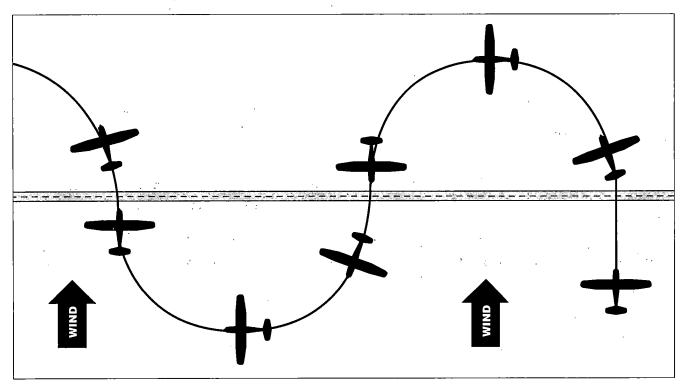

Figure 1-23. S-Turns

ALL, SPO

3202-1. Select the four flight fundamentals involved in maneuvering an aircraft.

A— Aircraft power, pitch, bank, and trim.
B— Starting, taxiing, takeoff, and landing.
C— Straight-and-level flight, turns, climbs, and descents.

The four flight fundamentals involved in maneuvering an aircraft are: straight-and-level flight, turns, climbs, and descents. (PLT219) — FAA-H-8083-3

ALL

3202-2. (Refer to Figure 62.) In flying the rectangular course, when would the aircraft be turned less than 90°?

A— Corners 1 and 4.
B— Corners 1 and 2.
C— Corners 2 and 4.

The airplane will turn less than 90 degrees at corners 1 and 4. At corner 1, the airplane turns to a heading that is crabbed into the wind, which makes the turn less than 90 degrees. At corner 4, the airplane is crabbed into the wind when the turn is started, and the turn will be less than 90 degrees. (PLT219) — FAA-H-8083-3

ALL

3202-3. (Refer to Figure 66.) While practicing S-turns, a consistently smaller half-circle is made on one side of the road than on the other, and this turn is not completed before crossing the road or reference line. This would most likely occur in turn

A— 1-2-3 because the bank is decreased too rapidly during the latter part of the turn.
B— 4-5-6 because the bank is increased too rapidly during the early part of the turn.
C— 4-5-6 because the bank is increased too slowly during the latter part of the turn.

In the half of an S-turn labeled 4-5-6, the bank should begin shallow and increase in steepness as the airplane turns crosswind and become steepest at point 6 where the turn is downwind. If the turn at point 4 is started with too steep a bank angle, the bank will increase too rapidly, and the upwind half of the S will be smaller than the downwind half. The turn will not be completed by the time the airplane is over the reference line. (PLT219) — FAA-H-8083-3

AIR, GLI, WSC, PPC

3202-4. If an emergency situation requires a downwind landing, pilots should expect a faster

A— airspeed at touchdown, a longer ground roll, and better control throughout the landing roll.
B— groundspeed at touchdown, a longer ground roll, and the likelihood of overshooting the desired touchdown point.
C— groundspeed at touchdown, a shorter ground roll, and the likelihood of undershooting the desired touchdown point.

A downwind landing, using the same airspeed as is used on a normal upwind landing, will result in a higher approach ground speed, with the likelihood of overshooting the desired touchdown point. The ground speed at touchdown will be higher than normal, and the ground roll will be longer. (PLT208) — FAA-H-8083-3

Answer (A) is incorrect because the airspeed will be the same, and the control throughout the landing roll will be less due to the higher ground speed. Answer (C) is incorrect because the ground roll will be longer, and there will be a greater likelihood of overshooting the touchdown point.

AIR

3202-5. When executing an emergency approach to land in a single-engine airplane, it is important to maintain a constant glide speed because variations in glide speed

A— increase the chances of shock cooling the engine.
B— assure the proper descent angle is maintained until entering the flare.
C— nullify all attempts at accuracy in judgment of gliding distance and landing spot.

A constant gliding speed should be maintained because variations of gliding speed nullify all attempts at accuracy in judgment of gliding distance and the landing spot. (PLT208) — FAA-H-8083-3

Answers

3202-1   [C]   3202-2   [A]   3202-3   [B]   3202-4   [B]   3202-5   [C]

Stalls and Spins

As the angle of attack is increased (to increase lift), the air will no longer flow smoothly over the upper wing surface but instead will become turbulent or "burble" near the trailing edge. A further increase in the angle of attack will cause the turbulent area to expand forward. At an angle of attack of approximately 18° to 20° (for most wings), turbulence over the upper wing surface decreases lift so drastically that flight can not be sustained and the wing **stalls**. *See* Figure 1-24.

The angle at which a stall occurs is called the **critical angle of attack**. An airplane can stall at any airspeed or any attitude, but will always stall at the same critical angle of attack. The indicated airspeed at which a given airplane will stall in a particular configuration, however, will remain the same regardless of altitude. Because air density decreases with an increase in altitude, the airplane has to be flown faster at higher altitudes to cause the same pressure difference between pitot impact pressure and static pressure.

An aircraft will **spin** only after it has stalled, and will continue to spin as long as the outside wing continues to provide more lift than the inside wing and the aircraft remains stalled.

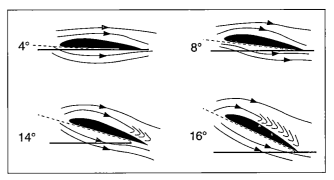

Figure 1-24. Flow of air over wing at various angles of attack

AIR, GLI, WSC, PPC

3263. As altitude increases, the indicated airspeed at which a given airplane stalls in a particular configuration will

A— decrease as the true airspeed decreases.
B— decrease as the true airspeed increases.
C— remain the same regardless of altitude.

An increase in altitude has no effect on the indicated airspeed at which an airplane stalls at altitudes normally used by general aviation aircraft. This means that the same indicated airspeed should be maintained during the landing approach regardless of the elevation or the density altitude at the airport of landing. (PLT477) — FAA-H-8083-25

Answer (A) is incorrect because true airspeed does not decrease with increased altitude, and indicated airspeed at which an airplane stalls does not change. Answer (B) is incorrect because the indicated airspeed of the stall does not decrease with increased altitude.

SPO

2233. The direct cause of every stall is excessive

A— angle of attack.
B— density altitude.
C— upward vertical velocity.

The direct cause of every stall is an excessive angle of attack. There are any number of flight maneuvers that may produce an increase in the angle of attack, but the stall does not occur until the angle of attack becomes excessive. (PLT477) — FAA-H-8083-25

AIR, GLI

3309. In what flight condition must an aircraft be placed in order to spin?

A— Partially stalled with one wing low.
B— In a steep diving spiral.
C— Stalled.

A spin results when a sufficient degree of rolling or yawing control input is imposed on an airplane in the stalled condition. If the wing is not stalled, a spin cannot occur. (PLT245) — FAA-H-8083-3

Answer (A) is incorrect because the aircraft must be at a full stall in order to spin. Answer (B) is incorrect because an airplane is not necessarily stalled when in a steep diving spiral.

Answers

3263   [C]   2233   [A]   3309   [C]

AIR, GLI
3310. During a spin to the left, which wing(s) is/are stalled?

A— Both wings are stalled.
B— Neither wing is stalled.
C— Only the left wing is stalled.

One wing is less stalled than the other, but both wings are stalled in a spin. (PLT245) — FAA-H-8083-3

Answer (B) is incorrect because both wings must be stalled through the spin. Answer (C) is incorrect because both wings are stalled; but the right wing is less fully stalled than the left.

AIR, GLI, WSC, PPC, LSA, LSG, LSW, LSP
3311. The angle of attack at which an airplane wing stalls will

A— increase if the CG is moved forward.
B— change with an increase in gross weight.
C— remain the same regardless of gross weight.

When the angle of attack is increased to between 18° and 20° (critical angle of attack) on most airfoils, the airstream can no longer follow the upper curvature of the wing because of the excessive change in direction. The airplane will stall if the critical angle of attack is exceeded. The indicated airspeed at which stall occurs will be determined by weight and load factor, but the stall angle of attack is the same. (PLT168) — FAA-H-8083-25

Answers (A) and (B) are incorrect because an airplane will always stall at the same angle of attack, regardless of the CG position or gross weight.

Flaps

Extending the flaps increases the wing camber and the angle of attack of a wing. This increases wing lift and also increases induced drag. *See* Figure 1-25.

The increased drag enables the pilot to make steeper approaches to a landing, without an increase in airspeed. VFR approaches to a landing at night should be made the same as during the daytime.

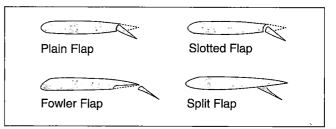

Plain Flap   Slotted Flap

Fowler Flap   Split Flap

Figure 1-25. Use of flaps increases lift and drag

AIR, GLI
3219. One of the main functions of flaps during approach and landing is to

A— decrease the angle of descent without increasing the airspeed.
B— permit a touchdown at a higher indicated airspeed.
C— increase the angle of descent without increasing the airspeed.

Flaps increase drag, allowing the pilot to make steeper approaches without increasing airspeed. (PLT473) — FAA-H-8083-25

Answer (A) is incorrect because extending the flaps increases drag, which enables the pilot to increase the angle of descent without increasing the airspeed. Answer (B) is incorrect because flaps increase lift at slow airspeed, which permits touchdown at a lower indicated airspeed.

AIR, GLI
3220. What is one purpose of wing flaps?

A— To enable the pilot to make steeper approaches to a landing without increasing the airspeed.
B— To relieve the pilot of maintaining continuous pressure on the controls.
C— To decrease wing area to vary the lift.

Flaps increase drag, allowing the pilot to make steeper approaches without increasing airspeed. (PLT473) — FAA-H-8083-25

Answer (B) is incorrect because trim tabs help relieve control pressures. Answer (C) is incorrect because wing area usually remains the same, except for certain specialized flaps which increase the wing area.

Answers

| 3310 | [A] | 3311 | [C] | 3219 | [C] | 3220 | [A] |

Ground Effect

Ground effect occurs when flying within one wingspan or less above the surface. The airflow around the wing and wing tips is modified and the resulting pattern reduces the downwash and the induced drag. These changes can result in an aircraft becoming airborne before reaching recommended takeoff speed or floating during an approach to land. *See* Figure 1-26.

An airplane leaving ground effect after takeoff will require an increase in angle of attack to maintain the same lift coefficient, which in turn will cause an increase in induced drag and therefore, require increased thrust.

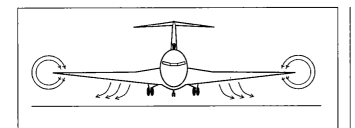

Figure 1-26. Ground effect phenomenon

ALL

3315. Ground effect is most likely to result in which problem?

A— Settling to the surface abruptly during landing.
B— Becoming airborne before reaching recommended takeoff speed.
C— Inability to get airborne even though airspeed is sufficient for normal takeoff needs.

Due to the reduced drag in ground effect, the airplane may seem capable of takeoff well below the recommended speed. It is important that no attempt be made to force the airplane to become airborne with a deficiency of speed. The recommended takeoff speed is necessary to provide adequate initial climb performance. (PLT131) — FAA-H-8083-25

Answer (A) is incorrect because the airplane gains lift from a reduction in induced drag while entering ground effect; therefore, it does not cause the airplane to settle abruptly. Answer (C) is incorrect because ground effect helps the airplane become airborne before the airspeed is sufficient for a normal takeoff.

AIR, GLI, RTC, WSC, PPC, LSA, LSR, LSG, LSW
3312. What is ground effect?

A— The result of the interference of the surface of the Earth with the airflow patterns about an airplane.
B— The result of an alteration in airflow patterns increasing induced drag about the wings of an airplane.
C— The result of the disruption of the airflow patterns about the wings of an airplane to the point where the wings will no longer support the airplane in flight.

Ground effect is the result of the interference of the surface of the Earth with the airflow patterns about an airplane. (PLT131) — FAA-H-8083-25

Answer (B) is incorrect because induced drag is decreased. Answer (C) is incorrect because the disruption of wing-tip vortices increases lift.

AIR, GLI, RTC, WSC, PPC
3313. Floating caused by the phenomenon of ground effect will be most realized during an approach to land when at

A— less than the length of the wingspan above the surface.
B— twice the length of the wingspan above the surface.
C— a higher-than-normal angle of attack.

When the wing is at a height equal to its span, the reduction in induced drag is only 1.4%. However, when the wing is at a height equal to one-fourth its span, the reduction in induced drag is 23.5% and when the wing is at a height equal to one-tenth its span, the reduction in induced drag is 47.6%. (PLT131) — FAA-H-8083-25

Answer (B) is incorrect because ground effect extends up to one wingspan length. Answer (C) is incorrect because floating will result from higher-than-normal angle of attack.

Answers
3315 [B]   3312 [A]   3313 [A]

AIR, GLI, RTC, WSC, LSA, LSG, LSR, LSW
3314. What must a pilot be aware of as a result of ground effect?

A— Wingtip vortices increase creating wake turbulence problems for arriving and departing aircraft.
B— Induced drag decreases; therefore, any excess speed at the point of flare may cause considerable floating.
C— A full stall landing will require less up elevator deflection than would a full stall when done free of ground effect.

The reduction of the wing-tip vortices, due to ground effect, alters the spanwise lift distribution and reduces the induced angle of attack, and induced drag causing floating. (PLT131) — FAA-H-8083-25

Answer (A) is incorrect because wing-tip vortices are decreased. Answer (C) is incorrect because a full stall landing will require more up-elevator deflection, due to the increased lift in ground effect.

RTC
3324. Which is a result of the phenomenon of ground effect?

A— The induced angle of attack of each rotor blade is increased.
B— The lift vector becomes more horizontal.
C— The angle of attack generating lift is increased.

In ground effect, as downwash velocity is reduced, the induced angle of attack is reduced and the lift vector becomes more vertical. Simultaneously, a reduction in induced drag occurs. In addition, as the induced angle of attack is reduced, the angle of attack generating lift is increased. The net result of these actions is a beneficial increase in lift and a lower power requirement to support a given weight. (PLT131) — FAA-H-8083-21

Answer (A) is incorrect because the induced angle of attack isn't described in the first place so we can't assume a change. Answer (B) is incorrect because if lift vector became more horizontal, lift would decrease but thrust would increase in the lateral direction.

RTC
3735. (Refer to Figure 46.) The airspeed range to avoid while flying in ground effect is

A— 25 – 40 MPH.
B— 25 – 57 MPH.
C— 40 MPH and above.

Use the following steps:

1. *Locate the ground effect unsafe area on FAA Figure 46.*
2. *Note that the ground effect altitude in the forward flight region is 40 feet.*
3. *The diagram depicts that a pilot should avoid flight of 40 MPH or greater at altitudes lower than 40 feet.*

(PLT285) — FAA-H-8083-21

LSA, LSR, LSG, LSW
2223-2. An aircraft leaving ground effect during takeoff will

A— experience a reduction in ground friction and require a slight power reduction.
B— experience an increase in induced drag and a decrease in performance.
C— require a lower angle of attack to maintain the same lift coefficient.

An airplane leaving ground effect will:

1. *Require an increase in angle of attack to maintain the same lift coefficient.*
2. *Experience an increase in induced drag and thrust required.*
3. *Experience a decrease in stability and a nose-up change in moments.*
4. *Produce a reduction in static source pressure and an increase in indicated airspeed.*

(PLT131) — FAA-H-8083-25

Answers
3314 [B]   3324 [C]   3735 [C]   2223-2 [B]

Wake Turbulence

All aircraft leave two types of **wake turbulence**: Prop or jet blast, and wing-tip vortices.

The prop or jet blast could be hazardous to light aircraft on the ground behind large aircraft which are either taxiing or running-up their engines. In the air, jet or prop blast dissipates rapidly.

Wing-tip vortices are a by-product of lift. When a wing is flown at a positive angle of attack, a pressure differential is created between the upper and lower wing surfaces, and the pressure above the wing will be lower than the pressure below the wing. In attempting to equalize the pressure, air moves outward, upward, and around the wing tip, setting up a **vortex** which trails behind each wing. *See* Figure 1-27.

The strength of a vortex is governed by the weight, speed, and the shape of the wing of the generating aircraft. Maximum vortex strength occurs when the generating aircraft is heavy, clean, and slow.

Vortices generated by large aircraft in flight tend to sink below the flight path of the generating aircraft. A pilot should fly at or above the larger aircraft's flight path in order to avoid the wake turbulence created by the wing-tip vortices. *See* Figure 1-28.

Close to the ground, vortices tend to move laterally. A crosswind will tend to hold the upwind vortex over the landing runway, while a tailwind may move the vortices of a preceding aircraft forward into the touchdown zone.

To avoid wake turbulence when landing, a pilot should note the point where a preceding large aircraft touched down and then land past that point. *See* Figure 1-29.

On takeoff, lift off should be accomplished prior to reaching the rotation point of a preceding large aircraft; the flight path should then remain upwind and above the preceding aircraft's flight path. *See* Figure 1-30.

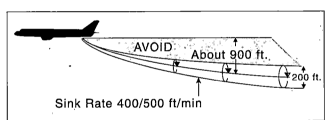

Figure 1-28. Vortices in cruise flight

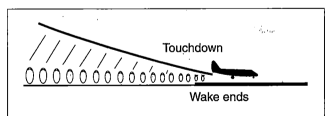

Figure 1-29. Touchdown and wake end

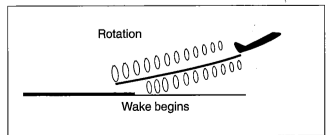

Figure 1-30. Rotation and wake beginning

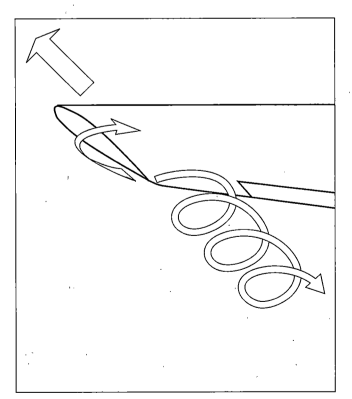

Figure 1-27. Wing-tip vortices

ALL

3829-2. When landing behind a large aircraft, which procedure should be followed for vortex avoidance?

A— Stay above its final approach flightpath all the way to touchdown.
B— Stay below and to one side of its final approach flightpath.
C— Stay well below its final approach flightpath and land at least 2,000 feet behind.

When landing behind a large aircraft, stay at or above the large aircraft's final approach path. Note its touchdown point and land beyond it. (PLT509) — FAA-H-8083-25

ALL

3829-3. How does the wake turbulence vortex circulate around each wingtip?

A— Inward, upward, and around each tip.
B— Inward, upward, and counterclockwise.
C— Outward, upward, and around each tip.

The vortex circulation is outward, upward, and around the wing tips when viewed from either ahead or behind the aircraft. (PLT509) — AIM ¶7-3-4

ALL

3827. When taking off or landing at an airport where heavy aircraft are operating, one should be particularly alert to the hazards of wingtip vortices because this turbulence tends to

A— rise from a crossing runway into the takeoff or landing path.
B— rise into the traffic pattern area surrounding the airport.
C— sink into the flightpath of aircraft operating below the aircraft generating the turbulence.

Flight tests have shown that the vortices from large aircraft sink at a rate of about 400 to 500 feet per minute. They tend to level off at a distance about 900 feet below the path of the generating aircraft. (PLT509) — FAA-H-8083-25

Answer (A) is incorrect because wing-tip vortices always trail behind an airplane and descend toward the ground; they will also drift with the wind. Answer (B) is incorrect because wing-tip vortices descend.

ALL, SPO

3824. Wingtip vortices are created only when an aircraft is

A— operating at high airspeeds.
B— heavily loaded.
C— developing lift.

Lift is generated by the creation of a pressure differential over the wing surface. The lowest pressure occurs over the wing surface and the highest pressure occurs under the wing. This pressure differential triggers the roll up of the airflow aft of the wing, resulting in wing-tip vortices. Vortices are generated from the moment an aircraft leaves the ground, since trailing vortices are a by-product of wing lift. (PLT509) — FAA-H-8083-25

Answer (A) is incorrect because the greatest turbulence is produced from an airplane developing lift at a slow airspeed. Answer (B) is incorrect because even though a heavily loaded airplane may produce greater turbulence, an airplane does not have to be heavily loaded in order to produce wing-tip vortices.

ALL, SPO

3825. The greatest vortex strength occurs when the generating aircraft is

A— light, dirty, and fast.
B— heavy, dirty, and fast.
C— heavy, clean, and slow.

The strength of the vortex is governed by the weight, speed, and shape of the wing of the generating aircraft. The greatest vortex strength occurs when the generating aircraft is heavy, clean and slow. (PLT509) — FAA-H-8083-25

Answer (A) is incorrect because light aircraft produce less vortex turbulence than heavy aircraft. Answer (B) is incorrect because in order to be fast, the wing tip must be at a lower angle of attack, thus producing less lift than during climbout. Also, being dirty presents less of a danger than when clean and/or slow.

ALL, SPO

3826. Wingtip vortices created by large aircraft tend to

A— sink below the aircraft generating turbulence.
B— rise into the traffic pattern.
C— rise into the takeoff or landing path of a crossing runway.

Flight tests have shown that the vortices from large aircraft sink at a rate of about 400 to 500 feet per minute. They tend to level off at a distance about 900 feet below the path of the generating aircraft. (PLT509) — FAA-H-8083-25

Answers (B) and (C) are incorrect because wing-tip vortices sink toward the ground; however, they may move horizontally depending on crosswind conditions.

Answers

3829-2 [A]	3829-3 [C]	3827 [C]	3824 [C]	3825 [C]	3826 [A]

ALL

3828. The wind condition that requires maximum caution when avoiding wake turbulence on landing is a

A— light, quartering headwind.
B— light, quartering tailwind.
C— strong headwind.

A tailwind condition can move the vortices of a preceding aircraft forward into the touchdown zone. A light quartering tailwind requires maximum caution. Pilots should be alert to large aircraft upwind from their approach and takeoff flight paths. (PLT509) — FAA-H-8083-25

Answer (A) is incorrect because headwinds push the vortices out of the touchdown zone when landing beyond the touchdown point of the preceding aircraft. Answer (C) is incorrect because strong winds help diffuse wake turbulence vortices.

ALL, SPO

3829. When landing behind a large aircraft, the pilot should avoid wake turbulence by staying

A— above the large aircraft's final approach path and landing beyond the large aircraft's touchdown point.
B— below the large aircraft's final approach path and landing before the large aircraft's touchdown point.
C— above the large aircraft's final approach path and landing before the large aircraft's touchdown point.

When landing behind a large aircraft stay at or above the large aircraft's final approach path. Note its touchdown point and land beyond it. (PLT509) — FAA-H-8083-25

Answer (B) is incorrect because below the flight path, you will fly into the sinking vortices generated by the large aircraft. Answer (C) is incorrect because by landing before the large aircraft's touchdown point, you will have to fly below the preceding aircraft's flight path, and into the vortices.

ALL

3830. When departing behind a heavy aircraft, the pilot should avoid wake turbulence by maneuvering the aircraft

A— below and downwind from the heavy aircraft.
B— above and upwind from the heavy aircraft.
C— below and upwind from the heavy aircraft.

When departing behind a large aircraft, note the large aircraft's rotation point, rotate prior to it, continue to climb above it, and request permission to deviate upwind of the large aircraft's climb path until turning clear of the aircraft's wake. (PLT509) — FAA-H-8083-25

SPO

2039. What wind condition prolongs the hazards of wake turbulence on a landing runway for the longest period of time?

A— Light quartering headwind.
B— Direct tailwind.
C— Light quartering tailwind.

A light wind with a cross runway component of 1 to 5 knots could result in the upwind vortex remaining in the touchdown zone for a period of time and hasten the drift of the downwind vortex toward another runway. Similarly, a tailwind condition can move the vortices of the preceding aircraft forward into the touchdown zone. The light quartering tailwind requires maximum caution. (PLT509) — AIM ¶7-3-4

SPO

2234-1. A go-around from a poor landing approach

A— should not be attempted unless circumstances make it absolutely necessary.
B— is preferable to last minute attempts to prevent a bad landing.
C— should not be attempted after the landing flare has been initiated regardless of airspeed.

It is safer to make a go-around than to touch down while drifting or while in a crab, or make a hard drop-in landing from a high round-out or a bounced landing. (PLT170) — FAA-H-8083-3

Answer (A) is incorrect because a go-around should be executed whenever unfavorable conditions exist. Answer (C) is incorrect because the go-around can be started at any time in the landing process.

Answers

3828 [B]   3829 [A]   3830 [B]   2039 [C]   2234-1 [B]

Chapter 2
Aircraft Systems

Reciprocating Engines

Most small airplanes are powered by **reciprocating** ("recip") **engines** made up, in part, of cylinders, pistons, connecting rods and a crankshaft. The pistons move back and forth within the cylinders. Connecting rods connect the pistons to the crankshaft, which converts the back and forth movements of the pistons to a rotary motion. It is this rotary motion which drives the propeller.

One cycle of the engine consists of two revolutions of the crankshaft. These two crankshaft revolutions require four strokes of the piston; namely, the **intake, compression, power**, and **exhaust** strokes.

The top end of the cylinder houses an intake valve, an exhaust valve, and two spark plugs.

During the intake stroke, the intake valve is open and the piston moves away from the top of the cylinder and draws in an air/fuel mixture (Figure 2-1A).

At the completion of the intake stroke, the intake valve closes and the piston returns to the top of the cylinder and compresses the air/fuel mixture (Figure 2-1B).

When the piston reaches a precise point near the top of its stroke, the spark plugs ignite the compressed mixture and the rapid expansion of the burning mixture forces the piston downward (Figure 2-1C).

As the piston completes the downward movement of the power stroke, the exhaust valve opens and the piston rises to the top of the cylinder. This exhaust stroke forces out the burned gases and completes one cycle of the engine (Figure 2-1D).

Because of the many moving parts in a reciprocating engine, as soon as the engine is started, power should be set to the RPM recommended for engine warm-up and the engine gauges checked for the desired indications.

Should it be necessary to start the engine by "**hand propping**," it is extremely important that a competent pilot be at the controls in the cockpit. In addition, the person turning the propeller should be thoroughly familiar with the procedure.

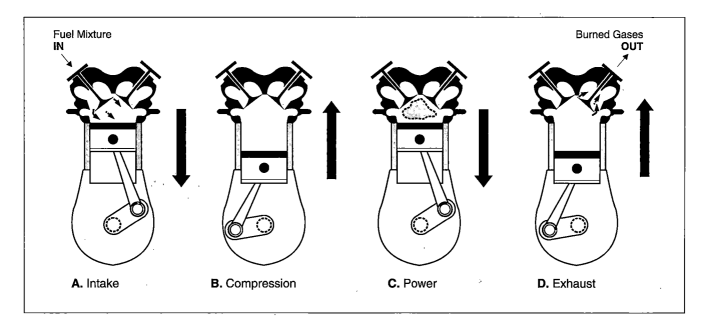

Figure 2-1. Four strokes of an internal combustion engine

AIR

3657. Should it become necessary to handprop an airplane engine, it is extremely important that a competent pilot

A— call "contact" before touching the propeller.
B— be at the controls in the cockpit.
C— be in the cockpit and call out all commands.

Because of the hazards involved in hand-starting airplane engines, it is extremely important that a competent pilot be at the controls in the cockpit and that all communications and procedures be agreed upon and rehearsed beforehand. (PLT479) — FAA-H-8083-25

Answer (A) is incorrect because the person propping the engine is not required to be a pilot, and calling "contact" is not required. Answer (C) is incorrect because a pilot must be in control of the aircraft, not only in the cockpit. Also, the person propping the engine calls out the commands.

AIR, RTC, WSC, PPC

3656. What should be the first action after starting an aircraft engine?

A— Adjust for proper RPM and check for desired indications on the engine gauges.
B— Place the magneto or ignition switch momentarily in the OFF position to check for proper grounding.
C— Test each brake and the parking brake.

As soon as the engine starts, check for unintentional movement of the aircraft and set power to the recommended warm-up RPM. The oil pressure should then be checked to determine that the oil system is functioning properly with pressure at recommended levels within the manufacturer's time limit. (PLT343) — FAA-H-8083-25

Answer (B) is incorrect because this is usually done at the end of the flight. Answer (C) is incorrect because brakes are checked when beginning to taxi.

AIR, RTC, WSC, PPC

3656-1. What is one purpose for using reciprocating engines?

A— Heat is distributed better.
B— To preserve cylinder head duration and maintain lower temperatures.
C— They are relatively simple and inexpensive to operate.

Most training aircraft use reciprocating engines because they are relatively simple and inexpensive to operate. (PLT141) — FAA-H-8083-25

Ignition and Electrical Systems

Most reciprocating engines used to power small aircraft incorporate two separate magneto ignition systems.

A **magneto** ("mag") is a self-contained source of electrical energy, so even if an aircraft loses total electrical power, the engine will continue to run.

When checking for magneto operation prior to flight, the engine should run smoothly when operating with the magneto selector set on "BOTH," and should experience a slight drop in revolutions per minute (RPM) when running on only one or the other magneto.

The main advantages of the dual ignition system are increased safety and improved engine performance.

AIR, WSC, PPC, LSA, LSR, LSW, LSP

3223. One purpose of the dual ignition system on an aircraft engine is to provide for

A— improved engine performance.
B— uniform heat distribution.
C— balanced cylinder head pressure.

The dual ignition system has two magnetos to supply the electrical current to two spark plugs for each combustion chamber. This provides both a redundancy of ignition and an improvement of engine performance. (PLT478) — FAA-H-8083-25

Answer (B) is incorrect because heat distribution is not affected by the ignition system. Answer (C) is incorrect because cylinder head pressure in not affected by the ignition system.

Answers

3657 [B]	3656 [A]	3656-1 [C]	3223 [A]

AIR, RTC, WSC, PPC, LSA, LSR, LSW, LSP

3223-1. An electrical system failure (battery and alternator) occurs during flight. In this situation, you would

A— experience avionics equipment failure.

B— probably experience failure of the engine ignition system, fuel gauges, aircraft lighting system, and avionics equipment.

C— probably experience engine failure due to the loss of the engine-driven fuel pump and also experience failure of the radio equipment, lights, and all instruments that require alternating current.

If you experience an inflight electrical system failure, you have an avionics equipment failure and cannot use your electrical fuel boost pump. (PLT208) — FAA-H-8083-25

Answer (B) is incorrect because the ignition system of an aircraft reciprocating engine is powered by two self-contained magnetos that are not dependent upon the aircraft electrical system. Answer (C) is incorrect because the engine-driven fuel pumps are mechanical and not dependent on the electrical system.

AIR, RTC, WSC, PPC

3223-2. If the ground wire between the magneto and the ignition switch becomes disconnected, the most noticeable result will be that the engine

A— will run very rough.

B— cannot be started with the switch in the ON position.

C— cannot be shut down by turning the switch to the OFF position.

If the ground wire between a magneto and the ignition switch becomes disconnected, the primary current cannot be directed to ground, and the engine cannot be shut down by turning the switch to the OFF position. (PLT478) — FAA-H-8083-25

LSA, LSR, LSW, LSP

2242. One purpose of the dual ignition system on a two-cycle engine is to provide for

A— system redundancy in the ignition system.

B— uniform heat distribution.

C— balanced cylinder head pressure.

The dual ignition system has two magnetos to supply the electrical current to two spark plugs for each combustion chamber. This provides both a redundancy of ignition and an improvement of engine performance. (PLT478) — FAA-H-8083-25

LSA, LSR, LSW, LSP

2238. An electrical system failure (battery and alternator) occurs in a magneto equipped aircraft during flight. In this situation, you would

A— probably experience engine failure due to the loss of the engine-driven fuel pump and also experience failure of the radio equipment, lights, and all instruments that require alternating current.

B— probably experience failure of the engine ignition system, fuel gauges, aircraft lighting system, and avionics equipment.

C— experience avionics equipment failure.

If you experience an inflight electrical system failure, you have an avionics equipment failure and cannot use your electrical fuel boost pump. (PLT207) — FAA-H-8083-25

Answer (A) is incorrect because the engine-driven fuel pumps are mechanical and not dependent on the electrical system. Answer (B) is incorrect because the ignition system of an aircraft reciprocating engine is powered by two self-contained magnetos that are not dependent upon the aircraft electrical system.

LSA, LSR, LSW, LSP

2364. Concerning the advantages of an aircraft generator or alternator, select the true statement.

A— A generator always provides more electrical current than an alternator.

B— An alternator provides more electrical power at lower engine RPM than a generator.

C— A generator charges the battery during low engine RPM; therefore, the battery has less chance to become fully discharged, as often occurs with an alternator.

One of the basic differences between a generator and an alternator used on an aircraft engine is the number of magnetic poles used to produce the electricity. Generators normally have 2 or 4 poles, while alternators have between 8 and 14 poles. Because of the greater number of poles, an alternator can provide more electrical power at a lower engine RPM than a generator. (PLT207) — FAA-H-8083-25

Answers

3223-1 [A]	3223-2 [C]	2242 [A]	2238 [C]	2364 [B]

Fuel Induction Systems

Most light airplane engines use either a carburetor or a fuel injection system to deliver an **air/fuel mixture** to the cylinders.

In a **carburetor induction system**, the float-type carburetor takes in air that flows through a restriction (venturi), which creates a low-pressure area. The pressure difference between the low-pressure area and outside air forces fuel into the airstream where it is mixed with the flowing air, drawn through an intake manifold, and delivered to the combustion chambers and ignited.

Carburetors are normally set to deliver the correct air/fuel mixture at sea level. Since air density decreases with altitude, a mixture control allows the pilot to decrease the fuel flow as altitude increases and thus maintain the correct mixture. Otherwise the mixture may become too "rich" at high altitudes.

When descending, air density increases. Unless fuel flow is increased, the mixture may become excessively "lean," i.e., the amount of fuel is too small for the amount of air reaching the cylinders. Modern 4-stroke engines may automatically adjust the mixture control. Two-stroke engines typically require main jet changes for operations at different altitudes.

In a **fuel injection system** the fuel and air are mixed just prior to entering the combustion chamber. No carburetor is used.

AIR, RTC, WSC, PPC

3225. The operating principle of float-type carburetors is based on the

A— automatic metering of air at the venturi as the aircraft gains altitude.
B— difference in air pressure at the venturi throat and the air inlet.
C— increase in air velocity in the throat of a venturi causing an increase in air pressure.

In a carburetor system, outside air flows into the carburetor and through a venturi (a narrow throat in the carburetor). When air flows rapidly through the venturi, a low pressure area is created. This low pressure allows the fuel to flow through the main fuel jet (located within the throat) and into the airstream where it mixes with the flowing air. (PLT191) — FAA-H-8083-25

Answer (A) is incorrect because fuel, rather than air, is metered manually with the mixture control. Answer (C) is incorrect because there is a decrease in air pressure.

AIR, RTC, WSC, PPC
3226. The basic purpose of adjusting the fuel/air mixture at altitude is to

A— decrease the amount of fuel in the mixture in order to compensate for increased air density.
B— decrease the fuel flow in order to compensate for decreased air density.
C— increase the amount of fuel in the mixture to compensate for the decrease in pressure and density of the air.

The mixture becomes richer as the airplane gains altitude, because the carburetor meters the same amount of fuel as at sea level. Leaning the mixture control prevents this by decreasing the rate of fuel discharge to compensate for the decrease in air density. (PLT249) — FAA-H-8083-25

Answer (A) is incorrect because the pilot would increase the amount of fuel to compensate for increased air density. Answer (C) is incorrect because the pilot would decrease the amount of fuel to compensate for decreased air density.

AIR, RTC, WSC, PPC
3228. While cruising at 9,500 feet MSL, the fuel/air mixture is properly adjusted. What will occur if a descent to 4,500 feet MSL is made without readjusting the mixture?

A— The fuel/air mixture may become excessively lean.
B— There will be more fuel in the cylinders than is needed for normal combustion, and the excess fuel will absorb heat and cool the engine.
C— The excessively rich mixture will create higher cylinder head temperatures and may cause detonation.

Air density increases in the descent, but the amount of fuel drawn into the carburetor remains the same. To re-establish a balanced fuel/air mixture in a descent, the mixture control must be adjusted toward "rich." (PLT249) — FAA-H-8083-25

Answer (B) is incorrect because the mixture will become too lean and the engine temperature will increase. Answer (C) is incorrect because an excessively lean mixture will result.

Answers

| 3225 | [B] | 3226 | [B] | 3228 | [A] |

Carburetor Ice

As air flows through a carburetor it expands rapidly. At the same time, fuel forced into the airstream is vaporized. Expansion of the air and vaporization of the fuel causes a sudden cooling of the mixture which may cause ice to form inside the carburetor. The possibility of icing should always be considered when operating in conditions where the temperature is between 20°F and 70°F, and the relative humidity is high.

Carburetor heat preheats the air before it enters the carburetor and either prevents carburetor ice from forming or melts any ice which may have formed. When carburetor heat is applied, the heated air that enters the carburetor is less dense. This causes the fuel/air mixture to become enriched, and this in turn decreases engine output and increases engine operating temperatures.

During engine runup prior to departure from a high-altitude airport, the pilot may notice a slight engine roughness which is not affected by the magneto check, but grows worse during the carburetor heat check. In this case, the air/fuel mixture may be too rich due to the lower air density at the high altitude, and applying carburetor heat decreases the air density even more. A leaner setting of the mixture control may correct this problem.

In an airplane with a fixed-pitch propeller, the first indication of carburetor ice would likely be a decrease in RPM as the air supply is choked off. Application of carburetor heat will decrease air density, causing the RPM to drop even lower. Then, as the carburetor ice melts, the RPM will rise gradually.

Fuel injection systems do not utilize a carburetor and are generally considered to be less susceptible to icing than carburetor systems are.

AIR

3227. During the run-up at a high-elevation airport, a pilot notes a slight engine roughness that is not affected by the magneto check but grows worse during the carburetor heat check. Under these circumstances, what would be the most logical initial action?

A— Check the results obtained with a leaner setting of the mixture.
B— Taxi back to the flight line for a maintenance check.
C— Reduce manifold pressure to control detonation.

When carburetor heat is applied, the air/fuel mixture of an engine will be enriched because any given volume of hot air is less dense than cold air of the same volume. This condition would be aggravated at high altitude where, because of decreased air density, the mixture is already richer than at sea level. (PLT253) — FAA-H-8083-25

Answer (B) is incorrect because the pilot should taxi back only if positive results were not obtained by leaning the mixture. Answer (C) is incorrect because detonation would not occur if the mixture was too rich, and a rich fuel mixture was the condition described in the question.

AIR, WSC, PPC

3231. If an aircraft is equipped with a fixed-pitch propeller and a float-type carburetor, the first indication of carburetor ice would most likely be

A— increase of RPM.
B— engine roughness.
C— loss of RPM.

For airplanes with a fixed-pitch propeller, the first indication of carburetor ice is loss of RPM. (PLT190) — FAA-H-8083-25

Answer (A) is incorrect because the RPM will decrease, not increase. Answer (B) is incorrect because this symptoms may develop, but only after a loss of RPM.

Answers

3227 [A]   3231 [C]

AIR, WSC, PPC

3235. The presence of carburetor ice in an aircraft equipped with a fixed-pitch propeller can be verified by applying carburetor heat and noting

A— an increase in RPM and then a gradual decrease in RPM.

B— a decrease in RPM and then a constant RPM indication.

C— a decrease in RPM and then a gradual increase in RPM.

When heat is applied there will be a drop in RPM in airplanes equipped with fixed-pitch propellers. If carburetor ice is present, there will normally be a rise in RPM after the initial drop. Then, when the carburetor heat is turned off, the RPM will rise to a setting greater than that before application of the heat. The engine should also run more smoothly after the ice has been removed. (PLT190) — FAA-H-8083-25

Answer (A) is incorrect because the warm air decreases engine RPM; melting ice also decreases RPM. Once the ice is gone, the RPM increases. Answer (B) is incorrect because this would happen if there was no carburetor ice to begin with.

AIR, RTC, WSC, PPC

3229. Which condition is most favorable to the development of carburetor icing?

A— Any temperature below freezing and a relative humidity of less than 50 percent.

B— Temperature between 32 and 50°F and low humidity.

C— Temperature between 20 and 70°F and high humidity.

If the temperature is between -7°C (20°F) and 21°C (70°F) with visible moisture or high humidity, the pilot should be constantly on the alert for carburetor ice. (PLT190) — FAA-H-8083-25

Answers (A) and (B) are incorrect because carburetor icing is more likely with high humidity.

AIR, RTC, WSC, PPC

3230. The possibility of carburetor icing exists even when the ambient air temperature is as

A— high as 70°F and the relative humidity is high.

B— high as 95°F and there is visible moisture.

C— low as 0°F and the relative humidity is high.

If the temperature is between -7°C (20°F) and 21°C (70°F) with visible moisture or high humidity, the pilot should be constantly on the alert for carburetor ice. (PLT253) — FAA-H-8083-25

Answer (B) is incorrect because icing is less likely to occur above 70°F. Answer (C) is incorrect because icing is less likely to occur below 20°F.

AIR, RTC, WSC, PPC

3230-1. Carburetor icing can occur with an OAT as high as

A— 100°F and visible moisture.

B— 20°C and high relative humidity.

C— 75°F and low relative humidity.

If the temperature is between –7°C (20°F) and 21°C (70°F), with visible moisture or high humidity, the pilot should constantly be on the alert for carburetor ice. (PLT253) — FAA-H-8083-25

AIR, RTC, WSC, PPC

3232. Applying carburetor heat will

A— result in more air going through the carburetor.

B— enrich the fuel/air mixture.

C— not affect the fuel/air mixture.

Carburetors are normally calibrated at sea level pressure to meter the correct fuel/air mixture. As altitude increases, air density decreases and the amount of fuel is too great for the amount of air — the mixture is "too rich." This same result may be brought about by the application of carburetor heat. The heated air entering the carburetor has less density than unheated air and the fuel/air mixture is enriched. (PLT189) — FAA-H-8083-25

Answer (A) is incorrect because applying carburetor heat decreases the density of air but does not affect the air going through the carburetor. Answer (C) is incorrect because the mixture is enriched by applying carburetor heat.

Answers

3235 [C]	3229 [C]	3230 [A]	3230-1 [B]	3232 [B]

AIR, RTC, WSC, PPC
3233. What change occurs in the fuel/air mixture when carburetor heat is applied?

A— A decrease in RPM results from the lean mixture.
B— The fuel/air mixture becomes richer.
C— The fuel/air mixture becomes leaner.

Carburetors are normally calibrated at sea level pressure to meter the correct fuel/air mixture. As altitude increases, air density decreases and the amount of fuel is too great for the amount of air—the mixture is "too rich." This same result may be brought about by the application of carburetor heat. The heated air entering the carburetor has less density than unheated air and the fuel/air mixture is enriched. (PLT253) — FAA-H-8083-25

Answers (A) and (C) are incorrect because the fuel/air mixture becomes richer.

AIR, RTC, WSC, PPC
3234. Generally speaking, the use of carburetor heat tends to

A— decrease engine performance.
B— increase engine performance.
C— have no effect on engine performance.

Use of carburetor heat tends to reduce the output of the engine and also to increase the operating temperature. (PLT189) — FAA-H-8083-25

AIR, RTC, WSC, PPC
3236. With regard to carburetor ice, float-type carburetor systems in comparison to fuel injection systems are generally considered to be

A— more susceptible to icing.
B— equally susceptible to icing.
C— less susceptible to icing.

Fuel injection systems are less susceptible to icing than carburetor systems because of the lack of the temperature drop caused by the venturi in a carburetor. Be aware that one can acquire carburetor ice even without easily visible moisture and, in the right circumstances, even at full power. (PLT136) — FAA-H-8083-25

Answers (B) and (C) are incorrect because the venturi throat of carburetors makes them more susceptible to icing than fuel injection systems.

LSA, LSR, LSW, LSP
2341. Which condition is most favorable to the development of carburetor icing?

A— Any temperature below freezing and a relative humidity of less than 50 percent.
B— Temperature between 32 and 50°F and low humidity.
C— Temperature between 20 and 70°F and high humidity.

If the temperature is between -7°C (20°F) and 21°C (70°F) with visible moisture or high humidity, the pilot should be constantly on the alert for carburetor ice. (PLT190) — FAA-H-8083-25

Answer (A) is incorrect because carburetor icing is more likely with high humidity. Answer (B) is incorrect because carburetor icing is more likely with high humidity.

Aviation Fuel

Fuel does two things for the engine; it acts both as an agent for combustion and as an agent for cooling (based on the mixture setting of the engine).

Aviation fuel is available in several grades. The proper grade for a specific engine will be listed in the aircraft flight manual. If the proper grade of fuel is not available, it is possible to use the next higher grade. A lower grade of fuel should never be used.

The use of low-grade fuel or an air/fuel mixture which is too lean may cause **detonation**, which is the uncontrolled spontaneous explosion of the mixture in the cylinder. Detonation produces extreme heat.

Preignition is the premature burning of the air/fuel mixture. It is caused by an incandescent area (such as a carbon or lead deposit heated to a red hot glow) which serves as an ignitor in advance of normal ignition.

Fuel can be contaminated by water and/or dirt. The air inside the aircraft fuel tanks can cool at night, and this cooling forms water droplets (through condensation) on the insides of the fuel tanks. These droplets then fall into the fuel. To avoid this problem, always fill the tanks completely when parking overnight.

Thoroughly drain all of the aircraft's sumps, drains, and strainers before a flight to get rid of all the water that might have collected.

Dirt can get into the fuel if refueling equipment is poorly maintained or if the refueling operation is sloppy. Use care when refueling an aircraft.

Two fuel pump systems are used on most airplanes. The main pump system is engine driven and an auxiliary electric driven pump is provided for use in the event the engine pump fails. The auxiliary pump,

commonly known as the "boost pump," provides added reliability to the fuel system, and is also used as an aid in engine starting. The electric auxiliary pump is controlled by a switch in the cockpit.

AIR, WSC, PPC, LSA, LSR, LSW, LSP

3224. On aircraft equipped with fuel pumps, when is the auxiliary electric driven pump used?

A— All the time to aid the engine-driven fuel pump.
B— In the event engine-driven fuel pump fails.
C— Constantly except in starting the engine.

Two fuel pump systems are used on most airplanes. The main pump system is engine driven and an auxiliary electric driven pump is provided for use in the event the engine pump fails. The auxiliary pump, commonly known as the "boost pump," provides added reliability to the fuel system, and is also used as an aid in engine starting. The electric auxiliary pump is controlled by a switch in the cockpit. (PLT253) — FAA-H-8083-25

AIR, RTC, WSC, PPC

3237. If the grade of fuel used in an aircraft engine is lower than specified for the engine, it will most likely cause

A— a mixture of fuel and air that is not uniform in all cylinders.
B— lower cylinder head temperatures.
C— detonation.

Using fuel of a lower rating is harmful under any circumstances because it may cause loss of power, excessive heat, burned spark plugs, burned and sticky valves, high oil consumption, and detonation. (PLT250) — FAA-H-8083-25

Answer (A) is incorrect because the carburetor will meter the lower-grade fuel the same as the proper fuel. Answer (B) is incorrect because lower-grade fuel raises cylinder head temperatures.

Answers

3224   [B]   3237   [C]

AIR, GLI, RTC, WSC

3238. Detonation may occur at high-power settings when

A— the fuel mixture ignites instantaneously instead of burning progressively and evenly.
B— an excessively rich fuel mixture causes an explosive gain in power.
C— the fuel mixture is ignited too early by hot carbon deposits in the cylinder.

Detonation or knock is a sudden explosion or shock to a small area of the piston top, rather than the normal smooth burn in the combustion chamber. (PLT115) — FAA-H-8083-25

Answer (B) is incorrect because detonation may occur with an excessively lean fuel mixture and a loss in power. Answer (C) is incorrect because this describes preignition.

AIR, RTC, WSC, PPC

3238-1. Detonation occurs in a reciprocating aircraft engine when

A— the spark plugs are fouled or shorted out or the wiring is defective.
B— hot spots in the combustion chamber ignite the fuel/air mixture in advance of normal ignition.
C— the unburned charge in the cylinders explodes instead of burning normally.

Detonation is a sudden explosion, or instantaneous combustion, of the fuel/air mixture in the cylinders, producing extreme heat and severe structural stresses on the engine. (PLT115) — FAA-H-8083-25

Answer (A) is incorrect because detonation does not have anything to do with the wiring. Answer (B) is incorrect because this describes preignition, not detonation.

AIR, RTC, WSC, PPC, LSA, LSR, LSW, LSP

3240. The uncontrolled firing of the fuel/air charge in advance of normal spark ignition is known as

A— combustion.
B— pre-ignition.
C— detonation.

Preignition is defined as ignition of the fuel prior to normal ignition. (PLT478) — FAA-H-8083-25

Answer (A) is incorrect because combustion is the normal engine process. Answer (C) is incorrect because detonation is the exploding of the fuel/air mixture.

AIR, RTC, WSC, PPC

3242. What type fuel can be substituted for an aircraft if the recommended octane is not available?

A— The next higher octane aviation gas.
B— The next lower octane aviation gas.
C— Unleaded automotive gas of the same octane rating.

If the proper grade of fuel is not available, it is possible (but not desirable), to use the next higher (aviation) grade as a substitute. (PLT250) — FAA-H-8083-25

Answer (B) is incorrect because burning lower octane fuel causes excessive engine temperatures. Answer (C) is incorrect because only aviation fuel should be used, except under special circumstances.

AIR, RTC, WSC, PPC, LSA, LSR, LSW, LSP

3243. Filling the fuel tanks after the last flight of the day is considered a good operating procedure because this will

A— force any existing water to the top of the tank away from the fuel lines to the engine.
B— prevent expansion of the fuel by eliminating airspace in the tanks.
C— prevent moisture condensation by eliminating airspace in the tanks.

Water in the fuel system is dangerous and the pilot must prevent contamination. The fuel tanks should be filled after each flight, or at least after the last flight of the day. This will prevent moisture condensation within the tank, since no air space will be left inside. (PLT250) — FAA-H-8083-25

Answer (A) is incorrect because water will settle to the bottom of a gas tank. Answer (B) is incorrect because fuel is allowed to expand by the fuel vent, whether the tanks are full or not.

AIR, RTC, LTA, WSC, PPC, LSA, LSR, LSW, LSP

3243-1. To properly purge water from the fuel system of an aircraft equipped with fuel tank sumps and a fuel strainer quick drain, it is necessary to drain fuel from the

A— fuel strainer drain.
B— lowest point in the fuel system.
C— fuel strainer drain and the fuel tank sumps.

Many aircraft are equipped with fuel strainers located at the lowest point in the fuel lines and sump drains installed at the lowest point in each fuel tank. In order to completely purge all of the liquid water from the fuel system, the fuel strainer drain and the sumps in all of the tanks must be drained. (PLT253) — FAA-H-8083-25

Answers

3238 [A]   3238-1 [C]   3240 [B]   3242 [A]   3243 [C]   3243-1 [C]

LSA, LSR

2353. During preflight in cold weather, crankcase breather lines should receive special attention because they are susceptible to being clogged by

A— congealed oil from the crankcase.
B— moisture from the outside air which has frozen.
C— ice from crankcase vapors that have condensed and subsequently frozen.

The crankcase breather requires special consideration when preparing for cold weather. Frozen breather lines can create numerous problems. When crankcase vapors cool, they may condense in the breather line and subsequently freeze it closed. Special care is recommended during the preflight to ensure that the breather system is free of ice. (PLT126) — FAA-H-8083-25

Answer (A) is incorrect because oil that lays in the bottom of the crankcase never gets into the breather lines. Answer (B) is incorrect because a low air temperature is usually associated with a low moisture content.

Engine Temperatures

Engine lubricating **oil** not only prevents direct metal-to-metal contact of moving parts, it also absorbs and dissipates some of the engine heat produced by internal combustion. If the engine oil level should fall too low, an abnormally high engine oil temperature indication may result.

On the ground or in the air, excessively high engine temperatures can cause excessive oil consumption, loss of power, and possible permanent internal engine damage.

If the engine oil temperature and cylinder head temperature gauges have exceeded their normal operating range, or if the pilot suspects that the engine (with a fixed-pitch propeller) is detonating during climb-out, the pilot may have been operating with either too much power and the mixture set too lean, using fuel of too low a grade, or operating the engine with an insufficient amount of oil in it. Reducing the rate of climb and increasing airspeed, enriching the fuel mixture, or retarding the throttle will aid in cooling an engine that is overheating.

The most important rule to remember in the event of a power failure after becoming airborne is to maintain safe airspeed.

AIR, WSC, LSA, LSR, LSW

3239. If a pilot suspects that the engine (with a fixed-pitch propeller) is detonating during climb-out after takeoff, the initial corrective action to take would be to

A— lean the mixture.
B— lower the nose slightly to increase airspeed.
C— apply carburetor heat.

To prevent detonation, the pilot should use the correct grade of fuel, maintain a sufficiently rich mixture, open the throttle smoothly, and keep the temperature of the engine within recommended operating limits. Some aircraft have an automatically enriched mixture for enhanced cooling in takeoff and climb-out at full throttle. Lowering the nose will allow the aircraft to gain airspeed, which eventually lowers the engine temperature. (PLT115) — FAA-H-8083-25

Answer (A) is incorrect because leaning the mixture increases engine temperatures; detonation results from excessively high engine temperatures. Answer (C) is incorrect because although a richer fuel mixture results from applying carburetor heat, the heat may offset the cooling effect of the mixture change. The most efficient initial action would be to increase airspeed.

AIR, RTC, WSC, PPC

3221. Excessively high engine temperatures will

A— cause damage to heat-conducting hoses and warping of the cylinder cooling fins.
B— cause loss of power, excessive oil consumption, and possible permanent internal engine damage.
C— not appreciably affect an aircraft engine.

Operating an engine at a higher temperature than it was designed for will cause loss of power, excessive oil consumption, and detonation. It will also lead to serious permanent injury to the engine including scoring of cylinder walls, damage to pistons and rings, and burning and warping of valves. (PLT342) — FAA-H-8083-25

Answer (A) is incorrect because internal engine damage is more likely to result before external damage occurs. Answer (C) is incorrect because excessively high engine temperatures seriously affect an aircraft engine.

Answers

2353 [C]	3239 [B]	3221 [B]

AIR, RTC, WSC, PPC
3221-1. Excessively high engine temperatures, either in the air or on the ground, will

A— increase fuel consumption and may increase power due to the increased heat.
B— result in damage to heat-conducting hoses and warping of cylinder cooling fans.
C— cause loss of power, excessive oil consumption, and possible permanent internal engine damage.

High engine temperatures can lead to loss of power, excessive oil consumption, detonation, and serious engine damage. (PLT253) — FAA-H-8083-25

AIR, RTC, WSC, PPC
3222. If the engine oil temperature and cylinder head temperature gauges have exceeded their normal operating range, the pilot may have been operating with

A— the mixture set too rich.
B— higher-than-normal oil pressure.
C— too much power and with the mixture set too lean.

Excessively high engine temperatures can result from insufficient cooling caused by too lean a mixture, too low a grade of fuel, low oil, or insufficient airflow over the engine. (PLT343) — FAA-H-8083-25

Answer (A) is incorrect because a richer fuel mixture will normally cool an engine. Answer (B) is incorrect because high oil pressure does not cause high engine temperatures.

AIR, RTC, WSC, PPC
3241. Which would most likely cause the cylinder head temperature and engine oil temperature gauges to exceed their normal operating ranges?

A— Using fuel that has a lower-than-specified fuel rating.
B— Using fuel that has a higher-than-specified fuel rating.
C— Operating with higher-than-normal oil pressure.

Excessively high engine temperatures result from insufficient cooling caused by too lean a mixture, too low a grade of fuel, low oil, or insufficient airflow over the engine. (PLT250) — FAA-H-8083-25

Answer (B) is incorrect because higher octane fuel will burn at lower temperatures, keeping the engine cooler. Answer (C) is incorrect because high oil pressure does not cause high engine temperatures.

AIR, RTC, WSC, PPC
3244. For internal cooling, reciprocating aircraft engines are especially dependent on

A— a properly functioning thermostat.
B— air flowing over the exhaust manifold.
C— the circulation of lubricating oil.

Oil, used primarily to lubricate the moving parts of the engine, also cools the internal parts of the engine as it circulates. (PLT342) — FAA-H-8083-25

Answer (A) is incorrect because most air-cooled aircraft engines do not have thermostats. Answer (B) is incorrect because, although air-cooling is important, internal cooling is more reliant on oil circulation. Air cools the cylinders, not the exhaust manifold.

LSA, LSR
2354. Which is true regarding preheating an aircraft during cold weather operations?

A— The cabin area as well as the engine should be preheated.
B— The cabin area should not be preheated with portable heaters.
C— Hot air should be blown directly at the engine through the air intakes.

Low temperatures may cause a change in the viscosity of engine oils, batteries may lose a high percentage of their effectiveness, and instruments may stick. Because of the above, preheating the engines as well as the cabin before starting is desirable in low temperatures. Extreme caution should be used in the preheat process to avoid fire. (PLT126) — FAA-H-8083-25

AIR, RTC, WSC, PPC
3245. An abnormally high engine oil temperature indication may be caused by

A— the oil level being too low.
B— operating with a too high viscosity oil.
C— operating with an excessively rich mixture.

Oil, used primarily to lubricate the moving parts of the engine, also helps reduce engine temperature by removing some of the heat from the cylinders. Therefore, if the oil level is too low, the transfer of heat to less oil would cause the oil temperature to rise. (PLT324) — FAA-H-8083-25

Answer (B) is incorrect because the higher the viscosity, the better the lubricating and cooling capability of the oil. Answer (C) is incorrect because a rich fuel/air mixture usually decreases engine temperature.

Answers

3221-1 [C]	3222 [C]	3241 [A]	3244 [C]	2354 [A]	3245 [A]

AIR, RTC, WSC, PPC

3651. What action can a pilot take to aid in cooling an engine that is overheating during a climb?

A— Reduce rate of climb and increase airspeed.
B— Reduce climb speed and increase RPM.
C— Increase climb speed and increase RPM.

To avoid excessive cylinder head temperatures, a pilot can open the cowl flaps, increase airspeed, enrich the mixture, or reduce power. Any of these procedures will aid in reducing the engine temperature. Establishing a shallower climb (increasing airspeed) increases the airflow through the cooling system, reducing high engine temperatures. (PLT342) — FAA-H-8083-25

Answer (B) is incorrect because reducing airspeed hinders cooling, and increasing RPM will further increase engine temperature. Answer (C) is incorrect because increasing RPM will increase engine temperature.

AIR, RTC, WSC, PPC

3652. What is one procedure to aid in cooling an engine that is overheating?

A— Enrichen the fuel mixture.
B— Increase the RPM.
C— Reduce the airspeed.

To avoid excessive cylinder head temperatures, a pilot can open the cowl flaps, increase airspeed, enrich the mixture, or reduce power. Any of these procedures will aid in reducing the engine temperature. (PLT342) — FAA-H-8083-25

Answer (B) is incorrect because increasing the RPM increases the engine's internal heat. Answer (C) is incorrect because reducing the airspeed decreases the airflow needed for cooling, thus increasing the engine's temperature.

AIR, RTC, WSC

3711. The most important rule to remember in the event of a power failure after becoming airborne is to

A— immediately establish the proper gliding attitude and airspeed.
B— quickly check the fuel supply for possible fuel exhaustion.
C— determine the wind direction to plan for the forced landing.

Maintaining the proper glide speed (safe airspeed) is the most important rule to remember in the event of a power failure. (PLT208) — FAA-H-8083-3

Answers (B) and (C) are incorrect because these steps should be taken only after establishing the proper glide speed.

Answers

3651   [A]   3652   [A]   3711   [A]

Propellers

A propeller provides thrust to propel the airplane through the air. Some aircraft are equipped with a **constant-speed propeller**. This type of propeller allows the pilot to select the most efficient propeller blade angle for each phase of flight. In these aircraft, the throttle controls the power output as registered on the manifold pressure gauge, and the propeller control regulates the engine RPM.

A pilot should avoid a high manifold pressure setting with low RPM on engines equipped with a constant-speed propeller. To avoid high manifold pressure combined with low RPM, reduce the manifold pressure before reducing RPM when decreasing power settings (or increase the RPM before increasing the manifold pressure when increasing power settings).

AIR
3653. How is engine operation controlled on an engine equipped with a constant-speed propeller?

A—The throttle controls power output as registered on the manifold pressure gauge and the propeller control regulates engine RPM.

B— The throttle controls power output as registered on the manifold pressure gauge and the propeller control regulates a constant blade angle.

C— The throttle controls engine RPM as registered on the tachometer and the mixture control regulates the power output.

On aircraft equipped with a constant-speed propeller, the throttle controls the engine power output which is registered on the manifold pressure gauge. The propeller control changes the pitch angle of the propeller and governs the RPM which is indicated on the tachometer. (PLT343) — FAA-H-8083-25

Answer (B) is incorrect because the propeller control does not maintain a constant pitch, it changes pitch in order to hold a constant RPM. Answer (C) is incorrect because the throttle does not directly control RPM, and mixture control does not regulate power.

AIR
3654. What is an advantage of a constant-speed propeller?

A— Permits the pilot to select and maintain a desired cruising speed.

B— Permits the pilot to select the blade angle for the most efficient performance.

C— Provides a smoother operation with stable RPM and eliminates vibrations.

A constant-speed propeller permits the pilot to select the blade angle that will result in the most efficient performance for a particular flight condition. A low blade angle allows higher RPM and horsepower, desirable for takeoffs. An intermediate position can be used for subsequent climb. After airspeed is attained during cruising flight, the propeller blade may be changed to a higher angle for lower RPM, reduced engine noise, generally lower vibration, and greater fuel efficiency. (PLT351) — FAA-H-8083-25

Answer (A) is incorrect because a constant-speed propeller is not used to maintain airspeed, but rather constant engine RPM. Answer (C) is incorrect because a constant-speed propeller may not be smoother or operate with less vibration than a fixed-pitch propeller.

AIR
3655. A precaution for the operation of an engine equipped with a constant-speed propeller is to

A— avoid high RPM settings with high manifold pressure.

B— avoid high manifold pressure settings with low RPM.

C— always use a rich mixture with high RPM settings.

On aircraft equipped with a constant-speed propeller, the throttle controls the engine power output which is registered on the manifold pressure gauge. The propeller control changes the pitch angle of the propeller and governs the RPM which is indicated on the tachometer. On most airplanes, for any given RPM, there is a manifold pressure that should not be exceeded. If an excessive amount of manifold pressure is carried for a given RPM, the maximum allowable pressure within the engine cylinders could be exceeded, thus putting undue strain on them. (PLT351) — FAA-H-8083-25

Answer (A) is incorrect because high manifold pressure is allowable with high RPM settings, within specification limits. Answer (C) is incorrect because the mixture should be leaned for best performance.

Answers

3653　[A]　　3654　[B]　　3655　[B]

Torque

An airplane of standard configuration has an insistent tendency to turn to the left. This tendency is called torque, and is a combination of four forces: namely, reactive force, spiraling slipstream, gyroscopic precession, and P-factor.

Reactive force is based on Newton's Law of action and reaction. A propeller rotating in a clockwise direction (as seen from the rear) produces a force which tends to roll the airplane in a counterclockwise direction. *See* Figure 2-2.

The **spiraling slipstream** is the reaction of the air to a rotating propeller. (The propeller forces the air to spiral in a clockwise direction around the fuselage.) This spiraling slipstream strikes the airplane's vertical stabilizer on the left side. This pushes the tail of the airplane to the right and the nose of the airplane to the left. *See* Figure 2-3. Weight-shift control and powered parachutes do not have this effect.

Gyroscopic precession is the result of a deflective force applied to a rotating body (such as a propeller). The resultant action occurs 90° later in the direction of rotation. *See* Figure 2-4.

Asymmetric propeller loading, called **P-factor**, is caused by the downward moving blade on the right side of the propeller having a higher angle of attack, a greater action and reaction, and therefore a higher thrust than the upward moving opposite blade. This results in a tendency for the aircraft to yaw to the left around the vertical axis. Additional left-turning tendency from torque will be greatest when the aircraft is operating at low airspeed with a high power setting.

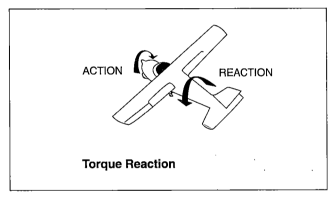

Torque Reaction

Figure 2-2. Reactive force

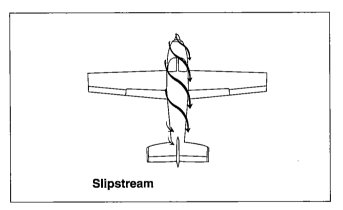

Slipstream

Figure 2-3. Spiraling slipstream

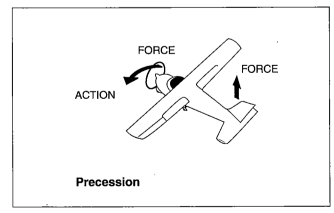

Precession

Figure 2-4. Gyroscopic precession

AIR, WSC, PPC

3207. In what flight condition is torque effect the greatest in a single-engine airplane?

A— Low airspeed, high power, high angle of attack.
B— Low airspeed, low power, low angle of attack.
C— High airspeed, high power, high angle of attack.

The effect of torque increases in direct proportion to the engine power, airspeed, and airplane attitude. If the power setting is high, the airspeed slow, and the angle of attack high (or a high deck angle for a PPC), the effect of torque is greater. (PLT243) — FAA-H-8083-25

Answer (B) is incorrect because the least amount of torque effect is produced under these conditions. Answer (C) is incorrect because torque effect is negligible at higher airspeeds due to increased stability generated by more airflow moving over all airfoils.

AIR, WSC, PPC

3208. The left turning tendency of an airplane caused by P-factor is the result of the

A— clockwise rotation of the engine and the propeller turning the airplane counter-clockwise.
B— propeller blade descending on the right, producing more thrust than the ascending blade on the left.
C— gyroscopic forces applied to the rotating propeller blades acting 90° in advance of the point the force was applied.

The downward-moving blade on the right side of the propeller has a higher angle of attack and greater action and reaction than the upward moving blade on the left. This results in a tendency for the airplane to yaw around the vertical axis to the left. (PLT243) — FAA-H-8083-25

Answer (A) is incorrect because it describes the characteristics involved with torque effect. Answer (C) is incorrect because it describes gyroscopic precession.

AIR, WSC, PPC

3209. When does P-factor cause the airplane to yaw to the left?

A— When at low angles of attack.
B— When at high angles of attack.
C— When at high airspeeds.

The effects of P-factor, or asymmetric propeller loading, usually occur when the airplane is flown at high angles of attack (or a high deck angle for a PPC) and at high power settings. (PLT243) — FAA-H-8083-25

Answer (A) is incorrect because the thrust differential between ascending and descending propeller blades at low angles of attack is slight. Answer (C) is incorrect because at higher airspeeds, an aircraft's angle of attack decreases in straight-and-level flight; therefore propeller-blade differential thrust becomes negligible.

Answers

3207 [A]   3208 [B]   3209 [B]

Preflight Inspection Procedures

A thorough **preflight inspection** should be performed on an aircraft to help ensure that the aircraft is prepared for safe flight and should be a thorough and systematic means by which the pilot determines the airplane is ready for safe flight. Prior to every flight, a pilot should at least perform a walk-around inspection of the aircraft.

After an aircraft has been stored for an extended period of time, a special check should be made during preflight for damage or obstructions caused by animals, birds, or insects.

The use of a written checklist for preflight inspection and starting the engine is recommended to ensure that all necessary items are checked in a logical sequence.

Although 14 CFR Part 91 places primary responsibility on the owner or operator for maintaining an aircraft in an airworthy condition, the pilot-in-command is responsible for determining whether that aircraft is in condition for safe flight.

ALL, SPO

3658. During the preflight inspection who is responsible for determining the aircraft is safe for flight?

A— The pilot in command.
B— The owner or operator.
C— The certificated mechanic who performed the annual inspection.

The pilot-in-command of an aircraft is responsible for determining whether that aircraft is in condition for safe flight. (PLT444) — FAA-H-8083-25

ALL

3659. How should an aircraft preflight inspection be accomplished for the first flight of the day?

A— Quick walk around with a check of gas and oil.
B— Thorough and systematic means recommended by the manufacturer.
C— Any sequence as determined by the pilot-in-command.

The preflight inspection should be a thorough and systematic means by which the pilot determines that the airplane is ready for safe flight. Most Aircraft Flight Manuals or Pilot's Operating Handbooks contain a section devoted to a systematic method of performing a preflight inspection that should be used by the pilot for guidance. (PLT445) — FAA-H-8083-25

ALL, SPO

3660. Who is primarily responsible for maintaining an aircraft in airworthy condition?

A— Pilot-in-command.
B— Owner or operator.
C— Mechanic.

14 CFR Part 91 places primary responsibility on the owner or operator for maintaining an aircraft in an airworthy condition. (PLT374) — FAA-H-8083-25

Answers

3658   [A]   3659   [B]   3660   [B]

Helicopter Systems

RTC
3318. (Refer to Figure 10.) During flight, if cyclic control pressure is applied which results in a maximum increase in pitch angle of the rotor blade at position A, the rotor disc will tilt

A— forward.
B— aft.
C— left.

Gyroscopic precession is the resultant action of a spinning object when a force is applied to the object. The action occurs approximately 90° later in the direction of rotation. Thus, if the maximum increase in angle of attack occurs at point A, maximum deflection takes place 90° later. This is maximum upward deflection at the rear, and the tip-path plane tips forward. (PLT199) — FAA-H-8083-21

RTC
3319. The lift differential that exists between the advancing main rotor blade and the retreating main rotor blade is known as

A— transverse flow effect.
B— dissymmetry of lift.
C— hunting tendency.

The difference in lift that exists between the advancing blade half of the disc and retreating blade half, created by horizontal flight or by wind during hovering flight, is called dissymmetry of lift. (PLT242) — FAA-H-8083-21

RTC
3320. During forward cruising flight at constant airspeed and altitude, the individual rotor blades, when compared to each other, are operating

A— with increased lift on the retreating blade.
B— with a decreasing angle of attack on the advancing blade.
C— at unequal airspeed, unequal angles of attack, and equal lift moment.

As the helicopter moves into forward flight, the relative wind moving over each rotor blade becomes a combination of the rotational speed of the rotor and the forward movement of the helicopter. Increased lift on the advancing blade will cause the blade to flap, decreasing the angle of attack. Decreased lift on the retreating blade will cause the blade to flap down, increasing the angle of attack. The combination of decreased angle of attack

on the advancing blade and increased angle of attack on the retreating blade through blade flapping action tends to equalize lift over the two halves of the rotor disc. (PLT470) — FAA-H-8083-21

RTC
3321. The upward bending of the rotor blades resulting from the combined forces of lift and centrifugal force is known as

A— coning.
B— blade slapping.
C— inertia.

As a vertical takeoff is made, two major forces are acting at the same time—centrifugal force acting outward, perpendicular to the rotor mast, and lift, acting upward and parallel to the mast. The result of these two forces is that the blades assume a conical path instead of remaining in the plane perpendicular to the mast. (PLT027) — FAA-H-8083-21

RTC
3322. When a blade flaps up, the CG moves closer to its axis of rotation giving that blade a tendency to

A— decelerate.
B— accelerate.
C— stabilize its rotational velocity.

When a rotor blade flaps up, the center of mass of that blade moves closer to the axis of rotation and blade acceleration takes place. (PLT197) — FAA-H-8083-21

RTC
3323. During a hover, a helicopter tends to drift to the right. To compensate for this, some helicopters have the

A— tail rotor tilted to the left.
B— tail rotor tilted to the right.
C— rotor mast rigged to the left side.

To counteract drift, the rotor mast in some helicopters is rigged slightly to the left side so that the tip-path plane has a built-in tilt to the left, thus producing a small sideward thrust. (PLT470) — FAA-H-8083-21

Answers

| 3318 | [A] | 3319 | [B] | 3320 | [C] | 3321 | [A] | 3322 | [B] | 3323 | [C] |

RTC
3325. Translational lift is the result of

A— decreased rotor efficiency.
B— airspeed.
C— both airspeed and groundspeed.

Translational lift is that additional lift obtained when entering horizontal flight due to the increased efficiency of the rotor system. Translational lift depends upon airspeed rather than ground speed. (PLT470) — FAA-H-8083-21

RTC
3326. The primary purpose of the tail rotor system is to

A— assist in making a coordinated turn.
B— maintain heading during forward flight.
C— counteract the torque effect of the main rotor.

The force that compensates for torque and keeps the fuselage from turning in the direction opposite to the main rotor is produced by means of an auxiliary rotor located on the end of the tail boom. (PLT470) — FAA-H-8083-21

RTC
3327. If RPM is low and manifold pressure is high, what initial corrective action should be taken?

A— Increase the throttle.
B— Lower the collective pitch.
C— Raise the collective pitch.

Lowering the collective pitch will reduce the manifold pressure, decrease drag on the rotor, and therefore increase the RPM. (PLT112) — FAA-H-8083-21

RTC
3328. The purpose of the lead-lag (drag) hinge in a three-bladed, fully articulated helicopter rotor system is to compensate for

A— Coriolis effect.
B— coning.
C— geometric unbalance.

In a fully-articulated rotor system, each rotor blade is attached to the hub by a vertical hinge called a drag or lag hinge that permits each blade, independently of the others, to move back and forth in the plane of the rotor disc. This movement is called dragging, lead-lag, or hunting. The purpose of the drag hinge and dampers is to absorb the acceleration and deceleration of the rotor blades caused by Coriolis effect. (PLT470) — FAA-H-8083-21

RTC
3329. High airspeeds, particularly in turbulent air, should be avoided primarily because of the possibility of

A— an abrupt pitchup.
B— retreating blade stall.
C— a low-frequency vibration developing.

A tendency for the retreating blade to stall in forward flight is a major factor in limiting a helicopter's forward airspeed. When operating at high airspeeds, stalls are more liable to occur under conditions of high gross weight, low RPM, high density altitude, steep or abrupt turns, and/or turbulent flight. (PLT470) — FAA-H-8083-21

RTC
3330. The maximum forward speed of a helicopter is limited by

A— retreating blade stall.
B— the rotor RPM red line.
C— solidity ratio.

A tendency for the retreating blade to stall in forward flight is a major factor in limiting a helicopter's forward airspeed. When operating at high airspeeds, stalls are more liable to occur under conditions of high gross weight, low RPM, high density altitude, steep or abrupt turns, and/or turbulent flight. (PLT470) — FAA-H-8083-21

RTC
3331. When operating at high forward airspeeds, retreating blade stalls are more likely to occur under which condition?

A— Low gross weight and low density altitude.
B— High RPM and low density altitude.
C— Steep turns in turbulent air.

A tendency for the retreating blade to stall in forward flight is a major factor in limiting a helicopter's forward airspeed. When operating at high airspeeds, stalls are more liable to occur under conditions of high gross weight, low RPM, high density altitude, steep or abrupt turns, and/or turbulent flight. (PLT470) — FAA-H-8083-21

Answers

3325	[B]	3326	[C]	3327	[B]	3328	[A]	3329	[B]	3330 [A]
3331	[C]									

RTC
3332. Ground resonance is most likely to develop when

A— on the ground and harmonic vibrations develop between the main and tail rotors.
B— a series of shocks causes the rotor system to become unbalanced.
C— there is a combination of a decrease in the angle of attack on the advancing blade and an increase in the angle of attack on the retreating blade.

When one landing gear of the helicopter strikes the surface first, a shock is transmitted through the fuselage to the rotor. This shock may cause the blades straddling the contact point to be forced closer together. When one of the other landing gears strikes, the unbalance could be aggravated. This sets up a resonance of the fuselage. (PLT259) — FAA-H-8083-21

RTC
3333. While in level cruising flight in a helicopter, a pilot experiences low-frequency vibrations (100 to 400 cycles per minute). These vibrations are normally associated with the

A— engine.
B— cooling fan.
C— main rotor.

Low-frequency vibrations are always associated with the main rotor. (PLT472) — FAA-H-8083-21

RTC
3334. Select the helicopter component that, if defective, would cause medium-frequency vibrations.

A— Tail rotor.
B— Main rotor.
C— Engine.

Medium-frequency vibrations are a result of trouble with the tail rotor in most helicopters. (PLT470) — FAA-H-8083-21

RTC
3335. The principal reason the shaded area of a Height vs. Velocity Chart should be avoided is

A— turbulence near the surface can dephase the blade dampers.
B— rotor RPM may decay before ground contact is made if an engine failure should occur.
C— insufficient airspeed would be available to ensure a safe landing in case of an engine failure.

The chart can be used to determine those altitude-airspeed combinations from which it would be impossible to successfully complete an autorotative landing. The altitude-airspeed combinations that should be avoided are represented by the shaded areas of the chart. (PLT285) — FAA-H-8083-21

RTC
3336. During surface taxiing, the collective pitch is used to control

A— drift during a crosswind.
B— rate of speed.
C— ground track.

Collective pitch is used to control rate of speed during taxi. The higher the collective pitch, the faster will be the taxi speed. (PLT112) — FAA-H-8083-21

RTC
3337. During surface taxiing, the cyclic pitch stick is used to control

A— forward movement.
B— heading.
C— ground track.

Cyclic pitch is used to control ground track during surface taxi. (PLT112) — FAA-H-8083-21

RTC, LSR
3338. If the pilot experiences ground resonance, and the rotor RPM is not sufficient for flight,

A— open the throttle full and liftoff.
B— apply the rotor brake and stop the rotor as soon as possible.
C— attempt to takeoff at that power setting.

Ground resonance is an aerodynamic phenomenon associated with fully-articulated rotor systems. It develops when the rotor blades move out of phase with each other and cause the rotor disc to become unbalanced. This condition can cause a helicopter to self-destruct in a matter of seconds. However, for this condition to occur, the helicopter must be in contact with the ground. If you experience ground resonance, and the rotor RPM is not yet sufficient for flight, apply the rotor brake to maximum and stop the rotor as soon as possible. If ground resonance occurs during takeoff, when rotor RPM is sufficient for flight, lift off immediately. (PLT265) — FAA-H-8083-21

Answers

3332	[B]	3333	[C]	3334	[A]	3335	[C]	3336	[B]	3337	[C]
3338	[B]										

LSR

2329. If ground resonance is experienced during rotor spin-up, what action should you take?

A— Taxi to a smooth area.
B— Make a normal takeoff immediately.
C— Close the throttle and slowly raise the spin-up lever.

A corrective action for ground resonance is an immediate takeoff if RPM is in proper range (for helicopters) or an immediate closing of the throttle and placing the blades in low pitch if the RPM is low. "During spin-up" implies low RPM, so closing the throttle is appropriate. (PLT259) — FAA-H-8083-21

RTC

3733. With calm wind conditions, which flight operation would require the most power?

A— A right-hovering turn.
B— A left-hovering turn.
C— Hovering out of ground effect.

During a hovering turn to the left, the RPM will decrease if throttle is not added. In a hovering turn to the right, RPM will increase if throttle is not reduced slightly. (This is due to the amount of engine power that is being absorbed by the tail rotor, which is dependent upon the pitch angle at which the tail rotor blades are operating.) (PLT268) — FAA-H-8083-21

RTC

3734. If the pilot were to make a near-vertical power approach into a confined area with the airspeed near zero, what hazardous condition may develop?

A— Ground resonance when ground contact is made.
B— A settling-with-power condition.
C— Blade stall vibration could develop.

The following combination of conditions are likely to cause settling with power:

1. A vertical, or nearly vertical, descent of at least 300 feet per minute. Actual critical rate depends on the gross weight, RPM, density altitude, and other pertinent factors.

2. The rotor system must be using some of the available engine power (from 20 to 100 percent).

3. The horizontal velocity must be no greater than approximately 10 miles per hour.

(PLT264) — FAA-H-8083-21

RTC

3736. (Refer to Figure 46.) Which airspeed/altitude combination should be avoided during helicopter operations?

A— 30 MPH/200 feet AGL.
B— 50 MPH/300 feet AGL.
C— 60 MPH/20 feet AGL.

Use the following steps:

1. Note the shaded "avoid operation" areas of FAA Figure 46.

2. Locate each of the three height-above-terrain and airspeed points on the diagram.

3. The 60 MPH/20 feet AGL point is located within the low-altitude high airspeed area.

(PLT285) — FAA-H-8083-21

RTC

3737. (Refer to Figure 46.) Which airspeed/altitude combination should be avoided during helicopter operations?

A— 20 MPH/200 feet AGL.
B— 35 MPH/175 feet AGL.
C— 40 MPH/75 feet AGL.

Use the following steps:

1. Note the shaded "avoid operation" areas of FAA Figure 46.

2. Locate each of the three height-above-terrain and airspeed points on the diagram.

3. The 20 MPH/200 feet AGL point is located within the high-altitude low airspeed area.

(PLT285) — FAA-H-8083-21

Answers

| 2329 [C] | 3733 [B] | 3734 [B] | 3736 [C] | 3737 [A] |

RTC
3738. If anti-torque failure occurred during the landing touchdown, what could be done to help straighten out a left yaw prior to touchdown?

A— A flare to zero airspeed and a vertical descent to touchdown should be made.
B— Apply available throttle to help swing the nose to the right just prior to touchdown.
C— A normal running landing should be made.

If sufficient forward speed is maintained, the fuselage remains fairly well streamlined. However, if descent is attempted at slow speeds, a continuous turning movement to the left can be expected. (Know the manufacturer's recommendations in case of tail rotor failure for each particular helicopter you fly. This information will generally be found under Emergency Procedures in the helicopter flight manual.) Directional control should be maintained primarily with cyclic control and, secondarily, by gently applying throttle momentarily, with needles joined, to swing the nose to the right. (PLT169) — FAA-H-8083-21

RTC
3739. Which flight technique is recommended for use during hot weather?

A— Use minimum allowable RPM and maximum allowable manifold pressure during all phases of flight.
B— During hovering flight, maintain minimum engine RPM during left pedal turns, and maximum engine RPM during right pedal turns.
C— During takeoff, accelerate slowly into forward flight.

The following techniques should be used in hot weather:

1. *Make full use of wind and translational lift.*

2. *Hover as low as possible and no longer than necessary.*

3. *Maintain maximum allowable engine RPM.*

4. *Accelerate very slowly into forward flight.*

5. *Employ running takeoffs and landings when necessary.*

6. *Use caution in maximum performance takeoffs and steep approaches.*

7. *Avoid high rates of descent in all approaches.*

(PLT222) — FAA-H-8083-21

RTC
3740. Under what condition should a helicopter pilot consider using a running takeoff?

A— When gross weight or density altitude prevents a sustained hover at normal hovering altitude.
B— When a normal climb speed is assured between 10 and 20 feet.
C— When the additional airspeed can be quickly converted to altitude.

A running takeoff is used when conditions of load and/ or density altitude prevent a sustained hover at normal hovering altitude. It is often referred to as a high-altitude takeoff. With insufficient power to hover at least momentarily or at a very low altitude, a running takeoff is not advisable. No takeoff should be attempted if the helicopter cannot be lifted off the surface momentarily at full power. (PLT222) — FAA-H-8083-21

RTC
3741. What action should the pilot take if engine failure occurs at altitude?

A— Open the throttle as the collective pitch is raised.
B— Reduce cyclic back stick pressure during turns.
C— Lower the collective pitch control, as necessary, to maintain rotor RPM.

By immediately lowering collective pitch (which must be done in case of engine failure), lift and drag will be reduced and the helicopter will begin an immediate descent, thus producing an upward flow of air through the rotor system. The impact of this upward flow of air provides sufficient thrust to maintain rotor RPM throughout the descent. (PLT208) — FAA-H-8083-21

Answers

3738 [B]   3739 [C]   3740 [A]   3741 [C]

RTC
3742. Which is a precaution to be observed during an autorotative descent?

A— Normally, the airspeed is controlled with the collective pitch.
B— Normally, only the cyclic control is used to make turns.
C— Do not allow the rate of descent to get too low at zero airspeed.

When making turns during an autorotative descent, generally use cyclic control only. Use of antitorque pedals to assist or speed the turn causes loss of airspeed and downward pitching of the nose. This is especially true when the left pedal is used. When the autorotation is initiated, sufficient right pedal pressure should be used to maintain straight flight and prevent yawing to the left. This pressure should not be changed to assist the turn. (PLT175) — FAA-H-8083-21

RTC
3743. The proper action to initiate a quick stop is to apply

A— forward cyclic and lower the collective pitch.
B— aft cyclic and raise the collective pitch.
C— aft cyclic and lower the collective pitch.

A quick stop is initiated by applying aft cyclic to reduce forward speed. Simultaneously, the collective pitch should be lowered as necessary, to counteract any climbing tendency. The timing must be exact. If too little down collective is applied for the amount of aft cyclic applied, a climb will result. If too much down collective is applied for the amount of aft cyclic applied, a descent will result. A rapid application of aft cyclic requires an equally rapid application of down collective. As collective pitch is lowered, the right pedal should be increased to maintain heading, and throttle should be adjusted to maintain RPM. (PLT217) — FAA-H-8083-21

RTC
3744. What is the procedure for a slope landing?

A— When the downslope skid is on the ground, hold the collective pitch at the same position.
B— Minimum RPM shall be held until the full weight of the helicopter is on the skid.
C— When parallel to the slope, slowly lower the upslope skid to the ground prior to lowering the downslope skid.

A downward pressure on the collective pitch will start the helicopter descending. As the upslope skid touches the ground, apply cyclic stick in the direction of the slope. This will hold the skid against the slope while the downslope skid is continuing to be let down with the collective pitch. (PLT170) — FAA-H-8083-21

RTC
3745. Takeoff from a slope is normally accomplished by

A— moving the cyclic in a direction away from the slope.
B— bringing the helicopter to a level attitude before completely leaving the ground.
C— moving the cyclic stick to a full up position as the helicopter nears a level attitude.

Recommended slope takeoff technique is to:

1. *Adjust throttle to obtain takeoff RPM and move the cyclic stick in the direction of the slope so that the rotor rotation is parallel to the true horizontal rather than the slope.*

2. *Apply up-collective pitch. As the helicopter becomes light on the skids, apply the pedal as needed to maintain heading.*

3. *As the downslope skid is rising and the helicopter approaches a level attitude, move the cyclic stick back to the neutral position, keeping the rotor disc parallel to the true horizon. Continue to apply up-collective pitch and take the helicopter straight up to a hover before moving away from the slope. In moving away from the slope, the tail should not be turned upslope because of the danger of the tail rotor striking the surface.*

(PLT170) — FAA-H-8083-21

RTC
3746. Which action would be appropriate for confined area operations?

A— Takeoffs and landings must be made into the wind.
B— Plan the flightpath over areas suitable for a forced landing.
C— A very steep angle of descent should be used to land on the selected spot.

In any type of confined area operation, plan a flight path over areas suitable for forced landings if possible. (PLT349) — FAA-H-8083-21

Answers

| 3742 | [B] | 3743 | [C] | 3744 | [C] | 3745 | [B] | 3746 | [B] |

RTC
3747. If possible, when departing a confined area, what type of takeoff is preferred?

A— A normal takeoff from a hover.
B— A vertical takeoff.
C— A normal takeoff from the surface.

If possible, a normal takeoff from a hover should be made when departing a confined area. (PLT222) — FAA-H-8083-21

RTC
3748. Which is a correct general rule for pinnacle and ridgeline operations?

A— Gaining altitude on takeoff is more important than gaining airspeed.
B— The approach path to a ridgeline is usually perpendicular to the ridge.
C— A climb to a pinnacle or ridgeline should be performed on the upwind side.

If necessary to climb to a pinnacle or ridgeline, the climb should be performed on the upwind side, when practicable, to take advantage of any updrafts. (PLT221) — FAA-H-8083-21

RTC
3749. Before beginning a confined area or pinnacle landing, the pilot should first

A— execute a high reconnaissance.
B— execute a low reconnaissance.
C— fly around the area to discover areas of turbulence.

The purpose of the high reconnaissance is to determine the suitability of an area for landing. In a high reconnaissance, the following items should be accomplished:

1. *Determine wind direction and speed.*
2. *Select the most suitable flight paths into and out of the area, with particular consideration being given to forced landing areas.*
3. *Plan the approach and select a point for touchdown.*
4. *Locate and determine the size of barriers, if any.*

The approach path should be generally into the wind. The purpose of the low reconnaissance is to verify what was seen in the high reconnaissance.

(PLT221) — FAA-H-8083-21

Glider Operations

GLI
3174. The minimum allowable strength of a towline used for an aerotow of a glider having a certificated gross weight of 700 pounds is

A— 560 pounds.
B— 700 pounds.
C— 1,000 pounds.

No person may operate a civil aircraft towing a glider unless the towline used has a breaking strength not less than 80% of the maximum certificated operating weight of the glider, and not greater than twice this operating weight unless safety links are used.

> 700 lbs
> x 0.80
> 560 lbs

(PLT496) — 14 CFR §91.309

GLI
3175. The minimum allowable strength of a towline used for an aerotow of a glider having a certificated gross weight of 1,040 pounds is

A— 502 pounds.
B— 832 pounds.
C— 1,040 pounds.

No person may operate a civil aircraft towing a glider unless the towline used has a breaking strength not less than 80% of the maximum certificated operating weight of the glider, and not greater than twice this operating weight unless safety links are used.

> 1,040 lbs
> x 0.80
> 832 lbs

(PLT496) — 14 CFR §91.309

Answers

3747 [A]	3748 [C]	3749 [A]	3174 [A]	3175 [B]

GLI
3177. When using a towline having a breaking strength more than twice the maximum certificated operating weight of the glider, an approved safety link must be installed at what point(s)?

A— Only the point where the towline is attached to the glider.
B— The point where the towline is attached to the glider and the point of attachment of the towline to the towplane.
C— Only the point where the towline is attached to the towplane.

The towline may have a breaking strength of more than twice the maximum certificated operating weight of the glider if a safety link is installed at the point of attachment of the towline to the glider, and a safety link is installed at the point of attachment of the towline to the towing aircraft. (PLT496) — 14 CFR §91.309

GLI
3176. For the aerotow of a glider that weighs 700 pounds, which towrope tensile strength would require the use of safety links at each end of the rope?

A— 850 pounds.
B— 1,040 pounds.
C— 1,450 pounds.

No person may operate a civil aircraft towing a glider unless the towline used has a breaking strength not less than 80% of the maximum certificated operating weight of the glider, and not greater than twice this operating weight unless safety links are used.

700 lbs
x 2
1,400 lbs

(PLT496) — 14 CFR §91.309

GLI
3340. What force provides the forward motion necessary to move a glider through the air?

A— Lift.
B— Centripetal force.
C— Gravity.

The pull of gravity provides the forward motion necessary to move the wings through the air. (PLT241) — FAA-H-8083-13

GLI
3341. To obtain maximum distance over the ground, the airspeed to use is the

A— minimum control speed.
B— best lift/drag speed.
C— minimum sink speed.

If the maximum distance over the ground is desired, the airspeed for best L/D should be used. (PLT132) — FAA-H-8083-13

GLI
3342. What effect would gusts and turbulence have on the load factor of a glider with changes in airspeed?

A— Load factor decreases as airspeed increases.
B— Load factor increases as airspeed increases.
C— Load factor increases as airspeed decreases.

Both positive and negative gust load factors increase with increasing airspeed. (PLT132) — FAA-H-8083-13

GLI
3343. (Refer to Figure 11.) Which yaw string and inclinometer illustrations indicate a slipping right turn?

A— 3 and 6.
B— 2 and 6.
C— 2 and 4.

In the case of a slipping right turn, the yaw string moves outside left and the ball moves inside, or right, as illustrated by 2 and 6 of FAA Figure 11. (PLT185) — FAA-H-8083-13

GLI
3344. (Refer to Figure 11.) Which of the illustrations depicts the excessive use of right rudder during the entry of a right turn?

A— 2 only.
B— 2 and 4.
C— 3 and 4.

In the case of a skidding right turn, the yaw string moves inside right and the ball moves outside, or left, as illustrated by 3 and 4 of FAA Figure 11. (PLT185) — FAA-H-8083-13

GLI
3345. A sailplane has a best glide ratio of 23:1. How many feet will the glider lose in 8 nautical miles?

A— 1,840 feet.
B— 2,100 feet.
C— 2,750 feet.

L/D is lift divided by drag. This significant ratio is numerically the same as glide ratio, the ratio of forward to downward motion. Hence, 23 to 1 glide ratio would indicate:

1. $\dfrac{23}{1} = \dfrac{6,000 \ (feet/NM - forward)}{X \ (feet/NM - downward)}$

2. $\dfrac{23}{1} \times X = 6,000$

3. *X = 261 feet downward for each 6,000 feet (1 NM) forward.*

4. *The total sink is 8 NM × 261 feet/NM or about 2,100 feet in 8 NM in calm air.*

(PLT006) — FAA-H-8083-13

GLI
3346. A sailplane has a best glide ratio of 30:1. How many nautical miles will the glider travel while losing 2,000 feet?

A— 10 nautical miles.
B— 15 nautical miles.
C— 21 nautical miles.

L/D is lift divided by drag. This significant ratio is numerically the same as glide ratio, the ratio of forward to downward motion. Hence, 30 to 1 glide ratio would indicate:

1. $\dfrac{30}{1} = \dfrac{X \ (feet/NM - forward)}{2,000 \ (feet/NM - downward)}$

2. $\dfrac{30}{1} \times 2,000 = X$

3. *X = 60,000 feet (10 NM) forward for each 2,000 feet downward.*

(PLT006) — FAA-H-8083-13

GLI
3347. A sailplane has lost 2,000 feet in 9 nautical miles. The best glide ratio for this sailplane is approximately

A— 24:1.
B— 27:1.
C— 30:1.

L/D is lift divided by drag. This significant ratio is numerically the same as glide ratio, the ratio of forward to downward motion. Assuming that 1 NM is approximately 6,000 feet, the glide ratio and L/D may be expressed as:

$$\dfrac{9 \times 6,000 \ feet \ forward}{2,000 \ feet \ downard} = \dfrac{54,000}{2,000} = \dfrac{54}{2} = \dfrac{27}{1} \ or \ 27:1$$

(PLT006) — FAA-H-8083-13

GLI
3348. How many feet will a sailplane sink in 15 nautical miles if its lift/drag ratio is 22:1?

A— 2,700 feet.
B— 3,600 feet.
C— 4,100 feet.

L/D is lift divided by drag. This significant ratio is numerically the same as glide ratio, the ratio of forward to downward motion. Hence, 22 to 1 glide ratio would indicate:

1. $\dfrac{22}{1} = \dfrac{6,000 \ (feet/NM - forward)}{X \ (feet/NM - downward)}$

2. $\dfrac{22}{1} \times X = 6,000$

3. *X = 273 feet downward for each 6,000 feet (1 NM) forward.*

4. *The total sink is 15 NM × 273 feet/NM, or about 4,095 feet in 15 NM in calm air.*

(PLT012) — FAA-H-8083-13

Answers

3345　[B]　　　3346　[A]　　　3347　[B]　　　3348　[C]

GLI
3349. How many feet will a glider sink in 10 nautical miles if its lift/drag ratio is 23:1?

A— 2,400 feet.
B— 2,600 feet.
C— 4,300 feet.

L/D is lift divided by drag. This significant ratio is numerically the same as glide ratio, the ratio of forward to downward motion. Hence, 23 to 1 glide ratio would indicate:

1. $\dfrac{23}{1} = \dfrac{6{,}000 \;(feet/NM - forward)}{X \;(feet/NM - downward)}$

2. $\dfrac{23}{1} \times X = 6{,}000$

3. X = 261 feet downward for each 6,000 feet (1 NM) forward.

4. The total sink is 10 NM × 261 feet/NM, or about 2,610 feet in 10 NM in calm air.

(PLT012) — FAA-H-8083-13

GLI
3750. What minimum upward current must a glider encounter to maintain altitude?

A— At least 2 feet per second.
B— The same as the glider's sink rate.
C— The same as the adjacent down currents.

Zero sink occurs when upward currents are just strong enough to hold altitude. For a sink rate of about 2 feet per second, there must be an upward air current of at least 2 feet per second. (PLT516) — AC 00-6

GLI
3751. On which side of a rocky knoll, that is surrounded by vegetation, should a pilot find the best thermals?

A— On the side facing the Sun.
B— On the downwind side.
C— Exactly over the center.

If a rocky knoll protrudes above a grassy plane, the most likely area for thermals to occur is over the eastern slope in the forenoon and over the western slope in the afternoon. (PLT494) — AC 00-6

GLI
3752. What is one recommended method for locating thermals?

A— Fly an ever increasing circular path.
B— Maintain a straight track downwind.
C— Look for converging streamers of dust or smoke.

Look for converging streamers of dust and smoke. (PLT494) — AC 00-6

GLI
3753. What is a recommended procedure for entering a dust devil for soaring?

A— Enter above 500 feet and circle the edge in the same direction as the rotation.
B— Enter below 500 feet and circle the edge opposite the direction of rotation.
C— Enter at or above 500 feet and circle the edge opposite the direction of rotation.

At around 500 feet, the pilot makes a circle on the outside of the dust devil against the direction of rotation. (PLT494) — AC 00-6

GLI
3754. What is an important precaution when soaring in a dust devil?

A— Avoid the eye of the vortex.
B— Avoid the clear area at the outside edge of the dust.
C— Maintain the same direction as the rotation of the vortex.

The rarefied air in the eye provides very little lift, and the wall of the hollow core is very turbulent. (PLT494) — AC 00-6

GLI
3755. What is the best visual indication of a thermal?

A— Fragmented cumulus clouds with concave bases.
B— Smooth cumulus clouds with concave bases.
C— Scattered to broken sky with cumulus clouds.

Look for a cumulus with a concave base, and with a firm, sharp, unfragmented outline. (PLT494) — AC 00-6

Answers
3349   [B]   3750   [B]   3751   [A]   3752   [C]   3753   [C]   3754   [A]
3755   [B]

GLI
3756. How can a pilot locate bubble thermals?

A— Look for wet areas where recent showers have occurred.
B— Look for birds that are soaring in areas of intermittent heating.
C— Fly the area just above the boundary of a temperature inversion.

Birds may be soaring in a "bubble" thermal that has been pinched off and forced upward through intermittent shading. (PLT494) — AC 00-6

GLI
3757. Where may the most favorable type thermals for cross-country soaring be found?

A— Just ahead of a warm front.
B— Along thermal streets.
C— Under mountain waves.

Thermal streeting is a real boon to speed and distance. (PLT494) — AC 00-6

GLI
3758. Where and under what condition can enough lift be found for soaring when the weather is generally stable?

A— On the upwind side of hills or ridges with moderate winds present.
B— In mountain waves that form on the upwind side of the mountains.
C— Over isolated peaks when strong winds are present.

Stability affects the continuity and extent of lift over hills or ridges, allowing relatively streamlined upslope flow. An upslope wind of 15 knots creates lift of about 6 feet per second. (PLT173) — AC 00-6

GLI
3857. Which is an advantage of using a CG hook for a winch tow rather than the nose hook?

A— A greater percent of the line length can be used to reach altitude.
B— Maximum release altitude is limited.
C— It is the safest method of launching.

A distinct advantage of a CG hook is that the sailplane can gain a greater altitude with a given line length. (PLT304) — FAA-H-8083-13

GLI
3858. To stop pitch oscillation (porpoising) during a winch launch, the pilot should .

A— release back pressure and then pull back against the cycle of pitching oscillation to get in phase with the undulations.
B— signal the ground crew to increase the speed of the tow.
C— relax the back pressure on the control stick and shallow the angle of climb.

"Porpoising" is caused by the horizontal stabilizer oscillating in and out of a stalled condition during a winch tow. The cure is to relax back pressure on the stick and shallow the climb angle. (PLT304) — FAA-H-8083-13

GLI
3859. A pilot plans to fly solo in the front seat of a two-place glider which displays the following placards on the instrument panel:

MINIMUM PILOT WEIGHT: 135 LB
MAXIMUM PILOT WEIGHT: 220 LB

NOTE: Seat ballast should be used as necessary.

The recommended towing speed for all tows is 55 – 65 knots. What action should be taken if the pilot's weight is 115 pounds?

A— Add 20 pounds of seat ballast to the rear seat.
B— Add 55 pounds of seat ballast to obtain the average pilot weight of 170 pounds.
C— Add 20 pounds of seat ballast.

Two criteria must be satisfied in the loading of a glider:

1. The total weight must be within limits, and

2. Within those limits, placement of the weight with respect to the aerodynamic center of the wing must satisfy total moment conditions (Weight × Arm = Moment).

To satisfy the conditions specified in the question, first calculate the weight required:

135 – 115 = 20 lbs

In order for that weight to provide the same moment as the "pilot weight" it replaces, it will also need to be at the same (that is, the forward) seat location. (PLT328) — FAA-H-8083-13

GLI

3860. A pilot plans to fly solo in the front seat of a two-place glider which displays the following placards on the instrument panel:

MINIMUM PILOT WEIGHT: 135 LB
MAXIMUM PILOT WEIGHT: 220 LB

NOTE: Seat ballast should be used as necessary.

The recommended towing speed for all tows is 55 – 65 knots. What action should be taken if the pilot's weight is 125 pounds?

A— Add 10 pounds of seat ballast to the rear seat.
B— Add 10 pounds of seat ballast.
C— Add 45 pounds of seat ballast to obtain the average pilot weight of 170 pounds.

Two criteria must be satisfied in the loading of a glider:

1. The total weight must be within limits, and

2. Within those limits, placement of the weight with respect to the aerodynamic center of the wing must satisfy total moment conditions (Weight × Arm = Moment).

To satisfy the conditions specified in the question, first calculate the weight required:

> *135 – 125 = 10 lbs*

In order for that weight to provide the same moment as the "pilot weight" it replaces, it will also need to be at the same (that is, the forward) seat location. (PLT328) — FAA-H-8083-13

GLI

3869. (Refer to Figure 55.) Illustration 2 means

A— release towline.
B— ready to tow.
C— hold position.

During all glider operations there should be a wing runner, if possible. Lowering the wing and raising the hands is the signal to hold position. (PLT502) — FAA-H-8083-13

GLI

3870. (Refer to Figure 55.) Illustration 3 means

A— stop operations.
B— release towline or stop engine now.
C— take up slack.

The wing runner moving his/her hand across the throat is the signal to release the towline or stop engine now. (PLT502) — FAA-H-8083-13

GLI

3871. (Refer to Figure 55.) Which illustration is a signal to stop operation?

A— 2.
B— 3.
C— 7.

Wing runners should use a paddle, flag or some signaling device that is easily visible to the tow pilot. Moving the signaling device and free hand back and forth over the head is the signal to stop operation. (PLT502) — FAA-H-8083-13

GLI

3872. (Refer to Figure 55.) Which illustration is a signal from the sailplane for the towplane to turn right?

A— 5.
B— 6.
C— 11.

To signal the towplane to turn, move the glider to the side opposite the direction of turn and gently pull the towplane's tail out. (PLT502) — FAA-H-8083-13

GLI

3873. (Refer to Figure 55.) Which illustration is a signal that the glider is unable to release?

A— 8.
B— 10.
C— 11.

If the glider cannot release, he/she should move to the left and rock the wings. (PLT502) — FAA-H-8083-13

GLI

3874. (Refer to Figure 55.) Which illustration is a signal to the towplane to reduce airspeed?

A— 7.
B— 10.
C— 12.

To signal the towplane or ground launch crew to reduce airspeed or ground launch speed, fishtail the glider. (PLT502) — FAA-H-8083-13

Answers

3860	[B]	3869	[C]	3870	[B]	3871	[C]	3872	[A]	3873	[B]
3874	[C]									

GLI
3875. (Refer to Figure 55.) Which illustration means the towplane cannot release?

A— 6.
B— 8.
C— 9.

After the glider has signaled that he/she cannot release, the towplane will attempt to release the glider. If the towplane cannot release, he/she should fishtail the towplane. A landing on tow will then be necessary. (PLT502) — FAA-H-8083-13

GLI, LSG
3876. What corrective action should the sailplane pilot take during takeoff if the towplane is still on the ground and the sailplane is airborne and drifting to the left?

A— Crab into the wind by holding upwind (right) rudder pressure.
B— Crab into the wind so as to maintain a position directly behind the towplane.
C— Establish a right wing low drift correction to remain in the flightpath of the towplane.

Crab into the wind to maintain a position directly behind the towplane. (PLT304) — FAA-H-8083-13

GLI
3877. An indication that the glider has begun a turn too soon on aerotow is that the

A— glider's nose is pulled to the outside of the turn.
B— towplane's nose is pulled to the outside of the turn.
C— towplane will pitch up.

When a turn is begun too soon, the towplane's nose is pulled to the outside of the turn. (PLT221) — FAA-H-8083-13

GLI
3878. The sailplane has become airborne and the towplane loses power before leaving the ground. The sailplane should release immediately,

A— and maneuver to the right of the towplane.
B— extend the spoilers, and land straight ahead.
C— and maneuver to the left of the towplane.

The glider should maneuver to the right of the towplane. The towplane should move over to the left. If there is a narrow runway, a full spoiler landing should be made as soon as possible. (PLT221) — FAA-H-8083-13

GLI
3879. What should a glider pilot do if a towline breaks below 200 feet AGL?

A— Turn into the wind, then back to the runway for a downwind landing.
B— Turn away from the wind, then back to the runway for a downwind landing.
C— Land straight ahead or make slight turns to reach a suitable landing area.

At low altitude, the only alternative to landing straight ahead may be slight turns in order to reach a suitable landing area. (PLT221) — FAA-H-8083-13

GLI
3880. A pilot unintentionally enters a steep diving spiral to the left. What is the proper way to recover from this attitude without overstressing the glider?

A— Apply up-elevator pressure to raise the nose.
B— Apply more up-elevator pressure and then use right aileron pressure to control the overbanking tendency.
C— Relax the back pressure and shallow the bank; then apply up-elevator pressure until the nose has been raised to the desired position.

The correct recovery from a spiral dive is to relax back pressure on the stick and at the same time reduce the bank angle with coordinated aileron and rudder. When the bank is less than 45°, the stick may be moved back while continuing to decrease bank. (PLT219) — FAA-H-8083-13

Answers

3875 [C]	3876 [B]	3877 [B]	3878 [A]	3879 [C]	3880 [C]

GLI

3881. What corrective action should be taken if, while thermalling at minimum sink speed in turbulent air, the left wing drops while turning to the left?

A— Apply more opposite (right) aileron pressure than opposite (right) rudder pressure to counteract the overbanking tendency.
B— Apply opposite (right) rudder pressure to slow the rate of turn.
C— Lower the nose before applying opposite (right) aileron pressure.

If a wing begins to drop during a turn, it is an indication of a stall. The nose of the sailplane should be lowered before applying coordinated opposite aileron and rudder to break the stall. (PLT494) — FAA-H-8083-13

GLI

3882. A sailplane pilot can differentiate between a spin and a spiral dive because in a spiral dive,

A— the speed remains constant.
B— the G loads increase.
C— there is a small loss of altitude in each rotation.

A spiral dive, as contrasted to a spin, can be recognized by rapidly increasing speed and G loading. (PLT245) — FAA-H-8083-13

GLI

3883. How are forward slips normally performed?

A— With the direction of the slip away from any crosswind that exists.
B— With dive brakes or spoilers fully open.
C— With rudder and aileron deflection on the same side.

When using the forward slip to increase an angle of descent without acceleration, the dive brakes or spoilers are normally fully open. (PLT221) — FAA-H-8083-13

GLI

3884. What would be a proper action or procedure to use if the pilot is getting too low on a cross-country flight in a sailplane?

A— Continue on course until descending to 1,000 feet above the ground and then plan the landing approach.
B— Fly directly into the wind and make a straight-in approach at the end of the glide.
C— Have a suitable landing area selected upon reaching 2,000 feet AGL, and a specific field chosen upon reaching 1,500 feet AGL.

It is always necessary to have a suitable landing site in mind. As altitude decreases, the plans have to get more specific. The area should be narrowed down at 2,000 feet and a specific field should be selected by 1,500 feet. (PLT221) — FAA-H-8083-13

Answers

| 3881 | [C] | 3882 | [B] | 3883 | [B] | 3884 | [C] |

Lighter-Than-Air Operations

LTA
3351. The part of a balloon that bears the entire load is the

A— envelope material.
B— envelope seams.
C— load tapes (or cords).

The load tape supports the weight of the balloon and minimizes the strain on the envelope fabric. (PLT177) — FAA-H-8083-11

LTA
3352. In hot air balloons, propane is preferred to butane or other hydrocarbons because it

A— is less volatile.
B— is slower to vaporize.
C— has a lower boiling point.

Propane is preferred over butane and other hydrocarbons in balloon design because propane has a lower boiling point (-44°F). (PLT253) — FAA-H-8083-11

LTA
3353. The initial temperature at which propane boils is

A— +32°F.
B— -44°F.
C— -60°F.

Propane is preferred over butane and other hydrocarbons in balloon design because propane has a lower boiling point (-44°F). (PLT253) — FAA-H-8083-11

LTA, LSL
3354. On cold days, it may be necessary to preheat the propane tanks because

A— the temperature of the liquid propane controls the burner pressure during combustion.
B— there may be ice in the lines to the burner.
C— the propane needs to be thawed from a solid to a liquid state.

On very cold days, it may be necessary to preheat the propane tanks since the temperature of the liquid propane controls the burner pressure during combustion. (PLT254) — FAA-H-8083-11

LTA
3355. When ample liquid propane is available, propane will vaporize sufficiently to provide proper operation between the temperatures of

A— +30 to +90°F.
B— -44 to +25°F.
C— -51 to +20°F.

When ample liquid propane is available, propane will vaporize sufficiently to provide proper operation between 30°F and 90°F. (PLT250) — FAA-H-8083-11

LTA, LSL
3356. If ample propane is available, within which temperature range will propane vaporize sufficiently to provide enough pressure for burner operation during flight?

A— 0 to 30°F.
B— 10 to 30°F.
C— 30 to 90°F.

When ample liquid propane is available, propane will vaporize sufficiently to provide proper operation between 30°F and 90°F. (PLT251) — FAA-H-8083-11

LTA
3357. The valve located on the top of the propane tank which opens automatically when the pressure in the tank exceeds maximum allowable pressure is the

A— pressure relief valve.
B— metering valve.
C— blast valve.

The pressure relief valve is located on top of the fuel tank and opens automatically when the pressure in the tank exceeds the maximum allowable pressure. (PLT254) — FAA-H-8083-11

Answers
3351 [C]   3352 [C]   3353 [B]   3354 [A]   3355 [A]   3356 [C]
3357 [A]

LTA
3358. The valve located on each tank that indicates when the tank is filled to 80 percent capacity is the

A— main tank valve.
B— vapor-bleed valve.
C— pilot valve.

A vapor-bleed valve, or "spit tube," is located on each tank and indicates when the tank is filled to 80% of capacity. (PLT254) — FAA-H-8083-11

LTA, LSL
3359. The lifting forces which act on a hot air balloon are primarily the result of the interior air temperature being

A— greater than ambient temperature.
B— less than ambient temperature.
C— equal to ambient temperature.

A hot air balloon derives lift from the fact that air inside the envelope is warmer and therefore, "lighter" than the air around the balloon. (PLT237) — FAA-H-8083-11

LTA, LSL
3360. Burner efficiency of a hot air balloon decreases approximately what percent for each 1,000 feet above MSL?

A— 4 percent.
B— 8 percent.
C— 15 percent.

Burner efficiency of a hot air balloon system decreases at approximately 4% per 1,000 feet above MSL. (PLT177) — FAA-H-8083-11

LTA, LSL
3361. While in flight, frost begins forming on the outside of the fuel tank in use. This would most likely be caused by

A— water in the fuel.
B— a leak in the fuel line.
C— vaporized fuel instead of liquid fuel being drawn from the tank into the main burner.

If large quantities of vapor are withdrawn rapidly from a propane cylinder, the cooling effect of the vaporization in the tank cools the propane and lowers the vapor pressure and the rate of vaporization. (PLT254) — FAA-H-8083-11

LTA
3362. For what reason is methanol added to the propane fuel of hot air balloons?

A— To check for fuel leaks.
B— As a fire retardant.
C— As an anti-icing additive.

Since propane holds little water in solution, there is a tendency for free water to collect in the bottom of the tanks where it may reach the dip tube, be piped into the burner system, and freeze up the regulators. If water contamination is suspected, methyl alcohol (methanol) should be added to the system. (PLT251) — FAA-H-8083-11

LTA, LSL
3363. On a balloon equipped with a blast valve, the blast valve is used for

A— climbs and descents only.
B— altitude control.
C— emergencies only.

The blast valve is located on the burner and controls ascent or descent by use of short bursts of power. When reaching the desired altitude, the pilot should reduce the frequency of blasts. As the envelope cools, the desired altitude can be maintained by using short blasts of heat evenly spaced. (PLT177) — FAA-H-8083-11

LTA, LSL
3364. The term "weigh-off" means to determine the

A— static equilibrium of the balloon as loaded for flight.
B— amount of gas required for an ascent to a preselected altitude.
C— standard weight and balance of the balloon.

A weigh-off is used to determine the static equilibrium of the balloon. (PLT123) — FAA-H-8083-11

Answers

3358	[B]	3359	[A]	3360	[A]	3361	[C]	3362	[C]	3363	[B]
3364	[A]									

LTA, LSL

3365. What causes false lift which sometimes occurs during launch procedures?

A— Closing the maneuvering vent too rapidly.
B— Excessive temperature within the envelope.
C— Venturi effect of the wind on the envelope.

False lift is caused by the venturi effect produced by the wind blowing across an inflated but stationary envelope. This is "dynamic lift" created by relative air movement. If the balloon is released, the relative wind decreases as the balloon accelerates to the speed of the wind and false lift decreases. (PLT237) — FAA-H-8083-11

LTA

3366. What is the relationship of false lift with the wind?

A— False lift increases as the wind accelerates the balloon.
B— False lift does not exist if the surface winds are calm.
C— False lift decreases as the wind accelerates the balloon.

False lift is caused by the venturi effect produced by the wind blowing across an inflated but stationary envelope. This is "dynamic lift" created by relative air movement. If the balloon is released, the relative wind decreases as the balloon accelerates to the speed of the wind and false lift decreases. (PLT237) — FAA-H-8083-11

LTA

3367. What would cause a gas balloon to start a descent if a cold air mass is encountered and the envelope becomes cooled?

A— A density differential.
B— A barometric pressure differential.
C— The contraction of the gas.

As the gas is cooled, it contracts and becomes more dense and so displaces less air. (PLT183) — FAA-H-8083-11

LTA, LSL

3368. Under which condition will an airship float in the air?

A— When buoyant force equals horizontal equilibrium existing between propeller thrust and airship drag.
B— When buoyant force is less than the difference between airship weight and the weight of the air volume being displaced.
C— When buoyant force equals the difference between airship weight and the weight of the air volume being displaced.

A lighter-than-air craft is in equilibrium when buoyancy equals weight. The buoyant force is equal to the weight of the air volume displaced. (PLT153) — Goodyear Airship Operations Manual

LTA, LSL

3369. During flight in an airship, when is vertical equilibrium established?

A— When buoyancy is greater than airship weight.
B— When buoyancy equals airship weight.
C— When buoyancy is less than airship weight.

A lighter-than-air craft is in equilibrium when buoyancy equals weight. The buoyant force is equal to the weight of the air volume displaced. (PLT153) — Goodyear Airship Operations Manual

LTA, LSL

3370. An airship descending through a steep temperature inversion will

A— show no change in superheat as altitude is lost.
B— show a decrease in superheat as altitude is lost.
C— become progressively lighter, thus becoming increasingly more difficult to drive down.

As the airship descends into the colder temperature of the inversion, the weight of the displaced air volume is increasing, thereby increasing buoyancy. (PLT153) — Goodyear Airship Operations Manual

Answers

| 3365 [C] | 3366 [C] | 3367 [C] | 3368 [C] | 3369 [B] | 3370 [C] |

LTA
3371. What is airship superheat?

A— A condition of excessive exterior temperature of the envelope.
B— The temperature of the lifting gas exceeding the red line.
C— The difference between outside air temperature and the temperature inside the envelope.

Superheat is the difference between outside air temperature and the temperature in the airship envelope. (PLT153) — Goodyear Airship Operations Manual

LTA
3372. In relation to the operation of an airship, what is the definition of aerostatics?

A— The gravitational factors involving equilibrium of a body freely suspended in the atmosphere.
B— The science of the dynamics involved in the expansion and contraction of hydrogen gas.
C— The expansion and contraction of the lifting gas helium.

Aerostatics are the gravitational factors involving equilibrium of a body freely suspended in the atmosphere. (PLT124) — Goodyear Airship Operations Manual

LTA
3373. Below pressure height, each 5°F of positive superheat amounts to approximately

A— 1 percent of gross lift.
B— 2 percent of net lift.
C— 2 percent of total lift.

Each 5°F amounts to about 1% of gross lift. (PLT153) — Goodyear Airship Operations Manual

LTA
3374. When the airship is at pressure height and superheat increases, constant pressure must be maintained by valving

A— gas from the envelope.
B— air from the envelope.
C— gas from the ballonets.

Expansion of the gas will cause the ballonets to completely deflate at pressure height. Gas must be valved from the envelope to maintain constant pressure. (PLT153) — Goodyear Airship Operations Manual

LTA
3375. How does the pilot know when pressure height has been reached?

A— Liquid in the gas manometer will rise and the liquid in the air manometer will fall below normal levels.
B— Liquid in the gas and air manometers will fall below the normal level.
C— Liquid in the gas manometer will fall and the liquid in the air manometer will rise above normal levels.

When pressure height has been reached, the liquid in the gas manometer will rise and the liquid in the air manometer will fall below normal levels. (PLT153) — Goodyear Airship Operations Manual

LTA, LSL
3376. The pressure height of an airship is the altitude at which

A— the airship would be unable to gain more altitude.
B— gas pressure would reach 3 inches of water.
C— the ballonet(s) would be empty.

Expansion of the gas will cause the ballonets to completely deflate at pressure height. Thus, no further increase in displaced air volume is possible. (PLT153) — Goodyear Airship Operations Manual

LTA, LSL
3377. The maximum altitude that a rigid airship can reach (under a given atmospheric condition) and then return safely to the surface is determined by

A— the disposable load.
B— ballonet capacity.
C— pressure altitude.

Expansion of the gas will cause the ballonets to completely deflate at pressure height. Thus, no further increase in displaced air volume is possible. (PLT153) — Goodyear Airship Operations Manual

LTA, LSL
3378. An unbalanced condition of an airship in flight must be overcome by

A— valving air from the ballonets.
B— valving gas from the envelope.
C— a negative or a positive dynamic force.

Dynamic force, created by movement through the air, must be used to overcome any out-of-equilibrium condition. (PLT153) — Goodyear Airship Operations Manual

Answers

| 3371 | [C] | 3372 | [A] | 3373 | [A] | 3374 | [A] | 3375 | [A] | 3376 | [C] |
| 3377 | [C] | 3378 | [C] | | | | | | | | | | |

LTA
3379. Air damper valves should normally be kept closed during climbs because any air forced into the system would

A— increase the amount of gas that must be exhausted to prevent the airship from ascending at an excessively high rate.
B— increase the amount of air to be exhausted, resulting in a lower rate of ascent.
C— decrease the purity of the gas within the envelope.

Any air entering the ballonets through the damper valves will have to be exhausted overboard as the gas expands. This slows the rate of ascent. (PLT221) — Goodyear Airship Operations Manual

LTA
3380. To check the gas pressures (pressure height) of an airship during a climb, the air damper valves should be

A— opened forward and closed aft.
B— opened aft and closed forward.
C— closed.

If damper valves are open, ram air pressure will keep the ballonets inflated longer than they should be inflated. (PLT158) — Goodyear Airship Operations Manual

LTA, LSL
3396. What condition does a rising barometer indicate for balloon operations?

A— Decreasing clouds and wind.
B— Chances of thunderstorms.
C— Approaching frontal activity.

Within a high-pressure system, flying conditions are generally more favorable than in low-pressure areas because there are normally fewer clouds, better visibility, calm or light winds, and less turbulence. (PLT516) — AC 00-6

LTA
3885. Why should propane tanks not be refueled in a closed trailer or truck?

A— Propane vapor is one and one-half times heavier than air and will linger in the floor of the truck or trailer.
B— The propane vapor is odorless and the refuelers may be overcome by the fumes.
C— Propane is very cold and could cause damage to the truck or trailer.

Since propane vapor is 1-1/2 times heavier than air, it can linger on the floor. (PLT254) — FAA-H-8083-11

LTA
3886. Why should special precautions be taken when filling the propane bottles?

A— Propane is transferred from the storage tanks to the propane bottles under high pressure.
B— During transfer, propane reaches a high temperature and can cause severe burns.
C— Propane vapor is super-cold and may cause severe freeze burns.

Precautions, such as wearing gloves, should be taken when filling the propane bottles because propane is super-cold and may cause severe freeze burns. (PLT250) — FAA-H-8083-11

LTA, LSL
3895. All fuel tanks should be fired during preflight to determine

A— the burner pressure and condition of the valves.
B— that the pilot light functions properly on each tank.
C— if there are any leaks in the tank.

Burner output is dependent on fuel pressure. Proper valve operation is critical to safety and control. (PLT177) — FAA-H-8083-11

Answers

3379 [B]	3380 [C]	3396 [A]	3885 [A]	3886 [C]	3895 [A]

LTA

3896. What is a recommended ascent upon initial launch?

A— Maximum ascent to altitude to avoid low-level thermals.

B— Shallow ascent to avoid flashbacks of flames as the envelope is cooled.

C— A moderate-rate ascent to determine wind directions at different levels.

A moderate-rate ascent is recommended initially to accurately determine the wind direction at various altitudes. (PLT304) — FAA-H-8083-11

LTA, LSL

3897. What is a potential hazard when climbing at maximum rate?

A— The envelope may collapse.

B— Deflation ports may be forced open.

C— The rapid flow of air may extinguish the burner and pilot light.

The positive pressure on the top of the envelope could force the deflation ports open. (PLT219) — FAA-H-8083-11

LTA

3898. How should a roundout from a moderate-rate ascent to level flight be made?

A— Reduce the amount of heat gradually as the balloon is approaching altitude.

B— Cool the envelope by venting and add heat just before arriving at altitude.

C— Vent at altitude and add heat upon settling back down to altitude.

The most efficient roundout is to reduce the frequency of blasts so that the envelope cools to a level flight temperature just as the balloon reaches the desired altitude. (PLT219) — FAA-H-8083-11

LTA

3899. What is one procedure for relighting the burner while in flight?

A— Open the regulator or blast valve full open and light the pilot light.

B— Close the tank valves, vent the fuel lines, reopen the tank valves, and light the pilot light.

C— Open another tank valve, open the regulator or blast valve, and light the main jets with reduced flow.

The pilot should open another tank valve, open the regular, or blast valve and light off the main jet with reduced flow. (PLT177) — FAA-H-8083-11

LTA

3900. The windspeed is such that it is necessary to deflate the envelope as rapidly as possible during a landing. When should the deflation port (rip panel) be opened?

A— The instant the gondola contacts the surface.

B— As the balloon skips off the surface the first time and the last of the ballast has been discharged.

C— Just prior to ground contact.

In a high-wind landing, the envelope should be ripped just prior to ground contact. (PLT184) — FAA-H-8083-11

LTA, LSL

3901. When landing a free balloon, what should the occupants do to minimize landing shock?

A— Be seated on the floor of the basket.

B— Stand with knees slightly bent, in the center of the gondola, facing the direction of movement.

C— Stand back-to-back and hold onto the load ring.

By facing forward with knees bent, the body is balanced and the legs act as springs, absorbing the landing shock. (PLT184) — FAA-H-8083-11

Answers

| 3896 [C] | 3897 [B] | 3898 [A] | 3899 [C] | 3900 [C] | 3901 [B] |

LTA
3902. Prior to a high-wind landing, the pilot in command should brief the passengers to prepare for the landing by

A— kneeling on the floor and facing aft.
B— crouching on the floor and jumping out of the basket upon contact with the ground.
C— crouching while hanging on in two places, and remaining in the basket until advised otherwise.

By facing forward with knees bent, the body is balanced and the legs act as springs absorbing the landing shock. It is important that everyone remain in the basket until the envelope cannot lift the balloon back into the air. (PLT208) — FAA-H-8083-11

LTA
3903. Which precaution should be exercised if confronted with the necessity of having to land a balloon when the air is turbulent?

A— Land in any available lake close to the upwind shore.
B— Land in the center of the largest available field.
C— Land in the trees to absorb shock forces, thus cushioning the landing.

At one time or another a balloonist will be faced with the necessity of having to land in turbulent air. When this happens, the landing should be attempted in the middle of the largest field available. (PLT486) — FAA-H-8083-11

LTA
3904. What action is most appropriate when an envelope over-temperature condition occurs?

A— Throw all unnecessary equipment overboard.
B— Descend; hover in ground effect until the envelope cools.
C— Land as soon as practical.

An envelope over-temperature can seriously degrade the strength of the envelope, so land as soon as is practical. (PLT208) — FAA-H-8083-11

LTA, LSL
3905. In addition to the required documents, what carry-on equipment should be accounted for during preflight?

A— Flotation gear.
B— Emergency locator transmitter.
C— Two means of burner ignition.

As a precaution against flameout, an ignitor must be carried to relight the burner. A second ignitor is necessary in case the first malfunctions or is lost overboard. (PLT473) — FAA-H-8083-11

LTA, LSL
3906. How should a balloon fuel system be checked for leaks prior to flight?

A— Listen and smell.
B— Check all connections with a lighted match.
C— Cover all connections and tubing with soapy water.

Propane is under pressure and has an artificial odor. If a leak exists, the fuel will "hiss" out and can be smelled. (PLT251) — FAA-H-8083-11

LTA, LSL
3907. In a balloon, best fuel economy in level flight can be accomplished by

A— riding the haze line in a temperature inversion.
B— short blasts of heat at high frequency.
C— long blasts of heat at low frequency.

The desired envelope temperature for level flight is best maintained by short blasts at high frequency. (PLT130) — FAA-H-8083-11

LTA
3908. The minimum size a launch site should be is at least

A— twice the height of the balloon.
B— 100 feet for every 1 knot of wind.
C— 500 feet on the downwind side.

A free balloon will move about 100 feet per minute for every knot of wind. A pilot should allow 100 feet of travel for each knot of wind speed. (PLT389) — Powerline Excerpts

Answers

| 3902 | [C] | 3903 | [B] | 3904 | [C] | 3905 | [C] | 3906 | [A] | 3907 | [B] |
| 3908 | [B] | | | | | | | | | | |

LTA, LSL

3909. What is a hazard of rapid descents?

A— Wind shear can cavitate one side of the envelope, forcing air out of the mouth.

B— The pilot light cannot remain lit with the turbulent air over the basket.

C— Aerodynamic forces may collapse the envelope.

Turbulent airflow may extinguish the pilot light. (PLT125)
— FAA-H-8083-11

LTA, LSL

3910. It may be possible to make changes in the direction of flight in a hot air balloon by

A— flying a constant atmospheric pressure gradient.

B— operating at different flight altitudes.

C— operating above the friction level, if there is no gradient wind.

A free balloon has no propulsion and so must take advantage of differing wind directions at various altitudes. (PLT219) — FAA-H-8083-11

LTA

3911. What action should be taken if a balloon encounters unforecast weather and shifts direction abruptly while in the vicinity of a thunderstorm?

A— Land immediately.

B— Descend to and maintain the lowest altitude possible.

C— Ascend to an altitude which will ensure adequate obstacle clearance in all directions.

Weather conditions during flight may take a sudden and unpredictable change. When this occurs and if powerful wind gusts, thermals, wind shears, or precipitation and lightning, are encountered, the appropriate action is to land as soon as possible. (PLT208) — Goodyear Operations Manual

LTA

3912. To land an airship that is 250 pounds heavy when the wind is calm, the best landing can usually be made if the airship is

A— in trim.

B— nose heavy approximately 20°.

C— tail heavy approximately 20°.

A heavy airship should be trimmed tail heavy to provide dynamic lift during approach. (PLT221) — Goodyear Operations Manual

LTA

3913. Which takeoff procedure is considered to be most hazardous for an airship?

A— Maintaining only 50 percent of the maximum permissible positive angle of inclination.

B— Failing to apply full engine power properly on all takeoffs, regardless of wind.

C— Maintaining a negative angle of inclination during takeoff after elevator response is adequate for controllability.

The most hazardous takeoff condition would be maintaining a negative angle of inclination during takeoff, after elevator response is adequate for stability. (PLT221) — Goodyear Operations Manual

LTA

3914. Which action is necessary in order to perform a normal descent in an airship?

A— Valve gas.

B— Valve air.

C— Take air into the aft ballonets.

An airship is normally flown heavy, so a power reduction would cause a descent. Air should be taken into the forward ballonets. (PLT133) — Goodyear Operations Manual

LTA, LSL

3915. If an airship should experience failure of both engines during flight and neither engine can be restarted, what initial immediate action must the pilot take?

A— The airship must be driven down to a landing before control and envelope shape are lost.

B— The emergency auxiliary power unit must be started for electrical power to the airscoop blowers so that ballonet inflation can be maintained.

C— Immediate preparations to operate the airship as a free balloon are necessary.

An airship without power must be operated as a free balloon. (PLT208) — Goodyear Operations Manual

Answers

| 3909 | [B] | 3910 | [B] | 3911 | [A] | 3912 | [C] | 3913 | [C] | 3914 | [A] |
| 3915 | [C] | | | | | | | | | | |

Powered Parachute and Weight-Shift Control Operations

The explanations for the answers given describe the concepts that should be understood before taking the test. Many of these questions are based on older weight-shift and PPC designs and unique characteristics of specific designs. The answers given are the best of the choices provided.

PPC, WSC, LSA, LSR, LSP, LSW

3958. The formation of ice in a carburetor's throat is indicated by

A— rough engine operation, followed by a decrease in oil pressure.
B— a rapid increase in RPM, followed by rough engine operation.
C— a drop in RPM, followed by rough engine operation.

Carb ice restricts the airflow into the engine reducing its power and resultant RPM, which also results in rough engine operation. (PLT190) — FAA-H-8083-29

Answers (A) and (B) are incorrect because oil pressure is not significantly affected by carb ice, and carb ice will not increase RPM.

PPC, WSC, LSA, LSR, LSP, LSW

3959. The purpose of the fuel tank vent system is to

A— remove dangerous vapors from the aircraft and prevent an explosion.
B— allow air to enter the tank as fuel is consumed.
C— ensure a proper fuel to air ratio.

Fuel tanks are not normally sealed systems; they need air venting because the fuel level is falling, therefore no vacuum builds up in the fuel tank. (PLT253) — FAA-H-8083-29

Answer (A) is incorrect because fuel tanks are isolated and fuel vapors are prevalent within the fuel tank confined area. Answer (C) relates to 2-stroke engines only. It is incorrect because fuel and oil are mixed either before the mixture is poured into the fuel tank (pre-mix), or after when oil is injected into the air/fuel mixture oil before it goes into the combustion chamber.

PPC, WSC, LSA, LSR, LSP, LSW

3960. A standby source of fuel to an engine in a powered parachute is typically

A— from an electrically powered pump.
B— through gravity feed.
C— from a pressurized fuel tank.

Some engines use an electric boost pump similar to an airplane to supply a back-up pump in case the engine-driven fuel pump fails when low to the ground. (PLT253) — FAA-H-8083-29

Answer (B) is incorrect because if a gravity feed system was used, then this would supply fuel and no standby pump would be needed. Answer (C) is incorrect because pressurized fuel tanks are not normally used for light-sport aircraft.

PPC, WSC, LSA, LSR, LSP, LSW

3961. The fuel vents on many powered parachutes and weight shift control aircraft are located

A— in the fuel cap.
B— adjacent to the crankcase breather.
C— in the fuel tank pressure relief valve.

The fuel vent in many but not all fuel tanks is in the fuel cap. (PLT253) — FAA-H-8083-29

Answer (B) is incorrect because the crankcase breather is used on a 4-stroke engine and has nothing to do with the fuel supply system on a 2-stroke engine. Answer (C) is incorrect because most PPCs do not have pressurized fuel tanks nor a fuel tank pressure relief valve.

PPC, WSC, LSA, LSR, LSP, LSW

3962. Combusted fuel is expelled from a 2-cycle engine through an

A— exhaust valve and exhaust port.
B— exhaust valve.
C— exhaust port.

All 2-stroke engines expel exhaust through a passage called the exhaust port. (PLT253) — FAA-H-8083-29

Answers (A) and (B) are incorrect because only some higher power engines use an exhaust valve, while all have an exhaust port.

Answers

3958 [C]	3959 [B]	3960 [A]	3961 [A]	3962 [C]

PPC, WSC, LSA, LSR, LSP, LSW
3963. Fuel enters a two-cycle engine through an

A— intake port and intake valve.
B— intake port and reed valve.
C— intake valve and reed valve.

The air/fuel/oil mixture enters the crankcase through an intake port that some types of valve systems use to close off the crankcase and pressurize the air/fuel/oil mixture, before it is ported up to the top of the piston. Many engines use the positioning of the piston as the intake valve system, others use a rotary valve, while still others use a one-way flow "reed" or "poppet" valve. (PLT253) — FAA-H-8083-29

Answer (B) is incorrect because not all two-stroke engines use a reed valve. Answer (C) is incorrect because you must have an intake port.

PPC, WSC, LSA, LSR, LSP, LSW
3964. The first indication of carburetor ice in an aircraft with a four-cycle engine and fixed-pitch propeller is

A— an increase in RPM.
B— a decrease in RPM.
C— a decrease in oil pressure.

The first symptom of carb ice in a 4-stroke engine is a reduction in engine RPM. (PLT190) — FAA-H-8083-29

Answer (A) is incorrect because carb ice reduces RPM. Answer (C) is incorrect because carb ice has no noticeable effect on oil pressure.

PPC, WSC, LSA, LSR, LSP, LSW
3965. Air cooled engines dissipate heat

A— through cooling fins on the cylinder and head.
B— by air flowing through the radiator fins.
C— through the cylinder head temperature probe.

Air cooled engines use fins on the cylinder and head, forcing air past them as the primary means to dissipate heat. (PLT342) — FAA-H-8083-29

Answer (B) is incorrect because air cooled engines do not have separate radiators; only water and oil coolers need a radiator. Answer (C) is incorrect because the probe is not used to dissipate heat.

PPC, WSC, LSA, LSR, LSP, LSW
3966. Coolant in a liquid cooled engine is normally circulated by

A— capillary attraction.
B— an electric pump.
C— an engine driven pump.

Most liquid-cooled systems are driven from some mechanical source or pump on the engine. (PLT342) — FAA-H-8083-29

Answer (A) is incorrect because capillary attraction is not normally used for engine cooling. Answer (B) is incorrect because electric pumps are usually used as coolant pumps.

PPC, WSC, LSA, LSR, LSP, LSW
3967. In order to improve engine efficiency, two-cycle engine exhaust systems are tuned to

A— close the exhaust valve to stop the fuel mixture from exiting the cylinder.
B— stop the fuel mixture from exiting the cylinder before combustion.
C— use a reed valve to stop the fuel mixture from exiting the cylinder.

If there is not an exhaust valve, tuned exhaust systems are designed to provide back pressure pulses at the exhaust port. The tuned exhaust bounces pressure back at the appropriate time, so the fuel mixture stays in the combustion chamber while both intake and exhaust ports are open. (PLT343) — FAA-H-8083-29

Answer (A) is incorrect because if the exhaust port has a valve, it is not as critical to have a tuned exhaust to provide back pressure at the exhaust port. There are not usually exhaust valves in a 2-stroke engine; however, some 2-stroke engines do have them. An example of this is the RAVE exhaust valve on the ROTAX 618. Answer (C) is incorrect because the reed valve is typically used for the intake air/fuel mixture.

Answers

3963 [A]	3964 [B]	3965 [A]	3966 [C]	3967 [B]

PPC, WSC, LSA, LSR, LSP, LSW

3968. 2-cycle engine thrust and fuel efficiency can be greatly compromised when

A— exhaust systems are installed that are not specifically tuned for an engine.
B— carbon deposits build up on exhaust valves.
C— intake valve lifters fail to pressurize and provide adequate fuel to the combustion chamber.

The exhaust systems should be tuned to the engine for maximum efficiency. (PLT343) — FAA-H-8083-29

Answer (B) is incorrect because most 2-stroke engines do not have exhaust valves. Answer (C) is incorrect because not all 2-stroke engines have intake valve lifters.

PPC, WSC, LSA, LSR, LSP, LSW

3969. The purpose of a kill switch is to

A— shut off the fuel to the carburetor.
B— ground the lead wire to the ignition coil shutting down the powerplant.
C— ground the battery eliminating current for the ignition system.

The kill switch shuts down the engine. (PLT207) — FAA-H-8083-29

Answer (A) is incorrect because a fuel valve shuts off fuel. Answer (C) is incorrect because the battery should already be grounded.

PPC, WSC, LSA, LSR, LSP, LSW

3970. A typical two-cycle engine ignition coil is powered by

A— a battery.
B— a battery or an alternator.
C— a magneto.

The magneto is an engine-driven generator that powers the ignition system and also supplies extra power to aircraft electrical system. (PLT478) — FAA-H-8083-29

Answers (A) and (B) are incorrect because the battery is further down the line, and is also powered by the magneto.

PPC, WSC, LSA, LSR, LSP, LSW

3971. Many 4-cycle engines utilize what type of lubrication system?

A— Forced.
B— Gravity.
C— Fuel/oil mixture.

Most 4-stroke engines have an oil pump that forces the oil through the system. (PLT343) — FAA-H-8083-29

Answer (B) is incorrect because gravity systems are not a typical oil supply system. Answer (C) is incorrect because a fuel/oil mixture system is on 2-stroke engines only.

PPC, WSC, LSA, LSR, LSP, LSW

3972. Adding more oil to the fuel than specified by the manufacturer of a 2-cycle engine will result in

A— increased engine performance.
B— increased carbon buildup and engine fouling.
C— increased engine lubrication and optimal performance.

Extra oil in the fuel would cause inefficient burning and more carbon buildup as a result. (PLT343) — FAA-H-8083-29

Answers (A) and (C) are incorrect because oil does not increase performance.

PPC, WSC, LSA, LSR, LSP, LSW

3973. Pilots should refrain from revving an engine with a reduction drive because

A— the crankshaft counterbalances may be dislodged and cause extreme engine vibration.
B— the propeller blade tips may exceed their RPM limits.
C— the torque exerted on the gears during excessive acceleration and deceleration can cause the gear box to self-destruct.

Revving the engine causes more stress than not revving it; it is good practice to not rev it unnecessarily. (PLT343) — FAA-H-8083-29

Answer (A) is incorrect because not all engines have counterbalances. Answer (B) is incorrect because the propeller is designed to not exceed its maximum RPM at full power.

Answers

| 3968 [A] | 3969 [B] | 3970 [C] | 3971 [A] | 3972 [B] | 3973 [C] |

PPC, WSC, LSA, LSR, LSP, LSW

3974. During preflight, the fuel vent system should always be checked

A— to ensure the vent is closed.
B— to ensure the vent is open.
C— to ensure the vent system pressure is in the green range.

The fuel vent needs to be open for flight for the air to fill the fuel tank as the fuel is consumed. (PLT253) — FAA-H-8083-29

Answer (A) is incorrect because a closed fuel vent would cause a power loss in flight when air is unable to fill the tank as fuel is used. Answer (C) is incorrect because there is no pressure in the fuel tank since it is vented.

PPC, WSC, LSA, LSR, LSP, LSW

3975. Carburetor ice can form

A— only at temperatures near freezing and the humidity near the saturation point.
B— when the outside air temperature is as high as 100 degrees F and the humidity is as low as 50%.
C— at any temperature or humidity level.

Carburetor ice can form when the outside air temperature is as high as 100°F and the humidity is as low as 50%. This is not the optimum conditions for the ice to form, but it can form under these conditions. (PLT190) — FAA-H-8083-29

Answer (A) is incorrect because carb ice can form when it is as high at 100°F. Answer (C) is incorrect because some moisture is needed to form the ice.

WSC, LSW

3976. As a weight shift aircraft wing approaches a stall, the wing tips

A— decrease the wing's angle of attack.
B— act in much the same way as ailerons on a three-axis aircraft.
C— increase the wing's angle of attack.

As the angle of attack of the wing is increased, the nose is at a higher angle of attack and therefore stalls first while the tips keep flying. This drops the nose and as a result, decreases the wing's angle of attack. (PLT214) — FAA-H-8083-5

Answer (B) is incorrect because the wing tips act the same way ailerons do while flying normally and while approaching a stall. Answer (C) is incorrect because the tips only increase the wing's angle of attack when the wing is at a low angle of attack, far from a stall.

WSC, LSW

3977. During a wing stall, the wing tips of a weight shift aircraft are

A— ineffective for stall recovery.
B— effective for stall recovery.
C— effective only when combined with maximum engine output.

Since the wing tips are at a lower angle of attack, they do not normally stall when the rest of the wing is stalled. They keep flying, creating an up-force in back of the CG—causing the nose to rotate down and decrease the angle of attack of the wing—therefore they are very effective for stall recovery. (PLT214) — FAA-H-8083-5

Answer (A) is incorrect because the tips are very effective for stall recovery, allowing the nose to fall through. Answer (C) is incorrect because the tips have more effect for stall recovery than the engine power.

WSC, LSW

3978. The crosstube is positioned by

A— a quick release pin.
B— self-locking bolts.
C— restraining cables attached to the rear of the keel.

The crossbar is pulled back to tension the airframe into the sail with the crossbar cables. These are attached to a connection point on the rear of the keel. (PLT346) — FAA-H-8083-5

Answers (A) and (B) are incorrect because these are fasteners and would only make smaller variations in the crossbar position if these fasteners were adjusted to different settings.

Answers

3974 [B]	3975 [B]	3976 [A]	3977 [B]	3978 [C]

WSC, LSW

3979. On some trikes, the hang point is part of

A— a variable trim arrangement that allows the pilot to adjust the aircraft center of gravity during flight to obtain the most favorable aircraft performance.

B— an adjustable trim arrangement that allows the pilot to adjust the aircraft center of gravity during flight to obtain the most favorable aircraft performance.

C— an adjustable trim arrangement that allows the center of gravity to shift fore and aft along the wing's keel.

Most trikes have an adjustment to move the position on the keel fore and aft on the ground. This is a common way to adjust the trim speed and bar position of the wing. (PLT214) — FAA-H-8083-5

Answers (A) and (B) are incorrect because although this is a viable design concept that has been and may be used for trikes, not many incorporate the complexity of a variable CG during flight.

WSC, LSW

3980. The keel pocket's purpose is to

A— act as a longitudinal stabilizer, keeping the wing from wandering left and right.

B— act as a roll stabilizer, keeping the wing from wandering left and right.

C— act as a yaw stabilizer, keeping the wing from wandering left and right.

The most significant effect a keel pocket could have on stability would be for yaw. This was an early design concept used in the development of the flex wing. Today, the wing sweep, washout, and airfoil shape are designed to optimize the tracking (yaw) for the vertical axis. Keel pockets today are a fabric channel in the sail material the keel is inserted into, to hold the keel in place at the root of the wing. (PLT346) — FAA-H-8083-5

Answers (A) and (B) are incorrect because the keel pocket does not supply this stability.

WSC, LSW

3981. How does the wing design feature "washout" affect the production of lift?

A— The wing tips continue producing lift when the main body of the wing is not producing lift.

B— The main body of the wing continues to produce lift when the wing tips are not producing lift.

C— The center of lift moves from the trailing edge of the wing, to the leading edge of the wing, as the wing begins to stall.

The washout/twist in the wing, starts with a high angle of attack at the root/nose, and decreases the angle of attack as the you approach each tip. This washout/twist, sweep, and airfoil shape is designed into the wing to make the nose lose lift first while the tips keep flying at high angles of attack. (PLT214) — FAA-H-8083-5

Answer (B) is incorrect because this happens only when the wing is at very low angles of attack where the wing is not near the critical angle of attack to stall. Answer (C) is incorrect because this is not the design of any trike wing and would produce a wing that would be unstable near the stall.

WSC, LSW

3982. The wing of a weight-shift aircraft twists so that the angle of attack

A— from the center of the wing to the wing tip is variable and can be adjusted by the pilot in flight to optimize performance.

B— changes from a low angle of attack at the center of the wing, to a high angle of attack at the tips.

C— changes from a high angle of attack at the center of the wing, to a low angle of attack at the tips.

The fundamental design of the flex wing is for the wing to twist from a high angle of attack at the nose, to a lower angle of attack at the tips. (PLT214) — FAA-H-8083-5

Answer (A) is incorrect because this would provide a wing that would be unstable and dangerous. Flex wings are not designed this way. Answer (B) is incorrect because this only applies for some wing designs but not all. Varying the twist in the wing is common to most high performance hang gliders in flight and used as one method to trim weight-shift wings as well.

Answers

3979　[C]　　　　3980　[C]　　　　3981　[A]　　　　3982　[C]

PPC, LSP
3983. During flight, advancing thrust will

A— increase airspeed.
B— cause the aircraft to climb.
C— cause the aircraft to increase airspeed and climb.

Throttle controls vertical speed in a PPC. Advancing the throttle will produce decreased descent rates or increased climb rates. Speed in a PPC is controlled by the weight and not the throttle. (PLT346) — FAA-H-8083-29

Answers (A) and (C) are incorrect because throttle does not affect airspeed.

PPC, LSP
3984. The torque effect of an engine that rotates clockwise in a powered parachute is counteracted by

A— increasing the length of the right and decreasing the length of the left riser cables.
B— decreasing the length of the left riser cables.
C— decreasing the length of right riser cables.

A clockwise or right-turning propeller when viewed from the rear creates an opposite reaction to turn the undercarriage aircraft to the left. Therefore, a slight right-hand turn needs to be built into the aircraft to accommodate for this torque. Many designs are used by manufacturers to accomplish this. Decreasing the length of the right-hand riser will accomplish this by bringing the right side of the wing down. (PLT346) — FAA-H-8083-29

Answers (A) and (B) are incorrect because they would create a turn in the wrong direction.

PPC, LSP
3985. The steering bars

A— are used during taxi operations with the parachute stowed.
B— control the outboard trailing edge of the parachute.
C— control the main landing gear brakes.

The steering bars are the main control to turning in flight. Pushing on the right-hand steering bar will pull the right control line, lower the trailing edge of the right wing, create more drag on the right side and turn the aircraft to the right. (PLT346) — FAA-H-8083-29

Answers (A) and (C) are incorrect because the steering bars control the wing and are not used for ground operations.

PPC, LSP
3986. The center of gravity tube is

A— lengthened for heavier pilots.
B— shortened for lighter pilots.
C— lengthened for lighter pilots.

The lighter the pilot, the more rearward the wing attachment should be for the hanging airframe to be balanced properly. Most modern designs have a number of wing attachment points fore and aft on the airframe. For the tube CG adjustment system, lengthening the CG tube moves the wing attachment point back to account for the lightweight person in the front. (PLT346) — FAA-H-8083-29

Answer (A) is incorrect because this would balance the airframe with the nose wheel too low. Answer (B) is incorrect because this would move the CG forward and the front wheel would be too high.

PPC, LSP
3987. The fan guard surrounds the propeller and

A— increases aerodynamic efficiency.
B— reduces "P" factor.
C— protects the parachute suspension lines from damage.

The purpose of the fan guard is to protect the parachute lines from hitting the prop. (PLT346) — FAA-H-8083-29

Answers (A) and (B) are incorrect because the fan guard reduces performance and has no effect on P factor.

PPC, LSP
3988. Cross ports in the parachute ribs aid in

A— weight reduction of the canopy.
B— the pressurization of the neighboring cells.
C— drying of the canopy.

Cross ports in the wing ribs allow air to flow sideways from cell to cell, called "cross flow" in the wing. This causes the cells next to each other to transfer pressure inside the wing and cells to pressurize neighboring cells. (PLT346) — FAA-H-8083-29

Answers

| 3983 [B] | 3984 [C] | 3985 [B] | 3986 [C] | 3987 [C] | 3988 [B] |

PPC, LSP

3989. Splicing severed suspension lines

A— is permissible if using the same size material as the original line.
B— is a very dangerous practice.
C— is an acceptable field repair.

Splicing lines is dangerous because you can change the airfoil; the lines could come loose and go through the prop. (PLT346) — FAA-H-8083-29

Answers (A) and (C) are incorrect because splicing is a dangerous practice.

PPC, LSP

3990. Tying a severed suspension line

A— will change the shape of the wing and is not permissible.
B— is permissible if it is shortened no more than six inches.
C— is an acceptable field repair.

Tying a severed suspension line would shorten it and create a discontinuity in the wing shape and is not acceptable. (PLT346) — FAA-H-8083-29

Answers (B) and (C) are incorrect because tying is a dangerous practice.

PPC, LSP

3991. What gives your powered parachute wing/canopy its airfoil shape?

A— The risers because, by decreasing the length of the right riser you will get the precise airfoil shape.
B— The suspension lines as they are precisely measured and fitted to a specific location.
C— The air as it enters the cell openings on the leading edge of the airfoil.

The precise lengths of the suspension lines determine the bottom shape of the airfoil. Airfoil-shaped ribs attached to the bottom of the airfoil where the suspension lines are attached define the top shape of the airfoil. (PLT346) — FAA-H-8083-29

Answer (A) is incorrect because the decreased length of the right riser is used to counteract torque on some designs, thus causing a turn. Answer (C) is incorrect because the air inflates the canopy to whatever airfoil shape the suspension lines and ribs define.

PPC, LSP

3992. Swapping wings from one brand or type of powered parachute to another is

A— permissible as long as the basic shape of the parachutes are similar.
B— dangerous since every wing is designed for a specific aircraft.
C— permissible if the overall area of the parachutes is the same.

Every wing is designed for a specific airframe configuration, engine torque and weight. (PLT346) — FAA-H-8083-29

Answers (A) and (C) are incorrect because there can be a different length in the lines between the right and left, which has nothing to do with the shape and area of the wing.

PPC, LSP

3993. Degradation of the parachute's protective polyurethane coating results in

A— increased takeoff distances, decreased maximum gross weight, and increased fuel consumption.
B— reduced takeoff distances, increased maximum gross weight, and reduced fuel consumption.
C— increased takeoff distances, increased maximum gross weight, and increased fuel consumption.

A degradation of the fabric results in air leaking through the fabric and a loss in performance since this creates more drag. (PLT346) — FAA-H-8083-29

Answers (B) and (C) are incorrect because there is no increased gross weight.

PPC, LSP

3994. Flaring allows the pilot to touchdown at a

A— higher rate of speed and a slower rate of descent.
B— lower rate of speed and a higher rate of descent.
C— lower rate of speed and a lower rate of descent.

Flaring slows you down and decreases your descent rate for a soft and slow landing. (PLT221) — FAA-H-8083-29

Answers (A) and (B) are incorrect because flaring does not produce a higher rate of speed or a higher rate of descent.

Answers

3989 [B]	3990 [A]	3991 [B]	3992 [B]	3993 [A]	3994 [C]

PPC, LSP
3995. Flaring during a landing

A— decreases the powered parachute's speed due to increased drag.
B— increases the powered parachute's speed due to reduced drag.
C— decreases the powered parachute's drag due to increased speed.

Flaring or pulling down on the trailing edge creates more drag and slows the aircraft similar to a flap on an airplane. (PLT221) — FAA-H-8083-29

Answers (B) and (C) are incorrect because flaring does not increase the speed of a PPC.

LSW
2347. One of the functions of the wing's crossbar is to

A— hold the wings open.
B— provide surface to grip and control the aircraft.
C— provide an attachment point for the carriage.

The purpose of the crosstube is to hold the leading edges open and therefore the wing. (PLT114) — FAA-H-8083-5

Answer (B) is incorrect because it is the control bar you grip to control the aircraft. Answer (C) is incorrect because the attachment point for the carriage is the keel, the carriage cannot be attached to the crossbar.

LSW
2348. Which aircraft component ensures the wing has a pitch-up tendency?

A— Keel pocket.
B— Luff lines.
C— Washout rod.

The luff lines can be used for pitch up stability in level flight by pulling the trailing edge up, creating a reflex in the training edge of the wing from the root out towards the tips. The luff lines also provide a positive pitch up tendency in a steep dive or slight negative angles of attack by increasing reflex in the airfoil by keeping the trailing edge pulled up in this unusual situation. (PLT114) — FAA-H-8083-5

Answer (A) is incorrect because the keel pocket simply holds the keel in place. Answer (C) is incorrect because the washout rods only provide a positive pitch-up moment when the aircraft is in a steep dive at zero angle of by holding the trailing edge up at the tips; the washout rods have no effect on the flight characteristics of the aircraft in normal flight conditions.

Gyroplane

LSR
2326. Why should gyroplane operations within the cross-hatched portion of a Height vs. Velocity chart be avoided?

A— The rotor RPM may build excessively high if it is necessary to flare at such low altitudes.
B— Sufficient airspeed may not be available to ensure a safe landing in case of an engine failure.
C— Turbulence near the surface can dephase the blade dampers causing geometric unbalanced conditions on the rotor system.

The chart can be used to determine those altitude-airspeed combinations from which it would be impossible to successfully complete an autorotative landing. The altitude-airspeed combinations that should be avoided are represented by the shaded areas of the chart. (PLT123) — FAA-H-8083-21

LSR
2327. The principal factor limiting the never-exceed speed (V_{NE}) of a gyroplane is

A— turbulence and altitude.
B— blade-tip speed, which must remain below the speed of sound.
C— lack of sufficient cyclic stick control to compensate for dissymmetry of lift or retreating blade stall, depending on which occurs first.

Retreating blade stall is the principal factor limiting the never-exceed speed. (PLT260) — FAA-H-8083-21

Answers

3995 [A]	2347 [A]	2348 [B]	2326 [B]	2327 [C]

Chapter 3
Flight Instruments

Pitot-Static Instruments

The pressure altimeter, vertical-speed indicator, and airspeed indicator operate in response to pressures through the **pitot-static system**. *See* Figure 3-1.

Static (atmospheric) **pressure** is taken from the static vents and is provided to all three instruments. Clogging of the static vents or line will cause all three instruments to become inoperative or to display erroneous readings.

Impact (ram) **pressure** is taken from the pitot tube and furnished to the airspeed indicator only. Clogging of the pitot opening will not affect operation of the altimeter or vertical speed indicator.

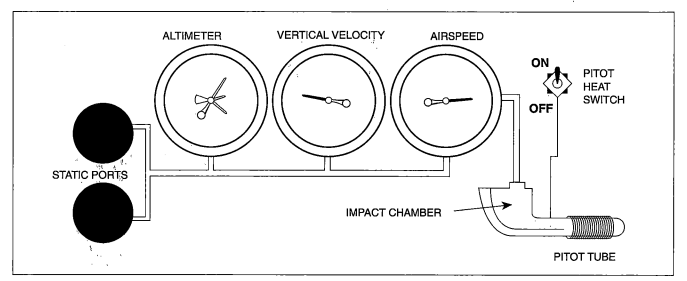

Figure 3-1. Pitot-static system

ALL
3248. Which instrument will become inoperative if the pitot tube becomes clogged?

A— Altimeter.
B— Vertical speed.
C— Airspeed.

The pitot tube provides input for the airspeed indicator only. (PLT337) — FAA-H-8083-25

Answers (A) and (B) are incorrect because the altimeter and vertical speed indicator operate off the static system and are not affected by a clogged pitot tube.

ALL
3249. Which instrument(s) will become inoperative if the static vents become clogged?

A— Airspeed only.
B— Altimeter only.
C— Airspeed, altimeter, and vertical speed.

Airspeed, altimeter and vertical speed all receive static input and would indicate inaccurately if the static sources became plugged. (PLT337) — FAA-H-8083-25

Answers
3248 [C]   3249 [C]

AIR, GLI, RTC, LSA, LSG, LSR, LSW

3247. If the pitot tube and outside static vents become clogged, which instruments would be affected?

A— The altimeter, airspeed indicator, and turn-and-slip indicator.

B— The altimeter, airspeed indicator, and vertical speed indicator.

C— The altimeter, attitude indicator, and turn-and-slip indicator.

Airspeed, altimeter and vertical speed all receive static input and would indicate inaccurately if the static sources became plugged. (PLT337) — FAA-H-8083-25

Answers (A) and (C) are incorrect because the turn-and-slip indicator and attitude indicator are gyroscopic instruments, and are not part of the pitot-static system.

AIR, GLI, RTC, LSA, LSG, LSR, LSW

3262. The pitot system provides impact pressure for which instrument?

A— Altimeter.

B— Vertical-speed indicator.

C— Airspeed indicator.

The pitot tube provides input for the airspeed indicator only. (PLT337) — FAA-H-8083-25

Answers (A) and (B) are incorrect because the altimeter and vertical speed indicator operate off the static system.

Airspeeds and the Airspeed Indicator

A pilot must be familiar with the following airspeed terms and abbreviations:

Indicated Airspeed (IAS)— the uncorrected reading obtained from the airspeed indicator.

Calibrated Airspeed (CAS)— indicated airspeed corrected for installation and instrument error.

True Airspeed (TAS)— calibrated airspeed corrected for temperature and pressure variations.

A number of airspeed limitations, abbreviated as "V" speeds, are indicated by color-coded marking on the airspeed indicator (*see* Figure 3-2):

V_{S0} — stall speed or minimum steady flight speed in the landing configuration (the lower limit of the white arc).

V_{FE}— maximum flap extended speed (the upper limit of the white arc). The entire white arc defines the flap operating range.

V_{S1}— the stall speed or minimum steady flight speed in a specified configuration (the lower limit of the green arc). The entire green arc defines the normal operating range.

V_{NO}— the maximum structural cruising speed (the upper limit of the green arc and lower limit of the yellow arc). The yellow arc defines the caution range, which should be avoided unless in smooth air.

V_{NE}— never exceed speed (the upper limit of the yellow arc) marked in red.

There are other important airspeed limitations that are not color-coded on the airspeed indicator:

V_{LE}— the maximum landing gear extended speed.

V_A— the design maneuvering speed. If rough air or severe turbulence is encountered, airspeed should be reduced to maneuvering speed or less to minimize stress on the airplane structure.

V_Y — the best rate-of-climb speed (the airspeed that will result in the most altitude in a given period of time).

V_X — the best angle-of-climb speed (the airspeed that will result in the most altitude in a given distance).

Answers

3247 [B]   3262 [C]

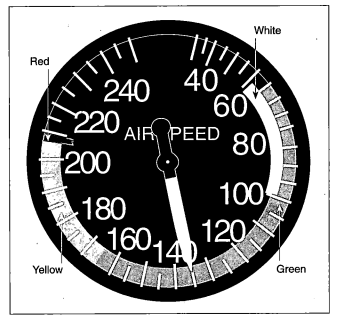

Figure 3-2. Airspeed indicator

AIR, GLI, RTC, WSC
3006. Which V-speed represents maneuvering speed?

A— V_A.
B— V_{LO}.
C— V_{NE}.

V_A is design maneuvering speed. (PLT506) — 14 CFR §1.2

Answer (B) is incorrect because this is the maximum landing gear operating speed. Answer (C) is incorrect because this is the never exceed speed.

AIR, GLI, RTC, WSC, LSA, LSG, LSR, LSW
3264. What does the red line on an airspeed indicator represent?

A— Maneuvering speed.
B— Turbulent or rough-air speed.
C— Never-exceed speed.

The upper end of the arc is marked by a red radial line which is the never-exceed speed (V_{NE}). (PLT132) — FAA-H-8083-25

Answers (A) and (B) are incorrect because the maneuvering speed and turbulent or rough-air speed is not indicated on the airspeed indicator.

AIR, GLI, RTC, WSC
3268. (Refer to Figure 4.) Which color identifies the never-exceed speed?

A— Upper limit of the green arc.
B— Upper limit of the white arc.
C— The red radial line.

The upper end of the arc is marked by a red radial line which is the never-exceed speed (V_{NE}). (PLT088) — FAA-H-8083-25

Answer (A) is incorrect because the upper limit of the green arc is the beginning of the caution range. Answer (B) is incorrect because the upper limit of the white arc is the maximum speed at which flaps may be extended.

AIR, WSC
3269. (Refer to Figure 4.) Which color identifies the power-off stalling speed in a specified configuration?

A— Upper limit of the green arc.
B— Upper limit of the white arc.
C— Lower limit of the green arc.

The green arc is the normal operating range. The lower end of the arc (V_{S1}) is the stalling speed in a specified configuration. (PLT088) — FAA-H-8083-25

Answer (A) is incorrect because the upper limit of the green arc indicates the maximum structural cruising speed. Answer (B) is incorrect because the upper limit of the white arc is the maximum flaps-extended speed.

AIR, WSC, PPC
3011. Which would provide the greatest gain in altitude in the shortest distance during climb after takeoff?

A— V_Y.
B— V_A.
C— V_X.

V_X (best angle) is the calibrated airspeed at which the aircraft will attain the highest altitude in a given horizontal distance. (PLT123) — 14 CFR §1.2

Answer (A) is incorrect because V_Y is best rate of climb. Answer (B) is incorrect because V_A is design maneuvering speed.

AIR, WSC

3012-1. After takeoff, which airspeed would the pilot use to gain the most altitude in a given period of time?

A— V_Y.
B— V_X.
C— V_A.

V_Y (best rate) is the calibrated airspeed at which the airplane will obtain the maximum increase in altitude per unit of time (feet per minute) after takeoff. (PLT123) — 14 CFR §1.2

Answer (B) is incorrect because V_X is the best angle of climb. Answer (C) is incorrect because V_A is the design maneuvering speed.

AIR

3265. (Refer to Figure 4.) What is the full flap operating range for the airplane?

A— 55 to 100 knots.
B— 55 to 208 knots.
C— 55 to 165 knots.

The flap operating range is marked by the white arc. The low end is V_{S0} (stall speed in a landing configuration), and the high end is V_{FE} (maximum flap extended speed). (PLT088) — FAA-H-8083-25

Answer (B) is incorrect because 55 to 208 knots is the entire operating range of this airplane, from the stall speed to the never-exceed speed. Answer (C) is incorrect because 55 to 165 knots is the normal operating range for this airplane (green arc).

AIR, WSC

3267. (Refer to Figure 4.) The maximum speed at which the airplane can be operated in smooth air is

A— 100 knots.
B— 165 knots.
C— 208 knots.

The caution range (yellow arc) includes speeds which should only be flown in smooth air; the maximum speed in the caution range is 208 knots for this airplane. (PLT088) — FAA-H-8083-25

Answer (A) is incorrect because 100 knots is the upper limit of the white arc, which is the maximum flaps-extended speed. Answer (B) is incorrect because 165 knots is the upper limit of the green arc, which is the maximum structural cruising speed.

AIR

3270. (Refer to Figure 4.) What is the maximum flaps-extended speed?

A— 65 knots.
B— 100 knots.
C— 165 knots.

The flap operating range is marked by the white arc. The high end is V_{FE} (maximum flap extended speed), which is 100 knots for this airplane. (PLT088) — FAA-H-8083-25

Answer (A) is incorrect because 65 knots is the lower limit of the green arc, which is the power-off stall speed, V_{S1}. Answer (C) is incorrect because 165 knots is the upper limit of the green arc, which is V_{NO}.

AIR

3271. (Refer to Figure 4.) Which color identifies the normal flap operating range?

A— The yellow arc.
B— The green arc.
C— The white arc.

The flap operating range is marked by the white arc. The low end is V_{S0} (stall speed in a landing configuration), and the high end is V_{FE} (maximum flap extended speed). (PLT088) — FAA-H-8083-25

Answer (A) is incorrect because the yellow arc is the caution range. Answer (B) is incorrect because the green arc indicates the normal operating range.

AIR

3272. (Refer to Figure 4.) Which color identifies the power-off stalling speed with wing flaps and landing gear in the landing configuration?

A— Upper limit of the green arc.
B— Upper limit of the white arc.
C— Lower limit of the white arc.

The flap operating range is marked by the white arc. The low end is V_{S0} (stall speed in a landing configuration). (PLT088) — FAA-H-8083-25

Answer (A) is incorrect because the upper limit of the green arc is V_{NO}. Answer (B) is incorrect because the upper limit of the white arc is V_{FE}.

Answers

3012-1 [A]	3265 [A]	3267 [C]	3270 [B]	3271 [C]	3272 [C]

AIR, WSC
3273. (Refer to Figure 4.) What is the maximum structural cruising speed?

A— 100 knots.
B— 165 knots.
C— 208 knots.

The green arc is the normal operating range. The upper end of the arc (V_{NO}) is defined as the "maximum structural cruising speed." (PLT088) — FAA-H-8083-25

Answer (A) is incorrect because 100 MPH is the upper limit of the white arc, which is the maximum flaps extended speed. Answer (C) is incorrect because 208 knots is the never-exceed speed.

AIR, WSC
3274. What is an important airspeed limitation that is not color coded on airspeed indicators?

A— Never-exceed speed.
B— Maximum structural cruising speed.
C— Maneuvering speed.

Maneuvering speed (V_A) is not displayed on the airspeed indicator. (PLT278) — FAA-H-8083-25

Answer (A) is incorrect because the never-exceed speed is indicated by a red line on the airspeed indicator. Answer (B) is incorrect because the maximum structural cruising speed can be found on the airspeed indicator by the upper limit of the green arc.

AIR, GLI
3007. Which V-speed represents maximum flap extended speed?

A— V_{FE}.
B— V_{LOF}.
C— V_{FC}.

V_{FE} is the highest calibrated airspeed permissible with the wing flaps in a prescribed extended position. (PLT506) — 14 CFR §1.2

Answer (B) is incorrect because this is the liftoff speed. Answer (C) is incorrect because this is the maximum speed for stability characteristics.

AIR, GLI
3008. Which V-speed represents maximum landing gear extended speed?

A— V_{LE}.
B— V_{LO}.
C— V_{FE}.

V_{LE} is the maximum calibrated airspeed at which the airplane can be safely flown with the landing gear extended. (PLT506) — 14 CFR §1.2

Answer (B) is incorrect because V_{LO} is maximum landing gear operating speed. Answer (C) is incorrect because V_{FE} is maximum flap extended speed.

AIR, GLI, WSC
3009. V_{NO} is defined as the

A— normal operating range.
B— never-exceed speed.
C— maximum structural cruising speed.

V_{NO} is the maximum calibrated airspeed for normal operation, or the maximum structural cruising speed. (PLT506) — 14 CFR §1.2

Answer (A) is incorrect because this is not designated a V-speed; but rather it is the green arc on the airspeed indicator. Answer (B) is incorrect because this is V_{NE}.

AIR, GLI
3010. V_{S0} is defined as the

A— stalling speed or minimum steady flight speed in the landing configuration.
B— stalling speed or minimum steady flight speed in a specified configuration.
C— stalling speed or minimum takeoff safety speed.

V_{S0} is the calibrated power-off stalling speed or the minimum steady-flight speed at which the aircraft is controllable in the landing configuration. (PLT506) — 14 CFR §1.2

Answer (B) is incorrect because this is V_{S1}. Answer (C) is incorrect because V_S is stalling speed, and V_2 is the minimum takeoff safety speed.

AIR, GLI, WSC
3266. (Refer to Figure 4.) What is the caution range of the airplane?

A— 0 to 60 knots.
B— 100 to 165 knots.
C— 165 to 208 knots.

The caution range (yellow arc) includes speeds which should only be flown in smooth air, and is 165 to 208 knots for this airplane. (PLT088) — FAA-H-8083-25

Answer (A) is incorrect because 0 to 60 knots is less than stall speed. Answer (B) is incorrect because 100 to 165 knots is the normal operating airspeed range from maximum flap extension speed to maximum structural cruising speed, the upper limit of the green arc and lower limit of the yellow arc.

Answers

3273	[B]	3274	[C]	3007	[A]	3008	[A]	3009	[C]	3010	[A]
3266	[C]										

The Altimeter and Altitudes

An **altimeter** is an instrument used to measure height (altitude) by responding to atmospheric pressure changes. *See* Figure 3-3 on the next page.

Altitude is indicated by three hands on the face of the altimeter. The shortest hand indicates altitude in tens of thousands of feet; the intermediate hand, in thousands of feet; and the longest hand in hundreds of feet. The altimeter is subdivided into 20-foot increments.

"Altitude" means elevation with respect to any assumed reference level, and different terms identify the reference level used. *See* Figure 3-4.

Indicated altitude — the altitude read on the altimeter after it is set to the current local altimeter setting.

Absolute altitude — the height above the surface.

True altitude — the true height above Mean Sea Level (MSL) normally measured in feet.

Pressure altitude — the altitude that is indicated whenever the altimeter setting dial (Kohlsman window) is adjusted to 29.92. This is the Standard Datum Plane; a theoretical level where air pressure is equal to 29.92 inches of mercury (in. Hg). The Standard Datum Plane may be above, at, or below sea level.

Density altitude — the pressure altitude corrected for nonstandard temperature and/or pressure. Rotating the setting knob on the altimeter simultaneously rotates the setting dial and the altimeter hands at a rate of one inch per 1,000 feet of altitude. Thus, increasing the setting dial from 29.15 to 29.85 would cause the hands of the altimeter to show an increase of 700 feet.

Prior to takeoff, the altimeter should be set to the current local altimeter setting. This is the value to which the scale of the altimeter is set so that the altimeter indicates true altitude at field elevation. If the altimeter setting is not available, the altimeter should be set to the elevation of the departure airport.

After takeoff, the altimeter should remain set to the current local altimeter setting until climbing through 18,000 feet MSL. At that time, the altimeter should be set to 29.92.

On a standard day (29.92" Hg and +15°C) at sea level, pressure altitude, true altitude, indicated altitude, and density altitude are all equal. Any variation from standard temperature or pressure will have an effect on the altimeter.

To compensate for the effect of nonstandard conditions, the altimeter must be set to the altimeter setting of a station within 100 NM of the aircraft (unless it is above 18,000 feet MSL).

If a flight is made from an area of low pressure/low temperature to an area of high pressure/high temperature without adjusting the altimeter setting, the altimeter will indicate *lower* than the actual altitude above ground level. If a flight is made from an area of high pressure/high temperature to an area of low pressure/low temperature without adjusting the altimeter setting, the altimeter will indicate *higher* than the actual altitude above mean sea level.

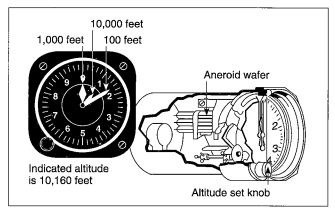

Figure 3-3. Altimeter components

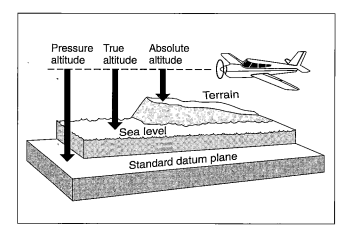

Figure 3-4. Types of altitude

ALL

3105. If an altimeter setting is not available before flight, to which altitude should the pilot adjust the altimeter?

A— The elevation of the nearest airport corrected to mean sea level.
B— The elevation of the departure area.
C— Pressure altitude corrected for nonstandard temperature.

The altimeter should be set to the elevation of the departure airport for airplanes, and the departure area for other aircraft. (PLT381) — 14 CFR §91.121

Answer (A) is incorrect because airport elevation is always expressed in feet above MSL. Answer (C) is incorrect because pressure altitude adjusted for nonstandard temperature is not true altitude, but density altitude.

ALL

3106. Prior to takeoff, the altimeter should be set to which altitude or altimeter setting?

A— The current local altimeter setting, if available, or the departure airport elevation.
B— The corrected density altitude of the departure airport.
C— The corrected pressure altitude for the departure airport.

The altimeter should be set to the elevation of the departure airport for airplanes, and the departure area for other aircraft. (PLT381) — 14 CFR §91.121

Answer (B) is incorrect because density altitude is pressure altitude corrected for nonstandard temperature variations and only concerns the performance of the aircraft. Answer (C) is incorrect because pressure altitude is the altitude indicated on the altimeter when the altimeter is set to 29.92.

ALL

3107. At what altitude shall the altimeter be set to 29.92, when climbing to cruising flight level?

A— 14,500 feet MSL.
B— 18,000 feet MSL.
C— 24,000 feet MSL.

*The altimeter should be set to 29.92" Hg at 18,000 feet MSL and above. **Note:** 18,000 feet is Class A airspace, which requires an instrument rating to operate in. (PLT381) — 14 CFR §91.121*

Answer (A) is incorrect because 14,500 feet is the base of Class E airspace, when not designated lower. Answer (C) is incorrect because 24,000 feet MSL is the altitude at which DME is required.

ALL

3254. Altimeter setting is the value to which the barometric pressure scale of the altimeter is set so the altimeter indicates

A— calibrated altitude at field elevation.
B— absolute altitude at field elevation.
C— true altitude at field elevation.

The local altimeter setting corrects for the difference between existing pressure and standard atmospheric pressure. Whether local pressure is higher or lower than standard, it will indicate true altitude (MSL) at ground level, when the aircraft altimeter is set to the local altimeter setting (assuming no setting scale error). (PLT041) — FAA-H-8083-25

Answer (A) is incorrect because "calibrated" does not apply to altitudes; it only applies to airspeeds. Answer (B) is incorrect because absolute altitude is the height above the ground.

Answers

3105 [B]   3106 [A]   3107 [B]   3254 [C]

ALL

3255. How do variations in temperature affect the altimeter?

A— Pressure levels are raised on warm days and the indicated altitude is lower than true altitude.

B— Higher temperatures expand the pressure levels and the indicated altitude is higher than true altitude.

C— Lower temperatures lower the pressure levels and the indicated altitude is lower than true altitude.

On a warm day, the expanded air is lighter than on a cold day, and consequently the pressure levels are raised. For example, the pressure level where the altimeter indicates 10,000 feet will be higher on a warm day than under standard conditions. On a cold day the reverse is true. (PLT165) — FAA-H-8083-25

Answer (B) is incorrect because raising the pressure levels would not cause the indicated altitude to be higher than the true altitude. Answer (C) is incorrect because lowering the pressure levels would not cause the indicated altitude to be lower than the true altitude.

ALL, SPO

3256. What is true altitude?

A— The vertical distance of the aircraft above sea level.

B— The vertical distance of the aircraft above the surface.

C— The height above the standard datum plane.

True altitude is height above sea level. Airport terrain and obstacle elevations found on aeronautical charts are true altitudes. (PLT023) — FAA-H-8083-25

Answer (B) is incorrect because the vertical distance above the surface is absolute altitude. Answer (C) is incorrect because the height above the standard datum plane is pressure altitude.

ALL

3392. Under what condition will true altitude be lower than indicated altitude?

A— In colder than standard air temperature.

B— In warmer than standard air temperature.

C— When density altitude is higher than indicated altitude.

True altitude will be lower than indicated altitude in colder than standard air temperature, even with an accurate altimeter set to 29.92. (PLT023) — AC 00-6

ALL, SPO

3257. What is absolute altitude?

A— The altitude read directly from the altimeter.

B— The vertical distance of the aircraft above the surface.

C— The height above the standard datum plane.

Absolute altitude is height above the surface. This height may be indicated directly on a radar altimeter. Absolute altitude may be approximately computed from indicated altitude and chart elevation data. (PLT023) — FAA-H-8083-25

Answer (A) is incorrect because the altitude read from the altimeter is indicated altitude. Answer (C) is incorrect because the height above the standard datum plane is pressure altitude.

ALL, SPO

3258. What is density altitude?

A— The height above the standard datum plane.

B— The pressure altitude corrected for nonstandard temperature.

C— The altitude read directly from the altimeter.

Under standard atmospheric conditions, each level of air in the atmosphere has a specific density, and under standard conditions, pressure altitude and density altitude identify the same level. At temperatures higher or lower than standard, density altitude cannot be determined directly from the altimeter. (PLT023) — FAA-H-8083-25

Answer (A) is incorrect because the height above the standard datum plane is pressure altitude. Answer (C) is incorrect because the altitude read from the altimeter is indicated altitude.

ALL, SPO

3259. What is pressure altitude?

A— The indicated altitude corrected for position and installation error.

B— The altitude indicated when the barometric pressure scale is set to 29.92.

C— The indicated altitude corrected for nonstandard temperature and pressure.

Answers

3255 [A]	3256 [A]	3392 [A]	3257 [B]	3258 [B]	3259 [B]

The pressure altitude can be determined by either of two methods:

1. *Setting the barometric scale of the altimeter to 29.92 and reading the indicated altitude, or*

2. *Applying a correction factor to the elevation (true altitude) according to the reported "altimeter setting."*

(PLT023) — FAA-H-8083-25

Answer (A) is incorrect because the altimeter is not corrected for position and installation error. Answer (C) is incorrect because indicated altitude corrected for nonstandard temperature and pressure defines density altitude.

ALL, SPO
3260. Under what condition is indicated altitude the same as true altitude?

A— If the altimeter has no mechanical error.
B— When at sea level under standard conditions.
C— When at 18,000 feet MSL with the altimeter set at 29.92.

On a standard day (29.92" Hg and +15°C) at sea level, pressure altitude, indicated altitude, and density altitude are all equal. Any variation from standard temperature or pressure will have an effect on the altimeter. (PLT023) — FAA-H-8083-25

Answer (A) is incorrect because mechanical error does not apply to true altitude. Answer (C) is incorrect because when the altimeter is set to 29.92, it indicates pressure altitude.

ALL, SPO
3261. If it is necessary to set the altimeter from 29.15 to 29.85, what change occurs?

A— 70-foot increase in indicated altitude.
B— 70-foot increase in density altitude.
C— 700-foot increase in indicated altitude.

When the knob on the altimeter is rotated, the pressure scale moves simultaneously with the altimeter pointers. The numerical values of pressure indicated in the window increase while the altimeter indicates an increase in altitude; or decrease while the altimeter indicates a decrease in altitude. This is contrary to the reaction on the pointers when air pressure changes, and is based solely on the mechanical makeup of the altimeter. The difference between the two settings is equal to 0.70" Hg (29.85 – 29.15). At the standard pressure lapse rate of 1" Hg = 1,000 feet in altitude, the amount of change equals 700 feet. (PLT166) — FAA-H-8083-25

ALL
3388. Under which condition will pressure altitude be equal to true altitude?

A— When the atmospheric pressure is 29.92" Hg.
B— When standard atmospheric conditions exist.
C— When indicated altitude is equal to the pressure altitude.

Pressure altitude is equal to true altitude under standard atmospheric conditions. (PLT023) — AC 00-6

ALL
3389. Under what condition is pressure altitude and density altitude the same value?

A— At sea level, when the temperature is 0°F.
B— When the altimeter has no installation error.
C— At standard temperature.

When conditions are standard, pressure altitude and density altitude are the same. (PLT345) — AC 00-6

Answer (A) is incorrect because standard temperature at sea level is 59°F. Answer (B) is incorrect because installation errors apply to airspeed indicators, not altimeters.

ALL
3390. If a flight is made from an area of low pressure into an area of high pressure without the altimeter setting being adjusted, the altimeter will indicate

A— the actual altitude above sea level.
B— higher than the actual altitude above sea level.
C— lower than the actual altitude above sea level.

If a flight is made from a high-pressure area to a low-pressure area without adjusting the altimeter, the actual altitude of the airplane will be lower than the indicated altitude, and when flying from a low-pressure area to high-pressure area, the actual altitude of the airplane will be higher than the indicated altitude. (PLT167) — AC 00-6

Answer (A) is incorrect because a correct altimeter setting must be used and/or standard atmospheric conditions must exist. Answer (B) is incorrect because the altimeter will indicate a lower altitude than actual.

Answers

| 3260 | [B] | 3261 | [C] | 3388 | [B] | 3389 | [C] | 3390 | [C] |

ALL

3391. If a flight is made from an area of high pressure into an area of lower pressure without the altimeter setting being adjusted, the altimeter will indicate

A— lower than the actual altitude above sea level.
B— higher than the actual altitude above sea level.
C— the actual altitude above sea level.

If a flight is made from a high-pressure area to a low-pressure area without adjusting the altimeter, the actual altitude of the airplane will be lower than the indicated altitude, and when flying from a low-pressure area to high-pressure area, the actual altitude of the airplane will be higher than the indicated altitude. (PLT167) — AC 00-6

Answer (A) is incorrect because this change would indicate a flight into a high-pressure area from a low-pressure area. Answer (C) is incorrect because the lack of change would indicate constant pressure, thus actual altitude.

ALL

3393. Which condition would cause the altimeter to indicate a lower altitude than true altitude?

A— Air temperature lower than standard.
B— Atmospheric pressure lower than standard.
C— Air temperature warmer than standard.

The altimeter will indicate a lower altitude than actually flown, in air temperature warmer than standard. (PLT023) — AC 00-6

Answer (A) is incorrect because if the air temperature was lower, this would indicate a higher indicated altitude and a lower true altitude. Answer (B) is incorrect because when atmospheric pressure is lower than standard, the same conditions exist as described in Answer (A).

ALL

3250. (Refer to Figure 3.) Altimeter 1 indicates

A— 500 feet.
B— 1,500 feet.
C— 10,500 feet.

On altimeter #1 the 10,000-foot pointer (shortest hand) is just above 10,000 feet, the 1,000-foot pointer (fat hand) is between 0 and 1,000 feet, and the 100-foot pointer is on 500 feet. (PLT041) — FAA-H-8083-25

ALL

3251. (Refer to Figure 3.) Altimeter 2 indicates

A— 1,500 feet.
B— 4,500 feet.
C— 14,500 feet.

On altimeter #2 the 10,000-foot pointer is between 10,000 feet and 20,000 feet. The 1,000-foot pointer is between 4,000 feet and 5,000 feet, and the 100-foot pointer is on 500 feet. (PLT041) — FAA-H-8083-25

ALL

3252. (Refer to Figure 3.) Altimeter 3 indicates

A— 9,500 feet.
B— 10,950 feet.
C— 15,940 feet.

On altimeter #3 the 10,000-foot pointer is not quite to 10,000 feet. The 1,000-foot pointer is halfway between 9,000 and 10,000 feet, and the 100-foot pointer is on 500 feet. (PLT041) — FAA-H-8083-25

ALL

3253. (Refer to Figure 3.) Which altimeter(s) indicate(s) more than 10,000 feet?

A— 1, 2, and 3.
B— 1 and 2 only.
C— 1 only.

The shortest hand (10,000 foot) in #1 is between 1 and 2, indicating 10,000 feet plus. The shortest hand in #2 also indicates 10,000 feet plus. The shortest hand in #3 indicates less than 10,000 feet. (PLT041) — FAA-H-8083-25

Answers

| 3391 | [B] | 3393 | [C] | 3250 | [C] | 3251 | [C] | 3252 | [A] | 3253 | [B] |

ALL
3253-1. (Refer to Figure 82.) Altimeter 3 is indicating a VFR cruising altitude for which direction?

A— 180°–359° magnetic.
B— 179° true.
C— 080° magnetic.

On altimeter 3, the 10,000-foot pointer is just before 10,000 feet. The 1,000-foot pointer is between 9,000 feet and 10,000 feet, and the 100-foot pointer is on 500 feet. The aircraft is at an altitude of 9,500 feet. A magnetic course of 0° to 179° should be flown at a VFR cruising altitude of odd-thousands plus 500 feet. (PLT041) — AIM ¶3-1-5

Answer (A) is incorrect because a VFR cruising altitude in a direction of 180°-359° should be flown at an even flight altitude plus 500 feet altitude. Answer (B) is incorrect because VFR cruising altitudes should be determined by magnetic direction, not true.

ALL
3387. If a pilot changes the altimeter setting from 30.11 to 29.96, what is the approximate change in indication?

A— Altimeter will indicate .15" Hg higher.
B— Altimeter will indicate 150 feet higher.
C— Altimeter will indicate 150 feet lower.

When the knob on the altimeter is rotated, the altimeter setting pressure scale moves simultaneously with the altimeter pointers. The numerical values of pressure indicated in the window increase while the altimeter indicates an increase in altitude, or decrease while the altimeter indicates a decrease in altitude. This is contrary to the reaction on the pointers when air pressure changes and is based solely on the mechanical makeup of the altimeter. The difference between the two settings is equal to 0.15" Hg (30.11 – 29.96 = 0.15). At the standard pressure lapse rate of 1" Hg = 1,000 feet in altitude, the amount of change equals 150 feet. (PLT167) — AC 00-6

Gyroscopic Instruments

Some aircraft instruments use gyroscopes. Simply stated, gyroscopes are rapidly spinning wheels or disks which resist any attempt to move them from their plane of rotation. This is called "rigidity in space." Three aircraft instruments which use gyroscopes are the **attitude indicator**, the **turn coordinator**, and the **heading indicator**.

Attitude Indicator

The rigidity in space principle makes the gyroscope an excellent "artificial horizon" around which the attitude indicator (and the airplane) pivot.

When viewing the attitude indicator, the direction of bank is determined by the relationship of the miniature airplane to the horizon bar. The miniature airplane may be moved up or down from the horizon with an adjustment knob. Normally, the miniature airplane will be adjusted so that the wings overlap the horizon bar whenever the airplane is in straight-and-level flight.

Turn Coordinator

The turn coordinator (also using the principle of the gyroscope) uses a miniature airplane to provide information concerning rate of roll and rate of turn. As the airplane enters a turn, movement of the miniature aircraft indicates rate of roll. When the bank is held constant, rate of turn is indicated. Simultaneously, the quality of turn, or movement about the yaw axis, is indicated by the ball of the inclinometer.

Heading Indicator

The heading indicator is a gyroscopic instrument designed to avoid many of the errors inherent in a magnetic compass. However, the heading indicator does suffer from precession, caused mainly by bearing friction. Because of this precessional error, the heading indicator must periodically be realigned with the magnetic compass during straight-and-level, unaccelerated flight.

Answers

3253-1 [C]   3387 [C]

AIR, RTC

3278. (Refer to Figure 7.) How should a pilot determine the direction of bank from an attitude indicator such as the one illustrated?

A— By the direction of deflection of the banking scale (A).

B— By the direction of deflection of the horizon bar (B).

C— By the relationship of the miniature airplane (C) to the deflected horizon bar (B).

The relationship of the miniature aircraft C to the horizon bar B is the same as the relationship of the real aircraft to the actual horizon. (PLT132) — FAA-H-8083-25

Answer (A) is incorrect because the bank scale shows degrees, and not direction of bank. Answer (B) is incorrect because the horizon line deflects opposite the direction of turn, in order to correct horizon representation.

AIR

3275. (Refer to Figure 5.) A turn coordinator provides an indication of the

A— movement of the aircraft about the yaw and roll axis.

B— angle of bank up to but not exceeding 30°.

C— attitude of the aircraft with reference to the longitudinal axis.

The movement of the miniature airplane on the instrument is proportional to the roll rate of the airplane. When the roll rate is reduced to zero, i.e., the bank is held constant, the instrument provides an indication of the rate of turn. This design features a realignment of the gyro in such a manner that it senses airplane movement about the yaw and roll axis. (PLT187) — FAA-H-8083-25

Answers (B) and (C) are incorrect because the miniature aircraft indicates rate of turn, not angle of bank or attitude.

AIR, RTC

3277. (Refer to Figure 7.) The proper adjustment to make on the attitude indicator during level flight is to align the

A— horizon bar to the level-flight indication.

B— horizon bar to the miniature airplane.

C— miniature airplane to the horizon bar.

The miniature airplane "C" is adjusted so that the wings overlap the horizon bar "B" when the airplane is in straight-and-level cruising flight. (PLT166) — FAA-H-8083-25

Answers (A) and (B) are incorrect because adjustment is only made to the miniature airplane.

AIR, RTC

3276. (Refer to Figure 6.) To receive accurate indications during flight from a heading indicator, the instrument must be

A— set prior to flight on a known heading.

B— calibrated on a compass rose at regular intervals.

C— periodically realigned with the magnetic compass as the gyro precesses.

Because the heading indicator is run by a gyroscope instead of a magnetic source, precession will cause creep or drift from a heading to which it is set. It is important to check the indications frequently and reset the heading indicator to align it with the magnetic compass when required. (PLT118) — FAA-H-8083-25

Answers (A) and (B) are incorrect because they don't do anything to correct for precession in flight.

Answers

| 3278 [C] | 3275 [A] | 3277 [C] | 3276 [C] |

Magnetic Compass (Northern Hemisphere)

Deviation is a compass error caused by magnetic disturbances from electrical and metal components in the aircraft. The correction for this error is displayed on a compass correction card placed near the magnetic compass in the aircraft. Variation is the angular difference between the true, or geographic, poles and the magnetic poles at a given point. The compass magnet is aligned with the magnetic poles, while aeronautical charts are oriented to the geographic poles. This variation must be taken into consideration when determining an aircraft's actual geographic location. Indicated on charts by isogonic lines, it is not affected by the airplane's heading.

The magnetic compass, attracted to a magnetic field in the earth, points down as well as north. This downward pointing tendency, called "**magnetic dip**," causes errors in compass indications.

When turning toward north from an easterly or westerly heading, the compass lags behind the actual aircraft heading. When a turn is initiated while on a northerly heading, the compass first indicates a turn in the opposite direction. The compass lags whenever turns are made to or from north.

When turning toward south from an easterly or westerly heading, the compass leads the actual aircraft heading. When a turn is initiated while on a southerly heading, the compass shows an immediate lead in the same direction as the turn. The compass leads whenever turns are made to or from south.

Accelerating or decelerating while heading either east or west will also cause compass errors. If acceleration occurs on a heading of east or west, the compass will indicate a turn to the north, while deceleration will cause an indication of a turn to the south. Therefore, it becomes apparent that the indications of a magnetic compass are accurate only during straight-and-level, unaccelerated flight.

The magnetic compass is also influenced by lines of force from magnetic fields within the aircraft. These errors are called deviations.

ALL
3279. Deviation in a magnetic compass is caused by the

A— presence of flaws in the permanent magnets of the compass.
B— difference in the location between true north and magnetic north.
C— magnetic fields within the aircraft distorting the lines of magnetic force.

Magnetic disturbances from magnetic fields produced by metals and electrical accessories in an aircraft disturb the compass card and produce an additional error which is referred to as deviation. (PLT215) — FAA-H-8083-25

Answer (A) is incorrect because deviation is not caused by magnet flaws. Answer (B) is incorrect because the difference between magnetic north and true north is called variation.

ALL
3279-1. The angular difference between true north and magnetic north is

A— magnetic deviation.
B— magnetic variation.
C— compass acceleration error.

The angular difference between magnetic north, the reference for the magnetic compass, and true north is variation. (PLT320) — FAA-H-8083-25

Answer (A) is incorrect because deviation is the error caused by magnetic fields produced by metal and electrical accessories within the airplane. Answer (C) is incorrect because compass acceleration errors are fluctuations in the compass during changes in speed.

Answers

3279   [C]   3279-1   [B]

ALL

3279-2. Deviation error of the magnetic compass is caused by :

A— northerly turning error.

B— certain metals and electrical systems within the aircraft.

C— the difference in location of true north and magnetic north.

Magnetic disturbances from magnetic fields produced by metals and electrical accessories in an aircraft disturb the compass card and produce an additional error which is referred to as deviation. (PLT215) — FAA-H-8083-25

Answer (A) is incorrect because this describes acceleration error. Answer (C) is incorrect because the difference between magnetic north and true north is called variation.

ALL

3282. In the Northern Hemisphere, a magnetic compass will normally indicate a turn toward the north if

A— an aircraft is decelerated while on an east or west heading.

B— a left turn is entered from a west heading.

C— an aircraft is accelerated while on an east or west heading.

*While on an east or west heading, an increase in airspeed or acceleration will cause the compass to indicate a turn toward the north and a deceleration will cause the compass to indicate a turn to the south. If on a north or south heading, no error will be apparent because of acceleration or deceleration. (Remember **ANDS** = Accelerate North Decelerate South). (PLT215) — FAA-H-8083-25*

ALL

3283. In the Northern Hemisphere, the magnetic compass will normally indicate a turn toward the south when

A— a left turn is entered from an east heading.

B— a right turn is entered from a west heading.

C— the aircraft is decelerated while on a west heading.

*While on an east or west heading, an increase in airspeed or acceleration will cause the compass to indicate a turn toward the north and a deceleration will cause the compass to indicate a turn to the south. If on a north or south heading, no error will be apparent because of acceleration or deceleration. (Remember **ANDS** = Accelerate North Decelerate South). (PLT215) — FAA-H-8083-25*

Answers (A) and (B) are incorrect because on east and west heading, turning error is negligible.

ALL

3283-1. What should be the indication on the magnetic compass as you roll into a standard rate turn to the right from a south heading in the Northern Hemisphere?

A— The compass will initially indicate a turn to the left.

B— The compass will indicate a turn to the right, but at a faster rate than is actually occurring.

C— The compass will remain on south for a short time, then gradually catch up to the magnetic heading of the airplane.

If you are on a southerly heading and roll into a standard-rate turn to the right, the compass will immediately indicate a turn toward the west (to the right) because of the northerly turning error. During the first part of the turn, it will show a faster rate of turn than you are actually making. (PLT215) — FAA-H-8083-25

Answer (A) is incorrect because the compass will initially indicate a turn to the left when rolling into a standard rate turn from a north heading in the Northern Hemisphere. Answer (C) is incorrect because the compass indication will lead the turn when rolling into a standard rate turn from a south heading in the Northern Hemisphere.

ALL

3284. In the Northern Hemisphere, if an aircraft is accelerated or decelerated, the magnetic compass will normally indicate

A— a turn momentarily.

B— correctly when on a north or south heading.

C— a turn toward the south.

*While on an east or west heading, an increase in airspeed or acceleration will cause the compass to indicate a turn toward the north and a deceleration will cause the compass to indicate a turn to the south. If on a north or south heading, no error will be apparent because of acceleration or deceleration. (Remember **ANDS** = Accelerate North Decelerate South). (PLT215) — FAA-H-8083-25*

Answers (A) and (C) are incorrect because acceleration error only occurs on an easterly/westerly heading; if accelerating, indicates a turn to the north and if decelerating, to the south.

Answers

3279-2	[B]	3282	[C]	3283	[C]	3283-1	[B]	3284	[B]

ALL
3280. In the Northern Hemisphere, a magnetic compass will normally indicate initially a turn toward the west if

A— a left turn is entered from a north heading.
B— a right turn is entered from a north heading.
C— an aircraft is accelerated while on a north heading.

If on a northerly heading and a turn is made toward east or west, the initial indication of the compass lags, or indicates a turn in the opposite direction. (PLT215) — FAA-H-8083-25

Answer (A) is incorrect because a left turn would indicate a turn toward the east, while turning west. Answer (C) is incorrect because acceleration error does not occur on a north or south heading.

ALL
3281. In the Northern Hemisphere, a magnetic compass will normally indicate initially a turn toward the east if

A— an aircraft is decelerated while on a south heading.
B— an aircraft is accelerated while on a north heading.
C— a left turn is entered from a north heading.

If on a northerly heading and a turn is made toward east or west, the initial indication of the compass lags, or indicates a turn in the opposite direction. (PLT215) — FAA-H-8083-25

Answers (A) and (B) are incorrect because acceleration error does not occur on north or south headings.

ALL
3286. During flight, when are the indications of a magnetic compass accurate?

A— Only in straight-and-level unaccelerated flight.
B— As long as the airspeed is constant.
C— During turns if the bank does not exceed 18°.

The magnetic compass should be read only when the aircraft is flying straight-and-level at a constant speed. This will help reduce errors to the minimum. (PLT215) — FAA-H-8083-25

Answer (B) is incorrect because airspeed can remain constant in a turn, and the compass is subject to turning errors. Answer (C) is incorrect because no matter how steep the turn, the compass is still susceptible to turning errors.

GLI
3285. In the Northern Hemisphere, if a glider is accelerated or decelerated, the magnetic compass will normally indicate

A— a turn toward north while decelerating on an east heading.
B— correctly only when on a north or south heading.
C— a turn toward south while accelerating on a west heading.

*While on an east or west heading, an increase in airspeed or acceleration will cause the compass to indicate a turn toward the north and a deceleration will cause the compass to indicate a turn to the south. If on a north or south heading, no error will be apparent because of acceleration or deceleration. (Remember **ANDS** = Accelerate North Decelerate South). (PLT215) — FAA-H-8083-25*

Answers

3280   [B]   3281   [C]   3286   [A]   3285   [B]

Chapter 4
Regulations

Introduction

Although "FAR" is used as the acronym for "Federal Aviation Regulations," and found throughout the regulations themselves and hundreds of other publications, the FAA is now actively discouraging its use. "FAR" also means "Federal Acquisition Regulations." To eliminate any possible confusion, the FAA cites the federal aviation regulations with reference to Title 14 of the Code of Federal Regulations. For example, "FAR Part 91.3" is referenced as "14 CFR Part 91 Section 3."

While **Federal Aviation Regulations** are many and varied, some are of particular interest to all pilots.

14 CFR Part 1 contains definitions and abbreviations of many terms commonly used in aviation. For example, the term "night" means "the time between the end of evening civil twilight and the beginning of morning civil twilight, as published in the American Air Almanac, converted to local time" and is used for logging night time.

14 CFR Part 61, entitled "Certification: Pilots, Flight Instructors and Ground Instructors," prescribes the requirements for issuing pilot and flight instructor certificates and ratings, the conditions of issue, and the privileges and limitations of those certificates and ratings.

14 CFR Part 91, entitled "General Operating and Flight Rules," describes rules governing the operation of aircraft (with certain exceptions) within the United States.

The **National Transportation Safety Board (NTSB)** has established rules and requirements for notification and reporting of aircraft accidents and incidents. These are contained in **NTSB Part 830**.

ALL, SPO

3005. The definition of nighttime is

A— sunset to sunrise.

B— 1 hour after sunset to 1 hour before sunrise.

C— the time between the end of evening civil twilight and the beginning of morning civil twilight.

Night is the time between the end of evening civil twilight and the beginning of morning civil twilight converted to local time, as published in the American Air Almanac. (PLT395) — 14 CFR §1.1

Answer (A) is incorrect because it refers to the time when lighted position lights are required. Answer (B) is incorrect because it refers to the currency requirement to carry passengers.

Pilot Certificate Privileges and Limitations

The types of pilot certificates and the attendant privileges are contained in 14 CFR Part 61 and are briefly stated as follows:

- The holder of a student pilot certificate is limited to solo flights or flights with an instructor.

- Recreational pilots may not carry more than one passenger, pay less than the pro rata share of the operating expenses of a flight with a passenger (provided the expenses involve only fuel, oil, airport expenses, or aircraft rental fees), fly an aircraft with more than 4 seats or high-performance characteristics, demonstrate an aircraft to a prospective buyer, fly between sunset and sunrise, or fly in airspace in which communication with air traffic control is required. Recreational pilots may fly beyond 50 NM from the departure airport with additional training and endorsements from an authorized instructor.

- A sport pilot may act as pilot-in-command of a light-sport aircraft, carry up to 1 passenger, during daylight hours, outside Class A, B, C, or D airspace (unless the sport pilot obtains further training and an endorsement), when visibilities are greater than 3 SM. Additional requirements are defined in 14 CFR §61.315

Continued

Answers

3005   [C]

- A private pilot has unlimited solo privileges, and may carry passengers or cargo as long as the flying is for the pilots' pleasure or personal business and is not done for hire. A private pilot may fly in conjunction with his/her job as long as that flying is incidental to his/her employment.

- A private pilot may not pay less than the pro rata share of the operating expenses of a flight with passengers, provided the expenses involve only fuel, oil, airport expenditures, or rental fees. The only time passengers may pay for the entire flight is if a donation is made by the passengers to the charitable organization which is sponsoring the flight.

- Commercial pilots may fly for compensation or hire.

- An Airline Transport Pilot may act as pilot-in-command (PIC) of airline and scheduled commuter operations.

- All pilot certificates (except student pilot) are valid indefinitely unless surrendered, superseded or revoked.

ALL
3064. In regard to privileges and limitations, a private pilot may

A— not pay less than the pro rata share of the operating expenses of a flight with passengers, provided the expenses involve only fuel, oil, airport expenditures, or rental fees.
B— act as pilot in command of an aircraft carrying a passenger for compensation if the flight is in connection with a business or employment.
C— not be paid in any manner for the operating expenses of a flight.

A private pilot may not pay less than the pro rata share of the operating expenses of a flight with passengers, provided the expenses involve only fuel, oil, airport expenditures, or rental fees. (PLT448) — 14 CFR §61.113

ALL
3065. According to regulations pertaining to privileges and limitations, a private pilot may

A— be paid for the operating expenses of a flight if at least three takeoffs and three landings were made by the pilot within the preceding 90 days.
B— not be paid in any manner for the operating expenses of a flight.
C— not pay less than the pro rata share of the operating expenses of a flight with passengers, provided the expenses involve only fuel, oil, airport expenditures, or rental fees.

A private pilot may not pay less than the pro rata share of the operating expenses of a flight with passengers, provided the expenses involve only fuel, oil, airport expenditures, or rental fees. (PLT448) — 14 CFR §61.113

ALL
3066. What exception, if any, permits a private pilot to act as pilot in command of an aircraft carrying passengers who pay for the flight?

A— If the passengers pay all the operating expenses.
B— If a donation is made to a charitable organization for the flight.
C— There is no exception.

A private pilot may act as pilot-in-command of an aircraft used in a passenger-carrying airlift sponsored by a charitable organization, and for which the passengers make a donation to the organization. This can be done if the sponsor of the airlift notifies the FAA General Aviation District Office having jurisdiction over the area concerned, at least 7 days before the flight, and furnishes any essential information that the office requests. (PLT448) — 14 CFR §61.113

ALL
3067. (Refer to Figure 74.) What minimum pilot certificate is required for a flight departing out of Hayward Executive (area 6)?

A— Student Pilot Certificate.
B— Private Pilot Certificate.
C— Sport Pilot Certificate.

Hayward Executive is located in Class D airspace up to but not including 1,500 feet MSL as depicted by the blue segmented line surrounding it. No specific pilot certification is required for flight within Class D airspace. A student pilot may operate within Class D airspace with appropriate solo endorsements. (PLT448) — AIM ¶3-2-5

Answer (B) and (C) are incorrect because no minimum pilot certificate is specified for operations in Class D airspace.

Answers

3064 [A]	3065 [C]	3066 [B]	3067 [A]

REC

3044. According to regulations pertaining to privileges and limitations, a recreational pilot may

A— be paid for the operating expenses of a flight.
B— not pay less than the pro rata share of the operating expenses of a flight with a passenger.
C— not be paid in any manner for the operating expenses of a flight.

A recreational pilot may not pay less than the pro rata share of the operating expenses of a flight with a passenger, provided the expenses involve only fuel, oil, airport expenditures, or rental fees. (PLT448) — 14 CFR §61.101

REC

3045. In regard to privileges and limitations, a recreational pilot may

A— fly for compensation or hire within 50 nautical miles from the departure airport with a logbook endorsement.
B— not be paid in any manner for the operating expenses of a flight from a passenger.
C— not pay less than the pro rata share of the operating expenses of a flight with a passenger.

A recreational pilot may not pay less than the pro rata share of the operating expenses of a flight with a passenger, provided the expenses involve only fuel, oil, airport expenditures, or rental fees. (PLT448) — 14 CFR §61.101

REC

3046. When may a recreational pilot act as pilot in command on a cross-country flight that exceeds 50 nautical miles from the departure airport?

A— After receiving ground and flight instructions on cross-country training and a logbook endorsement.
B— 12 calendar months after receiving his or her recreational pilot certificate and a logbook endorsement.
C— After attaining 100 hours of pilot-in-command time and a logbook endorsement.

A person who holds a recreational pilot certificate may act as pilot-in-command of an aircraft on a flight that exceeds 50 nautical miles from the departure airport, provided that person has received ground and flight training from an authorized instructor, been found proficient

in cross-country flying, and received an endorsement, which is carried in the person's possession in the aircraft. (PLT448) — 14 CFR §61.101

REC

3047. A recreational pilot may act as pilot in command of an aircraft that is certificated for a maximum of how many occupants?

A— Two.
B— Three.
C— Four.

A recreational pilot may not act as pilot-in-command of an aircraft that is certificated for more than four occupants. (PLT448) — 14 CFR §61.101

REC

3048. A recreational pilot may act as pilot in command of an aircraft with a maximum engine horsepower of

A— 160.
B— 180.
C— 200.

A recreational pilot may not act as pilot-in-command of an aircraft that is certificated with a powerplant of more than 180 horsepower. (PLT448) — 14 CFR §61.101

REC

3049. What exception, if any, permits a recreational pilot to act as pilot in command of an aircraft carrying a passenger for hire?

A— If the passenger pays no more than the operating expenses.
B— If a donation is made to a charitable organization for the flight.
C— There is no exception.

A recreational pilot may not act as pilot-in-command of an aircraft that is carrying a passenger or property for compensation or hire, in furtherance of a business, or for a charitable organization. (PLT448) — 14 CFR §61.101

Answer (A) is incorrect because the passenger may only pay an equal share of the operating expenses. Answer (B) is incorrect because a recreational pilot may not carry passengers for hire, even if the flight is a donation to a charitable organization.

Answers

3044 [B]	3045 [C]	3046 [A]	3047 [C]	3048 [B]	3049 [C]

REC
3050. May a recreational pilot act as pilot in command of an aircraft in furtherance of a business?

A— Yes, if the flight is only incidental to that business.
B— Yes, providing the aircraft does not carry a person or property for compensation or hire.
C— No, it is not allowed.

A recreational pilot may not act as pilot-in-command of an aircraft in furtherance of a business. (PLT448) — 14 CFR §61.101

REC
3051. With respect to daylight hours, what is the earliest time a recreational pilot may take off?

A— One hour before sunrise.
B— At sunrise.
C— At the beginning of morning civil twilight.

A recreational pilot may not act as pilot-in-command of an aircraft between sunset and sunrise. The earliest a recreational pilot may takeoff is at sunrise. (PLT467) — 14 CFR §61.101

REC
3052. If sunset is 2021 and the end of evening civil twilight is 2043, when must a recreational pilot terminate the flight?

A— 2021.
B— 2043.
C— 2121.

A recreational pilot may not act as pilot-in-command of an aircraft between sunset and sunrise. A recreational pilot must land by sunset. (PLT448) — 14 CFR §61.101

SPO
2130. If sunset is 2021 and the end of evening civil twilight is 2043, when must a sport pilot terminate the flight?

A— 2021.
B— 2043.
C— 2121.

A sport pilot may not act as pilot-in-command of an aircraft at night. A sport pilot must land by the end of evening twilight. (PLT448) — 14 CFR §61.315

REC
3052-1. When may a recreational pilot act as pilot in command of an aircraft at night?

A— When obtaining an additional certificate or rating under the supervision of an authorized instructor, provided the surface or flight visibility is at least 1 statute mile.
B— When obtaining an additional certificate or rating under the supervision of an authorized instructor, provided the surface or flight visibility is at least 3 statute miles.
C— When obtaining an additional certificate or rating under the supervision of an authorized instructor, provided the surface or flight visibility is at least 5 statute miles.

For the purpose of obtaining additional certificates or ratings while under the supervision of an authorized instructor, a recreational pilot may fly as the sole occupant of an aircraft between sunset and sunrise, provided the flight or surface visibility is at least 5 SM. (PLT448) — 14 CFR §61.101

REC
3053. When may a recreational pilot operate to or from an airport that lies within Class C airspace?

A— Anytime the control tower is in operation.
B— When the ceiling is at least 1,000 feet and the surface visibility is at least 2 miles.
C— After receiving training and a logbook endorsement from an authorized instructor.

A recreational pilot may not operate in airspace where air traffic control is required until they receive and log ground and flight training and an endorsement from an authorized instructor. (PLT161) — 14 CFR §61.101

REC
3054. Under what conditions may a recreational pilot operate at an airport that lies within Class D airspace and that has a part-time control tower in operation?

A— Between sunrise and sunset when the tower is in operation, the ceiling is at least 2,500 feet, and the visibility is at least 3 miles.
B— Any time when the tower is in operation, the ceiling is at least 3,000 feet, and the visibility is more than 1 mile.
C— Between sunrise and sunset when the tower is closed, the ceiling is at least 1,000 feet, and the visibility is at least 3 miles.

Answers

3050	[C]		3051	[B]		3052	[A]		2130	[B]	
3054	[C]										

2130 [B]   3052-1 [C]   3053 [C]

A recreational pilot may not act as pilot-in-command of an aircraft in airspace in which communication with ATC is required. If the tower is closed, no communication is required and it reverts to Class E airspace. The visibility and cloud clearances for Class E airspace require a ceiling at least 1,000 feet and the visibility at least 3 miles. (PLT161) — 14 CFR §61.101

Answers (A) and (B) are incorrect because a recreational pilot may not operate in airspace that requires communication with ATC.

REC
3055. When may a recreational pilot fly above 10,000 feet MSL?

A— When 2,000 feet AGL or below.
B— When 2,500 feet AGL or below.
C— When outside of controlled airspace.

A recreational pilot may not act as pilot-in-command of an aircraft at an altitude of more than 10,000 feet MSL or 2,000 feet AGL, whichever is higher. (PLT448) — 14 CFR §61.101

REC
3056. During daytime, what is the minimum flight or surface visibility required for recreational pilots in Class G airspace below 10,000 feet MSL?

A— 1 mile.
B— 3 miles.
C— 5 miles.

A recreational pilot may not act as pilot-in-command of an aircraft when the flight or surface visibility is less than 3 statute miles. (PLT163) — 14 CFR §61.101

REC
3057. During daytime, what is the minimum flight visibility required for recreational pilots in controlled airspace below 10,000 feet MSL?

A— 1 mile.
B— 3 miles.
C— 5 miles.

A recreational pilot may not act as pilot-in-command of an aircraft when the flight or surface visibility is less than 3 statute miles. (PLT163) — 14 CFR §61.101

REC
3058. Under what conditions, if any, may a recreational pilot demonstrate an aircraft in flight to a prospective buyer?

A— The buyer pays all the operating expenses.
B— The flight is not outside the United States.
C— None.

A recreational pilot may not act as pilot-in-command of an aircraft to demonstrate that aircraft in flight to a prospective buyer. (PLT448) — 14 CFR §61.101

REC
3059. When, if ever, may a recreational pilot act as pilot in command in an aircraft towing a banner?

A— If the pilot has logged 100 hours of flight time in powered aircraft.
B— If the pilot has an endorsement in his/her pilot logbook from an authorized flight instructor.
C— It is not allowed.

A recreational pilot may not act as pilot-in-command of an aircraft that is towing any object. (PLT401) — 14 CFR §61.101

REC
3043. How many passengers is a recreational pilot allowed to carry on board?

A— One.
B— Two.
C— Three.

A recreational pilot may not carry more than one passenger. (PLT448) — 14 CFR §61.101

SPO
2123. How many passengers is a sport pilot allowed to carry on board?

A— One.
B— Two.
C— Three.

Sport Pilots may not act as pilot in command of a light-sport aircraft while carrying more than one passenger. (PLT448) — 14 CFR §61.315

Answers

3055 [A]	3056 [B]	3057 [B]	3058 [C]	3059 [C]	3043 [A]
2123 [A]					

REC

3060. When must a recreational pilot have a pilot-in-command flight check?

A— Every 400 hours.
B— Every 180 days.
C— If the pilot has less than 400 total flight hours and has not flown as pilot in command in an aircraft within the preceding 180 days.

A recreational pilot who has logged fewer than 400 flight hours and who has not logged pilot-in-command time in an aircraft within the preceding 180 days may not act as pilot-in-command of an aircraft until flight instruction is received from an authorized flight instructor who certifies in the pilot's logbook that the pilot is competent to act as pilot-in-command of the aircraft. This requirement can be met in combination with the requirements of flight reviews, at the discretion of the instructor. (PLT448) — 14 CFR §61.101

REC

3061. A recreational pilot may fly as sole occupant of an aircraft at night while under the supervision of a flight instructor provided the flight or surface visibility is at least

A— 3 miles.
B— 4 miles.
C— 5 miles.

For the purpose of obtaining additional certificates or ratings, while under the supervision of an authorized flight instructor, a recreational pilot may fly as sole occupant of an aircraft between sunset and sunrise, provided the flight or surface visibility is at least 5 statute miles. (PLT448) — 14 CFR §61.101

REC

3134. What minimum visibility and clearance from clouds are required for a recreational pilot in Class G airspace at 1,200 feet AGL or below during daylight hours?

A— 1 mile visibility and clear of clouds.
B— 3 miles visibility and clear of clouds.
C— 3 miles visibility, 500 feet below the clouds.

Minimum flight or surface visibility for recreational pilots is 3 miles and minimum cloud clearance for all pilots in Class G airspace, below 1,200 AGL, is clear of clouds. (PLT163) — 14 CFR §61.101

Answer (A) is incorrect because this would be for private pilots. Answer (C) is incorrect because this is for controlled airspace.

REC

3135. Outside controlled airspace, the minimum flight visibility requirement for a recreational pilot flying VFR above 1,200 feet AGL and below 10,000 feet MSL during daylight hours is

A— 1 mile.
B— 3 miles.
C— 5 miles.

Minimum flight or surface visibility for recreational pilots is 3 miles. (PLT163) — 14 CFR §61.101

SPO

2061. Outside controlled airspace, the minimum flight visibility requirement for a sport pilot flying above 1,200 feet AGL and below 10,000 feet MSL during daylight hours is

A— 1 statute mile.
B— 3 statute miles.
C— 5 statute miles.

Minimum flight or surface visibility for sport pilots is 3 statute miles in all airspace at all times. (PLT467) — 14 CFR §61.315

SPO

2061-1. The minimum flight visibility requirement for a sport pilot is

A— 1 statute mile.
B— 3 statute miles.
C— 5 statute miles.

Minimum flight or surface visibility for sport pilots is 3 statute miles. (PLT163) — 14 CFR §61.315

Answers

| 3060 [C] | 3061 [C] | 3134 [B] | 3135 [B] | 2061 [B] | 2061-1 [B] |

Pilot Ratings

When a pilot certificate is issued, it lists the category, class, and type (if appropriate) of aircraft in which the certificate holder is qualified. *See* Figure 4-1.

The term "**category**" means a broad classification of aircraft, such as airplane, rotorcraft, glider, and lighter-than-air. The term "**class**" means a classification within a category having similar operating characteristics, such as single-engine, multi-engine, land, water, helicopter, and balloon. The term "**type**" means a specific make and basic model of aircraft, such as Cessna 172 or Gulfstream IV.

A type rating must be held by the pilot-in-command of a large aircraft. "Large aircraft" means aircraft of more than 12,500 pounds maximum certificated takeoff weight.

All turbojet-powered airplanes, regardless of weight, require the PIC to have a type rating.

In addition to the category, class, and type ratings, if a pilot wishes to fly IFR, an instrument rating is required.

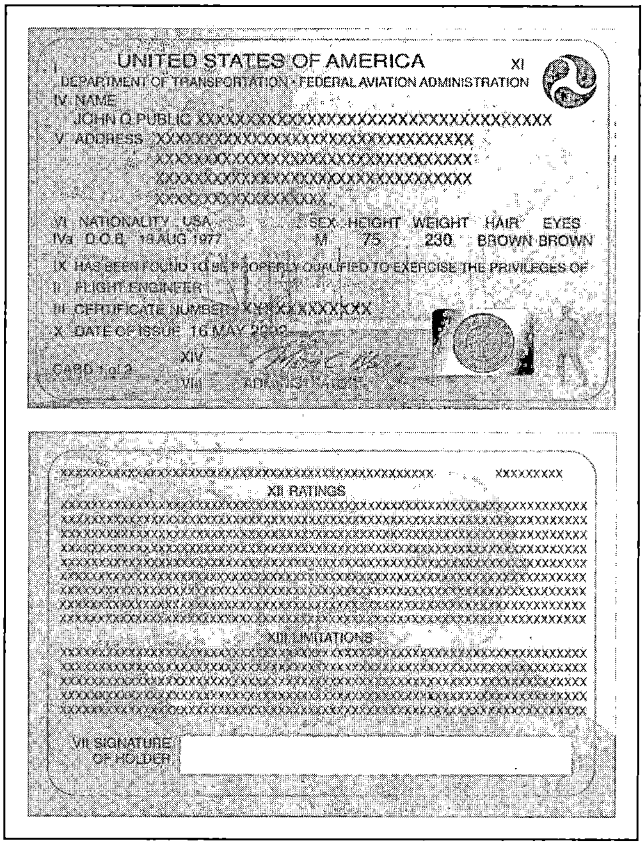

Figure 4-1. Airman certificate

ALL, SPO

3001. With respect to the certification of airmen, which are categories of aircraft?

A— Gyroplane, helicopter, airship, free balloon.
B— Airplane, rotorcraft, glider, lighter-than-air.
C— Single-engine land and sea, multiengine land and sea.

With respect to the certification of airmen, "category" means a broad classification of aircraft such as airplane, rotorcraft, glider, lighter-than-air, weight-shift control, and powered parachute. (PLT371) — 14 CFR §1.1

Answer (A) is incorrect because it refers to classes of rotorcraft and lighter-than-air craft. Answer (C) is incorrect because it refers to classes of airplanes.

ALL

3002. With respect to the certification of airmen, which are classes of aircraft?

A— Airplane, rotorcraft, glider, lighter-than-air.
B— Single-engine land and sea, multiengine land and sea.
C— Lighter-than-air, airship, hot air balloon, gas balloon.

With respect to the certification of airmen, a "class" refers to aircraft with similar operating characteristics such as single-engine land/sea and multi-engine land/sea, gyroplane, helicopter, airship, and free balloon. (PLT371) — 14 CFR §1.1

Answer (A) is incorrect because it refers to categories of aircraft. Answer (C) is incorrect because it refers to lighter-than-air category. Airship and free balloon are lighter-than-air class ratings, but hot air balloon and gas balloon are not.

Answers

3001 [B]   3002 [B]

AIR, RTC
3024. The pilot in command is required to hold a type rating in which aircraft?

A— Aircraft operated under an authorization issued by the Administrator.
B— Aircraft having a gross weight of more than 12,500 pounds.
C— Aircraft involved in ferry flights, training flights, or test flights.

A type rating is required in order for a pilot to act as pilot-in-command of a large aircraft (except lighter-than-air) which is further defined as more than 12,500 pounds maximum certificated takeoff weight or a turbojet-powered aircraft. (PLT451) — 14 CFR §61.31

Answers (A) and (C) are incorrect because they don't address the weight or type of propulsion.

Medical Certificates

Student pilot, recreational pilot, and private pilot operations, other than glider and balloon pilots, require a Third-Class Medical Certificate or compliance with BasicMed—which is detailed in 14 CFR Part 68.

The BasicMed privileges apply to persons exercising student, recreational, and private pilot privileges when acting as pilot in command (PIC). It also applies to persons exercising flight instructor privileges when acting as PIC. You cannot use BasicMed privileges to fly as a safety pilot, except when that pilot is acting as PIC. Pilots operating under BasicMed must hold a current and valid U.S. driver's license and comply with all medical requirements or restrictions associated with that license. Applicants operating under BasicMed regulations must also complete the comprehensive medical examination checklist (CMEC) in collaboration with a physical examination by a state-licensed physician. You physical must be completed within the last 48 months and the CMEC completed within the last 24 months. When operating under BasicMed, pilots are limited to:

1. Fly with no more than five passengers.

2. Fly an aircraft with a maximum certificated takeoff weight of no more than 6,000 lbs.

3. Fly an aircraft that is authorized to carry no more than 6 occupants.

4. Flights within the United States, at an indicated airspeed of 250 knots or less, and at an altitude at or below 18,000 feet mean sea level (MSL).

5. You may not fly for compensation or hire.

If operating beyond these limitations, pilots must obtain an FAA Medical Certificate. A Third-Class Medical Certificate expires at the end of:

1. The 60th month after the month of the date of the examination shown on the certificate if the person has not reached his or her 40th birthday on or before the date of examination; or

2. The 24th month after the month of the date of examination shown on the certificate if the person has reached his or her 40th birthday on or before the date of the examination.

The holder of a Second-Class Medical Certificate may exercise commercial privileges during the first 12 calendar months, but the certificate is valid only for private pilot privileges during the following (12 or 48) calendar months, depending on the applicant's age.

The holder of a First-Class Medical Certificate may exercise Airline Transport Pilot privileges during the first (6 or 12) calendar months, commercial privileges during the following (6 or 0) calendar months, and private pilot privileges during the following (12 or 48) calendar months, depending on the applicant's age. To state another way, a medical certificate may last 6 months to a year with first-class privileges, 12 months (from the date of the examination) with second-class privileges, and 2 or 5 years with third-class privileges—depending on whether the applicant is above or below 40 years of age.

Answers

3024 [B]

Each type of medical certificate is valid through the last day of the month (of the month it expires), regardless of the day the physical examination was given.

ALL
3039. A Third-Class Medical Certificate was issued to a 19-year-old pilot on August 10, this year. To exercise the privileges of a Recreational or Private Pilot Certificate, the medical certificate will expire at midnight on

A— August 10, 2 years later.
B— August 31, 5 years later.
C— August 31, 2 years later.

A Third-Class Medical Certificate expires at the end of the last day of the 60th month after the month of the date of the examination shown on the certificate if the person has not reached his or her 40th birthday on or before the date of examination, for operations requiring a Recreational or Private Pilot Certificate. (PLT447) — 14 CFR §61.23

ALL
3020. A Third-Class Medical Certificate is issued to a 36-year-old pilot on August 10, this year. To exercise the privileges of a Private Pilot Certificate, the medical certificate will be valid until midnight on

A— August 10, 3 years later.
B— August 31, 5 years later.
C— August 31, 3 years later.

A Third-Class Medical Certificate expires at the end of the last day of the 60th month after the month of the date of the examination shown on the certificate if the person has not reached his or her 40th birthday on or before the date of examination, for operations requiring a Recreational or Private Pilot Certificate. (PLT447) — 14 CFR §61.23

ALL
3021. A Third-Class Medical Certificate is issued to a 51-year-old pilot on May 3, this year. To exercise the privileges of a Private Pilot Certificate, the medical certificate will be valid until midnight on

A— May 3, 1 year later.
B— May 31, 1 year later.
C— May 31, 2 years later.

A Third-Class Medical Certificate expires at the end of the last day of the 24th month after the month of the date of the examination shown on the certificate if the person has reached his or her 40th birthday on or before the date of examination, for operations requiring a Private Pilot Certificate. (PLT447) — 14 CFR §61.23

ALL
3022. For private pilot operations, a Second-Class Medical Certificate issued to a 42-year-old pilot on July 15, this year, will expire at midnight on

A— July 15, 2 years later.
B— July 31, 1 year later.
C— July 31, 2 years later.

A Second-Class Medical Certificate expires at the end of the last day of the 24th month after the month of the date of the examination shown on the certificate if the person has reached his or her 40th birthday on or before the date of examination, for operations requiring a Private Pilot Certificate. (PLT447) — 14 CFR §61.23

ALL
3023. For private pilot operations, a First-Class Medical Certificate issued to a 23-year-old pilot on October 21, this year, will expire at midnight on

A— October 21, 2 years later.
B— October 31, next year.
C— October 31, 5 years later.

A First-Class Medical Certificate expires at the end of the last day of the 60th month after the month of the date of the examination shown on the certificate if the person has not reached his or her 40th birthday on or before the date of examination, for operations requiring a Recreational or Private Pilot Certificate. (PLT447) — 14 CFR §61.23

GLI
3062. Prior to becoming certified as a private pilot with a glider rating, the pilot must have in his or her possession what type of medical?

A— A statement from a designated medical examiner.
B— A third-class medical certificate.
C— A medical certificate is not required.

A person is not required to hold a medical certificate when exercising the privileges of a pilot certificate with a glider category rating. (PLT447) — 14 CFR §61.23

Answers

| 3039 [B] | 3020 [B] | 3021 [C] | 3022 [C] | 3023 [C] | 3062 [C] |

LTA
3063. Prior to becoming certified as a private pilot with a balloon rating, the pilot must have in his or her possession what class of medical?

A— A third-class medical certificate.
B— A medical certificate is not required.
C— A statement from a designated medical examiner.

A person is not required to hold a medical certificate when exercising the privileges of a pilot certificate with a balloon class rating. (PLT427) — 14 CFR §61.23

Required Certificates

When acting as pilot-in-command, a pilot must have a current pilot license, a photo ID, and a current medical certificate in his/her physical possession or readily accessible in the aircraft. Glider and balloon pilots do not need a medical certificate. A recreational pilot acting as PIC must have a current logbook endorsement in his/her personal possession within flights 50 NM from the departure airport.

A pilot must present his/her pilot license and medical certificate for inspection upon request of any FAA, NTSB or federal, state, or local law enforcement officer.

ALL
3016. What document(s) must be in your personal possession or readily accessible in the aircraft while operating as pilot in command of an aircraft?

A— Certificates showing accomplishment of a checkout in the aircraft and a current flight review.
B— A pilot certificate with an endorsement showing accomplishment of an annual flight review and a pilot logbook showing recency of experience.
C— An appropriate pilot certificate and an appropriate current medical certificate if required.

No person may act as pilot-in-command (PIC), or in any other capacity as a required pilot flight crewmember, of a civil aircraft of United States registry unless he/she has in possession or readily accessible in the aircraft a current pilot certificate and photo ID. Except for free balloon pilots piloting balloons and glider pilots piloting gliders, no person may act as pilot-in-command or in any other capacity as a required pilot flight crewmember of an aircraft unless he/she has in possession or readily accessible in the aircraft an appropriate current medical certificate or other documentation acceptable to the FAA. (PLT399) — 14 CFR §61.3

Answers (A) and (B) are incorrect because aircraft checkouts don't need to be recorded, and a flight review record and currency proof don't need to be in your possession.

ALL
3017. When must a current pilot certificate be in the pilot's personal possession or readily accessible in the aircraft?

A— When acting as a crew chief during launch and recovery.
B— Only when passengers are carried.
C— Anytime when acting as pilot in command or as a required crewmember.

No person may act as pilot-in-command (PIC), or in any other capacity as a required pilot flight crewmember, of a civil aircraft of United States registry unless he/she has in possession or readily accessible in the aircraft a current pilot certificate and a photo ID. (PLT399) — 14 CFR §61.3

Answers (A) and (B) are incorrect because a crew chief does not require a pilot certificate, and pilots must have certificates, regardless of whether carrying passengers or not.

ALL
3018. A recreational or private pilot acting as pilot in command, or in any other capacity as a required pilot flight crewmember, must have in their personal possession or readily accessible in the aircraft a current

A— logbook endorsement to show that a flight review has been satisfactorily accomplished.
B— medical certificate if required and an appropriate pilot certificate.
C— endorsement on the pilot certificate to show that a flight review has been satisfactorily accomplished.

Answers
3063　[B]　　　3016　[C]　　　3017　[C]　　　3018　[B]

No person may act as pilot-in-command (PIC), or in any other capacity as a required pilot flight crewmember, of a civil aircraft of United States registry unless he/she has in possession or readily accessible in the aircraft a current pilot certificate and a photo ID. Except for free balloon pilots piloting balloons and glider pilots piloting gliders, no person may act as pilot-in-command or in any other capacity as a required pilot flight crewmember of an aircraft unless he/she has in possession or readily accessible in the aircraft an appropriate current medical certificate or other documentation acceptable to the FAA. (PLT399) — 14 CFR §61.3

Answers (A) and (C) are incorrect because proof of a flight review does not need to be in your possession while acting as pilot-in-command.

ALL
3019. Each person who holds a pilot certificate or a medical certificate shall present it for inspection upon the request of the Administrator, the National Transportation Safety Board, or any

A— authorized representative of the Department of Transportation.
B— person in a position of authority.
C— federal, state, or local law enforcement officer.

Each person who holds a pilot or medical certificate shall present it for inspection upon the request of the FAA Administrator, an NTSB representative, or any federal, state, or local law enforcement officer. (PLT399) — 14 CFR §61.3

SPO
2129. Each person who holds a pilot certificate, a U.S. driver's license, or a medical certificate shall present it for inspection upon the request of the Administrator, the National Transportation Safety Board, or any

A— authorized representative of the Department of Transportation.
B— authorized representative of the Department of State.
C— federal, state, or local law enforcement officer.

Each person who holds a pilot or medical certificate shall present it for inspection upon the request of the FAA Administrator, an NTSB representative, or any Federal, State, or local law enforcement officer. (PLT399) — 14 CFR §61.3

REC
3038. A recreational pilot acting as pilot in command must have in his or her personal possession while aboard the aircraft

A— a current logbook endorsement to show that a flight review has been satisfactorily accomplished.
B— a current logbook endorsement that permits flights within 50 NM from the departure airport.
C— the pilot logbook to show recent experience requirements to serve as pilot in command have been met.

A recreational pilot may act as PIC on a flight within 50 NM from the departure airport, provided they receive from an authorized instructor a logbook endorsement, which is carried in the person's possession in the aircraft. (PLT448) — 14 CFR §61.101

Recent Flight Experience

No person may act as pilot-in-command of an aircraft unless within the preceding 24 calendar months he/she has accomplished a **flight review**. This review is given in an aircraft for which the pilot is rated by an appropriately-rated instructor or other person designated by the FAA. A logbook entry will document satisfactory accomplishment of this requirement. If the pilot takes a proficiency check (as for a certificate or a new rating), it counts for the flight review.

No person may act as PIC of an aircraft carrying passengers unless, within the preceding 90 days, he/she has made three takeoffs and three landings as the sole manipulator of the controls in an aircraft of the same category, class, and if a type rating is required, in the same type. Touch and go landings are acceptable unless the passengers are to be carried in a tailwheel airplane, in which case the landing must be to a full stop, and they must be in a tailwheel airplane.

Continued

Answers

3019   [C]   2129   [C]   3038   [B]

If passengers are to be carried during the period from 1 hour after sunset to 1 hour before sunrise, the PIC must have made, within the preceding 90 days, at least three takeoffs and three landings during that period. The landings must have been to a full stop and in the same category and class of aircraft to be used.

ALL
3028. To act as pilot in command of an aircraft carrying passengers, a pilot must show by logbook endorsement the satisfactory completion of a flight review or completion of a pilot proficiency check within the preceding

A— 6 calendar months.
B— 12 calendar months.
C— 24 calendar months.

Each pilot must complete a flight review every 24 calendar months. (PLT449) — 14 CFR §61.56

ALL
3029. If recency of experience requirements for night flight are not met and official sunset is 1830, the latest time passengers may be carried is

A— 1829.
B— 1859.
C— 1929.

No person may act as pilot-in-command of an aircraft carrying passengers during the period beginning one hour after sunset and ending one hour before sunrise (as published in the American Air Almanac) unless, within the preceding 90 days, he/she has made at least three takeoffs and three landings to a full stop during that period in the category and class of aircraft to be used.

1830 + 59 minutes = 1929

(PLT442) — 14 CFR §61.57

ALL
3030. To act as pilot in command of an aircraft carrying passengers, the pilot must have made at least three takeoffs and three landings in an aircraft of the same category, class, and if a type rating is required, of the same type, within the preceding

A— 90 days.
B— 12 calendar months.
C— 24 calendar months.

No person may act as pilot-in-command of an aircraft carrying passengers, unless, within the preceding 90 days, he/she has made three takeoffs and three landings as the sole manipulator of the flight controls in an aircraft of the same category and class and, if a type rating is required, of the same type. If the aircraft is a tailwheel airplane, the landings must have been made to a full stop. (PLT411) — 14 CFR §61.57

ALL
3030-1. Your cousin wants you to take him flying. In order to do this, you must have made at least three takeoffs and three landings in your aircraft within the preceding

A— 90 days.
B— 60 days.
C— 30 days.

No person may act as pilot-in-command of an aircraft carrying passengers, unless, within the preceding 90 days, he/she has made three takeoffs and three landings as the sole manipulator of the flight controls in an aircraft of the same category and class and, if a type rating is required, of the same type. If the aircraft is a tailwheel airplane, the landings must have been made to a full stop. (PLT411) – 14 CFR §61.57

ALL
3031. To act as pilot in command of an aircraft carrying passengers, the pilot must have made three takeoffs and three landings within the preceding 90 days in an aircraft of the same

A— make and model.
B— category and class, but not type.
C— category, class, and type, if a type rating is required.

No person may act as pilot-in-command of an aircraft carrying passengers, unless, within the preceding 90 days, he/she has made three takeoffs and three landings as the sole manipulator of the flight controls in an aircraft of the same category and class and, if a type rating is required, of the same type. If the aircraft is a tailwheel airplane, the landings must have been made to a full stop. (PLT442) — 14 CFR §61.57

Answers

3028 [C]	3029 [C]	3030 [A]	3030-1 [A]	3031 [C]

ALL

3034. To meet the recency of experience requirements to act as pilot in command carrying passengers at night, a pilot must have made at least three takeoffs and three landings to a full stop within the preceding 90 days in

A— the same category and class of aircraft to be used.
B— the same type of aircraft to be used.
C— any aircraft.

No person may act as pilot-in-command of an aircraft carrying passengers during the period beginning one hour after sunset and ending one hour before sunrise (as published in the American Air Almanac) unless, within the preceding 90 days, he/she has made at least three takeoffs and three landings to a full stop during that period in the category and class of aircraft to be used. (PLT442) — 14 CFR §61.57

ALL

3040. If a recreational or private pilot had a flight review on August 8, this year, when is the next flight review required?

A— August 8, 2 years later.
B— August 31, next year.
C— August 31, 2 years later.

Each pilot must have completed a biennial flight review since the beginning of the 24th calendar month before the month in which that pilot acts as pilot-in-command. A calendar month always ends at midnight of the last day of the month. If a pilot had a flight review on August 8, the next flight review would be due on August 31, two years later. (PLT442) — 14 CFR §61.56

ALL

3041. Each recreational or private pilot is required to have

A— a biennial flight review.
B— an annual flight review.
C— a semiannual flight review.

Each pilot must have completed a biennial flight review since the beginning of the 24th calendar month before the month in which that pilot acts as pilot-in-command. (PLT442) — 14 CFR §61.56

AIR

3032. The takeoffs and landings required to meet the recency of experience requirements for carrying passengers in a tailwheel airplane

A— may be touch and go or full stop.
B— must be touch and go.
C— must be to a full stop.

No person may act as pilot-in-command of an aircraft carrying passengers, unless, within the preceding 90 days, he/she has made three takeoffs and three landings as the sole manipulator of the flight controls in an aircraft of the same category and class and, if a type rating is required, of the same type. If the aircraft is a tailwheel airplane, the landings must have been made to a full stop. (PLT442) — 14 CFR §61.57

AIR, RTC, WSC, PPC

3033. The three takeoffs and landings that are required to act as pilot in command at night must be done during the time period from

A— sunset to sunrise.
B— 1 hour after sunset to 1 hour before sunrise.
C— the end of evening civil twilight to the beginning of morning civil twilight.

No person may act as pilot-in-command of an aircraft carrying passengers during the period beginning one hour after sunset and ending one hour before sunrise (as published in the American Air Almanac) unless, within the preceding 90 days, he/she has made at least three takeoffs and three landings to a full stop during that period in the category and class of aircraft to be used. (PLT442) — 14 CFR §61.57

Answer (A) is incorrect because this is the requirement for position lights. Answer (C) is incorrect because it refers to the time which may be logged as night flight.

Answers

3034 [A]   3040 [C]   3041 [A]   3032 [C]   3033 [B]

High-Performance Airplanes

No person holding a Private or Commercial Pilot Certificate may act as pilot-in-command of an airplane that has more than 200 horsepower, unless he/she has received instruction from an authorized flight instructor who has certified in his/her logbook that he/she is competent to pilot a high-performance airplane.

AIR
3025. What is the definition of a high-performance airplane?

A— An airplane with an engine of more than 200 horsepower.
B— An airplane with 180 horsepower, or retractable landing gear, flaps, and a fixed-pitch propeller.
C— An airplane with a normal cruise speed in excess of 200 knots.

A high-performance airplane is one with an engine of more than 200 horsepower. (PLT395) — 14 CFR §61.31

AIR
3026. Before a person holding a Private Pilot Certificate may act as pilot in command of a high-performance airplane, that person must have

A— passed a flight test in that airplane from an FAA inspector.
B— an endorsement in that person's logbook that he or she is competent to act as pilot in command.
C— received ground and flight instruction from an authorized flight instructor who then endorses that person's logbook.

No person holding a Private or Commercial pilot certificate may pilot a high-performance aircraft unless he or she has received instruction and has been certified competent in his/her logbook. (PLT448) — 14 CFR §61.31

Answer (A) is incorrect because a flight test is not required. Answer (B) is incorrect because instruction is required.

AIR
3027. In order to act as pilot in command of a high-performance airplane, a pilot must have

A— made and logged three solo takeoffs and landings in a high-performance airplane.
B— passed a flight test in a high-performance airplane.
C— received and logged ground and flight instruction in an airplane that has more than 200 horsepower.

A high-performance airplane is one with more than 200 horsepower. No person holding a Private or Commercial pilot certificate may pilot a high-performance aircraft unless he or she has received ground and flight instruction and has been certified proficient in his/her logbook. (PLT448) — 14 CFR §61.31

Answer (A) is incorrect because landings are only required in order to carry passengers, and they don't need to be solo. Answer (B) is incorrect because a flight test is not required.

Glider Towing

A private pilot may not act as pilot-in-command of an aircraft towing a glider unless at least 100 hours of pilot flight time is logged in the aircraft category, class, and type (if required), or 200 hours total pilot time. Also, within the preceding 24 months he/she has made at least three actual/simulated glider tows while accompanied by a qualified pilot or has made three flights as PIC of a towed glider.

Answers

3025   [A]   3026   [C]   3027   [C]

AIR, GLI, WSC

3036. A certificated private pilot may not act as pilot in command of an aircraft towing a glider unless there is entered in the pilot's logbook a minimum of

A— 100 hours of pilot flight time in any aircraft, that the pilot is using to tow a glider.
B— 100 hours of pilot-in-command time in the aircraft category, class, and type, if required, that the pilot is using to tow a glider.
C— 200 hours of pilot-in-command time in the aircraft category, class, and type, if required, that the pilot is using to tow a glider.

With a Private pilot certificate, no person may act as PIC of an aircraft towing a glider unless he/she has had, and entered in his/her logbook, at least:

1. 100 hours of pilot-in-command time in the aircraft category, class, and type (if required), or

2. 200 hours of pilot-in-command time in powered or other aircraft.

(PLT407) — 14 CFR §61.69

Answer (A) is incorrect because the 100 hours must be as PIC and in the proper category, class, and type, if required. Answer (C) is incorrect because the 200 hours of flight time can be in a combination of powered and other-than-powered aircraft.

AIR, GLI, WSC

3037. To act as pilot in command of an aircraft towing a glider, a pilot is required to have made within the preceding 24 months.

A— at least three flights as observer in a glider being towed by an aircraft.
B— at least three flights in a powered glider.
C— at least three actual or simulated glider tows while accompanied by a qualified pilot.

No person may act as a pilot-in-command of an aircraft towing a glider unless within the preceding 24 months he/she has—

1. Made at least three actual or simulated glider tows while accompanied by a qualified pilot who meets the requirements of 14 CFR §61.69, or

2. Made at least three flights as pilot-in-command of a glider towed by an aircraft.

(PLT407) — 14 CFR §61.69

GLI, LSG

3067-1. (Refer to Figure 73.) These glider hand signals are examples of

A— aerotow visual signals.
B— aerotow prelaunch signals.
C— aerotow emergency signals.

The glider hand signals displayed in the figure represent a few of the aerotow prelaunch signals used between pilots and launch crew members to facilitate a glider launch. (PLT407) – FAA-H-8083-13

Answer (A) is incorrect because aerotow visual signals are displayed inflight by the use of aircraft movements. Answer (C) is incorrect because the figure does not depict an emergency signal used in glider operations.

Change of Address

If a pilot changes his/her permanent mailing address without notifying the FAA Airmen's Certification Branch, in writing, within 30 days, then he/she may not exercise the privileges of his/her certificate.

ALL, SPO

3035. If a certificated pilot changes permanent mailing address and fails to notify the FAA Airmen Certification Branch of the new address, the pilot is entitled to exercise the privileges of the pilot certificate for a period of only

A— 30 days after the date of the move.
B— 60 days after the date of the move.
C— 90 days after the date of the move.

The holder of a Pilot or Flight Instructor Certificate who has made a change in his/her permanent mailing address may not, after 30 days from the date moved, exercise the privileges of his/her certificate unless he/she has notified in writing the Department of Transportation, Federal Aviation Administration, Airmen Certification Branch, Box 25082, Oklahoma City, OK 73125, of the new address. (PLT387) — 14 CFR §61.60

Answers

3036 [B]	3037 [C]	3067-1 [B]	3035 [A]

Responsibility and Authority of the Pilot-in-Command

The pilot-in-command (PIC) of an aircraft is directly responsible, and is the final authority, for the safety and operation of that aircraft. Should an emergency require immediate action, the PIC may deviate from 14 CFR Part 91 to the extent necessary in the interest of safety. Upon request, a written report of any deviation from the rules must be sent to the Administrator.

If a pilot receives a clearance that would cause a deviation from a rule, he/she should query the controller and request that the clearance be amended.

ALL
3070. The final authority as to the operation of an aircraft is the

A— Federal Aviation Administration.
B— pilot in command.
C— aircraft manufacturer.

The pilot-in-command of an aircraft is directly responsible for, and is the final authority as to the operation of that aircraft. (PLT444) — 14 CFR §91.3

ALL, SPO
3072. If an in-flight emergency requires immediate action, the pilot in command may

A— deviate from any rule of 14 CFR part 91 to the extent required to meet the emergency, but must submit a written report to the Administrator within 24 hours.
B— deviate from any rule of 14 CFR part 91 to the extent required to meet that emergency.
C— not deviate from any rule of 14 CFR part 91 unless prior to the deviation approval is granted by the Administrator.

If an emergency requires immediate action, the pilot-in-command may deviate from the operating rules of Part 91 to the extent necessary to meet that emergency. No report of such deviation is required unless the FAA requests one. (PLT444) — 14 CFR §91.3

ALL, SPO
3073. When must a pilot who deviates from a regulation during an emergency send a written report of that deviation to the Administrator?

A— Within 7 days.
B— Within 10 days.
C— Upon request.

*Each pilot-in-command who deviates from a rule in an emergency shall, **upon request**, send a written report of that deviation to the Administrator. (PLT440) — 14 CFR §91.3*

ALL, SPO
3074. Who is responsible for determining if an aircraft is in condition for safe flight?

A— A certificated aircraft mechanic.
B— The pilot in command.
C— The owner or operator.

The pilot-in-command of an aircraft is responsible for determining whether that aircraft is in condition for safe flight. The pilot shall discontinue the flight when unairworthy mechanical, electrical or structural conditions occur. (PLT444) — 14 CFR §91.7

LTA
3071. Pre-takeoff briefing of passengers for a flight is the responsibility of

A— all passengers.
B— the pilot.
C— a crewmember.

The pilot-in-command is responsible for briefing crewmembers and occupants in all areas of the flight, including inflation, tether, infight, landing, emergency, and recovery procedures. (PLT444) — 14 CFR §91.3

LSL
2308. The person directly responsible for the pre-launch briefing of passengers for a flight is the

A— safety officer.
B— pilot in command.
C— ground crewmember.

The pilot-in-command is responsible for briefing crewmembers and occupants in all areas of the flight, including inflation, tether, inflight, landing, emergency, and recovery procedures. (PLT444) — 14 CFR §91.3

Answers

| 3070 | [B] | 3072 | [B] | 3073 | [C] | 3074 | [B] | 3071 | [B] | 2308 | [B] |

Preflight Action

Before beginning a flight, the pilot-in-command is required to become familiar with all available information concerning that flight. This information must include the following:

1. Runway lengths, and

2. Takeoff and landing information for airports of intended use, including aircraft performance data.

If the flight will not be in the vicinity of the departure airport, the pilot must also consider the following:

1. Weather reports and forecasts,

2. Fuel requirements (enough fuel to fly to the first point of intended landing, and at normal cruising speed, to fly after that for at least 30 minutes if during the day, or for at least 45 minutes at night when in an airplane), and

3. Alternatives available if the flight cannot be completed as planned.

ALL, SPO

3080. Which preflight action is specifically required of the pilot prior to each flight?

A— Check the aircraft logbooks for appropriate entries.

B— Become familiar with all available information concerning the flight.

C— Review wake turbulence avoidance procedures.

Each pilot-in-command shall, before each flight, become familiar with all available information concerning that flight. This information must include:

(a) For a flight under IFR or a flight not in the vicinity of an airport, weather reports and forecasts, fuel requirements, alternatives available if the planned flight cannot be completed, and any known traffic delays of which the pilot has been advised by ATC;

(b) For any flight, runway lengths of airports of intended use, and the following takeoff and landing distance information:

1. For civil aircraft for which an approved airplane or rotorcraft flight manual containing takeoff and landing distance data is required, the takeoff and landing distance data contained therein; and

2. For civil aircraft other than those specified in paragraph (b)(1) of this section, other reliable information appropriate to the aircraft, relating to aircraft performance under expected values of airport elevation and runway slope, aircraft gross weight, and wind and temperature.

(PLT445) — 14 CFR §91.103

ALL, SPO

3081. Preflight action, as required for all flights away from the vicinity of an airport, shall include

A— the designation of an alternate airport.

B— a study of arrival procedures at airports/ heliports of intended use.

C— an alternate course of action if the flight cannot be completed as planned.

Each pilot-in-command shall, before each flight, become familiar with all available information concerning that flight. This information must include:

(a) For a flight under IFR or a flight not in the vicinity of an airport, weather reports and forecasts, fuel requirements, alternatives available if the planned flight cannot be completed, and any known traffic delays of which the pilot has been advised by ATC;

(b) For any flight, runway lengths of airports of intended use, and the following takeoff and landing distance information:

1. For civil aircraft for which an approved airplane or rotorcraft flight manual containing takeoff and landing distance data is required, the takeoff and landing distance data contained therein; and

2. For civil aircraft other than those specified in paragraph (b)(1) of this section, other reliable information appropriate to the aircraft, relating to aircraft performance under expected values of airport elevation and runway slope, aircraft gross weight, and wind and temperature.

(PLT445) — 14 CFR §91.103

Answers

3080 [B]   3081 [C]

ALL
3082. In addition to other preflight actions for a VFR flight away from the vicinity of the departure airport, regulations specifically require the pilot in command to

A— review traffic control light signal procedures.
B— check the accuracy of the navigation equipment and the emergency locator transmitter (ELT).
C— determine runway lengths at airports of intended use and the aircraft's takeoff and landing distance data.

Each pilot-in-command shall, before each flight, become familiar with all available information concerning that flight. This information must include:

(a) For a flight under IFR or a flight not in the vicinity of an airport, weather reports and forecasts, fuel requirements, alternatives available if the planned flight cannot be completed, and any known traffic delays of which the pilot has been advised by ATC;

(b) For any flight, runway lengths of airports of intended use, and the following takeoff and landing distance information:

1. For civil aircraft for which an approved airplane or rotorcraft flight manual containing takeoff and landing distance data is required, the takeoff and landing distance data contained therein; and

2. For civil aircraft other than those specified in paragraph (b)(1) of this section, other reliable information appropriate to the aircraft, relating to aircraft performance under expected values of airport elevation and runway slope, aircraft gross weight, and wind and temperature.

(PLT444) — 14 CFR §91.103

AIR, WSC, PPC
3132. What is the specific fuel requirement for flight under VFR at night in an airplane?

A— Enough to complete the flight at normal cruising speed with adverse wind conditions.
B— Enough to fly to the first point of intended landing and to fly after that for 30 minutes at normal cruising speed.
C— Enough to fly to the first point of intended landing and to fly after that for 45 minutes at normal cruising speed.

No person may begin a flight in an airplane under VFR unless (considering wind and forecast weather conditions) there is enough fuel to fly to the first point of intended landing and, assuming normal cruising speed, and night operations, to fly after that for at least 45 minutes. (PLT413) — 14 CFR §91.151

AIR, REC, WSC, PPC
3131. What is the specific fuel requirement for flight under VFR during daylight hours in an airplane?

A— Enough to complete the flight at normal cruising speed with adverse wind conditions.
B— Enough to fly to the first point of intended landing and to fly after that for 30 minutes at normal cruising speed.
C— Enough to fly to the first point of intended landing and to fly after that for 45 minutes at normal cruising speed.

No person may begin a flight in an airplane under VFR unless (considering wind and forecast weather conditions) there is enough fuel to fly to the first point of intended landing and, assuming normal cruising speed, and day operations, to fly after that for at least 30 minutes. (PLT413) — 14 CFR §91.151

RTC
3133. No person may begin a flight in a rotorcraft under VFR unless there is enough fuel to fly to the first point of intended landing and, assuming normal cruising speed, to fly thereafter for at least

A— 20 minutes.
B— 30 minutes.
C— 1 hour.

No person may begin a flight in a rotorcraft under VFR unless (considering wind and forecast weather conditions) there is enough fuel to fly to the first point of intended landing and, assuming normal cruising speed, to fly after that for at least 20 minutes. (PLT413) — 14 CFR §91.151

SPO
2033. How should an aircraft preflight inspection be accomplished for the first flight of the day?

A— Quick walk around with a check of gas and oil.
B— Any sequence as determined by the pilot-in-command.
C— Thorough and systematic means recommended by the manufacturer.

The preflight inspection should be a thorough and systematic means by which the pilot determines that the airplane is ready for safe flight. Most Aircraft Flight Manuals or Pilot's Operating Handbooks contain a section devoted to a systematic method of performing a preflight inspection that should be used by the pilot for guidance. (PLT444) — FAA-H-8083-25

Answers

| 3082 [C] | 3132 [C] | 3131 [B] | 3133 [A] | 2033 [C] |

Seatbelts

All required flight crewmembers must remain in their seats with seatbelts secured during the entire flight unless absent in connection with duties or physiological needs. When shoulder harnesses are installed they must be used during takeoffs and landings.

Prior to takeoff, the pilot-in-command must ensure that each person on board has been briefed on the use of seatbelts. In addition, he/she must ensure that the passengers are notified to fasten their seatbelts during taxi, takeoffs, and landings. A child who has not reached his/her second birthday may be held by an adult who is occupying a seat or berth.

ALL
3083. Flight crewmembers are required to keep their safety belts and shoulder harnesses fastened during

A— takeoffs and landings.
B— all flight conditions.
C— flight in turbulent air.

During takeoff and landing, and while en route, each required flight crewmember shall keep his/her seatbelt fastened while at the station. During takeoff and landing this includes shoulder harness (if installed) unless it interferes with required duties. (PLT440) — 14 CFR §91.105

ALL, SPO
3084. Which best describes the flight conditions under which flight crewmembers are specifically required to keep their safety belts and shoulder harnesses fastened?

A— Safety belts during takeoff and landing; shoulder harnesses during takeoff and landing.
B— Safety belts during takeoff and landing; shoulder harnesses during takeoff and landing and while en route.
C— Safety belts during takeoff and landing and while en route; shoulder harnesses during takeoff and landing.

During takeoff and landing, and while en route, each required flight crewmember shall keep his/her seatbelt fastened while at his/her station. During takeoff and landing this includes shoulder harness (if installed) unless it interferes with required duties. (PLT464) — 14 CFR §91.105

ALL
3085. With respect to passengers, what obligation, if any, does a pilot in command have concerning the use of safety belts?

A— The pilot in command must instruct the passengers to keep their safety belts fastened for the entire flight.
B— The pilot in command must brief the passengers on the use of safety belts and notify them to fasten their safety belts during taxi, takeoff, and landing.
C— The pilot in command has no obligation in regard to passengers' use of safety belts.

Unless otherwise authorized by the Administrator, no pilot may takeoff in a civil aircraft unless the pilot-in-command of that aircraft ensures that each person on board is briefed on how to fasten and unfasten that person's seatbelt, and that each person has been notified to fasten the seatbelt during taxi, takeoff and landing. (PLT465) — 14 CFR §91.107

ALL
3085-1. Pre-takeoff briefing of passengers about the use of seat belts for a flight is the responsibility of

A— all passengers.
B— the pilot-in-command.
C— the right-seat pilot.

Unless otherwise authorized by the Administrator, no pilot may takeoff in a civil aircraft unless the pilot-in-command of that aircraft ensures that each person on board is briefed on how to fasten and unfasten that person's seatbelt, and that each person has been notified to fasten the seatbelt during taxi, takeoff, and landing. (PLT384) – 14 CFR §91.107

Answers

3083 [A]   3084 [C]   3085 [B]   3085-1 [A]

ALL
3086. With certain exceptions, safety belts are required to be secured about passengers during

A— taxi, takeoffs, and landings.
B— all flight conditions.
C— flight in turbulent air.

During taxi, takeoff and landing, each person on board the aircraft must occupy a seat or berth with a seatbelt and shoulder harness, properly secured if installed. (PLT465) — 14 CFR §91.107

SPO
2232. The pilot in command is responsible for ensuring that each person on board applicable U.S. registered aircraft is briefed and instructed on how and when to

A— fasten and unfasten their seat belt and shoulder harness.
B— adjust their seat.
C— operate the fire extinguisher.

Unless otherwise authorized by the FAA, no pilot may takeoff in a civil aircraft unless the pilot-in-command ensures that each person on board is briefed on how to fasten and unfasten that person's seatbelt, and that each person has been notified to fasten the seatbelt during taxi, takeoff and landing. (PLT441) — 14 CFR §91.107

ALL, SPO
3087. Safety belts are required to be properly secured about which persons in an aircraft and when?

A— Pilots only, during takeoffs and landings.
B— Passengers, during taxi, takeoffs, and landings only.
C— Each person on board the aircraft during the entire flight.

During taxi, takeoff and landing, each person on board the aircraft must occupy a seat or berth with a safety belt and shoulder harness, properly secured if installed. However, a person who has not reached his/her second birthday may be held by an adult who is occupying a seat or a berth, and a person on board for the purpose of engaging in sport parachuting may use the floor of the aircraft as a seat. (PLT465) — 14 CFR §91.107

Alcohol and Drugs

No person may act as a crewmember on an aircraft under the following conditions:

1. Within 8 hours after the consumption of any alcoholic beverage;

2. While under the influence of alcohol (.04 percent by weight or more alcohol in the blood);

3. While using any drug that affects his/her faculties in any way contrary to safety.

Except in an emergency, no pilot of an aircraft may allow a person who appears to be intoxicated or under the influence of drugs (except a medical patient under proper care) to be carried in that aircraft.

A conviction for the violation of any law relating to drugs or alcohol is grounds for: (1) Denial of an application for any certificate, rating, or authorization issued under Part 61 for a period of up to 1 year after the date of final conviction; or (2) Suspension or revocation of any certificate, rating, or authorization issued under Part 61.

Pilots shall provide a written report of each alcohol- or drug-related motor vehicle action to the FAA, Civil Aviation Security Division (AMC-700) not later than 60 days after the motor vehicle action.

ALL
3077. A person may not act as a crewmember of a civil aircraft if alcoholic beverages have been consumed by that person within the preceding

A— 8 hours.
B— 12 hours.
C— 24 hours.

No person may act or attempt to act as a crewmember of a civil aircraft within 8 hours after the consumption of any alcoholic beverage. Remember "8 hours bottle to throttle." (PLT463) — 14 CFR §91.17

Answers

| 3086 [A] | 2232 [A] | 3087 [B] | 3077 [A] |

ALL
3078. Under what condition, if any, may a pilot allow a person who is obviously under the influence of drugs to be carried aboard an aircraft?

A— In an emergency or if the person is a medical patient under proper care.
B— Only if the person does not have access to the cockpit or pilot's compartment.
C— Under no condition.

Except in an emergency, or a medical patient under proper care, no pilot of a civil aircraft may allow a person who appears to be intoxicated, or who demonstrates by manner or physical indications that the individual is under the influence of drugs, to be carried in that aircraft. (PLT463) — 14 CFR §91.17

ALL, SPO
3079. No person may attempt to act as a crewmember of a civil aircraft with

A— .008 percent by weight or more alcohol in the blood.
B— .004 percent by weight or more alcohol in the blood.
C— .04 percent by weight or more alcohol in the blood.

No person may act, or attempt to act, as a crewmember of a civil aircraft while having .04 percent or more, by weight, alcohol in the blood. (PLT463) — 14 CFR §91.17

SPO
2087. Which is true regarding the presence of alcohol within the human body?

A— A small amount of alcohol increases vision acuity.
B— An increase in altitude decreases the adverse effect of alcohol.
C— Judgment and decision-making abilities can be adversely affected by even small amounts of alcohol.

As little as one ounce of liquor, one bottle of beer, or four ounces of wine can impair flying skills. (PLT205) — AIM ¶8-1-1

Answer (A) is incorrect because all mental and physical activities will be decreased with even small amounts of alcohol in the bloodstream. Answer (B) is incorrect because the adverse effects of alcohol are increased as altitude is increased.

ALL
3079-1. How soon after the conviction for driving while intoxicated by alcohol or drugs shall it be reported to the FAA, Civil Aviation Security Division?

A— No later than 60 days after the motor vehicle action.
B— No later than 30 working days after the motor vehicle action.
C— Required to be reported upon renewal of medical certificate.

Each person holding a pilot certificate shall provide a written report of each drug or alcohol-related motor vehicle action to the FAA, Civil Aviation Security Division (AMC-700), not later than 60 days after the motor vehicle action. (PLT463) — 14 CFR §61.15

SPO
2126. A pilot convicted of operating an aircraft under the influence of alcohol, or using drugs that affect the person's faculties, is grounds for a

A— denial of an application for an FAA certificate, rating, or authorization issued under 14 CFR part 61.
B— written notification to the FAA Civil Aeromedical Institute (CAMI) within 60 days after the conviction.
C— written report to be filed with the FAA Civil Aviation Security Division (AMC-700) not later than 60 day after the conviction.

A conviction for the violation of any Federal or State statute relating to drugs or alcohol is grounds for: (1) Denial of an application for any certificate, rating, or authorization issued under Part 61 for a period of up to 1 year after the date of final conviction; or (2) Suspension or revocation of any certificate, rating, or authorization issued under Part 61. (PLT463) — 14 CFR §61.15

Answer (B) is incorrect because the report must be filed with AMC-700. Answer (C) is incorrect because this applies to automobile convictions, not aircraft convictions.

SPO

2127. A pilot convicted for the violation of any Federal or State statute relating to the process, manufacture, transportation, distribution, or sale of narcotic drugs is grounds for

A— a written report to be filed with the FAA Civil Aviation Security Division (AMC-700) not later than 60 days after the conviction.

B— notification of this conviction to the FAA Civil Aeromedical Institute (CAMI) within 60 days after the conviction.

C— suspension or revocation of any certificate, rating, or authorization issued under 14 CFR part 61.

A conviction for the violation of any Federal or State statute relating to the growing, processing, manufacture, sale, disposition, possession, transportation, or importation of narcotic drugs, marijuana, or depressant or stimulant drugs or substances is grounds for: (1) Denial of an application for any certificate, rating, or authorization for a period of up to 1 year after the date of final conviction; or (2) Suspension or revocation of any certificate, rating, or authorization. (PLT463) — 14 CFR §61.15

Answers (A) and (B) are incorrect because a written report to AMC-700 is only necessary for motor vehicle actions.

SPO

2128. A pilot convicted of operating a motor vehicle while either intoxicated by, impaired by, or under the influence of alcohol or a drug is required to provide a

A— written report to the FAA Civil Aeromedical Institute (CAMI) within 60 days after the motor vehicle action.

B— written report to the FAA Civil Aviation Security Division (AMC-700) not later than 60 days after the conviction.

C— notification of the conviction to an FAA Aviation Medical Examiner (AME) not later than 60 days after the motor vehicle action.

Each person holding a pilot certificate shall provide a written report of each motor vehicle action to the FAA, Civil Aviation Security Division (AMC-700), not later than 60 days after the motor vehicle action. (PLT463) — 14 CFR §61.15

Right-of-Way Rules

When weather conditions permit, vigilance must be maintained so as to see and avoid other aircraft.

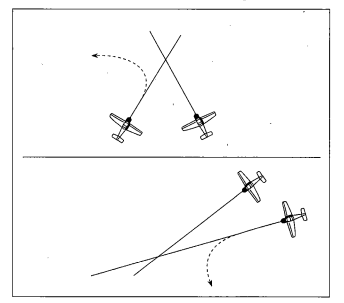

Figure 4-2. Aircraft on converging courses: Aircraft on the right has right-of-way — aircraft on the left must yield.

An aircraft in distress has the right-of-way over all other air traffic. When aircraft of the same category are converging at approximately the same altitude (except head-on, or nearly so), the aircraft on the other's right has the right-of-way. *See* Figure 4-2.

If the aircraft are of different categories, the following applies:

1. A balloon has the right-of-way over any other category of aircraft;

2. A glider has the right-of-way over an airship, airplane, rotorcraft, weight-shift control, or powered parachute; and

3. An airship has the right-of-way over an airplane, rotorcraft, weight-shift control, or powered parachute.

Answers

2127 [C]   2128 [B]

An aircraft towing or refueling other aircraft has the right-of-way over all other engine driven aircraft.

When aircraft are approaching each other head-on, or nearly so, each pilot of each aircraft (regardless of category), shall alter course to the right. *See* Figure 4-3.

An aircraft being overtaken has the right-of-way. The overtaking aircraft shall alter course to the right to pass well clear. *See* Figure 4-4.

When two or more aircraft are approaching an airport for landing, the aircraft at the lower altitude has the right-of-way, but it shall not take advantage of this rule to cut in front of, or overtake another aircraft.

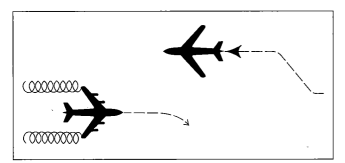

Figure 4-3. Aircraft approaching head-on

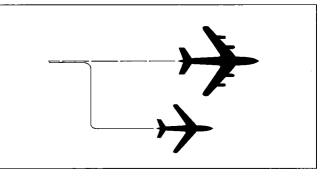

Figure 4-4. One aircraft overtaking another

ALL, SPO
3089. Which aircraft has the right-of-way over all other air traffic?

A— A balloon.
B— An aircraft in distress.
C— An aircraft on final approach to land.

An aircraft in distress has the right-of-way over all other air traffic. (PLT414) — 14 CFR §91.113

ALL, SPO
3090. What action is required when two aircraft of the same category converge, but not head-on?

A— The faster aircraft shall give way.
B— The aircraft on the left shall give way.
C— Each aircraft shall give way to the right.

When two aircraft of the same "right-of-way" category converge at approximately the same altitude, the aircraft to the other's right has the right-of-way. (PLT414) — 14 CFR §91.113

Answer (A) is incorrect because speed has nothing to do with right-of-way. Answer (C) is incorrect because "each aircraft giving way to the right" is the rule when approaching head-on.

ALL
3093. Which aircraft has the right-of-way over the other aircraft listed?

A— Glider.
B— Airship.
C— Aircraft refueling other aircraft.

A glider has the right-of-way over an airship, airplane, or rotorcraft. (PLT414) — 14 CFR §91.113

Answer (B) is incorrect because a glider has the right-of-way over powered aircraft. Answer (C) is incorrect because an aircraft refueling other aircraft only has right-of-way over other engine-driven aircraft.

ALL
3092. An airplane and an airship are converging. If the airship is left of the airplane's position, which aircraft has the right-of-way?

A— The airship.
B— The airplane.
C— Each pilot should alter course to the right.

An airship has the right-of-way over an airplane or rotorcraft. (PLT414) — 14 CFR §91.113

ALL
3091. Which aircraft has the right-of-way over the other aircraft listed?

A— Gyroplane.
B— Airship.
C— Aircraft towing other aircraft.

An aircraft towing or refueling other aircraft has the right-of-way over all other engine-driven aircraft. (PLT414) — 14 CFR §91.113

ALL
3095. When two or more aircraft are approaching an airport for the purpose of landing, the right-of-way belongs to the aircraft

A— that has the other to its right.
B— that is the least maneuverable.
C— at the lower altitude, but it shall not take advantage of this rule to cut in front of or to overtake another.

When two aircraft are approaching an airport for landing, the lower aircraft has the right-of-way. A pilot shall not take advantage of that rule to overtake or cut in front of another aircraft. (PLT414) — 14 CFR §91.113

AIR, WSC, PPC
3096. A seaplane and a motorboat are on crossing courses. If the motorboat is to the left of the seaplane, which has the right-of-way?

A— The motorboat.
B— The seaplane.
C— Both should alter course to the right.

For water operation, when aircraft, or an aircraft and a vessel, are on crossing courses, the aircraft or vessel to the other's right has the right-of-way. (PLT414) — 14 CFR §91.115

AIR, GLI, REC, WSC, PPC
3094. What action should the pilots of a glider and an airplane take if on a head-on collision course?

A— The airplane pilot should give way to the left.
B— The glider pilot should give way to the right.
C— Both pilots should give way to the right.

When two aircraft are approaching each other from head-on, or nearly so, each pilot must alter course to the right. This rule does not give right-of-way by categories. (PLT414) — 14 CFR §91.113

Parachutes

If any passengers are carried, the pilot of an aircraft may not intentionally exceed 60° of bank or 30° of pitch unless each occupant is wearing an approved parachute. However, this requirement does not apply when a Certified Flight Instructor is giving instruction in spins or any other flight maneuver required by regulations for a rating.

If the parachute is of the chair type, it must have been packed by a certificated and appropriately-rated parachute rigger within the preceding 180 days.

ALL
3172. An approved chair-type parachute may be carried in an aircraft for emergency use if it has been packed by an appropriately rated parachute rigger within the preceding

A— 120 days.
B— 180 days.
C— 365 days.

No pilot of a civil aircraft may allow a parachute that is available for emergency use to be carried in that aircraft unless, if a chair type, it has been packed by a certificated and appropriately-rated parachute rigger within the preceding 180 days. (PLT405) — 14 CFR §91.307

ALL
3173. With certain exceptions, when must each occupant of an aircraft wear an approved parachute?

A— When a door is removed from the aircraft to facilitate parachute jumpers.
B— When intentionally pitching the nose of the aircraft up or down 30° or more.
C— When intentionally banking in excess of 30°.

Unless each occupant of the aircraft is wearing an approved parachute, no pilot of a civil aircraft, carrying any person (other than a crewmember) may execute an intentional maneuver that exceeds 60° bank or 30° nose up or down, relative to the horizon. (PLT369) — 14 CFR §91.307

Answers

3091 [C]	3095 [C]	3096 [B]	3094 [C]	3172 [B]	3173 [B]

Deviation from Air Traffic Control Instructions

An ATC clearance is authorization for an aircraft to proceed under specified traffic conditions within controlled airspace. When an ATC clearance has been obtained, no pilot-in-command may deviate from that clearance, except in an emergency, unless he/she obtains an amended clearance. If a pilot does deviate from a clearance or ATC instruction during an emergency, he/she must notify ATC of the deviation as soon as possible. If, in an emergency, a pilot is given priority over other aircraft by ATC, he/she may be requested to submit a detailed report even though no deviation from a rule occurred. The requested report shall be submitted within 48 hours to the chief of the ATC facility which granted the priority.

ALL
3108. When an ATC clearance has been obtained, no pilot in command may deviate from that clearance, unless that pilot obtains an amended clearance. The one exception to this regulation is

A— when the clearance states "at pilot's discretion."
B— an emergency.
C— if the clearance contains a restriction.

Except in an emergency, no person may operate an aircraft contrary to an ATC clearance or instruction. (PLT444) — 14 CFR §91.123

ALL
3108-1. As Pilot in Command of an aircraft, under which situation can you deviate from an ATC clearance?

A— When operating in Class A airspace at night.
B— If an ATC clearance is not understood and in VFR conditions.
C— In response to a traffic alert and collision avoidance system resolution advisory.

The regulations authorize deviations from a clearance in response to a traffic alert and collision avoidance system resolution advisory. You must notify ATC as soon as possible following the deviation. (PLT444) — 14 CFR §91.123

Answers (A) and (B) are incorrect because neither of these are acceptable reasons to deviate from an ATC clearance.

ALL, SPO
3109. When would a pilot be required to submit a detailed report of an emergency which caused the pilot to deviate from an ATC clearance?

A— Within 48 hours if requested by ATC.
B— Immediately.
C— Within 7 days.

Each pilot-in-command who deviated from an ATC clearance during an emergency must submit a detailed report within 48 hours if requested by ATC. (PLT403) — 14 CFR §91.123

ALL
3110. What action, if any, is appropriate if the pilot deviates from an ATC instruction during an emergency and is given priority?

A— Take no special action since you are pilot in command.
B— File a detailed report within 48 hours to the chief of the appropriate ATC facility, if requested.
C— File a report to the FAA Administrator, as soon as possible.

Each pilot-in-command who (though not deviating from a rule of 14 CFR Part 91) is given priority by ATC in an emergency shall, if requested by ATC, submit a detailed report of that emergency within 48 hours to the chief of that ATC facility. (PLT444) — 14 CFR §91.123

ALL
3837. An ATC clearance provides

A— priority over all other traffic.
B— adequate separation from all traffic.
C— authorization to proceed under specified traffic conditions in controlled airspace.

An ATC Clearance is an authorization by air traffic control, for the purpose of preventing collisions between known aircraft, for an aircraft to proceed under specified traffic conditions within controlled airspace. (PLT370) — Pilot/Controller Glossary

Answer (A) is incorrect because a clearance does not provide priority. Answer (B) is incorrect because a clearance does not relieve the pilot of the responsibility for collision avoidance with aircraft not in instrument meteorological conditions (IMC).

Answers

| 3108 | [B] | 3108-1 | [C] | 3109 | [A] | 3110 | [B] | 3837 | [C] |

SPO

2003. An ATC clearance means an authorization by ATC for an aircraft to proceed under specified conditions within

A— controlled airspace.
B— uncontrolled airspace.
C— published Visual Flight Rules (VFR) routes.

An ATC clearance means an authorization by air traffic control for the purpose of preventing collision between known aircraft, for an aircraft to proceed under specified traffic conditions within controlled airspace. (PLT044) — Pilot/Controller Glossary

Answer (B) is incorrect because ATC does not provide clearances in uncontrolled airspace. Answer (C) is incorrect because an ATC clearance is not required to fly these routes.

ALL

2004. While on a VFR cross-country and not in contact with ATC, what frequency would you use in the event of an emergency?

A— 121.5 MHz.
B— 122.5 MHz.
C— 128.725 MHz.

Although the frequency in use or other frequencies assigned by ATC are preferable, the following emergency frequencies can be used for distress or urgency communications: 121.5 MHz, 243.0 MHz, or 406 MHz. (PLT391) — AIM ¶6-3-1

Minimum Safe Altitudes

No minimum altitude applies during takeoff or landing. During other phases of flight, however, the following minimum altitudes apply:

Anywhere—The pilot must maintain an altitude which, in the event of engine failure, will allow an emergency landing without undue hazard to persons or property on the surface.

Over congested areas—An altitude of at least 1,000 feet above the highest obstacle within a horizontal radius of 2,000 feet of the aircraft must be maintained over any congested area of a city, town, or settlement or over any open-air assembly of people.

Over other than congested areas—An altitude of 500 feet above the surface must be maintained except over open water or sparsely populated areas. In that case, the aircraft may not be operated closer than 500 feet to any person, vessel, vehicle or structure.

ALL, SPO

3101. Except when necessary for takeoff or landing, what is the minimum safe altitude for a pilot to operate an aircraft anywhere?

A— An altitude allowing, if a power unit fails, an emergency landing without undue hazard to persons or property on the surface.
B— An altitude of 500 feet above the surface and no closer than 500 feet to any person, vessel, vehicle, or structure.
C— An altitude of 500 feet above the highest obstacle within a horizontal radius of 1,000 feet.

Except when necessary for takeoff or landing, no person may operate an aircraft anywhere below an altitude allowing, if a power unit fails, an emergency landing without undue hazard to persons or property on the surface. (PLT430) — 14 CFR §91.119

AIR, GLI, LTA, REC, WSC, PPC

3102. Except when necessary for takeoff or landing, what is the minimum safe altitude required for a pilot to operate an aircraft over congested areas?

A— An altitude of 1,000 feet above any person, vessel, vehicle, or structure.
B— An altitude of 500 feet above the highest obstacle within a horizontal radius of 1,000 feet of the aircraft.
C— An altitude of 1,000 feet above the highest obstacle within a horizontal radius of 2,000 feet of the aircraft.

Except when necessary for takeoff or landing, no person may operate an aircraft over any congested area of a city, town, or settlement, or over any open air assembly of persons, below an altitude of 1,000 feet above the highest obstacle within a horizontal radius of 2,000 feet of the aircraft. (PLT430) — 14 CFR §91.119

Answers

2003 [A]	2004 [A]	3101 [A]	3102 [C]

AIR, GLI, LTA, REC, WSC, PPC
3103. Except when necessary for takeoff or landing, what is the minimum safe altitude required for a pilot to operate an aircraft over other than a congested area?

A— An altitude allowing, if a power unit fails, an emergency landing without undue hazard to persons or property on the surface.
B— An altitude of 500 feet AGL, except over open water or a sparsely populated area, which requires 500 feet from any person, vessel, vehicle, or structure.
C— An altitude of 500 feet above the highest obstacle within a horizontal radius of 1,000 feet.

Except when necessary for takeoff or landing, no person may operate an aircraft over other than congested areas below an altitude of 500 feet above the surface except over open water or sparsely populated areas. In that case, the aircraft may not be operated closer than 500 feet to any person, vessel, vehicle, or structure. (PLT430) — 14 CFR §91.119

AIR, GLI, LTA, REC, WSC, PPC
3104. Except when necessary for takeoff or landing, an aircraft may not be operated closer than what distance from any person, vessel, vehicle, or structure?

A— 500 feet.
B— 700 feet.
C— 1,000 feet.

Except when necessary for takeoff or landing, no person may operate an aircraft closer than 500 feet to any person, vessel, vehicle, or structure. (PLT430) — 14 CFR §91.119

Basic VFR Weather Minimums

Rules governing flight under **Visual Flight Rules (VFR)** have been adopted to assist the pilot in meeting his/her responsibility to see and avoid other aircraft. *See* the figure for Questions 3136 through 3147.

In addition, when operating within the lateral boundaries of the surface area of Class B, C, D or E airspace designated for an airport, the ceiling must not be less than 1,000 feet. If the pilot intends to land, take off, or enter a traffic pattern within such airspace, the ground visibility must be at least 3 miles at that airport. If ground visibility is not reported, 3 miles flight visibility is required in the pattern.

ALL
3136. During operations within controlled airspace at altitudes of less than 1,200 feet AGL, the minimum horizontal distance from clouds requirement for VFR flight is

A— 1,000 feet.
B— 1,500 feet.
C— 2,000 feet.

Minimum horizontal distance from clouds within Class C, D, or E airspace below 10,000 feet MSL is 2,000 feet. See the figure to the left. (PLT163) — 14 CFR §91.155

ALL
3138. What minimum flight visibility is required for VFR flight operations on an airway below 10,000 feet MSL?

A— 1 mile.
B— 3 miles.
C— 4 miles.

An airway below 10,000 feet MSL is in either Class B, C, or D, or E airspace, and requires 3 miles flight visibility. See the figure to the left. (PLT467) — 14 CFR §91.155

ALL
3139. The minimum distance from clouds required for VFR operations on an airway below 10,000 feet MSL is

A— remain clear of clouds.
B— 500 feet below, 1,000 feet above, and 2,000 feet horizontally.
C— 500 feet above, 1,000 feet below, and 2,000 feet horizontally.

An airway below 10,000 feet MSL is in either Class B, C, or D, or E airspace, and requires a cloud clearance of 500 feet below, 1,000 feet above, and 2,000 feet horizontally. See the figure to the left. (PLT468) — 14 CFR §91.155

Answers

| 3103 | [B] | 3104 | [A] | 3136 | [C] | 3138 | [B] | 3139 | [B] |

Airspace	Flight Visibility	Distance from Clouds
Class A	Not Applicable	Not Applicable
Class B	3 statute miles	Clear of clouds
Class C	3 statute miles	500 feet below 1,000 feet above 2,000 feet horizontal
Class D	3 statute miles	500 feet below 1,000 feet above 2,000 feet horizontal
Class E Less than 10,000 feet MSL	3 statute miles	500 feet below 1,000 feet above 2,000 feet horizontal
At or above 10,000 feet MSL	5 statute miles	1,000 feet below 1,000 feet above 1 statute mile horizontal

Class G
1,200 feet or less
  above the surface
  (regardless of
  MSL altitude)
Day, except as provided
  in §91.155(b)
	1 statute mile	Clear of clouds

Night, except as pro- vided in §91.155(b)	3 statute miles	500 feet below 1,000 feet above 2,000 feet horizontal

More than 1,200 feet
  above the surface
  but less than
  10,000 feet MSL
Day
	1 statute mile	500 feet below
		1,000 feet above
		2,000 feet horizontal

Night	3 statute miles	500 feet below 1,000 feet above 2,000 feet horizontal

More than 1,200 feet
  above the surface
  and at or above
  10,000 feet MSL
	5 statute miles	1,000 feet below
		1,000 feet above
		1 statute mile horizontal

Questions 3136 through 3147

ALL
3140. During operations within controlled airspace at altitudes of more than 1,200 feet AGL, but less than 10,000 feet MSL, the minimum distance above clouds requirement for VFR flight is

A— 500 feet.
B— 1,000 feet.
C— 1,500 feet.

Class B, C, D, and E airspace are all controlled airspace in which VFR flight is allowed, and requires a cloud clearance of 1,000 feet above at altitudes of more than 1,200 feet AGL, but less than 10,000 feet MSL. See the previous figure. (PLT468) — 14 CFR §91.155

ALL
3141. VFR flight in controlled airspace above 1,200 feet AGL and below 10,000 feet MSL requires a minimum visibility and vertical cloud clearance of

A— 3 miles, and 500 feet below or 1,000 feet above the clouds in controlled airspace.
B— 5 miles, and 1,000 feet below or 1,000 feet above the clouds at all altitudes.
C— 5 miles, and 1,000 feet below or 1,000 feet above the clouds only in Class A airspace.

With the exception of Class B airspace, VFR flight into controlled airspace requires 3 statute miles visibility and cloud clearance of 500 feet below and 1,000 feet above when operating above 1,200 feet AGL and below 10,000 feet MSL. See the previous figure. (PLT468) — 14 CFR §91.155

ALL
3145. The minimum flight visibility required for VFR flights above 10,000 feet MSL and more than 1,200 feet AGL in controlled airspace is

A— 1 mile.
B— 3 miles.
C— 5 miles.

Controlled airspace above 10,000 feet which allows VFR is Class E airspace, and requires 5 statute miles visibility above 10,000 feet MSL and more than 1,200 feet AGL. See the previous figure. (PLT163) — 14 CFR §91.155

ALL
3146. For VFR flight operations above 10,000 feet MSL and more than 1,200 feet AGL, the minimum horizontal distance from clouds required is

A— 1,000 feet.
B— 2,000 feet.
C— 1 mile.

Controlled airspace above 10,000 feet which allows VFR is Class E airspace, and requires cloud clearance of 1,000 feet below, 1,000 feet above, and 1 SM horizontal during operations above 10,000 feet MSL and more than 1,200 feet AGL. See the previous figure. (PLT163) — 14 CFR §91.155

Answers

3140 [B]   3141 [A]   3145 [C]   3146 [C]

ALL
3147. During operations at altitudes of more than 1,200 feet AGL and at or above 10,000 feet MSL, the minimum distance above clouds requirement for VFR flight is

A— 500 feet.
B— 1,000 feet.
C— 1,500 feet.

Controlled airspace above 10,000 feet which allows VFR is Class E airspace, and requires cloud clearance of 1,000 feet below, 1,000 feet above, and 1 SM horizontal during operations above 10,000 feet MSL and more than 1,200 feet AGL. See the previous figure. (PLT163) — 14 CFR §91.155

ALL
3620-1. (Refer to Figure 22, area 1.) The visibility and cloud clearance requirements to operate VFR during daylight hours over Sandpoint Airport at 1,200 feet AGL are

A— 1 mile and 1,000 feet above, 500 feet below, and 2,000 feet horizontally from each cloud.
B— 1 mile and clear of clouds.
C— 3 miles and 1,000 feet above, 500 feet below, and 2,000 feet horizontally from each cloud.

The Sandpoint Airport Class E airspace starts at 700 feet AGL. The visibility and cloud clearance requirements to operate VFR during daylight hours over Sandpoint Airport at 1,200 feet AGL are 3 SM, 500 feet below, 1,000 feet above, and 2,000 feet horizontal. (PLT064) — AIM ¶3-1-4

ALL
3620-2. (Refer to Figure 22, area 1.) The visibility and cloud clearance requirements to operate at night over Sandpoint Airport at less than 700 feet AGL are

A— 3 miles and 1,000 feet above, 500 feet below, and 2,000 feet horizontally from each cloud.
B— 3 miles and clear of clouds.
C— 1 mile and 1,000 feet above, 500 feet below, and 2,000 feet horizontally from each cloud.

The Sandpoint Airport Class E airspace starts at 700 feet AGL. Below 700 feet AGL, the visibility and cloud clearance requirements to operate VFR during daylight hours is 1 mile visibility and clear of clouds. At night, the requirements are 3 SM, 500 feet below, 1,000 feet above, and 2,000 feet horizontal. (PLT064) — AIM ¶3-1-4

ALL
3621-1. (Refer to Figure 26, area 2.) The visibility and cloud clearance requirements to operate VFR during daylight hours over the town of Cooperstown between 1,200 feet AGL and 10,000 feet MSL are

A— 1 mile and clear of clouds.
B— 1 mile and 1,000 feet above, 500 feet below, and 2,000 feet horizontally from clouds.
C— 3 miles and 1,000 feet above, 500 feet below, and 2,000 feet horizontally from clouds.

For VFR flight during daylight hours, between 1,200 feet AGL and 10,000 feet MSL, in Class E airspace, visibility and cloud clearances require 3 miles and 1,000 feet above, 500 feet below, and 2,000 feet horizontally. (PLT101) — AIM ¶3-1-4

ALL
3621-2. (Refer to Figure 26, area 2.) The day VFR visibility and cloud clearance requirements to operate over the town of Cooperstown after departing and climbing out of Cooperstown Airport at or below 700 feet AGL are

A— 3 miles and clear of clouds.
B— 1 mile and 1,000 feet above, 500 feet below, and 2,000 feet horizontally from clouds.
C— 1 mile and clear of clouds.

Cooperstown is in Class G airspace from the surface to 700 feet AGL. Therefore, the visibility and cloud clearance requirements are 1 mile and clear of clouds. (PLT064) — AIM ¶3-1-4

ALL
3621-3. (Refer to Figure 78.) What are the basic VFR weather minima required to takeoff from the Onawa, IA (K36) airport during the day?

A— 3 statute miles visibility, 500 feet below the clouds, 1,000 feet above the clouds and 2,000 feet horizontally from the clouds.
B— 0 statute miles, clear of clouds.
C— 1 statute mile, clear of clouds.

Onawa, IA (K36) is in the bottom right quadrant of the sectional excerpt. It is outside any shading or lines, indicating the airport is in Class G airspace. The basic VFR weather minima for a daytime departure from a Class G airport is 1 statute mile and clear of clouds. (PLT064) — AIM ¶3-1-4

Answers

3147 [B]   3620-1 [C]   3620-2 [A]   3621-1 [C]   3621-2 [C]   3621-3 [C]

ALL, SPO
3520. (Refer to Figure 26, area 2.) Inflight and approaching the Bryn (Pvt) Airstrip, the weather minimums are

A— 1 statute mile visibility.
B— 3 statute miles in all airspace.
C— no visibility, remain clear of clouds.

Bryn (PVT) Airstrip is located in Class G airspace. Therefore, the visibility and cloud clear requirements are 1 mile and clear of clouds. (PLT064) — AIM ¶3-1-4

ALL
3137. What minimum visibility and clearance from clouds are required for VFR operations in Class G airspace at 700 feet AGL or below during daylight hours?

A— 1 mile visibility and clear of clouds.
B— 1 mile visibility, 500 feet below, 1,000 feet above, and 2,000 feet horizontal clearance from clouds.
C— 3 miles visibility and clear of clouds.

Minimum visibility and cloud clearance for Class G airspace at 700 feet AGL or below during daylight hours is 1 mile visibility and clear of clouds. See the previous figure. (PLT163) — 14 CFR §91.155

Answer (B) is incorrect because this is for Class C, D, or E airspace. Answer (C) is incorrect because this is for Class B airspace.

ALL
3142. During operations outside controlled airspace at altitudes of more than 1,200 feet AGL, but less than 10,000 feet MSL, the minimum flight visibility for VFR flight at night is

A— 1 mile.
B— 3 miles.
C— 5 miles.

At altitudes of more than 1,200 feet AGL but less than 10,000 feet MSL, Class G airspace requires 3 miles visibility at night. See the previous figure. (PLT163) — 14 CFR §91.155

ALL
3143. Outside controlled airspace, the minimum flight visibility requirement for VFR flight above 1,200 feet AGL and below 10,000 feet MSL during daylight hours is

A— 1 mile.
B— 3 miles.
C— 5 miles.

At altitudes of more than 1,200 feet AGL but less than 10,000 feet MSL, Class G airspace requires 1 mile visibility during the day. See the previous figure. (PLT163) — 14 CFR §91.155

ALL
3144. During operations outside controlled airspace at altitudes of more than 1,200 feet AGL, but less than 10,000 feet MSL, the minimum distance below clouds requirement for VFR flight at night is

A— 500 feet.
B— 1,000 feet.
C— 1,500 feet.

At altitudes of more than 1,200 feet AGL but less than 10,000 feet MSL, Class G airspace requires a cloud clearance of 500 feet below, 1,000 feet above, and 2,000 feet horizontal, during both day and night flights. See the previous figure. (PLT163) — 14 CFR §91.155

ALL, SPO
3148. No person may take off or land an aircraft under basic VFR at an airport that lies within Class D airspace unless the

A— flight visibility at that airport is at least 1 mile.
B— ground visibility at that airport is at least 1 mile.
C— ground visibility at that airport is at least 3 miles.

Except for Special VFR procedures, no person may operate an aircraft under VFR within Class D airspace, beneath the ceiling when the ceiling is less than 1,000 feet. No person may takeoff or land an aircraft, or enter the traffic pattern of an airport under VFR, within Class D airspace unless ground visibility at that airport is at least 3 statute miles. (PLT163) — 14 CFR §91.155

ALL, SPO
3149. The basic VFR weather minimums for operating an aircraft within Class D airspace are

A— 500-foot ceiling and 1 mile visibility.
B— 1,000-foot ceiling and 3 miles visibility.
C— clear of clouds and 2 miles visibility.

Except for Special VFR procedures, no person may operate an aircraft under VFR within Class D airspace, beneath the ceiling when the ceiling is less than 1,000 feet. No person may takeoff or land an aircraft, or enter the traffic pattern of an airport under VFR, within Class D airspace unless ground visibility at that airport is at least 3 statute miles. (PLT163) — 14 CFR §91.155

Answers

| 3520 | [A] | 3137 | [A] | 3142 | [B] | 3143 | [A] | 3144 | [A] | 3148 | [C] |
| 3149 | [B] |

SPO
2137. During operations within Class E airspace at altitudes of less than 1,200 feet AGL, the minimum horizontal distance from clouds requirement for flight is

A— 500 feet.
B— 1,000 feet.
C— 2,000 feet.

Minimum horizontal distance from clouds within Class C, D, or E airspace below 10,000 feet is 2,000 feet. (PLT163) — 14 CFR §91.155

SPO
2040. Sport Pilot minimum flight visibility for Class E airspace less than 10,000 feet mean sea level (MSL) is

A— 2,000 feet horizontal.
B— 3 statute miles.
C— 3 nautical miles.

The minimum flight visibility for Class E airspace less than 10,000 feet MSL is 3 SM. (PLT163) — FAA-H-8083-25

Answer (A) is incorrect because this is the required distance from clouds, not flight visibility. Answer (C) is incorrect because flight visibility is based on statute miles, not nautical.

SPO
2203. You need to maintain this distance below clouds:

A— 500 feet.
B— 1,000 feet.
C— 2,000 feet.

Sport pilots need to maintain this distance from clouds: 500 feet below, 1,000 feet above, and 2,000 feet horizontal in all controlled airspace. (PLT163) — 14 CFR §91.155

Answer (B) is incorrect because this is the distance you must maintain above clouds. Answer (C) is incorrect because this is the distance you must maintain horizontally from clouds.

SPO
2186-1. (Refer to Figure 26.) In flight and approaching the Lowe Airstrip (area 1) the weather minimums are

A— 1 statute mile visibility.
B— 3 statute miles in all airspace.
C— no visibility, remain clear of clouds.

This airport lies in Class G airspace where you must have 3 miles of visibility and be clear of clouds to operate. (PLT163) — 14 CFR §91.155

Special VFR Weather Minimums

If an appropriate ATC clearance (**Special VFR**) has been received, an aircraft may be operated within the lateral boundaries of the surface area of Class B, C, D, or E airspace designated for an airport when the ceiling is less than 1,000 feet and/or the visibility is less than 3 miles.

Special VFR requires the aircraft to be operated clear of clouds with flight visibility of at least 1 statute mile.

For Special VFR operation between sunset and sunrise, the pilot must hold an instrument rating and the airplane must be equipped for instrument flight.

Requests for Special VFR arrival or departure clearance should be directed to the airport traffic control tower if one is in operation.

AIR, RTC, WSC, PPC
3150. A special VFR clearance authorizes the pilot of an aircraft to operate VFR while within Class D airspace when the visibility is

A— less than 1 mile and the ceiling is less than 1,000 feet.
B— at least 1 mile and the aircraft can remain clear of clouds.
C— at least 3 miles and the aircraft can remain clear of clouds.

No person may operate an aircraft (other than a helicopter) in a Class D airspace under Special VFR unless clear of clouds and flight visibility is at least 1 statute mile. (PLT376) — 14 CFR §91.157

Answers

2137 [C]	2040 [B]	2203 [A]	2186-1 [B]	3150 [B]

AIR, RTC, WSC, PPC

3151. What is the minimum weather condition required for airplanes operating under special VFR in Class D airspace?

A— 1 mile flight visibility.
B— 1 mile flight visibility and 1,000-foot ceiling.
C— 3 miles flight visibility and 1,000-foot ceiling.

No person may operate an aircraft (other than a helicopter) in a Class D airspace under special VFR unless clear of clouds and flight visibility is at least 1 statute mile. (PLT376) — 14 CFR §91.157

RTC

3152. Under what conditions, if any, may a private pilot operate a helicopter under special VFR at night within Class D airspace?

A— The helicopter must be fully instrument equipped and the pilot must be instrument rated.
B— The flight visibility must be at least 1 mile.
C— There are no conditions; regulations permit this.

There are no restrictions on helicopters for Special VFR operations within Class D airspace. (PLT161) — 14 CFR §91.157

AIR, WSC, PPC

3153. What are the minimum requirements for airplane operations under special VFR in Class D airspace at night?

A— The airplane must be under radar surveillance at all times while in Class D airspace.
B— The airplane must be equipped for IFR with an altitude reporting transponder.
C— The pilot must be instrument rated, and the airplane must be IFR equipped.

No person may operate an aircraft (other than a helicopter) in a Class D airspace under special weather minimums between sunset and sunrise unless the pilot and airplane are certified for instrument flight. (PLT161) — 14 CFR §91.157, §91.205

Answers (A) and (B) are incorrect because radar and transponder are not required in Class D airspace.

AIR

3154. No person may operate an airplane within Class D airspace at night under special VFR unless the

A— flight can be conducted 500 feet below the clouds.
B— airplane is equipped for instrument flight.
C— flight visibility is at least 3 miles.

No person may operate an aircraft (other than a helicopter) in a Class D airspace under special weather minimums between sunset and sunrise unless the airplane and pilot are certified for instrument flight. (PLT161) — 14 CFR §91.155

AIR, RTC, WSC, PPC

3813. What ATC facility should the pilot contact to receive a special VFR departure clearance in Class D airspace?

A— Automated Flight Service Station.
B— Air Traffic Control Tower.
C— Air Route Traffic Control Center.

When a control tower is in operation, requests for special VFR clearances should be to the tower. (PLT161) — AIM ¶4-4-6

VFR Cruising Altitudes

When operating an aircraft under VFR in level cruising flight more than 3,000 feet above the surface and below 18,000 feet MSL, a pilot is required to maintain an appropriate altitude in accordance with certain rules. This requirement is sometimes called the "Hemispherical Cruising Rule," and is based on magnetic course, not magnetic heading. *See* Figure 4-5.

Answers

3151   [A]   3152   [C]   3153   [C]   3154   [B]   3813   [B]

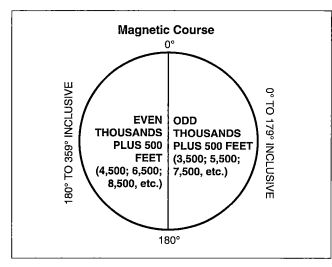

Magnetic Course

Figure 4-5. VFR cruising altitudes

AIR, RTC, WSC, PPC
3155. Which cruising altitude is appropriate for a VFR flight on a magnetic course of 135°?

A— Even thousandths.
B— Even thousandths plus 500 feet.
C— Odd thousandths plus 500 feet.

When operating below 18,000 feet MSL in VFR cruising flight more than 3,000 feet above the surface and on a magnetic course of 0° through 179°, any odd thousand-foot MSL altitude plus 500 feet (i.e., 3,500, 5,500, etc.) is appropriate. On a course of 180° through 359°, even thousands plus 500 feet (4,500, 6,500, etc.) is appropriate. (PLT467) — 14 CFR §91.159

AIR, RTC, WSC, PPC
3156. Which VFR cruising altitude is acceptable for a flight on a Victor Airway with a magnetic course of 175°? The terrain is less than 1,000 feet.

A— 4,500 feet.
B— 5,000 feet.
C— 5,500 feet.

When operating below 18,000 feet MSL in VFR cruising flight more than 3,000 feet above the surface and on a magnetic course of 0° through 179°, any odd thousand-foot MSL altitude plus 500 feet (i.e., 3,500, 5,500, etc.) is appropriate. On a course of 180° through 359°, even thousands plus 500 feet (4,500, 6,500, etc.) is appropriate. (PLT467) — 14 CFR §91.159

AIR, RTC, WSC, PPC
3157. Which VFR cruising altitude is appropriate when flying above 3,000 feet AGL on a magnetic course of 185°?

A— 4,000 feet.
B— 4,500 feet.
C— 5,000 feet.

When operating below 18,000 feet MSL in VFR cruising flight more than 3,000 feet above the surface and on a magnetic course of 0° through 179°, any odd thousand-foot MSL altitude plus 500 feet (i.e., 3,500, 5,500, etc.) is appropriate. On a course of 180° through 359°, even thousands plus 500 feet (4,500, 6,500, etc.) is appropriate. (PLT467) — 14 CFR §91.159

AIR, RTC, WSC, PPC
3158. Each person operating an aircraft at a VFR cruising altitude shall maintain an odd-thousand plus 500-foot altitude while on a

A— magnetic heading of 0° through 179°.
B— magnetic course of 0° through 179°.
C— true course of 0° through 179°.

When operating below 18,000 feet MSL in VFR cruising flight more than 3,000 feet above the surface and on a magnetic course of 0° through 179°, any odd thousand-foot MSL altitude plus 500 feet (i.e., 3,500, 5,500, etc.) is appropriate. On a course of 180° through 359°, even thousands plus 500 feet (4,500, 6,500, etc.) is appropriate. (PLT467) — 14 CFR §91.159

Answers (A) and (C) are incorrect because VFR altitudes are based on a magnetic course.

Answers
3155 [C]   3156 [C]   3157 [B]   3158 [B]

Categories of Aircraft

The term "**category**," when used with respect to the certification of aircraft, means a grouping of aircraft based upon intended use or operating limitations. Examples include normal, utility, aerobatic, restricted, experimental, transport, limited and provisional categories.

Both restricted and experimental category aircraft are prohibited from carrying persons or property for compensation or hire. In addition, both categories are normally prohibited from flying over densely populated areas or in congested airways.

ALL
3003. With respect to the certification of aircraft, which is a category of aircraft?

A— Normal, utility, acrobatic.
B— Airplane, rotorcraft, glider.
C— Landplane, seaplane.

With respect to the certification of aircraft, "a category of aircraft" means a grouping of aircraft based upon intended use or operating limitations. Examples include normal, utility, acrobatic, transport, limited, restricted, and provisional. (PLT371) — 14 CFR §1.1

Answer (B) is incorrect because it refers to the certification of air-men, not aircraft. Answer (C) is incorrect because it is not any kind of category.

ALL
3004. With respect to the certification of aircraft, which is a class of aircraft?

A— Airplane, rotorcraft, glider, balloon.
B— Normal, utility, acrobatic, limited.
C— Transport, restricted, provisional.

With respect to the certification of aircraft, "class" is a broad grouping of aircraft having similar means of propulsion, flight, or landing. Examples include airplane, rotorcraft, glider, balloon, landplane, and seaplane. (PLT371) — 14 CFR §1.1

Answers (B) and (C) are incorrect because they refer to category of aircraft rather than class.

ALL
3179. Unless otherwise specifically authorized, no person may operate an aircraft that has an experimental certificate

A— beneath the floor of Class B airspace.
B— over a densely populated area or in a congested airway.
C— from the primary airport within Class D airspace.

Unless otherwise authorized by the Administrator in special operating limitations, no person may operate an aircraft that has an experimental certificate over a densely populated area or in a congested airway. (PLT383) — 14 CFR §91.319

AIR, GLI, RTC, WSC, PPC
3178. Which is normally prohibited when operating a restricted category civil aircraft?

A— Flight under instrument flight rules.
B— Flight over a densely populated area.
C— Flight within Class D airspace.

No person may operate a restricted category civil aircraft within the United States:

1. *Over a densely populated area.*

2. *In a congested airway.*

3. *Near a busy airport where passenger transport operations are conducted.*

(PLT373) — 14 CFR §91.313

Answers

3003 [A]	3004 [A]	3179 [B]	3178 [B]

Formation Flight and Dropping Objects

Flying so close to another aircraft as to create a collision hazard is prohibited. If the intent is to fly formation, prior arrangement with the pilot-in-command of each aircraft is required. In any case, no person may operate an aircraft carrying passengers for hire in formation flight.

The PIC of an aircraft may not allow any object to be dropped while in flight unless reasonable precautions are taken to avoid injury or damage to persons or property on the surface.

ALL, SPO
3088. No person may operate an aircraft in formation flight

A— over a densely populated area.
B— in Class D airspace under special VFR.
C— except by prior arrangement with the pilot in command of each aircraft.

No person may operate an aircraft in formation flight except by arrangement with the pilot-in-command of each aircraft in the formation. The only restriction to formation flight is when carrying passengers for hire. (PLT431) — 14 CFR §91.111

ALL
3076. Under what conditions may objects be dropped from an aircraft?

A— Only in an emergency.
B— If precautions are taken to avoid injury or damage to persons or property on the surface.
C— If prior permission is received from the Federal Aviation Administration.

No pilot-in-command of a civil aircraft may allow any object to be dropped from an aircraft in flight that creates a hazard to persons or property. However, this does not prohibit the dropping of any object if reasonable precautions are taken to avoid injury or damage to persons or property. (PLT401) — 14 CFR §91.15

SPO
2133-1. Which is true with respect to formation flights? Formation flights are

A— authorized when carrying passengers for hire, with prior arrangement with the pilot in command of each aircraft in the formation.
B— not authorized, except by arrangement with the pilot in command of each aircraft.
C— not authorized, unless the pilot in command of each aircraft is trained and found competent in formation.

No person may operate an aircraft so close to another aircraft as to create a collision hazard. No person may operate an aircraft in formation flight except by arrangement with the pilot-in-command of each aircraft in the formation. No person may operate an aircraft, carrying passengers for hire, in formation flight. (PLT431) — 14 CFR §91.111

Answers

3088 [C]	3076 [B]	2133-1 [B]

VFR Flight Plans

Although filing a VFR flight plan is not mandatory (except under certain circumstances), it is considered good operating practice.

The pilot must close a VFR flight plan at the completion of a flight. This can be done by contacting the FAA upon landing.

ALL
3818. How should a VFR flight plan be closed at the completion of the flight at a controlled airport?

A— The tower will automatically close the flight plan when the aircraft turns off the runway.
B— The pilot must close the flight plan with the FAA upon landing.
C— The tower will relay the instructions to the nearest FSS when the aircraft contacts the tower for landing.

The pilot-in-command, upon canceling or completing the flight under the flight plan, shall notify an FAA Flight Service Station or ATC facility. (PLT225) — AIM ¶5-1-13

Speed Limits

The following maximum speed limits for aircraft have been established in the interest of safety:

1. Below 10,000 feet MSL, the speed limit is 250 knots indicated air speed (KIAS). *See* Figure 4-6a on the next page.

2. The speed limit within Class B airspace (Figure 4-6b) is also 250 KIAS.

3. The maximum speed authorized in a VFR corridor through Class B airspace (Figure 4-6c) or in airspace underlying Class B airspace (Figure 4-6d) is 200 KIAS.

4. In Class D airspace, aircraft are restricted to a maximum of 200 KIAS (Figure 4-6e).

5. Unless otherwise authorized or required by ATC, no person may operate an aircraft at or below 2,500 feet AGL within 4 NM of the primary airport of a Class C or Class D airspace area at an indicated airspeed of more than 200 knots.

AIR, RTC
3097. Unless otherwise authorized, what is the maximum indicated airspeed at which a person may operate an aircraft below 10,000 feet MSL?

A— 200 knots.
B— 250 knots.
C— 288 knots.

Maximum speed below 10,000 feet MSL is 250 knots. (PLT383) — 14 CFR §91.117

AIR, RTC
3098. Unless otherwise authorized, the maximum indicated airspeed at which aircraft may be flown when at or below 2,500 feet AGL and within 4 nautical miles of the primary airport of Class C airspace is

A— 200 knots.
B— 230 knots.
C— 250 knots.

Unless otherwise authorized or required by ATC, no person may operate an aircraft at or below 2,500 feet AGL within 4 NM of the primary airport of a Class C or Class D airspace area at an indicated airspeed of more than 200 knots. (PLT383) — 14 CFR §91.117

Answers

3818   [B]   3097   [B]   3098   [A]

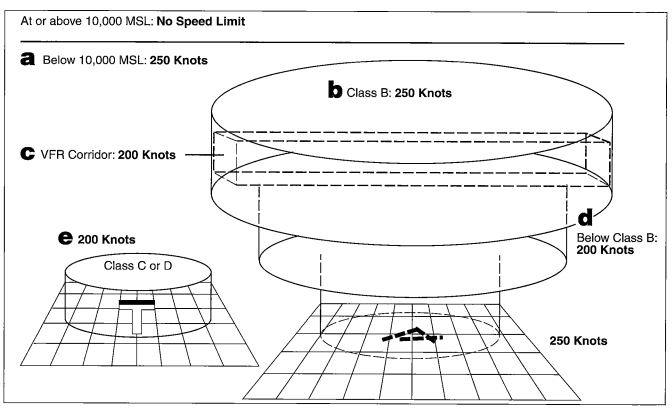

At or above 10,000 MSL: **No Speed Limit**

a Below 10,000 MSL: **250 Knots**

b Class B: **250 Knots**

c VFR Corridor: **200 Knots**

d Below Class B: **200 Knots**

e 200 Knots

Class C or D

250 Knots

Figure 4-6. Maximum speed limits

AIR, RTC

3099. When flying in the airspace underlying Class B airspace, the maximum speed authorized is

A— 200 knots.
B— 230 knots.
C— 250 knots.

No person may operate an aircraft in the airspace underlying Class B airspace at a speed of more than 200 knots. (PLT161) — 14 CFR §91.117

AIR, RTC

3100. When flying in a VFR corridor designated through Class B airspace, the maximum speed authorized is

A— 180 knots.
B— 200 knots.
C— 250 knots.

Maximum speed in a VFR corridor through Class B airspace is 200 KIAS. (PLT161) — 14 CFR §91.117

Answers

3099   [A]   3100   [B]

Airworthiness

Each aircraft is issued an Airworthiness Certificate, which remains valid as long as the aircraft is maintained and operated as required by regulations. This Airworthiness Certificate, along with the Aircraft Registration Certificate, operating limitations, and weight and balance must be aboard the aircraft during flight. Remember:

- **A**irworthiness
- **R**egistration
- **O**perating Limitations
- **W**eight and Balance

The aircraft's operating limitations may be found in the airplane flight manual, approved manual material, markings, and placards, or any combination thereof.

Summarized below are important points in understanding the definition of light-sport aircraft and the privileges associated with the Sport Pilot certificate:

- Two-place maximum (pilot and one passenger)
- Maximum gross takeoff weight 1,320 lbs (599 kg); 1,430 lbs for seaplanes
- Lighter-than-air light-sport aircraft maximum gross weight 660 lbs (300 kg)
- Maximum stall speed 51.8 mph (45 knots)
- Maximum speed in level flight with maximum continuous power 138 mph (120 knots)
- All LSA aircraft logbook signoffs are based on a specific make and model, allowing you to fly a similar "set" of performance and handling aircraft. Aircraft are organized by the FAA from large "Categories" of aircraft to specific "Sets" in the following order:

    Category and Class Light-Sport Aircraft — fixed wing/airplane category (land and sea classes), weight-shift control/trike category (land and sea classes), powered parachute category (land and sea classes), glider, rotorcraft category (gyroplane class), lighter-than-air category (balloon and airship classes).

    Sets are a more detailed breakdown of similar performance and handling.

    Make and Model — manufacturer specific that define/specify a set.

    Type — E-LSA or S-LSA.

- Single, non-turbine engine only, includes rotary or diesel engines
- Fixed or ground-adjustable propeller
- Unpressurized cabin with fixed landing gear
- Seaplanes with landing gear that can be configured so the wheels rotate for amphibious operation
- Will have FAA registration N number
- U.S. or foreign manufacture of light-sport aircraft is authorized
- (S-LSA) Special Light-Sport aircraft manufactured and sold ready-to-fly under a new certification without 14 CFR Part 23 compliance, but must meet ASTM consensus standards. Aircraft under this certification may be used for sport and recreation, flight training, and aircraft rental.
- (E-LSA) Experimental Light-Sport Aircraft is a kit built from an S-LSA design. May be used for sport and recreation and flight instruction for the owner of the aircraft.
- (E-LSA) Experimental Light-Sport Aircraft which was operated as an ultralight trainer or overweight single-place ultralight (fat ultralight). This existing fleet of ultralight trainers can be used for training until January 31, 2010.

- Aircraft with a standard airworthiness certificate (vintage production aircraft) that meet LSA specifications may be flown by sport pilots. However, that airworthiness certification category will not be changed to a light-sport aircraft. Maintenance must therefore be done by an A&P as it has in the past.
- Holders of a Sport Pilot Certificate may fly an aircraft with a standard airworthiness certificate if it meets the definition of a light-sport aircraft.
- May be operated at night if the aircraft is equipped per 14 CFR §91.209 and the pilot holds at least a Private Pilot certificate and a minimum of a third-class medical.
- E-LSA Experimental amateur-built, in which the builder completes 51% of the building of the aircraft.

ALL
3075. Where may an aircraft's operating limitations be found?

A— On the Airworthiness Certificate.
B— In the current, FAA-approved flight manual, approved manual material, markings, and placards, or any combination thereof.
C— In the aircraft airframe and engine logbooks.

No person may operate a civil aircraft without complying with the limitations found in the approved flight manual, markings, and placards. (PLT373) — 14 CFR §91.9

ALL
3075-1. Where may an aircraft's operating limitations be found if the aircraft has an Experimental or Special light-sport airworthiness certificate?

A— Attached to the Airworthiness Certificate.
B— In the current, FAA-approved flight manual.
C— In the aircraft airframe and engine logbooks.

Operating limitations for experimental and special light sport aircraft are attached to the airworthiness certificate. 14 CFR §21.190 and §91.319 describe the qualification for issuance and operating limitations. FAA Order 8130.2G specifically states that the operating limitations will be attached to FAA Form 8130-7. (PLT400) — 14 CFR §21.190, §91.319

ALL, SPO
3159. In addition to a valid Airworthiness Certificate, what documents or records must be aboard an aircraft during flight?

A— Aircraft engine and airframe logbooks, and owner's manual.
B— Radio operator's permit, and repair and alteration forms.
C— Operating limitations and Registration Certificate.

No person may operate an aircraft unless it has within it:

1. *An appropriate and current Airworthiness Certificate, displayed at the cabin or cockpit entrance so that it is legible to passengers or crew.*
2. *A Registration Certificate issued to its owner.*
3. *An approved flight manual, manual material, markings and placards or any combination thereof, which show the operating limitations of the aircraft.*

(PLT400) — 14 CFR §91.203

ALL, SPO
3187. How long does the Airworthiness Certificate of an aircraft remain valid?

A— As long as the aircraft has a current Registration Certificate.
B— Indefinitely, unless the aircraft suffers major damage.
C— As long as the aircraft is maintained and operated as required by Federal Aviation Regulations.

Unless sooner surrendered, suspended, revoked, or a termination date is otherwise established by the Administrator, Standard Airworthiness Certificates and Airworthiness Certificates issued for restricted or limited category aircraft are effective as long as the maintenance, preventive maintenance, and alterations are performed in accordance with Parts 43 and 91 and the aircraft are registered in the United States. (PLT377) — 14 CFR §21.181

Answers
3075 [B]   3075-1 [A]   3159 [C]   3187 [C]

Maintenance and Inspections

The owner or operator of an aircraft is primarily responsible for maintaining that aircraft in an airworthy condition, including compliance with airworthiness directives. He/she is also responsible for all records of maintenance, repairs, and alterations. (The pilot-in-command is responsible for determining that the aircraft is in an airworthy condition prior to flight.) The airworthiness of an aircraft can be determined by a preflight inspection and a review of the maintenance records.

The holder of a pilot certificate is allowed (within certain limits) to perform preventive maintenance on any aircraft owned and operated by that pilot. Preventive maintenance is limited to tasks such as replacing defective safety wire, servicing landing gear wheel bearings, replacing safety belts, and other tasks listed in 14 CFR Part 43, Appendix A. After preventive maintenance has been performed on an aircraft, the signature, certificate type and certificate number of the person approving the aircraft for return to service, and a description of the work, must be entered in the aircraft maintenance records.

An aircraft may not be operated unless, within the preceding 12 calendar months, it has had an annual inspection and has been approved for return to service. This will be indicated by the appropriate notation in the aircraft maintenance records. To determine the expiration date of the last annual inspection, refer to the aircraft maintenance records. For example, if the aircraft's last annual inspection was performed on July 12, 1993, the next annual inspection will be due no later than midnight, July 31, 1994.

If an aircraft is used to carry passengers for hire or used for flight instruction for hire, it must have, in addition to the annual inspection, an inspection each 100 hours of flight time. (An annual inspection may be substituted for the 100-hour inspection, but a 100-hour inspection may not be substituted for an annual inspection.) The 100-hour limitation may be exceeded by not more than 10 hours if necessary to reach a place at which the inspection can be done. The excess time should not be used in computing the next 100 hours of time in service. The next 100-hour inspection should be performed 100 hours after the previous inspection was due, not after the time the inspection was actually completed. For example: a 100-hour inspection was due at 3,302.5 hours on the hobbs meter. The 100-hour inspection was actually done at 3,309.5 hours. The next 100-hour inspection is due at 3,402.5 hours.

The transponder cannot be operated unless within the preceding 24 calendar months, it has been inspected and found satisfactory.

If an aircraft has been maintained, rebuilt, or altered in any manner that may have appreciably changed its flight characteristics or operation in flight, no passengers may be carried until it has been flight tested by an appropriately-rated pilot (with at least a Private Pilot Certificate) and approved for return to service.

Light-Sport Repairman Certificates

Two additional repairman certificates are available for working on light-sport aircraft: the maintenance and inspection ratings.

The **maintenance rating** allows repairmen to do maintenance, preventative maintenance, and alterations to E-LSA and S-LSA. The course is 120 hours (airplane category); 104 hours (weight-shift or powered parachute); 80 hours (glider or lighter-than-air). An A&P certificate counts towards these hour requirements for Light-Sport Aircraft qualifications, but additional training on specific category of aircraft will be required.

The **inspection rating** allows E-LSA repairmen/owners the ability to perform the annual inspection on their own aircraft. This course is 16 hours on the specific aircraft category and class. The 100-hour inspection required for training and hire for all E-LSA and S-LSA must be done by an appropriately-rated A&P mechanic or an LSA repairman with a maintenance rating.

Light-Sport Aircraft FAA Designated Airworthiness Representatives (DAR) must attend a three-day FAA course to inspect and issue experimental (E-LSA) and special (S-LSA) airworthiness certificates.

Special Light-Sport Airworthiness Certificated Aircraft (S-LSA) Maintenance

A certificated pilot (Sport Pilot rating or higher) can perform preventive maintenance as specified by the manufacturer (typically similar to 14 CFR Part 43 Appendix A) and return to service on his own aircraft with no sport pilot repairman certificate. However, the annual and 100-hour condition inspection must be completed by:

- An appropriately rated A&P mechanic;
- An appropriately rated repair station; or
- A light-sport repairman with a maintenance rating.

Experimental Light-Sport Airworthiness Certificated Aircraft (E-LSA) Maintenance

No rating is required to perform maintenance on (E-LSA). The annual condition inspection can be completed by:

- An appropriately-rated A&P mechanic;
- An appropriately-rated repair station;
- A light-sport repairman with a maintenance rating; or
- A light-sport repairman with an inspection rating (16 hour course) on their own aircraft.

ALL
3180-1. The responsibility for ensuring that an aircraft is maintained in an airworthy condition is primarily that of the

A— pilot-in-command.
B— owner or operator.
C— mechanic who performs the work.

The owner or operator of an aircraft is primarily responsible for maintaining the aircraft in an airworthy condition. The pilot-in-command of a civil aircraft is responsible for determining whether that aircraft is in condition for safe flight. (PLT374) — 14 CFR §91.403

ALL
3180-2. The airworthiness of an aircraft can be determined by a preflight inspection and a

A— statement from the owner or operator that the aircraft is airworthy.
B— log book endorsement from a flight instructor.
C— review of the maintenance records.

The airworthiness of an aircraft can be determined by a preflight inspection and a review of the maintenance records. Each owner or operator shall ensure that maintenance personnel make appropriate entries in the aircraft maintenance records indicating maintenance done and the aircraft has been approved for return to service. (PLT377) — 14 CFR §91.405

ALL
3181-1. The responsibility for ensuring that maintenance personnel make the appropriate entries in the aircraft maintenance records indicating the aircraft has been approved for return to service lies with the

A— owner or operator.
B— pilot in command.
C— mechanic who performed the work.

The registered owner or operator shall ensure that the aircraft maintenance records include the signature and the certificate number of the person approving the aircraft for return to service. (PLT374) — 14 CFR §91.417

ALL
3181-2. Who is responsible for ensuring appropriate entries are made in maintenance records indicating the aircraft has been approved for return to service?

A— Owner or operator.
B— Certified mechanic.
C— Repair station.

Each owner or operator shall ensure that maintenance personnel make appropriate entries in the aircraft maintenance records indicating maintenance done and the aircraft has been approved for return to service. (PLT374) — 14 CFR §91.405

Answers

3180-1 [B]   3180-2 [C]   3181-1 [A]   3181-2 [A]

ALL
3182. Completion of an annual condition inspection and the return of the aircraft to service should always be indicated by

A— the relicensing date on the Registration Certificate.
B— an appropriate notation in the aircraft maintenance records.
C— an inspection sticker placed on the instrument panel that lists the annual inspection completion date.

Each registered owner or operator shall keep records of the maintenance and alteration, and records of the 100-hour, annual, progressive, and other required or approved inspections, as appropriate, for each aircraft (including the airframe) and each engine, propeller, rotor, and appliance of an aircraft. The records must include:

1. A description (or reference to data acceptable to the Administrator) of the work performed;

2. The date of completion of the work performed; and

3. The signature and certificate number of the person approving the aircraft for return to service.

(PLT372) — 14 CFR §91.417

ALL
3185. An aircraft's annual condition inspection was performed on July 12, this year. The next annual inspection will be due no later than

A— July 1, next year.
B— July 13, next year.
C— July 31, next year.

No person may operate an aircraft unless, within the preceding 12 calendar months, it has had an annual inspection in accordance with Part 43 and has been approved for return to service by an authorized person. (PLT372) — 14 CFR §91.409

ALL
3186. To determine the expiration date of the last annual aircraft inspection, a person should refer to the

A— Airworthiness Certificate.
B— Registration Certificate.
C— aircraft maintenance records.

Each registered owner or operator shall keep records of the maintenance and alteration, and records of the 100-hour, annual, progressive, and other required or approved inspections, as appropriate, for each aircraft (including the airframe) and each engine, propeller, rotor, and appliance of an aircraft. (PLT372) — 14 CFR §91.417

ALL
3188. What aircraft inspections are required for rental aircraft that are also used for flight instruction?

A— Annual condition and 100-hour inspections.
B— Biannual condition and 100-hour inspections.
C— Annual condition and 50-hour inspections.

No person may operate an aircraft carrying any person for hire, and no person may give flight instruction for hire in an aircraft which that person provides, unless within the preceding 100 hours of time in service it has received an annual or 100-hour inspection and been approved for return to service. (PLT426) — 14 CFR §91.409

ALL
3191. No person may use an ATC transponder unless it has been tested and inspected within at least the preceding

A— 6 calendar months.
B— 12 calendar months.
C— 24 calendar months.

No person may use an ATC transponder unless within the preceding 24 calendar months, the ATC transponder has been tested and inspected and found to comply with Appendix F of Part 43. (PLT426) — 14 CFR §91.413

ALL
3192. Maintenance records show the last transponder inspection was performed on September 1, 2014. The next inspection will be due no later than

A— September 30, 2015.
B— September 1, 2016.
C— September 30, 2016.

No person may use an ATC transponder unless within the preceding 24 calendar months, the ATC transponder has been tested and inspected and found to comply with Appendix F of Part 43. (PLT508) — 14 CFR §91.413

Answers

3182 [B]	3185 [C]	3186 [C]	3188 [A]	3191 [C]	3192 [C]

ALL
3013-1. Preventive maintenance has been performed on an aircraft. What paperwork is required?

A— A full, detailed description of the work done must be entered in the airframe logbook.
B— The date the work was completed, and the name of the person who did the work must be entered in the airframe and engine logbook.
C— The signature, certificate number, and kind of certificate held by the person approving the work and a description of the work must be entered in the aircraft maintenance records.

Each registered owner or operator shall keep records of preventative maintenance. The records must include:

1. A description of the work performed;

2. The date of completion of the work performed; and

3. The signature and certificate number of the person approving the aircraft for return to service (could be pilot certificate number for Part 43 when you are doing your own preventative maintenance).

(PLT446) — 14 CFR §91.417

Answer (A) is incorrect because it is incomplete. Answer (B) is incorrect because it refers to who performed the work rather than who approved it.

ALL
3013-2. What regulation allows a private pilot to perform preventive maintenance?

A— 14 CFR Part 91.403.
B— 14 CFR Part 43.7.
C— 14 CFR Part 61.113.

14 CFR §43.7 Persons authorized to approve aircraft, airframes, aircraft engines, propellers, appliances, or component parts for return to service after maintenance, preventive maintenance, rebuilding, or alteration says a person holding at least a private pilot certificate may approve an aircraft for return to service after performing preventive maintenance under the provisions of §43.3(g). (PLT375) — 14 CFR §43.7

Answer (A) is incorrect because 14 CFR §91.403 explains that the owner or operator must maintain the aircraft in airworthy condition. Answer (C) is incorrect because 14 CFR §61.113 details the private pilot privileges and limitations while operating as pilot-in-command.

ALL
3013-3. Who may perform preventive maintenance on an aircraft and approve it for service?

A— Student or Recreational pilot.
B— Private or Commercial pilot.
C— None of the above.

A person holding at least a private pilot certificate may approve an aircraft for return to service after performing preventive maintenance. (PLT375) — 14 CFR §43.7

ALL
3014. Which operation would be described as preventive maintenance?

A— Replenishing hydraulic fluid.
B— Repair of portions of skin sheets by making additional seams.
C— Repair of landing gear brace struts.

Preventative maintenance items which can be performed by the pilot are listed in Part 43 and include such basic items as oil changes, wheel bearing lubrication, and hydraulic fluid (brakes, landing gear system) refills. (PLT446) — 14 CFR Part 43

Answers (B) and (C) are incorrect because they both list major maintenance.

ALL
3183. If an alteration or repair substantially affects an aircraft's operation in flight, that aircraft must be test flown by an appropriately-rated pilot and approved for return to service prior to being operated

A— by any private pilot.
B— with passengers aboard.
C— for compensation or hire.

No person may carry any person (other than crewmembers) in an aircraft that has been maintained, rebuilt, or altered in a manner that may have appreciably changed its flight characteristics or substantially affected its operation in flight until an appropriately-rated pilot with at least a Private Pilot Certificate flies the aircraft, makes an operational check of the maintenance performed or alteration made, and logs the flight in the aircraft records. (PLT375) — 14 CFR §91.407

Answers

| 3013-1 | [C] | 3013-2 | [B] | 3013-3 | [B] | 3014 | [A] | 3183 | [B] |

ALL
3184. Before passengers can be carried in an aircraft that has been altered in a manner that may have appreciably changed its flight characteristics, it must be flight tested by an appropriately-rated pilot who holds at least a

A— Commercial Pilot Certificate with an instrument rating.
B— Private Pilot Certificate.
C— Commercial Pilot Certificate and a mechanic's certificate.

No person may carry any person (other than crewmembers) in an aircraft that has been maintained, rebuilt, or altered in a manner that may have appreciably changed its flight characteristics or substantially affected its operation in flight until an appropriately-rated pilot with at least a Private Pilot Certificate flies the aircraft, makes an operational check of the maintenance performed or alteration made, and logs the flight in the aircraft records. (PLT375) — 14 CFR §91.407

AIR, RTC, WSC, PPC
3189. An aircraft had a 100-hour inspection when the tachometer read 1259.6. When is the next 100-hour inspection due?

A— 1349.6 hours.
B— 1359.6 hours.
C— 1369.6 hours.

The 100-hour limitation may be exceeded by not more than 10 hours if necessary to reach a place at which the inspection can be done. The excess time, however, is included in computing the next 100 hours in service.

   1259.6 *time at 100-hour inspection*
+ 100.0 *time in service*
   1359.6 *time next inspection due*

(PLT372) — 14 CFR §91.409

AIR, RTC, WSC, PPC
3190. A 100-hour inspection was due at 3302.5 hours. The 100-hour inspection was actually done at 3309.5 hours. When is the next 100-hour inspection due?

A— 3312.5 hours.
B— 3402.5 hours.
C— 3395.5 hours.

The 100-hour limitation may be exceeded by not more than 10 hours if necessary to reach a place at which the inspection can be done. The excess time, however, is included in computing the next 100 hours in service.

   3302.5 *time inspection was due*
+ 100.0 *time in service*
   3402.5 *time next inspection due*

(PLT372) — 14 CFR §91.409

ADs, ACs, and NOTAMs

Airworthiness Directives (ADs) identify unsafe aircraft conditions and prescribe regulatory actions (such as inspections or modifications) or limitations under which the affected aircraft may continue to be operated and are mandatory. Compliance with an applicable Airworthiness Directive must be entered in the appropriate aircraft maintenance records. The owner or operator is responsible for ensuring ADs are complied with. Pilots may operate an aircraft not in compliance with an AD, if the AD allows for this.

In addition to ADs, light-sport aircraft must comply with manufacturers' safety directives.

Advisory Circulars are issued by the FAA to inform the aviation community in a systematic way of non-regulatory material of interest. In many cases, they are the result of a need to fully explain a particular subject (wake turbulence, for example). They are issued in a numbered-subject system corresponding to the subject areas of the Federal Aviation Regulations. Advisory Circulars (some free, others at cost) may be obtained by ordering from the Government Printing Office (GPO).

The Aeronautical Information Manual (AIM) is the official guide to basic flight information and ATC procedures. It is updated every 180 days and is available from the FAA website.

Notices to Airmen (NOTAMs) provide the most current information available. They provide time-critical information on airports and changes that affect the national airspace system and are of concern to instrument flight rule (IFR) operations. NOTAM information is classified into four categories: NOTAM (D) or distant, Flight Data Center (FDC) NOTAMs, pointer NOTAMs, and military NOTAMs.

Answers

3184 [B]   3189 [B]   3190 [B]

NOTAM-Ds are attached to hourly weather reports and are available at flight service stations (AFSS/ FSS). FDC NOTAMs are issued by the National Flight Data Center and contain regulatory information, such as temporary flight restrictions or an amendment to instrument approach procedures.

Pointer NOTAMs highlight or point out another NOTAM, such as an FDC or NOTAM (D). This type of NOTAM will assist pilots in cross-referencing important information that may not be found under an airport or NAVAID identifier. Military NOTAMs pertain to U.S. Air Force, Army, Marine, and Navy NAVAIDs/ airports that are part of the NAS.

NOTAM-Ds and FDC NOTAMs are contained in the Notices to Airmen publication, which is issued every 28 days. Prior to any flight, pilots should check for any NOTAMs that could affect their intended flight.

An FDC NOTAM will be issued to designate a temporary flight restriction (TFR). The NOTAM will begin with the phrase "FLIGHT RESTRICTIONS" followed by the location of the temporary restriction, effective time period, area defined in statute miles, and altitudes affected. The NOTAM will also contain the FAA coordination facility and telephone number, the reason for the restriction, and any other information deemed appropriate. The pilot should check the NOTAMs as part of flight planning. Some of the purposes for establishing a temporary restriction are: protect persons and property in the air or on the surface from an existing or imminent hazard, provide a safe environment for the operation of disaster relief aircraft, prevent an unsafe congestion of sightseeing aircraft above an incident or event, which may generate a high degree of public interest, protect declared national disasters for humanitarian reasons in the State of Hawaii, protect the President, Vice President, or other public figures, provide a safe environment for space agency operations.

ALL
3193. Which records or documents shall the owner or operator of an aircraft keep to show compliance with an applicable Airworthiness Directive?

A— Aircraft maintenance records.
B— Airworthiness Certificate and Pilot's Operating Handbook.
C— Airworthiness and Registration Certificates.

Each registered owner or operator shall keep records of the maintenance and alteration, and records of the 100-hour, annual, progressive, and other required or approved inspections, as appropriate, for each aircraft (including the airframe) and each engine, propeller, rotor, and appliance of an aircraft. (PLT425) — 14 CFR §91.417

ALL
3012-2. What should an owner or operator know about Airworthiness Directives (AD's)?

A— For Informational purposes only.
B— They are mandatory.
C— They are voluntary.

Airworthiness Directives (ADs) are mandatory. No person may operate a product to which an airworthiness directive applies except in accordance with the requirements of that airworthiness directive. (PLT426) — 14 CFR §39.3

ALL, SPO
3012-3. May a pilot operate an aircraft that is not in compliance with an Airworthiness Directive (AD)?

A— Yes, under VFR conditions only.
B— Yes, AD's are only voluntary.
C— Yes, if allowed by the AD.

No person may operate a product to which an airworthiness directive applies except in accordance with the requirements of that airworthiness directive. (PLT378) — 14 CFR §39.3

ALL
3181-3. Who is responsible for ensuring Airworthiness Directives (ADs) are complied with?

A— Owner or operator.
B— Repair station.
C— Mechanic with inspection authorization (IA).

The owner or operator of an aircraft is primarily responsible for maintaining that aircraft in an airworthy condition, including compliance with the Airworthiness Directives (ADs) found in 14 CFR Part 39. (PLT374) — 14 CFR §91.403

Answers

3193 [A] 3012-2 [B] 3012-3 [C] 3181-3 [A]

ALL
3999. What information is contained in the Notices to Airman Publication (NTAP)?

A— Current NOTAM (D) and FDC NOTAMs.
B— All Current NOTAMs.
C— Current FDC NOTAMs.

The Notices to Airmen Publication (NTAP) is published by Air Traffic Publications every 28 days and contains all current NOTAM (D)s and FDC NOTAMs (except FDC NOTAMs for temporary flight restrictions) available for publication. (PLT323) — FAA-H-8083-25

ALL
3709. FAA advisory circulars (some free, others at cost) are available to all pilots and are obtained by

A— distribution from the nearest FAA district office.
B— ordering those desired from the Government Printing Office.
C— subscribing to the Federal Register.

Advisory circulars which are offered for sale or free may be ordered from the Superintendent of Documents, U.S. Government Printing Office. (PLT116) — AC 00-2

ALL
3854. FAA advisory circulars containing subject matter specifically related to Airmen are issued under which subject number?

A— 60.
B— 70.
C— 90.

Appendix II of the Advisory Circular Checklist contains the Circular Numbering System wherein advisory circular numbers relate to Federal Aviation Regulations subchapter titles and correspond to the Parts and/or sections of the regulations. The four to remember are:

20 — Aircraft;
60 — Airmen;
70 — Airspace; and
90 — Air Traffic and General Operating Rules

(PLT116) — AC 00-2

ALL
3855. FAA advisory circulars containing subject matter specifically related to Airspace are issued under which subject number?

A— 60.
B— 70.
C— 90.

Appendix II of the Advisory Circular Checklist contains the Circular Numbering System wherein advisory circular numbers relate to Federal Aviation Regulations subchapter titles and correspond to the Parts and/or sections of the regulations. The four to remember are:

20 — Aircraft;
60 — Airmen;
70 — Airspace; and
90 — Air Traffic and General Operating Rules

(PLT116) — AC 00-2

ALL, SPO
3856. FAA advisory circulars containing subject matter specifically related to Air Traffic Control and General Operations are issued under which subject number?

A— 60.
B— 70.
C— 90.

Appendix II of the Advisory Circular Checklist contains the Circular Numbering System wherein advisory circular numbers relate to Federal Aviation Regulations subchapter titles and correspond to the Parts and/or sections of the regulations. The four to remember are:

20 — Aircraft;
60 — Airmen;
70 — Airspace; and
90 — Air Traffic and General Operating Rules

(PLT116) — AC 00-2

SPO
2109. Unless incorporated into a regulation by reference, Advisory Circulars (ACs) are issued to inform the public of nonregulatory material

A— and are not binding.
B— but are binding.
C— and self-cancel after 1 year.

The FAA issues advisory circulars to inform the aviation public in a systematic way of nonregulatory material. Unless incorporated into a regulation by reference, the contents of an advisory circular are not binding on the public. (PLT116) — AC 00-2

Answers

3999 [A]	3709 [B]	3854 [A]	3855 [B]	3856 [C]	2109 [A]

SPO
2110. Some Advisory Circulars (ACs) are available free of charge while the remaining ACs must be purchased. All aviation safety ACs may be obtained by following the procedures in the AC Checklist (AC 00-2) or by

A— referring to the FAA internet home page and following the links to ACs.
B— contacting the local airport Fixed Base Operator and requesting the desired AC.
C— reading the ACs in the Aeronautical Information Manual (AIM).

A number of FAA organizations have made their ACs available on the Internet. These ACs may be found through the FAA home page at: www.faa.gov located under Regulatory/Advisory, select Advisory Circulars. (PLT116) — AC 00-2

Answers (B) and (C) are incorrect because FBOs are not responsible for distributing ACs, nor are they included as part of the AIM.

SPO
2117. The Federal Aviation Administration publication that provides the aviation community with basic flight information and Air Traffic Control procedures for use in the National Airspace System of the United States is the

A— Aeronautical Information Manual (AIM).
B— Chart Supplements U.S. (formerly A/FD).
C— Advisory Circular Checklist (AC 00-2).

The Aeronautical Information Manual (AIM) *is the official guide to basic flight information and ATC procedures. (PLT116) — AIM*

Answer (B) is incorrect because the Chart Supplements U.S. contains information on airports, communications, NAVAIDs, instrument landing systems, VOR receiver check points, preferred routes, Flight Service Station/Weather Service telephone numbers, Air Route Traffic Control Center (ARTCC) frequencies, part-time surface areas, and various other pertinent special notices essential to air navigation. Answer (C) is incorrect because AC 00-2 is the Advisory Circular checklist and status of other FAA publications, contains advisory circulars that are for sale as well as those distributed free-of-charge by the FAA.

SPO
2120. Flight Data Center (FDC) NOTAMS are issued by the National Flight Data Center and contain regulatory information, such as

A— temporary flight restrictions.
B— markings and signs used at airports.
C— standard communication procedures at uncontrolled airports.

FDC NOTAMs are issued by the National Flight Data Center and contain regulatory information, such as temporary flight restrictions. (PLT323) — FAA-H-8083-25

SPO
2121. Time-critical information on airports and changes that affect the national airspace system are provided by

A— Notices to Airmen (NOTAMS).
B— the Chart Supplements U.S. (formerly Airport/Facilities Directory or A/FD).
C— Advisory Circulars (ACs).

Notices to Airmen (NOTAMs) provide the most current information available. They provide time-critical information on airports and changes that affect the national airspace system. (PLT323) — FAA-H-8083-25

Answer (B) is incorrect because Chart Supplements U.S. are only revised every 8 weeks. Answer (C) is incorrect because the FAA issues ACs to inform the aviation public in a systematic way of non-regulatory material.

SPO
2053. One of the purposes for issuing a Temporary Flight Restriction (TFR) is to

A— announce Parachute Jump Areas.
B— protect public figures.
C— identify Airport Advisory Areas.

Temporary flight restrictions (TFR) are imposed in order to:

1. *Protect persons and property in the air or on the surface from an existing or imminent flight associated hazard;*

2. *Provide a safe environment for the operation of disaster relief aircraft;*

3. *Prevent an unsafe congestion of sightseeing aircraft above an incident;*

4. *Protect the President, Vice President, or other public figures; and,*

5. *Provide a safe environment for space agency operations.*

Pilots are expected to check appropriate NOTAMs during flight planning when conducting flight in an area where a temporary flight restriction is in effect. (PLT376) — FAA-H-8083-15, Glossary

Answer (A) is incorrect because this is done through NOTAMs. Answer (C) is incorrect because these are identified through the Sectional and Chart Supplements U.S.

Answers

2110 [A]	2117 [A]	2120 [A]	2121 [A]	2053 [B]

Accident Reporting Requirements

The National Transportation Security Board (NTSB) Part 830 contains rules pertaining to notification and reporting of aircraft accidents and incidents. It also addresses preservation of aircraft wreckage, mail, cargo, and records.

The term **accident** means "an occurrence in which any person suffers death or **serious injury**, or in which the aircraft receives **substantial damage**."

Serious injury means any injury which: (1) requires hospitalization for more than 48 hours, commencing within 7 days from the date the injury was received; (2) results in a fracture of any bone (except simple fractures of fingers, toes, or nose); (3) causes severe hemorrhages, nerve, muscle, or tendon damage; (4) involves any internal organ; or (5) involves second or third degree burns, or any burns affecting more than 5 percent of the body surface.

Substantial damage means damage or failure which adversely affects the structural strength, performance, or flight characteristics of the aircraft, and which would normally require major repair or replacement of the affected component. The following is **not** considered "substantial damage": engine failure, bent fairings or cowling, dented skin, small punctured holes in the skin or fabric, ground damage to rotor or propeller blades, and damage to landing gear, wheels, tires, flaps, engine accessories, brakes, or wingtips.

The term "incident" means "an occurrence other than an **accident**, which affects or could affect the safety of operations."

Immediate notification of the NTSB is required when an aircraft accident occurs, and any of a specified list of incidents, which include:

1. Inability of a flight crewmember to perform his/her duties due to illness or injury;

2. Infight fire;

3. An aircraft is overdue and believed to have been involved in an accident;

4. Flight control system malfunction or failure; or

5. When aircraft collide in flight or damage of more than $25,000 occurs to property other than the aircraft.

The operator of an aircraft involved in an accident or incident which requires notification of the NTSB is responsible for preserving the wreckage, mail, or cargo until the NTSB takes custody. These items may be moved to protect the wreckage from further damage.

The operator of an aircraft involved in an accident is required to file an accident report within 10 days. A report of an incident must be reported only upon request.

ALL, SPO
3194. If an aircraft is involved in an accident which results in substantial damage to the aircraft, the nearest NTSB field office should be notified

A— immediately.
B— within 48 hours.
C— within 7 days.

The operator of an aircraft shall immediately, and by the most expeditious means available, notify the nearest NTSB field office when an aircraft accident occurs. (PLT366) — NTSB §830.5

ALL
3195. Which incident requires an immediate notification to the nearest NTSB field office?

A— A forced landing due to engine failure.
B— Landing gear damage, due to a hard landing.
C— Flight control system malfunction or failure.

A flight control system malfunction or failure requires immediate NTSB notification. (PLT366) — NTSB §830.5

ALL
3196. Which incident would necessitate an immediate notification to the nearest NTSB field office?

A— An in-flight generator/alternator failure.
B— An in-flight fire.
C— An in-flight loss of VOR receiver capability.

Immediate notification of the NTSB is necessary if an inflight fire occurs. (PLT366) — NTSB §830.5

ALL
3197. Which incident requires an immediate notification be made to the nearest NTSB field office?

A— An overdue aircraft that is believed to be involved in an accident.
B— An in-flight radio communications failure.
C— An in-flight generator or alternator failure.

When an aircraft is overdue and believed to have been involved in an accident, the NTSB must be notified immediately. (PLT366) — NTSB §830.5

ALL, SPO
3198. May aircraft wreckage be moved prior to the time the NTSB takes custody?

A— Yes, but only if moved by a federal, state, or local law enforcement officer.
B— Yes, but only to protect the wreckage from further damage.
C— No, it may not be moved under any circumstances.

Prior to the time the Board and its authorized representative takes custody of aircraft wreckage, it may not be disturbed or moved except to remove persons injured or trapped, to protect the wreckage from further damage, or to protect the public from injury. (PLT366) — NTSB §830.10

ALL, SPO
3199. The operator of an aircraft that has been involved in an accident is required to file an NTSB accident report within how many days?

A— 5.
B— 7.
C— 10.

The operator of an aircraft shall file a report on Board Form 6120.1 or 6120.2 within 10 days of an accident. (PLT366) — NTSB §830.15

ALL, SPO
3200. The operator of an aircraft that has been involved in an incident is required to submit a report to the nearest field office of the NTSB

A— within 7 days.
B— within 10 days.
C— when requested.

A report on an incident for which notification is required shall be filed only as requested by an authorized representative of the Board. (PLT366) — NTSB §830.15

SPO
2189. While taxiing on the parking ramp, the landing gear, wheel, and tire are damaged by striking ground equipment. What action would be required to comply with NTSB Part 830?

A— A report must be filed with the nearest FAA field office within 7 days.
B— An immediate notification must be filed by the operator of the aircraft with the nearest NTSB field office.
C— No notification or report is required.

This unfortunate event would not require notification or a report with the NTSB, as it is not an accident or considered "substantial damage" per the regulations. (PLT366) — NTSB §830.2

Answer (A) is incorrect because a report must be filed within 7 days for certain accidents or injuries, of which the taxiing incident described here does not qualify. Answer (B) is incorrect because an immediate notification must be filed only when an aircraft accident occurs, of which the taxiing incident described here does not qualify.

Answers

3195 [C]   3196 [B]   3197 [A]   3198 [B]   3199 [C]   3200 [C]
2189 [C]

SPO

2211. Which publication covers the procedures required for aircraft accident and incident reporting responsibilities for pilots?

A— FAR Part 61.
B— FAR Part 91.
C— NTSB Part 830.

NTSB Part 830 contains regulations pertaining to notification and reporting of aircraft accidents or incidents and overdue aircraft, and preservation of aircraft wreckage, mail, cargo, and records. (PLT366) — NTSB Part 830

Answer (A) is incorrect because 14 CFR Part 61 contains regulations on certification of pilots. Answer (B) is incorrect because 14 CFR Part 91 contains regulations on general operating and flight rules.

SPO

2212. Notification to the NTSB is required when there has been substantial damage

A— which requires repairs to landing gear.
B— to an engine caused by engine failure in flight.
C— which adversely affects structural strength or flight characteristics.

The operator of an aircraft shall immediately, and by the most expeditious means available, notify the nearest NTSB field office when an aircraft accident occurs. An aircraft accident is an occurrence associated with the operation of an aircraft which takes place between the time any person boards the aircraft with the intention of flight and all such persons have disembarked, and in which any person suffers death or serious injury, or in which the aircraft receives substantial damage which adversely affects the structural strength, performance, or flight characteristics of the aircraft. (PLT366) — 49 CFR §830.2, §830.5

SPO

2213. What period of time must a person be hospitalized before an injury may be defined by the NTSB as a "serious injury"?

A— 10 days, with no other extenuating circumstances.
B— 48 hours; commencing within 7 days after date of the injury.
C— 72 hours; commencing within 10 days after date of the injury.

"Serious injury" means any injury requiring hospitalization for more than 48 hours, commencing within 7 days from the date the injury was received. (PLT395) — 49 CFR §830.2

SPO

2214. Which incident would require that the nearest NTSB field office be notified immediately?

A— In-flight fire.
B— Ground fire resulting in fire equipment dispatch.
C— Fire of the primary aircraft while in a hangar which results in damage to other property of more than $25,000.

The operator of an aircraft shall immediately and by the most expeditious means available notify the nearest NTSB field office of any infight fire. (PLT416) — 49 CFR §830.5

Answers (B) and (C) are incorrect because the regulation specifies "infight" fires only.

Answers

2211 [C]   2212 [C]   2213 [B]   2214 [A]

Chapter 5
Procedures and Airport Operations

Uncontrolled and Tower-Controlled Airports

Airport Traffic Control Towers (ATCT) are established to promote the safe, orderly, and expeditious flow of air traffic. The tower controller will issue instructions for aircraft to follow the desired flight path while in the airport traffic area whenever necessary by using terminology as shown in Figure 5-1.

The ATCT will also direct aircraft taxiing on the surface movement area of the airport. In all instances, an appropriate clearance must be received from the tower before taking off or landing.

At airports without an operating control tower, pilots of fixed-wing and weight-shift control aircraft must circle the airport to the left ("left traffic") unless visual indicators indicate right traffic.

A common visual indicator is the segmented circle system, which consists of the following components (*see* Figure 5-2):

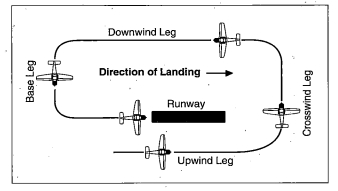

Figure 5-1

- The **segmented circle** is located in a position readily visible to pilots in the air and on the ground.
- A **tetrahedron** may be used to indicate the direction of landings and takeoffs. The small end of the tetrahedron points in the direction of landing. Pilots are cautioned against using the tetrahedron to determine wind direction, because it may not indicate the correct direction in light winds.
- A **wind cone, wind sock,** or **wind tee** may be installed near the operational runway to indicate wind direction. The large end of the wind cone or sock points into the wind as does the cross bar of the wind tee. *See* Figure 5-3.

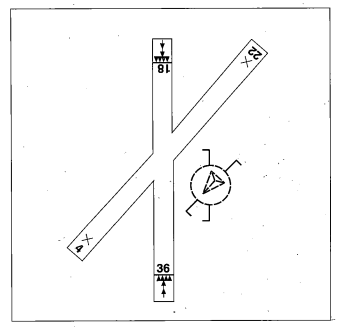

Figure 5-2. Segmented circle and landing direction indicator

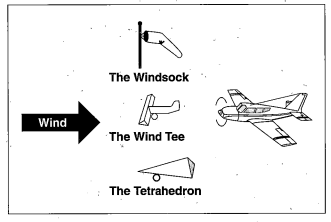

Figure 5-3. Wind/landing direction indicators

The tetrahedron, wind cone, wind sock, or wind tee may be located in the center of the segmented circle and may be lit for night operations.

Landing runway (landing strip) indicators are installed in pairs and used to show alignment of runways. *See* Figure 5-4(a). Traffic pattern indicators are installed in pairs in conjunction with landing strip indicators, and are used to indicate the direction of turns. *See* Figure 5-4(b).

Approaching to land at an airport without a control tower, or when the control tower is not in operation, the pilot should observe the indicator for the approach end of the runway to be used. VFR landings at night should be made the same as during daytime.

Aircraft departing an uncontrolled airport must comply with any FAA traffic pattern established for that airport.

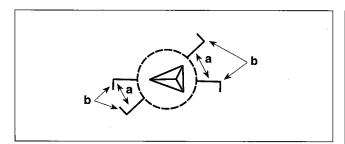

Figure 5-4. Landing runway and traffic pattern indicators

ALL, SPO
3123. Which is the correct traffic pattern departure procedure to use at a noncontrolled airport?

A— Depart in any direction consistent with safety, after crossing the airport boundary.
B— Make all turns to the left.
C— Comply with any FAA traffic pattern established for the airport.

In the case of an aircraft departing an airport without an operating control tower, comply with any FAA traffic pattern for that airport. (PLT201) — 14 CFR §91.127

ALL
3123-1. The recommended entry position to an airport traffic pattern is

A— 45° to the base leg just below traffic pattern altitude.
B— to enter 45° at the midpoint of the downwind leg at traffic pattern altitude.
C— to cross directly over the airport at traffic pattern altitude and join the downwind leg.

The recommended entry position for an airport traffic pattern is 45° to the midpoint of the downwind leg at traffic pattern altitude. (PLT150) — AIM ¶4-3-3

ALL
3807. (Refer to Figure 50.) The segmented circle indicates that the airport traffic is

A— left-hand for Runway 36 and right-hand for Runway 18.
B— left-hand for Runway 18 and right-hand for Runway 36.
C— right-hand for Runway 9 and left-hand for Runway 27.

The traffic pattern indicators on a segmented circle are used to indicate the direction of turns. The traffic pattern indicators, shown as extensions from the segmented circle, represent the base and final approach legs. (PLT039) — AIM ¶4-3-3

ALL, LSA, LSR, LSW, LSP
3808. (Refer to Figure 50.) The traffic patterns indicated in the segmented circle have been arranged to avoid flights over an area to the

A— south of the airport.
B— north of the airport.
C— southeast of the airport.

The segmented circle depicts the direction of landing for each airport; the long part of the "L" depicts the runway, and the short part depicts the airport traffic pattern for that runway. This figure indicates there are no flights that cross the southeast area of the airport. (PLT039) — AIM ¶4-3-3

Answers

3123 [C]	3123-1 [B]	3807 [A]	3808 [C]

ALL

3809. (Refer to Figure 50.) The segmented circle indicates that a landing on Runway 26 will be with a

A— right-quartering headwind.
B— left-quartering headwind.
C— right-quartering tailwind.

The large end of the wind cone (wind sock) points into the wind. The wind cone in FAA Figure 50 indicates a wind from the northwest. When landing on RWY 26, this would be a right quartering headwind. (PLT039) — AIM ¶4-3-3

ALL, SPO

3810. (Refer to Figure 50.) Which runway and traffic pattern should be used as indicated by the wind cone in the segmented circle?

A— Right-hand traffic on Runway 9.
B— Right-hand traffic on Runway 18.
C— Left-hand traffic on Runway 36.

The large end of the wind cone (wind sock) points into the wind. The wind cone in FAA Figure 50 indicates a wind from the northwest. Landing into the wind can be accomplished on either Runway 27 or Runway 36. The traffic pattern indicators require right traffic to Runway 27 and left traffic to Runway 36. (PLT039) — AIM ¶4-3-3

AIR, RTC, WSC, PPC

3719. VFR approaches to land at night should be accomplished

A— at a higher airspeed.
B— with a steeper descent.
C— the same as during daytime.

Inexperienced pilots often have a tendency to make approaches and landings at night with excessive airspeed. Every effort should be made to execute the approach and landing in the same manner as during the day. (PLT221) — FAA-H-8083-3

RTC, PPC

3122. Which is appropriate for a helicopter approaching an airport for landing?

A— Remain below the airplane traffic pattern altitude.
B— Avoid the flow of fixed-wing traffic.
C— Fly right-hand traffic.

Helicopters and powered parachutes must avoid the flow of fixed-wing aircraft. (PLT170) — 14 CFR §91.127, §91.129

SPO

2060. When approaching to land at an airport in Class G airspace that does not have light signals or other visual markings, an airplane pilot must make

A— a straight-in approach.
B— all turns to the right.
C— all turns to the left.

When approaching to land at an airport without an operating control tower in a Class G airspace area, each pilot of an airplane must make all turns of that airplane to the left unless the airport displays approved light signals or visual markings indicate otherwise. (PLT435) — 14 CFR §91.126

SPO

2194. When approaching to land at an airport, without an operating control tower, in Class G airspace, the pilot should

A— enter and fly a traffic pattern at 800 feet AGL.
B— make all turns to the left, unless otherwise indicated.
C— fly a left-hand traffic pattern at 800 feet AGL.

When approaching to land at an airport without an operating control tower in Class G airspace, each pilot of an airplane must make all turns to the left unless the airport displays approved light signals or visual markings indicating that turns should be made to the right. (PLT435) — 14 CFR §91.126

Answers (A) and (C) are incorrect because the traffic pattern altitude will vary for each airport and aircraft; however, all turns should be to the left unless otherwise indicated.

SPO

2002. Entries into traffic patterns while descending create specific collision hazards and

A— should be avoided.
B— should be used whenever possible.
C— are illegal.

Entries into traffic patterns while descending create specific collision hazards and should be avoided. (PLT170) — AIM ¶4-4-15

Answers

3809 [A]	3810 [C]	3719 [C]	3122 [B]	2060 [C]	2194 [B]
2002 [A]					

SPO

2007-1. Inbound to an airport with no tower, FSS, or UNICOM in operation, a pilot should self-announce on MULTICOM frequency

A— 123.0.

B— 122.9.

C— 122.7.

Where there is no tower, FSS, or UNICOM station on the airport, use MULTICOM frequency 122.9 for self-announce procedures. (PLT204) — AIM ¶4-1-9

SPO

2007-2. Inbound to an airport with no tower, FSS, or UNICOM in operation, a pilot should self-announce on MULTICOM frequency

A— 20 miles out.

B— 10 miles out.

C— 5 miles out.

Pilots of inbound traffic should monitor and communicate as appropriate on the designated frequency from 10 miles to landing. (PLT204) — AIM ¶4-1-9

SPO

2034-1. (Refer to Figure 20.) What is the recommended communications procedure for departure at Currituck County Airport (area 3)?

A— Broadcast intentions prior to taxi and announcing runway of departure.

B— Calling the Elizabeth City tower on 120.5.

C— Radio need not be used.

Pilots of departing aircraft should monitor/communicate on the appropriate frequency from start-up, during taxi, and until 10 miles from the airport unless regulations or local procedures require otherwise. (PLT435) — AIM ¶4-1-9

Answer (B) is incorrect because this is a nontowered airport; 120.5 is the CTAF. Answer (C) is incorrect because pilots should use the radio to announce intentions.

Airport Markings

Runway numbers and letters are determined from the approach direction. The number is the magnetic heading of the runway rounded to the nearest 10°. For example, an azimuth of 183° would result in a runway number of 18; a magnetic azimuth of 076° would result in a runway numbered 8. Runway letters differentiate between left (L), right (R), or center (C). *See* Figure 5-5.

The designated beginning of the runway that is available and suitable for the landing of aircraft is called the **threshold** (Figure 5-6a). A threshold that is not at the beginning of the full-strength runway pavement is a **displaced threshold**. The paved area behind the displaced threshold is marked by arrows (Figure 5-6b) and is available for taxiing, takeoff, and landing rollout, but is not to be used for landing, usually because of an obstruction in the approach path. *See* Figure 5-6.

Stopways are found extending beyond some usable runways. These areas are marked by chevrons, and while they appear usable, they are suitable only as overrun areas. *See* Figure 5-7.

A closed runway which is unusable and may be hazardous, even though it may appear usable, will be marked by an "X."

LAHSO is an acronym for "Land And Hold Short Operations." These operations include landing and holding short of an intersecting runway, an intersecting taxiway, or some other designated point on a runway other than an intersecting runway or taxiway. LAHSO is an air traffic control procedure that requires pilot participation to balance the needs for increased airport capacity and system efficiency, consistent with safety. Student pilots or pilots not familiar with LAHSO should not participate in the program. The pilot-in-command has the final authority to accept or decline any land and hold short clearance. The safety and operation of the aircraft remain the responsibility of the pilot. Pilots are expected to decline a

Answers

2007-1 [B]	2007-2 [B]	2034-1 [A]

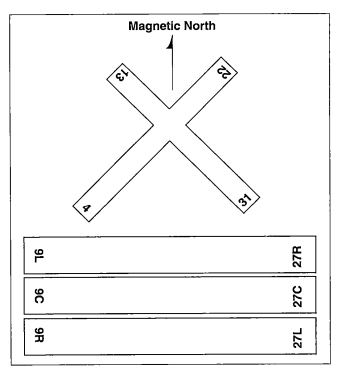

Figure 5-5. Runway numbers and letters

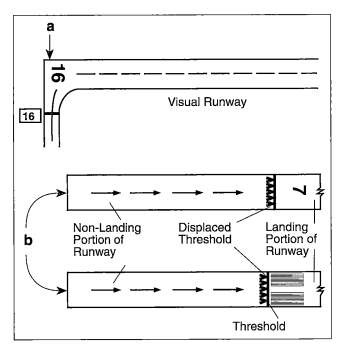

Figure 5-6. Threshold marking

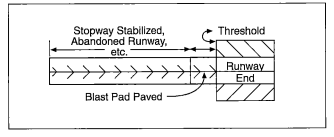

Figure 5-7. Stopway marking

LAHSO clearance if they determine it will compromise safety. Available Landing Distance (ALD) data are published in the special notices section of the Chart Supplements U.S. (previously Airport/Facility Directory, A/FD) and in the U.S. Terminal Procedures Publications. Pilots should only receive a LAHSO clearance when there is a minimum ceiling of 1,000 feet and 3 statute miles visibility. The intent of having "basic" VFR weather conditions is to allow pilots to maintain visual contact with other aircraft and ground vehicle operations.

Looking at FAA Figure 64 in the Computer Testing Supplement:

A is a surface painted runway marking

B is a stop bar/ILS hold

C is vehicle lanes

D is hold marking for land and hold short operations

E is taxiway/taxiway hold marking

F is taxiway edge marking (do not cross)

Looking at FAA Figure 65 in the Computer Testing Supplement:

A is a taxiway/runway hold position sign.

B is a runway approach hold position sign.

C is an ILS critical area hold position sign.

Continued

D is a no entry sign.

E is a taxiway location sign.

F is a runway location sign.

G is a runway safety area/obstacle free zone boundary.

H is an ILS critical area boundary.

I is an inbound destination sign.

J is an outbound destination sign.

K is a taxiway direction sign.

L is a runway distance remaining (in 1,000 foot increments).

M is a runway/runway hold position sign.

N is a taxiway ending marker.

A closed runway which is unusable and may be hazardous, even though it may appear usable, will be marked by an "X."

ALL
3778. The numbers 9 and 27 on a runway indicate that the runway is oriented approximately

A— 009° and 027° true.
B— 090° and 270° true.
C— 090° and 270° magnetic.

*The runway number is the whole number nearest one-tenth the **magnetic** azimuth of the centerline of the runway, measured clockwise from magnetic north. For example: 272° = RWY 27; 087° = RWY 9. (PLT141) — AIM ¶2-3-3*

SPO
2024. The numbers 35 and 17 on a runway indicate that the runway is oriented approximately

A— 035°; and 017°; magnetic heading.
B— 350°; and 170°; magnetic heading.
C— 350°; and 170°; true heading.

The runway number is the whole number nearest one-tenth the magnetic azimuth of the centerline of the runway, measured clockwise from magnetic north. For example: 352° = RWY 35; 172° = RWY 17. (PLT141) — AIM ¶2-3-3

Answer (A) is incorrect because runway numbers drop the last digit from the heading. Answer (C) is incorrect because runway numbers are based on magnetic direction.

ALL
3778-1. The numbers 8 and 26 on the approach ends of the runway indicate that the runway is orientated approximately

A— 008° and 026° true.
B— 080° and 260° true.
C— 080° and 260° magnetic.

The runway number is the whole number nearest one-tenth the magnetic azimuth of the centerline of the runway, measured clockwise from magnetic north. (PLT141) — AIM ¶2-3-3

ALL
3778-2. When turning onto a taxiway from another taxiway, what is the purpose of the taxiway directional sign?

A— Indicates direction to take-off runway.
B— Indicates designation and direction of exit taxiway from runway.
C— Indicates designation and direction of taxiway leading out of an intersection.

The taxiway directional sign identifies the designation(s) of the intersecting taxiway(s) leading out of the intersection that a pilot would normally be expected to turn onto or hold short of. (PLT141) — AIM ¶2-3-10

Answer (A) is incorrect because this is the purpose of the runway location sign. Answer (B) is incorrect because this is the purpose of the destination sign.

Answers

| 3778 | [C] | 2024 | [B] | 3778-1 | [C] | 3778-2 | [C] |

ALL, SPO

3778-3. (Refer to Figure 64.) Which symbol indicates a taxiway/taxiway intersection hold position marking?

A— B.
B— D.
C— E.

Symbol "E" indicates a taxiway/taxiway hold marking. (PLT141) — AIM ¶2-3-4

Answer (A) is incorrect because "B" is a stop bar/ILS hold marking. Answer (B) is incorrect because "D" is a hold marking for land and hold short operations.

ALL, SPO

3778-4. (See Figure 64.) Which marking indicates a vehicle lane?

A— A.
B— C.
C— E.

The vehicle roadway markings are used when necessary to define a pathway for vehicle operations on or crossing areas that are also intended for aircraft. These markings consist of a white solid line to delineate each edge of the roadway and a dashed line to separate lanes within the edges of the roadway. In lieu of the solid lines, zipper markings may be used to delineate the edges of the vehicle roadway. (PLT141) — AIM ¶2-3-6

ALL

3778-5. The "yellow demarcation bar" marking indicates

A— runway with a displaced threshold that precedes the runway.
B— a hold line from a taxiway to a runway.
C— the beginning of available runway for landing on the approach side.

A demarcation bar delineates a runway with a displaced threshold from a blast pad, stopway or taxiway that precedes the runway. A demarcation bar is 3 feet (1 m) wide and yellow, since it is not located on the runway. (PLT141) — AIM ¶2-3-3

ALL

3957. (Refer to the Runway Incursion Figure.) You have requested taxi instructions for takeoff using Runway 16. The controller issues the following taxi instructions: "N123, Taxi to runway 16." Where are you required to stop in order to be in compliance with the controller's insructions?

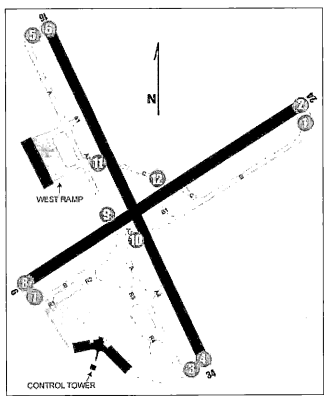

Runway Incursion

A— 5 (Five).
B— 6 (Six).
C— 9 (Nine).

When ATC clears an aircraft to "taxi to" an assigned takeoff runway, the absence of holding instructions does not authorize the aircraft to "cross" all runways which the taxi route intersects except the assigned takeoff runway. A clearance must be obtained prior to crossing any runway. It does not include authorization to "taxi onto" or "cross" the assigned takeoff runway at any point. You should taxi and hold short of runway 16, which is position 5. (PLT3957) — AIM ¶4-3-18

Answer (B) is incorrect because "taxi to" does not authorize the aircraft to "taxi onto" the assigned takeoff runway. Answer (C) is incorrect because the airplane should taxi the most direct route to the assigned runway unless instructed otherwise; position 9 would not be encountered for the airplane at the west ramp to taxi to runway 16.

Answers

3778-3   [C]   3778-4   [B]   3778-5   [A]   3957   [A]

ALL
3951. Who should not participate in the Land and Hold Short Operations (LAHSO) program?

A— Recreational pilots only.
B— Military pilots.
C— Student pilots.

Student pilots or pilots not familiar with LAHSO should not participate in the program. (PLT140) — AIM ¶4-3-11

ALL
3952. Who has final authority to accept or decline any land and hold short (LAHSO) clearance?

A— Pilot-in-command.
B— Air traffic controller.
C— Second-in-command.

The pilot-in-command has the final authority to accept or decline any land and hold short clearance. The safety and operation of the aircraft remain the responsibility of the pilot. (PLT444) — AIM ¶4-3-11

ALL
3953. When should pilots decline a land and hold short (LAHSO) clearance?

A— When it will compromise safety.
B— Only when the tower operator concurs.
C— Pilots can not decline clearance.

Pilots are expected to decline a LAHSO clearance if they determine it will compromise safety. (PLT140) — AIM ¶4-3-11

ALL
3954. Where is the "Available Landing Distance" (ALD) data published for an airport that utilizes Land and Hold Short Operations (LAHSO)?

A— Special Notices Section of the Chart Supplement U.S. (formerly Airport/Facility Directory or A/FD).
B— 14 CFR Part 91, General Operating and Flight Rules.
C— Aeronautical Information Manual (AIM).

ALD data are published in the special notices section of the Chart Supplements U.S. and in the U.S. Terminal Procedures Publications. (PLT140) — AIM ¶4-3-11

ALL
3955. What is the minimum visibility for a pilot to receive a land and hold short (LAHSO) clearance?

A— 3 nautical miles.
B— 3 statute miles.
C— 1 statute mile.

Pilots should only receive a LAHSO clearance when there is a minimum ceiling of 1,000 feet and 3 statute miles visibility. The intent of having "basic" VFR weather conditions is to allow pilots to maintain visual contact with other aircraft and ground vehicle operations. (PLT141) — AIM ¶4-3-11

ALL
3955-1. When approaching taxiway holding lines from the side with the continuous lines, the pilot

A— may continue taxiing.
B— should not cross the lines without ATC clearance.
C— should continue taxiing until all parts of the aircraft have crossed the lines.

When approaching the holding line from the side with the continuous lines, a pilot should not cross the holding line without ATC clearance at a controlled airport, or without making sure of adequate separation from other aircraft at uncontrolled airports. (PLT141) — AIM ¶2-3-5

Answers (A) and (C) are incorrect because no part of the aircraft may cross the hold line without ATC clearance.

ALL, SPO
3955-2. What is the purpose of the runway/runway hold position sign?

A— Denotes entrance to runway from a taxiway.
B— Denotes area protected for an aircraft approaching or departing a runway.
C— Denotes intersecting runways.

Mandatory instruction signs are used to denote an entrance to a runway or critical area and areas where an aircraft is prohibited from entering. The runway holding position sign is located at the holding position on taxiways that intersect a runway or on runways that intersect other runways. (PLT141) — AIM ¶2-3-8

Answers

| 3951 | [C] | 3952 | [A] | 3953 | [A] | 3954 | [A] | 3955 | [B] | 3955-1 | [B] |
| 3955-2 | [C] | | | | | | | | | | |

SPO
2026. The 'runway hold position' sign denotes

A— an entrance to a runway from a taxiway.
B— an area protected for an aircraft approaching a runway.
C— an entrance to a taxiway from a runway.

Mandatory instruction signs are used to denote an entrance to a runway or critical area and areas where an aircraft is prohibited from entering. The runway holding position sign is located at the holding position on taxiways that intersect a runway or on runways that intersect other runways. (PLT141) — AIM ¶2-3-8

SPO
2028. What is the purpose for the runway hold position markings on the taxiway?

A— Holds aircraft short of the runway.
B— Allows an aircraft permission onto the runway.
C— Identifies area where aircraft are prohibited.

Runway holding position markings on taxiways identify the locations on a taxiway where an aircraft is supposed to stop when it does not have clearance to proceed onto the runway. (PLT141) — AIM ¶2-3-5

SPO
2030. Holding position signs have

A— red inscriptions on white background.
B— white inscriptions on red background.
C— yellow inscriptions on red background.

Hold position signs have white inscriptions on red background. (PLT141) — AIM ¶2-3-5

Answers (A) and (C) are incorrect because these color combination are not used in airport signs.

SPO
2031. 'Runway hold position' markings on the taxiway

A— identifies where aircraft hold short of the runway.
B— identifies an area where aircraft are prohibited.
C— allows an aircraft permission onto the runway.

Runway holding position markings on taxiways identify the locations on a taxiway where an aircraft is supposed to stop when it does not have clearance to proceed onto the runway. (PLT141) — AIM ¶2-3-5

ALL
3955-3. What does the outbound destination sign identify?

A— Identifies entrance to the runway from a taxiway.
B— Identifies direction to take-off runways.
C— Identifies runway on which an aircraft is located.

Outbound destination signs provide information for locating the departure runway. (PLT141) — AIM ¶2-3-11

Answer (A) is incorrect because this is a runway marking. Answer (C) is incorrect because this is a runway location sign.

ALL, SPO
3955-4. What is the purpose of the No Entry sign?

A— Identifies a paved area where aircraft are prohibited from entering.
B— Identifies area that does not continue beyond intersection.
C— Identifies the exit boundary for the runway protected area.

The no entry sign prohibits an aircraft from entering an area. Typically, this sign would be located on a taxiway intended to be used in only one direction or at the intersection of vehicle roadways with runways, taxiways or aprons where the roadway may be mistaken as a taxiway or other aircraft movement surface. (PLT141) — AIM ¶2-3-8

Answer (B) is incorrect because this is the purpose of a hold position sign. Answer (C) is incorrect because this is the purpose of the runway boundary sign.

ALL
3955-5. (Refer to Figure 65.) Which airport marking is a runway safety area/obstacle free zone boundary?

A— G.
B— H.
C— N.

The runway boundary sign has a yellow background and a black inscription, with a graphic that depicts the pavement holding-position marking. This sign, which faces the runway and is visible to the pilot exiting the runway, is located adjacent to the holding-position marking on the pavement. The sign is intended to provide pilots with another visual cue they can use as a guide in deciding when they are "clear of the runway." (PLT141) — AIM ¶2-3-9

Answer (B) is incorrect because this is an ILS critical area boundary sign. Answer (C) is incorrect because this is a taxiway-ending marker.

Answers

2026 [A]	2028 [A]	2030 [B]	2031 [A]	3955-3 [B]	3955-4 [A]
3955-5 [A]					

SPO
2025. 'Runway hold position' markings on the taxiway

A— identify areas where aircraft are prohibited.
B— identify where aircraft hold short of the runway.
C— allow an aircraft permission onto the runway.

Runway holding position markings on taxiways identify the locations on a taxiway where an aircraft is supposed to stop when it does not have clearance to proceed onto the runway. (PLT141) — AIM ¶2-3-5

ALL, SPO
3773. (Refer to Figure 48.) That portion of the runway identified by the letter A may be used for

A— landing.
B— taxiing and takeoff.
C— taxiing and landing.

Thresholds are marked at the beginning of a full-strength runway surface able to endure landing impacts or at a point on the runway which will encourage pilots to avoid short approaches due to hidden noise or obstacle problems. Area A of FAA Figure 48 is marked with arrows which point towards a displaced threshold. Thus, the paved surface prior to the threshold is available for taxi, takeoff and landing rollout, but not for touchdown. (PLT077) — AIM ¶2-3-3

ALL
3774. (Refer to Figure 48.) According to the airport diagram, which statement is true?

A— Runway 30 is equipped at position E with emergency arresting gear to provide a means of stopping military aircraft.
B— Takeoffs may be started at position A on Runway 12, and the landing portion of this runway begins at position B.
C— The takeoff and landing portion of Runway 30 begins at position E.

Thresholds are marked at the beginning of a full-strength runway surface able to endure landing impacts or at a point on the runway which will encourage pilots to avoid short approaches due to hidden noise or obstacle problems. Area A of FAA Figure 48 is marked with arrows which point towards a displaced threshold. Thus, the paved surface prior to the threshold is available for taxi, takeoff and landing rollout, but not for touchdown. (PLT077) — AIM ¶2-3-3

ALL
3776. (Refer to Figure 48.) Area C on the airport depicted is classified as a

A— stabilized area.
B— multiple heliport.
C— closed runway.

An "X" painted on the end of runway means it is closed. (PLT077) — AIM ¶2-3-3

ALL, SPO
3777. (Refer to Figure 49.) The arrows that appear on the end of the north/south runway indicate that the area

A— may be used only for taxiing.
B— is usable for taxiing, takeoff, and landing.
C— cannot be used for landing, but may be used for taxiing and takeoff.

The paved area behind the displaced runway threshold is available for taxiing, landing rollout, and the takeoff of aircraft. (PLT141) — AIM ¶2-3-3

SPO
2206. Which publication contains an explanation of airport signs and markings?

A— Aeronautical Information Manual (AIM).
B— Advisory Circulars (AC).
C— Chart Supplements U.S. (formerly A/FD).

Both the Aeronautical Information Manual *(AIM) and the* Pilot's Handbook of Aeronautical Knowledge *(FAA-H-8083-25) contain explanations of airport signs and markings. (PLT141) — AIM Chapter 2, Section 3*

Answer (B) is incorrect because ACs provide information on non-regulatory material of interest. Answer (C) is incorrect because the Chart Supplements U.S. (formerly A/FD) provide only comprehensive information on a given airport (such as runway lengths, available services, lighting, etc.).

Answers

2025 [B]	3773 [B]	3774 [B]	3776 [C]	3777 [C]	2206 [A]

ALL

3805. (Refer to Figure 49.) Select the proper traffic pattern and runway for landing.

A— Left-hand traffic and Runway 18.
B— Right-hand traffic and Runway 18.
C— Left-hand traffic and Runway 22.

The small end of the tetrahedron points into the wind, indicating the direction of landing. The wind is coming from the southwest. However, the runway most nearly aligned into the wind is closed (X), leaving RWY 18 as the most suitable runway. The traffic pattern indicators on a segmented circle are used to indicate the direction of turns. The traffic pattern indicators, shown as extensions from the segmented circle, represent the base and final approach legs. The traffic pattern indicator shows right traffic for RWY 18. (PLT039) — AIM ¶4-3-4

ALL, SPO

3806. (Refer to Figure 49.) If the wind is as shown by the landing direction indicator, the pilot should land on

A— Runway 18 and expect a crosswind from the right.
B— Runway 22 directly into the wind.
C— Runway 36 and expect a crosswind from the right.

The small end of the tetrahedron points into the wind indicating the direction of landing. Landing to the south on RWY 18, the pilot could expect a right crosswind. (PLT077) — AIM ¶4-3-3

SPO

2029. (Refer to Figure 65) Which sign indicates the runway on which the aircraft is located?

A— E
B— F
C— L

"F" is a runway location sign, which identifies the runway on which the aircraft is located. (PLT141) — AIM ¶2-3-9

Answer (A) is incorrect because E is a taxiway location sign, which identifies the taxiway on which the aircraft is located. Answer (C) is incorrect because this is a runway distance remaining sign, which identifies the runway length remaining.

SPO

2218. The "taxiway ending" marker

A— indicates taxiway does not continue.
B— identifies area where aircraft are prohibited.
C— provides general taxiing direction to named taxiway.

Taxiway ending markers are used to indicate that the taxiway does not continue. (PLT141) — AIM ¶2-3-4

Answers

3805 [B]	3806 [A]	2029 [B]	2218 [A]

Airport Lighting

At night, the location of an airport can be determined by the presence of an airport **rotating beacon** light. The colors and color combinations that denote the type of airports are:

White and green .... Lighted land airport

*Green alone .... Lighted land airport

White and yellow .... Lighted water airport

*Yellow alone .... Lighted water airport

Green, yellow, white .... Lighted heliport

*Note: Green alone or amber alone is used only in connection with a white-and-green or white-and-amber beacon display, respectively.

A civil-lighted land airport beacon will show alternating white and green flashes. A military airfield will be identified by dual-peaked (two quick) white flashes between green flashes.

In Class B, C, D, or E airspace, operation of the airport beacon during the hours of daylight often indicates the ceiling is less than 1,000 feet and/or the visibility is less than 3 miles. However, pilots should not rely solely on the operation of the airport beacon to indicate if weather conditions are IFR or VFR.

Runway edge lights are used to outline the runway at night or during periods of low visibility. For the most part, runway edge lights are white, and may be high-, medium-, or low-intensity, while taxiways are outlined by blue omnidirectional lights.

Radio control of lighting is available at some airports, providing airborne control of lights by keying the aircraft's microphone. The control system is responsive to 7, 5, or 3 microphone clicks. Keying the microphone 7 times within 5 seconds will turn the lighting to its highest intensity; 5 times in 5 seconds will set the lights to medium intensity; low intensity is set by keying 3 times in 5 seconds.

ALL, SPO
3769. An airport's rotating beacon operated during daylight hours indicates

A— there are obstructions on the airport.
B— that weather at the airport located in Class D airspace is below basic VFR weather minimums.
C— the Air Traffic Control tower is not in operation.

In Class B, C, D or E airspace, operation of the airport beacon during the hours of daylight often indicates that the weather in the airspace is below basic VFR weather minimums (ground visibility is less than 3 miles and/or the ceiling is less than 1,000 feet). (PLT141) — AIM ¶2-1-9

AIR, RTC, WSC, PPC
3718. Airport taxiway edge lights are identified at night by

A— white directional lights.
B— blue omnidirectional lights.
C— alternate red and green lights.

A taxiway-edge lighting system consists of omnidirectional blue lights which outline the usable limits of taxi paths. (PLT141) — FAA-H-8083-3

Answers
3769 [B]   3718 [B]

AIR, RTC, WSC, PPC
3768. To set the high intensity runway lights on medium intensity, the pilot should click the microphone seven times, and then click it

A— one time within four seconds.
B— three times within three seconds.
C— five times within five seconds.

To save money at low-usage airports, pilot-controlled lighting is installed. Key the mike seven times to set the highest level, then adjust to medium with five clicks. (PLT462) — AIM ¶2-1-8

AIR, RTC, LTA, WSC, PPC
3770. A lighted heliport may be identified by a

A— green, yellow, and white rotating beacon.
B— flashing yellow light.
C— blue lighted square landing area.

A lighted heliport has a green, yellow and white beacon flashing 30 to 60 times per minute. A flashing yellow light identifies a lighted water port. (PLT141) — AIM ¶2-1-9

AIR, RTC, LTA, WSC, PPC
3771. A military air station can be identified by a rotating beacon that emits

A— white and green alternating flashes.
B— two quick, white flashes between green flashes.
C— green, yellow, and white flashes.

Military airport beacons flash alternately white and green, but are differentiated from civil beacons by dual-peaked (two quick) white flashes between the green flashes. (PLT141) — AIM ¶2-1-9

AIR, RTC, LTA, WSC, PPC
3772. How can a military airport be identified at night?

A— Alternate white and green light flashes.
B— Dual peaked (two quick) white flashes between green flashes.
C— White flashing lights with steady green at the same location.

Military airport beacons flash alternately white and green, but are differentiated from civil beacons by dual-peaked (two quick) white flashes between the green flashes. (PLT141) — AIM ¶2-1-9

Visual Approach Slope Indicator (VASI)

The **Visual Approach Slope Indicator (VASI)** is a lighting system arranged so as to provide visual-descent guidance information during approach to a runway. The lights are visible for up to 5 miles during the day. The VASI glide path provides obstruction clearance, while lateral guidance is provided by the runway or runway lights. When operating to an airport with an operating control tower, the pilot of an airplane approaching to land on a runway served by a VASI is required to maintain an altitude at or above the glide slope until a lower altitude is necessary for landing.

Most VASI installations consist of two bars, near and far, which provide one visual glide path. On final approach flying toward the runway of intended landing, if the pilot sees both bars as red, the aircraft is below the glide path (Figure 5-8A). Maintaining altitude, the pilot will see the near bar turn pink and then white, while the far bar remains red, indicating the glide path is being intercepted (Figure 5-8B). If the aircraft is above the glide path, the pilot will see both near and far bars as white (Figure 5-8C).

Pulsating VASIs normally consist of a single light unit projecting a two-color visual approach path. The below-glide path indication is normally

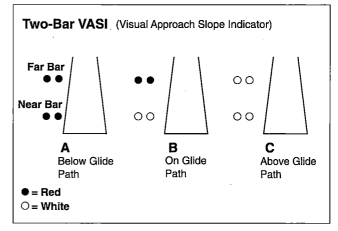

Figure 5-8. A 2-bar VASI

red or pulsating red, and the above-glide path indication is normally pulsating white. The on-glide path indication is usually steady white. *See* Figure 5-9.

The **Precision Approach Path Indicator (PAPI)** uses a single row of lights. Four white lights means "too high." One red light and three white lights means "slightly high," etc. *See* Figure 5-10.

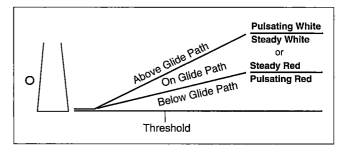

Figure 5-9. Pulsating VASI system

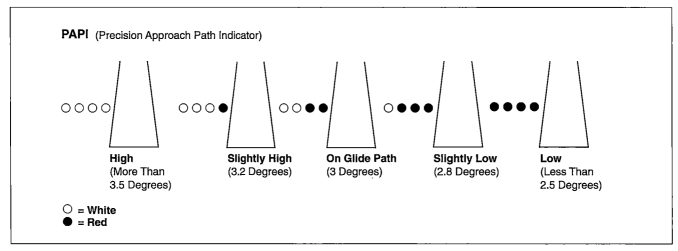

Figure 5-10. Precision approach path indicator (PAPI)

ALL

3762-1. Which approach and landing objective is assured when the pilot remains on the proper glidepath of the VASI?

A— Runway identification and course guidance.
B— Safe obstruction clearance in the approach area.
C— Lateral course guidance to the runway.

The VASI is a system of lights arranged to provide visual descent guidance information during the approach to a runway. These lights are visible from 3 to 5 miles during the day, and up to 20 miles or more at night. The visual glidepath of the VASI provides safe obstruction clearance within ±10° of the extended runway centerline, and to 4 NM from the runway threshold. (PLT147) — AIM ¶2-1-2

ALL, SPO

3764. A below glide slope indication from a pulsating approach slope indicator is a

A— pulsating white light.
B— steady white light.
C— pulsating red light.

Pulsating visual approach slope indicators normally consist of a single light unit projecting a two-color visual approach path. The below-glide path indication is red or pulsating red. The on-glide path indication is a steady white light for one type of system, while for another system it is an alternating red and white light. (PLT147) — AIM ¶2-1-2

Answers

3762-1   [B]   3764   [C]

ALL

3120. While operating in Class D airspace, each pilot of an aircraft approaching to land on a runway served by a visual approach slope indicator (VASI) shall

A— maintain a 3° glide until approximately 1/2 mile to the runway before going below the VASI.
B— maintain an altitude at or above the glide slope until a lower altitude is necessary for a safe landing.
C— stay high until the runway can be reached in a power-off landing.

An airplane approaching to land on a runway served by a visual approach indicator, shall maintain an altitude at or above the glide slope until a lower altitude is necessary for a safe landing. (PLT170) — 14 CFR §91.129

ALL

3121. When approaching to land on a runway served by a visual approach slope indicator (VASI), the pilot shall

A— maintain an altitude that captures the glide slope at least 2 miles downwind from the runway threshold.
B— maintain an altitude at or above the glide slope.
C— remain on the glide slope and land between the two-light bar.

An airplane approaching to land on a runway served by a visual approach indicator, shall maintain an altitude at or above the glide slope until a lower altitude is necessary for a safe landing. (PLT147) — 14 CFR §91.129

ALL

3760. A slightly high glide slope indication from a precision approach path indicator is

A— four white lights.
B— three white lights and one red light.
C— two white lights and two red lights.

The precision approach path indicator (PAPI) uses light units similar to the VASI but are installed in a single row of either two or four light units. Four white lights means you are above the glide slope, three white lights and one red light means you are slightly high, two red and two white lights means you are on the glide slope, three reds and one white light means you are slightly low and four red lights means you are below the glide slope. (PLT147) — AIM ¶2-1-2

ALL

3765. (Refer to Figure 47.) Illustration A indicates that the aircraft is

A— below the glide slope.
B— on the glide slope.
C— above the glide slope.

The two-bar VASI on-glide slope indication is red over white lights. (PLT147) — AIM ¶2-1-2

ALL

3766. (Refer to Figure 47.) VASI lights as shown by illustration C indicate that the airplane is

A— off course to the left.
B— above the glide slope.
C— below the glide slope.

The two-bar VASI above-glide slope indication is white over white lights. VASI lights do not give horizontal direction. (PLT147) — AIM ¶2-1-2

ALL, LSA, LSR, LSW, LSP

3767. (Refer to Figure 47.) While on final approach to a runway equipped with a standard 2-bar VASI, the lights appear as shown by illustration D. This means that the aircraft is

A— above the glide slope.
B— below the glide slope.
C— on the glide slope.

The below-glide slope indication from a two-bar VASI is red over red lights. (PLT147) — AIM ¶2-1-2

Answers

| 3120 | [B] | 3121 | [B] | 3760 | [B] | 3765 | [B] | 3766 | [B] | 3767 | [B] |

Surface Operations

Taxiing to or from the runway generally presents no problems during calm or light wind conditions. However, when taxiing in moderate to strong wind conditions, the airplane's control surfaces must be used to counteract the effects of wind. In airplanes equipped with a nose wheel (tricycle-gear), use the following taxi procedures:

1. The elevator should be in the neutral position when taxiing into a headwind.

2. The upwind aileron should be held in the up position when taxiing in a crosswind, (or the upwind wing will tend to be lifted).

3. The elevator should be held in the down position and the upwind aileron down when taxiing with a quartering tailwind (the most critical condition for a nosewheel-type airplane). See Figure 5-11.

   When an airplane equipped with a tailwheel is taxied into a headwind, the elevator should be held in the up position to hold the tail down. In a quartering tailwind, both the upwind aileron and the elevator should be in the down position.

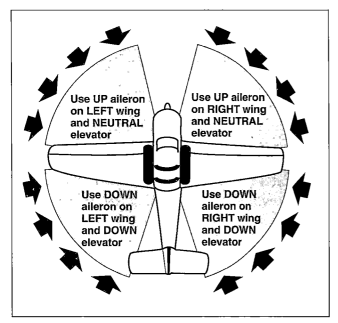

Figure 5-11. Control position while taxiing

AIR, REC, LSA

3302. When taxiing with strong quartering tailwinds, which aileron positions should be used?

A— Aileron down on the downwind side.
B— Ailerons neutral.
C— Aileron down on the side from which the wind is blowing.

Taxiing with a quartering tailwind provides the most hazardous conditions. In this case, the elevator should be in the down position and the aileron on the upwind side should also be in the down position to keep the wing from lifting. (PLT486) — FAA-H-8083-3

AIR, REC

3303. Which aileron positions should a pilot generally use when taxiing in strong quartering headwinds?

A— Aileron up on the side from which the wind is blowing.
B— Aileron down on the side from which the wind is blowing.
C— Ailerons neutral.

When taxiing a nosewheel aircraft in the presence of moderate to strong winds, extra caution should be taken. For a quartering headwind, the elevator should be held in the neutral position, and the aileron on the upwind side should be in the up position. (PLT486) — FAA-H-8083-3

Answers

3302 [C]   3303 [A]

AIR, REC
3304. Which wind condition would be most critical when taxiing a nosewheel equipped high-wing airplane?

A— Quartering tailwind.
B— Direct crosswind.
C— Quartering headwind.

When taxiing a nosewheel aircraft in the presence of moderate to strong winds, extra caution should be taken. Taxiing with a quartering tailwind produces the most hazardous conditions. (PLT486) — FAA-H-8083-3

AIR, REC
3305. (Refer to Figure 9, area A.) How should the flight controls be held while taxiing a tricycle-gear equipped airplane into a left quartering headwind?

A— Left aileron up, elevator neutral.
B— Left aileron down, elevator neutral.
C— Left aileron up, elevator down.

When taxiing a nosewheel aircraft in the presence of moderate to strong winds, extra caution should be taken. For a quartering headwind, the elevator should be held in the neutral position, and the aileron on the upwind side should be in the up position. (PLT112) — FAA-H-8083-3

AIR, REC
3306. (Refer to Figure 9, area B.) How should the flight controls be held while taxiing a tailwheel airplane into a right quartering headwind?

A— Right aileron up, elevator up.
B— Right aileron down, elevator neutral.
C— Right aileron up, elevator down.

When taxiing a tailwheel airplane with a quartering headwind, the aileron on the upwind side should be up, and the elevator held in the up position to hold the tail down. (PLT112) — FAA-H-8083-3

AIR, REC
3307. (Refer to Figure 9, area C.) How should the flight controls be held while taxiing a tailwheel airplane with a left quartering tailwind?

A— Left aileron up, elevator neutral.
B— Left aileron down, elevator neutral.
C— Left aileron down, elevator down.

When taxiing a tailwheel aircraft with a quartering tailwind, the upwind aileron should be down to keep that wing from lifting, and the elevator should also be down. (PLT112) — FAA-H-8083-3

AIR, REC
3308. (Refer to Figure 9, area C.) How should the flight controls be held while taxiing a tricycle-gear equipped airplane with a left quartering tailwind?

A— Left aileron up, elevator neutral.
B— Left aileron down, elevator down.
C— Left aileron up, elevator down.

Taxiing with a quartering tailwind produces the most hazardous conditions. In this case, the elevator should be in the down position, and the aileron on the upwind side should also be in the down position to keep the wing from lifting. (PLT112) — FAA-H-8083-3

AIR, GLI, REC
3308-1. To minimize the side loads placed on the landing gear during touchdown, the pilot should keep the

A— direction of motion of the aircraft parallel to the runway.
B— longitudinal axis of the aircraft parallel to the direction of its motion.
C— downwind wing lowered sufficiently to eliminate the tendency for the aircraft to drift.

It is extremely important that the touchdown occur with the airplane's longitudinal axis exactly parallel to the direction in which the airplane is moving along the runway. Failure to accomplish this imposes severe side loads on the landing gear. To avoid these side stresses, the pilot should not allow the airplane to touch down while turned into the wind or drifting. (PLT170) — FAA-H-8083-3

Answer (A) is incorrect because moving alongside the runway is not sufficient to reduce or eliminate side loads on the landing gear; the aircraft must be heading straight down the runway. Answer (C) is incorrect because this describes what happens on final approach, but the aircraft must be heading straight before it touches down.

Answers

| 3304 [A] | 3305 [A] | 3306 [A] | 3307 [C] | 3308 [B] | 3308-1 [B] |

LSR
2328. Select the true statement concerning gyroplane taxi procedures.

A— Taxi speed should be limited to no faster than a brisk walk in ideal conditions.
B— The cyclic stick should be held in the neutral position at all times.
C— The cyclic stick should be held slightly aft of neutral at all times.

A gyroplane should not be taxied in close proximity to people or obstructions while the rotor is turning. In addition, taxi speed should be limited to no faster than a brisk walk in ideal conditions, and adjusted appropriately according to the circumstances. (PLT149) — FAA-H-8083-21

LSR
2331. Select the true statement concerning gyroplane taxi procedures.

A— Avoid abrupt control movements when blades are turning.
B— The cyclic stick should be held in the neutral position at all times.
C— The cyclic stick should be held slightly aft of neutral at all times.

A gyroplane should not be taxied in close proximity to people or obstructions while the rotor is turning. In addition, taxi speed should be limited to no faster than a brisk walk in ideal conditions, and adjusted appropriately according to the circumstances. Avoid abrupt control motions while taxiing. (PLT149) — FAA-H-8083-21

LSR
2332. During the transition from pre-rotation to flight, all rotor blades change pitch

A— simultaneously to the same angle of incidence.
B— simultaneously but to different angles of incidence.
C— in sequence to the same angle of incidence.

Compensation for dissymmetry of lift requires constant change in the blade angle of incidence, with one increasing as another simultaneously decreases. During the transition from prerotation to flight (or any time there is dissymmetry of lift) all rotor blades change pitch simultaneously, but to different angles of incidence. (PLT260) — FAA-H-8083-21

RTC
3339. What precaution should be taken while taxiing a gyroplane?

A— The cyclic stick should be held in the neutral position at all times.
B— Avoid abrupt control movements when blades are turning.
C— The cyclic stick should be held slightly aft of neutral at all times.

Avoid abrupt control motions while taxiing. (PLT170) — FAA-H-8083-21

Answers

| 2328 | [A] | 2331 | [A] | 2332 | [B] | 3339 | [B] |

Chart Supplements U.S. (previously A/FD)

The Chart Supplements U.S. (formerly Airport/Facility Directory or A/FD) is a publication designed primarily as a pilot's operational manual containing all airports, seaplane bases, and heliports open to the public including communications data, navigational facilities, and certain special notices and procedures. Directories are reissued in their entirety each 56 days.

Because of the wealth of information provided, an extensive legend is required for the Chart Supplements Airport/Facility section. *See* FAA Legends 2–19.

ALL, SPO
3619. (Refer to Figure 71, area 4 and Legend 1.) For information about the parachute jumping operations at Lincoln Regional/Harder (LHM) Airport, refer to

A— notes on the border of the chart.
B— the Chart Supplements U.S.
C— the Notices to Airmen (NOTAM) publication.

Tabulations of parachute jump areas in the U.S. are contained in the Chart Supplements U.S. (formerly Airport/Facility Directory or A/FD). (PLT064) — AIM ¶3-5-4

ALL
3619-1. Information concerning parachute jumping sites may be found in the

A— NOTAMs.
B— Chart Supplements U.S.
C— Graphic Notices and Supplemental Data.

Tabulations of parachute jump areas in the U.S. are contained in the Chart Supplements U.S. (formerly Airport/Facility Directory or A/FD). (PLT281) — AIM ¶3-5-4

ALL
3841. (Refer to Figure 52.) Where is Loup City Municipal located with relation to the city?

A— Northeast approximately 3 miles.
B— Northwest approximately 1 mile.
C— East approximately 7 miles.

Airport location is expressed as distance and direction from the center of the associated city in NM and cardinal points. The first item in parentheses is the airport identifier and the second item is the relation from the city. In this case, "1 NW." (PLT078) — Chart Supplements U.S. Legend

ALL
3842. (Refer to Figure 52.) Traffic patterns in effect at Lincoln Municipal are

A— to the right on Runway 18 and Runway 36.
B— to the right on Runway 18 and Runway 35; to the left on Runway 36.
C— to the right on Runways 14 – 32.

Traffic is to the left unless otherwise stated in the Chart Supplements U.S. (formerly A/FD) as "Rgt tfc." (PLT078) — Chart Supplements U.S. Legend

ALL, SPO
3513. (Refer to Figure 63.) What is the length of the displaced threshold for runway 22 at Toledo (TDZ)?

A— 25 feet.
B— 100 feet.
C— 380 feet.

The Chart Supplements U.S. for Toledo Executive (TDZ) shows a displaced threshold (Thld dsplcd) of 380 feet for runway 22. (PLT078) – Chart Supplements U.S. Legend

Answer (A) is incorrect because 25 feet is the touchdown zone height for runway 22. Answer (B) is incorrect because 100 feet is the displaced threshold for runway 4.

ALL
3838-1. (Refer to Figures 76 and 77.) Inbound to Pierre Regional (PIR) from the South-West, with wind 240 at 12 knots, expect to make

A — left traffic for runway 25.
B — right traffic for runway 25.
C — left traffic for runway 07.

Unless otherwise noted in the Chart Supplements U.S. airport traffic patterns are left traffic for the stated runway. Wind is 240 at 12 knots resulting in a landing into the wind on runway 25. (PLT078) – 14 CFR 91.127, Chart Supplements U.S. Legend

Answer (B) is incorrect because the Chart Supplements U.S. does not list or specify right traffic for runway 25. Answer (C) is incorrect because landing on runway 07 would result in a significant tailwind landing.

Answers

3619 [B]	3619-1 [B]	3841 [B]	3842 [B]	3513 [C]	3838-1 [A]

ALL

3841-1. (Refer to Figure 78, 79 and Legend 3.) Where in relation to the airfield is the airport beacon located for Sioux City (SUX) airport?

A — West of runway 17-35.

B — East of runway 17-35.

C — Approach end of runway 31.

Using Legend 3, you can determine that an airport beacon is depicted by a star feature. In both Figure 78 and on the airport diagram of Figure 79, locate the star feature on the east side of the airport or east of runway 17-35. (PLT064) – Chart Supplements U.S. Legend

AIR, RTC, WSC, PPC

3838. (Refer to Figure 52.) When approaching Lincoln Municipal from the west at noon for the purpose of landing, initial communications should be with

A— Lincoln Approach Control on 124.0 MHz.

B— Minneapolis Center on 128.75 MHz.

C— Lincoln Tower on 118.5 MHz.

Arriving aircraft landing at airports within Class C airspace should contact Approach Control from outside the Class C airspace on the specified frequency.

1. *Figure 52 shows UTC-6(-5DT). This means that local time is 6 hours behind UTC time, and 5 hours behind during daylight saving time. In order to convert local time to UTC time, add this difference to local time:*

    1200 *local*
    + 0600 *UTC conversion*
    ────────────────
    1800 *Z*

    Lincoln Muni approach should be contacted since its hours of operation are 1130 – 0630Z.

2. *Identify the appropriate frequency for the aircraft's arrival from the west, 270°. Two frequencies are available. Aircraft approaching from any direction between 170° and 349° should make contact on 124.0 MHz.*

(PLT078) — AIM ¶3-2-4

AIR, RTC, WSC, PPC

3839. (Refer to Figure 52.) Which type radar service is provided to VFR aircraft at Lincoln Municipal?

A— Sequencing to the primary Class C airport and standard separation.

B— Sequencing to the primary Class C airport and conflict resolution so that radar targets do not touch, or 1,000 feet vertical separation.

C— Sequencing to the primary Class C airport, traffic advisories, conflict resolution, and safety alerts.

Radar service in Class C airspace consists of sequencing to the primary airport, standard IFR/IFR separation, IFR/VFR separation (so that targets do not touch or have less than 500-foot separation), and providing traffic advisories and safety alerts. (PLT078) — AIM ¶3-2-4

AIR, RTC, REC, WSC, PPC

3840. (Refer to Figure 52.) What is the recommended communications procedure for landing at Lincoln Municipal during the hours when the tower is not in operation?

A— Monitor airport traffic and announce your position and intentions on 118.5 MHz.

B— Contact UNICOM on 122.95 MHz for traffic advisories.

C— Monitor ATIS for airport conditions, then announce your position on 122.95 MHz.

At an airport where the tower is operated on a part-time basis, a pilot should self-announce on the CTAF. (PLT078) — AIM ¶4-1-9

SPO

2107. The Chart Supplements U.S. (formerly Airport/Facility Directory, A/FD) will generally have the latest information pertaining to airport elevation, runway facilities, and control tower frequencies. If there are differences, it should be used in preference to the information

A— on the sectional chart.

B— in the Pilot's Handbook of Aeronautical Knowledge.

C— in the Aeronautical Information Manual (AIM).

Chart Supplements U.S. (formerly A/FDs) are revised every 8 weeks; sectional charts are revised semiannually. If there are differences, the Chart Supplements U.S. should be relied upon since they are more current. (PLT078) — FAA-H-8083-25

Answers (B) and (C) are incorrect because these publications do not have airport specific information.

Answers

3841-1   [B]   3838   [A]   3839   [C]   3840   [A]   2107   [A]

SPO
2118. The most comprehensive information on a given airport is provided by

A— the Chart Supplements U.S. (formerly Airport/ Facility Directory, A/FD).
B— Notices to Airmen (NOTAMS).
C— sectional charts.

The Chart Supplements U.S. (formerly Airport/Facility Directory, A/FD) provides the most comprehensive information on a given airport. (PLT281) — FAA-H-8083-25

Answer (B) is incorrect because NOTAMs provide time-critical information on airports and changes that affect the national airspace system. Answer (C) is incorrect because sectional charts provide broad information on airport services and airspace.

SPO
2119. For a complete listing of information provided in Chart Supplements U.S. (formerly Airport/Facility Directory, A/FD) and how the information may be decoded, refer to the

A— "Directory Legend Sample" located in the front of each Chart Supplements U.S.
B— Aeronautical Information Manual (AIM).
C— legend on sectional and VFR terminal area charts.

For a complete listing of information provided in Chart Supplements U.S. and how the information may be decoded, refer to the "Directory Legend Sample" located in the front of each Chart Supplements U.S. (PLT078) — FAA-H-8083-25

Fitness for Flight

Pilot performance can be seriously degraded by a number of physiological factors. While some of the factors may be beyond the control of the pilot, awareness of cause and effect can help minimize any adverse effects.

Hypoxia, a state of oxygen deficiency, impairs functions of the brain and other organs. Headache, drowsiness, dizziness, and euphoria are all symptoms of hypoxia.

For optimum protection, pilots should avoid flying above 10,000 feet MSL for prolonged periods without using supplemental oxygen. Federal Aviation Regulations require that when operating an aircraft at cabin pressure altitudes above 12,500 feet MSL up to and including 14,000 feet MSL, **supplemental oxygen** shall be used by the minimum flight crew during that time in excess of 30 minutes at those altitudes. Every occupant of the aircraft must be provided with supplemental oxygen above 15,000 feet.

Aviation-breathing oxygen should be used to replenish an aircraft oxygen system for high-altitude flight. Oxygen used for medical purposes or welding normally should not be used because it may contain too much water. The excess water could condense and freeze in oxygen lines when flying at high altitudes. This could block oxygen flow. Also, constant use of oxygen containing too much water may cause corrosion in the system. Specifications for "aviators' breathing oxygen" are 99.5% pure oxygen and not more than .005 mg. of water per liter of oxygen.

Hyperventilation, a deficiency of carbon dioxide within the body, can be the result of rapid or extra deep breathing due to emotional tension, anxiety, or fear. Symptoms will subside after the rate and depth of breathing are brought under control. A pilot should be able to overcome the symptoms or avoid future occurrences of hyperventilation by talking aloud, breathing into a bag, or slowing the breathing rate.

Carbon monoxide is a colorless, odorless, and tasteless gas contained in exhaust fumes. Symptoms of carbon monoxide poisoning include headache, drowsiness, or dizziness. Large accumulations of carbon monoxide in the human body result in a loss of muscular power. Susceptibility increases as altitude increases.

A pilot who detects symptoms of carbon monoxide poisoning should immediately shut off the heater and open air vents.

Continued

Answers

2118   [A]   2119   [A]

Various complex motions, forces, and visual scenes encountered in flight may result in misleading information being sent to the brain by various sensory organs. Spatial disorientation may result if these body signals are used to interpret flight attitude. The best way to overcome **spatial disorientation** is by relying on the flight instruments rather than taking a chance on the sensory organs. Weight-shift control and powered parachutes can use the compass heading as an instrument indication.

ALL

3163. When operating an aircraft at cabin pressure altitudes above 12,500 feet MSL up to and including 14,000 feet MSL, supplemental oxygen shall be used during

A— the entire flight time at those altitudes.
B— that flight time in excess of 10 minutes at those altitudes.
C— that flight time in excess of 30 minutes at those altitudes.

No person may operate civil aircraft at cabin pressure altitudes above 12,500 feet MSL up to and including 14,000 feet MSL, unless the required minimum flight crew uses supplemental oxygen for that part of the flight at those altitudes that is more than 30 minutes duration. (PLT438) — 14 CFR §91.211

ALL

3164. Unless each occupant is provided with supplemental oxygen, no person may operate a civil aircraft of U.S. registry above a maximum cabin pressure altitude of

A— 12,500 feet MSL.
B— 14,000 feet MSL.
C— 15,000 feet MSL.

No person may operate a civil aircraft at cabin pressure altitudes above 15,000 feet MSL unless each occupant is provided with supplemental oxygen. (PLT438) — 14 CFR §91.211

ALL, SPO

3832. Large accumulations of carbon monoxide in the human body result in

A— tightness across the forehead.
B— loss of muscular power.
C— an increased sense of well-being.

A large accumulation of carbon monoxide in the body results in loss of muscular power, vomiting, convulsions, and coma. (PLT097) — FAA-H-8083-25

Answers (A) and (C) are incorrect because hypoxia gives you an increased sense of well-being; stress could result in tightness across the forehead.

ALL

3844. Which statement best defines hypoxia?

A— A state of oxygen deficiency in the body.
B— An abnormal increase in the volume of air breathed.
C— A condition of gas bubble formation around the joints or muscles.

Hypoxia is an oxygen deficiency in the body usually caused by flight at higher altitudes. For optimum protection from hypoxia, pilots are encouraged to use supplemental oxygen above 10,000 feet during the day, and above 5,000 feet at night. (PLT330) — AIM ¶8-1-2

Answer (B) is incorrect because it describes hyperventilation. Answer (C) is incorrect because it describes the bends.

ALL

3845. When a stressful situation is encountered in flight, an abnormal increase in the volume of air breathed in and out can cause a condition known as

A— hyperventilation.
B— aerosinusitis.
C— aerotitis.

An abnormal increase in the volume of air breathed in and out of the lungs flushes an excessive amount of carbon dioxide from the lungs and blood, causing hyperventilation. (PLT332) — AIM ¶8-1-3

ALL, SPO

3846. Which would most likely result in hyperventilation?

A— Emotional tension, anxiety, or fear.
B— The excessive consumption of alcohol.
C— An extremely slow rate of breathing and insufficient oxygen.

Hyperventilation is most likely to occur during periods of stress or anxiety. (PLT332) — AIM ¶8-1-3

Answers

3163 [C]	3164 [C]	3832 [B]	3844 [A]	3845 [A]	3846 [A]

ALL
3847. A pilot experiencing the effects of hyperventilation should be able to restore the proper carbon dioxide level in the body by

A— slowing the breathing rate, breathing into a paper bag, or talking aloud.
B— breathing spontaneously and deeply or gaining mental control of the situation.
C— increasing the breathing rate in order to increase lung ventilation.

The symptoms of hyperventilation subside within a few minutes after the rate and depth of breathing are consciously brought back under control. The buildup of carbon dioxide in the body can be hastened by controlled breathing in and out of a paper bag held over the nose and mouth. Talking aloud often helps, while normally-paced breathing at all times prevents hyperventilation. (PLT332) — AIM ¶8-1-3

ALL
3848. Susceptibility to carbon monoxide poisoning increases as

A— altitude increases.
B— altitude decreases.
C— air pressure increases.

Susceptibility to carbon monoxide poisoning increases with altitude. As altitude increases, air pressure decreases and the body has difficulty getting oxygen. Add carbon monoxide, which further deprives the body of oxygen, and the situation can become critical. (PLT097) — FAA-H-8083-25

ALL
3850. The danger of spatial disorientation during flight in poor visual conditions may be reduced by

A— shifting the eyes quickly between the exterior visual field and the instrument panel.
B— having faith in the instruments rather than taking a chance on the sensory organs.
C— leaning the body in the opposite direction of the motion of the aircraft.

Even if the natural horizon or surface reference is clearly visible, rely on instrument indications to overcome the effects of spatial disorientation. Shifting the eyes quickly from outside to inside, and leaning, will only compound the problem. (PLT334) — AIM ¶8-1-5

ALL
3851. A lack of orientation with regard to the position, attitude, or movement of the aircraft in space is defined as

A— spatial disorientation.
B— hyperventilation.
C— hypoxia.

Spatial disorientation is the state of confusion due to misleading information being sent to the brain from various sensory organs, resulting in a lack of awareness of the aircraft position in relation to a specific reference point. (PLT334) — FAA-H-8083-2

ALL
3852. Pilots are more subject to spatial disorientation if

A— they ignore the sensations of muscles and inner ear.
B— visual cues are taken away, as they are in instrument meteorological conditions (IMC).
C— eyes are moved often in the process of cross-checking the flight instruments.

Sight, supported by other senses, allows the pilot to maintain orientation. However, during periods of low visibility, the supporting senses sometimes conflict with what is seen. When this happens, a pilot is particularly vulnerable to disorientation and must rely more on flight instruments. (PLT334) — FAA-H-8083-25

ALL
3853. If a pilot experiences spatial disorientation during flight in a restricted visibility condition, the best way to overcome the effect is to

A— rely upon the aircraft instrument indications.
B— concentrate on yaw, pitch, and roll sensations.
C— consciously slow the breathing rate until symptoms clear and then resume normal breathing rate.

Even if the natural horizon or surface reference is clearly visible, rely on instrument indications to overcome the effects of spatial disorientation. Shifting the eyes quickly from outside to inside, and leaning, will only compound the problem. (PLT334) — AIM ¶8-1-6

Answers

| 3847 [A] | 3848 [A] | 3850 [B] | 3851 [A] | 3852 [B] | 3853 [A] |

SPO
2202. Which will almost always affect your ability to fly?

A— Over-the-counter analgesics and antihistamines.
B— Antibiotics and anesthetic drugs.
C— Prescription analgesics and antihistamines.

Pilot performance can be seriously degraded by both prescribed and over-the-counter medications, as well as by the medical conditions for which they are taken. Flying is almost always precluded while using prescription analgesics since these drugs may cause side effects such as mental confusion, dizziness, headaches, nausea, and vision problems. Depressants, including antihistamines, lower blood pressure, reduce mental processing, and slow motor and reaction responses. (PLT098) — FAA-H-8083-25

Answer (A) is incorrect because over-the-counter analgesics such as aspirin, Tylenol and Advil, and antihistamines have few side effects when taken in the correct dosage. Answer (B) is incorrect because these drugs do not typically limit flying (but the medical conditions for which they are being taken may indeed limit flying activities).

SPO
2089. As a pilot, flying for long periods in hot summer temperatures increases the susceptibility of dehydration since the

A— dry air at altitude tends to increase the rate of water loss from the body.
B— moist air at altitude helps retain the body's moisture.
C— temperature decreases with altitude.

As a pilot, flying for long periods in hot summer temperatures or at high altitudes increases the susceptibility of dehydration since the dry air at altitude tends to increase the rate of water loss from the body. If this fluid is not replaced, fatigue progresses to dizziness, weakness, nausea, tingling of hands and feet, abdominal cramps, and extreme thirst. (PLT098) — FAA-H-8083-25

SPO
2091. A pilot should be able to overcome the symptoms or avoid future occurrences of hyperventilation by

A— closely monitoring the flight instruments to control the airplane.
B— slowing the breathing rate or breathing into a bag.
C— increasing the breathing rate in order to increase lung ventilation.

The symptoms of hyperventilation subside within a few minutes after the rate and depth of breathing are consciously brought back under control. The buildup of carbon dioxide in the body can be hastened by controlled breathing in and out of a paper bag held over the nose and mouth. Talking aloud often helps, while normally-paced breathing at all times prevents hyperventilation. (PLT332) — AIM ¶8-1-3

SPO
2090. If advice is needed concerning possible flight with an illness, a pilot should contact

A— an Aviation Medical Examiner.
B— their family doctor.
C— the nearest hospital.

The safest rule is not to fly while suffering from any illness. If this rule is considered too stringent for a particular illness, the pilot should contact an Aviation Medical Examiner for advice. (PLT098) — AIM ¶8-1-1

SPO
2092. As hyperventilation progresses a pilot can experience

A— decreased breathing rate and depth.
B— heightened awareness and feeling of well being.
C— symptoms of suffocation and drowsiness.

As hyperventilation "blows off" excessive carbon dioxide from the body, a pilot can experience symptoms of light-headedness, suffocation, drowsiness, tingling in the extremities, and coolness and react to them with even greater hyperventilation. Incapacitation can eventually result from uncoordination, disorientation, and painful muscle spasms. Finally, unconsciousness can occur. (PLT332) — AIM ¶8-1-3

SPO
2093. To overcome the symptoms of hyperventilation, a pilot should

A— swallow or yawn.
B— slow the breathing rate.
C— increase the breathing rate.

The symptoms of hyperventilation subside within a few minutes after the rate and depth of breathing are consciously brought back under control. The buildup of carbon dioxide in the body can be hastened by controlled breathing in and out of a paper bag held over the nose and mouth. (PLT332) — AIM ¶8-1-3

Answers

| 2202 [C] | 2089 [A] | 2091 [B] | 2090 [A] | 2092 [C] | 2093 [B] |

SPO
2097. A state of temporary confusion resulting from misleading information being sent to the brain by various sensory organs is defined as

A— spatial disorientation. ·
B— hyperventilation.
C— hypoxia.

Disorientation, or vertigo, is actually a state of temporary spatial confusion resulting from misleading information sent to the brain by various sensory organs. (PLT334) — AIM ¶8-1-5

Aeronautical Decision Making

The pilot is responsible for determining whether he/she is fit to fly for a particular flight. Most preventable accidents have one common factor: human error, rather than a mechanical malfunction. Good aeronautical decision making (ADM) is necessary to prevent human error. ADM is a systematic approach to the mental process used by aircraft pilots to consistently determine the best course of action in response to a given set of circumstances.

The ADM process addresses all aspects of decision making in the cockpit and identifies the steps involved in good decision making. Steps for good decision making are:

1. Identifying personal attitudes hazardous to safe flight.
2. Learning behavior modification techniques.
3. Learning how to recognize and cope with stress.
4. Developing risk assessment skills.
5. Using all resources in a multicrew situation.
6. Evaluating the effectiveness of one's ADM skills.

There are a number of classic behavioral traps into which pilots have been known to fall. Pilots, particularly those with considerable experience, as a rule always try to complete a flight as planned, please passengers, meet schedules, and generally demonstrate that they have the "right stuff." These tendencies ultimately may lead to practices that are dangerous and often illegal, and may lead to a mishap. All experienced pilots have fallen prey to, or have been tempted by, one or more of these tendencies in their flying careers. These dangerous tendencies or behavior patterns, which must be identified and eliminated, include:

Peer Pressure. Poor decision making based upon emotional response to peers rather than evaluating a situation objectively.

Mind Set. The inability to recognize and cope with changes in the situation different from those anticipated or planned.

Get-There-Itis. This tendency, common among pilots, clouds the vision and impairs judgment by causing a fixation on the original goal or destination combined with a total disregard for any alternative course of action.

Duck-Under Syndrome. The tendency to sneak a peek by descending below minimums during an approach. Based on a belief that there is always a built-in "fudge" factor that can be used or on an unwillingness to admit defeat and shoot a missed approach.

Scud Running. Pushing the capabilities of the pilot and the aircraft to the limits by trying to maintain visual contact with the terrain while trying to avoid physical contact with it. This attitude is characterized by the old pilot's joke: "If it's too bad to go IFR, we'll go VFR."

Answers

2097 [A]

Continuing Visual Flight Rules (VFR) into instrument conditions often leads to spatial disorientation or collision with ground/obstacles. It is even more dangerous if the pilot is not instrument qualified or current.

Getting Behind the Aircraft. Allowing events or the situation to control your actions rather than the other way around. Characterized by a constant state of surprise at what happens next.

Loss of Positional or Situation Awareness. Another case of getting behind the aircraft which results in not knowing where you are, an inability to recognize deteriorating circumstances, and/or the misjudgment of the rate of deterioration.

Operating Without Adequate Fuel Reserves. Ignoring minimum fuel reserve requirements, either VFR or Instrument Flight Rules (IFR), is generally the result of overconfidence, lack of flight planning, or ignoring the regulations.

Descent Below the Minimum Enroute Altitude. The duck-under syndrome (mentioned above) manifesting itself during the enroute portion of an IFR flight.

Flying Outside the Envelope. Unjustified reliance on the (usually mistaken) belief that the aircraft's high performance capability meets the demands imposed by the pilot's (usually overestimated) flying skills.

Neglect of Flight Planning, Preflight Inspections, Checklists, etc. Unjustified reliance on the pilot's short- and long-term memory, regular flying skills, repetitive and familiar routes, etc.

Each ADM student should take the Self-Assessment Hazardous Attitude Inventory Test in order to gain a realistic perspective on his/her attitudes toward flying. The inventory test requires the pilot to provide a response which most accurately reflects the reasoning behind his/her decision. The pilot must choose one of the five given reasons for making that decision, even though the pilot may not consider any of the five choices acceptable. The inventory test presents extreme cases of incorrect pilot decision making in an effort to introduce the five types of hazardous attitudes.

ADM addresses the following five hazardous attitudes:

1. **Antiauthority (don't tell me!).** This attitude is found in people who do not like anyone telling them what to do. In a sense they are saying "no one can tell me what to do." They may be resentful of having someone tell them what to do or may regard rules, regulations, and procedures as silly or unnecessary. However, it is always your prerogative to question authority if you feel it is in error. The antidote for this attitude is: Follow the rules. They are usually right.

2. **Impulsivity (do something quickly!).** is the attitude of people who frequently feel the need to do something — *anything* — immediately. They do not stop to think about what they are about to do, they do not select the best alternative, and they do the first thing that comes to mind. The antidote for this attitude is: Not so fast. Think first.

3. **Invulnerability (it won't happen to me).** Many people feel that accidents happen to others, but never to them. They know accidents can happen, and they know that anyone can be affected. They never really feel or believe that they will be personally involved. Pilots who think this way are more likely to take chances and increase risk. The antidote for this attitude is: It could happen to me.

4. **Macho (I can do it).** Pilots who are always trying to prove that they are better than anyone else are thinking "I can do it — I'll show them." Pilots with this type of attitude will try to prove themselves by taking risks in order to impress others. While this pattern is thought to be a male characteristic, women are equally susceptible. The antidote for this attitude is: taking chances is foolish.

5. **Resignation (what's the use?).** Pilots who think "what's the use?" do not see themselves as being able to make a great deal of difference in what happens to them. When things go well, the pilot is apt to think that's good luck. When things go badly, the pilot may feel that "someone is out to get me," or attribute it to bad luck. The pilot will leave the action to others, for better or worse. Sometimes, such pilots will even go along with unreasonable requests just to be a "nice guy." The antidote for this attitude is: I'm not helpless. I can make a difference.

Hazardous attitudes which contribute to poor pilot judgment can be effectively counteracted by redirecting that hazardous attitude so that appropriate action can be taken. Recognition of hazardous thoughts is the first step in neutralizing them in the ADM process. Pilots should become familiar with a means of counteracting hazardous attitudes with an appropriate antidote thought. When a pilot recognizes a thought as hazardous, the pilot should label that thought as hazardous, then correct that thought by stating the corresponding antidote.

If you hope to succeed at reducing stress associated with crisis management in the air or with your job, it is essential to begin by making a personal assessment of stress in all areas of your life. Good **cockpit stress management** begins with good life stress management. Many of the stress coping techniques practiced for life stress management are not usually practical in flight. Rather, you must condition yourself to relax and think rationally when stress appears. The following checklist outlines some thoughts on cockpit stress management.

1. Avoid situations that distract you from flying the aircraft.

2. Reduce your workload to reduce stress levels. This will create a proper environment in which to make good decisions.

3. If an emergency does occur, be calm. Think for a moment, weigh the alternatives, then act.

4. Maintain proficiency in your aircraft; proficiency builds confidence. Familiarize yourself thoroughly with your aircraft, its systems, and emergency procedures.

5. Know and respect your own personal limits.

6. Do not let little mistakes bother you until they build into a big thing. Wait until after you land, then "debrief" and analyze past actions.

7. If flying is adding to your stress, either stop flying or seek professional help to manage your stress within acceptable limits.

The DECIDE Model, comprised of a six-step process, is intended to provide the pilot with a logical way of approaching decision making. The six elements of the DECIDE Model represent a continuous loop decision process which can be used to assist a pilot in the decision making process when he/she is faced with a change in a situation that requires a judgment. This DECIDE Model is primarily focused on the intellectual component, but can have an impact on the motivational component of judgment as well. If a pilot practices the DECIDE Model in all decision making, its use can become very natural and could result in better decisions being made under all types of situations.

1. **Detect.** The decisionmaker detects the fact that change has occurred.

2. **Estimate.** The decisionmaker estimates the need to counter or react to the change.

3. **Choose.** The decisionmaker chooses a desirable outcome (in terms of success) for the flight.

4. **Identify.** The decisionmaker identifies actions which could successfully control the change.

5. **Do.** The decisionmaker takes the necessary action.

6. **Evaluate.** The decisionmaker evaluates the effect(s) of his/her action countering the change.

ALL, SPO
3931. What is it often called when a pilot pushes his or her capabilities and the aircraft's limits by trying to maintain visual contact with the terrain in low visibility and ceiling?

A— Scud running.
B— Mind set.
C— Peer pressure.

Scud running is pushing the capabilities of the pilot and the aircraft to the limits by trying to maintain visual contact with the terrain while trying to avoid physical contact with it. (PLT104) — FAA-H-8083-25

ALL, SPO
3932. What antidotal phrase can help reverse the hazardous attitude of "antiauthority"?

A— Rules do not apply in this situation.
B— I know what I am doing.
C— Follow the rules.

The antiauthority (don't tell me!) attitude is found in people who do not like anyone telling them what to do. The antidote for this attitude is: follow the rules, they are usually right. (PLT103) — FAA-H-8083-25

ALL
3933. What antidotal phrase can help reverse the hazardous attitude of "impulsivity"?

A— It could happen to me.
B— Do it quickly to get it over with.
C— Not so fast, think first.

Impulsivity (do something quickly!) is the attitude of people who frequently feel the need to do something, anything, immediately. They do not stop to think about what they are about to do, they do not select the best alternative, and they do the first thing that comes to mind. The antidote for this attitude is: Not so fast. Think first. (PLT103) — FAA-H-8083-25

ALL
3931-1. Hazardous attitudes occur to every pilot to some degree at some time. What are some of these hazardous attitudes?

A— Poor risk management and lack of stress management.
B— Antiauthority, impulsivity, macho, resignation, and invulnerability.
C— Poor situational awareness, snap judgments, and lack of a decision making process.

ADM addresses the following five hazardous attitudes: Antiauthority (don't tell me!), Impulsivity (do something quickly!), Invulnerability (it won't happen to me!), Macho (I can do it!), Resignation (what's the use?). (PLT103) — FAA-H-8083-25

ALL, SPO
3931-2. In the aeronautical decision making (ADM) process, what is the first step in neutralizing a hazardous attitude?

A— Making a rational judgement.
B— Recognizing hazardous thoughts.
C— Recognizing the invulnerability of the situation.

Hazardous attitudes which contribute to poor pilot judgment can be effectively counteracted by redirecting that hazardous attitude so that appropriate action can be taken. Recognition of hazardous thoughts is the first step in neutralizing them in the ADM process. (PLT103) — FAA-H-8083-25

ALL, SPO
3931-3. Risk management, as part of the aeronautical decision making (ADM) process, relies on which features to reduce the risks associated with each flight?

A— Application of stress management and risk element procedures.
B— Situational awareness, problem recognition, and good judgment.
C— The mental process of analyzing all information in a particular situation and making a timely decision on what action to take.

Risk management is the part of the decision making process which relies on situational awareness, problem recognition, and good judgment to reduce risks associated with each flight. (PLT271) — FAA-H-8083-25

ALL, SPO
3934. What antidotal phrase can help reverse the hazardous attitude of "invulnerability"?

A— It will not happen to me.
B— It can not be that bad.
C— It could happen to me.

Invulnerability (it won't happen to me) is found in people who think accidents happen to others, but never to them. Pilots who think this way are more likely to take chances and increase risk. The antidote for this attitude is: It could happen to me. (PLT103) — FAA-H-8083-25

Answers

| 3931 | [A] | 3932 | [C] | 3933 | [C] | 3931-1 | [B] | 3931-2 | [B] | 3931-3 | [B] |
| 3934 | [C] | | | | | | | | | | |

ALL
3935. What antidotal phrase can help reverse the hazardous attitude of "macho"?

A— I can do it.
B— Taking chances is foolish.
C— Nothing will happen.

Macho (I can do it) is the attitude found in pilots who are always trying to prove they are better than anyone else. Pilots with this type of attitude will try to prove themselves by taking risks in order to impress others. The antidote for this attitude is: taking chances is foolish. (PLT103) — FAA-H-8083-25

ALL
3936. What antidotal phrase can help reverse the hazardous attitude of "resignation"?

A— What is the use.
B— Someone else is responsible.
C— I am not helpless.

Resignation (what's the use?) is the attitude in pilots who do not see themselves as being able to make a great deal of difference in what happens to them. When things go well, the pilot is apt to think it's due to good luck. When things go badly, the pilot may feel that "someone is out to get me," or attribute it to bad luck. The antidote for this attitude is: I'm not helpless. I can make a difference. (PLT103) — FAA-H-8083-25

ALL
3937. Who is responsible for determining whether a pilot is fit to fly for a particular flight, even though he or she holds a current medical certificate?

A— The FAA.
B— The medical examiner.
C— The pilot.

The pilot is responsible for determining whether he/she is fit to fly for a particular flight. (PLT443) — FAA-H-8083-25

SPO
2078. Who is responsible for determining whether a pilot is fit to fly for a particular flight, even though the pilot holds a current and valid U.S. driver's license?

A— The FAA.
B— The pilot.
C— The medical examiner.

The pilot is responsible for determining whether he/she is fit to fly for a particular flight. (PLT443) — FAA-H-8083-25

ALL, SPO
3938. What is the one common factor which affects most preventable accidents?

A— Structural failure.
B— Mechanical malfunction.
C— Human error.

Most preventable accidents have one common factor: human error, rather than a mechanical malfunction. (PLT104) — FAA-H-8083-25

ALL
3939. What often leads to spatial disorientation or collision with ground/obstacles when flying under Visual Flight Rules (VFR)?

A— Continual flight into instrument conditions.
B— Getting behind the aircraft.
C— Duck-under syndrome.

Continuing visual flight rules (VFR) into instrument conditions often leads to spatial disorientation or collision with ground/obstacles. It is even more dangerous if the pilot is not instrument qualified or current. (PLT334) — FAA-H-8083-25

ALL, SPO
3940. What is one of the neglected items when a pilot relies on short and long term memory for repetitive tasks?

A— Checklists.
B— Situation awareness.
C— Flying outside the envelope.

Unjustified reliance on the pilot's short and long term memory, regular flying skills, repetitive and familiar routes usually results in neglect of flight planning, preflight inspections, and checklists. (PLT104) — FAA-H-8083-25

Answers

3935 [B]	3936 [C]	3937 [C]	2078 [B]	3938 [C]	3939 [A]
3940 [A]					

ALL
3940-1. A pilot and two passengers landed on a 2,100 foot east-west gravel strip with an elevation of 1,800 feet. The temperature is warmer than expected and after computing the density altitude it is determined the takeoff distance over a 50 foot obstacle is 1,980 feet. The airplane is 75 pounds under gross weight. What would be the best choice?

A— Takeoff off into the headwind will give the extra climb-out time needed.
B— Try a takeoff without the passengers to make sure the climb is adequate.
C— Wait until the temperature decreases, and recalculate the takeoff performance.

The conditions described provide only 120 feet for a margin of error between required takeoff distance and available runway. This is too risky; the pilot should wait until conditions improve and there is a larger margin of safety between available and needed runway distance. (PLT011) — FAA-H-8083-2

SPO
2073. A series of judgmental errors which can lead to a human factors-related accident is sometimes referred to as the

A— error chain.
B— course of action.
C— DECIDE model.

The poor judgment chain, sometimes referred to as the "error chain," is a term used to describe this concept of contributing factors in a human factors-related accident. Breaking one link in the chain normally is all that is necessary to change the outcome of the sequence of events. (PLT271) — FAA-H-8083-25

SPO
2085. Which of the following is the first step of the Decide Model for effective risk management and Aeronautical Decision Making?

A— Identify.
B— Detect.
C— Evaluate.

The DECIDE Model, comprised of a six-step process, is intended to provide the pilot with a logical way of approaching decision making: Detect, Estimate, Choose, Identify, Do, and Evaluate. (PLT022) — FAA-H-8083-25

SPO
2074. What are some of the hazardous attitudes dealt with in Aeronautical Decision Making (ADM)?

A— Risk management, stress management, and risk elements.
B— Poor decision making, situational awareness, and judgment.
C— Antiauthority (don't tell me), impulsivity (do something quickly without thinking), macho (I can do it).

ADM addresses the following five hazardous attitudes: Antiauthority (don't tell me!), Impulsivity (do something quickly!), Invulnerability (it won't happen to me), Macho (I can do it), Resignation (what's the use?). (PLT103) — FAA-H-8083-25

SPO
2195. What should a pilot do when recognizing a thought as hazardous?

A— Label that thought as hazardous, then correct that thought by stating the corresponding learned antidote.
B— Avoid developing this hazardous thought.
C— Develop this hazardous thought and follow through with modified action.

When a pilot recognizes a thought as hazardous, the pilot should label that thought as hazardous, then correct that thought by stating the corresponding antidote. (PLT103) — FAA-H-8083-25

SPO
2176. Pilots should be familiar with positive alternatives to

A— Counteract hazardous attitudes.
B— Ensure the right choices have been made.
C— Ensure they are applying the appropriate antidote.

The pilot must examine decisions carefully to ensure choices have not been influenced by hazardous attitudes and be familiar with positive alternatives to counteract the hazardous attitudes (referred to as antidotes). (PLT103) — FAA-H-8083-25

Answers

3940-1 [C]	2073 [A]	2085 [B]	2074 [C]	2195 [A]	2176 [A]

SPO
2079. Aeronautical Decision Making (ADM) is a

A— mental process of analyzing all information in a particular situation and making a timely decision on what action to take.
B— systematic approach to the mental process used by pilots to consistently determine the best course of action for a given set of circumstances.
C— decision making process which relies on good judgment to reduce risks associated with each flight.

ADM is a systematic approach to the mental process used by aircraft pilots to consistently determine the best course of action in response to a given set of circumstances. (PLT022) — FAA-H-8083-25

SPO
2083. Ignoring minimum fuel reserve requirements is generally the result of overconfidence, disregarding applicable regulations, or

A— lack of flight planning.
B— impulsivity.
C— physical stress.

Ignoring minimum fuel reserve requirements is generally the result of overconfidence, lack of flight planning, or disregarding applicable regulations. (PLT104) — FAA-H-8083-25

SPO
2196. The basic drive for a pilot to demonstrate the "right stuff" can have an adverse effect on safety, by

A— a total disregard for any alternative course of action.
B— generating tendencies that lead to practices that are dangerous, often illegal, and may lead to a mishap.
C— allowing events, or the situation, to control his or her actions.

Pilots, particularly those with considerable experience, as a rule always try to complete a flight as planned, please passengers, meet schedules, and generally demonstrate that they have the "right stuff." These tendencies ultimately may lead to practices that are dangerous and often illegal, and may lead to a mishap. (PLT103) — FAA-H-8083-25

SPO
2197. A pilot who relies on short- and long-term memory for repetitive tasks often neglects

A— flying outside the envelope.
B— checklists.
C— situation awareness.

Unjustified reliance on the pilot's short- and long-term memory, regular flying skills, repetitive and familiar routes usually results in neglect of flight planning, preflight inspections, and checklists. (PLT104) — FAA-H-8083-25

SPO
2063. Consistent adherence to approved checklists is a sign of a

A— disciplined and competent pilot.
B— pilot who lacks the required knowledge.
C— low-time pilot.

To avoid missing important steps, always use the appropriate checklists whenever they are available. Consistent adherence to approved checklists is a sign of a disciplined and competent pilot. (PLT122) — FAA-H-8083-25

SPO
2069. The positive three-step process in the exchange of flight controls between pilots includes these verbal steps: (1) You have the flight controls, (2) I have the flight controls and (3)

A— You have the flight controls.
B— I have the aircraft.
C— I have the flight controls.

There must always be a clear understanding who has control of the aircraft. Prior to flight, a briefing should be conducted that includes the procedure for the exchange of flight controls. A positive three-step process in the exchange of flight controls between pilots is a proven procedure: You have the flight controls, I have the flight controls, You have the flight controls. (PLT340) — FAA-H-8083-9

Answers

2079 [B]	2083 [A]	2196 [B]	2197 [B]	2063 [A]	2069 [A]

SPO

2068. To avoid missing important steps, always use the

A— appropriate checklists.
B— placarded airspeeds.
C— airworthiness certificate.

To avoid missing important steps, always use the appropriate checklists whenever they are available. Consistent adherence to approved checklists is a sign of a disciplined and competent pilot. (PLT122) — FAA-H-8083-25

SPO

2082. An extreme case of a pilot getting behind the aircraft can lead to the operational pitfall of

A— loss of situational awareness.
B— loss of workload.
C— internal stress.

Getting behind the aircraft can result in not knowing where you are, an inability to recognize deteriorating circumstances, and/or the misjudgment of the rate of deterioration. (PLT104) — FAA-H-8083-25

Collision Avoidance

Vision is the most important body sense for safe flight. Major factors that determine how effectively vision can be used are the level of illumination and the technique of scanning the sky for other aircraft.

Atmospheric haze reduces the ability to see traffic or terrain during flight, making all features appear to be farther away than they actually are.

In preparation for a night flight, the pilot should avoid bright white lights for at least 30 minutes before the flight.

Scanning the sky for other aircraft is a key factor in collision avoidance. Pilots must develop an effective scanning technique which maximizes visual capabilities. Because the eyes focus only on a narrow viewing area, effective scanning is accomplished with a series of short, regularly spaced eye movements. Each movement should not exceed 10°, and each area should be observed for at least one second. At night, scan slowly to permit the use of off-center vision.

Prior to starting any maneuver, a pilot should visually scan the entire area for collision avoidance. Any aircraft that appears to have no relative motion and stays in one scan quadrant is likely to be on a collision course. If a target shows neither lateral nor vertical motion, but increases in size, take evasive action.

When climbing or descending VFR on an airway, execute gentle banks, right and left, to provide for visual scanning of the airspace.

ALL, SPO

3710-1. Most midair collision accidents occur during

A— hazy days.
B— clear days.
C— cloudy nights.

The FAA Near Mid-Air Collision Report indicates that 81% of the incidents occurred in clear skies and unrestricted visibility conditions. (PLT194) — AC 90-48

ALL, SPO

3710. Prior to starting each maneuver, pilots should

A— check altitude, airspeed, and heading indications.
B— visually scan the entire area for collision avoidance.
C— announce their intentions on the nearest CTAF.

Scanning the sky for other aircraft is a key factor in collision avoidance. (PLT194) — FAA-H-8083-25

Answer (A) is incorrect because checking your instruments is important but secondary to collision avoidance. Answer (C) is incorrect because announcing your intentions on the nearest CTAF does not guarantee that anyone is listening.

Answers

| 2068 [A] | 2082 [A] | 3710-1 [B] | 3710 [B] |

ALL, SPO
3833. What effect does haze have on the ability to see traffic or terrain features during flight?

A— Haze causes the eyes to focus at infinity.
B— The eyes tend to overwork in haze and do not detect relative movement easily.
C— All traffic or terrain features appear to be farther away than their actual distance.

Atmospheric haze can create the illusion of being at a greater distance from objects on the ground and in the air. (PLT333) — AIM ¶8-1-5

SPO
2240. Haze creates which of the following atmospheric illusions?

A— Being at a greater distance from the runway.
B— Being at a closer distance from the runway.
C— Haze creates no atmospheric illusions.

Atmospheric haze can create the illusion of being at a greater distance from objects on the ground and in the air. (PLT280) — AIM ¶8-1-5

SPO
2066. Pilots who become apprehensive for their safety for any reason should

A— request assistance immediately.
B— reduce their situational awareness.
C— change their mindset.

Pilots who become apprehensive for their safety for any reason should request assistance immediately. Ready and willing help is available in the form of radio, radar, direction finding stations and other aircraft. Delay has caused accidents and cost lives. Safety is not a luxury! Take action! (PLT116) — AIM ¶6-1-2

SPO
2064. To scan properly for traffic, a pilot should

A— slowly sweep the field of vision from one side to the other at intervals.
B— concentrate on any peripheral movement detected.
C— use a series of short, regularly spaced eye movements that bring successive areas of the sky into the central visual field.

Effective scanning is accomplished with a series of short, regularly spaced eye movements that bring successive areas of the sky into the central visual field. Each movement should not exceed 10°, and each area should be observed for at least one second to enable detection. (PLT194) — AIM ¶8-1-6

SPO
2062. Guy wires, which support antenna towers, can extend horizontally; therefore, the towers should be avoided horizontally by at least

A— 2,000 feet horizontally.
B— 300 feet horizontally.
C— 1,000 feet horizontally.

Most skeletal structures are supported by guy wires which are very difficult to see in good weather and can be invisible at dusk or during periods of reduced visibility. These wires can extend about 1,500 feet horizontally from a structure; therefore, all skeletal structures should be avoided horizontally by at least 2,000 feet. (PLT116) — AIM ¶7-5-3

ALL
3834. The most effective method of scanning for other aircraft for collision avoidance during daylight hours is to use

A— regularly spaced concentration on the 3-, 9-, and 12-o'clock positions.
B— a series of short, regularly spaced eye movements to search each 10-degree sector.
C— peripheral vision by scanning small sectors and utilizing offcenter viewing.

Effective scanning is accomplished with a series of short, regularly spaced eye movements that bring successive areas of the sky into the central visual field. Each movement should not exceed 10°, and each area should be observed for at least one second to enable detection. (PLT194) — AIM ¶8-1-6

Answers

| 3833 | [C] | 2240 | [A] | 2066 | [A] | 2064 | [C] | 2062 | [A] | 3834 | [B] |

ALL
3835. Which technique should a pilot use to scan for traffic to the right and left during straight-and-level flight?

A— Systematically focus on different segments of the sky for short intervals.
B— Concentrate on relative movement detected in the peripheral vision area.
C— Continuous sweeping of the windshield from right to left.

Effective scanning is accomplished with a series of short, regularly spaced eye movements that bring successive areas of the sky into the central visual field. Each movement should not exceed 10°, and each area should be observed for at least one second to enable detection. (PLT194) — AIM ¶8-1-6

ALL, SPO
3836. How can you determine if another aircraft is on a collision course with your aircraft?

A— The other aircraft will always appear to get larger and closer at a rapid rate.
B— The nose of each aircraft is pointed at the same point in space.
C— There will be no apparent relative motion between your aircraft and the other aircraft.

Any aircraft that appears to have no relative motion and stays in one scan quadrant is likely to be on a collision course. (PLT194) — AIM ¶8-1-8

ALL
3849. What preparation should a pilot make to adapt the eyes for night flying?

A— Wear sunglasses after sunset until ready for flight.
B— Avoid red lights at least 30 minutes before the flight.
C— Avoid bright white lights at least 30 minutes before the flight.

Exposure to total darkness for at least 30 minutes is required for complete dark adaptation. Any degree of dark adaptation is lost within a few seconds of viewing a bright light. Red lights do not affect night vision. (PLT333) — AIM ¶8-1-6

AIR, RTC, LTA, WSC, PPC
3712. What is the most effective way to use the eyes during night flight?

A— Look only at far away, dim lights.
B— Scan slowly to permit offcenter viewing.
C— Concentrate directly on each object for a few seconds.

During daylight, an object can be seen best by looking directly at it, but at night, a scanning procedure to permit "off-center" viewing of the object is more effective. In addition, the pilot should consciously practice moving the eyes more slowly than in daylight to optimize night vision. Off-center viewing must be utilized during night flying because of the distribution of rods and cones in the eye. (PLT099) — FAA-H-8083-25

AIR, RTC, LTA, WSC, PPC
3713. The best method to use when looking for other traffic at night is to

A— look to the side of the object and scan slowly.
B— scan the visual field very rapidly.
C— look to the side of the object and scan rapidly.

During daylight, an object can be seen best by looking directly at it, but at night, a scanning procedure to permit "off-center" viewing of the object is more effective. In addition, the pilot should consciously practice moving the eyes more slowly than in daylight to optimize night vision. Off-center viewing must be utilized during night flying because of the distribution of rods and cones in the eye. (PLT099) — FAA-H-8083-25

AIR, RTC, LTA, WSC, PPC
3714. The most effective method of scanning for other aircraft for collision avoidance during nighttime hours is to use

A— regularly spaced concentration on the 3-, 9-, and 12-o'clock positions.
B— a series of short, regularly spaced eye movements to search each 30-degree sector.
C— peripheral vision by scanning small sectors and utilizing offcenter viewing.

During daylight, an object can be seen best by looking directly at it, but at night, a scanning procedure to permit "off-center" viewing of the object is more effective. In addition, the pilot should consciously practice moving the eyes more slowly than in daylight to optimize night vision. Off-center viewing must be utilized during night flying because of the distribution of rods and cones in the eye. (PLT099) — FAA-H-8083-3

Answers

3835 [A]	3836 [C]	3849 [C]	3712 [B]	3713 [A]	3714 [C]

SPO
2096. The most effective method of scanning for other aircraft for collision avoidance during daylight hours is to use

A— regularly spaced concentration on the 3-, 9-, and 12-o'clock positions.
B— a series of short, regularly spaced eye movements to search each 10-degree sector.
C— peripheral vision by scanning small sectors and utilizing offcenter viewing.

Effective scanning is accomplished with a series of short, regularly spaced eye movements that bring successive areas of the sky into the central visual field. Each movement should not exceed 10°, and each area should be observed for at least one second to enable detection. (PLT099) — AIM ¶8-1-6

Aircraft Lighting

When an aircraft is being operated during the period from sunset to sunrise (except in Alaska), it must display lighted position lights and an anticollision light. The anticollision light may be either aviation red or aviation white. *See* Figure 5-12.

For collision avoidance, a pilot must know where each colored light is located on an aircraft. For example, if a pilot observes a steady red light and a flashing red light ahead and at the same altitude, the other aircraft is crossing to the left; a steady white and a flashing red light indicates that the other aircraft is headed away from the observer; and steady red and green lights at the same altitude as the observer indicates that the other aircraft is approaching head-on.

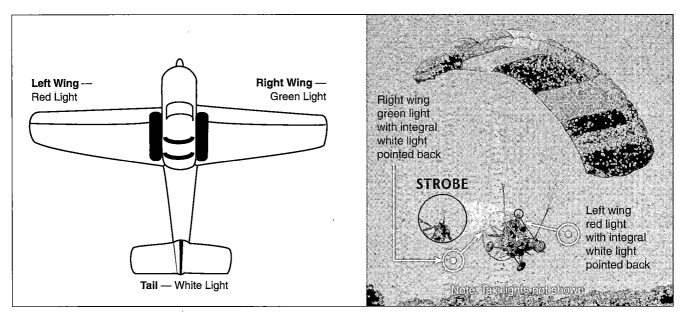

Figure 5-12. Aircraft lighting

ALL
3162. Except in Alaska, during what time period should lighted position lights be displayed on an aircraft?

A— End of evening civil twilight to the beginning of morning civil twilight.
B— 1 hour after sunset to 1 hour before sunrise.
C— Sunset to sunrise.

An aircraft must display lighted position lights from sunset to sunrise. (PLT119) — 14 CFR §91.209

Answer (A) is incorrect because it applies to logging of night time. Answer (B) is incorrect because it applies to the night landing requirement.

ALL
3916. Pilots are encouraged to turn on their landing lights when operating below 10,000 feet, day or night, and when operating within

A— Class B airspace.
B— 10 miles of any airport.
C— within 15 miles of a towered airport.

Pilots are encouraged to turn on their landing lights when operating below 10,000 feet, day or night, especially when operating within 10 miles of any airport or in conditions of reduced visibility and in areas where flocks of birds may be expected. (PLT119) — AIM ¶4-3-23

ALL
3916-1. The Aeronautical Information Manual (AIM) specifically encourages pilots to turn on their landing lights when operating below 10,000 feet, day or night, and especially when operating

A— in Class B airspace.
B— in conditions of reduced visibility.
C— within 15 miles of a towered airport.

Pilots are encouraged to turn on their landing lights when operating below 10,000 feet, day or night, especially when operating within 10 miles of any airport or in conditions of reduced visibility and in areas where flocks of birds may be expected. (PLT119) — AIM ¶4-3-23

AIR, RTC, LTA, WSC, PPC
3715. During a night flight, you observe a steady red light and a flashing red light ahead and at the same altitude. What is the general direction of movement of the other aircraft?

A— The other aircraft is crossing to the left.
B— The other aircraft is crossing to the right.
C— The other aircraft is approaching head-on.

Airplanes have a red light on the left wing tip, a green light on the right wing tip and a white light on the tail. The flashing red light is the rotating beacon which can be seen from all directions around the aircraft. If the only steady light seen is red, then the airplane is crossing from right to left in relation to the observing pilot. (PLT119) — FAA-H-8083-3

AIR, RTC, LTA, WSC, PPC
3716. During a night flight, you observe a steady white light and a flashing red light ahead and at the same altitude. What is the general direction of movement of the other aircraft?

A— The other aircraft is flying away from you.
B— The other aircraft is crossing to the left.
C— The other aircraft is crossing to the right.

Airplanes have a red light on the left wing tip, a green light on the right wing tip and a white light on the tail. The flashing red light is the rotating beacon which can be seen from all directions around the aircraft. When the only steady light seen is white, then the airplane is headed away from the observing pilot. (PLT119) — FAA-H-8083-3

AIR, RTC, LTA, WSC, PPC
3717. During a night flight, you observe steady red and green lights ahead and at the same altitude. What is the general direction of movement of the other aircraft?

A— The other aircraft is crossing to the left.
B— The other aircraft is flying away from you.
C— The other aircraft is approaching head-on.

When both a red and green light of another airplane are observed, the airplane would be flying in a general direction toward you. Airplanes have a red light on the left wing tip, a green light on the right wing tip and a white light on the tail. (PLT119) — FAA-H-8083-3

Answers

3162 [C]	3916 [B]	3916-1 [B]	3715 [A]	3716 [A]	3717 [C]

SPO

2020. Pilots must operate the anti-collision lights

A— at night or in inclement weather.
B— at night when the visibility is less than three miles and flying in Class B airspace.
C— day and night, except when the pilot-in-command determines that they constitute a hazard to safety.

Aircraft equipped with an anti-collision light system are required to operate that light system during all types of operations (day and night). However, the pilot-in-command may determine that the anti-collision lights should be turned off when their operation would constitute a hazard to safety. (PLT119) — 14 CFR §91.209

Answers

2020   [C]

Chapter 6
Weather

The Heating of the Earth

The major source of all weather is the sun. Changes or variations of weather patterns are caused by the unequal heating of the Earth's surface.

Every physical process of weather is accompanied by or is a result of unequal heating of the Earth's surface. The heating of the Earth (and therefore the heating of the air surrounding the Earth) is unequal around the entire planet. Both north or south of the equator, one square foot of sunrays is not concentrated over one square foot of the surface, but over a larger area. This lower concentration of sunrays produces less radiation of heat over a given surface area; therefore, less atmospheric heating takes place in that area.

The unequal heating of the Earth's atmosphere creates a large air-cell circulation pattern (wind) because the warmer air has a tendency to rise (low pressure) and the colder air has a tendency to settle or descend (high pressure) and replace the rising warmer air. This unequal heating, which causes pressure variations, will also cause variations in altimeter settings between weather reporting points.

Because the Earth rotates, this large, simple air-cell circulation pattern is greatly distorted by a phenomenon known as the **Coriolis force**. When the wind (which is created by high pressure trying to flow into low pressure) first begins to move at higher altitudes, the Coriolis force deflects it to the right (in the Northern Hemisphere) causing it to flow parallel to the isobars (lines of equal pressure). These deflections of the large-cell circulation pattern create general wind patterns as depicted in Figure 6-1.

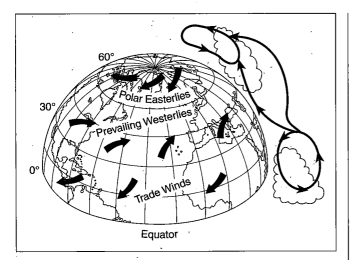

Figure 6-1. Prevailing wind systems

ALL, SPO
3381. Every physical process of weather is accompanied by, or is the result of, a

A— movement of air.
B— pressure differential.
C— heat exchange.

Every physical process of weather is accompanied by, or is a result of, unequal heating of the Earth's surface. (PLT512) — AC 00-6

ALL, SPO
3382. What causes variations in altimeter settings between weather reporting points?

A— Unequal heating of the Earth's surface.
B— Variation of terrain elevation.
C— Coriolis force.

All altimeter settings are corrected to sea level. Unequal heating of the Earth's surface causes pressure differences. (PLT165) — AC 00-6

GLI
3448. The development of thermals depends upon

A— a counterclockwise circulation of air.
B— temperature inversions.
C— solar heating.

Thermals are updrafts in convective currents dependent on solar heating. A temperature inversion would result in stable air with very little, if any, convective activity. (PLT494) — AC 00-6

Answers
3381　[C]　　　　3382　[A]　　　　3448　[C]

GLI
3647. (Refer to Figure 20.) Over which area should a glider pilot expect to find the best lift under normal conditions?

A—2.
B—7.
C—5.

One fundamental point is that dry areas get hotter than moist areas. Dry fields or dry ground of any nature are better thermal sources than moist areas. This applies to woods or forests, which are poor sources of thermals because of the large amount of moisture given off by foliage. (PLT064) — FAA-H-8083-13

Circulation and Wind

The general circulation and wind rules in the Northern Hemisphere are as follows:

1. Air circulates in a clockwise direction around a high;

2. Air circulates in a counterclockwise direction around a low;

3. The closer the isobars are together, the stronger the wind speed; and

4. Due to surface friction (up to about 2,000 feet AGL), surface winds do not exactly parallel the isobars, but move outward from the center of the high toward lower pressure. *See* Figure 6-2.

Knowing that air flows out of the high in a clockwise direction and into the low in a counterclockwise direction is useful in preflight planning. Assume a flight from point A to point B as shown in Figure 6-3. Going direct would involve fighting the wind flowing around the low. However, by traveling south of the low-pressure area, the circulation pattern could help instead of hinder. Generally speaking, in the Northern Hemisphere, when traveling west to east, the most favorable winds can be found by flying north of high-pressure areas and south of low-pressure areas. Conversely, when flying east to west, the most favorable winds can be found south of high-pressure areas and north of low-pressure areas.

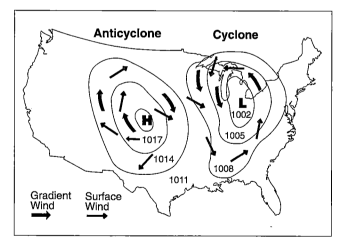

Figure 6-2. Gradient and surface wind

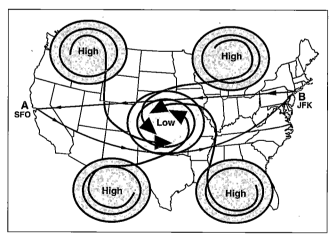

Figure 6-3. Circulation and wind

ALL
3395. The wind at 5,000 feet AGL is southwesterly while the surface wind is southerly. This difference in direction is primarily due to

A— stronger pressure gradient at higher altitudes.
B— friction between the wind and the surface.
C— stronger Coriolis force at the surface.

Friction between the wind and the surface slows the wind. The Coriolis force has less affect on slower winds, therefore there will be less deflection with surface winds than with winds at 5,000 feet AGL. (PLT516) — AC 00-6

Answer (A) is incorrect because pressure gradient is not the reason for wind direction differences; it is the force which causes wind. Answer (C) is incorrect because slower wind speed results in weaker Coriolis force at the surface.

ALL
3450. Convective circulation patterns associated with sea breezes are caused by

A— warm, dense air moving inland from over the water.
B— water absorbing and radiating heat faster than the land.
C— cool, dense air moving inland from over the water.

Caused by the heating of land on warm, sunny days, the sea breeze usually begins during early forenoon, reaches a maximum during the afternoon, and subsides around dusk after the land has cooled. The leading edge of the cool sea breeze forces warmer air inland to rise. Rising air from over land returns seaward at higher altitude to complete the convective cell. (PLT516) — AC 00-6

Answer (A) is incorrect because there will be cooler air over the water. Answer (B) is incorrect because land absorbs and radiates heat faster.

GLI
3350. What is the proper airspeed to use when flying between thermals on a cross-country flight against a headwind?

A— The best lift/drag speed increased by one-half the estimated wind velocity.
B— The minimum sink speed increased by one-half the estimated wind velocity.
C— The best lift/drag speed decreased by one-half the estimated wind velocity.

When gliding into a headwind, maximum distance will be achieved by adding approximately one-half the estimated headwind velocity to the best L/D speed. (PLT303) — FAA-H-8083-13

Temperature

In aviation, temperature is measured in degrees Celsius (°C). The standard temperature at sea level is 59°F (15°C). The average decrease in temperature with altitude (standard lapse rate) is 2°C (3.5°F) per 1,000 feet. Since this is an average, the exact value seldom exists; in fact, temperature sometimes increases with altitude (an inversion). The most frequent type of ground- or surface-based **temperature inversion** is one that is produced by terrestrial radiation on a clear, relatively still night.

ALL
3383. A temperature inversion would most likely result in which weather condition?

A— Clouds with extensive vertical development above an inversion aloft.
B— Good visibility in the lower levels of the atmosphere and poor visibility above an inversion aloft.
C— An increase in temperature as altitude is increased.

An increase in temperature with altitude is defined as an inversion. An inversion often develops near the ground on clear, cool nights when wind is light. The ground radiates heat and cools much faster than the overlying air. Air in contact with the ground becomes cold while the temperature a few hundred feet above changes very little. Thus, the temperature increases with height. A ground-based inversion usually means poor visibility. (PLT301) — AC 00-6

Answer (A) is incorrect because a temperature inversion will not result in vertical development, since warm air will not rise if the air above is warmer. Answer (B) is incorrect because a temperature inversion will trap dust, smoke, and other particles, thus causing reduced visibilities.

Answers

3395 [B]	3450 [C]	3350 [A]	3383 [C]

ALL
3384. The most frequent type of ground or surface-based temperature inversion is that which is produced by

A—terrestrial radiation on a clear, relatively still night.
B—warm air being lifted rapidly aloft in the vicinity of mountainous terrain.
C—the movement of colder air under warm air, or the movement of warm air over cold air.

An inversion often develops near the ground on clear, cool nights when wind is light. The ground radiates heat and cools much faster than the overlying air. Air in contact with the ground becomes cold while the temperature a few hundred feet above changes very little. Thus, the temperature increases with height. (PLT301) — AC 00-6

Answer (B) is incorrect because this is an example of convective activity. Answer (C) is incorrect because this describes a cold front and a warm front.

Moisture

Air has moisture (water vapor) in it. The water vapor content of air can be expressed in two different ways. The two commonly used terms are **relative humidity** and **dew point**.

Relative humidity relates the actual water vapor present in the air to that which could be present in the air. Temperature largely determines the maximum amount of water vapor air can hold. Warm air can hold more water vapor than can cold air. *See* Figure 6-4.

Air with 100% relative humidity is said to be saturated, and less than 100% is unsaturated.

Dew point is the temperature to which air must be cooled to become saturated by the water already present in the air. *See* Figure 6-5.

Moisture can be added to the air by either evaporation or sublimation. Moisture is removed from the air by either condensation or sublimation.

When water vapor condenses on large objects such as leaves, windshields, or airplanes, it will form **dew**; and when it condenses on microscopic particles such as salt, dust, or combustion by-products (condensation nuclei), it will form clouds or fog.

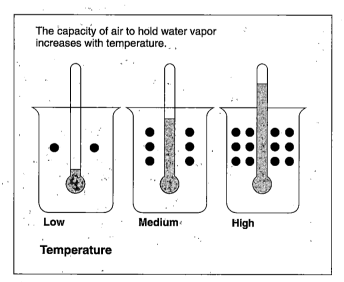

Figure 6-4. Capacity of air to hold water

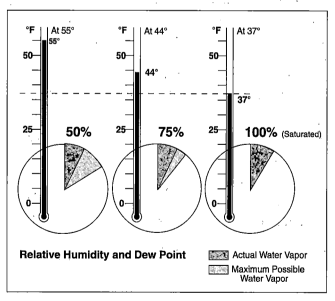

Figure 6-5. Relative humidity and dew point

To summarize, relative humidity can be increased either by lowering the air temperature or by increasing the amount of moisture in the air. If the temperature and dew point spread is small and decreasing, condensation is about to occur. If the temperature is above freezing, the weather most likely to develop will be fog or low clouds.

ALL, SPO
3397. What is meant by the term "dewpoint"?

A— The temperature at which condensation and evaporation are equal.
B— The temperature at which dew will always form.
C— The temperature to which air must be cooled to become saturated.

Dew point is the temperature to which air must be cooled to become saturated by the water vapor already present in the air. (PLT512) — AC 00-6

Answer (A) is incorrect because evaporation is not directly related to the dew point. Answer (B) is incorrect because dew will form only when an object cools below the dew point of the surrounding air.

ALL
3398. The amount of water vapor which air can hold depends on the

A— dewpoint.
B— air temperature.
C— stability of the air.

Temperature largely determines the maximum amount of water vapor air can hold. (PLT512) — AC 00-6

ALL, SPO
3399. Clouds, fog, or dew will always form when

A— water vapor condenses.
B— water vapor is present.
C— relative humidity reaches 100 percent.

As water vapor condenses or sublimates on condensation nuclei, liquid or ice particles begin to grow. Some condensation nuclei have an affinity for water and can induce condensation or sublimation even when air is almost, but not completely, saturated. (PLT512) — AC 00-6

Answer (B) is incorrect because the presence of water vapor does not result in clouds, fog, or dew unless condensation occurs. Answer (C) is incorrect because it is possible to have 100% humidity without the occurrence of condensation, which is necessary for clouds, fog, or dew to form.

ALL
3400. What are the processes by which moisture is added to unsaturated air?

A— Evaporation and sublimation.
B— Heating and condensation.
C— Supersaturation and evaporation.

Evaporation is the changing of liquid water to invisible water vapor. Sublimation is the changing of solid water directly to the vapor phase or water vapor to ice, by passing the liquid state in each process. (PLT512) — AC 00-6

Answer (B) is incorrect because heating and condensation alone do not add moisture to unsaturated air. Answer (C) is incorrect because "supersaturation" does not fit the context of the question.

SPO
2369. Moisture is added to air by

A— sublimation and condensation.
B— evaporation and condensation.
C— evaporation and sublimation.

Evaporation is the changing of liquid water to invisible water vapor. Sublimation is the changing of ice directly to water vapor. (PLT512) — AC 00-6

Answers (A) and (B) are incorrect because condensation removes moisture from the air.

ALL
3444. If the temperature/dewpoint spread is small and decreasing, and the temperature is 62°F, what type weather is most likely to develop?

A— Freezing precipitation.
B— Thunderstorms.
C— Fog or low clouds.

With a small temperature/dew point spread, the air is close to saturation. This will usually result in fog or low clouds. Anticipate fog when the temperature/dew point spread is 5°F or less and decreasing. (PLT512) — AC 00-6

Answer (A) is incorrect because precipitation will not freeze at a temperature of 62°F. Answer (B) is incorrect because temperature/dew point spread does not relate to the development of thunderstorms.

Answers

3397 [C]	3398 [B]	3399 [A]	3400 [A]	2369 [C]	3444 [C]

Air Masses and Fronts

When a body of air comes to rest on, or moves slowly over, an extensive area having fairly uniform properties of temperature and moisture, the air takes on these properties. The area over which the air mass acquires its identifying distribution of temperature and moisture is its "source region." As this air mass moves from its source region, it tends to take on the properties of the new underlying surface. The trend toward change is called air mass modification.

A **ridge** is an elongated area of high pressure. A **trough** is an elongated area of low pressure. All fronts lie in troughs. A **cold front** is the leading edge of an advancing cold air mass. A **warm front** is the leading edge of an advancing warm air mass. Warm fronts move about half as fast as cold fronts. **Frontal waves** and **cyclones** (areas of low pressure) usually form on slow-moving cold fronts or stationary fronts. Figure 6-6 shows the symbols that would appear on a weather map.

The physical manifestations of a warm or cold front can be different with each front. They vary with the speed of the air mass on the move and the degree of stability of the air mass being overtaken. A stable air mass forced aloft will continue to exhibit stable characteristics, while an unstable air mass forced to ascend will continue to be characterized by cumulus clouds, turbulence, showery precipitation, and good visibility.

Frontal passage will be indicated by the following discontinuities:

1. A temperature change (the most easily recognizable discontinuity);

2. A continuous decrease in pressure followed by an increase as the front passes; and

3. A shift in the wind direction, speed, or both.

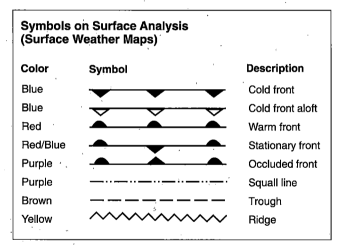

Symbols on Surface Analysis (Surface Weather Maps)

Color	Symbol	Description
Blue		Cold front
Blue		Cold front aloft
Red		Warm front
Red/Blue		Stationary front
Purple		Occluded front
Purple		Squall line
Brown		Trough
Yellow		Ridge

Figure 6-6. Weather map symbols

ALL
3422. One of the most easily recognized discontinuities across a front is

A— a change in temperature.
B— an increase in cloud coverage.
C— an increase in relative humidity.

Temperature is one of the most easily recognized discontinuities across a front. (PLT511) — AC 00-6

Answer (B) is incorrect because cloud coverage is not always present across a front. Answer (C) is incorrect because relative humidity is not an easily recognized discontinuity across a front.

ALL
3423. One weather phenomenon which will always occur when flying across a front is a change in the

A— wind direction.
B— type of precipitation.
C— stability of the air mass.

Wind direction always changes across a front. (PLT511) — AC 00-6

Answer (B) is incorrect because precipitation does not always exist with a front. Answer (C) is incorrect because the stability on both sides of the front may be the same.

Answers
3422 [A] 3423 [A]

GLI
3451. During which period is a sea breeze front most suitable for soaring flight?

A— Shortly after sunrise.
B— During the early forenoon.
C— During the afternoon.

A sea breeze begins during early afternoon and reaches a maximum in the afternoon, subsiding around dusk. (PLT516) — AC 00-6

Stability of the Atmosphere

Atmospheric stability is defined as the resistance of the atmosphere to vertical motion. A stable atmosphere resists any upward or downward movement. An unstable atmosphere allows an upward or downward disturbance to grow into a vertical (convective) current.

Determining the stability of the atmosphere requires measuring the difference between the actual existing (ambient) temperature lapse rate of a given parcel of air and the dry adiabatic (3°C per 1,000 feet) lapse rate.

A stable layer of air would be associated with a temperature inversion. Warming from below, on the other hand, would decrease the stability of an air mass.

The conditions shown in Figure 6-7 can be characteristic of stable or unstable air masses.

Unstable Air	Stable Air
Cumuliform clouds	Stratiform clouds and fog
Showery precipitation	Continuous precipitation
Rough air (turbulence)	Smooth air
Good visibility except in blowing obstructions	Fair to poor visibility in haze and smoke

Figure 6-7

ALL
3385. Which weather conditions should be expected beneath a low-level temperature inversion layer when the relative humidity is high?

A— Smooth air, poor visibility, fog, haze, or low clouds.
B— Light wind shear, poor visibility, haze, and light rain.
C— Turbulent air, poor visibility, fog, low stratus type clouds, and showery precipitation.

A ground-based inversion leads to poor visibility by trapping fog, smoke, and other restrictions into low levels of the atmosphere. The layer is stable and convection is suppressed. (PLT301) — AC 00-6

Answer (B) is incorrect because wind shears would occur above the inversion. Answer (C) is incorrect because showery precipitation and turbulent air are not associated with the presence of a low-level temperature inversion.

ALL
3403. What measurement can be used to determine the stability of the atmosphere?

A— Atmospheric pressure.
B— Actual lapse rate.
C— Surface temperature.

The difference between the existing lapse rate of a given mass of air and the adiabatic rates of cooling in upward moving air determines if the air is stable or unstable. (PLT173) — AC 00-6

ALL
3404. What would decrease the stability of an air mass?

A— Warming from below.
B— Cooling from below.
C— Decrease in water vapor.

When air near the surface is warm and moist, suspect instability. Surface heating, cooling aloft, converging or upslope winds, or an invading mass of colder air may lead to instability and cumuliform clouds. (PLT173) — AC 00-6

Answer (B) is incorrect because cooling from the air below would increase the stability of the air. Answer (C) is incorrect because an increase in water vapor will result in a decrease in stability.

Answers
3451   [C]   3385   [A]   3403   [B]   3404   [A]

ALL, SPO
3405. What is a characteristic of stable air?

A— Stratiform clouds.
B— Unlimited visibility.
C— Cumulus clouds.

Since stable air resists convection, clouds in stable air form in horizontal, sheet-like layers or "strata." (PLT173) — AC 00-6

Answers (B) and (C) are incorrect because unlimited visibility and cumulus clouds are characteristics of unstable air.

ALL
3408. What feature is associated with a temperature inversion?

A— A stable layer of air.
B— An unstable layer of air.
C— Chinook winds on mountain slopes.

If the temperature increases with altitude through a layer (an inversion), the layer is stable and convection is suppressed. (PLT492) — AC 00-6

ALL, SPO
3412. What are characteristics of a moist, unstable air mass?

A— Cumuliform clouds and showery precipitation.
B— Poor visibility and smooth air.
C— Stratiform clouds and showery precipitation.

Characteristics of a moist, unstable air mass include cumuliform clouds, showery precipitation, rough air (turbulence), and good visibility (except in blowing obstructions). (PLT511) — AC 00-6

ALL
3413. What are characteristics of unstable air?

A— Turbulence and good surface visibility.
B— Turbulence and poor surface visibility.
C— Nimbostratus clouds and good surface visibility.

Characteristics of an unstable air mass include cumuliform clouds, showery precipitation, rough air (turbulence), and good visibility (except in blowing obstructions). (PLT511) — AC 00-6

ALL
3414. A stable air mass is most likely to have which characteristic?

A— Showery precipitation.
B— Turbulent air.
C— Poor surface visibility.

Characteristics of a stable air mass include stratiform clouds and fog, continuous precipitation, smooth air, and fair to poor visibility in haze and smoke. (PLT511) — FAA-H-8083-25

Clouds

Stability determines which of two types of clouds will be formed: **cumuliform** or **stratiform**.

Cumuliform clouds are the billowy-type clouds having considerable vertical development, which enhances the growth rate of precipitation. They are formed in unstable conditions, and they produce showery precipitation made up of large water droplets. *See* Figure 6-8.

Stratiform clouds are the flat, more evenly based clouds formed in stable conditions. They produce steady, continuous light rain and drizzle made up of much smaller raindrops. *See* Figure 6-9.

Steady precipitation (in contrast to showery) preceding a front is an indication of stratiform clouds with little or no turbulence.

Clouds are divided into four families according to their height range: low, middle, high, and clouds with extensive vertical development. *See* Figure 6-10.

The first three families — low, middle, and high — are further classified according to the way they are formed. Clouds formed by vertical currents (unstable) are cumulus (heap) and are billowy in appearance. Clouds formed by the cooling of a stable layer are stratus (layered) and are flat and sheet-like in appearance. A further classification is the prefix "nimbo-" or suffix "-nimbus," which means raincloud.

Answers

| 3405 [A] | 3408 [A] | 3412 [A] | 3413 [A] | 3414 [C] |

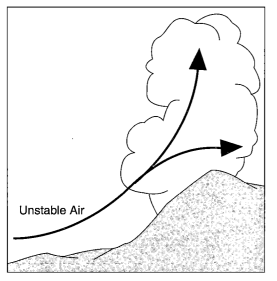

Figure 6-8. Cumulus clouds

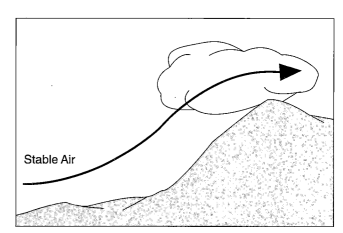

Figure 6-9. Stratiform clouds

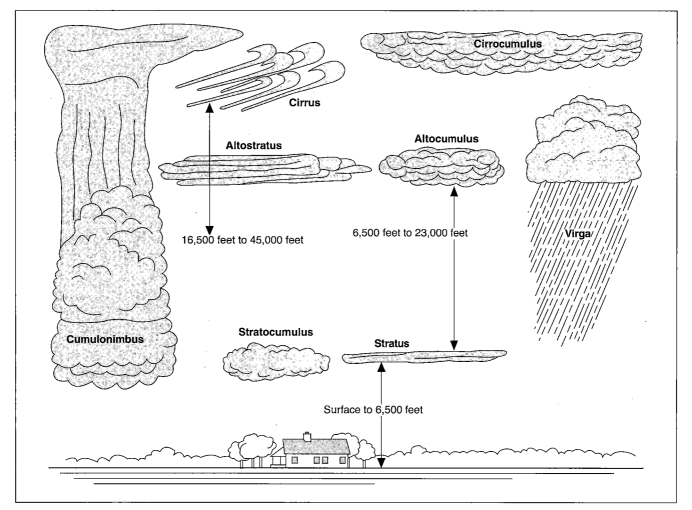

Figure 6-10. Cloud families

High clouds, called **cirrus**, are composed mainly of ice crystals; therefore, they are least likely to contribute to structural icing (since it requires water droplets).

The base of a cloud (AGL) that is formed by vertical currents (cumuliform clouds) can be roughly calculated by dividing the difference between the surface temperature and dew point by 4.4 and multiplying the rounded result by 1,000. The convergence of the temperature and the dew point lapse rate is 4.4°F per 1,000 feet.

Problem: What is the approximate base of the cumulus clouds if the surface air temperature is 70°F and the dew point is 61°F?

Solution:

Use the following steps:

1.   70°F (Temperature)
   <u>– 61°F</u> (Dew point)
      9°F

2. 9 ÷ 4.4 = 2.05 or 2

3. 2 x 1,000 = 2,000 feet (base of cloud, AGL)

ALL
3406. Moist, stable air flowing upslope can be expected to
A— produce stratus type clouds.
B— cause showers and thunderstorms.
C— develop convective turbulence.

When stable air is forced upward the air tends to retain horizontal flow and any cloudiness is flat and stratified. (PLT192) — AC 00-6

ALL, SPO
3407. If an unstable air mass is forced upward, what type clouds can be expected?
A— Stratus clouds with little vertical development.
B— Stratus clouds with considerable associated turbulence.
C— Clouds with considerable vertical development and associated turbulence.

When unstable air is forced upward, the disturbance grows. Any resulting cloudiness shows extensive vertical development. (PLT192) — AC 00-6

ALL
3424. Steady precipitation preceding a front is an indication of
A— stratiform clouds with moderate turbulence.
B— cumuliform clouds with little or no turbulence.
C— stratiform clouds with little or no turbulence.

Precipitation from stratiform clouds is usually steady and there is little or no turbulence. (PLT511) — AC 00-6

ALL
3433. The conditions necessary for the formation of cumulonimbus clouds are a lifting action and
A— unstable air containing an excess of condensation nuclei.
B— unstable, moist air.
C— either stable or unstable air.

For a cumulonimbus cloud or thunderstorm to form, the air must have:

1. Sufficient water vapor,

2. An unstable lapse rate, and

3. An initial upward boost (lifting) to start the storm process in motion.

(PLT192) — AC 00-6

Answers

3406 [A]	3407 [C]	3424 [C]	3433 [B]

ALL
3409. What is the approximate base of the cumulus clouds if the surface air temperature at 1,000 feet MSL is 70°F and the dewpoint is 48°F?

A— 4,000 feet MSL.
B— 5,000 feet MSL.
C— 6,000 feet MSL.

When lifted, unsaturated air cools at approximately 5.4°F per 1,000 feet. The dew point cools at approximately 1°F per 1,000 feet. Therefore, the convergence of the temperature and dew point lapse rates is 4.4°F per 1,000 feet. The base of a cloud (AGL) that is formed by vertical currents can be roughly calculated by dividing the difference between the surface temperature and the dew point by 4.4 and multiplying the rounded result by 1,000.

1.   70°F surface temperature
*   – 48°F dew point*
*   22°F*

2. 22 ÷ 4.4 = 5

3. 5 x 1,000 = 5,000 feet AGL

4.   5,000 feet AGL
*   + 1,000 feet field elevation*
*   6,000 feet MSL*

(PLT512) — AC 00-6

ALL
3410. At approximately what altitude above the surface would the pilot expect the base of cumuliform clouds if the surface air temperature is 82°F and the dewpoint is 38°F?

A— 9,000 feet AGL.
B— 10,000 feet AGL.
C— 11,000 feet AGL.

When lifted, unsaturated air cools at approximately 5.4°F per 1,000 feet. The dew point cools at approximately 1°F per 1,000 feet. Therefore, the convergence of the temperature and dew point lapse rates is 4.4°F per 1,000 feet. The base of a cloud (AGL) that is formed by vertical currents can be roughly calculated by dividing the difference between the surface temperature and the dew point by 4.4 and multiplying the rounded result by 1,000.

1.   82°F surface temperature
*   – 38°F dew point*
*   44°F*

2. 44 ÷ 4.4 = 10

3. 10 x 1,000 = 10,000 feet AGL

(PLT512) — AC 00-6

ALL, SPO
3415. The suffix "nimbus," used in naming clouds, means

A— a cloud with extensive vertical development.
B— a rain cloud.
C— a middle cloud containing ice pellets.

The prefix "nimbo-" or suffix "-nimbus" means rain cloud. (PLT192) — AC 00-6

ALL
3416. Clouds are divided into four families according to their

A— outward shape.
B— height range.
C— composition.

For identification purposes, clouds are divided into four families: high clouds, middle clouds, low clouds, and clouds with extensive vertical development. (PLT192) — AC 00-6

Answers

| 3409 | [C] | 3410 | [B] | 3415 | [B] | 3416 | [B] |

Turbulence

Cumulus clouds are formed by convective currents (heating from below); therefore, a pilot can expect turbulence below or inside cumulus clouds, especially towering cumulus clouds. The greatest turbulence could be expected inside cumulonimbus clouds.

If severe turbulence is encountered either inside or outside of clouds, the airplane's airspeed should be reduced to maneuvering speed and the pilot should attempt to maintain a level flight attitude because the amount of excess load that can be imposed on the wing will be decreased. Any attempt to maintain a constant altitude will greatly increase the stresses that are applied to the aircraft.

ALL
3419. What clouds have the greatest turbulence?

A— Towering cumulus.
B— Cumulonimbus.
C— Nimbostratus.

Cumulonimbus are the ultimate manifestation of instability. They are vertically-developed clouds of large dimensions with dense boiling tops, often crowned with thick veils of dense cirrus (the anvil). Nearly the entire spectrum of flying hazards are contained in these clouds including violent turbulence. (PLT192) — AC 00-6

ALL
3417. An almond or lens-shaped cloud which appears stationary, but which may contain winds of 50 knots or more, is referred to as

A— an inactive frontal cloud.
B— a funnel cloud.
C— a lenticular cloud.

Crests of standing waves may be marked by stationary, lens-shaped clouds known as standing lenticular clouds. (PLT192) — AC 00-6

ALL
3418. Crests of standing mountain waves may be marked by stationary, lens-shaped clouds known as

A— mammatocumulus clouds.
B— standing lenticular clouds.
C— roll clouds.

Crests of standing waves may be marked by stationary, lens-shaped clouds known as standing lenticular clouds. (PLT192) — AC 00-6

ALL, SPO
3420. What cloud types would indicate convective turbulence?

A— Cirrus clouds.
B— Nimbostratus clouds.
C— Towering cumulus clouds.

Towering cumulus signifies a relatively deep layer of unstable air. They show considerable vertical development and have billowing cauliflower tops. Showers can result from these clouds. Expect very strong turbulence, and perhaps some clear icing above the freezing level. (PLT192) — AC 00-6

ALL
3425. Possible mountain wave turbulence could be anticipated when winds of 40 knots or greater blow

A— across a mountain ridge, and the air is stable.
B— down a mountain valley, and the air is unstable.
C— parallel to a mountain peak, and the air is stable.

Always anticipate possible mountain wave turbulence when strong winds of 40 knots or greater blow across a mountain or ridge and the air is stable. (PLT263) — AC 00-6

SPO
2159. One of the most dangerous features of mountain waves is the turbulent areas in and

A— below rotor clouds.
B— above rotor clouds.
C— below lenticular clouds.

Rotor clouds appear to remain stationary, parallel the range, and stand a few miles leeward of the mountains. Turbulence is most frequent and most severe in and below the standing rotors just beneath the wave crests at or below mountaintop levels. (PLT501) — AC 00-6

Answers

3419 [B]	3417 [C]	3418 [B]	3420 [C]	3425 [A]	2159 [A]

ALL

3442. Upon encountering severe turbulence, which flight condition should the pilot attempt to maintain?

A— Constant altitude and airspeed.
B— Constant angle of attack.
C— Level flight attitude.

The primary concern is to avoid undue stress on the airframe. This can best be done by attempting to maintain a constant attitude while keeping the airspeed below design maneuvering speed (V$_A$). (PLT263) — AC 00-6

Answer (A) is incorrect because attempting to maintain a constant altitude or airspeed may result in overstressing the aircraft. Answer (B) is incorrect because a constant angle of attack would be impossible to maintain with the wind shear and shifts encountered in severe turbulence.

Thunderstorms

Thunderstorms present many hazards to flying. Three conditions necessary to the formation of a thunderstorm are:

1. Sufficient water vapor;

2. An unstable lapse rate; and

3. An initial upward boost (lifting).

The initial upward boost can be caused by heating from below, frontal lifting, or by mechanical lifting (wind blowing air upslope on a mountain).

There are three stages of a thunderstorm: the cumulus, mature, and dissipating stages. *See* Figure 6-11.

The **cumulus stage** is characterized by continuous updrafts, and these updrafts create low-pressure areas. Thunderstorms reach their greatest intensity during the **mature stage**, which is characterized by updrafts and downdrafts inside the cloud. Precipitation inside the cloud aids in the development of these downdrafts, and the start of rain from the base of the cloud signals the beginning of the mature stage. The precipitation that evaporates before it reaches the ground is called **virga**. The **dissipating stage** of a thunderstorm is characterized predominantly by downdrafts.

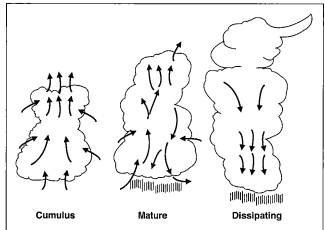

Figure 6-11. Stages of thunderstorms

Lightning is always associated with a thunderstorm.

Hail is formed inside thunderstorms by the constant freezing, melting, and refreezing of water as it is carried about by the up- and downdrafts.

A pilot should always expect the hazardous and invisible atmospheric phenomena called **wind shear turbulence** when operating anywhere near a thunderstorm (within 20 NM).

Thunderstorms that generally produce the most intense hazard to aircraft are called **squall-line thunderstorms**. These non-frontal, narrow bands of thunderstorms often develop ahead of a cold front.

Embedded thunderstorms are those that are obscured by massive cloud layers and cannot be seen.

Answers

3442 [C]

ALL

3434. What feature is normally associated with the cumulus stage of a thunderstorm?

A— Roll cloud.
B— Continuous updraft.
C— Frequent lightning.

The key feature of the cumulus stage is an updraft. Precipitation beginning to fall from the cloudbase is the signal that a downdraft has developed also and a cell has entered the mature stage. (PLT495) — AC 00-6

Answer (A) is incorrect because a roll cloud is associated with a mountain wave. Answer (C) is incorrect because frequent lightning may be present in any stage.

ALL

3435. Which weather phenomenon signals the beginning of the mature stage of a thunderstorm?

A— The appearance of an anvil top.
B— Precipitation beginning to fall.
C— Maximum growth rate of the clouds.

The key feature of the cumulus stage is an updraft. Precipitation beginning to fall from the cloudbase is the signal that a downdraft has developed also and the cell has entered the mature stage. (PLT495) — AC 00-6

Answer (A) is incorrect because the appearance of an anvil top is characteristic of the dissipating stage. Answer (C) is incorrect because the maximum growth rate of the clouds is during the mature stage of a thunderstorm, but it does not signal the beginning of that stage.

ALL, SPO

3436. What conditions are necessary for the formation of thunderstorms?

A— High humidity, lifting force, and unstable conditions.
B— High humidity, high temperature, and cumulus clouds.
C— Lifting force, moist air, and extensive cloud cover.

For a cumulonimbus cloud or thunderstorm to form, the air must have:

1. Sufficient water vapor,

2. An unstable lapse rate, and

3. An initial upward boost (lifting) to start the storm process in motion.

(PLT495) — AC 00-6

ALL

3437. During the life cycle of a thunderstorm, which stage is characterized predominately by downdrafts?

A— Cumulus.
B— Dissipating.
C— Mature.

Downdrafts characterize the dissipating stage of the thunderstorm cell and the storm dies rapidly. (PLT495) — AC 00-6

Answer (A) is incorrect because updrafts occur during the cumulus stage. Answer (C) is incorrect because both updrafts and downdrafts occur during the mature stage.

ALL, SPO

3438. Thunderstorms reach their greatest intensity during the

A— mature stage.
B— downdraft stage.
C— cumulus stage.

All thunderstorm hazards reach their greatest intensity during the mature stage. (PLT495) — AC 00-6

ALL, SPO

3439. Thunderstorms which generally produce the most intense hazard to aircraft are

A— squall line thunderstorms.
B— steady-state thunderstorms.
C— warm front thunderstorms.

A squall line is a non-frontal, narrow band of active thunderstorms. The line may be too long to easily detour and too wide and severe to penetrate. It often contains severe steady-state thunderstorms and presents the single, most intense weather hazard to aircraft. (PLT495) — AC 00-6

ALL, SPO

3521. The mature stage of a thunderstorm begins with

A— formation of the anvil top.
B— the start of precipitation.
C— continuous downdrafts.

The mature stage of a thunderstorm is characterized by updrafts and downdrafts inside the cloud and the start of rain. (PLT495) — AC 00-6

Answer (A) is incorrect because this represents the cumulus stage. Answer (C) is incorrect because this represents the dissipating stage.

Answers

3434 [B]	3435 [B]	3436 [A]	3437 [B]	3438 [A]	3439 [A]
3521 [B]					

ALL
3440. A nonfrontal, narrow band of active thunderstorms that often develop ahead of a cold front is known as a

A— prefrontal system.
B— squall line.
C— dry line.

A squall line is a nonfrontal, narrow band of active thunderstorms. The line may be too long to easily detour and too wide and severe to penetrate. It often contains severe steady-state thunderstorms and presents the single, most intense weather hazard to aircraft. (PLT495) — AC 00-6

ALL
3441. If there is thunderstorm activity in the vicinity of an airport at which you plan to land, which hazardous atmospheric phenomenon might be expected on the landing approach?

A— Precipitation static.
B— Wind-shear turbulence.
C— Steady rain.

Wind shear is an invisible hazard associated with all thunderstorms. Shear turbulence has been encountered 20 miles laterally from a severe storm. (PLT495) — AC 00-6

Answer (A) is incorrect because precipitation static is not considered a hazardous atmospheric phenomenon. Answer (C) is incorrect because showery precipitation is a characteristic of thunderstorm activity.

ALL
3452. Which weather phenomenon is always associated with a thunderstorm?

A— Lightning.
B— Heavy rain.
C— Hail.

A thunderstorm is, in general, a local storm invariably produced by a cumulonimbus cloud, and is always accompanied by lightning and thunder. (PLT495) — AC 00-6

GLI, LSG
3449. Which is considered to be the most hazardous condition when soaring in the vicinity of thunderstorms?

A— Static electricity.
B— Lightning.
C— Wind shear and turbulence.

During the mature stage of a thunderstorm, updrafts and downdrafts in close proximity create strong vertical shears and a very turbulent environment. A lightning strike can puncture the skin of an aircraft and damage communication and navigation equipment. (PLT120) — AC 00-6

Answers

3440 [B]   3441 [B]   3452 [A]   3449 [C]

Wind Shear

Wind shear is defined as a change in wind direction and/or speed over a very short distance in the atmosphere. This can occur at any level of the atmosphere and can be detected by the pilot as a sudden change in airspeed.

Low-level (low-altitude) **wind shear** can be expected during strong temperature inversions, on all sides of a thunderstorm and directly below the cell. A pilot can expect a wind shear zone in a temperature inversion whenever the wind speed at 2,000 feet to 4,000 feet above the surface is at least 25 knots.

Low-level wind shear can also be found near frontal activity because winds can be significantly different in the two air masses which meet to form the front.

In warm front conditions, the most critical period is before the front passes. Warm front shear may exist below 5,000 feet for about 6 hours before surface passage of the front. The wind shear associated with a warm front is usually more extreme than that found in cold fronts.

The shear associated with cold fronts is usually found behind the front. If the front is moving at 30 knots or more, the shear zone will be 5,000 feet above the surface 3 hours after frontal passage.

Basically, there are two potentially hazardous shear situations—the loss of a tailwind or the loss of a headwind.

A tailwind may shear to either a calm or headwind component. The airspeed initially increases, the aircraft pitches up, and altitude increases. Lower than normal power would be required initially, followed by a further decrease as the shear is encountered, and then an increase as the glide slope is regained. *See* Figure 6-12.

A headwind may shear to a calm or tailwind component. Initially, the airspeed decreases, the aircraft pitches down, and altitude decreases. *See* Figure 6-13.

Some airports can report boundary winds as well as the wind at the tower. When a tower reports a boundary wind which is significantly different from the airport wind, there is a possibility of hazardous wind shear.

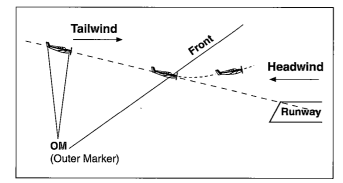

Figure 6-12. Tailwind shearing to headwind or calm

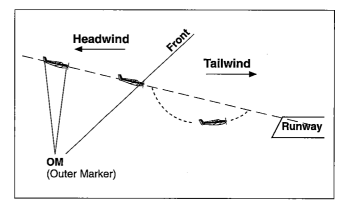

Figure 6-13. Headwind shearing to tailwind or calm

ALL, SPO

3426. Where does wind shear occur?

A— Only at higher altitudes.
B— Only at lower altitudes.
C— At all altitudes, in all directions.

Wind shear may be associated with either a wind shift or a wind speed gradient at any level in the atmosphere. (PLT518) — AC 00-6

ALL, SPO

3427. When may hazardous wind shear be expected?

A— When stable air crosses a mountain barrier where it tends to flow in layers forming lenticular clouds.
B— In areas of low-level temperature inversion, frontal zones, and clear air turbulence.
C— Following frontal passage when stratocumulus clouds form indicating mechanical mixing.

Hazardous wind shear can occur near the ground with either thunderstorms or a strong temperature inversion. (PLT518) — AC 00-6

Answer (A) is incorrect because turbulence can be expected when stable air crosses a mountain barrier. Answer (C) is incorrect because turbulence can be expected following frontal passage when stratocumulus clouds form, indicating mechanical mixing.

ALL, SPO

3428. A pilot can expect a wind-shear zone in a temperature inversion whenever the windspeed at 2,000 to 4,000 feet above the surface is at least

A— 10 knots.
B— 15 knots.
C— 25 knots.

An increase in temperature with altitude is defined as a temperature inversion. A pilot can be relatively certain of a shear zone in the inversion if the pilot knows the wind at 2,000 to 4,000 feet is 25 knots or more. (PLT518) — AC 00-6

SPO

2163. If a temperature inversion is encountered immediately after takeoff or during an approach to a landing, a potential hazard exists due to

A— wind shear.
B— strong surface winds.
C— strong convective currents.

When taking off or landing in calm wind under clear skies within a few hours before or after sunrise, be prepared for a temperature inversion near the ground. You can be relatively certain of a shear zone in the inversion if you know the wind at 2,000 to 4,000 feet is 25 knots or more. Allow a margin of airspeed above normal climb or approach speed to alleviate danger of stall in event of turbulence or sudden change in wind velocity. (PLT518) — AC 00-6

Icing

Structural icing occurs on an aircraft whenever supercooled condensed droplets of water make contact with any part of the aircraft that is also at a temperature below freezing. An inflight condition necessary for structural icing to form is visible moisture (clouds or raindrops).

Icing in precipitation (rain) is of concern to the VFR pilot because it can occur outside of clouds. Aircraft structural ice will most likely have the highest accumulation in freezing rain which indicates warmer temperature at a higher altitude. *See* Figure 6-14. The effects of structural icing on an aircraft may be seen in Figure 6-15.

The presence of ice pellets at the surface is evidence that there is freezing rain at a higher altitude, while wet snow indicates that the temperature at your altitude is above freezing. A situation conducive to any icing would be flying in the vicinity of a front.

Answers

3426 [C]   3427 [B]   3428 [C]   2163 [A]

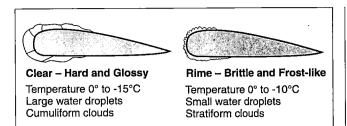

Clear – Hard and Glossy

Temperature 0° to -15°C
Large water droplets
Cumuliform clouds

Rime – Brittle and Frost-like

Temperature 0° to -10°C
Small water droplets
Stratiform clouds

Figure 6-14. Clear and rime ice

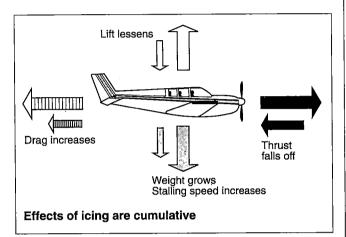

Lift lessens

Drag increases

Thrust falls off

Weight grows
Stalling speed increases

Effects of icing are cumulative

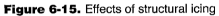

Figure 6-15. Effects of structural icing

ALL
3402. The presence of ice pellets at the surface is evidence that there

A— are thunderstorms in the area.
B— has been cold frontal passage.
C— is a temperature inversion with freezing rain at a higher altitude.

Ice pellets always indicate freezing rain at higher altitude. (PLT301) — AC 00-6

AIR, GLI, RTC, WSC, PPC
3429. One in-flight condition necessary for structural icing to form is .

A— small temperature/dewpoint spread.
B— stratiform clouds.
C— visible moisture.

Two conditions are necessary for structural icing in flight:

1. The aircraft must be flying through visible water such as rain or cloud droplets, and

2. The temperature at the point where the moisture strikes the aircraft must be 0°C (32°F) or colder.

(PLT274) — AC 00-6

AIR, GLI, RTC, WSC, PPC
3430. In which environment is aircraft structural ice most likely to have the highest accumulation rate?

A— Cumulus clouds with below freezing temperatures.
B— Freezing drizzle.
C— Freezing rain.

A condition favorable for rapid accumulation of clear icing is freezing rain below a frontal surface. (PLT274) — AC 00-6

Answers (A) and (B) are incorrect because although cumulus clouds with below-freezing temperatures and freezing drizzle are conducive to structural icing, they will not have as high an accumulation rate as freezing rain.

ALL
3956. During a cross-country flight you picked up rime icing which you estimate is 1/2" thick on the leading edge of the wings. You are now below the clouds at 2,000 feet AGL and are approaching your destination airport under VFR. Visibility under the clouds is more than 10 miles, winds at the destination airport are 8 knots right down the runway, and the surface temperature is 3°C. You decide to:

A— use a faster than normal approach and landing speed.
B— approach and land at your normal speed since the ice is not thick enough to have any noticeable effect.
C— fly your approach slower than normal to lessen the "wind chill" effect and break up the ice.

Ice will accumulate unevenly on the airplane. It will add weight and drag, and decrease thrust and lift. With ice accumulations, landing approaches should be made with a minimum wing flap setting and with an added margin of airspeed. Sudden and large configuration and airspeed changes should be avoided. (PLT128) — FAA-H-8083-3

Answer (B) is incorrect because ice having a thickness similar to sandpaper on the leading edge and upper surface of a wing can reduce wing lift by as much as 30% and increase drag by 40%. Answer (C) is incorrect because ice will increase drag, requiring additional lift (airspeed); "wind chill" effect cannot be relied upon to melt/remove the ice that has already accumulated; flying slower than normal increases the possibility of a stall due to the decreased lift.

Answers

| 3402 | [C] | 3429 | [C] | 3430 | [C] | 3956 | [A] |

Fog

Fog is a surface-based cloud (restricting visibility) composed of either water droplets or ice crystals. Fog may form by cooling the air to its dew point or by adding moisture to the air near the ground. A small temperature/dew point spread is essential to the formation of fog. An abundance of condensation nuclei from combustion products makes fog prevalent in industrial areas.

Fog is classified by the way it is formed.

Radiation fog (ground fog) is formed when terrestrial radiation cools the ground, which in turn cools the air in contact with it. When the air is cooled to its dew point (or within a few degrees), fog will form. This fog will form most readily in warm, moist air over low, flatland areas on clear, calm (no wind) nights.

Advection fog (sea fog) is formed when warm, moist air moves (wind is required) over colder ground or water (e.g., an air mass moving inland from the coast in winter).

Upslope fog is formed when moist, stable air is cooled to its dew point as it moves (wind is required) up sloping terrain. Cooling will be at the dry adiabatic lapse rate of approximately 3°C per 1,000 feet.

Precipitation (rain or drizzle)-induced fog is most commonly associated with frontal activity and is formed by relatively warm drizzle or rain falling through cooler air. Evaporation from the precipitation saturates the cool air and fog forms. This fog is especially critical because it occurs in the proximity of precipitation and other possible hazards such as icing, turbulence, and thunderstorms.

Steam fog forms in the winter when cold, dry air passes from land areas over comparatively warm ocean waters. Low-level turbulence can occur and icing can become hazardous in a steam fog.

ALL
3443. What situation is most conducive to the formation of radiation fog?

A— Warm, moist air over low, flatland areas on clear, calm nights.
B— Moist, tropical air moving over cold, offshore water.
C— The movement of cold air over much warmer water.

Conditions favorable for radiation fog are clear sky, little or no wind, and small temperature/dew point spread (high relative humidity). Radiation fog is restricted to land because water surfaces cool little from nighttime radiation. (PLT226) — AC 00-6

Answers (B) and (C) are incorrect because radiation fog will not form over water since water surfaces cool little from nighttime radiation.

ALL
3445. In which situation is advection fog most likely to form?

A— A warm, moist air mass on the windward side of mountains.
B— An air mass moving inland from the coast in winter.
C— A light breeze blowing colder air out to sea.

Advection fog forms when moist air moves over colder ground or water. It is most common along coastal areas. This fog frequently forms offshore as a result of cold water, then is carried inland by the wind. (PLT226) — AC 00-6

Answer (A) is incorrect because a warm, moist air mass on the windward side of mountains will form upslope fog and/or rain. Answer (C) is incorrect because a light breeze blowing colder air out to sea will form steam fog.

Answers

3443 [A]   3445 [B]

ALL

3446. What types of fog depend upon wind in order to exist?

A— Radiation fog and ice fog.
B— Steam fog and ground fog.
C— Advection fog and upslope fog.

Advection fog forms when moist air moves over colder ground or water. It is most common along coastal areas, but often develops deep in continental areas. Advection fog deepens as wind speed increases up to about 15 knots. Wind much stronger than 15 knots lifts the fog into a layer of low stratus or stratocumulus. Upslope fog forms as a result of moist, stable air being cooled adiabatically as it moves up sloping terrain. Once upslope wind ceases, the fog dissipates. (PLT226) — AC 00-6

Answer (A) is incorrect because radiation fog and ice fog do not depend upon wind in order to exist. Answer (B) is incorrect because ground fog does not depend on wind in order to exist.

ALL

3447. Low-level turbulence can occur and icing can become hazardous in which type of fog?

A— Rain-induced fog.
B— Upslope fog.
C— Steam fog.

Steam fog forms in the winter when cold, dry air passes from land areas over comparatively warm ocean waters. Low-level turbulence can occur and icing can become hazardous in a steam fog. (PLT226) — AC 00-6

Frost

Frost is described as ice deposits formed by sublimation on a surface when the temperature of the collecting surface is at or below the dew point of the adjacent air and the dew point is below freezing.

Frost causes early airflow separation on an airfoil resulting in a loss of lift. Therefore, all frost should be removed from the lifting surfaces of an airplane before flight or it may prevent the airplane from becoming airborne.

ALL

3401. Which conditions result in the formation of frost?

A— The temperature of the collecting surface is at or below freezing when small droplets of moisture fall on the surface.
B— The temperature of the collecting surface is at or below the dewpoint of the adjacent air and the dewpoint is below freezing.
C— The temperature of the surrounding air is at or below freezing when small drops of moisture fall on the collecting surface.

Frost forms in much the same way as dew. The difference is that the dew point of surrounding air must be colder than freezing. (PLT493) — AC 00-6

Answers (A) and (C) are incorrect because ice will form in these situations.

AIR

3432. How does frost affect the lifting surfaces of an airplane on takeoff?

A— Frost may prevent the airplane from becoming airborne at normal takeoff speed.
B— Frost will change the camber of the wing, increasing lift during takeoff.
C— Frost may cause the airplane to become airborne with a lower angle of attack at a lower indicated airspeed.

The roughness of the surface of frost spoils the smooth flow of air, thus causing a slowing of the airflow. This slowing of the air causes early air flow separation over the affected airfoil, resulting in a loss of lift. Even a small amount of frost on airfoils may prevent an aircraft from becoming airborne at normal takeoff speed. (PLT128) — AC 00-6

Answer (B) is incorrect because frost does not change the basic aerodynamic shape of the airfoil. Answer (C) is incorrect because frost may prevent the aircraft from becoming airborne at normal takeoff speed and will not lower the angle of attack.

Answers

3446   [C]   3447   [C]   3401   [B]   3432   [A]

AIR, GLI

3206. How will frost on the wings of an airplane affect takeoff performance?

A— Frost will disrupt the smooth flow of air over the wing, adversely affecting its lifting capability.

B— Frost will change the camber of the wing, increasing its lifting capability.

C— Frost will cause the airplane to become airborne with a higher angle of attack, decreasing the stall speed.

The roughness of the surface of frost spoils the smooth flow of air, thus causing a slowing of the airflow. This slowing of the air causes early air flow separation over the affected airfoil, resulting in a loss of lift. Even a small amount of frost on airfoils may prevent an aircraft from becoming airborne at normal takeoff speed. (PLT134) — FAA-H-8083-25

Answer (B) is incorrect because frost will not change the shape of the wing. Answer (C) is incorrect because frost on the wings of an airplane will increase the stall speed.

AIR, GLI, RTC, WSC, PPC

3431. Why is frost considered hazardous to flight?

A— Frost changes the basic aerodynamic shape of the airfoils, thereby increasing lift.

B— Frost slows the airflow over the airfoils, thereby increasing control effectiveness.

C— Frost spoils the smooth flow of air over the wings, thereby decreasing lifting capability.

The roughness of the surface of frost spoils the smooth flow of air, thus causing a slowing of the airflow. This slowing of the air causes early air flow separation over the affected airfoil, resulting in a loss of lift. Even a small amount of frost on airfoils may prevent an aircraft from becoming airborne at normal takeoff speed. (PLT128) — AC 00-6

Answer (A) is incorrect because frost does not change the basic aerodynamic shape of the airfoil, nor does it increase lift. Answer (B) is incorrect because frost does not have an effect on the control effectiveness.

SPO

2170. Which is true with respect to a high- or low-pressure system?

A— A high-pressure area or ridge is an area of rising air.

B— A low-pressure area or trough is an area of descending air.

C— A high-pressure area or ridge is an area of descending air.

Highs and ridges are areas of descending air. (PLT517) — AC 00-6

Answer (A) is incorrect because a high or ridge is an area of descending air. Answer (B) is incorrect because a low or trough is an area of rising air.

LSG

2312. During which period is a sea breeze front most suitable for soaring flight?

A— Shortly after sunrise.

B— During the middle of the morning.

C— During the afternoon.

A sea breeze begins during early afternoon and reaches a maximum in the afternoon, subsiding around dusk. (PLT511) — AC 00-6

Answers

| 3206 | [A] | 3431 | [C] | 2170 | [C] | 2312 | [C] |

Chapter 7
Weather Services

Aviation Routine Weather Report (METAR)

An international weather reporting code is used for weather reports (METAR) and forecasts (TAFs) worldwide. The reports follow the format shown in Figure 7-1.

For aviation purposes, the ceiling is the lowest broken or overcast layer, or vertical visibility into an obscuration.

Key to Aerodrome Forecast (TAF) and Aviation Routine Weather Report (METAR)

TAF	KPIT 091730Z 0918/1024 15005KT 5SM HZ FEW020 WS010/31022KT
	FM091930 30015G25KT 3SM SHRA OVC015
	TEMPO 0920/0922 1/2SM +TSRA OVC008CB
	FM100100 27008KT 5SM SHRA BKN020 OVC040
	PROB30 1004/1007 1SM -RA BR
	FM101015 18005KT 6SM -SHRA OVC020
	BECMG 1013/1015 P6SM NSW SKC

Note: Users are cautioned to confirm *DATE* and *TIME* of the TAF. For example FM100000 is 0000Z on the **10th**. Do not confuse with *1000Z!*

METAR KPIT 091955Z COR 22015G25KT 3/4SM R28L/2600FT TSRA OVC010CB 18/16 A2992 RMK SLP045 T01820159

Forecast	Explanation	Report
TAF	Message type: TAF: routine or TAF AMD: amended forecast; METAR: hourly; SPECI: special or TESTM: noncommissioned ASOS report	METAR
KPIT	ICAO location indicator	KPIT
091730Z	Issuance time: ALL times in UTC "Z", 2-digit date; 4-digit time	091955Z
0918/1024	Valid period: Either 24 hours or 30 hours. The first two digits of EACH four-digit number indicate the date of the valid period, the final two digits indicate the time (valid from 18Z on the 9th to 24Z on the 10th).	
	In U.S. METAR: CORrected ob; or AUTOmated ob for automated report with no human intervention; omitted when observer logs on.	COR
15005KT	Wind: 3-digit true-north direction, nearest 10 degrees (or VaRiaBle); next 2-3 digits for speed and unit, KT (KMH or MPS); as needed, Gust and maximum speed; 00000KT for calm; for METAR, if direction varies 60 degrees or more, Variability appended, e.g., 180V260	22015G25KT
5SM	Prevailing visibility: In U.S., Statute Miles and fractions; above 6 miles in TAF Plus6SM. (Or, 4-digit minimum visibility in meters and as required, lowest value with direction.)	3/4SM
	Runway Visual Range: R; 2-digit runway designator Left, Center, or Right as needed; "/"; Minus or Plus in U.S., 4-digit value, FeeT in U.S. (usually meters elsewhere); 4-digit value Variability, 4-digit value (and tendency Down, Up or No change)	R28L/2600FT
HZ	Significant present, forecast and recent weather: See table (to the right)	TSRA
FEW020	Cloud amount, height and type: SKy Clear 0/8, FEW >0/8-2/8, SCaTtered 3/8-4/8, BroKeN 5/8-7/8, OVerCast 8/8; 3-digit height in hundreds of feet; Towering CUmulus or CumulonimBus in METAR; in TAF, only CB. Vertical Visibility for obscured sky and height "VV004". More than 1 layer may be reported or forecast. In automated METAR reports only, CLeaR for "clear below 12,000 feet."	OVC010CB
	Temperature: Degrees Celsius; first 2 digits, temperature "/" last 2 digits, dewpoint temperature; Minus for below zero, e.g., M06	18/16
	Altimeter setting: Indicator and 4 digits; in U.S., A: inches and hundredths; (Q: hectoPascals, e.g., Q1013)	A2992
	Continued	

Key to Aerodrome Forecast (TAF) and Aviation Routine Weather Report (METAR)

Forecast	Explanation	Report
WS010/ 31022KT	In U.S. TAF, nonconvective low-level (≤2,000 feet) Wind Shear; 3-digit height (hundreds of feet); "/"; 3-digit wind direction and 2-3 digit wind speed above the indicated height, and unit, KT	
	In METAR, ReMarK indicator and remarks. For example: Sea-Level Pressure in hectoPascals and tenths, as shown: 1004.5 hPa; Temp/ dewpoint in tenths °C, as shown: temp. 18.2°C, dewpoint 15.9°C	RMK SLP045 T01820159
FM091930	FroM: Changes are expected at: 2-digit date, 2-digit hour, and 2-digit minute beginning time: indicates significant change. Each FM starts on a new line, indented 5 spaces	
TEMPO 0920/0922	TEMPOrary: Changes expected for <1 hour and in total, < half of the period between the 2-digit date and 2-digit hour beginning, and 2-digit date and 2-digit hour ending time	
PROB30 1004/1007	PROBability and 2-digit percent (30 or 40): Probable condition in the period between the 2-digit date and 2-digit hour beginning time, and the 2-digit date and 2-digit hour ending time	
BECMG 1013/1015	BECoMinG: Change expected in the period between the 2-digit date and 2-digit hour beginning time, and the 2-digit date and 2-digit hour ending time	

Table of Significant Present, Forecast and Recent Weather—Grouped in categories and used in the order listed below; or as needed in TAF, No Significant Weather

QUALIFIERS

Intensity or Proximity

"–" = Light   No sign = Moderate   "+" = Heavy

"VC" = Vicinity, but not at aerodrome. In the U.S. METAR, 5 to 10 SM from the point of observation. In the U.S. TAF, 5 to 10 SM from the center of the runway complex. Elsewhere, within 8000m.

Descriptor

BC Patches	BL Blowing	DR Drifting	FZ Freezing
MI Shallow	PR Partial	SH Showers	TS Thunderstorm

WEATHER PHENOMENA

Precipitation

DZ Drizzle	GR Hail	GS Small hail or snow pellets
IC Ice crystals	PL Ice pellets	RA Rain SG Snow grains
SN Snow	UP Unknown precipitation in automated observations	

Obscuration

BR Mist (≥5/8SM)	DU Widespread dust	FG Fog (<5/8SM)	FU Smoke
HZ Haze	PY Spray	SA Sand	VA Volcanic ash

Other

DS Dust storm	FC Funnel cloud	+FC Tornado or waterspout
PO Well-developed dust or sand whirls	SQ Squall	SS Sandstorm

• Explanations in parentheses "( )" indicate different worldwide practices.
• Ceiling is not specified; defined as the lowest broken or overcast layer, or the vertical visibility.
• NWS TAFs exclude BECMG groups and temperature forecasts, NWS TAFs do not use PROB in the first 9 hours of a TAF; NWS METARs exclude trend forecasts. U.S. Military TAFs include Turbulence and Icing groups.

Figure 7-1. TAF/METAR weather card

ALL, SPO

3462. (Refer to Figure 12.) Which of the reporting stations have VFR weather?

A— All.
B— KINK, KBOI, and KJFK.
C— KINK, KBOI, and KLAX.

IFR conditions are a ceiling less than 1,000 feet and/or visibility less than 3 miles.

KINK: Visibility is 15 statute miles and the sky is clear: VFR.

KBOI: Visibility is 30 statute miles and sky is scattered at 15,000 feet: VFR.

KLAX: Visibility is 6 statute miles with mist and the sky is scattered at 700 feet (SCT does not constitute a ceiling): VFR.

KMDW: Visibility is 1-1/2 statute miles with rain and the ceiling is overcast at 700 feet: IFR.

KJFK: Visibility is 1/2 statute mile with fog and the ceiling is overcast at 500 feet: IFR.

(PLT059) — AC 00-45

ALL, SPO

3463. For aviation purposes, ceiling is defined as the height above the Earth's surface of the

A— lowest reported obscuration and the highest layer of clouds reported as overcast.
B— lowest broken or overcast layer or vertical visibility into an obscuration.
C— lowest layer of clouds reported as scattered, broken, or thin.

For aviation purposes, the ceiling is the lowest broken or overcast layer, or vertical visibility into an obscuration. (PLT026) — AC 00-45

ALL, SPO

3464. (Refer to Figure 12.) The wind direction and velocity at KJFK is from

A— 180° true at 4 knots.
B— 180° magnetic at 4 knots.
C— 040° true at 18 knots.

The wind is reported as a five-digit group (six digits if speed is over 99 knots). The first three digits is the direction the wind is blowing from rounded to the nearest tens of degrees relative to true north, or "VRB" if the direction is variable. The next two digits is the speed in knots, or if over 99 knots, the next three digits. If the wind is gusty, it is reported as a "G" after the speed followed by the highest gust reported. The abbreviation "KT" is appended to denote the use of knots for wind speed. The wind group for KJFK is 18004KT which means the wind is from 180° at 4 knots. (PLT059) — AC 00-45

ALL

3465. (Refer to Figure 12.) What are the wind conditions at Wink, Texas (KINK)?

A— Calm.
B— 110° at 12 knots, gusts 18 knots.
C— 111° at 2 knots, gusts 18 knots.

The wind is reported as a five-digit group (six digits if speed is over 99 knots). The first three digits is the direction the wind is blowing from rounded to the nearest tens of degrees relative to true north, or "VRB" if the direction is variable. The next two digits is the speed in knots, or if over 99 knots, the next three digits. If the wind is gusty, it is reported as a "G" after the speed followed by the highest gust reported. The abbreviation "KT" is appended to denote the use of knots for wind speed. The wind group for KINK is 11012G18KT which means the wind is from 110° at 12 knots, with gusts to 18 knots. (PLT059) — AC 00-45

ALL

3466. (Refer to Figure 12.) The remarks section for KMDW has RAB35 listed. This entry means

A— blowing mist has reduced the visibility to 1-1/2 SM.
B— rain began at 1835Z.
C— the barometer has risen .35" Hg.

The entry RAB35 means that rain began 35 minutes past the hour. (PLT059) — AC 00-45

Answer (A) is incorrect because mist is reported as BR. Answer (C) is incorrect because there is no format for reporting a change in altimeter in a METAR.

Answers

3462 [C]   3463 [B]   3464 [A]   3465 [B]   3466 [B]

ALL
3467. (Refer to Figure 12.) What are the current conditions depicted for Chicago Midway Airport (KMDW)?

A— Sky 700 feet overcast, visibility 1-1/2 SM, rain
B— Sky 7000 feet overcast, visibility 1-1/2 SM, heavy rain
C— Sky 700 feet overcast, visibility 11, occasionally 2 SM, with rain.

The current conditions at KMDW are 1-1/2 SM visibility (1-1/2 SM) with rain (RA), ceiling overcast at 700 feet (OVC007). (PLT059) — AC 00-45

Pilot Weather Reports (PIREPs) (UA)

Aircraft in flight are the only means of directly observing cloud tops, icing, and turbulence; therefore, no observation is more timely than one made from the cockpit. While the FAA encourages pilots to report inflight weather, a report of any unforecast weather is required by regulation. A **PIREP** (identified by the letters "UA") is usually transmitted in a prescribed format. *See* Figure 7-2.

PIREP FORM

Pilot Weather Report
→ = Space Symbol

3-Letter SA Identifier
1. **UA→** _____ **UUA→** _____
_____ _____ →
Routine Report / Urgent Report

2. **/OV** → Location:

3. **/TM** → Time:

4. **/FL** → Altitude/Flight Level:

5. **/TP** → Aircraft Type:

Items 1 through 5 are mandatory for all PIREPs

6. **/SK** → Sky Cover:

7. **/WX** → Flight Visibility and Weather:

8. **/TA** → Temperature (*Celsius*):

9. **/WV** → Wind:

10. **/TB** → Turbulence:

11. **/IC** → Icing:

12. **/RM** → Remarks:

FAA FORM 7110-2 (1-85) Supersedes Previous Edition
(Side A)

Encoding Pilot Weather Reports (PIREP)

1. **UA** - Routine PIREP, **UUA** - Urgent PIREP

2. **/OV** - **Location:** Use 3-letter or 4-letter NAVAID idents only.
   a. Fix: /OV ABC, /OV ABC 090025.
   b. Fix to fix: /OV ABC-DEF, /OV ABC-DEF 120020, /OV ABC 045020-DEF 120005, /OV ABC-DEF-GHI..

3. **/TM** - **Time:** 4 digits in UTC: /TM 0915

4. **/FL** - **Altitude/Flight Level:** 3 digits for hundreds of feet. If not known, use UNKN: /FL095, /FL310, /FLUNKN.

5. **/TP** - **Type aircraft:** 4 digits maximum. If not known use UNKN: /TP L329./TP B727 /TP UNKN

6. **/SK** - **Sky cover:** Describe as follows:
   a. Height of cloud base in hundreds of feet. If unknown, use UNKN.
   b. Cloud cover symbol.
   c. Height of cloud tops in hundreds of feet.
   d. Use solidus (/) to separate layers.
   e. Use a space to separate each sub element.
   f. Examples: /SK 038 BKN. /SK 038 OVC 045, /SK 055 SCT 073/085 BKN 105, /SK UNKN OVC

7. **/WX** - **Flight Visibility and Weather:** Flight visibility reported first. Use standard weather symbols. /WX FV02 R H, /WX FV01 TRW.

8. **/TA** - **Air temperature in Celsius:** If below zero, prefix with an "M." /TA 15, /TA -M06.

9. **/WV** - **Wind:** Direction and speed. /WV 27045, /WV 280110.

10. **/TB** - **Turbulence:** Use standard contractions for intensity and type (use CAT or CHOP when appropriate). Include altitude only if different from /FL. /TB EXTRM, /TB LGT-MDT BLO-090.

11. **/IC** - **Icing:** Describe using standard intensity and type contractions. Include altitude only if different than /FL: /IC LGT-MDT RIME, /IC SVR CLR 028-045.

12. **/RM** - **Remarks:** Use free form to clarify the report. Most hazardous element first: /RM LLWS - 15KT SFC-003 DURGC RNWY 22 JFK.

Examples of Completed PIREPS

UUA /OV ABQ090045/TM 1430/FL130/TP BE30/TB SEV/RM BROKE ALL THE BOTTLES IN THE BAR

UA /OV KMRB-KPIT/TM 1600/FL100/TP BE55/SK BKN024-TOP032/BKN-OVC043-TOPUNKN/TA M12/IC LGT-MOD RIME 055-080

Figure 7-2

UA/OV KOKC-KTUL/TM 1800/FL120/TP BE90//SK BKN018-TOP055/OVC072-TOP089/CLR ABV/TA M7/WV 08021/TB LGT 055-072/IC LGT-MOD RIME 072-089.

Decodes as follows:

Pilot report, Oklahoma City to Tulsa at 1800Z at 12,000 feet.

Type of aircraft is a Beech King Air 90.

The first cloud layer has a base of 1,800 feet broken, with tops at 5,500 feet.

The second cloud layer base is 7,200 feet overcast with tops at 8,900 feet.

It is clear above.

Outside air temperature is -7° Celsius.

The wind is 080° at 21 knots.

There is light turbulence between 5,500 feet and 7,200 feet.

There is light to moderate rime icing reported between 7,200 feet and 8,900 feet.

ALL
3472. (Refer to Figure 14.) The base and tops of the overcast layer reported by a pilot are

A— 1,800 feet MSL and 5,500 feet MSL. .
B— 5,500 feet AGL and 7,200 feet MSL.
C— 7,200 feet MSL and 8,900 feet MSL.

Cloud layers in a PIREP are found after the "SK" heading. Height of the cloud base is given in hundreds of feet, then the cloud cover symbol (SCT, BKN, etc.) is given, followed by the height of cloud tops in hundreds of feet. A diagonal slash is used to separate cloud layers.

The base of the broken (BKN) layer was reported to be 1,800 feet and tops at 5,500 feet (BKN018-TOP055).

The question is asking for the overcast (OVC) layer that has a reported base at 7,200 feet and tops at 8,900 feet. All cloud heights in a PIREP are MSL (OVC072-TOP089). (PLT061) — AC 00-45

ALL
3473. (Refer to Figure 14.) The wind and temperature at 12,000 feet MSL as reported by a pilot are

A— 090° at 21 MPH and -9°F.
B— 090° at 21 knots and -9°C.
C— 080° at 21 knots and -7°C.

Winds are given after the "WV" heading. Wind direction is listed first, followed by wind speed in knots. WV 08021/ means wind from 080° at 21 knots. Air temperature is given in 2 digits, (in degrees Celsius), after the "TA" heading. If below zero, it will be prefixed with an "M." Therefore, /TA M7/ means that the outside air temperature is -7°C. (PLT061) — AC 00-45

ALL
3474. (Refer to Figure 14.) If the terrain elevation is 1,295 feet MSL, what is the height above ground level of the base of the ceiling?

A— 505 feet AGL.
B— 1,295 feet AGL.
C— 6,586 feet AGL.

Cloud layers in a PIREP are found after the "SK" heading. Height of the cloud base is given in hundreds of feet, then the cloud cover symbol (SCT, BKN, etc.) is given, followed by the height of the cloud tops in hundreds of feet. All cloud heights in a PIREP are MSL.

The first cloud layer was reported by a pilot to have bases at 1,800 feet and tops at 5,500 feet with broken (BKN) cloud cover (a broken cloud layer does constitute a ceiling).

If the field elevation is 1,295 feet MSL and the base of the first cloud layer (BKN) is 1,800 feet MSL, then the base of the ceiling is 505 feet AGL.

1,800 MSL
− 1,295 MSL
505 AGL

(PLT061) — AC 00-45

ALL
3475. (Refer to Figure 14.) The intensity of the turbulence reported at a specific altitude is

A— moderate from 5,500 feet to 7,200 feet.
B— moderate at 5,500 feet and at 7,200 feet.
C— light from 5,500 feet to 7,200 feet.

Turbulence in a PIREP is found after the "TB" heading. /TB LGT 055-072/ means light turbulence between 5,500 feet MSL and 7,200 feet MSL. (PLT061) — AC 00-45

ALL
3476. (Refer to Figure 14.) The intensity and type of icing reported by a pilot is

A— light to moderate.
B— light to moderate rime.
C— light to moderate clear.

The intensity and type of icing is listed in a PIREP after the "IC" heading. /IC LGT-MOD RIME 072-089 means light (LGT) to moderate (MOD) rime icing from 7,200 feet MSL to 8,900 feet MSL. (PLT061) — AC 00-45

Terminal Aerodrome Forecast (TAF)

A Terminal Aerodrome Forecast (TAF) is a concise statement of the expected meteorological conditions at an airport during a specified period (usually 24 hours). TAFs use the same code used in the METAR weather reports (*See* Figure 7-1).

TAFs are issued in the following format:

TYPE / LOCATION / ISSUANCE TIME / VALID TIME / FORECAST

Note: The "/" above are for separation purposes and do not appear in the actual TAFs.

ALL, SPO
3479. (Refer to Figure 15.) What is the valid period for the TAF for KMEM?

A— 12th 1800Z to 13th 2400Z.
B— 12th at 1700Z.
C— 1218Z to 1324Z.

The valid period of the TAF is 1218/1324. The first two numbers in each four number grouping identify the date followed by the time in Zulu. It reads as 12th at 1800Z to the 13th at 2400Z. (PLT072) — AC 00-45

ALL
3480. (Refer to Figure 15.) In the TAF for KMEM, what does "SHRA" stand for?

A— Rain showers.
B— A shift in wind direction is expected.
C— A significant change in precipitation is possible.

"SH" stands for showers, and "RA" stands for rain. (PLT072) — AC 00-45

Answers (B) and (C) are incorrect because a permanent change in existing conditions during the valid period of the TAF is indicated by the change groups FMHH (FroM) and BECMG (BECoMinG) HHhh.

ALL
3481. (Refer to Figure 15.) Between 1000Z and 1200Z the visibility at KMEM is forecast to be

A— 1/2 statute mile.
B— 3 statute miles.
C— 6 statute miles.

Between 1000Z and 1200Z, the visibility at KMEM is forecast to be 3 statute miles (BECMG 1310/1312 00000KT...3SM). (PLT072) — AC 00-45

ALL
3482. (Refer to Figure 15.) What is the forecast wind for KMEM from 1600Z until the end of the forecast?

A— No significant wind.
B— Variable in direction at 4 knots.
C— Variable in direction at 6 knots.

From 1600Z until the end of the forecast, wind will be variable in direction at 6 knots (VRB06KT). (PLT072) — AC 00-45

Answers

3475 [C]	3476 [B]	3479 [A]	3480 [A]	3481 [B]	3482 [C]

ALL
3483. (Refer to Figure 15.) In the TAF from KOKC, the "FM (FROM) Group" is forecast for the hours from 1600Z to 2200Z with the wind from

A— 160° at 10 knots.
B— 180° at 10 knots, becoming 200° at 13 knots.
C— 180° at 10 knots.

The FROM group is forecast for the hours from 1600 (051600) to 2200Z (BECMG 0522/0524) with the wind from 180 degrees at 10 knots (18010KT). (PLT072) — AC 00-45

Answer (A) is incorrect because 18010 indicates the wind will be from 180. Answer (B) is incorrect because "BECMG" indicates another change group; the wind will change from 200 at 13 knots between 2200 and 2400Z.

ALL
3484. (Refer to Figure 15.) In the TAF from KOKC, the clear sky becomes

A— overcast at 2,000 feet during the forecast period between 2200Z and 2400Z.
B— overcast at 200 feet with a 40% probability of becoming overcast at 600 feet during the forecast period between 2200Z and 2400Z.
C— overcast at 200 feet with the probability of becoming overcast at 400 feet during the forecast period between 2200Z and 2400Z.

Between 2200Z and 2400Z (BECMG 0522/0524), the sky will be overcast at 2,000 feet (OVC020). (PLT072) — AC 00-45

ALL
3485. (Refer to Figure 15.) During the time period from 0600Z to 0800Z, what visibility is forecast for KOKC?

A— Greater than 6 statute miles.
B— Not forecasted.
C— Possibly 6 statute miles.

During the period from 0600Z to 0800Z (0606/0608), the visibilities are forecast to be greater than 6 statute miles (P6SM). (PLT072) — AC 00-45

ALL
3486. (Refer to Figure 15.) The only cloud type forecast in TAF reports is

A— nimbostratus.
B— cumulonimbus.
C— scattered cumulus.

Cumulonimbus clouds are the only cloud types forecast in TAFs. (PLT072) — AC 00-45

Graphical Forecasts for Aviation (GFA)

The GFA at the Aviation Weather Center (AWC) website is an interactive display providing continuously updated observed and forecast weather information over the continental United States (CONUS). It is intended to give users a complete picture of weather critical to aviation safety. The GFA display shows user-selected weather categories, each containing multiple fields of interest at altitudes from the surface up to FL480. Depending on the field of interest chosen, weather information is available from -6 in the past (observed) to +15 hours in the future (forecast).

The GFA is not considered a weather product but an aggregate of several existing weather products. The information and data from the various weather products are overlaid on a high-resolution basemap of the United States: **www.aviationweather.gov/gfa**. The user selects flight levels and current time period for either observed or forecast weather information. Mouse-clicking or hovering over the map provides additional information in textual format, such as current METAR or TAF for a selected airport. The GFA replaces the textual area forecast (FA) for the CONUS and Hawaii with a more modern digital solution for obtaining weather information. The Aviation Surface Forecast and Aviation Cloud Forecast graphics are snapshot images derived from a subset of the aviation weather forecasts.

Answers

3483   [C]   3484   [A]   3485   [A]   3486   [B]

ALL, SPO
3487. To best determine general forecast weather conditions covering a flight information region, the pilot should refer to

A— Graphical Forecasts for Aviation (GFA).
B— Weather Depiction Charts.
C— Satellite Maps.

The Graphical Forecasts for Aviation (GFA) is intended to provide the necessary aviation weather information to give users a complete picture of the weather that may impact flight in the continental U.S. (CONUS). (PLT514) — AC 00-45

Winds and Temperatures Aloft Forecast (FB)

The winds and temperatures aloft forecast is displayed in a 6-digit format (DDffTT). It shows wind direction (DD), wind velocity (ff), and the temperature (TT) that is forecast to exist at specified levels. For example, "234502" decodes as: winds from 230 degrees true north, at 45 knots, temperatures 02°C.

When the wind speed (ff) is between 100 and 199 knots, the wind direction (DD) portion of the code will be greater than 50. In cases such as this, you will need to subtract 50 from the coded wind direction, and add 100 to the coded wind speed in order to decipher the code. For example, "734502" decodes as: winds from 230 degrees true north at 145 knots, temperature 02 degrees C.

Temperatures with a negative symbol in front of them (DDff-37) are negative. For flight levels above 24,000, temperatures are always negative and will not have a negative symbol. Light and variable winds or wind speeds below 5 knots are indicated by 9900, followed by the forecast temperature. For example, the coded winds aloft forecast for flight level FL270 (flight level 27,000) is "990017" and decodes as: winds are light and variable, temperature negative 17.

The observed winds aloft chart shows temperature, wind direction, and speed at selected stations. Arrows with pennants and barbs indicate wind direction and speed. Each pennant is 50 knots, each barb is 10 knots, and each half barb is 5 knots. Wind direction is shown by an arrow drawn to the nearest 10 degrees, with the second digit of the coded direction entered at the outer end of the arrow. Thus, a wind in the northwest quadrant with the digit 3 indicates 330 degrees, and a wind in the southwest quadrant with the digit 3 indicates 230 degrees.

ALL, SPO
3500. (Refer to Figure 17.) What wind is forecast for STL at 9,000 feet?

A— 230° true at 32 knots.
B— 230° magnetic at 25 knots.
C— 230° true at 25 knots.

A six-digit group shows wind directions (in reference to true north) in the first two digits, wind speed (in knots) in the second two digits, and temperature (in Celsius) in the last two digits. In this case, 2332+02 means 230° at 32 knots, and the temperature is 2°C. (PLT076) — AC 00-45

ALL
3501. (Refer to Figure 17.) What wind is forecast for STL at 12,000 feet?

A— 230° true at 56 knots.
B— 230° magnetic at 56 knots.
C— 230° true at 39 knots.

A six-digit group shows wind directions (in reference to true north) in the first two digits, wind speed (in knots) in the second two digits, and temperature (in Celsius) in the last two digits. In this case, 2339-04 means 230° at 39 knots, and the temperature is -4°C. (PLT076) — AC 00-45

Answers

3487 [A]	3500 [A]	3501 [C]

ALL
3502. (Refer to Figure 17.) Determine the wind and temperature aloft forecast for DEN at 9,000 feet.

A— 230° magnetic at 53 knots, temperature 47°C.
B— 230° true at 53 knots, temperature -47°C.
C— 230° true at 21 knots, temperature -4°C.

A six-digit group shows wind directions (in reference to true north) in the first two digits, wind speed (in knots) in the second two digits, and temperature (in Celsius) in the last two digits. In this case, 2321-04 means 230° at 21 knots, and the temperature is -4°C. (PLT076) — AC 00-45

ALL
3503. (Refer to Figure 17.) Determine the wind and temperature aloft forecast for MKC at 6,000 feet.

A— 200° true at 6 knots, temperature +3°C.
B— 050° true at 7 knots, temperature missing.
C— 200° magnetic at 6 knots, temperature +3°C.

A six-digit group shows wind directions (in reference to true north) in the first two digits, wind speed (in knots) in the second two digits, and temperature (in Celsius) in the last two digits. In this case, 2006+03 means 200° at 6 knots, and the temperature is 3°C. (PLT076) — AC 00-45

ALL
3505. What values are used for Winds Aloft Forecasts?

A— Magnetic direction and knots.
B— Magnetic direction and miles per hour.
C— True direction and knots.

A six-digit group shows wind directions (in reference to true north) in the first two digits, wind speed (in knots) in the second two digits, and temperature (in Celsius) in the last two digits. (PLT284) — AC 00-45

ALL
3506. When the term "light and variable" is used in reference to a Winds Aloft Forecast, the coded group and windspeed is

A— 0000 and less than 7 knots.
B— 9900 and less than 5 knots.
C— 9999 and less than 10 knots.

When the forecast speed is less than 5 knots, the coded group is "9900" and reads "light and variable" on the Winds Aloft Forecast. (PLT284) — AC 00-45

Inflight Weather Advisories (WA, WS, WST)

Inflight Weather Advisories advise enroute pilots of the possibility of encountering hazardous flying conditions that may not have been forecast at the time of the preflight weather briefing.

AIRMETs (WA) contain information on weather that may be hazardous to single engine, other light aircraft, and VFR pilots. The items covered are moderate icing or turbulence, sustained winds of 30 knots or more at the surface, widespread areas of IFR conditions, and extensive mountain obscurement.

SIGMETs (WS) advise of weather potentially hazardous to all aircraft. The items covered are severe icing, severe or extreme turbulence, and widespread sandstorms, dust storms or volcanic ash lowering visibility to less than 3 miles.

SIGMETs and AIRMETs are broadcast upon receipt and at 30-minute intervals (H + 15 and H + 45) during the first hour. If the advisory is still in effect after the first hour, an alert notice will be broadcast. Pilots may contact the nearest FSS to ascertain whether the advisory is pertinent to their flights.

Convective SIGMETs (WST) cover weather developments such as tornadoes, lines of thunderstorms, and embedded thunderstorms, and they also imply severe or greater turbulence, severe icing, and low-level wind shear. When a SIGMET forecasts embedded thunderstorms, it indicates that the thunderstorms are obscured by massive cloud layers and cannot be seen. Convective SIGMET bulletins are issued hourly at H + 55. Unscheduled convective SIGMETs are broadcast upon receipt and at 15-minute intervals for the first hour (H + 15; H + 30; H + 45).

Answers

3502 [C]	3503 [A]	3505 [C]	3506 [B]

ALL
3495. What is indicated when a current CONVECTIVE SIGMET forecasts thunderstorms?

A— Moderate thunderstorms covering 30 percent of the area.
B— Moderate or severe turbulence.
C— Thunderstorms obscured by massive cloud layers.

Convective SIGMETs include: severe thunderstorms, embedded thunderstorms, line of thunderstorms, thunderstorms greater than or equal to VIP (Digital Video Interrogator and Processor) level "A" affecting 40% or more of an area of 3,000 square miles. (PLT290) — AC 00-45

ALL
3496. What information is contained in a CONVEC-TIVE SIGMET?

A— Tornadoes, embedded thunderstorms, and hail 3/4 inch or greater in diameter.
B— Severe icing, severe turbulence, or widespread dust storms lowering visibility to less than 3 miles.
C— Surface winds greater than 40 knots or thunderstorms equal to or greater than video integrator processor (VIP) level 4.

Any convective SIGMET implies severe or greater turbulence, severe icing, and low-level wind shear. The forecast may be issued for any of the following:

Severe thunderstorms due to—

1. Surface winds greater than or equal to 50 knots, or

2. Hail at the surface greater than or equal to 3/4 inch in diameter, or

3. Tornadoes, embedded thunderstorms, lines of thunderstorms.

(PLT290) — AC 00-45

ALL, SPO
3497. SIGMETs are issued as a warning of weather conditions hazardous to which aircraft?

A— Small aircraft only.
B— Large aircraft only.
C— All aircraft.

A SIGMET advises of weather potentially hazardous to all aircraft. (PLT290) — AC 00-45

ALL
3498. Which in-flight advisory would contain information on severe icing not associated with thunderstorms?

A— Convective SIGMET.
B— SIGMET.
C— AIRMET.

A SIGMET advises of weather potentially hazardous to all aircraft other than convective activity. Some items included are severe icing, and severe or extreme turbulence. (PLT290) — AC 00-45

ALL
3499. AIRMET's are advisories of significant weather phenomena but of lower intensities than SIGMET's and are intended for dissemination to

A— only IFR pilots.
B— all pilots.
C— only VFR pilots.

AIRMETs are intended for dissemination to all pilots in the preflight and enroute phase of flight to enhance safety. (PLT290) — AC 00-45

Answers
3495 [C]   3496 [A]   3497 [C]   3498 [B]   3499 [B]

Obtaining a Telephone Weather Briefing

When telephoning a weather briefing facility for preflight weather information, pilots should:

- Identify themselves as pilots;
- State whether they intend to fly VFR or IFR;
- State the intended route, destination, and type of aircraft;
- Request a standard briefing to get a "complete" weather briefing;
- Request an abbreviated briefing to supplement mass disseminated data or when only one or two items are needed; and
- Request an outlook briefing whenever the proposed departure time is 6 or more hours from the time of briefing.

ALL

3455. When telephoning a weather briefing facility for preflight weather information, pilots should state

A— whether they intend to fly VFR only.
B— that they possess a current pilot certificate.
C— the full name and address of the formation commander.

When requesting a preflight weather briefing, identify yourself as a pilot or the tail number of the aircraft to be flown and provide the type of flight planned (e.g., VFR or IFR). (PLT514) — FAA-H-8083-25

ALL

3456. To get a complete weather briefing for the planned flight, the pilot should request

A— a general briefing.
B— an abbreviated briefing.
C— a standard briefing.

You should request a standard briefing any time you are planning a flight and you have not received a previous briefing. (PLT514) — AC 00-45

ALL, SPO

3457. Which type weather briefing should a pilot request, when departing within the hour, if no preliminary weather information has been received?

A— Outlook briefing.
B— Abbreviated briefing.
C— Standard briefing.

You should request a standard briefing any time you are planning a flight and you have not received a previous briefing. (PLT514) — AC 00-45

ALL, SPO

3458. Which type of weather briefing should a pilot request to supplement mass disseminated data?

A— An outlook briefing.
B— A supplemental briefing.
C— An abbreviated briefing.

Request an abbreviated briefing when you need information to supplement mass disseminated data, update a previous briefing, or when you need only one or two specific items. (PLT514) — AC 00-45

ALL, SPO

3459. To update a previous weather briefing, a pilot should request

A— an abbreviated briefing.
B— a standard briefing.
C— an outlook briefing.

Request an abbreviated briefing when you need information to supplement mass disseminated data, update a previous briefing, or when you need only one or two specific items. (PLT514) — AC 00-45

ALL

3460. A weather briefing that is provided when the information requested is 6 or more hours in advance of the proposed departure time is

A— an outlook briefing.
B— a forecast briefing.
C— a prognostic briefing.

Answers

| 3455 [A] | 3456 [C] | 3457 [C] | 3458 [C] | 3459 [A] | 3460 [A] |

You should request an outlook briefing whenever your proposed time of departure is 6 or more hours from the time of the briefing. This type of briefing is provided for planning purposes only. You should obtain a standard or abbreviated briefing prior to departure in order to obtain such items as current conditions, updated forecasts, winds aloft and NOTAMs. (PLT514) — AC 00-45

ALL
3461. When requesting weather information for the following morning, a pilot should request

A— an outlook briefing.
B— a standard briefing.
C— an abbreviated briefing.

You should request an outlook briefing whenever your proposed time of departure is 6 or more hours from the time of the briefing. This type of briefing is provided for planning purposes only. You should obtain a standard or abbreviated briefing prior to departure in order to obtain such items as current conditions, updated forecasts, winds aloft and NOTAMs. (PLT514) — AC 00-45

ALL
3526. What should pilots state initially when telephoning a weather briefing facility for preflight weather information?

A— The intended route of flight radio frequencies.
B— The address of the pilot in command.
C— The intended route of flight and destination.

When requesting a briefing, pilots should identify themselves and provide as much information regarding the proposed flight as possible. (PLT445) — FAA-H-8083-25

Answer (A) is incorrect because the pilot only needs to identify the route of flight. Answer (B) is incorrect because the caller only needs to provide an aircraft number or pilot's name.

ALL, SPO
3527. What should pilots state initially when telephoning a weather briefing facility for preflight weather information?

A— Tell the number of occupants on board.
B— Identify themselves as pilots.
C— State their total flight time.

When requesting a briefing, pilots should identify themselves and provide as much information regarding the proposed flight as possible. The information received will depend on the type of briefing requested. The following would be helpful to the briefer.

1. *Type of flight, visual flight rule (VFR) or instrument operating rule (IFR)*
2. *Aircraft number or pilot's name*
3. *Aircraft type*
4. *Departure point*
5. *Route of flight*
6. *Destination*
7. *Flight altitude(s)*
8. *Estimated time of departure*
9. *Estimated time en route or estimated time of arrival*

(PLT514) — FAA-H-8083-25

ALL
3528. When telephoning a weather briefing facility for preflight weather information, pilots should state

A— the aircraft identification or the pilot's name.
B— true airspeed.
C— fuel on board.

When requesting a briefing, make known you are a pilot. Give clear and concise facts about your flight:

1. *Type of flight: VFR or IFR*
2. *Aircraft identification or pilot's name*
3. *Aircraft type*
4. *Departure point*
5. *Route-of-flight*
6. *Destination*
7. *Altitude*
8. *Estimated time of departure*
9. *Estimated time en route or estimated time of arrival*

(PLT514) — FAA-H-8083-25

Answers (B) and (C) are incorrect because these are necessary when filing a flight plan, but not when obtaining a weather briefing.

Answers

3461 [A]	3526 [C]	3527 [B]	3528 [A]

ALL
3528-1. When speaking to a Flight Service weather briefer, you should state

A— the pilot-in-command's full name and address.
B— a summary of your qualifications.
C— whether the flight is VFR or IFR.

When requesting a briefing, make known you are a pilot. Give clear and concise facts about your flight:

1. *Type of flight: VFR or IFR*

2. *Aircraft identification or pilot's name*

3. *Aircraft type*

4. *Departure point*

5. *Route of flight*

6. *Destination*

7. *Altitude*

8. *Estimated time of departure*

9. *Estimated time en route or estimated time of arrival*

(PLT514) – FAA-H-8083-25

GLI
3525. In addition to the standard briefing, what additional information should be asked of the weather briefer in order to evaluate soaring conditions?

A— The upper soundings to determine the thermal index at all soaring levels.
B— Dry adiabatic rate of cooling to determine the height of cloud bases.
C— Moist adiabatic rate of cooling to determine the height of cloud tops.

Since thermals depend on sinking cold air forcing warm air upward, strength of thermals depends on the temperature difference between the sinking air and the rising air—the greater the temperature difference, the stronger the thermals. To arrive at an approximation of this difference, a thermal index is computed. A thermal index may be computed for any level using upper soundings. (PLT514) — AC 00-45

GLI
3470. (Refer to Figure 13.) What effect do the clouds mentioned in the weather briefing have on soaring conditions?

A— All thermals stop at the base of the clouds.
B— Thermals persist to the tops of the clouds at 25,000 feet.
C— The scattered clouds indicate thermals at least to the tops of the lower clouds.

The telephone weather briefing indicates a few scattered clouds at 5,000 feet AGL, with higher scattered cirrus at 25,000 feet MSL. This briefing shows two different clouds bases and does not give cloud tops. Thermals are a product of instability. The height of thermals depends on the depth of the unstable layer, and their strength depends on the degree of instability. A cloud grows with a rising thermal and scattered cumulus clouds are positive signs of thermals. Whereas an abundant convective cloud cover reduces thermal activity, thermals will exist at least to the tops of the scattered clouds, especially if the outline is firm and sharp, indicating a growing cumulus. (PLT316) — AC 00-45

GLI
3471. (Refer to Figure 13.) At what time will thermals begin to form?

A— Between 1300Z and 1500Z while the sky is clear.
B— By 1500Z (midmorning) when scattered clouds begin to form.
C— About 2000Z (early afternoon) when the wind begins to increase.

The telephone weather briefing indicates there should be a few scattered clouds at 5,000 feet AGL by 15Z. The sky must be clear enough for the sun to warm the earth's surface in order for thermals to develop. (PLT494) — AC 00-45

Answers

| 3528-1 | [C] | 3525 | [A] | 3470 | [C] | 3471 | [A] |

GLI
3471-1. (Refer to Figure 13.) When are the thermals at the best?

A— Between 1300Z and 1500Z while the sky is clear.
B— By 1500Z (midmorning) when scattered clouds begin to form.
C— About 2000Z (early afternoon) when the wind begins to form.

The telephone weather briefing indicates there should be a few scattered clouds at 5,000 feet AGL by 15Z. Thermals are a product of instability. A cloud grows with a rising thermal and scattered cumulus clouds are positive signs of thermals. Whereas abundant convective cloud cover reduces thermal activity, thermals will exist at least to the tops of the scattered clouds—especially if the outline is firm and sharp, indicating a growing cumulus. (PLT494) — AC 00-45

LTA
3411. What early morning weather observations indicate the possibility of good weather conditions for balloon flight most of the day?

A— Clear skies and surface winds, 10 knots or less.
B— Low moving, scattered cumulus clouds and surface winds, 5 knots or less.
C— Overcast with stratus clouds and surface winds, 5 knots or less.

Stratiform clouds indicate no turbulence and 5 knots or less winds are well within safety parameters. (PLT173) — AC 00-6

LTA
3468. (Refer to Figure 13.) According to the weather briefing, the most ideal time to launch balloons is

A— as soon as possible after 1300Z.
B— at 1500Z when the ground will be partially shaded.
C— at 2000Z when there is enough wind for cross-country.

The telephone weather briefing given at 13Z indicates no clouds until 15Z, and no wind until after 20Z. The ideal time to launch balloons is as soon after 13Z as possible before the clouds and wind develop. (PLT316) — AC 00-45

LTA
3469. (Refer to Figure 13.) According to the weather briefing, good balloon weather will begin to deteriorate

A— soon after 1300Z as the wind starts to increase.
B— about 1500Z when the lower scattered clouds begin to form.
C— at 2000Z due to sharp increase in wind conditions.

The telephone weather briefing given at 13Z indicates only a few scattered clouds at 5,000 feet AGL, with higher scattered cirrus at 25,000 feet MSL to form by 15Z. After 20Z, however, the wind should pick up to about 15 knots from the south. The marked increase of wind at 20Z indicates deteriorating ballooning weather. (PLT316) — AC 00-45

LTA
3477. Which weather reports and forecasts are most important for local area balloon operations?

A— Winds Aloft Forecasts and Radar Summary Charts.
B— Winds Aloft Forecasts and Surface Analysis Charts.
C— Winds Aloft Forecasts and Aviation Routine Weather Reports.

Local information is provided by the Aviation Routine Weather Report (METAR). (PLT515) — AC 00-45

Answer (A) is incorrect because it is a local flight. Answer (B) is incorrect because Surface Analysis Charts are a nationwide reference.

Chapter 8
Aircraft Performance

Weight and Balance

Even though an aircraft has been certificated for flight at a specified maximum gross weight, it may not be safe to take off with that load under all conditions. High altitude, high temperature, and high humidity are additional factors which may require limiting the load to some weight less than the maximum allowable.

Some of the problems caused by overloading an aircraft are:

- The aircraft will need a higher takeoff speed, which results in a longer takeoff run.
- Both the rate and angle of climb will be reduced.
- The service ceiling will be lowered.
- The cruising speed will be reduced.
- The cruising range will be shortened.
- Maneuverability will be decreased.
- A longer landing roll will be required because the landing speed will be higher.
- Excessive loads will be imposed on the structure, especially the landing gear.

The **empty weight** is obtained from appropriate charts. It includes the airframe, engine, all fixed equipment, and unusable fuel and oil. Some aircraft include all oil in the aircraft empty weight. The **useful load** includes the pilot, passengers, baggage, fuel and oil. The **takeoff weight** is the empty weight plus the useful load. The **landing weight** is the takeoff weight minus any fuel used.

The **arm** is the horizontal distance measured in inches from the datum line to a point on the aircraft. If measured aft, toward the tail, the arm is given a positive (+) value; if measured forward, toward the nose, the arm is given a negative (-) value. *See* Figure 8-1.

The **moment** is the product of the weight of an object multiplied by its arm and is expressed in pound-inches (lbs-in). A formula that is used to find moment is usually expressed as follows:

Weight × Arm = Moment

The **moment index** is a moment divided by a constant such as 100 or 1,000. It is used to simplify computations where heavy items and long arms result in large, unmanageable numbers. This is usually expressed as Moment/100 or Mom/1,000, etc.

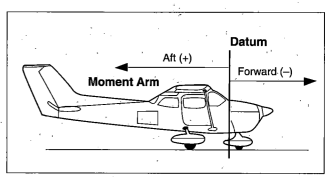

Figure 8-1. Positive and negative arm

The center of gravity (CG) is the point about which an aircraft will balance, and it is expressed in inches from datum. The center of gravity is found by dividing the total moment by the total weight, and the formula is usually expressed as follows:

$$\frac{\text{Total Moment}}{\text{Total Weight}} = \text{CG (inches aft of datum)}$$

Continued

Standard weights have been established for numerous items involved in weight and balance computations. These weights should not be used if actual weights are available. Some of the standard weights are:

Item	Weight
General aviation crew and passenger	190 lbs each
Gasoline	6 lbs/U.S. gallon
Oil	7.5 lbs/U.S. gallon
Water	8.35 lbs/U.S. gallon

Airplane

In addition to considering the weight to be carried, the pilot must ensure that the load is arranged to keep the aircraft in balance. The balance point, or Center of Gravity ( ), is the point at which all of the weight of the airplane is considered to be concentrated. For an aircraft to be safe to fly, the center of gravity must fall between specified limits. All aircraft categories have unique balance requirements; some need to be balanced precisely while others are less sensitive to fore and aft weight distribution. The specific balance requirements for each aircraft category are covered in the Pilot Operating Handbook (POH) and will be tested on during the practical (checkride). To keep the CG within safe limits it may be necessary to move weight toward the nose of the aircraft (forward), which moves the CG forward, or toward the tail (aft) which moves the CG aft.

The specified forward and aft points within which the CG must be located for safe flight are called the center of gravity limits. These limits are specified by the manufacturer. The distance between the forward and aft CG limits is called the center of gravity range.

Weight-Shift Control

Weight and loading is typically used for weight-shift control. The cart normally does not have balance requirements, but the attachment point to the cart is specified in the Pilot's Operating Handbook.

Powered Parachute

Weight and loading is used for powered parachutes. The POH procedure for the fore and aft attachment points of the wing to the cart must be followed so that the cart will obtain the proper deck angle (the angle of the cart bottom with the horizontal plane).

ALL
3663-1. (Refer to Figure 61.) If 50 pounds of weight is located at point X and 100 pounds at point Z, how much weight must be located at point Y to balance the plank?

A— 30 pounds.
B— 50 pounds.
C— 300 pounds.

Find the moments left and right of the fulcrum, and set them equal to one another.

> *Left = right*
>
> *50(50) + Y(25) = 100(100)*
>
> *2,500 + 25Y = 10,000*
>
> *Y = 300 pounds*

(PLT021) — FAA-H-8083-25

ALL
3663-2. (Refer to Figure 60.) How should the 500-pound weight be shifted to balance the plank on the fulcrum?

A— 1 inch to the left.
B— 1 inch to the right.
C— 4.5 inches to the right.

1. *Find the moments left and right of the fulcrum, and set them equal to one another.*

> *left = right*
>
> *500(X) = 250(20) + 200(15)*
>
> *500X = 8,000*
>
> *X = 16 inches*

2. *The 500-pound weight must be 16 inches from the fulcrum to be in balance. It is currently located at 15 inches, therefore the weight should be shifted 1 inch to the left.*

(PLT092) — FAA-H-8083-25

AIR, REC
3815. (Refer to Figure 67.) What effect does a 30-gallon fuel burn have on the weight and balance if the airplane weighed 2,784 pounds and the MOM/100 was 2,222 at takeoff?

A— No effect on CG.
B— Moment will increase to 2,357 in-lb.
C— Moment will decrease to 2,087 in-lb.

The original CG is 2,222 / 2,784 = 79.8. Figure 67 includes a table summarizing fuel weights and moments. Burning 30 gallons of fuel will result in a 180-pound

reduction, making the new airplane weigh 2,604 pounds (2,784 – 180). The moment is reduced by 135, making the new MOM/100 = 2,087 (2,222 – 135). The new CG is 2,222 / 2604 = 85.3. (PLT021) – FAA-H-8083-25

Answer (A) is incorrect because the CG will increase from 79.8 to 85.3. Answer (B) is incorrect because 2,357 is an increase of 135 in-lb.

ALL, LSA, LSR, LSW, LSP
3661. Which items are included in the empty weight of an aircraft?

A— Unusable fuel and undrainable oil.
B— Only the airframe, powerplant, and optional equipment.
C— Full fuel tanks and engine oil to capacity.

Empty weight consists of the airframe, engines, and all items of operating equipment that have fixed locations and are permanently installed in the airplane. It includes optional and special equipment, fixed ballast, hydraulic fluid, unusable (residual) fuel, and undrainable (residual) oil. (PLT328) — FAA-H-8083-25

Answer (B) is incorrect because empty weight also includes operating fluids and unusable fuel. Answer (C) is incorrect because empty weight does not include full fuel.

AIR, RTC, WSC, PPC
3662. An aircraft is loaded 110 pounds over maximum certificated gross weight. If fuel (gasoline) is drained to bring the aircraft weight within limits, how much fuel should be drained?

A— 15.7 gallons.
B— 16.2 gallons.
C— 18.4 gallons.

1. *Determine the total weight to be removed (110 pounds) and the weight per gallon of gasoline (6 pounds).*

2. *Calculate the amount of gasoline to be drained using the formula:*

$$Gallons = \frac{Pounds}{Pounds/Gallon}$$

or:

$$\frac{110}{6} = 18.33 \ gallons$$

When "rounding" an answer, do so in the sense that will provide the greater flight safety. In this case, round to 18.4. (PLT021) — FAA-H-8083-25

Answers

3663-1   [C]   3663-2   [A]   3815   [C]   3661   [A]   3662   [C]

AIR, RTC, WSC, PPC

3663. If an aircraft is loaded 90 pounds over maximum certificated gross weight and fuel (gasoline) is drained to bring the aircraft weight within limits, how much fuel should be drained?

A— 10 gallons.
B— 12 gallons.
C— 15 gallons.

1. Determine the total weight to be removed (90 pounds) and the weight per gallon of gasoline (6 pounds).
2. Calculate the amount of gasoline to be drained using the formula:

$$Gallons = \frac{Pounds}{Pounds/Gallon}$$

or:

$$\frac{90}{6} = 15 \text{ gallons}$$

(PLT021) — FAA-H-8083-25

SPO

2371. (Refer to Figure 72.) The positive limit load factor is represented by the

A— vertical dashed line from E to F.
B— vertical solid line from D to G.
C— horizontal dashed line from C to point E.

C to E is the maximum positive load limit. In this case it is 3.8 Gs, which is appropriate for normal category airplanes. (PLT074) — FAA-H-8083-25

Answer (A) is incorrect because the vertical dashed line from E to F is the never-exceed airspeed (V_{NE}). Answer (B) is incorrect because the vertical solid line from D to G is the high end for normal operations.

Computing Weight and Balance Problems Using a Table

Problem:

Determine if the airplane weight and balance is within limits.

Front seat occupants.............................. 340 lbs
Rear seat occupants............................... 295 lbs
Fuel (main wing tanks) .... 44 gal
Baggage .... 56 lbs

Solution:

1. Determine the total weight. Using the information provided in the question, enter the items and the weights:

Item	Weight (lbs)	Arm (in)	Moment (lbs-in)
Front seat occupants	340		
Rear seat occupants	295		
Fuel (main wing tanks)	264 *		
Baggage	56		
Empty weight	+ 2,015 **		
	2,970 lbs		

*44 gal x 6 lbs/gal   **found in FAA Figure 33

2. Fill in the arms (found in FAA Figure 32) and calculate the moments. Moments are determined by multiplying in each row: weight x arm. Then divide that moment by 100 to keep the number a manageable size, and finally, total all moments.

Item	Weight (lbs)	Arm (in)	Moment/100 (lbs-in)
Front seat occupants	340	85	289.0
Rear seat occupants	295	121	357.0
Fuel (main wing tanks)	264	75	198.0
Baggage	56	140	78.4
Empty weight	+ 2,015		1,554.0
	2,970 lbs		2,476.4 lbs-in

3. Determine the balance conditions. Looking at FAA Figure 33, notice that the table stops at the maximum weight of 2,950. Even though the weight is off the scale, the Moment of 2,476.4 is between the minimum and maximum Moment limits given in the table. Therefore, we are 20 pounds overweight and within balance limits.

AIR
3664. GIVEN:

	WEIGHT (LB)	ARM (IN)	MOMENT (LB-IN)
Empty weight	1,495.0	101.4	151,593.0
Pilot and passengers	380.0	64.0	—
Fuel (30 gal usable— no reserve)	—	96.0	—

The CG is located how far aft of datum?

A— CG 92.44.
B— CG 94.01.
C— CG 119.8.

1. Compute the total weight and moment using the formula:

   Weight x Arm = Moment
   or:

Item	Weight	Arm	Moment
Empty weight	1,495.0	101.4	151,593.0
Pilot & passenger	380.0	64.0	24,320.0
Fuel (30 x 6)	180.0	96.0	17,280.0
Total	2,055.0 lbs		193,193.0

2. Compute the center of gravity using the formula:

$$CG = \frac{Total\ Moment}{Total\ Weight}$$
   or:

$$CG = \frac{193,193}{2,055} = 94.01\ inches\ aft\ of\ datum$$

(PLT021) — FAA-H-8083-25

AIR
3665. (Refer to Figures 32 and 33.) Determine if the airplane weight and balance is within limits.

Front seat occupants...340 lb
Rear seat occupants..295 lb
Fuel (main wing tanks).......................................44 gal
Baggage...56 lb

A— 20 pounds overweight, CG aft of aft limits.
B— 20 pounds overweight, CG within limits.
C— 20 pounds overweight, CG forward of forward limits.

When multiplying a weight by its arm you must divide by 100 to get moment index (Moment/100). Moments listed in FAA Figures 32 and 33 are already divided by 100, and are therefore moment indexes.

1. *Calculate weight and moment index using the information from the question and from FAA Figures 32 and 33 and the formula:*

   Weight x Arm ÷ 100 = Moment/Index

Item	Weight	Arm	Moment/100
Empty weight	2,015 lbs		1,554.0 lbs-in
Front seat	340 lbs	85	289.0 lbs-in
Rear seat	295 lbs	121	357.0 lbs-in
Fuel (44 x 6)	264 lbs	75	198.0 lbs-in
Baggage	56 lbs	140	78.4 lbs-in
Total	2,970 lbs		2,476.4 lbs-in

2. *Consult the Moment Limits vs. Weight Table, FAA Figure 33. The aircraft weight is 2,970 pounds or 20 pounds in excess of the maximum weight on the chart. The moment of 2,476.4 lbs-in would be within limits if the chart went to 2,970 pounds gross weight.*

(PLT121) — FAA-H-8083-25

Answers

3664   [B]   3665   [B]

AIR
3666. (Refer to Figures 32 and 33.) What is the maximum amount of baggage that can be carried when the airplane is loaded as follows?

Front seat occupants... 387 lb
Rear seat occupants.. 293 lb
Fuel... 35 gal

A— 45 pounds.
B— 63 pounds.
C— 220 pounds.

1. *When multiplying a weight times its arm you must divide by 100 to get moment index. Calculate total weight and total moment index using the information from the question and from FAA Figures 32 and 33 and the formula:*

Weight x Arm ÷ 100 = Moment/Index

Item	Weight	Arm	Moment/100
Empty weight	2,015 lbs		1,554.0 lbs-in
Front seat	387 lbs	85	329.0 lbs-in
Rear seat	293 lbs	121	354.5 lbs-in
Fuel (35 x 6)	210 lbs	75	157.5 lbs-in
Total	2,905 lbs		2,395.0 lbs-in

2. *The maximum takeoff weight is 2,950 pounds. Calculate what the allowed baggage weight would be:*

2,950 – 2,905 = 45 pounds

3. *Verify that the CG would remain within the allowable range with this much baggage by calculating the new weight and moment index.*

Item	Weight	Arm	Moment/100
Original total	2,905 lbs		2,395.0 lbs-in
Baggage	+ 45 lbs	140	+ 63.0 lbs-in
New Total	2,950 lbs		2,458.0 lbs-in

4. *Consult the Moment Limit vs. Weight Table, FAA Figure 33. For a weight of 2,950 pounds, the range of allowable moments is 2,422 to 2,499. The new total moment index of 2,458.0 is acceptable.*

(PLT021) — FAA-H-8083-25

AIR
3667. (Refer to Figures 32 and 33.) Calculate the weight and balance and determine if the CG and the weight of the airplane are within limits.

Front seat occupants... 350 lb
Rear seat occupants.. 325 lb
Baggage .... 27 lb
Fuel... 35 gal

A— CG 81.7, out of limits forward.
B— CG 83.4, within limits.
C— CG 84.1, within limits.

Use the following steps:

1. *Calculate weight and moment index using the information from the problem and from FAA Figures 32 and 33 and the formula:*

Weight x Arm ÷ 100 = Moment/Index

Item	Weight	Arm	Moment/100
Empty weight	2,015 lbs		1,554.0 lbs-in
Front seat	350 lbs	85	297.5 lbs-in
Rear seat	325 lbs	121	393.3 lbs-in
Baggage	27 lbs	140	37.8 lbs-in
Fuel (35 x 6)	210 lbs	75	157.5 lbs-in
Total	2,927 lbs		2,440.1 lbs-in

2. *Calculate the position of CG using the formula:*

$$CG = \frac{Total\ Mom\ Ind}{Total\ Weight} \times Reduction\ Factor$$

or:

$$CG = \frac{2,440.1}{2,927} \times 100 = 83.4\ inches\ aft\ of\ datum$$

(PLT021) — FAA-H-8083-25

Answers

3666   [A]   3667   [B]

AIR
3668. (Refer to Figures 32 and 33.) Determine if the airplane weight and balance is within limits.

Front seat occupants .... 415 lb
Rear seat occupants .... 110 lb
Fuel, main tanks .... 44 gal
Fuel, aux. tanks .... 19 gal
Baggage .... 32 lb

A— 19 pounds overweight, CG within limits.
B— 19 pounds overweight, CG out of limits forward.
C— Weight within limits, CG out of limits.

Use the following steps:

1. *Calculate weight and moment index using the information from the problem and from FAA Figures 32 and 33, and the formula:*

   Weight x Arm ÷ 100 = Moment/Index

Item	Weight	Arm	Moment/100
Empty weight	2,015 lbs		1,554.0 lbs-in
Front seat	415 lbs	85	352.8 lbs-in
Rear seat	110 lbs	121	133.1 lbs-in
Fuel main 44 x 6	264 lbs	75	198.0 lbs-in
Fuel aux. 19 x 6	114 lbs	94	107.2 lbs-in
Baggage	32 lbs	140	44.8 lbs-in
Total	2,950 lbs		2,389.9 lbs-in

2. *Calculate the CG using the formula:*

$$CG = \frac{Total\ Mom\ Ind}{Total\ Weight} \times Reduction\ Factor$$

   or:

$$CG = \frac{2,389.9}{2,950} \times 100 = 81.0\ inches\ aft\ of\ datum$$

3. *Consult the Moment Limits vs. Weight Table (FAA Figure 33). A CG of 81 inches is 1.1 inches forward of the forward CG limit for a weight (allowed) of 2,950 pounds (2,422 ÷ 2,950 = 82.1); (82.1 – 81 = 1.1 inches forward).*

(PLT121) — FAA-H-8083-25

AIR
3674. (Refer to Figures 32 and 33.) Upon landing, the front passenger (180 pounds) departs the airplane. A rear passenger (204 pounds) moves to the front passenger position. What effect does this have on the CG if the airplane weighed 2,690 pounds and the MOM/100 was 2,260 just prior to the passenger transfer?

A— The CG moves forward approximately 3 inches.
B— The weight changes, but the CG is not affected.
C— The CG moves forward approximately 0.1 inch.

Use the following steps:

1. *Consider the effect on the total weight.*

Item	Weight
Original weight	2,690 pounds
Deplaned passenger	– 180 pounds
New Weight	2,510 pounds

2. *Consider the effect on the total moment index using the arms given in FAA Figure 32, and the formula:*

   Weight x Arm ÷ 100 = Moment/Index

Item	Weight	Arm	Moment/100
Original weight & Mom Ind	2,690		2,260.0 lbs-in
Passenger exiting, front	-180	85	-153.0 lbs-in
Passenger exiting, rear	-204	121	-246.8 lbs-in
Passenger into front	+ 204	85	+ 173.4 lbs-in
New Total Weight & Moment	2,510		2,033.6 lbs-in

3. *Determine both the original and new CG using the formula:*

$$CG = \frac{Total\ Mom\ Ind}{Total\ Weight} \times Reduction\ Factor$$

   or:

   a. *Original CG =*

$$\frac{2,260}{2,690} \times 100 = 84.0\ inches\ aft\ of\ datum$$

   b. *New CG =*

$$\frac{2,033.6}{2,510} \times 100 = 81.0\ inches\ aft\ of\ datum$$

4. *Calculate the change in CG:*

   84 – 81 = 3 inches (forward)

(PLT021) — FAA-H-8083-25

AIR
3675. (Refer to Figures 32 and 33.) Which action can adjust the airplane's weight to maximum gross weight and the CG within limits for takeoff?

Front seat occupants... 425 lb
Rear seat occupants.. 300 lb
Fuel, main tanks... 44 gal

A— Drain 12 gallons of fuel.
B— Drain 9 gallons of fuel.
C— Transfer 12 gallons of fuel from the main tanks to the auxiliary tanks.

Use the following steps:

1. *Calculate the original weights and moment index using the information from the problem and FAA Figures 32 and 33, and the formula:*

   Weight x Arm ÷ 100 = Moment/Index

Item	Weight	Arm	Moment/100
Empty weight	*2,015 lbs*		*1,554.0 lbs-in*
Front seat	*425 lbs*	*85*	*361.3 lbs-in*
Rear seat	*300 lbs*	*121*	*363.0 lbs-in*
Fuel (44 x 6)	*264 lbs*	*75*	*198.0 lbs-in*
Total	*3,004 lbs*		*2,476.3 lbs-in*

2. *If the aircraft has a maximum allowable takeoff weight of 2,950 lbs, compute the weight to be removed to reach an acceptable takeoff weight.*

   3,004 – 2,950 = 54 pounds

3. *Compute the amount of fuel (in gallons) that totals 54 lbs:*

   54 ÷ 6 = 9 gallons

4. *Compute the revised weight and moment index:*

Item	Weight	Arm	Moment/100
Original totals	*3,004 lbs*		*2,476.3 lbs-in*
Fuel	*– 54 lbs*	*75*	*– 40.5 lbs-in*
New Total	*2,950 lbs*		*2,435.8 lbs-in*

5. *Consult the Moment Limits vs. Weight Chart. At 2,950 lbs takeoff weight, 2,435.8 is within the Moments Limits.*

(PLT021) — FAA-H-8083-25

AIR
3676. (Refer to Figures 32 and 33.) What effect does a 35-gallon fuel burn (main tanks) have on the weight and balance if the airplane weighed 2,890 pounds and the MOM/100 was 2,452 at takeoff?

A— Weight is reduced by 210 pounds and the CG is aft of limits.
B— Weight is reduced by 210 pounds and the CG is unaffected.
C— Weight is reduced to 2,680 pounds and the CG moves forward.

Use the following steps:

1. *Calculate the change in both weight and moment index caused by a burn of 35 gallons, using the information from FAA Figures 32 and 33.*

   Weight x Arm ÷ 100 = Moment/Index

Item	Weight	Arm	Moment
Fuel (35 x 6)	*210 lbs*	*75*	*158 lbs-in*

2. *Determine the effect of burn on total weight and moment index:*

Item	Weight	Arm	Moment/100
Original total	*2,890 lbs*		*2,452.0 lbs-in*
Fuel burn	*–210 lbs*	*75*	*– 158.0 lbs-in*
New Total	*2,680 lbs*		*2,294.0 lbs-in*

3. *Consult the Moment Limits vs. Weight Table (FAA Figure 33). The allowed range of moment indexes for a weight of 2,680 lbs is 2,123 to 2,287 lbs-in/100. Hence the new moment index exceeds the maximum allowed and the CG is aft of limits.*

(PLT021) — FAA-H-8083-25

Answers

3675 [B]   3676 [A]

AIR

3677. (Refer to Figures 32 and 33.) With the airplane loaded as follows, what action can be taken to balance the airplane?

Front seat occupants..411 lb
Rear seat occupants.. 100 lb
Main wing tanks... 44 gal

A— Fill the auxiliary wing tanks.
B— Add a 100-pound weight to the baggage compartment.
C— Transfer 10 gallons of fuel from the main tanks to the auxiliary tanks.

Use the following steps:

1. *Calculate the weights and moments using the information from the problem and FAA Figures 32 and 33, and the formula:*

   Weight x Arm ÷ 100 = Moment/Index

Item	Weight	Arm	Moment/100
Empty weight	2,015 lbs		1,554.0 lbs-in
Front seat	411 lbs	85	349.4 lbs-in
Rear seat	100 lbs	121	121.0 lbs-in
Fuel 44 x 6	264 lbs	75	198.0 lbs-in
Total	2,790 lbs		2,222.4 lbs-in

2. *Consulting the Moment Limits vs. Weight Table (FAA Figure 33), the allowed range of moments for 2,790 lbs is between 2,243 and 2,374 lbs-in/100.*

3. *Since the moment index is too small, add weight, and for maximum increase in moment index with minimum weight penalty, as far aft as practical. Add 100 lbs in the baggage compartment and recompute weight and moment index:*

Item	Weight	Arm	Moment/100
Original totals	2,790 lbs		2,222.4 lbs-in
Add weight	+ 100 lbs	140	+ 140.0 lbs-in
New Totals	2,890 lbs		2,362.4 lbs-in

4. *Consult the Moment Limits vs. Weight Table. The allowed range of moments for 2,890 pounds is 2,354 to 2,452 lbs-in/100. The new moment is now within limits.*

(PLT021) — FAA-H-8083-25

Answers

3677   [B]

Computing Weight and Balance Problems Using a Graph

Problem:

Referring to FAA Figure 34, determine the maximum amount of baggage that may be loaded aboard the airplane for the CG to remain within the loading envelope.

Item	Weight (lbs)	Moment/1,000 (lbs-in)
Empty weight	1,350	51.5
Pilot, front passenger	250	—
Rear passengers	400	—
Baggage	—	—
Fuel 30 gal.	—	—
Oil 8 qt.	—	—

Solution:

1. Determine the total weight. Using the information provided in the question, enter the items and the weights:

Item	Weight (lbs)	Moment/1,000 (lbs-in)
Pilot, front passenger	250	
Rear passengers	400	
Fuel	180 *	
Oil	15 **	
Baggage	—	
Empty weight	+ 1,350 †	
	2,195 lbs	

*30 gal x 6 lbs/gal   **given in the note in the middle of FAA Figure 34   † given in problem

2. Determine the moments. Using FAA Figure 34, locate the moments for all the given weights:

Item	Weight (lbs)	Moment/1,000 (lbs-in)
Pilot, front passenger	250	9.3
Rear passengers	400	29.3
Fuel	180	8.7
Oil	15	-0.2 *
Baggage	—	—
Empty weight	+ 1,350	51.5
	2,195 lbs	98.6 lbs-in

*from note in center of FAA Figure 34

3. From the Center of Gravity Moment Envelope, bottom of FAA Figure 34, determine the maximum allowable gross weight of the aircraft, as indicated by the top of the "Normal Category" envelope (2,300 pounds). Comparing the total weight of this problem with the maximum allowable weight shows that 105 pounds of baggage could be carried:

```
  2,300
- 2,195
    105
```

4. From the Loading Graph, determine the Mom/1,000 of 105 pounds of baggage. Add that amount to the previous total Mom/1,000:

Item	Weight (lbs)	Moment/1,000 (lbs-in)
Totals	2,195	98.6
Baggage	+ 105	+ 10.0
New Totals	2,300 lbs	108.6 lbs-in

5. Enter the Center of Gravity Moment Envelope Graph at the total Mom/1,000 (108.6) and the maximum allowable gross weight line at 2,300 pounds. The point of intersection falls within the "Normal Category" envelope and acceptable weight and balance conditions.

AIR
3669. (Refer to Figure 34.) What is the maximum amount of baggage that may be loaded aboard the airplane for the CG to remain within the moment envelope?

	WEIGHT (LB)	MOM/1000
Empty weight	1,350	51.5
Pilot and front passenger	250	—
Rear passengers	400	—
Baggage	—	—
Fuel, 30 gal	—	—
Oil, 8 qt	—	-0.2

A— 105 pounds.
B— 110 pounds.
C— 120 pounds.

Use the following steps:

1. *Find total weight and moment index (except baggage) by using the loading graphs in FAA Figure 34. Note that the reduction factor is 1,000 in this problem. The standard weight for gasoline is 6 lbs/U.S. gallon, and for oil, 7.5 lbs/U.S. gallon.*

Item	Weight	Moment/1,000
B.E.W.	1,350 lbs	51.5 lbs-in
Pilot & Pax (a)	250 lbs	9.3 lbs-in
Rear Pax (b)	400 lbs	29.3 lbs-in
Fuel (30 x 6) (c)	180 lbs	8.7 lbs-in
Oil	15 lbs	-0.2 lbs-in
Total	2,195 lbs	98.6 lbs-in

2. *Calculate the maximum allowable weight for baggage:*
   2,300 – 2,195 = 105 pounds

3. *Add baggage and calculate the new totals for weight and moment index.*

Weight	Moment/1,000
2,195 lbs	98.6 lbs-in
+ 105 lbs	10.0 lbs-in
2,300 lbs	108.6 lbs-in

4. *Plot the position of the point determined by 2,300 pounds and the moment of 108.6 lbs-in/1,000 on the center of gravity moment envelope graph. The point is in the normal category envelope.*

(PLT092) — FAA-H-8083-25

AIR
3670. (Refer to Figure 34.) Calculate the moment of the airplane and determine which category is applicable.

	WEIGHT (LB)	MOM/1000
Empty weight	1,350	51.5
Pilot and front passenger	310	—
Rear passengers	96	—
Fuel, 38 gal	—	—
Oil, 8 qt	—	-0.2

A— 79.2, utility category.
B— 80.8, utility category.
C— 81.2, normal category.

Use the following steps:

1. *Find total weight and moment index by using the loading graph (FAA Figure 34). The standard weight for gasoline is 6 lbs/U.S. gallons and for oil, 7.5 lbs U.S. gallon.*

Item	Weight	Moment/1,000
B.E.W.	1,350 lbs	51.5 lbs-in
Pilot & Pax (a)	310 lbs	11.5 lbs-in
Rear Pax (b)	96 lbs	7.0 lbs-in
Fuel (38 x 6) (c)	228 lbs	11.0 lbs-in
Oil	15 lbs	-0.2 lbs-in
Total	1,999 lbs	80.8 lbs-in

2. *Plot the position of the point determined by 1,999 pounds and a moment of 80.8 lbs-in/1,000. The point is just inside the utility category envelope.*

(PLT092) — FAA-H-8083-25

Answer (A) is incorrect because this answer choice doesn't have any significance. Answer (C) is incorrect because the oil moment needs to be subtracted.

AIR
3671. (Refer to Figure 34.) What is the maximum amount of fuel that may be aboard the airplane on takeoff if loaded as follows?

	WEIGHT (LB)	MOM/1000
Empty weight	1,350	51.5
Pilot and front passenger	340	—
Rear passengers	310	—
Baggage	45	—
Oil, 8 qt	—	—

A— 24 gallons.
B— 32 gallons.
C— 40 gallons.

1. Find the total weight and moment index (except fuel) by using the loading graph in FAA Figure 34.

Item	Weight	Moment/1,000
B.E.W.	1,350 lbs	51.5 lbs-in
Pilot & Pax (a)	340 lbs	12.6 lbs-in
Rear Pax (b)	310 lbs	22.6 lbs-in
Baggage (c)	45 lbs	4.2 lbs-in
Oil (d)	15 lbs	-0.2 lbs-in
Total	2,060 lbs	90.7 lbs-in

2. Calculate the additional fuel weight which can be added:

   2,300 – 2,060 = 240 lbs

3. Calculate the number of gallons of fuel at 6 lbs/gallon:

   240 ÷ 6 = 40 gallons

4. Calculate the added fuel moment index from the graph (40 gal fuel – 11.5 MOM/1,000).

5. Calculate the new total weight and moment index:

Weight	Moment/1,000
2,060 lbs	90.7 lbs-in
+ 240 lbs	11.5 lbs-in
2,300 lbs	102.2 lbs-in

6. Plot the position of the point determined by 2,300 pounds and a moment index of 102.2 lbs-in/1,000. The point lies on the normal category envelope.

(PLT092) — FAA-H-8083-25

AIR
3673. (Refer to Figure 34.) Determine the aircraft loaded moment and the aircraft category.

	WEIGHT (LB)	MOM/1000
Empty weight	1,350	51.5
Pilot and front passenger	380	—
Fuel, 48 gal	288	—
Oil, 8 qt	—	—

A— 78.2, normal category.
B— 79.2, normal category.
C— 80.4, utility category.

Use the following steps:

1. Find the total weight and moment index by using the loading graph from FAA Figure 34.

Item	Weight	Moment/1,000
B.E.W.	1,350 lbs	51.5 lbs-in
Pilot & Pax (a)	380 lbs	14.0 lbs-in
Fuel (b)	288 lbs	13.8 lbs-in
Oil (c)	15 lbs	-0.2 lbs-in
Total	2,033 lbs	79.1 lbs-in

2. Plot the position of the point determined by 2,033 lbs. and a moment of 79.1 lbs-in/1,000. The point is within the normal category envelope.

(PLT092) — FAA-H-8083-25

AIR, WSC
3672. (Refer to Figure 34.) Determine the moment with the following data:

	WEIGHT (LB)	MOM/1000
Empty weight	1,350	51.5
Pilot and front passenger	340	—
Fuel (std tanks)	Capacity	—
Oil, 8 qt	—	—

A— 69.9 pound-inches.
B— 74.9 pound-inches.
C— 77.6 pound-inches.

1. Find the total weight and moment index by using the loading graph from FAA Figure 34.

Item	Weight	Moment/1,000
B.E.W.	1,350 lbs	51.5 lbs-in
Pilot & Pax (a)	340 lbs	12.6 lbs-in
Fuel (Std. Tanks) (b)	228 lbs	11.0 lbs-in
Oil (c)	15 lbs	-0.2 lbs-in
Total	1,933 lbs	74.9 lbs-in

(PLT003) — FAA-H-8083-25

Answers

3671 [C]	3673 [B]	3672 [B]

RTC
3720. (Refer to Figure 43.) What action, if any, should be taken for lateral balance if the helicopter is loaded as follows?

Gross weight.. 1,800 lb
Pilot...................... 140 lb, 13.5 in. left of "0" MOM arm
Copilot .... 180 lb, 13.5 in. right of "0" MOM arm

A— Add 10 pounds of weight to the pilot's side.
B— Decrease the gross weight 50 pounds.
C— No action is required.

Use the following steps:

1. *Compute the left and right moments using the formula:*

   Weight x Arm = Moment

Item	Weight	Arm	Moment
Pilot	140 lbs	13.5	1,890 lbs-in (left)
Copilot	180 lbs	13.5	2,430 lbs-in (right)

2. *Find the offset to the left or right:*

   2,430.0 lbs-in (right)
   − 1,890.0 lbs-in (left)
   540.0 lbs-in offset (right)

3. *Enter the bottom of the Lateral Offset Moment Graph at 540 lbs-in right of the zero point. Proceed upward until intercepting the 1,800-pound gross weight line. The point of intercept lies inside the envelope.*

(PLT021) — FAA-H-8083-21

RTC
3721. (Refer to Figure 43.) What action should be taken for lateral balance if the helicopter is loaded as follows?

Gross weight.. 1,800 lb
Pilot...................... 100 lb, 13.5 in. left of "0" MOM arm
Copilot .... 200 lb, 13.5 in. right of "0" MOM arm

A— Add 50 pounds of weight to the pilot's side.
B— Decrease the gross weight 50 pounds.
C— No action is required.

Use the following steps:

1. *Compute the left and right moments using the formula:*

   Weight x Arm = Moment

Item	Weight	Arm	Moment
Copilot	200 lbs	13.5	2,700 lbs-in (right)
Pilot	100 lbs	13.5	1,350 lbs-in (left)

2. *Find the offset to the right or left:*

   2,700.0 lbs-in (right)
   − 1,350.0 lbs-in (left)
   1,350.0 lbs-in offset (right)

3. *Enter the bottom of the Lateral Offset Moment Envelope Graph of FAA Figure 43 at 1,350 right of the zero point. Proceed upward until intercepting the 1,800-pound gross weight line. The point of intercept falls outside the envelope to the right.*

4. *Try adding 50 pounds to the pilot's side and do the same computations:*

   Copilot   200 x 13.5 = 2,700 (right)
   Pilot   150 x 13.5 = 2,025 (left)

   2,700 (right)
   − 2,025 (left)
   675 (right)

Plot the new values on the lateral offset envelope graph of FAA Figure 43.

(PLT021) — FAA-H-8083-21

RTC
3722. (Refer to Figure 41.) Determine the weight and balance of the helicopter.

	WEIGHT (LB)	ARM (IN)	MOMENT (LB-IN)
Empty weight	1,495.0	—	151,593.0
Pilot and one passenger	350.0	64.0	—
Fuel (40 gal usable)	—	96.0	—

A— Over gross weight limit, but within CG limit.
B— Within gross weight limit and at the aft CG limit.
C— Over gross weight limit and exceeds the aft CG limit.

Use the following steps:

1. *Calculate the weight and moment using the information given in the problem and the formula:*

   Weight x Arm = Moment

   Note: The standard weight of gasoline is 6 lbs/U.S. gallon.

Item	Weight	Arm	Moment
Empty weight	1,495 lbs		151,593.0 lbs-in
Pilot & Pax	350 lbs	64	22,400.0 lbs-in
Fuel 40 x 6	240 lbs	96	23,040.0 lbs-in
Total	2,085 lbs		197,033.0 lbs-in

   Continued

Answers

3720 [C]   3721 [A]   3722 [B]

2. Determine the position of the CG using the formula:

$$CG = \frac{Total\ Moment}{Total\ Weight}$$

or:

$$CG = \frac{197,033}{2,085} = 94.5\ inches\ aft\ of\ datum$$

3. Locate the point on FAA Figure 41 defined by a weight of 2,085 pounds and a CG of 94.5 inches, and find the aircraft within gross weight limit and at the aft CG limit.

(PLT021) — FAA-H-8083-21

RTC
3723. (Refer to Figure 42.) Determine if the helicopter's CG is within limits.

	WEIGHT (LB)	MOMENT (lb-in)
Empty weight (including oil)	1,025	102,705
Pilot and passenger	345	—
Fuel, 35 gal	—	—

A— Out of limits forward.
B— Within limits.
C— Out of limits aft.

Use the following steps:

1. Calculate the weights and moments using the information from the problem and the Loading Chart of FAA Figure 42. Use the formula:

Weight x Arm = Moment

Note: The standard weight of gasoline is 6 lbs/U.S gallon.

Item	Weight	Arm	Moment
Empty weight	1,025 lbs		102,705.0 lbs-in
Pilot & Pax (a)	345 lbs	83.90	28,945.5 lbs-in
Fuel 35 x 6 (b)	210 lbs	107.0	22,470.0 lbs-in
Total	1,580 lbs		154,120.5 lbs-in

2. Determine the position of the CG using the formula:

$$CG = \frac{Total\ Moment}{Total\ Weight}$$

or:

$$CG = \frac{154,120.5}{1,580} = 97.54\ inches\ aft\ of\ datum$$

3. Plot the point determined by a weight of 1,580 pounds and a moment of 154,120.5 lbs-in on the CG limit graph of FAA Figure 42. The point is within the forward and aft limits.

(PLT021) — FAA-H-8083-21

RTC
3724. (Refer to Figure 42.) What effect does adding a 185-pound passenger have on the CG, if prior to boarding the passenger, the helicopter weighed 1,380 pounds and the moment is 136,647.5 pound-inches?

A— The CG is moved forward 1.78 inches.
B— The CG is moved aft 1.78 inches.
C— The CG is moved forward 2.36 inches.

Use the following steps:

1. Calculate the original position of the CG using the formula:

$$CG = \frac{Total\ Moment}{Total\ Weight}$$

or:

$$CG = \frac{136,647.5}{1,380} = 99.02\ inches\ aft\ of\ datum$$

2. Determine the revised weight and moment. The station for the passenger is 83.90 inches as shown on the Loading Chart of FAA Figure 42. Use the following formula:

Weight x Arm = Moment

Item	Weight	Arm	Moment
Original total	1,380 lbs		136,647.5 lbs-in
Passenger	+185 lbs	83.9	15,521.5 lbs-in
New Total	1,565 lbs		152,169.0 lbs-in

3. Calculate the new CG:

$$CG = \frac{152,169}{1,565} = 97.23\ inches\ aft\ of\ datum$$

4. Compute the change in CG:

Original CG	99.02	inches aft of datum
minus new CG	– 97.23	inches aft of datum
Movement	1.79	inches (forward)

(PLT021) — FAA-H-8083-21

RTC
3725. How is the CG of the helicopter affected after a fuel burn of 20 gallons?

Gross weight prior to fuel burn .... 2,050 lb
Moment .... 195,365 lb-in
Fuel arm .... 96.9 in

A— CG shifts forward 1.0 inch.
B— CG shifts forward 0.1 inch.
C— CG shifts aft 1.0 inch.

Answers

3723 [B] 3724 [A] 3725 [B]

Use the following steps:

1. *Calculate the original position of the CG using the formula:*

$$CG = \frac{Total\ Moment}{Total\ Weight}$$

or:

$$CG = \frac{195,365}{2,050} = 95.3\ inches\ aft\ of\ datum$$

2. *Determine the revised weight and moment. The station for the fuel is 96.9 inches as shown on the question which contradicts FAA Figure 43. Use the following formula:*

Weight x Arm = Moment

Item	Weight		Arm	Moment	
Original total	2,050	lbs		195,365	lbs-in
Fuel burn	– 120	lbs	96.9	11,628	lbs-in
New Total	1,930	lbs		183,737	lbs-in

3. *Calculate the new CG:*

$$CG = \frac{183,737}{1,930} = 95.2\ inches\ aft\ of\ datum$$

4. *Compute the change in CG:*

Original CG	*95.3*	*inches aft of datum*
minus new CG	*– 95.2*	*inches aft of datum*
Movement	*.1*	*inch (forward)*

(PLT021) — FAA-H-8083-21

RTC
3726. (Refer to Figure 42.) How is the CG of the helicopter affected when all of the auxiliary fuel is burned off?

Gross weight prior to fuel burn .... 1,660 lb
Moment... 159,898.5 lb-in

A— CG moves aft 0.12 inch.
B— CG moves forward 0.78 inch.
C— CG moves forward 1.07 inches.

Use the following steps:

1. *Calculate the original position of the CG using the formula:*

$$CG = \frac{Total\ Moment}{Total\ Weight}$$

or:

$$CG = \frac{159,898.5}{1,660} = 96.32\ inches\ aft\ of\ datum$$

2. *Determine the revised weight and moment. The auxiliary fuel burn is 19 gallons (the dotted line goes from 44 to 25). 19 x 6 = 114 lbs. The station for the fuel is 107 inches as shown on the Loading Chart of FAA Figure 42. Use the following formula:*

Weight x Arm = Moment

Item	Weight		Arm	Moment	
Original total	1,660	lbs		159,898.5	lbs-in
Fuel burn	– 114	lbs	107	–12,198	lbs-in
New Total	1,546	lbs		147,700.5	lbs-in

3. *Calculate the new CG:*

147,700.5 ÷ 1,546 = 95.54 inches aft of datum

4. *Compute the change in CG:*

Original CG	*96.32*	*inches aft of datum*
minus new CG	*– 95.54*	*inches aft of datum*
Movement	*.78*	*inches (forward)*

(PLT021) — FAA-H-8083-21

RTC
3728. (Refer to Figure 43.) Determine if the helicopter weight and balance is within limits.

	WEIGHT (LB)	ARM (IN)	MOMENT (100)
Empty weight	1,495.0	101.4	1,515.93
Oil, 8 qt	—	100.5	—
Fuel, 40 gal	—	96.0	—
Pilot and copilot	300.0	64.0	—

A— CG 95.2 inches, within limits.
B— CG 95.3 inches, weight and CG out of limits.
C— CG 95.4 inches, within limits.

Use the following steps:

1. *Calculate the weights and moment indexes using the information from the problem and the formula:*

Weight x Arm ÷ Reduction Factor = Moment/Index

Note: The standard weight for gasoline is 6 lbs/U.S. gallon and for oil, 7.5 lbs/U.S. gallon.

Item	Weight		Arm	Moment/100	
Empty weight	*1,495*	*lbs*	*101.4*	*1,515.93*	*lbs-in*
Oil, 8 qts (2 x 7.5)	*15*	*lbs*	*100.5*	*15.08*	*lbs-in*
Fuel (40 x 6)	*240*	*lbs*	*96.0*	*230.40*	*lbs-in*
Pilots	*300*	*lbs*	*64.0*	*192*	*lbs-in*
Total	*2,050*	*lbs*		*1,953.41*	*lbs-in*

Continued

Answers

3726 [B]　　　3728 [B]

2. Determine the position of the CG using the formula:

$$CG = \frac{Total\ Mom/Ind}{Total\ Weight} \times Reduction\ Factor$$

or:

$$\frac{1,953.41}{2,050} \times 100 = 95.29\ inches\ aft\ of\ datum$$

3. Plot the point determined by a weight of 2,050 pounds and a CG of 95.29 inches on the longitudinal CG envelope of FAA Figure 43. The point is outside the allowable limits.

(PLT021) — FAA-H-8083-21

RTC

3727. (Refer to Figure 43.) Calculate the weight and balance of the helicopter, and determine if the CG is within limits.

	WEIGHT (LB)	ARM (IN)	MOMENT (100)
Empty weight	1,495.0	101.4	1,515.93
Oil, 8 qt	—	100.5	—
Fuel, 40 gal	—	96.0	—
Pilot	160.0	64.0	—

A— CG 90.48 inches, out of limits forward.
B— CG 95.32 inches, within limits.
C— CG 97.58 inches, within limits.

This problem uses a reduction factor so we arrive at moment index instead of moment.

Use the following steps:

1. Calculate the weights and moment indexes using the information from the problem and the formula:

Weight x Arm ÷ Reduction Factor =
Moment Index

Note: The standard weight for gasoline is 6 lbs/U.S. gallon and for oil, 7.5 lbs/U.S. gallon.

Item	Weight	Arm	Moment/100
Empty weight	1,495 lbs	101.4	1,515.93 lbs-in
Oil, 8 qts (2 x 7.5)	15 lbs	100.5	15.08 lbs-in
Fuel (40 x 6)	240 lbs	96.0	230.40 lbs-in
Pilot	160 lbs	64.0	102.40 lbs-in
Total	1,910 lbs		1,863.81 lbs-in

2. Determine the position of the CG using the formula:

$$CG = \frac{Total\ Mom/Ind}{Total\ Weight} \times Reduction\ Factor$$

or:

$$\frac{1,863.81}{1,910} \times 100 = 97.58\ inches\ aft\ of\ datum$$

3. Plot the point determined by a weight of 1,910 pounds and a CG of 97.58 inches on the longitudinal CG envelope of FAA Figure 43. The point is within the allowable limits.

(PLT021) — FAA-H-8083-21

RTC

3729. (Refer to Figures 44 and 45.) What is the new CG of the gyroplane after a 10-gallon fuel burn if the original weight was 1,450 pounds and the MOM/1000 was 108 pound-inches?

A— Out of limits forward.
B— Out of limits aft.
C— Within limits near the forward limit.

Use the following steps:

1. Determine the change in load moment resulting from 10 gallons of fuel burned by entering the Loading Chart at the 10 gallon point on the fuel line, drawing a line downward and reading the moment for 10 gallons of fuel (5.3 x 1,000 lbs-in).

2. Calculate the new weight and moment:

Item	Weight	Moment/1,000
Original total	1,450.0 lbs	108.0 lbs-in
Fuel (10 x 6)	− 60.0 lbs	− 5.3 lbs-in
New Total	1,390.0 lbs	102.7 lbs-in

3. Plot the point determined by 1,390 and 102.7 lbs-in/1,000 on the center of gravity moment envelope graph. The point is outside (to the left or forward) of the center of gravity moment envelope.

(PLT003) — FAA-H-8083-21

Answers

3727 [C]　　　　3729 [A]

RTC
3730. (Refer to Figures 44 and 45.) What is the condition of the weight and balance of the gyroplane as loaded?

	WEIGHT (LB)	MOMENT (1000)
Empty weight	1,074	85.6
Oil, 6 qt	—	1.0
Pilot and passenger	247	—
Fuel, 12 gal	—	—
Baggage	95	—

A— Within limits.
B— Overweight.
C— Out of limits aft.

Use the following steps:

1. *Calculate the total weight and moments using the information in the problem and FAA Figure 45. The standard weight for oil is 7.5 lbs/U.S. gallon, and for gasoline it is 6 lbs/U.S. gallon.*

Item	Weight	Moment/1,000
Empty weight	1,074 lbs	85.6 lbs-in
Oil, 6 qts (1.5 X 7.5)	11.25 lbs	1.0 lbs-in
Pilot and Pax (seat aft)	247 lbs	14.1 lbs-in
Fuel (12 x 6)	72 lbs	6.3 lbs-in
Baggage	95 lbs	5.7 lbs-in
Total	1,499 lbs	112.7 lbs-in

2. *Plot the point determined by 1,499 pounds and 112.7 x 1,000 lbs-in on FAA Figure 44. The point is within the envelope (Answer A).*

3. *Now, consider the effect of pilot and passenger in the forward position. The moment would now be 13.3 x 1,000 lbs-in and the resulting total moment would be reduced to 111.9 x 1,000 lbs-in. When plotted on the Center of Gravity Moment Envelope Graph SEAT FWD, the weight-moment is slightly outside the envelope. Note that the manufacturer uses an aft position in presenting sample weight and balance calculations for this aircraft.*

(PLT021) — FAA-H-8083-21

RTC
3731. (Refer to Figures 44 and 45.) Approximately how much baggage, if any, may be carried in the gyroplane, without exceeding weight and balance limits?

	WEIGHT (LB)	MOMENT (1000)
Empty weight	1,074	85.6
Oil, 6 qt	—	1.0
Fuel, Full	—	—
Pilot (FWD)	224	—

A— None, overweight.
B— 70 pounds.
C— 100 pounds.

Use the following steps:

1. *Calculate the total weight and moment using the information in the problem and the Loading Chart. The standard weight for oil is 7.5 pounds per gallon and for gasoline is 6.0 pounds per gallon.*

Item	Weight	Moment/1,000
Empty weight	1,074 lbs	85.6 lbs-in
Oil, 6 qts. (1.5 x 7.5)	11.25 lbs	1.0 lbs-in
Pilot (a)	224 lbs	12.1 lbs-in
Fuel (full) (b)	119 lbs	10.2 lbs-in
Totals	1,428 lbs	108.9 lbs-in

2. *Consider adding enough baggage to approach the maximum takeoff weight 1,500 pounds.*

   1,500 – 1,428 = 72 or about 70 pounds
   (Answer B)
   (This remains within the weight limit.)

3. *Determine the moment of the 70 pounds of added baggage (4.2 x 1,000 lbs-in).*

4. *Compute the new weight and moment.*

Item	Weight	Moment
Original Total	1,428	108.9
Baggage	+ 70	+ 4.2
New Total	1,498	113.1

5. *Plot the point determined by 1,498 lbs and 113.1 x 1,000 lbs-in on the Center of Gravity Moment Envelope Graph of FAA Figure 44. The point is within the envelope.*

(PLT021) — FAA-H-8083-21

Answers

3730   [A]   3731   [B]

GLI

3861. (Refer to Figure 53.) Calculate the weight and balance of the glider, and determine if the CG is within limits.

Pilot (fwd seat).. 160 lb
Passenger (aft seat) .... 185 lb

A— CG 71.65 inches aft of datum—out of limits forward.
B— CG 79.67 inches aft of datum – within limits.
C— CG 83.43 inches aft of datum – within limits.

Use the following steps:

1. Calculate the total weight and moment using the information in the question and in FAA Figure 53, and the formula:

Weight x Arm = Moment

Item	Weight	Arm	Moment
Empty weight	610	96.47	58,846.7 lbs-in
Pilot (fwd seat)	160	43.80	7,008.0 lbs-in
Passenger (aft seat)	185	74.70	13,819.5 lbs-in
Totals	955		79,674.2 lbs-in

2. Calculate the position of the CG using the formula:

$$CG = \frac{Total\ Moment}{Total\ Weight}$$

or:

$$CG = \frac{79,674.2}{955} = 83.43 \text{ inches aft of datum}$$

3. Compare the calculated value to the allowed range for the position of the CG, 78.20 to 86.10. The calculated position is within the allowed range of both maximum weight and CG.

(PLT021) — FAA-H-8083-13

GLI

3862. (Refer to Figure 53.) How is the CG affected if radio and oxygen equipment weighing 35 pounds is added at station 43.8? The glider weighs 945 pounds with a moment of 78,000.2 pound-inches prior to adding the equipment.

A— CG shifts forward 0.79 inch – out of limits forward.
B— CG shifts forward 1.38 inches – within limits.
C— CG shifts aft 1.38 inches – out of limits aft.

Use the following steps:

1. Calculate the weight and moment of the equipment to be added using the formula:

Weight x Arm = Moment

Item	Weight	Arm	Moment
Added equip.	35 lbs	43.8	1,533.0 lbs-in

2. Calculate the new total weight and moment.

Item	Weight	Moment
Old	945	78,000.2 lbs-in
Added	35	1,533.0 lbs-in
New Total	980	79,533.2 lbs-in

3. Calculate the old and new positions of the center of gravity using the formula:

$$CG = \frac{Total\ Moment}{Total\ Weight}$$

Original CG =

$$\frac{78,000.2}{945} = 82.54 \text{ inches aft of datum}$$

$$New\ CG = \frac{79,533.2}{980} = 81.16 \text{ inches aft of datum}$$

4. Compute change and direction of change of the CG.

Original CG   82.54
New CG   – 81.16
           1.38 inches closer to datum (forward)

5. Compare the calculated values of weight and CG position to the allowed range shown in FAA Figure 53. The allowed CG range is 78.20 to 86.10 and the calculated value is within these limits.

(PLT256) — FAA-H-8083-13

Answers

3861   [C]   3862   [B]

GLI

3863. (Refer to Figure 53.) What is the CG of the glider if the pilot and passenger each weigh 215 pounds?

A— 74.69 inches aft of datum – out of limits forward.
B— 81.08 inches aft of datum – within limits.
C— 81.08 inches aft of datum – over maximum gross weight.

Use the following steps:

1. Calculate the total weight and moment using the information in the question and in FAA Figure 53, and the formula:

Weight x Arm = Moment

Item	Weight	Arm	Moment
Empty weight	610	96.47	58,846.7 lbs-in
Pilot (fwd seat)	215	43.80	9,417.0 lbs-in
Passenger (aft seat)	215	74.70	16,060.5 lbs-in
Totals	1,040		84,324.2 lbs-in

2. Calculate the position of the CG using the formula:

$$CG = \frac{Total\ Moment}{Total\ Weight}$$

or:

$$CG = \frac{84,324.2}{1,040} = 81.08\ inches\ aft\ of\ datum$$

3. Compare the calculated value to the allowed range for the position of the CG, 78.20 to 86.10. The calculated position is within the allowed range of both maximum weight and CG.

(PLT021) — FAA-H-8083-13

LTA, LSL

3887. What constitutes the payload of a balloon?

A— Total gross weight.
B— Total weight of passengers, cargo, and fuel.
C— Weight of the aircraft and equipment.

Payload is the total weight of passengers, cargo, and fuel an aircraft can legally carry on a given flight, excluding weight of the aircraft and equipment. (PLT177) — FAA-H-8083-11

LTA

3888. (Refer to Figure 56.) The gross weight of the balloon is 1,350 pounds and the outside air temperature (OAT) is +51°F. The maximum height would be

A— 5,000 feet.
B— 8,000 feet.
C— 10,000 feet.

Use the following steps:

1. Locate the gross weight, 1,350 pounds, on the bottom of the graph in FAA Figure 56.
2. From that point, draw a line upward through the graph.
3. Locate the OAT +51°F on the left side of the graph.
4. From that point, draw a line to the right through the graph.
5. Note the point of intersection of the two lines, which in this case falls on the 10,000-foot curve.

(PLT057) — FAA-H-8083-11

LTA

3889. (Refer to Figure 56.) The gross weight of the balloon is 1,200 pounds and the maximum height the pilot needs to attain is 5,000 feet. The maximum temperature to achieve this performance is

A— +37°F.
B— +70°F.
C— +97°F.

Use the following steps:

1. Locate the gross weight, 1,200 pounds, on the bottom of the graph in FAA Figure 56.
2. From that point, draw a line upward to the 5,000-foot pressure altitude line.
3. From there, draw a line to the left to the air temperature scale and read the maximum temperature, 100°F.

(PLT057) — FAA-H-8083-11

Answers

3863 [B]   3887 [B]   3888 [C]   3889 [C]

LTA

3890. (Refer to Figure 57.) Determine the maximum payload for a balloon flying at 2,500 feet at an ambient temperature of 91°F.

A— 420 pounds.
B— 465 pounds.
C— 505 pounds.

Payload is the total weight of passengers, cargo and fuel an aircraft can legally carry on a given flight, excluding weight of the aircraft and equipment. Using FAA Figure 57, perform the following steps:

1. *Enter the chart at an ambient temperature of 91°F. From that point, proceed upward to the 2,500-foot pressure altitude point (halfway between sea level and 5,000 feet).*

2. *From the point of intersection, proceed to the left to determine the gross weight for 2,500 feet (840 pounds).*

3. *Note that the empty weight is 335 pounds. Compute the payload using the formula:*

   Payload = Gross Weight − Empty Weight
   Payload = 840 lbs − 335 lbs
   Payload = 505 lbs

(PLT057) — FAA-H-8083-11

LTA

3893. (Refer to Figure 57.) Determine the maximum weight allowable for pilot and passenger for a flight at approximately 1,000 feet with a temperature of 68°F. Launch with 20 gallons of propane.

A— 580 pounds.
B— 620 pounds.
C— 720 pounds.

Use FAA Figure 57, and the following steps:

(The standard weight of propane is 4.23 pounds per gallon.)

1. *Enter the chart at the 68°F ambient temperature value. Move upward to a point about 1/5 of the distance between the sea level and 5,000-foot pressure altitude curves.*

2. *From that point, draw a line to the left and read the gross weight as 1,040 pounds.*

3. *Calculate the weight of 20 gallons of propane:*

   20 x 4.23 = 85 pounds

4. *Compute the available lift:*

Item	*Weight*	
Gross weight	*1,040*	*lbs*
Empty weight	*-335*	*lbs*
Fuel weight	*-85*	*lbs*
Pilot and passengers	*620*	*lbs*

(PLT057) — FAA-H-8083-11

LTA

3894. (Refer to Figure 57.) What is the maximum weight allowed for pilot and passengers for a flight at 5,000 feet with a standard temperature? Launch with 20 gallons of propane.

A— 670 pounds.
B— 760 pounds.
C— 1,095 pounds.

Use FAA Figure 57, and the following steps:

(The standard weight of propane is 4.23 pounds per gallon.)

1. *Enter the chart where 5,000 feet and the standard temperature line intersect.*

2. *From that point, draw a line to the left and read the gross weight as 1,090 pounds.*

3. *Calculate the weight of 20 gallons of propane:*

   20 x 4.23 = 85 pounds

4. *Compute the available lift:*

Item	*Weight*	
Gross weight	*1,090*	*lbs*
Empty weight	*-335*	*lbs*
Fuel weight	*-85*	*lbs*
Pilot and passengers	*670*	*lbs*

(PLT057) — FAA-H-8083-11

Answers

3890　[C]　　　　3893　[B]　　　　3894　[A]

SPO

2174. Problems caused by overloading an aircraft include

A— reduced climb rate, excessive structural loads, and shortened cruising range.
B— increased service ceiling, increased angle of climb, and increased cruising speed.
C— slower takeoff speed, increased maneuverability, and shorter takeoff roll.

Some of the problems caused by overloading an aircraft are:

* *The aircraft will need a higher takeoff speed, which results in a longer takeoff run.*

* *Both the rate and angle of climb will be reduced.*

* *The service ceiling will be lowered.*

* *The cruising speed will be reduced.*

* *The cruising range will be shortened.*

* *Maneuverability will be decreased.*

* *A longer landing roll will be required because the landing speed will be higher.*

* *Excessive loads will be imposed on the structure, especially the landing gear.*

(PLT313) — FAA-H-8083-1

SPO

2182. Most aircraft are so designed that if all seats are occupied, all baggage allowed by the baggage compartment structure is carried, and all the fuel tanks are full, the aircraft will be

A— grossly overloaded.
B— under maximum gross weight.
C— at maximum gross weight.

The maximum allowable gross weight for an aircraft is determined by design considerations. However, the maximum operational weight may be less than the maximum allowable due to such considerations as high density altitude or high-drag field conditions caused by wet grass or water on the runway. The maximum gross weight may also be limited by the departure or arrival airport's runway length. One important preflight consideration is the distribution of the load in the aircraft. Loading an aircraft so the gross weight is less than the maximum allowable is not enough. This weight must be distributed to keep the CG within the limits specified in the POH or AFM. (PLT313) — FAA-H-8083-1

SPO

2183. When operating an aircraft, the pilot-in-command is responsible for using

A— the most current weight and balance data.
B— weight and balance data from the factory.
C— recent weight and balance data.

It is the responsibility of the pilot in command to use the most current weight and balance data when planning a flight and operating the aircraft. (PLT328) — FAA-H-8083-1

LSA, LSR

2350. (Refer to Figures 44 and 45.) GIVEN:

	Weight	Moment
Gyroplane basic weight	1,150	92
Pilot (seat forward)	155	?
Passenger (seat forward)	125	?
Fuel, 15 gallons	?	?

The CG is located

A— outside the CG envelope; the maximum gross weight is exceeded.
B— outside the CG envelope; the maximum gross weight and the gross-weight moment are exceeded.
C— within the CG envelope; neither maximum gross weight nor gross-weight moment is exceeded.

Total the weights and moments to determine if the CG is within limits.

Item	Weight	Moment
Gyroplane basic weight	1,150	92
Pilot (seat forward)	155	8.4
Passenger (seat forward)	125	6.8
Fuel, 15 gallons	+ 100	+ 8.8
Total	1,530	116

Weight exceeds the maximum gross weight by 30 pounds and the gross-weight moment is forward of limits. (PLT021) — FAA-H-8083-1

Answers

2174 [A]	2182 [A]	2183 [A]	2350 [B]

LSA, LSR
2351. (Refer to Figures 44 and 45.) GIVEN:

	Weight	Moment
Gyroplane basic weight	1,150	92
Pilot (seat forward)	160	?
Passenger (seat forward)	110	?
Fuel, 10 gallons	?	?

The CG is located

A— outside the CG envelope; the maximum gross weight is exceeded.

B— outside the CG envelope; the maximum gross weight and the gross-weight moment are exceeded.

C— within the CG envelope; neither maximum gross weight nor gross-weight moment is exceeded.

Total the weights and moments to determine if the CG is within limits.

Item	Weight	Moment
Gyroplane basic weight	*1,150*	*92*
Pilot (seat forward)	*160*	*8.6*
Passenger (seat forward)	*110*	*6*
Fuel, 10 gallons	*+ 70*	*+ 6*
Total	*1,490*	*112.6*

Both gross weight and moment are within limits. (PLT021) — FAA-H-8083-1

Density Altitude and Aircraft Performance

Aircraft performance charts show a pilot what can be expected of an airplane (rate of climb, takeoff roll, etc.) under stipulated conditions. Prediction of performance is based upon a sea level temperature of +15°C (+59°F) and atmospheric pressure of 29.92" Hg (1013.2 mb). This combination of temperature and pressure is called a "standard day." When the air is at a "standard density," temperature and/or pressure deviations from standard will change the air density, or the density altitude, which affects aircraft performance. Performance charts allow the pilot to predict how an aircraft will perform.

Relative humidity also affects density altitude, but is not considered when the performance charts are formulated. A combination of high temperature, high humidity, and high altitude result in a density altitude higher than the pressure altitude which, in turn, results in reduced aircraft performance.

Problem:

Using the Density Altitude Chart shown in FAA Figure 8, and the following conditions, determine the density altitude.

Conditions:

Altimeter Setting .... 30.35"
Airport Temperature...................................+25°F
Airport Elevation .... 3,894 feet

Solution:

1. Determine the applicable altitude correction for the altimeter setting of 30.35" Hg. *See* FAA Figure 8. That setting is not shown on the chart, so it is necessary to interpolate between the correction factors shown for 30.30" Hg and 30.40" Hg. To interpolate, add the two factors and divide by 2:

    -348 + (-440) = -788

    -788 ÷ 2 = -394

Answers

2351   [C]

Since the result is a negative number, subtract that value from the given airport elevation:

3,894 feet
− 394 feet
3,500 feet

2. Along the bottom of the chart, locate the given OAT (+25°F). From that point, proceed upward until intersecting the pressure altitude line that is equal to the corrected airport elevation (3,500 feet). From that point, proceed to the left and read the density altitude (2,000 feet).

Note that high-density altitude reduces propeller efficiency as well as overall aircraft performance.

ALL, SPO
3289. If the outside air temperature (OAT) at a given altitude is warmer than standard, the density altitude is

A— equal to pressure altitude.
B— lower than pressure altitude.
C— higher than pressure altitude.

If the temperature is above standard, the density altitude will be higher than pressure altitude. (PLT206) — FAA-H-8083-25

ALL
3294. (Refer to Figure 8.) Determine the density altitude for these conditions:

Altimeter setting...29.25
Runway temperature...+81°F
Airport elevation.......................................5,250 ft MSL

A— 4,600 feet MSL.
B— 5,877 feet MSL.
C— 8,500 feet MSL.

Referencing FAA Figure 8, use the following steps:

1. *Since the altimeter setting that is given is not shown in FAA Figure 8, interpolation is necessary. Locate the settings immediately above and below the given value of 29.25" Hg:*

Altimeter Setting	Conversion Factor
29.20	673 feet
29.30	579 feet

2. *Determine the difference between the two conversion factors:*

   673 − 579 = 94 feet

3. *Determine the amount of difference to be added to the 29.30" Hg conversion factor:*

   94 × .5 = 47 feet

4. *Add the amount of difference to the amount shown for the 29.30" Hg conversion factor:*

   579 + 47 = 626 feet

5. *Add the correction factor to the airport elevation to find pressure altitude:*

   5,250
   + 626
   5,876 feet MSL (pressure altitude)

6. *Determine the density altitude by entering the chart at +81°F; move upward to the 5,876 pressure altitude line; from the point of intersection, move to the left and read a density altitude of 8,500 feet.*

(PLT005) — FAA-H-8083-25

ALL
3295. (Refer to Figure 8.) Determine the pressure altitude at an airport that is 3,563 feet MSL with an altimeter setting of 29.96.

A— 3,527 feet MSL.
B— 3,556 feet MSL.
C— 3,639 feet MSL.

Referencing FAA Figure 8, use the following steps:

1. *Since the altimeter setting that is given is not shown in FAA Figure 8, interpolation is necessary. Locate the settings immediately above and below the given value of 29.96" Hg:*

Altimeter Setting	Conversion Factor
29.92	0 feet
30.00	-73 feet

2. *Determine the difference between the two conversion factors:*

   0 − 73 = -73 feet

   The setting 29.96 is halfway between the two values, so:

   -73 ÷ 2 = -36.5 feet

3. *Determine the amount of difference to be subtracted from the 30.00" Hg conversion factor.*

   Continued

Answers

3289	[C]	3294	[C]	3295	[A]

4. *Subtract the correction factor from the airport elevation to find pressure altitude:*

> 3,563.0
> − 36.5
> ───────
> 3,526.5 *feet MSL (pressure altitude)*

(PLT019) — FAA-H-8083-25

3298. (Refer to Figure 8.) Determine the density altitude for these conditions:

Altimeter setting 30.35
Runway temperature .... +25°F
Airport elevation .... 3,894 ft MSL

A— 2,000 feet MSL.
B— 2,900 feet MSL.
C— 3,500 feet MSL.

Referencing FAA Figure 8, use the following steps:

1. *Since the altimeter setting that is given is not shown in FAA Figure 8, interpolation is necessary. Locate the settings immediately above and below the given value of 30.35" Hg:*

Altimeter Setting	Conversion Factor
30.30	-348 feet
30.40	-440 feet

2. *Determine the difference between the two factors:*

> *-440 + 348 = -92 feet*

3. *Determine amount of difference to be added to the 30.30" Hg conversion factor:*

> *-92.0 x .5 = -46.0 feet*

4. *Add the amount of difference to the amount shown for the 30.30" Hg conversion factor:*

> *-348 + (-46) = -394 feet*

5. *Subtract the correction factor from the airport elevation to find pressure altitude:*

> 3,894
> − 394
> ───────
> 3,500 *feet MSL (pressure altitude)*

6. *Determine the density altitude by entering the chart at +25°F; proceed upward to the 3,500-foot pressure altitude line; from the point of intersection move to the left edge of the chart and read a density altitude of 2,000 feet.*

(PLT019) — FAA-H-8083-25

3299. (Refer to Figure 8.) What is the effect of a temperature decrease and a pressure altitude increase on the density altitude from 90°F and 1,250 feet pressure altitude to 55°F and 1,750 feet pressure altitude?

A— 1,700-foot increase.
B— 1,300-foot decrease.
C— 1,700-foot decrease.

Referencing FAA Figure 8, use the following steps:

1. *Determine the density altitude when the temperature is +90°F and the pressure altitude is 1,250 feet. Enter the density altitude chart at +90°F and proceed upward to the 1,250-foot pressure altitude line. From the point of intersection move to the left edge of the chart and read a density altitude of 3,600 feet.*

2. *Determine the density altitude when the temperature is +55°F and the pressure altitude is 1,750 feet. Enter the density altitude chart at +55°F and proceed upward to the 1,750-foot pressure altitude line. From the point of intersection move to the left edge of the chart. Read a density altitude of 1,900 feet.*

3. *Determine the change in density altitude:*

> *3,600 − 1,900 = 1,700 foot (decrease)*

(PLT124) — FAA-H-8083-25

3386. What are the standard temperature and pressure values for sea level?

A— 15°C and 29.92" Hg.
B— 59°C and 1013.2 millibars.
C— 59°F and 29.92 millibars.

Standard sea level pressure is 29.92 inches of mercury. Standard sea level temperature is 15°C. (PLT345) — FAA-H-8083-25

3394. Which factor would tend to increase the density altitude at a given airport?

A— An increase in barometric pressure.
B— An increase in ambient temperature.
C— A decrease in relative humidity.

On a hot day, the air becomes "thinner" or lighter, and its density is equivalent to a higher altitude in the standard atmosphere, thus the term "high density altitude." (PLT206) — AC 00-6

Answer (A) is incorrect because an increase in barometric pressure would decrease density altitude. Answer (C) is incorrect because a decrease in relative humidity would decrease density altitude.

Answers

3298 [A]   3299 [C]   3386 [A]   3394 [B]

AIR, RTC, WSC, PPC, SPO
3290. Which combination of atmospheric conditions will reduce aircraft takeoff and climb performance?

A— Low temperature, low relative humidity, and low density altitude.
B— High temperature, low relative humidity, and low density altitude.
C— High temperature, high relative humidity, and high density altitude.

An increase in air temperature or humidity, or a decrease in air pressure (which results in a higher density altitude), will significantly decrease both power output and propeller efficiency. (PLT124) — FAA-H-8083-25

Answer (A) is incorrect because all of these conditions improve performance. Answer (B) is incorrect because low humidity and low density altitude improve performance.

AIR, RTC, WSC, PPC, SPO
3291. What effect does high density altitude have on aircraft performance?

A— It increases engine performance.
B— It reduces climb performance.
C— It increases takeoff performance.

An increase in air temperature or humidity, or a decrease in air pressure (which results in a higher density altitude), will significantly decrease both power output and propeller efficiency. (PLT127) — FAA-H-8083-25

AIR, RTC, WSC, PPC
3292. (Refer to Figure 8.) What is the effect of a temperature increase from 25 to 50°F on the density altitude if the pressure altitude remains at 5,000 feet?

A— 1,200-foot increase.
B— 1,400-foot increase.
C— 1,650-foot increase.

Referencing FAA Figure 8, use the following steps:

1. *Enter the density altitude chart at 25°F. Proceed upward to intersect the 5,000-foot pressure altitude line. From the point of intersection, move left to the edge of the chart and read a density altitude of 3,850 feet.*

2. *Enter the density altitude chart at 50°F. Proceed upward to the 5,000-foot pressure altitude line. From the point of intersection, move left to the edge of the chart and read a density altitude of 5,500 feet.*

3. *Determine the change in density altitude:*
   5,500 – 3,850 = 1,650 feet (increase)
(PLT005) — FAA-H-8083-25

AIR, RTC, WSC, PPC
3293. (Refer to Figure 8.) Determine the pressure altitude with an indicated altitude of 1,380 feet MSL with an altimeter setting of 28.22 at standard temperature.

A— 2,991 feet MSL.
B— 2,913 feet MSL.
C— 3,010 feet MSL.

Referencing FAA Figure 8, use the following steps:

1. *Since the altimeter setting that is given is not shown in FAA Figure 8, interpolation is necessary. Locate the settings immediately above and below the given value of 28.22" Hg:*

Altimeter Setting	Conversion Factor
28.2	1,630 feet
28.3	1,533 feet

2. *Determine the difference in the two conversion factors:*
   1,630 – 1,533 = 97 feet

3. *Determine the amount of the difference to be subtracted from the 28.20" Hg conversion factor (2/10 of 97).*
   97.0 x .2 = 19.4

4. *Subtract the amount of difference from the amount shown for the 28.20" Hg conversion factor:*
   1,630.0 – 19.4 = 1,610.6

5. *Add the correction factor to the indicated altitude to find the pressure altitude:*
   1,610.6
   + 1,380.0
   2,990.6 feet MSL (pressure altitude)

(PLT019) — FAA-H-8083-25

Answers

3290 [C]   3291 [B]   3292 [C]   3293 [A]

AIR, RTC, WSC, PPC
3296. (Refer to Figure 8.) What is the effect of a temperature increase from 35 to 50°F on the density altitude if the pressure altitude remains at 3,000 feet MSL?

A— 1,000-foot increase.
B— 1,100-foot decrease.
C— 1,300-foot increase.

Referencing FAA Figure 8, use the following steps:

1. Enter the density altitude chart at 35°F. Proceed upward to the 3,000-foot pressure altitude line. From the point of intersection, move left to the edge of the chart and read a density altitude of 2,000 feet.

2. Enter the density altitude chart at 50°F. Proceed upward to the 3,000-foot pressure altitude line. From the point of intersection, move left to the edge of the chart and read a density altitude of 2,950 feet.

3. Find the difference between the two values: 2,950 – 2,000 = 950 foot (increase).

(PLT124) — FAA-H-8083-25

SPO
2356. (Refer to Figure 8.) What is the effect of a temperature increase from 30 to 50°F on the density altitude if the pressure altitude remains at 3,000 feet MSL?

A— 900-foot increase.
B— 1,100-foot decrease.
C— 1,300-foot increase.

Referencing FAA Figure 24, use the following steps:

1. Enter the density altitude chart at 30°F. Proceed upward to the 3,000-foot pressure altitude line. From the point of intersection, move left to the edge of the chart and read a density altitude of 1,650 feet.

2. Enter the density altitude chart at 50°F. Proceed upward to the 3,000-foot pressure altitude line. From the point of intersection, move left to the edge of the chart and read a density altitude of 2,950 feet.

3. Find the difference between the two values: 2,950 – 1,650 = 1,300 foot (increase)

(PLT005) — FAA-H-8083-25

AIR, RTC, WSC, PPC, SPO
3297. (Refer to Figure 8.) Determine the pressure altitude at an airport that is 1,386 feet MSL with an altimeter setting of 29.97.

A— 1,341 feet MSL.
B— 1,451 feet MSL.
C— 1,562 feet MSL.

Referencing FAA Figure 8, use the following steps:

1. Since the altimeter setting that is given is not shown in FAA Figure 8, interpolation is necessary. Locate the settings immediately above and below the given value of 29.97" Hg:

Altimeter Setting	Conversion Factor
29.92	*0 feet*
30.00	*-73 feet*

2. Determine the difference between the two conversion factors:

0 – 73 = -73 feet

3. Determine the amount of the difference to be subtracted from the 29.92" Hg conversion factor:

(-73 ÷ 8) x 5 = -45.6 or 46 feet

4. Subtract the conversion factor from the airport elevation to determine the pressure altitude:

1,386
– 46
1,340 feet MSL (pressure altitude)

(PLT019) — FAA-H-8083-25

AIR, RTC, WSC, PPC, SPO
3300. What effect, if any, does high humidity have on aircraft performance?

A— It increases performance.
B— It decreases performance.
C— It has no effect on performance.

An increase in air temperature or humidity, or a decrease in air pressure (which results in a higher density altitude) will significantly decrease both power output and propeller efficiency. If an air mass is humid, there is more water in it, therefore, less oxygen. (PLT124) — FAA-H-8083-25

Answers

3296 [A]	2356 [C]	3297 [A]	3300 [B]

AIR, LTA, WSC, PPC, SPO

3246. What effect does high density altitude, as compared to low density altitude, have on propeller efficiency and why?

A— Efficiency is increased due to less friction on the propeller blades.
B— Efficiency is reduced because the propeller exerts less force at high density altitudes than at low density altitudes.
C— Efficiency is reduced due to the increased force of the propeller in the thinner air.

The propeller produces thrust in proportion to the mass of air being accelerated through the rotating blades. If the air is less dense, propeller efficiency is decreased. (PLT351) — FAA-H-8083-25

RTC, LSR

3702. (Refer to Figure 39.) Determine the total takeoff distance required for a gyroplane to clear a 50-foot obstacle if the temperature is 95°F and the pressure altitude is 1,700 feet.

A— 1,825 feet.
B— 1,910 feet.
C— 2,030 feet.

Use the following steps:

1. Locate the 1,700-foot pressure altitude on the Take-Off Distance Graph (right).

2. Draw a horizontal line from the 1,700-foot position to the 95°F OAT point.

3. Draw a vertical line downward from the point of intersection to the total Take-Off Distance Scale. Note the distance 2,030 feet.

(PLT011) — FAA-H-8083-21

SPO

2067. Density altitude, and its effect on landing performance, is defined by

A— pressure altitude and ambient temperature.
B— headwind and landing weight.
C— humidity and braking friction forces.

The effect of pressure altitude and ambient temperature is to define density altitude and its effect on landing performance. (PLT127) — FAA-H-8083-25

LTA

3891. (Refer to Figure 57.) What is the maximum altitude for the balloon if the gross weight is 1,100 pounds and standard temperature exists at all altitudes?

A— 1,000 feet.
B— 4,000 feet.
C— 5,500 feet.

Use FAA Figure 57, and the following steps:

1. Enter the graph at the 1,100-pound gross weight point and proceed to the right to intercept the standard temperature curve.

2. Note that the intercept is between sea level and the 5,000-foot limit lines, and is much closer to the 5,000-foot line (4,000 feet).

(PLT057) — FAA-H-8083-11

LTA

3892. (Refer to Figure 57.) What is the maximum altitude for the balloon if the gross weight is 1,000 pounds and standard temperature exists at all altitudes?

A— 4,000 feet.
B— 5,500 feet.
C— 11,000 feet.

Use FAA Figure 57, and the following steps:

1. Enter the graph at the 1,000-pound gross weight point and proceed to the right to intercept the standard temperature curve.

2. Note that the intercept is just over 10,000 feet (11,000 feet).

(PLT057) — FAA-H-8083-11

Answers

3246 [B]	3702 [C]	2067 [A]	3891 [B]	3892 [C]

Takeoff Distance

The Takeoff Distance Graph, FAA Figure 40, allows the pilot to determine the ground roll required for takeoff under various conditions. It also shows the total distance required for a takeoff and climb to clear a 50-foot obstacle.

Problem:

Using the Takeoff Distance Graph shown in FAA Figure 40, determine the approximate ground roll distance for takeoff and the total distance for a takeoff to clear a 50-foot obstacle under the following conditions:

Outside air temperature (OAT)	90°F
Pressure altitude	2,000 feet
Takeoff weight	2,500 lbs
Headwind component	20 knots

Solution:

1. Locate the OAT, 90°F, on the graph.

2. From that point, draw a line upward to the line representing the pressure altitude of 2,000 feet.

3. From the point of intersection, draw a line to the right to the reference line.

4. From that point, proceed downward and to the right (remaining proportionally between the existing guide lines) to the vertical line representing 2,500 pounds.

5. From there, draw a line to the right to the second reference line.

6. Then proceed down and to the right (remaining proportionally between the existing guide lines) to the line representing the 20-knot headwind component line.

7. From there, draw a line to the right to the third reference line.

8. From here, move to the right and read approximate ground roll for takeoff of 650 feet.

9. Proceed upward and to the right (remaining proportionately between the existing guide lines) to the vertical line representing a 50-foot obstacle and read the approximate total distance to clear a 50-foot obstacle (1,100 feet).

AIR
3705. (Refer to Figure 40.) Determine the total distance required for takeoff to clear a 50-foot obstacle.

OAT ....Std
Pressure altitude... 4,000 ft
Takeoff weight.. 2,800 lb
Headwind component...Calm

A— 1,500 feet.
B— 1,750 feet.
C— 2,000 feet.

Use the following steps:

1. Locate the ISA curve on FAA Figure 40.

2. Note the intersection of the ISA curve with the pressure altitude, 4,000 feet.

3. From that point, draw a line to the right to the first reference line.

4. From there, proceed downward and to the right (remaining proportionally between the existing lines) to the vertical line representing 2,800 pounds.

5. Then proceed to the right to the second reference line.

6. In this case the reference line is also the vertical line representing the 0 MPH wind component.

7. From that point, continue to the right to the third vertical reference line.

8. From there, proceed upward and to the right (remaining proportionally between the existing lines) to the vertical line representing the obstacle height, 50 feet.

9. Read the distance (approximately 1,750 feet).

(PLT011) — FAA-H-8083-25

AIR
3706. (Refer to Figure 40.) Determine the total distance required for takeoff to clear a 50-foot obstacle.

OAT ....Std
Pressure altitude.. Sea level
Takeoff weight.. 2,700 lb
Headwind component...Calm

A— 1,000 feet.
B— 1,400 feet.
C— 1,700 feet.

Use the following steps:

1. Locate the OAT, 59°F, on FAA Figure 40.

2. From that point, draw a line upward to the line representing the pressure altitude, 0 feet (SL).

3. From that point, draw a line to the right to the first reference line.

4. From there, proceed downward and to the right (remaining proportionally between the existing lines) to the vertical line representing 2,700 pounds.

5. Then draw a line to the right to the second reference line.

6. In this case, the reference line is also the vertical line representing the 0-knot wind component.

7. From that point, continue a horizontal line to the third vertical reference line.

8. Finally, proceed upward and to the right (remaining proportionally between the existing lines) to the vertical line representing the obstacle height, 50 feet and read the distance (approximately 1,400 feet).

(PLT011) — FAA-H-8083-25

AIR
3707. (Refer to Figure 40.) Determine the approximate ground roll distance required for takeoff.

OAT ....100°F
Pressure altitude.. 2,000 ft
Takeoff weight.. 2,750 lb
Headwind component...Calm

A— 1,150 feet.
B— 1,300 feet.
C— 1,800 feet.

Use the following steps:

1. Locate the OAT, 100°F, on FAA Figure 40.

2. From that point, draw a line upward to the line representing the pressure altitude, 2,000 feet.

3. From that point, draw a line to the right to the first reference line.

4. From there, proceed downward and to the right (remaining proportionally between the existing lines) to the vertical line representing 2,750 pounds.

Continued

Answers

3705   [B]   3706   [B]   3707   [A]

5. Then draw a line to the right to the second reference line.

6. In this case, the reference line is also the vertical line representing the 0-knot wind component.

7. Then draw a horizontal line to the third vertical reference line.

8. In this case, the reference line is also the vertical line representing the obstacle height, 0 feet.

9. From that point, draw a horizontal line to the right and read the distance (approximately 1,150 feet).

(PLT011) — FAA-H-8083-25

AIR

3708. (Refer to Figure 40.) Determine the approximate ground roll distance required for takeoff.

OAT	95°F
Pressure altitude	2,000 ft
Takeoff weight	2,500 lb
Headwind component	20 kts

A— 650 feet.
B— 850 feet.
C— 1,000 feet.

Use the following steps:

1. Locate the OAT, 95°F, on FAA Figure 40.

2. From that point, draw a line upward to the line representing the pressure altitude of 2,000 feet.

3. Form the point of intersection, draw a line to the right to the reference line and stop.

4. From that point, proceed downward and to the right (remaining proportionally between the existing guide lines) to the vertical line representing 2,500 pounds.

5. From there, draw a line to the right to the second reference line.

6. Then proceed down and to the right (remaining proportionally between the existing guide lines) to the line representing the 20-knot headwind component line.

7. From that point, draw a line to the right to the third reference line.

8. From there, move to the right and read an approximate ground roll for takeoff (650 feet).

(PLT011) — FAA-H-8083-25

RTC

3703. (Refer to Figure 39.) Determine the total takeoff distance required for a gyroplane to clear a 50-foot obstacle if the temperature is standard at sea level pressure altitude.

A— 950 feet.
B— 1,090 feet.
C— 1,200 feet.

1. On the sea level line of FAA Figure 39 locate the intersection of the +59°F point.

2. Read takeoff distance of 1,200 feet.

(PLT011) — FAA-H-8083-25

RTC

3704. (Refer to Figure 39.) Approximately how much additional takeoff distance will be required for a gyroplane to clear a 50-foot obstacle if the temperature increases from 75 to 90°F at a pressure altitude of 2,300 feet?

A— 160 feet.
B— 200 feet.
C— 2,020 feet.

Use the following steps:

1. Locate the 2,300-foot pressure altitude on FAA Figure 39.

2. Draw a horizontal line from the 2,300-foot position to the 75°F and the 90°F OAT points.

3. From these points, draw vertical lines downward to the takeoff distance scale and note the distances (2,025 and 2,185, respectively).

4. The difference is the increase in takeoff distance.

    2,185 – 2,025 = 160 feet

(PLT011) — FAA-H-8083-25

Answers

3708   [A]   3703   [C]   3704   [A]

SPO

2199. What effect does an uphill runway slope have on takeoff performance?

A— Increases takeoff speed.
B— Increases takeoff distance.
C— Decreases takeoff distance.

The effect of runway slope on takeoff distance is due to the component of weight along the inclined path of the aircraft. An upslope would contribute a retarding force component, while a downslope would contribute an accelerating force component. In the case of an upslope, the retarding force component adds to drag and rolling friction to reduce the net accelerating force. (PLT129) — FAA-H-8083-25

Answer (A) is incorrect because runway slope has no effect on the takeoff speed. Answer (C) is incorrect because an upslope will increase the takeoff distance required.

LSA, LSG, LSR, LSW, LSP
2283. The most critical conditions of takeoff performance are the result of some combination of high gross weight, altitude, temperature, and

A— unfavorable wind.
B— obstacles surrounding the runway.
C— powerplant systems.

The most critical conditions of takeoff performance are the result of some combination of high gross weight, altitude, temperature, and unfavorable wind. In all cases, the pilot must make an accurate prediction of takeoff distance from the performance data of the AFM/POH, regardless of the runway available, and strive for a polished, professional takeoff procedure. (PLT134) — FAA-H-8083-25

SPO

2234. The most critical conditions of takeoff performance are the result of some combination of high gross weight, altitude, temperature, and

A— unfavorable wind.
B— obstacles surrounding the runway.
C— powerplant systems.

The most critical conditions for takeoff performance are the result of some combination of high gross weight, altitude, temperature, and unfavorable wind. In all cases, the pilot must make an accurate prediction of takeoff distance from the performance data of the AFM or POH, regardless of the runway available, and strive for a polished, professional takeoff procedure. (PLT134) — FAA-H-8083-25

RTC
3732. (Refer to Figure 46.) What is the best rate-of-climb speed for the helicopter?

A— 24 MPH.
B— 40 MPH.
C— 57 MPH.

Use the following steps:

1. *Locate the recommended takeoff profile on FAA Figure 46.*

2. *Note that the best rate-of-climb speed at sea level is designated by the arrow pointing to the vertical line.*

3. *Interpret the diagram. The vertical line is most closely aligned with an IAS of about 57 MPH.*

(PLT285) — FAA-H-8083-21

Answers

2199 [B]   2283 [A]   2234 [A]   3732 [C]

Cruise Power Setting Table

The Cruise Power Setting Table (FAA Figure 35) may be used to forecast fuel flow and true airspeed and, therefore allow a pilot to determine the amount of fuel required and the estimated time en route.

Problem:

Using the Cruise Power Setting Table shown in FAA Figure 35, determine the expected fuel consumption for a 1,000-statute-mile flight under the following conditions:

Pressure altitude................................. 8,000 feet

Temperature ....-19°C

Manifold pressure...................................19.5" Hg

Wind ....Calm

Solution:

1. Find the fuel flow and TAS. Enter the chart at the 8,000-foot pressure altitude line and proceed to the right and identify the chart which represents an indicated outside air temperature (IOAT) of -19°C at 8,000 feet (the chart for ISA -20°C). Continue reading to the right, noting the manifold pressure of 19.5" Hg, the fuel flow per engine will be 6.6 pounds per square inch or 11.5 gallons per hour (GPH), and the TAS will be 157 knots or 181 miles per hour (MPH).

2. Calculate the time flown. Using a flight computer, calculate the time en route:

    1,000 SM at 181 MPH = 5.52 hours

3. Calculate the fuel consumption. Using a flight computer, calculate the fuel burned in this time:

    5.52 hours × 11.5 GPH = 63.48 gallons consumed

AIR
3678. (Refer to Figure 35.) Approximately what true airspeed should a pilot expect with full throttle at 10,500 feet with a temperature of 36°F above standard?

A— 190 kts.
B— 159 kts.
C— 165 kts.

Use the following steps:

1. Locate +36°F (ISA +20°C) on FAA Figure 35. Notice that the stated altitude of 10,500 feet does not appear on the chart so it is necessary to interpolate.

2. Read across the 10,000-foot pressure altitude line and determine the TAS (166 knots).

3. Read across the 12,000-foot pressure altitude line and determine the TAS (163 knots).

4. Interpolate between the values for 10,000 feet and 12,000 feet to determine a TAS for 10,500 feet.

a. 166 knots (10,000 feet) – 163 knots (12,000 feet) = 3 knots difference in speed

b. Interpolate to find one-quarter of difference for 10,500 feet: 3 × .25 = .75

c. Subtract the difference to the speed for 10,000 feet to find TAS for 10,500 feet: 166 – .75 = 165.25

(PLT012) — FAA-H-8083-25

AIR
3679. (Refer to Figure 35.) What is the expected fuel consumption for a 1,000-nautical mile flight under the following conditions?

Pressure altitude.. 8,000 ft
Temperature ....22°C
Manifold pressure... 20.8" Hg
Wind ....Calm

A— 60.2 gallons.
B— 70.1 gallons.
C— 73.2 gallons.

Use the following steps:

1. *Locate the pressure altitude of 8,000 feet on FAA Figure 35. Read to the right and identify the chart which presents an indicated outside temperature of 22°C at 8,000 feet (the chart for ISA +20°C).*

2. *On this chart, read across the 8,000-foot line, 22°C, 20.8" Hg manifold pressure line. The fuel flow is 11.5 GPH and the TAS is 164 knots.*

3. *Using a flight computer, calculate the time en route:*

   Distance is 1,000 NM
   TAS is 164 knots, with no wind

   Therefore, the time en route is 6 hours, 6 minutes.

4. *Using a flight computer, calculate the fuel consumption:*
   Time en route is 6 hours, 6 minutes
   Fuel burn is 11.5 GPH

   Therefore, the fuel consumption is 70.1 gallons.

(PLT012) — FAA-H-8083-25

AIR
3680. (Refer to Figure 35.) What is the expected fuel consumption for a 500-nautical mile flight under the following conditions?

Pressure altitude.. 4,000 ft
Temperature ....+29°C
Manifold pressure... 21.3" Hg
Wind ....Calm

A— 31.4 gallons.
B— 36.1 gallons.
C— 40.1 gallons.

Use the following steps:

1. *Locate the pressure altitude of 4,000 feet on FAA Figure 35. Read to the right and identify the chart which presents an indicated outside temperature of +29°C at 4,000 feet (in this case, the chart for ISA +20°C).*

2. *On this chart, read across the 4,000-foot line, +29°C, 21.3" Hg manifold pressure line. The fuel flow is 11.5 GPH and the TAS is 159 knots.*

3. *Using a flight computer, calculate the time en route:*

   Distance is 500 NM
   TAS is 159 knots, with no wind

   Therefore, the time en route is 3 hours, 9 minutes.

4. *Using a flight computer, calculate the fuel consumption:*

   Time en route is 3 hours, 9 minutes
   Fuel burn is 11.5 GPH

   Therefore, the fuel consumption is 36.2 gallons.

(PLT012) — FAA-H-8083-25

AIR
3681. (Refer to Figure 35.) What fuel flow should a pilot expect at 11,000 feet on a standard day with 65 percent maximum continuous power?

A— 10.6 gallons per hour.
B— 11.2 gallons per hour.
C— 11.8 gallons per hour.

Use the following steps:

1. *Locate the Standard Day (ISA) Chart on FAA Figure 35. Notice that the stated altitude, 11,000 feet, does not appear on the chart, so it is necessary to interpolate.*

2. *Read across the 10,000-foot pressure altitude line and determine the fuel flow at that altitude (11.5 GPH).*

3. *Read across the 12,000-foot pressure altitude line and determine the fuel flow at that altitude (10.9 GPH).*

4. *To determine the flow at 11,000 feet, add the two flows and divide by two.*

$$\text{Fuel Flow} = \frac{(11.5 + 10.9)}{2} = \frac{22.4}{2} = 11.2 \text{ gallons per hr}$$

(PLT012) — FAA-H-8083-25

Answers

3679 [B]   3680 [B]   3681 [B]

AIR

3682. (Refer to Figure 35.) Determine the approximate manifold pressure setting with 2,450 RPM to achieve 65 percent maximum continuous power at 6,500 feet with a temperature of 36°F higher than standard.

A— 19.8" Hg.
B— 20.8" Hg.
C— 21.0" Hg.

Use the following steps:

1. *Locate the +36°F (ISA + 20°C) Chart on FAA Figure 35. Notice that the stated altitude of 6,500 feet does not appear on the chart, so it is necessary to interpolate.*

2. *Read across the 6,000-foot pressure altitude line and determine the manifold pressure at that altitude (21.0" Hg).*

3. *Read across the 8,000-foot pressure altitude line and determine the manifold pressure at that altitude (20.8" Hg).*

4. *The altitude, 6,500 feet, is closer to the 6,000-foot value of 21.0" Hg.*

(PLT278) — FAA-H-8083-25

Landing Distance Graphs and Tables

Some landing distance graphs such as the one shown in FAA Figure 37, are used in the same manner as the takeoff distance graph.

Another type of landing distance table is shown in FAA Figure 38.

Problem:

Using the Landing Distance Table shown in FAA Figure 38, determine the total distance required to land over a 50-foot obstacle.

Pressure altitude.................................. 5,000 feet

Headwind...8 knots

Temperature ....41°F

Runway...Hard surface

Solution:

Enter FAA Figure 38 at 5,000 feet and 41°F to find 1,195 feet is required to clear a 50-foot obstacle. Note #1 states an additional correction is necessary for the headwind, 10% for each 4 knots. This would mean 20% for 8 knots. 20% of 1,195 feet is 239 feet, resulting in 956 feet — total distance required to land:

    1,195 x .20 = 239 feet

    1,195 − 239 = 956 feet

Answers

3682 [C]

AIR, WSC
3698. (Refer to Figure 38.) Determine the approximate landing ground roll distance.

Pressure altitude... 1,250 ft
Headwind...8 kts
Temperature ....Std

A— 275 feet.
B— 366 feet.
C— 470 feet.

Use the following steps:

1. Locate the tables for sea level and 2,500 feet. Note that 1,250 feet is midway between sea level and 2,500 feet.

2. Interpolate between charts for 2,500 feet pressure altitude and sea level to find ground roll:

   (445 + 470) ÷ 2 = 457.5 ground roll

3. Apply Note 1 to account for the 8-knot headwind (a 20% decrease in distance):

   457.5 x .20 = 91.5 feet
   457.5 – 91.5 = 366 feet

(PLT008) — FAA-H-8083-25

AIR, WSC
3689. (Refer to Figure 37.) Determine the total distance required to land.

OAT ....32°F
Pressure altitude... 8,000 ft
Weight .... 2,600 lb
Headwind component...20 kts
Obstacle .... 50 ft

A— 850 feet.
B— 1,400 feet.
C— 1,750 feet.

Use the following steps:

1. Enter FAA Figure 37 at the point where the vertical 32°F temperature line intersects the 8,000-foot pressure altitude line.

2. From there, proceed to the right to the first vertical reference line.

3. From that point, proceed down and to the right (remaining proportionally between the existing lines) to the vertical line representing 2,600 pounds.

4. Then, proceed to the right to the second vertical reference line.

5. Then, proceed down and to the right (remaining proportionally between the existing headwind lines) to the vertical line representing 20 knots.

6. From that point, proceed to the right to the third reference line.

7. Finally, proceed up and to the right (remaining proportionally between the existing lines) to the 50-foot obstacle line at the end of the graph and read the landing distance (approximately 1,400 feet).

(PLT008) — FAA-H-8083-25

AIR, WSC
3690. (Refer to Figure 37.) Determine the total distance required to land.

OAT ....Std
Pressure altitude.. 10,000 ft
Weight .... 2,400 lb
Wind component..Calm
Obstacle .... 50 ft

A— 750 feet.
B— 1,925 feet.
C— 1,450 feet.

Use the following steps:

1. Enter the graph at the point where the ISA line intercepts the 10,000-foot pressure altitude line.

2. From that point, proceed to the right to the first vertical reference line.

3. From there, proceed down to the right (remaining proportionally between the existing lines), to the vertical line representing 2,400 pounds.

4. Then proceed to the right to the second vertical reference line.

5. Since the wind is calm, continue to the right to the third vertical reference line.

6. From there, proceed upward and to the right (remaining proportionally between the existing lines) to the vertical line representing the required 50-foot obstacle height. Read the landing distance from the vertical scale (approximately 1,900 feet).

(PLT008) — FAA-H-8083-25

Answers

3698　[B]　　　　3689　[B]　　　　3690　[B]

AIR, WSC

3691. (Refer to Figure 37.) Determine the total distance required to land.

OAT	90°F
Pressure altitude	3,000 ft
Weight	2,900 lb
Headwind component	10 kts
Obstacle	50 ft

A— 1,450 feet.
B— 1,550 feet.
C— 1,725 feet.

Use the following steps:

1. *Enter FAA Figure 37 at the point where the vertical 90°F temperature line intersects the 3,000-foot pressure altitude line. (The point must be visualized midway between the 2,000- and 4,000-foot pressure altitude lines.)*

2. *From that point, proceed to the right to the first vertical reference line.*

3. *From there, proceed downward and to the right (remaining proportionally between the existing lines), to the vertical line representing 2,900 pounds.*

4. *Then proceed to the right to the second vertical reference line.*

5. *Since there is a 10-knot headwind, proceed downward and to the right (remaining proportionally between the existing lines) to the vertical line representing 10 knots.*

6. *From that point, proceed to the right to the third vertical reference line.*

7. *From there, proceed upward and to the right (remaining proportionally between the existing lines) to the vertical line representing the required 50-foot obstacle height. Read the landing distance from the vertical scale (approximately 1,725 feet).*

(PLT008) — FAA-H-8083-25

AIR, WSC

3692. (Refer to Figure 37.) Determine the approximate total distance required to land over a 50-foot obstacle.

OAT	90°F
Pressure altitude	4,000 ft
Weight	2,800 lb
Headwind component	10 kts

A— 1,525 feet.
B— 1,775 feet.
C— 1,950 feet.

Use the following steps:

1. *Enter FAA Figure 37 at the point where the vertical 90°F temperature line intersects the 4,000-foot pressure altitude line.*

2. *From that point, proceed to the right to the first vertical reference line.*

3. *From there, proceed downward and to the right (remaining proportionally between the existing lines), to the vertical line representing 2,800 pounds.*

4. *Then proceed to the right to the intersection with the second vertical reference line.*

5. *Since there is a 10-knot headwind component, proceed downward and to the right (remaining proportionally between the existing lines) to the vertical line representing 10 knots.*

6. *From that point, proceed to the right to the third vertical reference line.*

7. *Proceed upward to the right following the diagonal line for the 50-foot obstacle and then continue to read the landing distance (approximately 1,775 feet).*

(PLT008) — FAA-H-8083-25

Answers

3691   [C]   3692   [B]

AIR, WSC

3693. (Refer to Figure 38.) Determine the approximate landing ground roll distance.

Pressure altitude.. Sea level
Headwind...4 kts
Temperature ....Std

A— 356 feet.
B— 401 feet.
C— 490 feet.

Use the following steps:

1. Locate the sea level portion of FAA Figure 38.

2. Read the landing ground roll distance (445 feet).

3. Note 1 requires that the distances shown be decreased by 10% for each 4 knots of headwind.

> *445 x .10 = 44.5 feet*
> *445.0 – 44.5 = 400.5 or 401 feet*

(PLT008) — FAA-H-8083-25

AIR, WSC

3694. (Refer to Figure 38.) Determine the total distance required to land over a 50-foot obstacle.

Pressure altitude.. 7,500 ft
Headwind...8 kts
Temperature ....32°F
Runway...Hard surface

A— 1,004 feet.
B— 1,205 feet.
C— 1,506 feet.

Use the following steps:

1. Locate the portion of FAA Figure 38 that is applicable to a pressure altitude of 7,500 feet. The standard temperature at 7,500 feet is approximately 32°F, based on a temperature lapse rate of 3.5°F/1,000 feet.

2. Determine from the table that the basic distance to clear a 50-foot obstacle is 1,255 feet.

3. Apply Note 1 to account for an 8-knot headwind (a 20% decrease in distance):

> *1,255 x .20 = 251 feet*
> *1,255 – 251 = 1,004 feet*

(PLT008) — FAA-H-8083-25

AIR, WSC

3695. (Refer to Figure 38.) Determine the total distance required to land over a 50-foot obstacle.

Pressure altitude... 5,000 ft
Headwind...8 kts
Temperature ....41°F
Runway...Hard surface

A— 837 feet.
B— 956 feet.
C— 1,076 feet.

Use the following steps:

1. Locate the table applicable to a pressure altitude of 5,000 feet and ambient temperature of 41°F on FAA Figure 38.

2. Read the total distance required to clear a 50-foot obstacle (1,195 feet).

3. Apply Note 1 to account for an 8-knot headwind (a 20% decrease in distance):

> *1,195 x .20 = 239 feet*
> *1,195 – 239 = 956 feet*

(PLT008) — FAA-H-8083-25

AIR, WSC

3696. (Refer to Figure 38.) Determine the approximate landing ground roll distance.

Pressure altitude... 5,000 ft
Headwind...Calm
Temperature ....101°F

A— 495 feet.
B— 545 feet.
C— 445 feet.

Use the following steps:

1. Locate the table which applies to a pressure altitude of 5,000 feet on FAA Figure 38.

2. Read the ground roll of 495 feet.

3. Apply Note 2 to account for the temperature difference between 101°F ambient and the 41°F value on which the table is based.

> *495 x .10 = 49.5 feet*
> *495 + 49.5 = 544.5 feet*

(PLT008) — FAA-H-8083-25

Answers

3693	[B]	3694	[A]	3695	[B]	3696	[B]

AIR, WSC

3697. (Refer to Figure 38.) Determine the total distance required to land over a 50-foot obstacle.

Pressure altitude..3,750 ft
Headwind...12 kts
Temperature ....Std

A— 794 feet.
B— 836 feet.
C— 816 feet.

Use the following steps:

1. *Locate the 2,500-foot and 5,000-foot tables.*

2. *Interpolate (3,750 is midway between 2,500 feet and 5,000 feet) to obtain a landing distance:*

    (1,135 + 1,195) ÷ 2 = 1,165 feet ground roll

3. *Apply Note 1 to account for the 12-knot headwind.*

    12 ÷ 4 = 3
    3.00 x .10 = .30
    1,165 x .30 = 349.5
    1,165 – 349.5 = 815.5 feet

(PLT008) — FAA-H-8083-25

RTC, LSR

3699. (Refer to Figure 39.) Determine the total landing distance to clear a 50-foot obstacle in a gyroplane. The outside air temperature (OAT) is 75°F and the pressure altitude at the airport is 2,500 feet.

A— 521 feet.
B— 525 feet.
C— 529 feet.

Use the following steps:

1. *Locate the horizontal line corresponding to 2,500 feet pressure altitude on FAA Figure 39.*

2. *Draw vertical lines through the points of intersection of the 2,500-foot pressure altitude line with the 75°F point. Note the landing distance of 525 feet.*

(PLT008) — FAA-H-8083-21

RTC

3700. (Refer to Figure 39.) Approximately how much additional landing distance will be required for a gyroplane to clear a 50-foot obstacle with an increase in temperature from 40 to 60°F at 3,200 feet pressure altitude?

A— 4 feet.
B— 8 feet.
C— 12 feet.

Use the following steps:

1. *Locate the 3,200-foot pressure altitude point on FAA Figure 39.*

2. *Select any two adjacent temperature lines (which are separated by 20°F increments). Note the points of intersection of each line with the 3,200-foot pressure altitude.*

3. *Read downward from each of the two intersections to the distance scale.*

4. *Note the difference between the two distances (4 feet).*

(PLT008) — FAA-H-8083-25

RTC

3701. (Refer to Figure 39.) Determine the total landing distance to clear a 50-foot obstacle in a gyroplane. The outside air temperature (OAT) is 80°F and the pressure altitude is 3,500 feet.

A— 521 feet.
B— 526 feet.
C— 531 feet.

Use the following steps:

1. *Locate the horizontal line corresponding to 3,500 feet pressure altitude on FAA Figure 39.*

2. *Draw vertical lines through the points of intersection of the 3,500-foot pressure altitude line with the 80°F point. Note the landing distance of 531 feet.*

(PLT008) — FAA-H-8083-25

Answers

3697   [C]   3699   [B]   3700   [A]   3701   [C]

GLI
3864. (Refer to Figure 54.) How many feet will the glider sink in 1 statute mile at 53 MPH in still air?

A— 144 feet.
B— 171 feet.
C— 211 feet.

Use the following steps:

1. *Read the L/D ratio (which is numerically the same as the glide ratio) for a speed of 53 MPH from the graph (30.9:1).*

2. *Using the glide ratio of 30.9 feet forward for each foot of vertical sink, calculate the sink encountered in one statute mile (5,280 feet):*

$$\frac{Distance}{L/D\ Ratio} = Vertical\ Sink$$

$$\frac{5,280}{30.9} = 171\ feet\ vertical\ sink$$

(PLT054) — FAA-H-8083-13

GLI
3865. (Refer to Figure 54.) At what speed will the glider attain a sink rate of 5 feet per second in still air?

A— 75 MPH.
B— 82 MPH.
C— 84 MPH.

Use the following steps:

1. *Locate the sinking speed (V$_S$) curve and its associated scale (on the right side) of FAA Figure 54.*

2. *Read to the left from the 5 FPS position to the sinking speed curved scale.*

3. *Interpreting the horizontal scale gives a speed of 82 MPH forward.*

(PLT054) — FAA-H-8083-13

GLI
3866. (Refer to Figure 54.) How many feet will the glider descend at minimum sink speed for 1 statute mile in still air?

A— 132 feet.
B— 170 feet.
C— 180 feet.

Use the following steps:

1. *Locate the minimum sink speed (2.2 FPS at 44 MPH) on FAA Figure 54.*

2. *Determine the L/D (glide ratio) at 44 MPH by reading up from 44 MPH (on the V$_S$ coordinate) to the intersection with the L/D curve. Read from that intersection to the left (L/D) coordinate. At 44 MPH the L/D ratio is 29.3:1.*

3. *Using the glide ratio of 29.3 feet forward for each foot of vertical sink, calculate the sink encountered in 5,280 feet (one statue mile):*

$$\frac{Distance}{L/D\ Ratio} = Vertical\ Sink$$

$$\frac{5,280}{29.3} = 180\ feet\ vertical\ sink$$

(PLT054) — FAA-H-8083-13

GLI
3867. (Refer to Figure 54.) At what speed will the glider gain the most distance while descending 1,000 feet in still air?

A— 44 MPH.
B— 53 MPH.
C— 83 MPH.

The L/D ratio is numerically the same as the glide ratio. Hence, the best forward distance attained per foot of descent will be at the velocity which gives the maximum L/D. (PLT054) — FAA-H-8083-13

GLI, LSG
3868. (Refer to Figure 54.) What approximate lift/drag ratio will the glider attain at 68 MPH in still air?

A— 10.5:1.
B— 21.7:1.
C— 28.5:1.

Use the following steps:

1. *Locate 68 MPH on the V coordinate (at the bottom) on FAA Figure 54.*

2. *Read upward from the 68 MPH point to the intersection with the L/D curve.*

3. *Read to the left, from the point of intersection, to the L/D scale and read L/D, 28.5:1.*

(PLT054) — FAA-H-8083-13

Answers

3864　[B]　　　　3865　[B]　　　　3866　[C]　　　　3867　[B]　　　　3868　[C]

Headwind and Crosswind Component Graph

In general, taking off into a wind improves aircraft performance, and reduces the length of runway required to become airborne. The stronger the wind, the better the aircraft performs. Crosswinds, however, may make the aircraft difficult or impossible to control. The aircraft manufacturer determines the safe limit for taking off or landing with a crosswind and establishes the maximum allowable crosswind component. The graph shown in FAA Figure 36 is used to determine what extent a wind of a given direction and speed is felt as a headwind and/or crosswind.

Problem:

The wind is reported to be from 085° at 30 knots, and you plan to land on Runway 11. What will the headwind and crosswind components be?

Solution:

1. Determine the angular difference between the wind direction and the runway:

$$\begin{array}{rl} 110° & \text{runway} \\ -085° & \text{wind} \\ \hline 25° & \text{difference} \end{array}$$

2. Find the intersection of the 25°-angle radial line and the 30-knot wind speed arc on the graph shown in FAA Figure 36. From the intersection move straight down to the bottom of the chart and read that the crosswind component equals 13 knots. From the point of intersection move horizontally left and read that the headwind component equals 27 knots.

AIR, RTC, WSC, PPC

3688. (Refer to Figure 36.) What is the crosswind component for a landing on Runway 18 if the tower reports the wind as 220° at 30 knots?

A— 19 knots.
B— 23 knots.
C— 30 knots.

Use the following steps:

1. *Determine the relative wind angle (WA) from the difference between the runway heading (RH) and the wind direction (WD).*

   $WA = WD - RH$
   $WA = 220° - 180°$
   $WA = 40°$

2. *Locate the arc corresponding to a 30-knot wind velocity.*

3. *Find the point of intersection of the 40° line with the 30-knot wind speed arc.*

4. *Draw a line downward from the intersection to the crosswind component scale and read the resulting velocity of 19 knots.*

(PLT013) — FAA-H-8083-25

Answer (B) is incorrect because this is the headwind component.
Answer (C) is incorrect because this is the wind speed.

AIR, RTC, WSC, PPC

3683. (Refer to Figure 36.) What is the headwind component for a landing on Runway 18 if the tower reports the wind as 220° at 30 knots?

A— 19 knots.
B— 23 knots.
C— 26 knots.

Use the following steps:

1. *Determine the relative wind angle (WA) from the difference between the runway heading (RH) and the wind direction (WD):*

   $WA = WD - RH$
   $WA = 220° - 180°$
   $WA = 40°$

2. *Locate the arc corresponding to a 30-knot wind on FAA Figure 36.*

3. *Find the point of intersection of the 40° line with the 30-knot wind speed arc.*

4. *Draw a line to the left from the intersection to the headwind component scale and read the resulting velocity of 23 knots.*

(PLT013) — FAA-H-8083-25

Answers

3688   [A]   3683   [B]

AIR, RTC, WSC, PPC

3684. (Refer to Figure 36.) Determine the maximum wind velocity for a 45° crosswind if the maximum crosswind component for the airplane is 25 knots.

A— 25 knots.
B— 29 knots.
C— 35 knots.

Use the following steps:

1. *Locate the 45° wind angle in FAA Figure 36.*

2. *Locate the vertical line representing a 25-knot crosswind component and its point of intersection with the 45° wind angle line.*

3. *Interpret the intersection point as lying on an arc midway between the 30- and 40-knot wind velocity arcs, or 35 knots.*

(PLT013) — FAA-H-8083-25

AIR, RTC, WSC, PPC

3685. (Refer to Figure 36.) What is the maximum wind velocity for a 30° crosswind if the maximum crosswind component for the airplane is 12 knots?

A— 16 knots.
B— 20 knots.
C— 24 knots.

Use the following steps:

1. *Locate the 30° wind angle line on FAA Figure 36.*

2. *Locate the vertical line representing the maximum crosswind component of 12 knots and its point of intersection with the 30° wind angle line.*

3. *Interpret the point of intersection as lying on an arc slightly less than midway between the 20- and 30-knot wind velocity arcs or about 24 knots.*

(PLT013) — FAA-H-8083-25

AIR, RTC, WSC, PPC

3686. (Refer to Figure 36.) With a reported wind of north at 20 knots, which runway (6, 29, or 32) is acceptable for use for an airplane with a 13-knot maximum crosswind component?

A— Runway 6.
B— Runway 29.
C— Runway 32.

Use the following steps:

1. *Locate the 20-knot wind velocity arc on FAA Figure 36.*

2. *Draw a line upward from the 13-knot crosswind component (maximum crosswind).*

3. *Note that in this case, acceptable crosswind components will result anytime the relative wind angle is equal to or less than about 40° (the intersection of the 13-knot vertical line and the 20-knot wind arc).*

4. *Calculate the relative wind angle between the north wind (0°) and the runway headings:*

RWY	Relative Angle	Landing
6	60°	Upwind
29	70°	Upwind
32	40°	Upwind

Only runway 32 provides a crosswind component that would be in acceptable limits for the airplane specified.
(PLT013) — FAA-H-8083-25

Answers

3684 [C]   3685 [C]   3686 [C]

AIR, RTC, WSC, PPC

3687. (Refer to Figure 36.) With a reported wind of south at 20 knots, which runway (10, 14, or 24) is appropriate for an airplane with a 13-knot maximum crosswind component?

A— Runway 10.
B— Runway 14.
C— Runway 24.

Use the following steps:

1. *Locate the 20-knot wind velocity arc on FAA Figure 36.*

2. *Draw a line upward from the 13-knot crosswind component (maximum crosswind).*

3. *Note that in this case, acceptable crosswind components will result anytime the relative wind angle is equal to or less than 40° (the intersection of the 13-knot vertical line and the 20-knot wind arc).*

4. *Calculate the relative wind angle between the south wind (180°) and the runway headings:*

RWY	Relative Angle	Landing
10	80°	Downwind
14	40°	Upwind
24	60°	Upwind

(PLT013) — FAA-H-8083-25

Maximum Range Performance

LSA, LSW, LSR

2230. Maximum endurance is obtained at the point of minimum power to maintain the aircraft

A— in steady, level flight.
B— in a long range descent.
C— at its slowest possible indicated airspeed.

The maximum endurance condition is obtained at the point of minimum power required since this would require the lowest fuel flow to keep the airplane in steady, level flight. Maximum range condition occurs where the proportion between speed and power required is greatest. (PLT015) — FAA-H-8083-25

LSA, LSW, LSR

2236. When range and economy of operation are the principal goals, the pilot must ensure that the airplane will be operated at the recommended

A— specific endurance.
B— long-range cruise performance.
C— equivalent airspeed.

Total range is dependent on both fuel available and specific range. When range and economy of operation are the principal goals, the pilot must ensure that the airplane is operated at the recommended long-range cruise condition. By this procedure, the airplane will be capable of its maximum design-operating radius, or can achieve lesser flight distances with a maximum of fuel reserve at the destination. (PLT501) — FAA-H-8083-25

Answers

| 3687 | [B] | 2230 | [A] | 2236 | [B] |

Chapter 9
Enroute Flight

Pilotage

Air navigation is the art of directing an aircraft along a desired course and being able to determine its geographical position at any time. Such navigation may be accomplished by pilotage, dead reckoning, or using radio navigational aids.

Pilotage is the use of visible landmarks to maintain a desired course, and is the basic form of navigation for the beginning pilot operating under Visual Flight Rules (VFR). Visible landmarks which can be identified on aeronautical charts allow the pilot to proceed from one check point to the next.

The aeronautical charts most commonly used by VFR pilots are the **VFR Sectional Aeronautical Chart**, the **VFR Terminal Area Chart**, and the **World Aeronautical Chart**. All three charts include aeronautical information such as airports, airways, special use airspace, and other pertinent data.

The scale of the VFR Sectional Aeronautical Chart is 1:500,000 (1 inch = 6.86 NM). Designed for visual navigation of slow speed aircraft in VFR conditions, this chart portrays terrain relief and checkpoints such as populated places, roads, railroads, and other distinctive landmarks. These charts have the best detail and are revised every 6 months.

Information found on the VFR Terminal Area Chart is similar to that found on the VFR Sectional Chart, but the scale on this chart is 1:250,000 (1 inch = 3.43 NM). These charts are for a specific city with Class B airspace. They show much detail, but have small coverage.

The World Aeronautical Chart has a scale of 1:1,000,000, which is more convenient for use in navigation by moderate speed aircraft. It depicts cities, railroads, and distinctive landmarks, etc. These charts have less detail and are revised no more than once a year.

To identify a point on the surface of the earth, a geographic coordinate, or "grid" system was devised. By reference to meridians of **longitude** and parallels of **latitude**, any position may be accurately located when using the grid system.

Equidistant from the poles is an imaginary circle called the **equator**. The lines running east and west, parallel to the equator are called parallels of latitude, and are used to measure angular distance north or south of the equator. From the equator to either pole is 90°, with 0° being at the equator; while 90° north latitude describes the location of the North Pole. *See* Figure 9-1.

Lines called meridians of longitude are drawn from pole to pole at right angles to the equator. The **prime meridian**, used as the zero degree line, passes through Greenwich, England. From this line, measurements are made in degrees both easterly and westerly up to 180°.

Any specific geographical point can be located by reference to its longitude and latitude. For example, Washington, DC is approximately 39° north of the equator and 77° west of the prime meridian and would be stated as 39°N 77°W. Note that latitude is stated first.

In order to describe a location more precisely, each degree (°) is subdivided into 60 minutes (') and each minute further divided into 60 seconds ("), although seconds are not shown. Thus, the location of the airport at Elk City, Oklahoma is described as being at 35°25'55"N 99°23'15"W (35 degrees, 25 minutes, 55 seconds north latitude; 99 degrees, 23 minutes, 15 seconds west longitude). Degrees of west longitude increase from east to west. Degrees of north latitude increase from south to north.

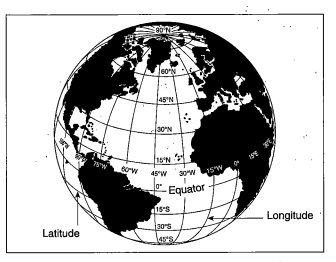

Figure 9-1. Meridians of longitude and parallels of latitude

ALL
3530-1. Which statement about longitude and latitude is true?

A— Lines of longitude are parallel to the Equator.
B— Lines of longitude cross the Equator at right angles.
C— The 0° line of latitude passes through Greenwich, England.

Meridians of longitude encircle the earth from pole to pole, and all meridians cross the equator at right angles. (PLT101) — FAA-H-8083-25

Answer (A) is incorrect because lines of latitude are parallel to the equator. Answer (C) is incorrect because the 0° line of longitude passes through Greenwich, England.

ALL
3530. (Refer to Figure 20, area 3.) Determine the approximate latitude and longitude of Currituck County Airport.

A— 36°24'N – 76°01'W.
B— 36°48'N – 76°01'W.
C— 47°24'N – 75°58'W.

Graticules on Sectional Aeronautical Charts are the lines dividing each 30 minutes of latitude and each 30 minutes of longitude. Each tick mark represents one minute of latitude or longitude. Latitude increases northward, west longitude increases going westward. The approximate latitude and longitude of Currituck County Airport is 36°24'N, 76°01'W. (PLT064) — FAA-H-8083-25

ALL, SPO
3535. (Refer to Figure 21, area 2.) Which airport is located at approximately 47°35'30"N latitude and 100°43'00"W longitude?

A— Turtle Lake.
B— Makeeff.
C— Johnson.

Graticules on Sectional Aeronautical Charts are the lines dividing each 30 minutes of latitude and each 30 minutes of longitude. Each tick mark represents one minute of latitude or longitude. Latitude increases northward, west longitude increases going westward. The Makeeff (Pvt) airport is located at approximately 47°35'30"N latitude and 100°43'00"W longitude. (PLT064) — FAA-H-8083-25

ALL
3536. (Refer to Figure 21, area 3.) Which airport is located at approximately 47°21'N latitude and 101°01'W longitude?

A— Lorentzen.
B— Johnson.
C— Washburn.

Graticules on Sectional Aeronautical Charts are the lines dividing each 30 minutes of latitude and each 30 minutes of longitude. Each tick mark represents one minute of latitude or longitude. Latitude increases northward, west longitude increases going westward. Washburn is located at approximately 47°21'N latitude and 101°01'W longitude. (PLT064) — FAA-H-8083-25

ALL
3543. (Refer to Figure 22, area 3.) Determine the approximate latitude and longitude of Shoshone County Airport.

A— 47°02'N – 116°11'W
B— 47°33'N – 116°11'W
C— 47°32'N – 116°41'W

Graticules on Sectional Aeronautical Charts are the lines dividing each 30 minutes of latitude and each 30 minutes of longitude. Each tick mark represents one minute of latitude or longitude. Latitude increases northward, west longitude increases going westward. The approximate latitude and longitude of Shoshone County Airport is 47°33'N, 116°11'W. (PLT064) — FAA-H-8083-25

ALL
3567. (Refer to Figure 26, area 2.) What is the approximate latitude and longitude of Cooperstown Airport?

A— 47°25'N – 98°06'W.
B— 47°25'N – 99°54'W.
C— 47°55'N – 98°06'W.

Graticules on Sectional Aeronautical Charts are the lines dividing each 30 minutes of latitude and each 30 minutes of longitude. Each tick mark represents one minute of latitude or longitude. Latitude increases northward, west longitude increases going westward. Cooperstown airport is approximately at 47°25'N latitude, and 98°06'W longitude. (PLT064) — FAA-H-8083-25

Answers

3530-1 [B]	3530 [A]	3535 [B]	3536 [C]	3543 [B]	3567 [A]

SPO
2106. During VFR navigation without radio instruments, heading and groundspeed, as calculated by dead reckoning, should be constantly monitored and corrected by

A— pilotage as observed from checkpoints.
B— the wind triangle.
C— wet compass and the groundspeed indicator.

Except for flights over water, dead reckoning is usually used with pilotage. The heading and ground speed as calculated is constantly monitored and corrected by pilotage as observed from checkpoints. (PLT116) — FAA-H-8083-25

SPO
2108. For cross-country flights over land, navigation without radio instruments is usually accomplished using dead reckoning and

A— pilotage.
B— the wind triangle.
C— compass heading.

Except for flights over water, dead reckoning is usually used with pilotage. The heading and ground speed as calculated is constantly monitored and corrected by pilotage as observed from checkpoints. (PLT116) — FAA-H-8083-25

SPO
2178. Using pilotage, a pilot can keep from drifting too far off course by

A— flying the flight plan heading.
B— filing a flight plan.
C— referring to selected features or checkpoints.

Pilotage is navigation by reference to landmarks or checkpoints. The checkpoints selected should be prominent features common to the area of the flight and be readily identified by other features such as roads, rivers, and power lines. Select features that will make useful boundaries or brackets on each side of the course, such as highways, rivers, railroads, and mountains. (PLT335) — FAA-H-8083-25

Time

Time is measured in relation to the rotation of the earth. A day is defined as the time required for the earth to make one complete revolution of 360°. Since the day is divided into 24 hours, it follows that the earth revolves at the rate of 15° each hour. Thus, longitude may be expressed as either 90° or 6 hours west of Greenwich.

Twenty-four time zones have been established. Each time zone is 15° of longitude in width, with the first zone centered on the meridian of Greenwich. Each zone uses the local time of its central meridian as shown in FAA Figure 27.

For example, when the sun is above the 90th meridian, it is noon central standard time (CST). At the same time it is 6 p.m. Greenwich, 11 a.m. mountain standard time (MST), and 1 p.m. eastern standard time (EST). When daylight saving time (DST) is in effect, the sun is over the 75th meridian at noon CST.

Most aviation operations time is expressed in terms of the 24-hour clock, (for example, 8 a.m. is expressed as 0800; 2 p.m. is 1400; 11 p.m. is 2300) and may be either local or **Coordinated Universal Time (UTC)**. UTC is the time at the prime meridian and is represented in aviation operations by the letter "Z," referred to as "**Zulu time**." For example, 1500Z would be read as "one five zero zero Zulu."

In the United States, conversion from local time to UTC is made in accordance with the table in the lower left corner of FAA Figure 27.

Continued

Answers

2106　[A]　　　　2108　[A]　　　　2178　[C]

Problem: An aircraft departs an airport in the Pacific standard time zone at 1030 PST for a 4-hour flight to an airport located in the central standard time zone. The landing should be at what coordinated universal time (UTC)?

Solution: Use the conversion table in FAA Figure 27 and the following steps:

1. Convert 1030 PST to UTC:

    1030   PST (takeoff time)
  + 0800   (conversion)
    1830   (UTC)

2. Add the flight time.

    1830   (UTC)
  + 0400   (flight time)
    2230   UTC (time the aircraft should land)

ALL
3571. (Refer to Figure 27.) An aircraft departs an airport in the eastern daylight time zone at 0945 EDT for a 2-hour flight to an airport located in the central daylight time zone. The landing should be at what coordinated universal time?

A— 1345Z.
B— 1445Z.
C— 1545Z.

Use the following steps:

1. Convert the EDT takeoff time to UTC:

    0945   *EDT takeoff time*
  + 0400   *conversion*
    1345 Z *UTC (also called "ZULU" time)*

2. Add the flight time to the ZULU time of takeoff:

    1345 Z *takeoff time*
  + 0200
    1545 Z *time of landing*

(PLT012) — FAA-H-8083-25

ALL
3572. (Refer to Figure 27.) An aircraft departs an airport in the central standard time zone at 0930 CST for a 2-hour flight to an airport located in the mountain standard time zone. The landing should be at what time?

A— 0930 MST.
B— 1030 MST.
C— 1130 MST.

Use the following steps:

1. Change the CST takeoff time to UTC:

    0930   *CST takeoff time*
  + 0600   *conversion*
    1530 Z *UTC (also called "ZULU" time)*

2. Add the flight time to the time of takeoff:

    1530 Z *takeoff time*
  + 0200   *flight time*
    1730 Z *time of landing*

3. Convert UTC to MST:

    1730 Z *UTC*
  – 0700   *conversion*
    1030   *MST time of landing*

(PLT012) — FAA-H-8083-25

ALL
3573. (Refer to Figure 27.) An aircraft departs an airport in the central standard time zone at 0845 CST for a 2-hour flight to an airport located in the mountain standard time zone. The landing should be at what coordinated universal time?

A— 1345Z.
B— 1445Z.
C— 1645Z.

Use the following steps:

1. Convert the CST takeoff time to UTC:

  0845 CST takeoff time
 + 0600 conversion
  1445 Z UTC (also called "ZULU" time)

2. Add the flight time to the ZULU time of takeoff:

  1445 Z takeoff time
 + 0200 flight time
  1645 Z the time of landing

(PLT012) — FAA-H-8083-25

ALL
3574. (Refer to Figure 27.) An aircraft departs an airport in the mountain standard time zone at 1615 MST for a 2-hour 15-minute flight to an airport located in the Pacific standard time zone. The estimated time of arrival at the destination airport should be

A— 1630 PST.
B— 1730 PST.
C— 1830 PST.

Use the following steps:

1. Convert the MST takeoff time to UTC:

  1615 MST takeoff time
 + 0700 conversion
  2315 Z UTC (also called "ZULU" time)

2. Add the flight time to the ZULU time of takeoff:

  2315 Z takeoff time
 + 0215 flight time
  0130 Z time of landing

3. Convert UTC to PST:

  0130 Z UTC
 – 0800 conversion
  1730 PST time of landing

(PLT012) — FAA-H-8083-25

ALL
3575. (Refer to Figure 27.) An aircraft departs an airport in the Pacific standard time zone at 1030 PST for a 4-hour flight to an airport located in the central standard time zone. The landing should be at what coordinated universal time?

A— 2030Z.
B— 2130Z.
C— 2230Z.

Use the following steps:

1. Convert the PST takeoff time to UTC:

  1030 PST takeoff time
 + 0800 conversion
  1830 Z UTC (also called "ZULU" time)

2. Add the flight time to the ZULU takeoff time:

  1830 Z takeoff time
 + 0400 flight time
  2230 Z time of landing

(PLT012) — FAA-H-8083-25

ALL
3576. (Refer to Figure 27.) An aircraft departs an airport in the mountain standard time zone at 1515 MST for a 2-hour 30-minute flight to an airport located in the Pacific standard time zone. What is the estimated time of arrival at the destination airport?

A— 1645 PST.
B— 1745 PST.
C— 1845 PST.

Use the following steps:

1. Convert the MST takeoff time to UTC:

  1515 MST takeoff time
 + 0700 conversion
  2215 Z UTC (also called "ZULU" time)

2. Add the flight time to the ZULU takeoff time:

  2215 Z takeoff time
 + 0230 flight time
  2445 Z (0045) Z time of landing

3. Convert UTC to PST:

  2445 Z (0045) Z
 – 0800 conversion
  1645 PST time of landing

(PLT012) — FAA-H-8083-25

Answers

3573 [C]   3574 [B]   3575 [C]   3576 [A]

Topography

A VFR Sectional Aeronautical Chart is a pictorial representation of a portion of the Earth's surface upon which lines and symbols in a variety of colors represent features and/or details that can be seen on the Earth's surface. Contour lines, shaded relief, color tints, obstruction symbols, and maximum elevation figures are all used to show topographical information. Explanations and examples may be found in the chart legend. Pilots should become familiar with all of the information provided in each Sectional Chart Legend, found in FAA Legend 1.

ALL, SPO

3637-1. Which is true concerning the blue and magenta colors used to depict airports on Sectional Aeronautical Charts?

A— Airports with control towers underlying Class A, B, and C airspace are shown in blue, Class D and E airspace are magenta.

B— Airports with control towers underlying Class C, D, and E airspace are shown in magenta.

C— Airports with control towers underlying Class B, C, D, and E airspace are shown in blue.

Reference FAA Legend 1. Airports having control towers are shown in blue, all others in magenta. (PLT101) — Sectional Chart Legend

Answer (A) is incorrect because Class A airspace is not depicted on a Sectional; Class C airspace is magenta; and Class E airspace is both blue and magenta depending on where the floor of the airspace starts. Answer (B) is incorrect because airports with control towers are shown in blue.

ALL

3637. (Refer to Figure 23, area 3.) What is the height of the lighted obstacle approximately 6 nautical miles southwest of Savannah International?

A— 1,500 feet MSL.

B— 1,531 feet AGL.

C— 1,545 feet MSL.

Reference FAA Legend 1. The top number, printed in bold, is the height of the obstruction above mean sea level. The second number, printed in parentheses, is the height of the obstruction above ground level. The obstruction is shown as 1,545 feet MSL and 1,532 feet AGL. (PLT064) — Sectional Chart Legend

ALL

3638. (Refer to Figure 23, area 3.) The top of the group obstruction approximately 11 nautical miles from the Savannah VORTAC on the 009° radial is

A— 400 feet AGL.

B— 454 feet MSL.

C— 432 feet MSL.

Reference FAA Legend 1. On Figure 24, area 3, the group obstruction near the 009° radial has the word "stacks" below 454. The bold number (454) indicates the height of the obstruction above mean sea level. (PLT064) — Sectional Chart Legend

ALL

3639. (Refer to Figure 24, area 1.) What minimum altitude is necessary to vertically clear the obstacle on the northeast side of Airpark East Airport by 500 feet?

A— 1,010 feet MSL.

B— 1,273 feet MSL.

C— 1,283 feet MSL.

The elevation of the top of the obstacle is shown as 773 feet above mean sea level (MSL). Add the 500-foot vertical clearance specified by the question to the height (MSL) of the obstacle:

> 773   feet MSL
> + 500
> ――――――――――
> 1,273   feet MSL minimum altitude

(PLT064) — Sectional Chart Legend

Answers

| 3637-1 | [C] | 3637 | [C] | 3638 | [B] | 3639 | [B] |

ALL, SPO
3640. (Refer to Figure 24, area 2.) What minimum altitude is necessary to vertically clear the obstacle on the southeast side of Winnsboro Airport by 500 feet?

A— 823 feet MSL.
B— 1,013 feet MSL.
C— 1,403 feet MSL.

The elevation of the top of the obstacle is shown as 903 feet above mean sea level (MSL). Add the 500-foot ver-tical clearance specified by the question to the height (MSL) of the obstacle:

903 feet MSL
+ 500
1,403 feet MSL

(PLT064) — Sectional Chart Legend

ALL
3631. (Refer to Figure 20, area 5.) The CAUTION box denotes what hazard to aircraft?

A— Unmarked balloon on cable to 3,008 feet MSL.
B— Unmarked balloon on cable to 3,008 feet AGL.
C— Unmarked blimp hangers at 308 feet MSL.

Reference FAA Legend 1. The boxed caution reads, "CAUTION: UNMARKED BALLOON ON CABLE TO 3,008 MSL." (PLT064) — Sectional Chart Legend

ALL, SPO
3632. (Refer to Figure 20, area 2.) The flag symbol at Lake Drummond represents a

A— compulsory reporting point for Norfolk Class C airspace.
B— compulsory reporting point for Hampton Roads Airport.
C— visual checkpoint used to identify position for initial callup to Norfolk Approach Control.

Reference FAA Legend 1. The flag symbol represents a visual checkpoint used to identify position for initial call-up to Norfolk Approach Control. (PLT064) — Sectional Chart Legend

ALL
3633. (Refer to Figure 20, area 2.) The elevation of the Chesapeake Regional Airport is

A— 19 feet.
B— 55 feet.
C— 230 feet.

Reference FAA Legend 1. The airport elevation is noted in the airport information, beneath the airport symbol. The elevation of Chesapeake Regional Airport is 19 feet. (PLT064) — Sectional Chart Legend

ALL
3634. (Refer to Figure 21.) The terrain elevation of the light tan area between Minot (area 1) and Audubon Lake (area 2) varies from

A— sea level to 2,000 feet MSL.
B— 2,000 feet to 2,500 feet MSL.
C— 2,000 feet to 2,700 feet MSL.

Reference FAA Legend 1. The contour line which borders the tan area is labeled 2,000 feet. There are no higher contour levels depicted inside the tan area. (PLT012) — Sectional Chart Legend

Answer (A) is incorrect because the light tan area indicates terrain between 2,000–3,000 feet MSL. Answer (C) is incorrect because contour intervals are 500 feet, not 700.

ALL
3635. (Refer to Figure 21.) Which public use airports depicted are indicated as having fuel?

A— Minot Intl. (area 1) and Garrison (area 2).
B— Minot Intl. (area 1).
C— Mercer County Regional Airport (area 3) and Garrison (area 2).

Reference FAA Legend 1. Minot International is depicted as having fuel, as indicated by the ticks around the basic airport symbol. (PLT064) — Sectional Chart Legend

ALL

3636. (Refer to Figure 23.) The flag symbols at States-boro Bullock County Airport, Claxton-Evans County Airport, and Ridgeland Airport are

A— outer boundaries of Savannah Class C airspace.
B— airports with special traffic patterns.
C— visual checkpoints to identify position for initial callup prior to entering Savannah Class C airspace.

Reference FAA Legend 1. "Visual check point" is the name for the flag symbol. (PLT064) — Sectional Chart Legend

ALL, SPO

3642. (Refer to Figure 25, area 8.) What minimum altitude is required to fly over the Cedar Hill TV towers in the congested area south of Dallas Executive (RBD)?

A— 2,655 feet MSL.
B— 3,549 feet MSL.
C— 3,449 feet MSL.

The height of the tower is 2,549 MSL. A 1,000-foot clearance is required between obstructions and aircraft over a congested area.

> *2,549 MSL*
> *+ 1,000*
> *3,549 MSL*

(PLT101) — 14 CFR §91.119

LTA, LSL

3644. (Refer to Figure 20, area 4.) A balloon launched at the town of Edenton drifts northeasterly along the railroad. What minimum altitude must it maintain to clear all of the obstacles in the vicinity of Hertford by at least 500 feet?

A— 805 feet MSL.
B— 1,000 feet MSL.
C— 1,015 feet MSL.

Use the following steps:

1. Locate the towns of Edenton and Hertford.

2. Note the highest obstruction in the vicinity of Hertford (515 feet MSL).

3. Calculate the minimum altitude (MSL) by adding the required 500-foot clearance to the obstacle height.

> *515 feet*
> *+ 500 feet*
> *1,015 feet MSL*

(PLT064) — Sectional Chart Legend

LTA, LSL

3645. (Refer to Figure 21, area 1.) A balloon launched at Flying S Airport drifts southward towards the lighted obstacle. If the altimeter was set to the current altimeter setting upon launch, what should it indicate if the balloon is to clear the obstacle at 500 feet above the top?

A— 1,531 feet MSL.
B— 1,809 feet MSL.
C— 3,649 feet MSL.

The height of the lit obstacle is 3,149 feet MSL. The altimeter will indicate 3,649 (3,149 + 500) if set to the current altimeter setting upon launch. (PLT064) — Sectional Chart Legend

LTA

3646. (Refer to Figure 22, area 1.) A balloon, launched at CX Airport located near the east end of Lake Pend Oreille, drifts south-southwest. What is the approximate elevation of the highest terrain for 20 miles along its path?

A— 2,000 – 4,000 feet MSL.
B— 4,000 – 6,000 feet MSL.
C— 6,000 – 7,000 feet MSL.

On Sectional Aeronautical Charts, color tints are used to depict bands of elevation. These colors range from light green for the lowest elevations to brown for the higher elevations. Note the terrain height of 6,405 feet MSL within the tan shading south-southwest of CX airport. (PLT064) — Sectional Chart Legend

---

Answers

3636 [C]   3642 [B]   3644 [C]   3645 [C]   3646 [C]

Dead Reckoning

Dead reckoning is the method used for determining position with a heading indicator and calculations based on speed, elapsed time, and wind effect from a known position. The instruments used for dead reckoning navigation include the outside air temperature gauge, the airspeed indicator, the altimeter, the clock, and the magnetic compass system or slaved gyro system. These instruments provide information concerning direction, airspeed, altitude, and time, and must be correctly interpreted for successful navigation.

Plotting Courses

A course is the direction of flight measured in degrees clockwise from north. Meridians of longitude run from the south pole to the north pole. This alignment is called true north. When a course is plotted on a chart in relation to the lines of longitude and/or latitude it is called a **true course (TC)**, and will be expressed in three digits. North may be either 360° or 000°; east is 090°; south is 180°; and west is 270°. Any attempt to project lines of latitude and longitude onto a flat surface such as a chart results in a certain amount of distortion. When plotting a course on a sectional aeronautical chart, this distortion may be minimized by measuring true course in reference to the meridian nearest to the halfway point between the departure point and the destination.

A common type of plotter that is used to plot a course is shown in Figure 9-2 on the next page. This plotter is a semi-circular protractor with a straight edge attached to it. The straight edge has distance scales that match various charts and these scales may depict both statute and nautical miles. A small hole at the base of the protractor portion indicates the center of the arc of the angular scale. Two complete scales cover the outer edge of the protractor, and they are graduated in degrees. An inner scale measures the angle from the vertical.

To determine true course (TC), use the plotter in the following manner:

1. Using the straight edge of the plotter as a guide, draw a line from the point of departure to the destination.

2. Place the top straight edge of the plotter parallel to the plotted course and move the plotter along the course line as necessary to place the small center hole over a meridian as near to the halfway point of the course as possible. *See* Figure 9-2a.

3. The true course is the angle measured between the meridian and the course line. *See* Figure 9-2b. The outer scale is used to read all angles between north through east to south, and the inner scale is used to read all angles between south through west to north. In Figure 9-2 the true course from point (a) to point (b) is 115° as read at point (c).

4. Course lines which fall within 30° of true north or south can be more easily measured by sliding the plotter along the course line until the hole falls over a horizontal latitude line; use the partial protractor scale for these measurements.

Continued

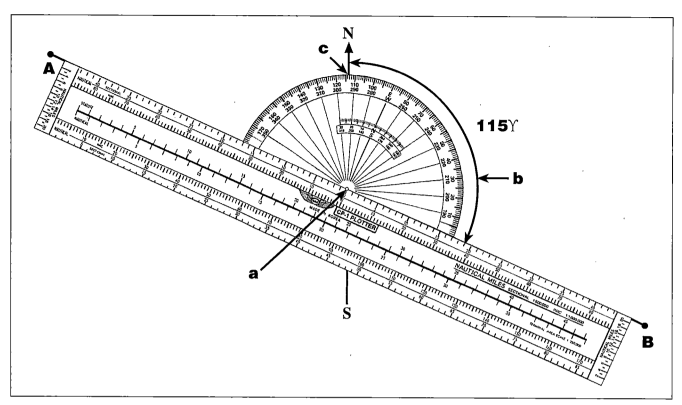

Figure 9-2. Placing the plotter on the course line

Magnetic Variation

The north pole where all meridians converge is **true north**. The north pole which attracts the needle of a compass is **magnetic north**. These two poles are not in the same place. At any point where magnetic north and true north are in line with each other, the compass needle points both to magnetic north, and coincidentally, true north. The line along which this occurs is known as the **agonic line**. When positioned west of the agonic line, a compass will point right (east) of true north. When positioned east of the agonic line, a compass will point left (west) of true north. This angular difference between true north and magnetic north is called **magnetic variation (VAR)**. West of the agonic line, variation is "easterly." East of the agonic line, variation is "westerly."

The amount and direction of variation is depicted on sectional charts as dashed magenta colored lines connecting points of equal variation, called isogonic lines.

A course measured on a sectional chart is a true course: it is measured from a meridian, which runs from the south pole to the north pole. Since a magnetic compass is used to maintain a course while flying, this true course must now be converted to a **magnetic course (MC)**. This conversion is made by either adding or subtracting the variation. To convert a true course to a magnetic course, subtract easterly variation, and add westerly variation: "East is least, west is best."

TC ± VAR = MC

ALL

3531. (Refer to Figure 20.) Determine the magnetic course from First Flight Airport (area 5) to Hampton Roads Airport (area 2).

A— 141°.
B— 321°.
C— 332°.

Use the following steps:

1. *Plot the course from First Flight Airport to Hampton Roads Airport.*

2. *Measure the true course angle at the approximate midpoint of the route. The true course is 321°.*

3. *Note that the variation is 11°W as shown on the isogonic line.*

4. *Using the formula:*
   $$MC = TC \pm VAR$$
   $$MC = 321° + 11°W$$
   $$MC = 332°$$

(PLT064) — FAA-H-8083-25

ALL

3556. (Refer to Figure 24.) Determine the magnetic course from Airpark East Airport (area 1) to Winnsboro Airport (area 2). Magnetic variation is 6°30'E.

A— 075°.
B— 082°.
C— 091°.

Use the following steps:

1. *Plot the course from Airpark East Airport to Winns-boro Airport.*

2. *Measure the true course angle at the approximate midpoint of the route (082°).*

3. *Calculate the magnetic course by subtracting the magnetic variation (6°30') from the true course (082°).*
   $$MC = TC \pm VAR$$
   $$MC = 082° - 6°30'E$$
   $$MC = 75°30' \text{ (075° is the closest answer)}$$

(PLT012) — FAA-H-8083-25

ALL

3568. (Refer to Figure 26.) Determine the magnetic course from Tomlinson Airport (area 1) to Jamestown Airport (area 4).

A— 153°.
B— 154°.
C— 159°.

Use the following steps:

1. *Plot the course from Tomlinson Airport to Jamestown Airport.*

2. *Measure the true course angle at the approximate midpoint of the route (158°).*

3. *Note that the variation is 5° E as shown on the dashed isogonic line.*

4. *Using the formula:*
   $$MC = TC \pm VAR$$
   $$MC = 158 - 5° \text{ East}$$
   $$MC = 153°$$

(PLT012) — FAA-H-8083-25

SPO

2201. Heading and groundspeed are calculated using dead reckoning procedures. In flight, they are constantly monitored and corrected by

A— pilotage as observed from checkpoints.
B— the wind triangle.
C— the wet compass and the groundspeed indicator.

Dead reckoning is navigation solely by means of computations based on time, airspeed, distance, and direction. The products derived from these variables, when adjusted by windspeed and velocity, are heading and ground speed. Except for flights over water, dead reckoning is usually used with pilotage for cross-country flying. The heading and ground speed as calculated is constantly monitored and corrected by pilotage as observed from checkpoints. (PLT335) — FAA-H-8083-25

SPO

2102. The course measured on a sectional chart by reference to a meridian is known as the

A— true course.
B— magnetic course.
C— true heading.

The course measured on the chart is known as the true course. (PLT320) — FAA-H-8083-25

Answer (B) is incorrect because magnetic course adds variation to the course measured on the chart. Answer (C) is incorrect because true heading accounts for wind.

Answers

3531 [C]	3556 [A]	3568 [A]	2201 [A]	2102 [A]

Magnetic Deviation

The magnetic compass is affected by influences within the aircraft such as electrical circuits, radios, engines, magnetized metal parts, etc., which cause the compass needle to be deflected from its normal reading. This deflection is known as **deviation (DEV)**, and it must be applied to convert a magnetic course to a **compass course (CC)** to make it usable in flight.

Deviation, which is different for each aircraft, may also vary for different courses in the same airplane. To let the pilot know the appropriate correction, a correction card is mounted near the compass.

To determine the actual compass reading to be followed during flight, it is necessary to apply the corrections for both variation and deviation:

True Course ± Variation = Magnetic Course ± Deviation = Compass Course

or,

TC ± VAR = MC ± DEV = CC.

Wind and Its Effects

An additional computation, common to both pilotage and dead reckoning, is necessary to compensate for the effect of wind.

Wind direction is reported as the direction from which the wind blows, i.e., wind blowing from the west to the east is a west wind. Wind speed is the rate of motion without regard to direction. In the United States, wind speed is usually expressed in knots. Wind velocity includes both direction and speed of the wind; for example, a west wind of 25 knots.

Downwind movement is with the wind; upwind movement is against the wind. Moving air exerts a force in the direction of its motion on any object within it. Objects that are free to move in air will move in a downwind direction at the speed of the wind.

If a powered aircraft is flying in a 20-knot wind, it will move 20 nautical miles downwind in 1 hour in addition to its forward movement through the air. The path of an aircraft over the earth is determined both by the motion of the aircraft through the air and by the motion of the air over the earth's surface. Direction and movement through the air is governed both by the direction that the aircraft nose is pointing and by aircraft speed.

The sideward displacement of an aircraft caused by wind is called drift. Drift can be determined by measuring the angle between the heading (the direction in which the nose is pointing) and the track (the actual path of the aircraft over the earth). *See* Figure 9-3.

For example, Figure 9-3 shows an aircraft which departs point A on a heading of 360° and flies for 1 hour in a wind of 270° at 20 knots. Under a no-wind condition the aircraft would arrive at point B at the end of 1 hour. However, this example has a wind of 20 knots, and the aircraft moves with the wind; so at the end of 1 hour, the aircraft is at point C, 20 nautical miles downwind from B. From A to B is the intended path of the aircraft, from B to C is the motion of the body of air, and from A to C is the actual path of the aircraft over the earth (the track).

A given wind will cause a different drift on each aircraft heading and it will also affect the distance traveled over the ground in a given time. With a given wind, the ground speed varies with each different aircraft heading. Figure 9-4 illustrates how a wind of 270° at 20 knots would affect the ground speed and track of an aircraft on various headings. In this particular illustration, on a heading of 360°, drift would be to the right; on a heading of 180°, drift would be to the left. With a 90° crosswind and no heading correction applied, there would be little effect on ground speed. On a heading of 090°, no left or right

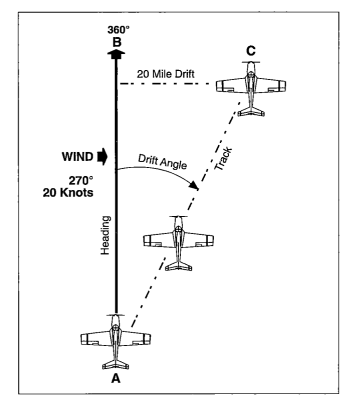

Figure 9-3. Drift

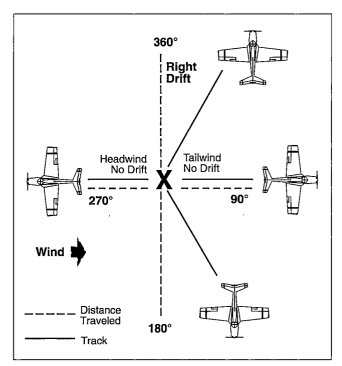

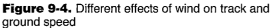

Figure 9-4. Different effects of wind on track and ground speed

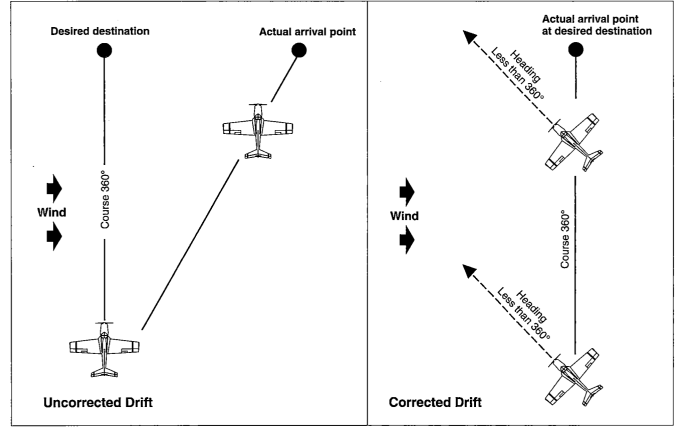

Figure 9-5. Compensating for wind drift

drift would be experienced; instead, the ground speed would be increased by the tailwind. On a 270° heading, the ground speed would be reduced by the headwind.

By determining the amount of drift, a pilot can counteract the effect of wind and make the track of the aircraft coincide with the desired course. For example, if the wind is from the left, the correction would be made by pointing the aircraft to the left a certain number of degrees, thereby compensating for wind drift. This is the Wind Correction Angle (WCA), and it is expressed as degrees left or right of the course. *See* Figure 9-5.

Any course, true, magnetic, or compass, becomes a heading when it is corrected for wind. *See* Figure 9-6.

Course				Heading
True	±	WCA	=	True
±				±
Variation				Variation
=				=
Magnetic	±	WCA	=	Magnetic
±				±
Deviation				Deviation
=				=
Compass	±	WCA	=	Compass

Figure 9-6

SPO
2177. If proper correction has been made for the wind, ground track will be identical with

A— drift angle.
B— course.
C— heading.

If proper correction has been made for the wind, track and course will be identical. (PLT198) — FAA-H-8083-25

SPO
2103. Motion of the air affects the speed with which aircraft move

A— over the Earth's surface.
B— through the air.
C— in a turn.

Motion of the air affects the speed with which airplanes move over the Earth's surface. (PLT198) — FAA-H-8083-25

SPO
2104. If a flight is to be made on a course to the east, with a wind blowing from northeast, the aircraft must be headed

A— somewhat to the north of east to counteract drift.
B— south of east to counteract drift.
C— north to counteract torque.

If the mass of air is moving across the course from the left, the airplane will drift to the right, and a correction must be made by heading the airplane sufficiently to the left to offset this drift. (PLT198) — FAA-H-8083-25

Answers
2177　[B]　　　　2103　[A]　　　　2104　[A]

The Wind Triangle

True course is determined by measuring the course on an aeronautical chart. **True airspeed** is known by applying the appropriate correction to the indication of the airspeed indicator. The wind direction and velocity are known from reports or forecasts from the Flight Service Stations.

The true heading and the ground speed can be found by drawing a wind triangle of vectors. One side of the triangle is the wind direction and velocity, one side is the true heading and true airspeed, the final side is the track, or true course, and the ground speed. Each side of a wind triangle is the vector sum of the other two sides.

ALL
3816. (Refer to Figure 68.) The line from point A to point B of the wind triangle represents

A— true heading and airspeed.
B— true course and ground speed.
C— ground speed and true heading.

The line A to B of the wind triangle represents true heading and the true airspeed. It is the vector sum of the lines C to B (the true course and ground speed) and C to A (the wind direction and speed). (PLT012) – FAA-H-8083-25

Answer (B) is incorrect because this is represented by the line from point C to B. Answer (C) is incorrect because these values are defined by separate lines of the wind triangle.

ALL
3817. (Refer to Figure 68.) The line from point C to point B of the wind triangle represents

A— airspeed and heading.
B— ground speed and true course.
C— true heading and ground speed.

The line from point C to B of the wind triangle represents the ground speed and true course. (PLT012) – FAA-H-8083-25

Answer (A) is incorrect because this is represented by the line from point A to B. Answer (C) is incorrect because these values are defined by separate lines of the wind triangle.

ALL
2001. (Refer to Figure 68.) The line from point C to point A of the wind triangle represents

A— wind direction and velocity.
B— true course and ground speed.
C— true heading and ground speed.

The line from point C to A of the wind triangle represents the wind direction and speed (velocity). (PLT012) – FAA-H-8083-25

Answer (B) is incorrect because this is represented by the line from point C to B. Answer (C) is incorrect because these are the values found by using the wind triangle.

Answers

3816	[A]	3817	[B]	2001	[A]

The Flight Computer (E6-B)

Note: ASA's CX-2 Pathfinder is an electronic flight computer and can be used in place of the E6-B. This aviation computer can solve all flight planning problems, as well as perform standard mathematical calculations.

Finding Wind Correction Angle (WCA) and Ground Speed

The Wind Correction Angle (WCA) required to change a course to a heading can be found by using the wind face of the E6-B. Ground speed can also be determined as a part of this procedure.

The wind face of the E6-B consists of a transparent, rotatable plotting disk mounted in a frame as shown in Figure 9-7 on the next page. A compass rose is located around the plotting disk (Figure 9-7a). A correction scale on the top of the frame is graduated in degrees left and right of the true index (Figure 9-7b), and it is used for calculating drift correction. A small reference circle, called a grommet, is located at the center of the plotting disk (Figure 9-7c).

A sliding grid (Figure 9-7d) inserted behind the plotting disk is used for wind computations. The slide has converging lines (track or drift lines) which indicate degrees left or right of center (Figure 9-7e). Concentric arcs (speed circles) on the slide are used for calculations of speed (Figure 9-7f). The wind correction angle and ground speed may be found when true course, true airspeed, wind speed and wind direction (relative to true north) are known.

Problem: Using a flight computer and the following conditions, find the wind correction angle (WCA), the true heading (TH), and the ground speed (GS).

Conditions:

True course (TC) .... 090°
True airspeed (TAS) .... 120 knots
True wind direction .... 160°
Wind speed .... 30 knots

Solution:

1. Using the wind face side of the E6-B, set the true wind direction (160°) under the true index (Figure 9-8a).

2. Plot the wind speed above the grommet 30 units (wind speed). *Note:* The sliding grid can be at any value for this step. Place a wind dot within a circle at this point (Figure 9-8b).

3. Rotate the plotting disk and set the true course (090°) under the true index (Figure 9-9a).

4. Adjust the sliding grid so that the TAS arc (120 knots) is at the wind dot (Figure 9-9b). Note the wind dot is 14° right of centerline (Figure 9-9c), so the WCA = 14°R.

5. Under the grommet, read the ground speed (GS) of 106 knots (Figure 9-9d).

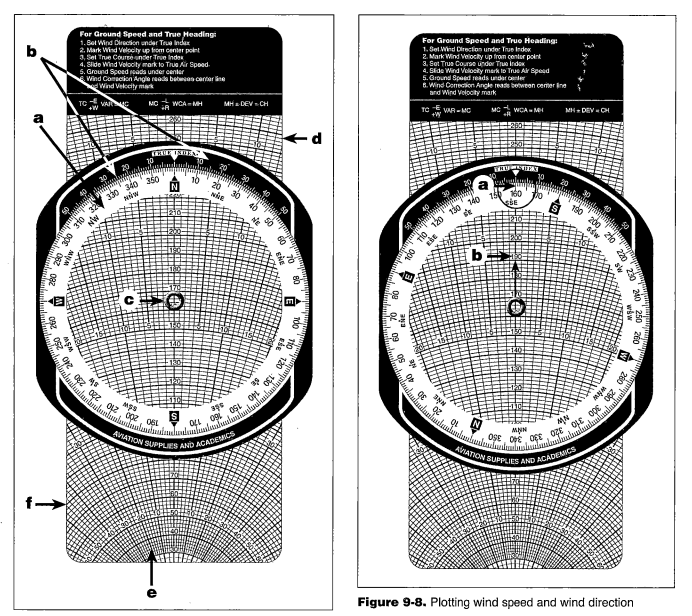

Figure 9-7. Wind face of E6-B computer

Figure 9-8. Plotting wind speed and wind direction

6. Determine the true heading by applying the formula:

TC + WCA = TH

In this case the wind correction is to the right, so it will be added to the true course:

$$
\begin{array}{ll}
090° & \text{(TC)} \\
+ 14° & \text{(WCA)} \\
\hline
104° & \text{(TH)}
\end{array}
$$

Flight Computer Calculator Face

Opposite the windface of the flight computer is a circular slide rule or calculator face. The outer scale, called the miles scale, is stationary (Figure 9-10a). The inner circle rotates and is called the minutes scale (Figure 9-10b).

The numbers on the computer scale represent multiples of 10, of the values shown. For example, the number 24 on either scale may be 0.24, 2.4, 24, 240, etc. On the inner scale, minutes may be converted to hours by reference to the adjacent hours scale. In Figure 9-10c, for example, 4 hours is found adjacent to 24, meaning 240 minutes.

Relative values must be kept in mind. For example, the numbers 21 and 22 are separated by divisions, each space representing 2 units. Thus, the second division past 21 will be read as 21.4, 214, or 2,140. Between 80 and 90 are 10 divisions, each space representing 1 unit. Thus, the second division past 80 will be read as 8.2, 82 or 820.

There are three index marks on the miles (outer) scale which are used for converting statute miles (SM), nautical miles (NM) and kilometers (KM). The E6-B computer has a scale for converting statute

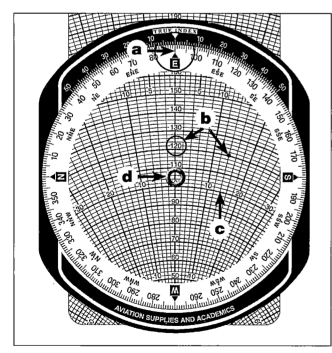

Figure 9-9. Determining the wind correction angle and ground speed

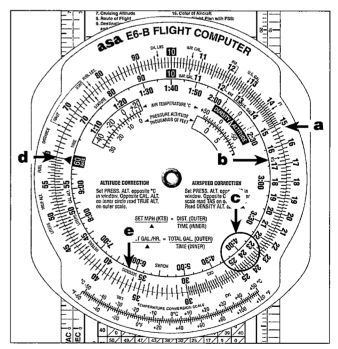

Figure 9-10. Slide rule (calculator) face

miles, nautical miles, and kilometers. Place the known figure on the inner scale under "naut," "stat," or "KM," as appropriate, and read the equivalent value under the other indexes. For example, to convert 85 statute miles to kilometers and nautical miles, place 85 on the inner scale under the "stat" index. Under the "KM" index, read 137; under the "naut" index read 74.

Each scale has a 10-index used as a reference mark for multiplication and division. The 10-index on the inner scale can also be used as a rate index representing 1 hour. Also on the inner scale is a 60-index, representing 60 minutes and usually used for computation instead of the 10 or 1 hour index (Figure 9-10d) and a 36 or "seconds" index (3,600 seconds = 1 hour) (Figure 9-10e).

Finding Time, Rate, and Distance

The flight computer will commonly be used to solve problems of time, rate, and distance. When two factors are known, the third can be found using the proportion:

$$\text{RATE (speed)} = \frac{\text{DISTANCE}}{\text{TIME}}$$

Problem: How far does an aircraft travel in 2 hours and 15 minutes at a ground speed of 138 knots?

Solution: Use the formula:

Distance = Ground Speed x Time, or use the flight computer in the following manner:

1. Place the 60 (speed) index (inner scale) under 138 (outer scale).

2. Over the time of 135 minutes or 2 hours +15 minutes (inner scale), read 310 NM (on the outer scale). *See* Figure 9-11.

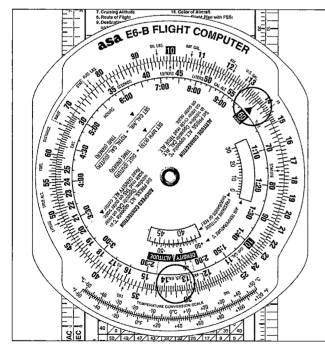

Figure 9-11. Computing distance on the E6-B

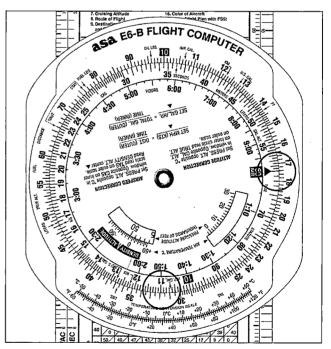

Figure 9-12. Determining time required on the E6-B

Problem: How much time is required to fly 320 nautical miles at a ground speed of 174 knots?

Solution: Use the formula:

Time = Distance ÷ Ground Speed, or use the flight computer in the following manner:

1. Set the 60 (speed) index under 174 (outer scale).
2. Under 320 (outer scale), read 110 minutes or 1 hour 50 minutes (inner scale). *See* Figure 9-12.

Problem: What is the ground speed if it takes 40 minutes to fly 96 nautical miles?

Solution: Use the formula: *Ground Speed = Distance ÷ Time,* or use the flight computer in the following manner:

1. Place 40 minutes (inner scale) under 96 (outer scale).
2. Over the 60 (speed) index, read 144 knots (outer scale). *See* Figure 9-13.

Problem: If 50 minutes are required to fly 120 nautical miles, how many minutes are required to fly 86 nautical miles at the same rate?

Solution:

1. Set 50 (inner scale) under 120 (outer scale).
2. Under 86 (outer scale), read 36 minutes required (inner scale). *See* Figure 9-14.

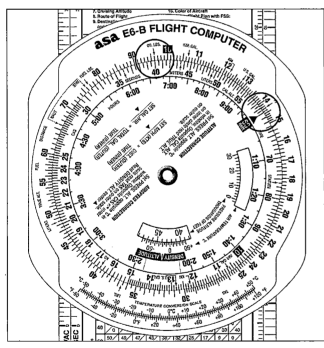

Figure 9-13. Determining groundspeed on the E6-B

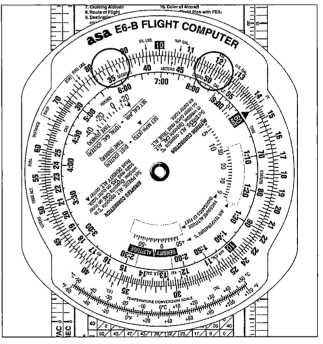

Figure 9-14. Determining time-rate-distance on the E6-B

Calculating Fuel Consumption

Fuel consumption problems are solved in the same manner as Time-Rate-Distance problems.

Problem: If 18 gallons of fuel are consumed in 1 hour, how much fuel will be used in 2 hours 20 minutes?

Solution:

1. Set the 60-index (inner scale) under 18 (outer scale).

2. Over 2 hour 20 minute (inner scale), read 42 gallons (outer scale). *See* Figure 9-15.

Problem: What is the rate of fuel consumption if 30 gallons of fuel are consumed in 111 minutes?

Solution:

1. Set 111 (inner scale) under 30 (outer scale).

2. Over the 60-index (inner scale), read 16.2 gallons per hour (outer scale). *See* Figure 9-16.

Problem: Forty gallons of fuel have been consumed in 135 minutes (2 hours and 15 minutes) flying time. How much longer can the aircraft continue to fly if 25 gallons of available fuel remain and the rate of consumption remains the same?

Solution:

1. Set 135 (inner scale) under 40 (outer scale).

2. Under 25 (outer scale), read 84.5 minutes of fuel remaining. *See* Figure 9-17.

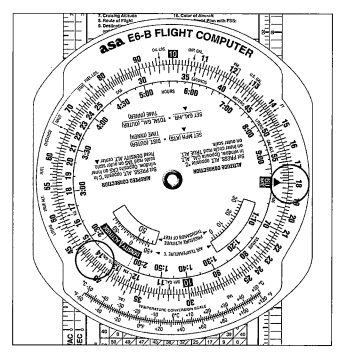

Figure 9-15. Determining total fuel consumed on the E6-B

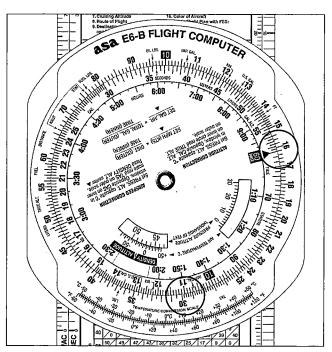

Figure 9-16. Determining rate of consumption on the E6-B

Finding True Airspeed and Density Altitude

The calculator (slide rule) side of the computer may also be used to determine true airspeed by correcting calibrated airspeed for temperature and pressure altitude. Density altitude is computed simultaneously.

Problem: Using a flight computer and the following conditions, find the true airspeed (TAS) and the density altitude (DA).

Conditions:

True Air Temperature .... +10°C
Pressure Altitude (PA) .... 10,000 feet
Calibrated Airspeed (CAS) .... 140 knots

Solution:

1. Using the window marked "for airspeed and density altitude computations," place the true air temperature over the pressure altitude (Figure 9-18a).

2. In the density altitude window read the density altitude of 11,800 feet. (Figure 9-18b).

3. Over 140 knots CAS (inner scale) read the TAS of 167 knots (outer scale). *See* Figure 9-18c.

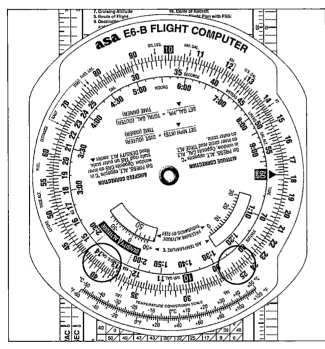

Figure 9-17. Determining flight time remaining on the E6-B

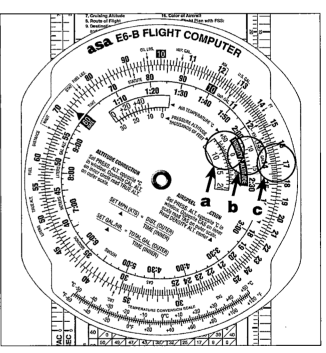

Figure 9-18. Determining true airspeed and density altitude on the E6-B

AIR, RTC, GLI, WSC, PPC

3529-1. If a true heading of 135° results in a ground track of 130° and a true airspeed of 135 knots results in a groundspeed of 140 knots, the wind would be from

A— 019° and 12 knots.
B— 200° and 13 knots.
C— 246° and 13 knots.

You are heading to the southeast (135°) at 135 knots. The wind is blowing you left of course (130°) and giving you a faster ground speed which means the wind is blowing from the southwest. Use your manual or electronic flight computer to determine the wind direction and speed at 246° and 13 knots. (PLT012) — FAA-H-8083-25

Answer (A) is incorrect because a wind from 019° would blow you right of course (resulting in a ground track of 140°). Answer (B) is incorrect because a wind from 200° would be a right quartering headwind which wouldn't increase your ground speed.

AIR, RTC, GLI, WSC, PPC, SPO

3529-2. When converting from true course to magnetic heading, a pilot should

A— subtract easterly variation and right wind correction angle.
B— add westerly variation and subtract left wind correction angle.
C— subtract westerly variation and add right wind correction angle.

When converting a true course to a true heading, subtract a left wind correction angle or add a right wind correction angle. When converting from a true heading to a magnetic heading, add westerly variation or subtract easterly variation. (PLT198) — FAA-H-8083-25

Answer (A) is incorrect because right wind correction is added. Answer (C) is incorrect because westerly variation is added.

AIR, RTC, GLI, WSC, PPC

3529-3. How far will an aircraft travel in 2-1/2 minutes with a groundspeed of 98 knots?

A— 2.45 NM.
B— 3.35 NM.
C— 4.08 NM.

To find the distance flown in a given time, multiply ground speed by time. The distance flown in 2-1/2 minutes (convert to hours by dividing by 60) at a ground speed of 98 knots is .04 x 98 = 4.08 NM. (PLT012) — FAA-H-8083-25

ALL

3529-4. How far will an aircraft travel in 7.5 minutes with a ground speed of 114 knots?

A— 14.25 NM.
B— 15.00 NM.
C— 14.50 NM.

To find the distance flown in a given time, multiply ground speed by time. The distance flown in 7.5 minutes (convert to hours by dividing by 60) at a ground speed of 114 knots is .125 x 114 = 14.25 NM. (PLT012) — FAA-H-8083-25

AIR, RTC, WSC, PPC

3565. (Refer to Figure 25.) Determine the magnetic heading for a flight from Fort Worth Meacham (area 4) to Denton Muni (area 1). The wind is from 330° at 25 knots, the true airspeed is 110 knots, and the magnetic variation is 7° east.

A— 004°.
B— 017°.
C— 023°.

Use the following steps:

1. *Plot a course from Meacham to Denton, and measure the course (021°).*

2. *Using the wind obtained, calculate a correction angle. This angle will be the difference between the course bearing and the heading required to maintain that course. Wind correction angle is 10° to the left.*

3. *Add course bearing and wind correction angle to obtain true heading.*

    021 + -010 = 011° (true heading)

4. *Find the magnetic heading by adding the variation to the true heading.*

    011 + -7 = 004° (magnetic heading)

(PLT012) — FAA-H-8083-25

Answers

3529-1　[C]　　　3529-2　[B]　　　3529-3　[C]　　　3529-4　[A]　　　3565　[A]

AIR, RTC, WSC, PPC

3551. (Refer to Figures 23 and 58.) Determine the compass heading for a flight from Claxton-Evans County Airport (area 2) to Hampton Varnville Airport (area 1). The wind is from 280° at 08 knots, the true airspeed is 85 knots, and the magnetic variation is 5° west.

A— 033°.
B— 042°.
C— 038°.

Use the following steps:

1. *Plot the course from Claxton-Evans County Airport to Hampton Varnville Airport.*

2. *Measure the true course angle at the approximate midpoint of the route (044°).*

3. *Use a flight computer to find the true heading:*

   Wind direction is 280° (given in question)
   Wind speed is 8 knots (given in question)
   True course is 044° (found in Step 2)
   True airspeed is 85 knots (given in question)

   Therefore, the true heading is 40°.

4. *Calculate the magnetic heading by adding the westerly variation (5°W) to the true heading (40°).*

   $MH = TH \pm VAR$
   $MH = 40° + 5°W$
   $MH = 045°$

5. *Note the compass deviation card in Figure 58 indicates that in order to fly a magnetic course of 030°, the pilot must steer a compass heading of 027° or a 3° compass deviation. To fly a magnetic course of 060°, the pilot must steer a compass heading of 056° or a 4° compass deviation. Interpolate between these to find the compass correction for 045° (3.5°). Calculate the compass heading (CH) by subtracting the compass deviation (3.5°) from the magnetic heading (045°).*

   $CH = MH \pm DEV$
   $CH = 045° - 3.5°$
   $CH = 41.5°$

(PLT012) — FAA-H-8083-25

AIR, RTC, WSC, PPC

3538. (Refer to Figure 21.) Determine the magnetic heading for a flight from Mercer County Regional Airport (area 3) to Minot International (area 1). The wind is from 330° at 25 knots, the true airspeed is 100 knots, and the magnetic variation is 10° east.

A— 002°
B— 012°.
C— 352°.

Use the following steps:

1. *Plot the course from Mercer County Regional Airport to Minot Airport.*

2. *Measure the true course angle at the approximate midpoint of the route. The true course (TC) is 011°.*

3. *Find the true heading using a flight computer:*

   Wind direction is 330° (given in question)
   Wind speed is 25 knots (given in question)
   True course is 011° (found in Step 2)
   True airspeed is 100 knots (given in question)

   Therefore, the true heading is 002°.

4. *Calculate the magnetic heading by subtracting the easterly variation (10°) from the true heading (002°).*

   $MH = TH \pm VAR$
   $MH = 002° - 10°E$
   $MH = 352°$

(PLT012) — FAA-H-8083-25

Answers

3551   [B] ·   3538   [C]

AIR, RTC, WSC, PPC
3545. (Refer to Figure 22.) Determine the magnetic heading for a flight from Sandpoint Airport (area 1) to St. Maries Airport (area 4). The wind is from 215° at 25 knots and the true airspeed is 125 knots.

A— 172°.
B— 349°.
C— 187°.

Use the following steps:

1. *Plot the course from Sandpoint Airport to St. Maries Airport.*

2. *Measure the true course angle at the approximate midpoint of the route (181°).*

3. *Find true heading, using a flight computer:*

> *Wind direction is 215° (given in question)*
> *Wind speed is 25 knots (given in question)*
> *True course is 181° (found in Step 2)*
> *True airspeed is 125 knots (given in question)*

> *Therefore, the true heading is 187°.*

4. *Calculate the magnetic heading by subtracting the easterly variation (15°) from the true heading (187°).*

> *MH = TH ± VAR*
> *MH = 187° – 15°E*
> *MH = 172°*

(PLT012) — FAA-H-8083-25

AIR, RTC, WSC, PPC
3546. (Refer to Figure 22.) What is the magnetic heading for a flight from Priest River Airport (area 1) to Shoshone County Airport (area 3)? The wind is from 030° at 12 knots and the true airspeed is 95 knots.

A— 121°.
B— 143°.
C— 136°.

Use the following steps:

1. *Plot the course from Priest River to Shoshone County Airport.*

2. *Measure the true course angle at the approximate midpoint of the route (143°).*

3. *Find the true heading using a flight computer:*

> *Wind direction is 030° (given in question)*
> *Wind speed is 12 knots (given in question)*
> *True course is 143° (found in Step 2)*
> *True airspeed is 95 knots (given in question)*

> *Therefore, the true heading is 136°.*

4. *Calculate the magnetic heading by subtracting the easterly variation (15°E, as shown on the dashed isogonic line) from the true heading (136°).*

> *MH = TH ± VAR*
> *MH = 136° – 15°E*
> *MH = 121°*

(PLT012) — FAA-H-8083-25

Answers

3545   [A]   3546   [A]

AIR, RTC, WSC, PPC

3547. (Refer to Figure 22.) Determine the magnetic heading for a flight from St. Maries Airport (area 4) to Priest River Airport (area 1). The wind is from 340° at 10 knots, and the true airspeed is 90 knots.

A— 345°.
B— 329°.
C— 327°.

Use the following steps:

1. *Plot the course from St. Maries Airport to Priest River Airport.*

2. *Measure the true course angle at the approximate midpoint of the route (345°).*

3. *Use a flight computer to find true heading:*

   Wind direction is 340° (given in question)
   Wind speed is 10 knots (given in question)
   True course is 345° (found in Step 2)
   True airspeed is 90 knots (given in question)

   Therefore, the true heading is 344°.

4. *Calculate the magnetic heading by subtracting the easterly variation (15°E, as shown on the dashed isogonic line) from the true heading (344°).*

   MH = TH ± VAR
   MH = 344° − 15°E
   MH = 329°

(PLT012) — FAA-H-8083-25

AIR, RTC, WSC, PPC

3550. (Refer to Figure 23.) Determine the magnetic heading for a flight from Allendale County Airport (area 1) to Claxton-Evans County Airport (area 2). The wind is from 090° at 16 knots, the true airspeed is 90 knots, and the magnetic variation is 6° west.

A— 209°.
B— 230°.
C— 212°.

Use the following steps:

1. *Plot the course from Allendale County Airport to Claxton-Evans County Airport.*

2. *Measure the true course angle at the approximate midpoint of the route (212°).*

3. *Find true heading, using a flight computer:*

   Wind direction is 090° (given in question)
   Wind speed is 16 knots (given in question)
   True course is 212° (found in Step 2)

True airspeed is 90 knots (given in question)

Therefore, the true heading is 203°.

4. *Calculate the magnetic heading by adding the westerly variation (6°W, as shown on the dashed isogonic line) from the true heading (203°).*

   MH = TH ± VAR
   MH = 203° + 6°W
   MH = 209°

(PLT012) — FAA-H-8083-25

AIR, RTC, WSC, PPC

3550-1. On a cross-country flight, point A is crossed at 1500 hours and the plan is to reach point B at 1530 hours. Use the following information to determine the indicated airspeed required to reach point B on schedule.

Distance between A and B...............................70 NM
Forecast wind.. 310° at 15 kts
Pressure altitude.. 8,000 ft
Ambient temperature..-10°C
True course ....270°

The required indicated airspeed would be approximately

A— 126 knots.
B— 137 knots.
C— 152 knots.

Use your CX-2 electronic flight computer to find the answer:

1. *Find the ground speed that must be made between points A and B (GS on CX-2 menu).*

   Distance...70 NM
   Time to travel..30 min.
   Ground speed...140 kts

2. *Find the true airspeed (Hdg/TAS).*

   Wind direction...310°
   Wind speed..15 kts
   Course...270°
   Ground speed...140 kts
   True airspeed...151.8 kts
   True heading...274°

3. *Find the required indicated (or calibrated) airspeed (ReqCAS).*

   Pressure altitude... 8,000 ft
   Temperature ....-10°C
   True airspeed..151.8 kts
   Indicated airspeed......................................137.1 kts
   (same as calibrated)

(PLT012) — FAA-H-8083-25

Answers

3547   [B]   3550   [A]   3550-1   [B]

AIR, RTC, GLI, WSC, PPC

3564. (Refer to Figure 25.) Determine the magnetic heading for a flight from Dallas Executive (area 3) to Fort Worth Meacham (area 4). The wind is from 030° at 10 knots, the true airspeed is 135 knots, and the magnetic variation is 7° east.

A— 266°.

B— 286°.

C— 312°.

Use the following steps:

1. *Plot a course from Dallas Executive to Meacham, and measure the course (289°).*

2. *Using the wind obtained, calculate a correction angle. This angle will be the difference between the course bearing and the heading required to maintain that course. Wind correction angle is 4° to the right.*

3. *Add course bearing and wind correction angle to obtain true heading.*

> *289° course bearing*
> *+ 4° wind correction angle*
> *293° true heading*

4. *Find the magnetic heading by adding the variation to the true heading.*

> *293° true heading*
> *− 007° variation (E)*
> *286° magnetic heading*

(PLT012) — FAA-H-8083-25

AIR, RTC, LSA

3564-1. (Refer to Figure 75.) What is the time en route from the Gila Bend VORTAC to Buckeye VOR along V461 at a TAS of 125 knots with forecasted winds from 180 at 17 knots?

A— Approximately 14 minutes.

B— Approximately 15 minutes.

C— Approximately 13 minutes.

Use your CX-2 electronic flight computer to find the answer:

1. *Your course along V461 can be determined by using Figure 75 and identifying the 332° to Buckeye.*

2. *Next determine your ground speed using your CX-2 and the following information: course 332°, TAS 125 knots, wind direction 180, and wind speed of 17 knots. This results in a GS of 140 knots.*

3. *The distance along V461 is determined by the number 31.*

4. *Determine your time en route using your CX-2: 31 NM at 140 knots results in 13 minutes and 18 seconds.*

(PLT012) — FAA-H-8083-25

ALL

3564-2. (Refer to Figure 21.) What is the estimated time en route from Mercer County Regional Airport (area 3) to Minot International (area 1)? The wind is from 330° at 25 knots and the true airspeed is 100 knots. Add 3-1/2 minutes for departure and climb-out.

A— 48 minutes.

B— 44 minutes.

C— 52 minutes.

Use your CX-2 electronic flight computer to find the answer:

1. *Use your plotter on Figure 21 to identifying the distance (52 NM) and course (12 degrees) between Mercer and Minot airports.*

2. *Next determine your ground speed using your CX-2 and the following information: distance 52 NM, TAS 100 knots, course 15 degrees, wind direction 330, and wind speed 25 knots. This results in a GS of 81 knots.*

3. *Determine your time enroute using your CX-2, 39 minutes.*

4. *Add 3-1/2 minutes per the question requirements, 42-1/2 minutes.*

(PLT012) – FAA-H-8083-25

Answers

3564   [B]   3564-1   [C]   3564-2   [B]

GLI

3650. (Refer to Figure 26, areas 5 and 6.) What minimum altitude should be used for a go-ahead point at Eckelson in order to arrive at Barnes County Airport at 1,000 feet AGL if the glide ratio is 22:1 in no wind conditions? Use the recommended safety factor.

A— 5,959 feet MSL.
B— 7,960 feet MSL.
C— 9,359 feet MSL.

Use the following steps:

1. *A safety margin is provided to allow for any performance degradation. Use one-half the published L/D ratio for planning purposes. In this case use 11 to 1 (no wind).*

2. *Determine the distance from Eckelson to Barnes County Airport (14.5 SM).*

3. *If 1 SM = 5,280 feet, calculate the total sink in 14.5 SM at a glide ratio of 11:1.*

     5,280 ÷11= 480 feet sink per SM
     480.0 x 14.5 = 6,960.0 feet total sink

4. *Calculate the arrival altitude (MSL) by adding 1,000 feet AGL to the Barnes County elevation of 1,400 feet.*

     1,400 Barnes County elevation
     + 1,000 arrival (AGL)
     ──────
     2,400 arrival (MSL)

5. *Determine the go-ahead minimum by adding total sink to the required arrival altitude.*

     6,960 feet total sink
     + 2,400 feet MSL arrival altitude
     ──────
     9,360 feet MSL go-ahead minimum altitude

(PLT303) — *Soaring Flight Manual*

LTA, LSL

3537. (Refer to Figure 21.) An airship crosses over Minot VORTAC (area 1) at 1056 and over the creek 8 nautical miles south-southeast on Victor 15 at 1108. What should be the approximate position on Victor 15 at 1211?

A— Over Lake Nettie National Wildlife Refuge.
B— Crossing the road east of Underwood.
C— Over the powerlines east of Washburn Airport.

This is a time/speed/distance problem.

1. *The distance is 8 NM (given in the question).*

2. *The time is:*

     11:08 – 10:56 = 12 minutes

3. *Use:* $\dfrac{Distance}{Time}$ *x 60 = Ground speed*

     $\dfrac{8\ NM}{12\ min.}$ *x 60 = 40 knots*

4. *Calculate the distance traveled on the next leg at this speed by 12:11.*

     12:11 – 11:08 = :63 minutes

5. *Use:* $\dfrac{Speed}{60}$ *x Time = Distance*

     $\dfrac{40\ kts}{60\ min.}$ *x 63 min. = 42 NM*

6. *Locate the 8 NM creek and measure an additional 42 NM along V15. You are east of Underwood; it is west of your position. The legs were 8 NM and 42 NM, total 50 NM.*

(PLT012) — *FAA-H-8083-25*

LTA

3558. (Refer to Figure 24.) Determine the magnetic heading for a flight from Majors Airport (area 1) to Winnsboro Airport (area 2). The wind is from 340° at 12 knots, the true airspeed is 36 knots, and the magnetic variation is 6°30'E.

A— 078°.

B— 091°.

C— 101°.

Use the following steps:

1. *Plot the course from Majors Airport to Winnsboro Airport.*

2. *Measure the true course angle at the approximate midpoint of the route (100°).*

3. *Find true heading, using a flight computer:*

   Wind direction is 340° (given in question)
   Wind speed is 12 knots (given in question)
   True course is 100° (found in Step 2)
   True airspeed is 36 knots (given in question)

   Therefore, the true heading is 083°.

4. *Calculate the magnetic heading by subtracting the easterly variation (6°30'E) from the true heading (084°).*

   $$MH = TH \pm VAR$$
   $$MH = 084° - 6°30'E$$
   $$MH = 78°$$

(PLT012) — FAA-H-8083-25

LTA

3569. (Refer to Figure 26, area 5.) A balloon drifts over the town of Eckelson on a magnetic course of 014° at 10 MPH. If wind conditions remain constant, where will the balloon be after 2 hours 30 minutes?

A— Cooperstown airport.

B— West of Dazey.

C— Hannaford.

Use the following steps:

1. *Calculate the distance traveled at 10 MPH during 2-1/2 hours.*

   Distance = Speed x Time
   Distance = 10 MPH x 2.5 H = 25 SM

2. *Locate Eckelson in FAA Figure 27.*

3. *Note that the magnetic variation near Eckelson, as shown on the dashed isogonic line, is 5°E.*

4. *Calculate the true course from the magnetic course:*

   TC ± VAR = MC
   TC – 5° = 14°
   TC = 019°

5. *Plot a true course of 019° from Eckelson extending 25 statute miles. The balloon would be over the town of Hannaford.*

(PLT012) — FAA-H-8083-25

SPO

2099. If an aircraft is consuming 3 gallons of fuel per hour at a cruising altitude of 500 feet and the groundspeed is 45 mph, how much fuel is required to travel 75 SM?

A— 6 gallons.

B— 5 gallons.

C— 3 gallons.

To determine the fuel required for a given flight, the time required for the flight must be known. Time in flight multiplied by rate of consumption gives the quantity of fuel required. For example, a flight of 75 SM at a ground speed of 45 mph requires 1.67 hours (distance divided by ground speed = time). If the plane consumes 3 gallons an hour, the total consumption will be 1.67 x 3, or 5 gallons. (PLT012) — FAA-H-8083-25

SPO

2105. To find the distance flown in a given time, multiply time by

A— groundspeed.

B— indicated airspeed.

C— equivalent airspeed.

Distance D = GS x T: To find the distance flown in a given time, multiply ground speed by time. (PLT012) — FAA-H-8083-25

Answers

3558 [A]	3569 [C]	2099 [B]	2105 [A]

SPO
2101. Given:

True course 050
True Heading...040
True airspeed ....75 kts
Groundspeed...65 kts

Determine the wind direction and speed.

A— 105°; and 16 knots
B— 355°; and 16 knots
C— 355°; and 10 knots

Using an E6-B computer:

1. *Turn compass azimuth so 050° is at the true index.*

2. *Slide board so grommet is on the ground speed arc, 65 knots.*

3. *Determine the wind correction angle (WCA) by comparing course to heading.*
   050° – 040° = 10° left

4. *Plot WCA at TAS arc with a pencil dot, 75 knots.*

5. *Rotate compass azimuth so pencil dot is on the centerline.*

6. *Read wind direction under true index and wind speed as number of units between grommet and pencil dot, 354° and 16 knots.*

Alternate method, using CX-2 computer:

1. *Go to FLIGHT menu, select 5. Act Leg.*

2. *Select 3. Unknown Wind, and enter 40 for THdg input, press ENT.*

3. *GS input 65 knots, press ENT.*

4. *TCrs input 50 for true course, press ENT.*

5. *TAS input 75 for true airspeed, press ENT.*

6. *Read unknown wind direction of 354° at 15.8 kts.*

Alternate method: using logic to find answer.

1. *Picture your true course flying northeast.*

2. *Picture your heading 10 degrees to the north.*

3. *This indicates a crosswind from your left.*

4. *Note your ground speed is lower than your airspeed. This indicates a headwind rather than a tailwind.*

5. *From items 3 and 4 above, the wind can be determined from the northwest.*

6. *Your true airspeed and ground speed are exactly 10 knots apart; since you are crabbed, the wind must be stronger than 10 knots overall.*

7. *You pick answer B because the wind is from the estimated direction, and the speed is above 10 knots.*

8. *Looking at the answer and determining direction and speed, this confirms your assumptions and the correct answer.*

(PLT012) — FAA-H-8083-25

LSL
2222. (Refer to Figure 71, point 1.)

Given:

Departure point................... Georgetown Airport (E36)
Departure time..0637
Winds aloft forecast (FD) at your altitude............1008
Airspeed ....8 kts

At 0755, the aircraft should be

A— over Auburn Airport (AUN).
B— over the town of Auburn.
C— slightly west of the town of Garden Valley.

1. *Calculate time en route:*
   0755 – 0637 = 1:18 = 1.3 hours

2. *Compute distance traveled:*
   Distance = Speed x Time
   8 x 1.3 = 10.4 NM

3. *Plot course of 100° + 180° = 280° out to a distance of 10.4 NM from Georgetown Airport (E36), point 1. The aircraft should be just south of there.*

(PLT012) — FAA-H-8083-25

SPO
2175. Why should you file a VFR flight plan with FSS?

A— You are required to do so when flying beyond 25 NM from an airport.
B— To provide traffic reports with Flight Service.
C— To provide search and rescue in the event of an emergency.

Filing a flight plan is not required by regulations; however, it is a good operating practice, since the information contained in the flight plan can be used in search and rescue in the event of an emergency. (PLT225) — FAA-H-8083-25

Answers

2101 [B]   2222 [A]   2175 [C]

Airspace

Controlled airspace, that is, airspace within which some or all aircraft may be subject to air traffic control, consists of those areas designated as Class A, Class B, Class C, Class D, and Class E airspace.

Much of the controlled airspace begins at either 700 feet or 1,200 feet above the ground. The lateral limits and floors of Class E airspace of 700 feet are defined by a magenta vignette; while the lateral limits and floors of 1,200 feet are defined by a blue vignette if it abuts uncontrolled airspace. Floors other than 700 feet or 1,200 feet are indicated by a number indicating the floor.

Class A — Class A airspace extends from 18,000 feet MSL up to and including FL600 and is not depicted on VFR sectional charts. No flight under visual flight rules (VFR), including VFR-On-Top, is authorized in Class A airspace.

Class B — Class B airspace consists of controlled airspace extending upward from the surface or higher to specified altitudes. Each Class B airspace sector, outlined in blue on the sectional aeronautical chart, is labeled with its delimiting altitudes. On the Terminal Area Chart, each Class B airspace sector is, again, outlined in blue and is labeled with its delimiting arcs, radials, and altitudes. Each Class B airspace location will contain at least one primary airport. An ATC clearance is required prior to operating within Class B airspace. A pilot landing or taking off from one of a group of 12 specific, busy airports must hold at least a Private Pilot Certificate. At other airports, a student pilot may not operate an aircraft on a solo flight within Class B airspace or to, from, or at an airport located within Class B airspace unless both ground and flight instruction has been received from an authorized instructor to operate within that Class B airspace or at that airport, and the flight and ground instruction has been received within that Class B airspace or at the specific airport for which the solo flight is authorized. The student's logbook must be endorsed within the preceding 90 days by the instructor who gave the flight training and the endorsement must specify that the student has been found competent to conduct solo flight operations in that Class B airspace or at that specific airport. Each airplane operating within Class B airspace must be equipped with a two-way radio with appropriate ATC frequencies, and a 4096 code transponder with Mode C automatic altitude-reporting capability.

Class C — All Class C airspace has the same dimensions with minor site variations. They are composed of two circles both centered on the primary airport. The inner circle (now called surface area) has a radius of 5 nautical miles and extends from the surface up to 4,000 feet above the airport. The outer circle (now called shelf area) has a radius of 10 nautical miles and extends vertically from 1,200 feet AGL up to 4,000 feet above the primary airport. In addition to the Class C airspace proper, there is an outer area with a radius of 20 nautical miles and vertical coverage from the lower limits of the radio/radar coverage up to the top of the approach control facility's delegated airspace. Within the outer area, pilots are encouraged to participate but it is not a VFR requirement. Class C airspace service to aircraft proceeding to a satellite airport will be terminated at a sufficient distance to allow time to change to the appropriate tower or advisory frequency. Aircraft departing satellite airports within Class C airspace shall establish two-way communication with ATC as soon as practicable after takeoff. On aeronautical charts, Class C airspace is depicted by solid magenta lines.

Class D — Class D airspace extends upward from the surface to approximately 2,500 feet AGL (the actual height is as needed). Class D airspace may include one or more airports and is normally 4 nautical miles in radius. The actual size and shape is depicted by a blue dashed line and numbers showing the top. When the ceiling of Class D airspace is less than 1,000 feet and/or the visibility is less than 3 statute miles, pilots wishing to take off or land must hold an instrument rating, must have filed an instrument flight plan, and must have received an appropriate clearance from ATC. In addition, the aircraft must be equipped for instrument flight. At some locations, a pilot who does not hold an instrument rating may be authorized to take off or land when the weather is less than that required for visual flight rules. When special VFR flight is prohibited, it will be depicted by "No SVFR" above the airport information on the chart.

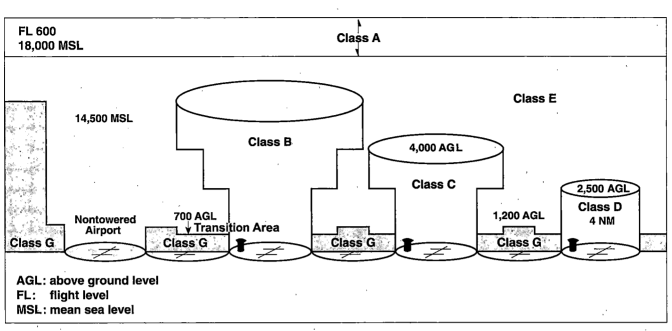

Figure 9-19

Class E — Magenta shading identifies Class E airspace starting at 700 feet AGL, and no shading (or blue if next to Class G airspace) identifies Class E airspace starting at 1,200 feet AGL. It may also start at other altitudes. All airspace from 14,500 feet to 17,999 feet is Class E airspace. It also includes the surface area of some airports with an instrument approach but no control tower.

An **airway** is a corridor of controlled airspace extending from 1,200 feet above the surface (or as designated) up to and including 17,999 feet MSL, and 4 nautical miles either side of the centerline. The airway is indicated by a centerline, shown in blue.

Class G — Class G airspace is airspace within which Air Traffic Control (ATC) has neither the authority nor responsibility to exercise any control over air traffic. Class G airspace typically extends from the surface to the base of the overlying controlled (Class E) airspace which is normally 700 or 1,200 feet AGL. In some areas of the western U.S. and Alaska, Class G airspace may extend from the surface to 14,500 feet MSL. An exception to this rule occurs when 14,500 feet MSL is lower than 1,500 feet AGL.

Prohibited Areas are blocks of airspace within which the flight of aircraft is prohibited.

Restricted Areas denote the presence of unusual, often invisible, hazards to aircraft such as artillery firing, aerial gunnery, or guided missiles. Penetration of Restricted Areas without authorization of the using or controlling agency may be extremely hazardous to the aircraft and its occupants.

Warning Areas contain the same hazardous activities as those found in Restricted Areas, but are located in international airspace. Prohibited, restricted, or warning areas are depicted as shown in FAA Legend 1.

Military Operations Areas (MOAs) consist of airspace established for the purpose of separating certain military training activities from instrument flight rules (IFR) traffic. Pilots operating under VFR should exercise extreme caution while flying within an active MOA. Any Flight Service Station (FSS) within 100 miles of the area will provide information concerning MOA hours of operation. Prior to entering an active MOA, pilots should contact the controlling agency for traffic advisories.

Continued

Alert Areas may contain a high volume of pilot training activities or an unusual type of aerial activity, neither of which is hazardous to aircraft. Pilots of participating aircraft as well as pilots transiting the area are equally responsible for collision avoidance.

Aircraft are requested to remain at least 2,000 feet above the surface of National Parks, National Monuments, Wilderness and Primitive Areas, and National Wildlife Refuges.

Military Training Routes (MTRs) have been developed for use by the military for the purpose of conducting low-altitude, high-speed training. Generally, MTRs are established below 10,000 feet MSL for operations at speeds in excess of 250 knots.

IFR Military Training Routes (IR) operations are conducted in accordance with instrument flight rules (IFRs), regardless of weather conditions. **VFR Military Training Routes (VR)** operations are conducted in accordance with visual flight rules (VFRs). IR and VR at and below 1,500 feet AGL (with no segment above 1,500) will be identified by four digit numbers, e.g., VR1351, IR1007. IR and VR above and below 1,500 feet AGL (segments of these routes may be below 1,500) will be identified by three digit numbers, e.g., IR341, VR426.

ALL, SPO
3599. (Refer to Figure 25, area 4.) The floor of Class B airspace overlying Hicks Airport (T67) north-northwest of Fort Worth Meacham Field is

A— at the surface.
B— 3,200 feet MSL.
C— 4,000 feet MSL.

The thick blue lines on the sectional chart indicate the boundaries of the overlying Class B airspace. Within each segment, the floor and ceiling are denoted by one number over a second number or the letters SFC. The floor of the Class B airspace is 4,000 feet MSL. (PLT040) — AIM ¶3-2-3

ALL, SPO
3600. (Refer to Figure 25, area 2.) The floor of Class B airspace at Addison Airport is

A— at the surface.
B— 3,000 feet MSL.
C— 3,100 feet MSL.

The thick blue lines on the sectional chart indicate the boundaries of the overlying Class B airspace. Within each segment, the floor and ceiling are denoted by one number over a second number or the letters SFC. The floor of the Class B airspace is 3,000 feet MSL. (PLT040) — AIM ¶3-2-3

ALL
3126. What minimum pilot certification is required for operation within Class B airspace?

A— Commercial Pilot Certificate.
B— Private Pilot Certificate or Student Pilot Certificate with appropriate logbook endorsements.
C— Private Pilot Certificate with an instrument rating.

It is generally true that no person may operate a civil aircraft within Class B airspace unless the pilot-in-command holds at least a Private Pilot Certificate or is a student pilot that has the proper logbook endorsements. However, there are certain Class B airports which never permit students, even if they have the proper endorsements. (PLT161) — 14 CFR §91.131

Answer (A) is incorrect because Private pilots may operate in Class B airspace. Answer (C) is incorrect because only some airports restrict student pilots, and none require an instrument rating.

Answers
3599 [C]   3600 [B]   3126 [B]

ALL
3127. What minimum pilot certification is required for operation within Class B airspace?

A— Private Pilot Certificate or Student Pilot Certificate with appropriate logbook endorsements.
B— Recreational Pilot Certificate.
C— Private Pilot Certificate with an instrument rating.

It is generally true that no person may operate a civil aircraft within Class B airspace unless the pilot-in-command holds at least a Private Pilot Certificate or a student pilot has the proper logbook endorsements. However, there are some Class B airports which never permit students, even if they have the proper endorsements. (PLT161) — 14 CFR §61.95, §91.131

Answer (B) is incorrect because the PIC must hold at least a private pilot certificate. Answer (C) is incorrect because an instrument rating is not required to operate within Class B airspace.

ALL
3128. What minimum radio equipment is required for VFR operation within Class B airspace?

A— Two-way radio communications equipment and a 4096-code transponder.
B— Two-way radio communications equipment, a 4096-code transponder, and an encoding altimeter.
C— Two-way radio communications equipment, a 4096-code transponder, an encoding altimeter, and a VOR or TACAN receiver.

Unless otherwise authorized by ATC, no person may operate an aircraft within Class B airspace unless that aircraft is equipped with an operable two-way radio capable of communications with ATC, a transponder with applicable altitude reporting equipment, and an encoding altimeter. (PLT161) — 14 CFR §91.131

ALL
3628. (Refer to Figure 25.) At which airports is fixed-wing Special VFR not authorized?

A— Fort Worth Meacham and Fort Worth Spinks.
B— Dallas-Fort Worth International and Dallas Love Field.
C— Addison and Dallas Executive.

Special VFR operations by fixed-wing aircraft are prohibited in some Class B, C, and D airspaces due to the volume of IFR traffic. These airspaces are depicted by the notation "No SVFR" over the airport information. (PLT064) — AIM ¶4-4-6

ALL, SPO
3117. A blue segmented circle on a Sectional Chart depicts which class airspace?

A— Class B.
B— Class C.
C— Class D.

A blue segmented circle on a sectional chart depicts Class D airspace which means a control tower is in operation. (PLT101) — 14 CFR §1.1

Answer (A) is incorrect because Class B airspace is depicted by a solid blue line. Answer (B) is incorrect because Class C airspace is depicted by a solid magenta line.

ALL, SPO
3118. Airspace at an airport with a part-time control tower is classified as Class D airspace only

A— when the weather minimums are below basic VFR.
B— when the associated control tower is in operation.
C— when the associated Flight Service Station is in operation.

Class D airspace means a control tower is in operation. If the tower closes, it reverts to Class E airspace. (PLT161) — 14 CFR §1.1

Answer (A) is incorrect because weather minimums have nothing to do with airspace classifications. Answer (C) is incorrect because an FSS has nothing to do with the class of airspace.

ALL
3787. The lateral dimensions of Class D airspace are based on

A— the number of airports that lie within the Class D airspace.
B— 5 statute miles from the geographical center of the primary airport.
C— the instrument procedures for which the controlled airspace is established.

The dimensions of Class D airspace are as needed for each individual circumstance. The airspace may include extensions necessary for IFR arrival and departure paths. (PLT161) — AIM ¶3-2-5

Answers

| 3127 | [A] | 3128 | [B] | 3628 | [B] | 3117 | [C] | 3118 | [B] | 3787 | [C] |

ALL
3787-1. When a control tower, located on an airport within Class D airspace, ceases operation for the day, what happens to the airspace designation?

A— The airspace designation normally will not change.

B— The airspace remains Class D airspace as long as a weather observer or automated weather system is available.

C— The airspace reverts to Class E or a combination of Class E and G airspace during the hours the tower is not in operation.

By definition, Class D airspace surrounds airports that have an operational control tower. Class D airspace reverts to Class E airspace (if the weather observer is present or the weather system is automated) or Class G airspace (at the airports where the tower controllers are also the weather observers). (PLT162) — AIM ¶3-2-5

Answer (A) is incorrect because the tower must be operational for the airspace to be designated Class D. Answer (B) is incorrect because the airspace will revert to Class E if the tower is closed but the weather observer is present or an automated weather system is available.

ALL
3788. A non-tower satellite airport, within the same Class D airspace as that designated for the primary airport, requires radio communications be established and maintained with the

A— satellite airport's UNICOM.

B— associated Flight Service Station.

C— primary airport's control tower.

Radio communications must be established and maintained with the primary control tower even when operating to and from a non-tower airport located within the lateral limits of Class D airspace. On takeoff from a satellite airport, communication must be established as soon as practicable after takeoff. (PLT162) — AIM ¶3-2-5

ALL
3124. Two-way radio communication must be established with the Air Traffic Control facility having jurisdiction over the area prior to entering which class airspace?

A— Class C.

B— Class E.

C— Class G.

Two-way radio communication must be established with the ATC facility having jurisdiction over the Class C airspace prior to entry and thereafter as instructed by ATC. (PLT434) — 14 CFR §91.130

Answers (B) and (C) are incorrect because airports within Class E and G airspace only require two-way radio communication when a control tower is present.

ALL, SPO
3799. Which initial action should a pilot take prior to entering Class C airspace?

A— Contact approach control on the appropriate frequency.

B— Contact the tower and request permission to enter.

C— Contact the FSS for traffic advisories.

Radio contact is required to operate in Class C airspace, but permission is not required. (PLT161) — AIM ¶3-2-4

ALL, SPO
3779. The vertical limit of Class C airspace above the primary airport is normally

A— 1,200 feet AGL.

B— 3,000 feet AGL.

C— 4,000 feet AGL.

Class C airspace consists of two circles, both centered on the primary/Class C airspace airport. The surface area has a radius of 5 NM. The shelf area usually has a radius of 10 NM. The airspace of the surface area usually extends from the surface of the Class C airspace airport up to 4,000 feet above that airport. The airspace area between the 5 and 10 NM rings usually begins at a height of 1,200 feet AGL and extends to the same altitude cap as the inner circle. These dimensions may be varied to meet individual situations. (PLT161) — AIM ¶3-2-4

Answers

3787-1 [C]	3788 [C]	3124 [A]	3799 [A]	3779 [C]

ALL, SPO

3780. The radius of the procedural Outer Area of Class C airspace is normally

A— 10 NM.
B— 20 NM.
C— 30 NM.

The normal radius of the outer area will be 20 NM. (PLT161) — AIM ¶3-2-4

ALL

3781. All operations within Class C airspace must be in

A— accordance with instrument flight rules.
B— compliance with ATC clearances and instructions.
C— an aircraft equipped with a 4096-code transponder with Mode C encoding capability.

Aircraft operating in Class C airspace must have a Mode C transponder. (PLT161) — AIM ¶3-2-4

Answer (A) is incorrect because visual flight rules are also used within Class C airspace. Answer (B) is incorrect because an ATC clearance is not required to operate within Class C airspace.

ALL

3782. Under what condition may an aircraft operate from a satellite airport within Class C airspace?

A— The pilot must file a flight plan prior to departure.
B— The pilot must monitor ATC until clear of the Class C airspace.
C— The pilot must contact ATC as soon as practicable after takeoff.

For aircraft departing a satellite airport, two-way radio communication must be established as soon as practicable and thereafter maintained with ATC while within the area. (PLT161) — AIM ¶3-2-4

Answers (A) and (B) are incorrect because Class C airspace does not require flight plans, and a pilot must maintain contact with ATC in Class C airspace.

ALL

2122. (Refer to Figure 69.) What minimum equipment is required for a flight from Kleberg Co. Airport (area 7) to Corpus Christi Intl. Airport (area 3)?

A— ADS-B.
B— Two-way radio equipment.
C— Two-way radio and Mode C transponder with altitude reporting equipment.

A flight from Kleberg County Airport to Corpus Christi International requires flight into Class C airspace. This is shown by the magenta circle around Corpus Christi International Airport. Minimum required equipment for flight into Class C airspace is two-way radio and Mode C transponder with automatic altitude reporting equipment. (PLT393) — AIM ¶3-2-4

Answer (A) is incorrect because ADS-B is not required equipment for flight into Class C airspace. Answer (B) is incorrect because besides a two-way radio, a Mode C transponder with altitude reporting equipment is also required.

ALL, SPO

3626. (Refer to Figure 23, area 3.) What is the floor of the Savannah Class C airspace at the shelf area (outer circle)?

A— 1,300 feet AGL.
B— 1,300 feet MSL.
C— 1,700 feet MSL.

Within the outer magenta circle of Savannah Class C airspace, there is a number 41 directly above the number 13. These depict the floor and ceiling of the Class C airspace; the floor being 1,300 feet MSL and the ceiling being 4,100 feet MSL. (PLT161) — AIM ¶3-2-4

ALL

3627. (Refer to Figure 20, area 1.) What minimum radio equipment is required to land and take off at Norfolk International?

A— Mode C transponder and omnireceiver.
B— Mode C transponder and two-way radio.
C— Mode C transponder, omnireceiver, and DME.

Norfolk International is in Class C airspace. To operate within Class C airspace, an aircraft must have (1) two-way communications capability and (2) a Mode C transponder. (PLT064) — AIM ¶3-2-4

Answers

| 3780 | [B] | 3781 | [C] | 3782 | [C] | 2122 | [C] | 3626 | [B] | 3627 | [B] |

ALL
3125. What minimum radio equipment is required for operation within Class C airspace?

A— Two-way radio communications equipment and a 4096-code transponder.
B— Two-way radio communications equipment, a 4096-code transponder, and DME.
C— Two-way radio communications equipment, a 4096-code transponder, and an encoding altimeter.

Class C requires two-way radio communications equipment, a transponder, and an encoding altimeter. (PLT393) — 14 CFR §91.130 and §91.215

ALL
3069. Normal VFR operations in Class D airspace with an operating control tower require the ceiling and visibility to be at least

A— 1,000 feet and 1 mile.
B— 1,000 feet and 3 miles.
C— 2,500 feet and 3 miles.

Except as provided in 14 CFR §91.157, no person may operate an aircraft, under VFR, within the lateral boundaries of the surface areas of Class B, Class C, Class D, or Class E airspace designated for an airport when the ceiling is less than 1,000 feet. The flight visibility and cloud clearance for VFR operations in Class D airspace is 3 statute miles visibility, and 500 feet below, 1,000 feet above, 2,000 feet horizontal from all clouds. (PLT163) — 14 CFR §91.155

ALL
3119. Unless otherwise authorized, two-way radio communications with Air Traffic Control are required for landings or takeoffs

A— at all tower controlled airports regardless of weather conditions.
B— at all tower controlled airports only when weather conditions are less than VFR.
C— at all tower controlled airports within Class D airspace only when weather conditions are less than VFR.

No person may operate an aircraft to, from, or on an airport having a control tower operated by the United States unless two-way radio communications are maintained between that aircraft and the control tower. (PLT044) — 14 CFR §91.126, §91.127, and §91.129

ALL, SPO
3625. (Refer to Figure 25, area 4.) The airspace directly overlying Fort Worth Meacham is

A— Class B airspace to 10,000 feet MSL.
B— Class C airspace to 5,000 feet MSL.
C— Class D airspace to 3,200 feet MSL.

A blue segmented circle depicts Class D airspace which extends from the surface to 3,200 feet MSL, in this case as shown by the blue number 32 surrounded by the blue segmented box. (PLT101) — AIM ¶3-2-5

Answer (A) is incorrect because although Class B airspace does overlie Fort Worth Meacham to 10,000 feet MSL, its base is 4,000 feet MSL. Answer (B) is incorrect because Class C airspace does not exist around Fort Worth Meacham.

ALL, SPO
3421. (Refer to Figure 59, area 3.) The airspace directly overlying the town of Findlay is

A— Class E airspace from 700 feet AGL.
B— surface area Class E airspace.
C— Class E airspace from 1,200 feet AGL.

The town of Findlay is outlined in yellow just north of Findlay (FDY) Airport. Findlay's magenta segmented line depicts surface area Class E airspace. (PLT101) — FAA-H-8083-25

ALL, SPO
3068. Unless otherwise specified, Federal Airways include that Class E airspace extending upward from

A— 700 feet above the surface up to and including 17,999 feet MSL.
B— 1,200 feet above the surface up to and including 17,999 feet MSL.
C— the surface up to and including 18,000 feet MSL.

Federal airways are part of Class B, C, D, or E airspace. They are eight miles wide, four miles either side of centerline. They usually begin at 1,200 AGL and continue up to but not including 18,000 feet MSL, or FL180. (PLT161) — 14 CFR §71.71

Answers
3125 [C]   3069 [B]   3119 [A]   3625 [C]   3421 [B]   3068 [B]

ALL

3068-1. With certain exceptions, Class E airspace extends upward from either 700 feet or 1,200 feet AGL to, but does not include,

A— 10,000 feet MSL.
B— 14,500 feet MSL.
C— 18,000 feet MSL.

Class E airspace extends upward to (but not including) 18,000 feet MSL. (PLT161) — 14 CFR §71.71

ALL, SPO

3068-2. (Refer to Figure 20, area 1.) The NALF Fentress (NFE) Airport is in what type of airspace?

A— Class C.
B— Class E.
C— Class G.

The Nalf Fentress (NFE) airport is halfway between areas 1 and 2 in Figure 20. It is inside a magenta dashed line indicating Class E airspace starts at the surface. (PLT064) — AIM ¶3-2-6

Answer (A) is incorrect because Class C airspace is indicated with a solid magenta line. Answer (C) is incorrect because Class G airspace would be indicated with solid (shaded) magenta or blue lines.

ALL, SPO

3629. (Refer to Figure 22, area 3.) The vertical limits of that portion of Class E airspace designated as a Federal Airway over Magee Airport are

A— 700 feet MSL to 12,500 feet MSL.
B— 7,500 feet MSL to 17,999 feet MSL.
C— 1,200 feet AGL to 17,999 feet MSL.

The VOR and L/MF Airway System consists of airways designated from 1,200 feet above the surface (in some instances higher) up to, but not including, 18,000 feet MSL. (PLT064) — AIM ¶3-2-6

ALL, SPO

3622. (Refer to Figure 26, area 1.) Identify the airspace over Tomlinson Airport.

A— Class G airspace – surface up to but not including 18,000 feet MSL.
B— Class G airspace – surface up to but not including 1,200 feet AGL, Class E airspace – 1,200 feet AGL up to but not including 18,000 feet MSL.
C— Class G airspace – surface up to but not including 700 feet MSL, Class E airspace – 700 feet to 14,500 feet MSL.

The blue shading in the bottom left corner of Figure 26 indicates Tomlinson Airport lies in Class G airspace from the surface to 1,200 feet AGL, and Class E airspace from 1,200 feet AGL to 18,000 feet MSL. The blue shading of the Victor airways indicates Class E airspace from 1,200 feet AGL. (PLT161) — AIM ¶3-2-1

ALL, SPO

3623. (Refer to Figure 26, area 5.) The airspace overlying and within 5 miles of Barnes County Airport is

A— Class D airspace from the surface to the floor of the overlying Class E airspace.
B— Class E airspace from the surface to 1,200 feet MSL.
C— Class G airspace from the surface to 700 feet AGL.

The Barnes County Airport is depicted inside the magenta shading, which is controlled airspace from 700 feet AGL up to but not including 18,000 feet. Therefore, the airspace below 700 feet AGL is Class G. (PLT040) — AIM ¶3-2-1

ALL, SPO

3624. (Refer to Figure 25, area 7.) The airspace overlying Collin Co RGL McKinney (TKI) is controlled from the surface to

A— 2,500 feet MSL.
B— 2,900 feet MSL.
C— 700 feet AGL.

The [29] indicates the Class D airspace around McKinney (TKI) goes from the surface to 2,900 feet MSL. (PLT101) — AIM ¶3-2-1

Answers

| 3068-1 [C] | 3068-2 [B] | 3629 [C] | 3622 [B] | 3623 [C] | 3624 [B] |

ALL, SPO

3601. (Refer to Figure 20, area 4.) What hazards to aircraft may exist in restricted areas such as R-5302B?

A— Military training activities that necessitate acrobatic or abrupt flight maneuvers.
B— Unusual, often invisible, hazards such as aerial gunnery or guided missiles.
C— High volume of pilot training or an unusual type of aerial activity.

Restricted areas denote the presence of unusual, often invisible, hazards to aircraft such as artillery firing, aerial gunnery, or guided missiles. Penetration of restricted areas without authorization of the using or controlling agency may be extremely hazardous to the aircraft and its occupants. (PLT064) — AIM ¶3-4-3

Answer (A) is incorrect because this defines a military operations area. Answer (C) is incorrect because this defines an alert area.

ALL, SPO

3602. (Refer to Figure 26, area 2.) What hazards to aircraft may exist in areas such as Devils Lake East MOA?

A— Unusual, often invisible, hazards to aircraft such as artillery firing, aerial gunnery, or guided missiles.
B— High volume of pilot training or an unusual type of aerial activity.
C— Military training activities that necessitate acrobatic or abrupt flight maneuvers.

A Military Operations Area (MOA) contains military training activities such as aerobatics, and calls for extreme caution. (PLT393) — AIM ¶3-4-5

ALL

3783. Under what condition, if any, may pilots fly through a restricted area?

A— When flying on airways with an ATC clearance.
B— With the controlling agency's authorization.
C— Regulations do not allow this.

Restricted areas can be penetrated but only with the permission of the controlling agency. No person may operate an aircraft within a restricted area contrary to the restrictions imposed unless he/she has the permission of the using or controlling agency as appropriate. Penetration of restricted areas without authorization from the using or controlling agency may be fatal to the aircraft and its occupants. (PLT393) — AIM ¶3-4-3

ALL

3783-1. Flight through a restricted area should not be accomplished unless the pilot has

A— filed an IFR flight plan.
B— received prior authorization from the controlling agency.
C— received prior permission from the commanding officer of the nearest military base.

Restricted areas denote the existence of unusual, often invisible hazards to aircraft such as artillery firing, aerial gunnery, or guided missiles. Authorization must be received prior to entering any restricted areas. (PLT393) — AIM ¶3-4-3

ALL

3785. What action should a pilot take when operating under VFR in a Military Operations Area (MOA)?

A— Obtain a clearance from the controlling agency prior to entering the MOA.
B— Operate only on the airways that transverse the MOA.
C— Exercise extreme caution when military activity is being conducted.

Pilots operating under VFR should exercise extreme caution while flying within a MOA when military activity is being conducted. No clearance is necessary to enter a MOA. (PLT393) — AIM ¶3-4-5

ALL

3786. Responsibility for collision avoidance in an alert area rests with

A— the controlling agency.
B— all pilots.
C— Air Traffic Control.

All activity within an Alert Area shall be conducted in accordance with FAA regulations, without waiver, and pilots of participating aircraft, as well as pilots transiting the area, shall be equally responsible for collision avoidance. (PLT444) — AIM ¶3-4-6

Answers

3601 [B]	3602 [C]	3783 [B]	3783-1 [B]	3785 [C]	3786 [B]

ALL
3603. (Refer to Figure 21, area 3.) What type military flight operations should a pilot expect along IR 644?

A— IFR training flights above 1,500 feet AGL at speeds in excess of 250 knots.
B— VFR training flights above 1,500 feet AGL at speeds less than 250 knots.
C— Instrument training flights below 1,500 feet AGL at speeds in excess of 150 knots.

IR644 begins at the lower left (eastbound) and turns northeast as a thin gray line. IR644 has three digits, which mean: generally above 1,500 feet AGL (but some segments below), operations under IFR, and (as with all MTRs) may be over 250 knots. (PLT064) — AIM ¶3-5-2

ALL, SPO
3618. (Refer to Figure 26, area 3.) When flying over Arrowwood National Wildlife Refuge, a pilot should fly no lower than

A— 2,000 feet AGL.
B— 2,500 feet AGL.
C— 3,000 feet AGL.

All aircraft are requested to maintain a minimum altitude of 2,000 feet above the surface of national parks, monuments, seashores, lakeshores, recreation areas, and scenic riverways administered by the National Park Service, National Wildlife Refuges, Big Game Refuges, Game Ranges and Wildlife Ranges administered by the U.S. Fish and Wildlife Service, and Wilderness and Primitive areas administered by the U.S. Forest Service. (PLT376) — AIM ¶7-4-6

ALL
3831. Pilots flying over a national wildlife refuge are requested to fly no lower than

A— 1,000 feet AGL.
B— 2,000 feet AGL.
C— 3,000 feet AGL.

All aircraft are requested to maintain a minimum altitude of 2,000 feet above the surface of the following: national parks, monuments, seashores, lakeshores, recreation areas and scenic riverways administered by the National Park Service, National Wildlife Refuges, Big Game Refuges, Game Ranges and Wildlife Ranges administered by the U.S. Fish and Wildlife Service, and Wilderness and Primitive areas administered by the U.S. Forest Service. (PLT064) — AIM ¶7-4-6

AIR, GLI, WSC, PPC
3130. In which type of airspace are VFR flights prohibited?

A— Class A.
B— Class B.
C— Class C.

No person may operate an aircraft within Class A airspace unless that aircraft is operated under IFR at a specific flight level assigned by ATC. (PLT161) — 14 CFR §91.135

LTA, LSL
3784. A balloon flight through a restricted area is

A— permitted at certain times, but only with prior permission by the appropriate authority.
B— permitted anytime, but caution should be exercised because of high-speed military aircraft.
C— never permitted.

Restricted areas can be penetrated but only with the permission of the controlling agency. No person may operate an aircraft within a restricted area contrary to the restrictions imposed unless he/she has the permission of the using or controlling agency as appropriate. Penetration of restricted areas without authorization from the using or controlling agency may be fatal to the aircraft and its occupants. (PLT393) — AIM ¶3-4-3

SPO
2192. Which is true regarding flight operations in Class B airspace?

A— The pilot must receive an ATC clearance before operating an aircraft in that area.
B— Flight under VFR is not authorized unless the pilot in command is instrument rated.
C— Solo student pilot operations are not authorized.

No person may operate an aircraft within Class B airspace unless the operator first receives an ATC clearance from the ATC facility having jurisdiction for that area. (PLT162) — 14 CFR §91.131

Answer (B) is incorrect because a Private pilot certificate without an instrument rating is sufficient to operate in Class B airspace. Answer (C) is incorrect because with the proper training and endorsements, a student pilot may operate in Class B airspace.

Answers

| 3603 | [A] | 3618 | [A] | 3831 | [B] | 3130 | [A] | 3784 | [A] | 2192 | [A] |

SPO
2193. Which is true regarding flight operations in Class B airspace?

A— The pilot in command must hold at least a private pilot certificate with an instrument rating.
B— The pilot in command must hold at least a student pilot certificate.
C— The aircraft must be equipped with an ATC transponder and altitude reporting equipment.

You may not operate an aircraft in Class B airspace unless the aircraft is equipped with an operating transponder and automatic altitude reporting equipment or you have requested a waiver at least one hour before the proposed operation. Both 14 CFR §§91.130 and 91.131 have provisions to allow any aircraft to operate in the airspace without transponders. (PLT162) — 14 CFR §91.131

Answer (A) is incorrect because a private pilot certificate without an instrument rating is sufficient to operate in Class B airspace. Answer (B) is incorrect because Class B airspace requires the pilot-in-command hold a private pilot certificate or have a logbook endorsement confirming that the necessary training was received.

SPO
2043. Which is true regarding flight operations to a satellite airport, without an operating control tower, within Class C airspace?

A— Prior to entering that airspace, a Sport Pilot must contact the FSS.
B— Prior to entering that airspace, a Sport Pilot must contact the primary airport tower.
C— Prior to entering that airspace, a Sport Pilot must receive the appropriate logbook endorsement.

A Sport Pilot must receive ground training and a logbook endorsement to operate in Class B, C, and D airspace. (PLT162) — 14 CFR §61.94

Answer (A) is incorrect because airports in Class C airspace have a control tower; all communications must be established with this facility, not FSS. Answer (B) is incorrect because the Sport Pilot must first have specific ground training and a logbook endorsement before attempting to enter Class C airspace.

SPO
2049. What designated airspace associated with an airport becomes inactive when the control tower at that airport is not in operation?

A— Class D, which then becomes Class C.
B— Class D, which then becomes Class E.
C— Class B.

Class D airspace means a control tower is in operation. If the tower closes, it reverts to Class E airspace. (PLT161) — 14 CFR §1.1

SPO
2050. (Refer to Figure 70, point 5) What minimum altitude is required to avoid the Livermore Airport (LVK) Class D airspace?

A— 2,503 feet MSL.
B— 2,901 feet MSL.
C— 3,297 feet MSL.

The Class D airspace at Livermore has a top of 2,900 feet MSL, indicated by the [29] within the blue segmented circle. Therefore, the minimum altitude to fly over and avoid the Class D airspace is 2,901 feet MSL. (PLT040) — AIM ¶3-2-5

Answer (A) is incorrect because 2,503 feet MSL would place you within the Class D airspace. Answer (C) is incorrect because although 3,297 feet MSL would keep you outside the Class D airspace, it is not the minimum altitude required to avoid it.

SPO
2052. The purpose of Military Training Routes, charted as VFR Military Training Routes (VR) and IFR Military Training Routes (IR) on sectional charts, is to ensure the greatest practical level of safety for all flight operations and to allow the military to conduct

A— low altitude, high-speed training.
B— radar instrument training.
C— air-to-air refueling training.

The military services must train in a wide range of airborne tactics. One phase of this training involves "low level" combat tactics. The required maneuvers and high speeds are such that they may occasionally make the see-and-avoid aspect of VFR flight more difficult without increased vigilance in areas containing such operations. In an effort to ensure the greatest practical level of safety for all flight operations, the Military Training Route (MTR) program was conceived. (PLT116) — AIM ¶3-5-2

Answers

| 2193 | [C] | 2043 | [C] | 2049 | [B] | 2050 | [B] | 2052 | [A] |

SPO
2056. Who is responsible for collision avoidance in a Military Operations Area (MOA)?

A— Each pilot.
B— ATC controllers.
C— Military controllers.

Pilots operating under VFR should exercise extreme caution while flying within a MOA when military activity is being conducted. No clearance is necessary to enter a MOA. (PLT162) — AIM ¶3-4-5

SPO
2059. (Refer to Figure 24, point 6) The floor of the Class E airspace over the town of Commerce is

A— 1,200 feet MSL.
B— 700 feet AGL.
C— 1,200 feet AGL.

The magenta shading around Commerce indicates the floor of the Class E airspace starts 700 feet above the surface. (PLT064) — Sectional Chart

Answers (A) and (C) are incorrect because 1,200 feet AGL (not MSL) is indicated with blue shading.

SPO
2198. Which is true concerning the colors used to depict airports on Sectional Aeronautical Charts?

A— Airports with control towers underlying Class D and E airspace are magenta.
B— Airports with control towers are shown in magenta.
C— Airports with control towers are shown in blue.

Reference FAA Legend 1 in the Computer Testing Supplement. Airports having control towers are shown in blue, all others in magenta. (PLT064) — Sectional Chart

SPO
2115. (Refer to Figure 71, point 6) Sky Way Airport is

A— an airport restricted to use by private and recreational pilots.
B— a restricted military stage field within restricted airspace.
C— a nonpublic use airport.

The "Pvt" after the airport names indicates Sky Way airport is a restricted or non-public use airport. (PLT064) — Sectional Chart

Answer (A) is incorrect because the R in the circle indicates the airport is a nonpublic-use airport. Answer (B) is incorrect because the blue box near Sky Way airport indicates an alert area.

SPO
2204. (Refer to Figure 71, point 1.) The floor of the Class E airspace above Georgetown Airport (E36) is at

A— the surface.
B— 700 feet AGL.
C— 3,823 feet MSL.

Georgetown Airport is outside the magenta shaded area, which indicates the floor of Class E airspace is at 1,200 feet AGL. The airport elevation is given in the airport data as 2,623 feet MSL. Therefore, the Class E airspace above Georgetown Airport is 3,823 feet MSL (2,623 + 1,200). (PLT064) — Sectional Chart

Answer (A) is incorrect because Class E airspace begins at the surface only when surrounded by a magenta segmented circle. Answer (B) is incorrect because Class E airspace begins at 700 feet AGL inside the magenta shaded areas.

SPO
2138. (Refer to Figure 22, area 1.) The visibility and cloud clearance requirements for a Sport Pilot to operate over Sandpoint Airport at less than 700 feet AGL are

A— 3 miles and clear of clouds.
B— 1 mile and 1,000 feet above, 500 feet below, and 2,000 feet horizontally from each cloud.
C— 3 miles and 1,000 feet above, 500 feet below, and 2,000 feet horizontally from each cloud.

The Sandpoint Airport Class E airspace starts at 700 feet AGL (indicated by the magenta shading). Class G airspace exists below this. The Sport Pilot clearance requirements are 3 miles visibility and clear of clouds. (PLT163) — 14 CFR §61.315

SPO
2179. Airports with control towers are shown in

A— magenta.
B— blue.
C— brown.

Reference FAA Legend 1. Airports having control towers are shown in blue, all others in magenta. (PLT064) — Sectional Chart

Answers

| 2056 | [A] | 2059 | [B] | 2198 | [C] | 2115 | [C] | 2204 | [C] | 2138 | [A] |
| 2179 | [B] | | | | | | | | | | |

SPO
2055-1. (Refer to Figure 26.) The Devils Lake East MOA (area 1) is a

A— meteorological observation area.
B— military observation area.
C— military operations area.

A military operations area (MOA) contains military training activities such as aerobatics, and calls for extreme caution. (PLT064) — AIM ¶3-4-5

SPO
2367. (Refer to Figure 26.) The floor of the Class E airspace over the Jamestown airport is

A— surface.
B— 700 feet AGL.
C— 1,200 feet AGL.

The magenta shading around Jamestown indicates the floor of the Class E airspace starts 700 feet above the surface. The dashed area means the Class E goes all the way to the surface (PLT064) — Sectional Chart

Answer (B) is incorrect because 700 feet AGL is indicated with magenta shading; however, there is a dashed line as well near the airport bringing Class E to the surface. Answer (C) is incorrect because 1,200 feet AGL would require blue shading around the airport.

SPO
2113-1. (Refer to Figure 25, area 7.) What is the base of Class B airspace at Air Park-Dallas (F69)?

A— 3000.
B— 4000.
C— 1700.

The thick blue lines on the sectional chart indicate the boundaries of the overlying Class B airspace. Within each segment, the floor and ceiling are denoted by one number over a second number or the letters SFC. The floor of the Class B airspace at F69 airport is 3,000 feet MSL. (PLT011) — AIM ¶3-2-3

SPO
2138-1. (Refer to Figure 75.) The airspace surrounding the Gila Bend AF AUX Airport (GXF) (area 6) is classified as Class

A— B.
B— C.
C— D.

The GXF airport is surrounded by a dashed blue line which indicates it is within Class D airspace. (PLT040) — Sectional Chart

SPO
2138-2. (Refer to Figure 22.) Weather information is available at the Coeur d'Alene (COE) Airport (area 2)

A— over the nearest VOR.
B— from AWOS 3 135.075.
C— from UNICOM (CTAF) on 122.8.

Automated Surface Weather Observing System (AWOS) is available on 135.075. (PLT116) — Sectional Chart Legend

---

Answers

2055-1 [C]   2367 [A]   2113-1 [A]   2138-1 [C]   2138-2 [B]

Chapter 10
Navigation

VHF Omnidirectional Range (VOR)

The **VHF Omnidirectional Range (VOR)** is the backbone of the National Airway System, and this radio aid to navigation (**NAVAID**) provides guidance to pilots operating under visual flight rules as well as those flying instruments.

On sectional aeronautical charts, VOR locations are shown by blue symbols centered in a blue compass rose which is oriented to Magnetic North. A blue identification box adjacent to the VOR symbol lists the name and frequency of the facility, its three-letter identifier and Morse Code equivalent, and other information as appropriate. For example: a small solid blue square in the bottom right hand corner indicates Hazardous Inflight Weather Advisory Service (HIWAS) are available. *See* the "Radio Aids to Navigation and Communications Box" information in FAA Legend 1.

Some VORs have a voice identification alternating with the Morse Code identifier. Absence of the identifier indicates the facility is unreliable or undergoing routine maintenance; in either case, it should not be used for navigation. Some VORs also transmit a T-E-S-T code when undergoing maintenance.

The VOR station continuously transmits navigation signals, providing 360 magnetic courses to or radials from the station. Courses are TO the station and radials are FROM the station.

TACAN, a military system which provides directional guidance, also informs the pilot of the aircraft's distance from the TACAN Station. When a VOR and a TACAN are co-located, the facility is called a VORTAC. Civil pilots may receive both azimuth and distance information from a VORTAC.

At some VOR sites, additional equipment has been installed to provide pilots with distance information. Such an installation is termed a VOR/DME (for "distance measuring equipment").

AIR, RTC
3643. (Refer to Figure 25, area 5.) The navigation facility at Dallas-Ft. Worth International (DFW) is a

A— VOR.
B— VORTAC.
C— VOR/DME.

Reference FAA Legend 1. There is a VOR/DME at DFW. (PLT101) — Sectional Chart Legend

VOR Orientation

Cockpit display of VOR information is by means of an indicator as shown in Figure 10-1.

The **Omni Bearing Selector (OBS)** is an azimuth dial which can be rotated to select a course or to determine which radial the aircraft is on. The **TO/FROM indicator** shows whether flying the selected course would take the aircraft to or from the VOR station. A TO indication shows the radial selected is on the far side of the VOR station, while a FROM indication means the aircraft and the selected course are on the same side.

The **Course Deviation Indicator (CDI)**, when centered, indicates the aircraft is on the selected course, or, when not centered, whether that course is to the left or right of the aircraft. For example,

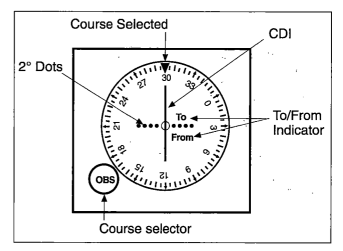

Figure 10-1. The VOR indicator

Answers
3643 [C]

Figure 10-2 is indicating that a course of 030° would take the aircraft to the selected station, and to get on that course, the aircraft would have to fly to the left of 030°.

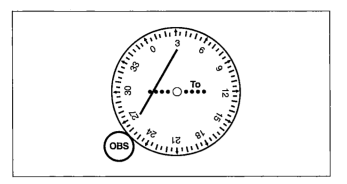

Figure 10-2. Interpreting the OBS and CDI indications

To determine position in relation to one or more VOR stations, first tune and identify the selected station. Next, rotate the OBS until the CDI centers with a FROM indication. The OBS reading is the magnetic course from the VOR station to the aircraft. With reference to Figure 10-3, the line of position is established on the 265° radial of the XYZ VOR.

Repeat the procedure using a second VOR. The aircraft is located at the point where the two lines of position cross. *See* Figure 10-4.

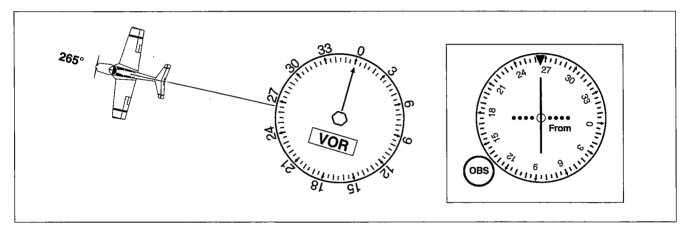

Figure 10-3. Aircraft on the 265° radial of a VOR

AIR, RTC

3552. (Refer to Figure 23.) What is the approximate position of the aircraft if the VOR receivers indicate the 320° radial of Savannah VORTAC (area 3) and the 184° radial of Allendale VOR (area 1)?

A— Southeast of Guyton.
B— Town of Springfield.
C— Over Briggs Airport.

Use the following steps:

1. *Plot the 320° radial (magnetic course FROM) of the Savannah VORTAC.*

2. *Plot the 184° radial of the Allendale VOR.*

3. *Note the intersection of the two plotted radials southeast of the town of Guyton.*

(PLT335) — FAA-H-8083-25

AIR, RTC

3559. (Refer to Figure 24.) What is the approximate position of the aircraft if the VOR receivers indicate the 245° radial of Sulphur Springs VOR-DME (area 5) and the 140° radial of Bonham VORTAC (area 3)?

A— Weese Intl. Airport.
B— Glenmar Airport.
C— Majors Airport.

Use the following steps:

1. *Plot the 245° radial (magnetic course FROM) of the Sulphur Springs VOR-DME.*

2. *Plot the 140° radial (magnetic course FROM) of the Bonham VORTAC.*

3. *Note the intersection of the two plotted radials over the Glenmar Airport (Pvt).*

(PLT101) — FAA-H-8083-25

Answers
3552 [A]   3559 [B]

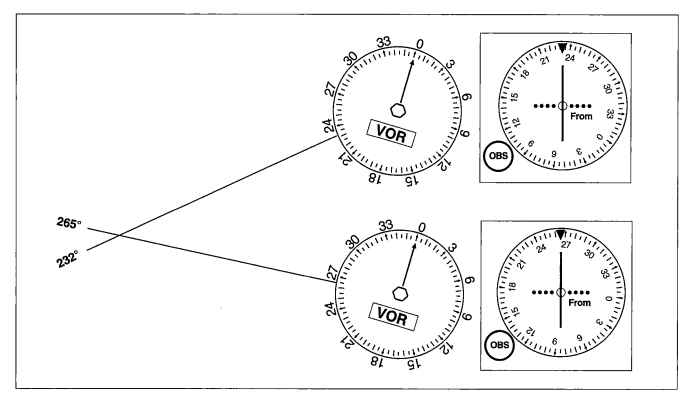

Figure 10-4. VOR orientation using two VORs

AIR, RTC

3566. (Refer to Figure 25, area 5.) The VOR is tuned to the VOR-DME at the Dallas-Fort Worth airport. The omnibearing selector (OBS) is set on 253°, with a TO indication, and a right course deviation indicator (CDI) deflection. What is the aircraft's position from the VOR-DME?

A— East–northeast.
B— North–northeast.
C— West–southwest.

The course selected is 253° and the TO/FROM indicator has a TO flag, which means the aircraft is south of the course but north of the VOR. The CDI needle is deflected to the right, which means the aircraft is left (or east) of the course. Therefore, the aircraft must be to the east northeast of the station to satisfy the VOR indications. (PLT101) — FAA-H-8083-25

AIR, RTC

3577. (Refer to Figure 28, illustration 4.) The VOR receiver has the indications shown. What is the aircraft's position relative to the station?

A— North.
B— East.
C— South.

The course selected is 210° and the TO/FROM indicator is showing TO with a left deflection. This means the aircraft is right of the course and north of the station. (PLT090) — FAA-H-8083-25

AIR, RTC

3578. (Refer to Figure 28, illustration 7.) The VOR receiver has the indications shown. What is the aircraft's position relative to the station?

A— East.
B— Southeast.
C— West.

Observe from illustration #7 of FAA Figure 28, that there is no TO/FROM indication and the CDI is deflected left with an OBS set on 030°. The aircraft is somewhere along the perpendicular line (120/300°). The CDI left means the 030° radial is to the left, or west, of the aircraft position. Answer B is the only one placing the aircraft on the 120° radial, or southeast of the station. (PLT090) — FAA-H-8083-25

Answers

3566 [A]   3577 [A]   3578 [B]

AIR, RTC
3579. (Refer to Figure 28, illustration 5.) The VOR receiver has the indications shown. What radial is the aircraft crossing?

A— 030°.
B— 210°.
C— 300°.

The CDI is centered with the OBS set to 210° with a TO indication. Therefore, the aircraft is located on the 030° radial. (PLT090) — FAA-H-8083-25

Course Determination

To determine the course to be flown to a VOR station on the sectional aeronautical chart, first draw a line from the starting point to the VOR symbol in the center of the compass rose. At the point where the course line crosses the compass rose, read the radial. The course to the station is the reciprocal of that radial. *See* Figure 10-5.

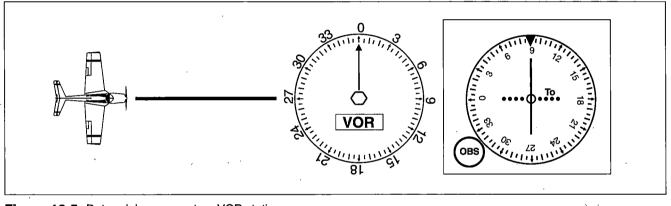

Figure 10-5. Determining course to a VOR station

AIR, RTC
3553. (Refer to Figure 23.) On what course should the VOR receiver (OBS) be set to navigate direct from Hampton Varnville Airport (area 1) to Savannah VOR-TAC (area 3)?

A— 003°.
B— 195°.
C— 200°.

Use the following steps:

1. *Plot the course direct from Hampton Varnville Airport to the Savannah VORTAC.*

2. *Note the radial (magnetic course from Savannah) on which the plotted course lies (015°).*

3. *Determine the course TO the VORTAC by finding the reciprocal:*

   TO = FROM + 180°
   TO = 015° + 180°
   TO = 195°

(PLT064) — FAA-H-8083-25

AIR, RTC
3560. (Refer to Figure 24.) On what course should the VOR receiver (OBS) be set in order to navigate direct from Majors Airport (area 1) to Quitman VOR-DME (area 2)?

A— 101°.
B— 108°.
C— 281°.

Use the following steps:

1. *Plot the course direct from Majors Airport to Quitman VOR-DME.*

2. *Note the radial (magnetic course FROM) of Quitman VOR-DME on which the plotted course lies (281°).*

3. *Determine the course TO the VOR-DME by finding the reciprocal:*

   TO = FROM + 180°
   TO = 281° + 180°
   TO = 461° – 360° = 101°

(PLT090) — FAA-H-8083-25

Answers
3579 [A]   3553 [B]   3560 [A]

AIR, RTC

3533. (Refer to Figure 20, area 3; and Figure 28.) The VOR is tuned to Elizabeth City VOR/DME, and the aircraft is positioned over Shawboro, a small town 3 NM west of Currituck County Regional (ONX). Which VOR indication is correct?

A— 2.
B— 5.
C— 8.

1. Locate the Shawboro Airport and the Elizabeth City VOR in FAA Figure 20. Draw the radial (magnetic course FROM) of the Elizabeth City VOR on which Shawboro lies (030°).

2. When over Shawboro on the 030 radial, the CDI should be centered with a 030 FROM indication or a 210 TO indication (the reciprocal). Dials 5 and 9 satisfy these conditions.

(PLT090) — FAA-H-8083-25

AIR, RTC

3561. (Refer to Figure 24 and Figure 28.) The VOR is tuned to Bonham VORTAC (area 3), and the aircraft is positioned over the town of Sulphur Springs (area 5). Which VOR indication is correct?

A— 1.
B— 7.
C— 8.

Use the following steps:

1. Locate and draw the magnetic course from Bonham VORTAC to Sulphur Springs (120°).

2. Notice that the OBS selections of all the dials in FAA Figure 28 are 030° or 210°, both of which are at 90° with respect to the 120° radial. Therefore, when over Sulphur Springs, the flag should indicate neither TO nor FROM and the course needle should have a full deflection either side.

3. Both dials 3 and 7 of FAA Figure 28 are at 90° from the correct radial of 120°. However, only dial 7 is a valid answer option.

(PLT090) — FAA-H-8083-25

AIR, RTC

3570. (Refer to Figure 26, areas 4 and 2; and Figure 28.) The VOR is tuned to Jamestown VOR, and the aircraft is positioned over Cooperstown Airport. Which VOR indication is correct?

A— 2.
B— 5.
C— 8.

1. Locate the Cooperstown Airport and the Jamestown VOR in FAA Figure 26. Draw the radial (magnetic course FROM) of the Jamestown VOR on which Cooperstown Airport lies (030°).

2. When over Cooperstown Airport on the 030 radial, the CDI should have a 030 FROM indication or a 210 TO indication (the reciprocal). Dial 5 satisfies these conditions.

(PLT090) — FAA-H-8083-25

AIR, RTC

3539. (Refer to Figure 21.) What course should be selected on the omnibearing selector (OBS) to make a direct flight from Mercer County Regional Airport (area 3) to the Minot VORTAC (area 1) with a TO indication?

A— 001°.
B— 359°.
C— 179°.

Use the following steps:

1. Plot a direct course from Mercer Airport to the Minot Airport VORTAC.

2. Note the radial (magnetic course FROM Minot VORTAC) on which the plotted course lies (179°).

3. Determine the course TO Minot VORTAC by finding the reciprocal:

TO = FROM + 180°
TO = 179° + 180°
TO = 359°

(PLT012) — FAA-H-8083-25

Answers

3533	[B]	3561	[B]	3570	[B]	3539	[B]

SPO

2100. True course measurements on a Sectional Aeronautical Chart should be made at a meridian near the midpoint of the course because the

A— values of isogonic lines change from point to point.

B— angles formed by isogonic lines and lines of latitude vary from point to point.

C— angles formed by lines of longitude and the course line vary from point to point.

Sectional Aeronautical Charts are made on grid in which the meridians of longitude are nonparallel straight lines that all meet at the earth's poles. When planning a flight, measure the true course from the mid-meridian to get an average true course. (PLT200) — FAA-H-8083-25

VOR Airways

The routes established between VORs are depicted by blue-tinted bands showing the airway number following the letter "V," and are called "Victor airways." *See* Figure 10-6.

When approaching a VOR where airways converge, a pilot must exercise extreme vigilance for other aircraft. In addition, when climbing or descending VFR on an airway, it is considered good operating practice to execute gentle banks left and right for continuous visual scanning of the airspace.

ALL

3814. What procedure is recommended when climbing or descending VFR on an airway?

A— Execute gentle banks, left and right for continuous visual scanning of the airspace.

B— Advise the nearest FSS of the altitude changes.

C— Fly away from the centerline of the airway before changing altitude.

During climbs and descents in flight conditions which permit visual detection of other traffic, pilots should execute gentle banks, left and right, at a frequency which permits continuous visual scanning of the airspace about them. (PLT125) — AIM ¶4-4-15

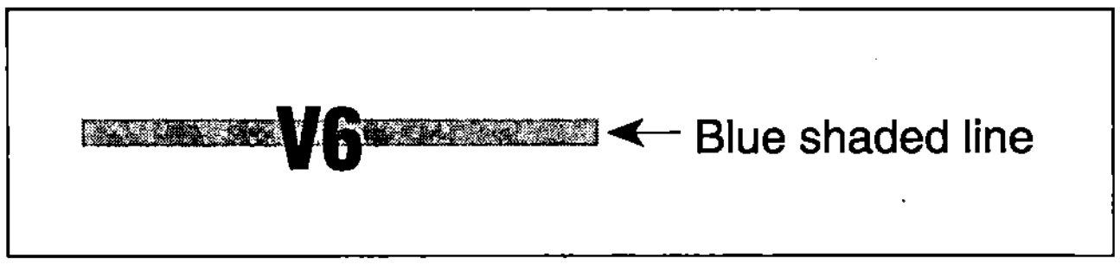

Figure 10-6

Answers

2100   [C]   3814   [A]

VOR Receiver Check Points

VOR receiver accuracy may be checked by means of a VOR Test Facility (VOT), ground check points, or airborne check points.

VOTs transmit only the 360° radial signal. Thus, when the OBS is set to 360°, the CDI will center with a FROM indication; while the reciprocal, 180°, will cause the CDI to center with a TO indication. An accuracy factor of plus or minus 4° is allowed when using a VOT facility.

AIR, RTC

3598-1. When the course deviation indicator (CDI) needle is centered during an omnireceiver check using a VOR test signal (VOT), the omnibearing selector (OBS) and the TO/FROM indicator should read

A— 180° FROM, only if the pilot is due north of the VOT.

B— 0° TO or 180° FROM, regardless of the pilot's position from the VOT.

C— 0° FROM or 180° TO, regardless of the pilot's position from the VOT.

To use the VOT service, tune in the VOT frequency on the VOR receiver. With the CDI centered, the OBS should read 0° with the TO/FROM indication showing "FROM" or the OBS should read 180° with the TO/FROM indication showing "TO." (PLT300) — AIM ¶1-1-4

Global Positioning System (GPS)

GPS is a United States satellite-based radio navigational, positioning, and time transfer system operated by the Department of Defense (DOD). The system provides highly accurate position and velocity information and precise time on a continuous global basis to an unlimited number of properly-equipped users. The GPS constellation of satellites is designed so that a minimum of five are always observable by a user anywhere on earth. The GPS receiver uses data from a minimum of four satellites to yield a three dimensional position (latitude, longitude, and altitude) and time solution.

The GPS receiver verifies the integrity (usability) of the signals received from the GPS satellites through receiver autonomous integrity monitoring (RAIM) to determine if a satellite is providing corrupted information. Without RAIM capability, the pilot has no assurance of the accuracy of the GPS position. If RAIM is not available, another type of navigation and approach system must be used, another destination selected, or the trip delayed until RAIM is predicted to be available on arrival.

ALL
3598-3. If receiver autonomous integrity monitoring (RAIM) capability is lost in flight,

A— the pilot may still rely on GPS derived altitude for vertical information.
B— the pilot has no assurance of the accuracy of the GPS position.
C— GPS position is reliable provided at least 3 GPS satellites are available.

The GPS receiver verifies the integrity (usability) of the signals received from the GPS constellation through receiver autonomous integrity monitoring (RAIM) to determine if a satellite is providing corrupted information. At least one satellite, in addition to those required for navigation, must be in view for the receiver to perform the RAIM function; thus, RAIM needs a minimum of 5 satellites in view, or 4 satellites and a barometric altimeter (baro-aiding) to detect an integrity anomaly. For receivers capable of doing so, RAIM needs 6 satellites in view (or 5 satellites with baro-aiding) to isolate the corrupt satellite signal and remove it from the navigation solution. GPS derived altitude should not be relied upon to determine aircraft altitude since the vertical error can be quite large and no integrity is provided. (PLT354) — AIM ¶1-1-19

ALL
3598-4. How many Global Positioning System (GPS) satellites are required to yield a three dimensional position (latitude, longitude, and altitude) and time solution?

A— 5.
B— 6.
C— 4.

The GPS receiver uses data from a minimum of four satellites to yield a three-dimensional position (latitude, longitude, and altitude) and time solution. (PLT354) — FAA-H-8083-25

Answers
3598-3   [B]   3598-4   [C]

Chapter 11
Communication Procedures

Phraseology, Techniques, and Procedures

Automatic Terminal Information Service (ATIS) is a continuous broadcast of non-control information in selected high-activity terminal areas. To relieve frequency congestion, pilots are urged to listen to ATIS, and on initial contact, to advise controllers that the information has been received by repeating the alphabetical code word appended to the broadcast. For example: "information Sierra received." The phrase "have numbers" does not indicate receipt of the ATIS broadcast.

When transmitting an altitude to ATC (up to but not including 18,000 feet MSL), state the separate digits of the thousands, plus the hundreds. For example, 13,500 is "one three thousand five hundred" and 4,500 is "four thousand five hundred."

At airports with operating air traffic control towers (ATCT), approval must be obtained prior to moving an aircraft onto the movement area. Ground control frequencies are provided to reduce congestion on the tower frequency. They are used for issuance of taxi information, clearances and other necessary contacts. If instructed by ground control to "taxi to" a particular runway, the pilot must stop prior to crossing any runway. A clearance must be obtained prior to crossing any runway.

Aircraft arriving at an airport where a control tower is in operation should not change to ground control frequency until directed to do so by ATC.

The key to operating at an airport without an operating control tower is selection of the correct **Common Traffic Advisory Frequency (CTAF)**. The CTAF is identified in appropriate aeronautical publications and on the sectional chart. If the airport has a part-time air traffic control tower (ATCT), the CTAF is usually a tower frequency. If a flight service station (FSS) is located on the airport, they will usually monitor that frequency and provide advisories when the tower is closed. Where there is no tower or FSS, UNICOM, (if available) is usually the CTAF. UNICOM is limited to the necessities of safe and expeditious operation of private aircraft pertaining to runways and wind conditions, types of fuel available, weather, and dispatching. Secondarily, communications may be transmitted concerning ground transportation, food, lodging and services available during transit. When no tower, FSS, or UNICOM is available, use MULTICOM frequency 122.9 for self-announce procedures. *See* Figure 11-1.

Facility at Airport	Frequency Use	Communication/Broadcast Procedures		
		Outbound	*Inbound*	*Practice Instrument Approach*
1 UNICOM (No Tower or FSS)	Communicate with UNICOM station on published CTAF frequency (122.7, 122.8, 122.725, 122.975, or 123.0). If unable to contact UNICOM station, use self-announce procedures on CTAF.	Before taxiing and before taxiing on the runway for departure.	10 miles out. Entering downwind, base, and final. Leaving the runway.	
2 No Tower, FSS, or UNICOM	Self-announce on MULTICOM frequency 122.9.	Before taxiing and before taxiing on the runway for departure.	10 miles out. Entering downwind, base, and final. Leaving the runway.	Departing final approach fix (name) or on final approach segment inbound.
3 No Tower in operation, FSS open	Communicate with FSS on CTAF frequency.	Before taxiing and before taxiing on the runway for departure.	10 miles out. Entering downwind, base, and final. Leaving the runway.	Approach completed/terminated.
4 FSS closed (No Tower)	Self-announce on CTAF.	Before taxiing and before taxiing on the runway for departure.	10 miles out. Entering downwind, base, and final. Leaving the runway.	
5 Tower or FSS not in operation	Self-announce on CTAF.	Before taxiing and before taxiing on the runway for departure.	10 miles out. Entering downwind, base, and final. Leaving the runway.	

Figure 11-1. Summary of recommended communications procedures

ALL

3613. When flying HAWK N666CB, the proper phraseology for initial contact with McAlester Flight Service is

A— "MC ALESTER RADIO, HAWK SIX SIX SIX CHARLIE BRAVO, RECEIVING ARDMORE VORTAC, OVER."

B— "MC ALESTER STATION, HAWK SIX SIX SIX CEE BEE, RECEIVING ARDMORE VORTAC, OVER."

C— "MC ALESTER FLIGHT SERVICE STATION, HAWK NOVEMBER SIX CHARLIE BRAVO, RECEIVING ARDMORE VORTAC, OVER."

The term "initial radio contact," or "initial callup," means the first radio call you make to a given facility, or the first call to a different controller or Flight Service specialist within a facility. Use the following format:

1. Name of facility being called;

2. Your full aircraft identification as filed in the flight plan;

3. Type of message to follow or your request if it is short, and

4. The word "over," if required.

Example: "New York Radio, Mooney Three One One Echo."

When the aircraft manufacturer's name or model is stated, the prefix "N" is dropped. The first two characters of the call sign may be dropped only after ATC calls you by your last three letters/numbers. (PLT204) — AIM ¶4-2-3

ALL

3614. The correct method of stating 4,500 feet MSL to ATC is

A— "FOUR THOUSAND FIVE HUNDRED."

B— "FOUR POINT FIVE."

C— "FORTY-FIVE HUNDRED FEET MSL."

Up to but not including 18,000 feet MSL, state the separate digits of the thousands, plus the hundreds, if appropriate. Example: "4,500—four thousand, five hundred." (PLT204) — AIM ¶4-2-9

Answers

3613 [A]   3614 [A]

ALL
3615. The correct method of stating 10,500 feet MSL to ATC is

A— "TEN THOUSAND, FIVE HUNDRED FEET."
B— "TEN POINT FIVE."
C— "ONE ZERO THOUSAND, FIVE HUNDRED."

Up to but not including 18,000 feet MSL, state the separate digits of the thousands, plus the hundreds, if appropriate. Example: "10,500—one zero thousand, five hundred." (PLT204) — AIM ¶4-2-9

ALL, SPO
3604. (Refer to Figure 20, area 3.) What is the recommended communications procedure for a landing at Currituck County Airport?

A— Transmit intentions on 122.9 MHz when 10 miles out and give position reports in the traffic pattern.
B— Contact Elizabeth City FSS for airport advisory service.
C— Contact New Bern FSS for area traffic information.

Where there is no tower, Flight Service, or UNICOM station on the airport, use MULTICOM frequency 122.9 for self-announce procedures. Such airports will be identified in the appropriate aeronautical information publications. (PLT435) — AIM ¶4-1-9

ALL
3630. (Refer to Figure 21.) On what frequency can a pilot receive Hazardous Inflight Weather Advisory Service (HIWAS) in the vicinity of area 1?

A— 117.1 MHz.
B— 118.0 MHz.
C— 122.0 MHz.

The reversed-out H in the upper-right corner indicates HIWAS on the VOR frequency. (PLT064) — AIM ¶7-1-9

ALL
3605. (Refer to Figure 21, area 2.) The CTAF/MULTI-COM frequency for Garrison Airport is

A— 122.8 MHz.
B— 122.9 MHz.
C— 123.0 MHz.

Where there is no tower, Flight Service, or UNICOM station on the airport, use MULTICOM frequency 122.9 for self-announce procedures. Such airports will be identified in the appropriate aeronautical information publications. (PLT435) — AIM ¶4-1-9

ALL
3998. When should pilots state their position on the airport when calling the tower for takeoff?

A— When visibility is less than 1 mile.
B— When parallel runways are in use.
C— When departing from a runway intersection.

Pilots should state their position on the airport when calling the tower for takeoff from a runway intersection. (PLT222) — AIM ¶4-3-10

ALL
3605-1. As standard operating practice, all inbound traffic to an airport without a control tower should continuously monitor the appropriate facility from a distance of

A— 25 miles.
B— 20 miles.
C— 10 miles.

Pilots of inbound traffic should monitor and communicate as appropriate on the designated CTAF from 10 miles to landing. Pilots of departing aircraft should monitor/communicate on the appropriate frequency from start-up, during taxi, and until 10 miles from the airport unless the CFRs or local procedures require otherwise. (PLT435) — AIM ¶4-1-9

ALL
3605-2. Absence of the sky condition and visibility on an ATIS broadcast indicates that

A— weather conditions are at or above VFR minimums.
B— the sky condition is clear and visibility is unrestricted.
C— the ceiling is at least 5,000 feet and visibility is 5 miles or more.

The absence of a sky condition or ceiling and/or visibility on ATIS indicates a ceiling of 5,000 feet or above and visibility of 5 miles or more. (PLT196) — AIM ¶4-1-13

Answers

3615	[C]		3604	[A]		3630	[A]	3605	[B]	3998 [C]	3605-1 [C]
3605-2	[C]									

ALL
3606. (Refer to Figure 22, area 2; and Figure 31.) At Coeur D'Alene, which frequency should be used as a Common Traffic Advisory Frequency (CTAF) to self-announce position and intentions?

A— 122.05 MHz.
B— 122.1/108.8 MHz.
C— 122.8 MHz.

CTAF (Common Traffic Advisory Frequency) is a frequency designed for the purpose of carrying out airport advisory practices and/or position reporting at an uncontrolled airport (which may also occur during hours when a tower is closed). The CTAF may be a UNICOM, MULTICOM, FSS, or tower frequency and is identified in the appropriate aeronautical publications. A solid dot with the letter "C" inside indicates the Common Traffic Advisory Frequency. When the control tower operates part time and a UNICOM frequency is provided, use the UNICOM frequency. (PLT064) — AIM ¶4-1-9

ALL, SPO
3607. (Refer to Figure 22, area 2; and Figure 31.) At Coeur D'Alene, which frequency should be used as a Common Traffic Advisory Frequency (CTAF) to monitor airport traffic?

A— 122.05 MHz.
B— 135.075 MHz.
C— 122.8 MHz.

CTAF (Common Traffic Advisory Frequency) is a frequency designed for the purpose of carrying out airport advisory practices and/or position reporting at an uncontrolled airport (which may also occur during hours when a tower is closed). The CTAF may be a UNICOM, MULTICOM, FSS, or tower frequency and is identified in the appropriate aeronautical publications. A solid dot with the letter "C" inside indicates Common Traffic Advisory Frequency. When the control tower operates part time and a UNICOM frequency is provided, use the UNICOM frequency. (PLT064) — AIM ¶4-1-9

SPO
2014. (Refer to Figure 22, area 2; and Figure 31.) What is the correct UNICOM frequency to be used at Coeur D'Alene?

A— 135.075 MHz.
B— 122.05 MHz.
C— 122.8 MHz.

The sectional chart and Chart Supplements U.S. both list the UNICOM frequency as 122.8. The UNICOM frequency is depicted in the airport information in the lower right-hand corner. (PLT064) — AIM ¶4-1-11

Answer (A) is incorrect because 135.075 is used to listen to AWOS. Answer (B) is incorrect because 122.05 is the remote communication outlet (RCO) frequency to contact Boise FSS in the Coeur D'Alene vicinity.

ALL
3608. (Refer to Figure 22, area 2; and Figure 31.) What is the correct UNICOM frequency to be used at Coeur D'Alene to request fuel?

A— 135.075 MHz.
B— 122.1/108.8 MHz.
C— 122.8 MHz.

The sectional chart and Chart Supplements U.S. both list the UNICOM frequency as 122.8. This is the appropriate frequency to use to contact UNICOM. The UNICOM frequency is depicted in the airport information in the lower right-hand corner. (PLT064) — AIM ¶4-1-11

ALL
3609. (Refer to Figure 25, area 3.) If Dallas Executive (RBD) Tower is not in operation, which frequency should be used as a Common Traffic Advisory Frequency (CTAF) to monitor airport traffic?

A— 127.25 MHz.
B— 122.95 MHz.
C— 126.35 MHz.

A solid dot with the letter "C" inside indicates the Common Traffic Advisory Frequency. (PLT064) — AIM ¶4-1-9

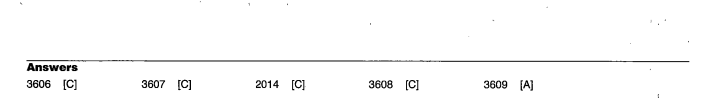

Answers

| 3606 | [C] | 3607 | [C] | 2014 | [C] | 3608 | [C] | 3609 | [A] |

ALL·
3641. (Refer to Figure 25, area 2.) The control tower frequency for Addison Airport is

A— 122.95 MHz.
B— 126.0 MHz.
C— 133.4 MHz.

The correct answer is found in the explanatory box for Addison airport in area 2: 126.0 MHz. (PLT101) — Sectional Chart Legend

ALL
3610. (Refer to Figure 26, area 2.) What is the recommended communication procedure when inbound to land at Cooperstown Airport?

A— Broadcast intentions when 10 miles out on the CTAF/MULTICOM frequency, 122.9 MHz.
B— Contact UNICOM when 10 miles out on 122.8 MHz.
C— Circle the airport in a left turn prior to entering traffic.

MULTICOM frequency is always 122.9 MHz, and the correct procedure is to broadcast intentions when 10 miles from the airport. (PLT064) — AIM ¶4-1-9

ALL·
3611. (Refer to Figure 26, area 4.) The CTAF/UNICOM frequency at Jamestown Airport is

A— 122.0 MHz.
B— 123.0 MHz.
C— 123.6 MHz.

CTAF (Common Traffic Advisory Frequency) is a frequency designed for the purpose of carrying out airport advisory practices and/or position reporting at an uncontrolled airport (which may also occur during hours when a tower is closed). The CTAF may be a UNICOM, MULTICOM, FSS, or tower frequency and is identified in the appropriate aeronautical publications. A solid dot with the letter "C" inside indicates Common Traffic Advisory Frequency; it may be a UNICOM, MULTICOM, FSS, or tower frequency. (PLT064) — AIM ¶4-1-9

ALL
3612. (Refer to Figure 26, area 5.) What is the CTAF/UNICOM frequency at Barnes County Airport?

A— 122.0 MHz.
B— 122.8 MHz.
C— 123.6 MHz.

CTAF (Common Traffic Advisory Frequency) is a frequency designed for the purpose of carrying out airport advisory practices and/or position reporting at an uncontrolled airport (which may also occur during hours when a tower is closed). The CTAF may be a UNICOM, MULTICOM, FSS, or tower frequency and is identified in the appropriate aeronautical publications. A solid dot with the letter "C" inside indicates Common Traffic Advisory Frequency. (PLT064) — AIM ¶4-1-9

ALL
3791. Automatic Terminal Information Service (ATIS) is the continuous broadcast of recorded information concerning

A— pilots of radar-identified aircraft whose aircraft is in dangerous proximity to terrain or to an obstruction.
B— nonessential information to reduce frequency congestion.
C— noncontrol information in selected high-activity terminal areas.

ATIS is the continuous broadcast of recorded non-control information in selected high-activity terminal areas. (PLT196) — AIM ¶4-1-13

ALL
3790. Select the UNICOM frequencies normally assigned to stations at landing areas used exclusively as heliports.

A— 122.75 and 123.65 MHz.
B— 123.0 and 122.95 MHz.
C— 123.05 and 123.075 MHz.

Frequencies used solely for heliports are 123.050 and 123.075. (PLT204) — AIM ¶4-1-11

Answers

3641 [B]   3610 [A]   3611 [B]   3612 [B]   3791 [C]   3790 [C]

AIR, RTC, WSC, PPC
3811. After landing at a tower-controlled airport, when should the pilot contact ground control?

A— When advised by the tower to do so.
B— Prior to turning off the runway.
C— After reaching a taxiway that leads directly to the parking area.

A pilot who has just landed should not change from tower to ground frequency until advised to do so by the controller. (PLT044) — AIM ¶4-3-14

AIR, RTC, WSC, PPC
3812. If instructed by ground control to taxi to Runway 9, the pilot may proceed

A— via taxiways and across runways to, but not onto, Runway 9.
B— to the next intersecting runway where further clearance is required.
C— via taxiways and across runways to Runway 9, where an immediate takeoff may be made.

When ATC clears an aircraft to "taxi to" an assigned takeoff runway, the absence of holding instructions does not authorize the aircraft to "cross" all runway which the taxi route intersects except the assigned takeoff runway. A clearance must be obtained prior to crossing any runway. It does not include authorization to "taxi on to" or "cross" the assigned takeoff runway at any point. (PLT502) — AIM ¶4-3-18

SPO
2205. What services will a FSS provide?

A— Fuel pricing.
B— Assistance during an emergency.
C— Clearance to taxi for takeoff.

Flight Service Stations (FSS's) are air traffic facilities that provide pilot briefings, enroute communications and VFR search-and-rescue services, assist lost aircraft and aircraft in emergency situations, relay ATC clearances, originate Notices to Airmen, broadcast aviation weather and National Airspace System (NAS) information, receive and process IFR flight plans, and monitor navigational aids (NAVAIDs). In addition, at selected locations FSS's provide En Route Flight Advisory Service (Flight Watch), take weather observations, issue airport advisories, and advise Customs and Immigration of transborder flights. (PLT172) — AIM ¶4-1-3

Answer (A) is incorrect because this is done by UNICOM. Answer (C) is incorrect because this is done by Ground Control or Tower Control.

SPO
2006. When outbound from an airport with a UNICOM station on the published common traffic advisory frequency (CTAF) and there is no tower or Flight Service Station (FSS), the pilot should contact UNICOM or use self-announce procedures on CTAF before

A— engine start.
B— taxiing and before taxiing on the runway.
C— the preflight inspection.

Pilots should contact UNICOM before taxiing, crossing any runway, and again before taxiing on the runway for departure. (PLT435) — AIM ¶4-1-9

SPO
2007. When outbound from an airport without a UNICOM station, tower or Flight Service Station (FSS), the pilot should self-announce on frequency

A— 122.7
B— 122.9
C— 122.8

Where there is no tower, FSS, or UNICOM station on the airport, use MULTICOM frequency 122.9 for self-announce procedures. (PLT435) — AIM ¶4-1-9

Answers (A) and (C) are incorrect because these are both CTAF frequencies used to communicate with a UNICOM station.

SPO
2015. You have just landed at a towered airport and the tower tells you to contact ground control when clear of the runway. You are considered clear of the runway when

A— all parts of the aircraft have crossed the hold line.
B— the aircraft cockpit is clear of the hold line.
C— the tail of the aircraft is clear of the runway edge.

An aircraft exiting a runway is not clear of the runway until all parts of the aircraft have crossed the applicable holding position marking. (PLT112) — AIM ¶2-3-5

Answers

| 3811 [A] | 3812 [B] | 2205 [B] | 2006 [B] | 2007 [B] | 2015 [A] |

SPO

2016. Pilots should state their position on the airport when calling the tower for takeoff

A— from a runway intersection, during instrument conditions.

B— from a runway intersection or the end of the runway.

C— from a runway intersection, only at night.

Pilots should state their position on the airport when calling the tower for takeoff from a runway intersection. **Example:** *Cleveland Tower, Apache Three Seven Two Two Papa, at the intersection of taxiway Oscar and runway two three right, ready for departure. (PLT486) — AIM ¶4-3-10*

Answers (A) and (C) are incorrect because this rule applies to all operations.

SPO

2017. After landing at a tower controlled airport a pilot should contact ground control

A— when advised by the tower.

B— prior to turning off the runway.

C— after reaching a taxiway that leads directly to the parking area.

A pilot who has just landed should not change from the tower frequency to the ground control frequency until directed to do so by the controller. (PLT170) — AIM ¶4-3-14

Airport Traffic Area Communications and Light Signals

Unless otherwise authorized, aircraft are required to maintain two-way radio communication with the airport traffic control towers (ATCT) when operating to, from, or on the controlled airport, regardless of the weather. If radio contact cannot be maintained, ATC will direct traffic by means of light gun signals as shown in Figure 11-2.

If the aircraft radios fail while inbound to a tower-controlled airport, the pilot should remain outside or above the airport traffic area until the direction and flow of traffic has been determined and then join the airport traffic pattern and watch the tower for light signals.

The general warning signal (alternating red and green) may be followed by any other signal. For example, while on final approach for landing, an alternating red and green light followed by a flashing red light is received from the control tower. Under these circumstances, the pilot should abandon the approach, realizing the airport is unsafe for landing.

Color & Type of Signal	Movement of Vehicles, Equipment & Personnel	Aircraft on the Ground	Aircraft in Flight
Steady green	Cleared to cross, proceed or go	Cleared for takeoff	Cleared to land
Flashing green	Not applicable	Cleared for taxi	Return for landing (to be followed by steady green at the proper time)
Steady red	STOP	STOP	Give way to other aircraft and continue circling
Flashing red	Clear the taxiway/runway	Taxi clear of the runway in use	Airport unsafe, do not land
Flashing white	Return to starting point on airport	Return to starting point on airport	Not applicable
Alternating red and green	Exercise extreme caution	Exercise extreme caution	Exercise extreme caution

Figure 11-2

ALL, SPO

3111. A steady green light signal directed from the control tower to an aircraft in flight is a signal that the pilot

A— is cleared to land.
B— should give way to other aircraft and continue circling.
C— should return for landing.

A steady green light signal directed to an aircraft in flight means that the pilot is cleared to land. (PLT141) — 14 CFR §91.125

Answer (B) is incorrect because this would be a steady red signal. Answer (C) is incorrect because this would be a flashing green signal.

ALL

3115. An alternating red and green light signal directed from the control tower to an aircraft in flight is a signal to

A— hold position.
B— exercise extreme caution.
C— not land; the airport is unsafe.

An alternating red and green light signal means to exercise extreme caution. (PLT141) — 14 CFR §91.125

Answer (A) is incorrect because you can't hold position in flight. Answer (C) is incorrect because this would be a flashing red signal.

AIR, RTC, WSC, PPC
3112. Which light signal from the control tower clears a pilot to taxi?

A— Flashing green.
B— Steady green.
C— Flashing white.

A flashing green light signal clears a pilot to taxi. (PLT141) — 14 CFR §91.125

Answer (B) is incorrect because this means cleared to takeoff/land. Answer (C) is incorrect because this means return to starting point on airport.

AIR, RTC, WSC, PPC
3113. If the control tower uses a light signal to direct a pilot to give way to other aircraft and continue circling, the light will be

A— flashing red.
B— steady red.
C— alternating red and green.

A steady red signal directed to an aircraft in flight indicates the pilot should give way to other aircraft and continue circling. (PLT141) — 14 CFR §91.125

Answer (A) is incorrect because this means the airport is unsafe. Answer (C) is incorrect because this means the pilot should exercise extreme caution.

AIR, RTC, WSC, PPC
3114. A flashing white light signal from the control tower to a taxiing aircraft is an indication to

A— taxi at a faster speed.
B— taxi only on taxiways and not cross runways.
C— return to the starting point on the airport.

A flashing white light signal to a taxiing aircraft is an indication to return to the starting point on the airport. (PLT141) — 14 CFR §91.125

Answers (A) and (B) are incorrect because there are no light signals for these instructions.

AIR, RTC, WSC, PPC
3116. While on final approach for landing, an alternating green and red light followed by a flashing red light is received from the control tower. Under these circumstances, the pilot should

A— discontinue the approach, fly the same traffic pattern and approach again, and land.
B— exercise extreme caution and abandon the approach, realizing the airport is unsafe for landing.
C— abandon the approach, circle the airport to the right, and expect a flashing white light when the airport is safe for landing.

An alternating red and green light means to exercise extreme caution. A flashing red light means the airport is unsafe, do not land. (PLT141) — 14 CFR §91.125

Answer (A) is incorrect because the flashing red light indicates the airport is unsafe for landing. Answer (C) is incorrect because a flashing white is not applicable in flight.

AIR, RTC, WSC, PPC
3804. If the aircraft's radio fails, what is the recommended procedure when landing at a controlled airport?

A— Observe the traffic flow, enter the pattern, and look for a light signal from the tower.
B— Enter a crosswind leg and rock the wings.
C— Flash the landing lights and cycle the landing gear while circling the airport.

When a transmitter, receiver, or both have become inoperative, an aircraft should observe the traffic flow, enter the pattern, and look for a light signal from the tower, when landing at a controlled airport. (PLT150) — AIM ¶4-2-13

Answers (B) and (C) are incorrect because entering on the crosswind is not required and rocking the wings is used to acknowledge light signals during the day. Flashing the lights is used to acknowledge light signals during night, and a fixed gear airplane would not be able to cycle the gear.

SPO
2012. A steady red light from the tower, for an aircraft on the ground indicates

A— Give way to other aircraft and continue circling.
B— Stop.
C— Taxi clear of the runway in use.

A steady red light from the tower, for an aircraft on the ground indicates the aircraft should stop. (PLT044) — 14 CFR §91.125

Answer (A) is incorrect because this would be issued to an aircraft in flight. Answer (C) is incorrect because this would be a flashing red light.

Answers

3112 [A]	3113 [B]	3114 [C]	3116 [B]	3804 [A]	2012 [B]

Radar Assistance to VFR Aircraft

Radar-equipped ATC facilities provide traffic advisories and limited vectoring (called "basic radar service") to VFR aircraft, provided the aircraft can communicate with the facility, is within radar coverage, and can be radar-identified.

Stage II service provides radar advisories and sequencing for VFR aircraft. Arriving aircraft should initiate contact with approach control. Approach control will assume Stage II service is requested, unless the pilot states that the service is not wanted. Pilots of departing VFR aircraft should request Stage II terminal radar advisory service from ground control on initial contact.

At some locations Stage III service has been established to provide separation between all participating VFR aircraft and all IFR aircraft in the terminal radar service area (TRSA). Unless the pilot states "negative Stage III" on initial contact with approach control, the service will be provided.

Traffic advisories given by a radar service will refer to the other aircraft by azimuth in terms of the 12-hour clock, with 12 o'clock being the direction of flight (track), not aircraft heading. Each hour is equal to 30°. For example, an aircraft heading 090° is advised of traffic at the 3 o'clock position. The pilot should look 90° to the right of the direction of flight, or to the south. In Figure 11-3, traffic information would be issued to the pilot of aircraft A as 12 o'clock. The actual position of the traffic as seen by the pilot of aircraft A would be 2 o'clock. Traffic information issued to aircraft B would also be given as 12 o'clock, but in this case, the pilot of B would see traffic at 10 o'clock.

These radar programs are not to be interpreted as relieving pilots of their responsibilities to see and avoid other traffic operating in basic VFR weather conditions, to maintain appropriate terrain and obstruction clearance, or to remain in weather conditions equal to or better than the minimum required by FAA regulations. Whenever compliance with an assigned route, heading, and/or altitude is likely to compromise pilot responsibilities respecting terrain, obstruction clearance, and weather minimums, the controller should be so advised and a revised clearance or instruction obtained.

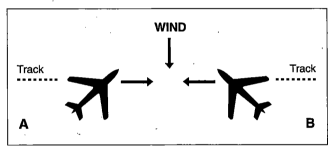

Figure 11-3. Traffic advisory

ALL
3792-1. When an air traffic controller issues radar traffic information in relation to the 12-hour clock, the reference the controller uses is the aircraft's

A— true course.
B— ground track.
C— magnetic heading.

Azimuth information given by ATC is based on the ground track of an aircraft as it is observed. The pilot must apply a correction to the reported azimuth using a drift-correction angle in order to maintain the track. (PLT044) — AIM ¶4-1-15

ALL
3792. An ATC radar facility issues the following advisory to a pilot flying on a heading of 090°:

"TRAFFIC 3 O'CLOCK, 2 MILES, WESTBOUND..."

Where should the pilot look for this traffic?

A— East.
B— South.
C— West.

Traffic information will be given in azimuth from the aircraft in terms of the 12-hour clock. Thus, each hour would constitute an angle of 30°. Picture a clock in your lap; 3 o'clock is to your right, 9 o'clock is to your left,

Answers
3792-1   [B]   3792   [B]

12 o'clock is straight ahead, and 6 o'clock is behind you. If an aircraft is proceeding on a heading of 090° (east), traffic located at the 3 o'clock position would be 90° right of the nose, south of the aircraft. (PLT194) — AIM ¶4-1-15

ALL
3793. An ATC radar facility issues the following advisory to a pilot flying on a heading of 360°:

"TRAFFIC 10 O'CLOCK, 2 MILES, SOUTHBOUND..."

Where should the pilot look for this traffic?

A— Northwest.
B— Northeast.
C— Southwest.

If an aircraft is proceeding on a heading of 360° (north), traffic located at the 10 o'clock position would be 60° (left) of the nose, or to the northwest. (PLT194) — AIM ¶4-1-15

ALL
3798. TRSA Service in the terminal radar program provides

A— IFR separation (1,000 feet vertical and 3 miles lateral) between all aircraft.
B— warning to pilots when their aircraft are in unsafe proximity to terrain, obstructions, or other aircraft.
C— sequencing and separation for participating VFR aircraft.

TRSA Service provides separation of participating VFR aircraft and all IFR aircraft operating within the airspace. (PLT370) — AIM ¶4-1-18

ALL
3794. An ATC radar facility issues the following advisory to a pilot during a local flight:

"TRAFFIC 2 O'CLOCK, 5 MILES, NORTHBOUND..."

Where should the pilot look for this traffic?

A— Between directly ahead and 90° to the left.
B— Between directly behind and 90° to the right.
C— Between directly ahead and 90° to the right.

Traffic information issued to the pilot as "2 o'clock" would mean approximately 60° right. (PLT194) — AIM ¶4-1-15

SPO
2054. An ATC radar facility issues the following advisory to a pilot flying on a heading of 270°: 'TRAFFIC 3 O'CLOCK, 2 MILES, EASTBOUND...' Where should the pilot look for this traffic?

A— North.
B— South.
C— West.

Traffic information will be given in azimuth from the aircraft in terms of the 12-hour clock. Thus, each hour would constitute an angle of 30°. Picture a clock in your lap; 3 o'clock is to your right, 9 o'clock is to your left, 12 o'clock is straight ahead, and 6 o'clock is behind you. If an aircraft is proceeding on a heading of 270° (west), traffic located at the 3 o'clock position would be 90° right of the nose, north of the aircraft. (PLT194) — AIM ¶4-1-15

ALL
3795. An ATC radar facility issues the following advisory to a pilot flying north in a calm wind:

"TRAFFIC 9 O'CLOCK, 2 MILES, SOUTHBOUND..."

Where should the pilot look for this traffic?

A— South.
B— North.
C— West.

An aircraft flying north in calm wind would be heading 360°. When advised of traffic at the 9 o'clock position, the pilot should look 90° left of the nose, to the west. (PLT194) — AIM ¶4-1-15

ALL
3796. Basic radar service in the terminal radar program is best described as

A— safety alerts, traffic advisories and limited vectoring to VFR aircraft.
B— mandatory radar service provided by the Automated Radar Terminal System (ARTS) program.
C— wind-shear warning at participating airports.

In addition to the use of radar for the control of IFR aircraft, all commissioned radar facilities provide safety alerts, traffic advisories and limited vectoring (on a workload-permitting basis) to VFR aircraft. Radar facilities are not responsible for weather information and the service is not mandatory. (PLT172) — AIM ¶4-1-18

ALL

3797. From whom should a departing VFR aircraft request radar traffic information during ground operations?

A— Clearance delivery.
B— Tower, just before takeoff.
C— Ground control, on initial contact.

Pilots of departing VFR aircraft are encouraged to request radar traffic information by notifying ground control on initial contact with their request and proposed direction of flight. (PLT204) — AIM ¶4-1-18

SPO

2226. During departure, when visual separation is employed by Air Traffic Control (ATC), traffic is no longer a factor when

A— the other aircraft turns away or is on a diverging course.
B— visual contact with the other aircraft is lost.
C— the other aircraft is passed.

Traffic is no longer a factor when during approach phase the other aircraft is in the landing phase of flight or executes a missed approach; and during departure or en route, when the other aircraft turns away or is on a diverging course. (PLT116) — AIM ¶4-4-14

Transponder

A transponder is an airborne radar beacon transmitter-receiver that automatically receives signals from a ground-based radar beacon transmitter-receiver (interrogator). The transponder selectively replies (with a specific code) only to those interrogations being received on the mode to which it is set. Civil Mode A transponders have 4,096 discrete four-digit codes. This return signal is displayed on a radarscope on the ground, and a controller can then identify and pinpoint the position of each aircraft (target) under his/her control.

Some transponders are also equipped with a Mode C automatic altitude-reporting capability. This system converts aircraft altitude (in 100-foot increments) to coded digital information which is transmitted back to the interrogating radar system. With Mode C, the controller has information on the aircraft's altitude as well as its position. The IDENT feature should not be activated unless requested by ATC. Mode C, which should be operated at all times unless ATC requests otherwise, is also required for all flights above 10,000 feet MSL.

The transponder code for VFR flight is 1200. When changing transponder codes, avoid inadvertent selection of codes 7500 (hijack), 7600 (lost communications), 7700 (emergency), and 7777 (military interceptor operations).

Operation in Class A, Class B, and Class C airspace requires a transponder with Mode A/C capability and 4,096 codes available.

If air traffic control advises that radar service is being terminated, the transponder should be set to code 1200.

Answers

3797   [C]   2226   [A]

ALL
3165. An operable 4096-code transponder with an encoding altimeter is required in which airspace?

A— Class A, Class B (and within 30 miles of the Class B primary airport), and Class C.
B— Class D and Class E (below 10,000 feet MSL).
C— Class D and Class G (below 10,000 feet MSL).

Class A, B (and within 30 miles of the Class B primary airport), and C airspace require a Mode C transponder. (PLT161) — 14 CFR §91.215

ALL
3129. An operable 4096-code transponder and Mode C encoding altimeter are required in

A— Class B airspace and within 30 miles of the Class B primary airport.
B— Class D airspace.
C— Class E airspace below 10,000 feet MSL.

Encoding transponders are required within all Class B airspace and within 30 miles of the primary airport even if you are below a Class B airspace layer. (PLT497) — 14 CFR §91.131, §91.215

Answers (B) and (C) are incorrect because transponders are not required in Class D airspace, or below 10,000 feet unless in Class B or C airspace.

ALL
3801. When operating under VFR below 18,000 feet MSL, unless otherwise authorized, what transponder code should be selected?

A— 1200.
B— 7600.
C— 7700.

Unless otherwise instructed by an ATC facility, adjust the transponder to reply on Mode 3/A, code 1200, regardless of altitude. (PLT497) — AIM ¶4-1-20

ALL
3996. When operating the transponder on the VFR code (1200), what is the minimum mode the transponder must be in?

A— Mode A.
B— Mode C.
C— Mode F.

When operating on the VFR code 1200, adjust the transponder to reply on Mode A unless otherwise instructed by an ATC facility. (PLT497) — AIM ¶4-1-20

Answer (B) is incorrect because while altitude-reporting Mode C should be used if it is installed, it is not required to squawk 1200. Answer (C) is incorrect because F is not a transponder mode.

ALL
3803. If Air Traffic Control advises that radar service is terminated when the pilot is departing Class C airspace, the transponder should be set to code

A— 0000.
B— 1200.
C— 4096.

When VFR, unless otherwise instructed by an ATC facility, adjust transponder to reply code 1200 regardless of altitude. (PLT161) — AIM ¶4-1-20

ALL
3166. With certain exceptions, all aircraft within 30 miles of a Class B primary airport from the surface upward to 10,000 feet MSL must be equipped with

A— an operable VOR or TACAN receiver and an ADF receiver.
B— instruments and equipment required for IFR operations.
C— an operable transponder having either Mode S or 4096-code capability with Mode C automatic altitude reporting capability.

With certain exceptions, all aircraft need encoding transponders under the 30-mile veil of Class B airspace. (PLT161) — 14 CFR §91.215

Answers (A) and (B) are incorrect because they apply to IFR flight.

Answers

| 3165 [A] | 3129 [A] | 3801 [A] | 3996 [A] | 3803 [B] | 3166 [C] |

ALL
3800. When making routine transponder code changes, pilots should avoid inadvertent selection of which codes?

A— 0700, 1700, 7000.
B— 1200, 1500, 7000.
C— 7500, 7600, 7700.

When making routine code changes, pilots should avoid selecting codes 7500, 7600 or 7700, thereby preventing false alarms at automated ground facilities. (PLT497) — AIM ¶4-1-20

ALL
3800-1. When making routine transponder code changes, pilots should avoid inadvertent selection of which code?

A— 7200.
B— 7000.
C— 7500.

When making routine code changes, pilots should avoid selecting codes 7500, 7600 or 7700, thereby preventing false alarms at automated ground facilities. (PLT497) — AIM ¶4-1-20

ALL
3802. Unless otherwise authorized, if flying a transponder equipped aircraft, a pilot should squawk which VFR code?

A— 1200.
B— 7600.
C— 7700.

It is important for pilots to operate the transponder and encoder so radar controllers will know the aircraft's position and altitude—even if not in communication with ATC. (PLT497) — AIM ¶4-1-20

GLI
3802-1. If your glider is equipped with 4096 code radar beacon transponder, the code uitlized for normal operations is

A— 1202.
B— 1200.
C— 7700.

Gliders not in contact with an ATC facility should squawk 1202 in lieu of 1200. (PLT161) — AIM ¶4-1-20

SPO
2005. When a distress or urgency condition is encountered, the pilot of an aircraft with a coded radar beacon transponder, who desires to alert a ground radar facility, should squawk code

A— 7700
B— 7600
C— 7500

When a distress or urgency condition is encountered, the pilot of an aircraft with a coded radar beacon transponder, who desires to alert a ground radar facility, should squawk Code 7700 and then immediately establish communications with the ATC facility. (PLT497) — AIM ¶6-2-2

Answer (B) is incorrect because 7600 is used for lost communications. Answer (C) is incorrect because 7500 is used to indicate a hijack situation.

Answers
3800 [C]   3800-1 [C]   3802 [A]   3802-1 [A]   2005 [A]

Emergency Locator Transmitter (ELT)

Emergency Locator Transmitters (ELT) have been developed as a means of locating downed aircraft. Transmitting on 121.5 and 406 MHz, the ELT will operate continuously for at least 48 hours.

To prevent false alarms, the ELT should be tested only during the first 5 minutes after any hour and only for one to three sweeps. False alarms can also be minimized by monitoring 121.5 or 406 MHz prior to engine shutdown at the end of each flight.

Non-rechargeable batteries used in ELTs must be replaced when 50% of their useful life has expired, or when the transmitter has been in use for more than 1 cumulative hour.

ALL
3819. When activated, an emergency locator transmitter (ELT) transmits on

A— 118.0 and 118.8 MHz.
B— 121.5 and 406 MHz.
C— 123.0 and 119.0 MHz.

ELTs transmit an audio tone on 121.5, 243.0, and 406 MHz. (PLT402) — AIM ¶6-2-4

ALL
3819-1. When activated, an emergency locator transmitter (ELT) transmits on

A— 118.0 and 118.8 MHz.
B— 121.5 and 243.0 MHz.
C— 123.0 and 119.0 MHz.

ELTs transmit an audio tone on 121.5, 243.0, and 406 MHz. ELTs operating on 121.5 and 243.0 MHz are analog devices. The newer 406 MHz ELT is a digital transmitter that can be encoded with the owner's contact information or aircraft data. (PLT402) — AIM ¶6-2-4

ALL
3160. When must batteries in an emergency locator transmitter (ELT) be replaced or recharged, if rechargeable?

A— After any inadvertent activation of the ELT.
B— When the ELT has been in use for more than 1 cumulative hour.
C— When the ELT can no longer be heard over the airplane's communication radio receiver.

ELT batteries must be replaced after 1 hour of cumulative use or when 50% of their useful life has expired, whichever comes first. (PLT402) — 14 CFR §91.207

ALL
3161. When are non-rechargeable batteries of an emergency locator transmitter (ELT) required to be replaced?

A— Every 24 months.
B— When 50 percent of their useful life expires.
C— At the time of each 100-hour or annual inspection.

ELT batteries must be replaced after 1 hour of cumulative use or when 50% of their useful life has expired, whichever comes first. (PLT402) — 14 CFR §91.207

ALL
3820. When must the battery in an emergency locator transmitter (ELT) be replaced (or recharged if the battery is rechargeable)?

A— After one-half the battery's useful life.
B— During each annual and 100-hour inspection.
C— Every 24 calendar months.

ELT batteries must be replaced after 1 hour of cumulative use or when 50% of their useful life has expired, whichever comes first. (PLT402) — AIM ¶6-2-4

Answers
3819 [B]   3819-1 [B]   3160 [B]   3161 [B]   3820 [A]

ALL

3821. When may an emergency locator transmitter (ELT) be tested?

A— Anytime.
B— At .15 and 45 minutes past the hour.
C— During the first 5 minutes after the hour.

An ELT test should be conducted only during the first 5 minutes after any hour and then only for three audible sweeps. (PLT402) — AIM ¶6-2-4

ALL

3822. Which procedure is recommended to ensure that the emergency locator transmitter (ELT) has not been activated?

A— Turn off the aircraft ELT after landing.
B— Ask the airport tower if they are receiving an ELT signal.
C— Monitor 121.5 before engine shutdown.

Immediately after hard landings and before parking, check radio frequency 121.5 MHz. (PLT402) — AIM ¶6-2-4

Answers

3821   [C]   3822   [C]

Cross-Reference A
Question Number and Page Number

The following list of the numbered questions included in this ASA Test Prep is given in sequential order; however, as a result of our ongoing review of FAA test question databases, some question numbers may have been removed due to changes in the database. **All currently existing questions are accounted for in this list.** For more information about the questions included in ASA Test Preps, please read Pages vii–xix in the front matter for this book.

Question Number	Page Number	Question Number	Page Number	Question Number	Page Number	Question Number	Page Number
2001	9–17	2063	5–33	2121	4–49	2206	5–12
2002	5–5	2064	5–35	2122	9–38	2211	4–52
2003	4–28	2066	5–35	2123	4–7	2212	4–52
2004	4–28	2067	8–29	2126	4–23	2213	4–52
2005	11–16	2068	5–34	2127	4–24	2214	4–52
2006	11–8	2069	5–33	2128	4–24	2215	1–9
2007	11–8	2073	5–32	2129	4–13	2216	1–9
2007-1	5–6	2074	5–32	2130	4–6	2218	5–13
2007-2	5–6	2078	5–31	2133-1	4–37	2222	9–32
2012	11–11	2079	5–33	2137	4–33	2223-2	1–22
2014	11–6	2082	5–34	2138	9–44	2225	1–5
2015	11–8	2083	5–33	2138-1	9–45	2225-1	1–5
2016	11–9	2085	5–32	2138-2	9–45	2226	11–14
2017	11–9	2087	4–23	2159	6–14	2229	1–9
2020	5–39	2089	5–26	2163	6–19	2230	8–44
2024	5–8	2090	5–26	2170	6–23	2232	4–22
2025	5–12	2091	5–26	2174	8–23	2233	1–19
2026	5–11	2092	5–26	2175	9–32	2234	8–33
2028	5–11	2093	5–26	2176	5–32	2234-1	1–25
2029	5–13	2096	5–37	2177	9–16	2236	8–44
2030	5–11	2097	5–27	2178	9–5	2238	2–5
2031	5–11	2099	9–31	2179	9–44	2239	1–9
2033	4–20	2100	10–8	2182	8–23	2240	5–35
2034-1	5–6	2101	9–32	2183	8–23	2242	2–5
2039	1–25	2102	9–13	2186-1	4–33	2283	8–33
2040	4–33	2103	9–16	2189	4–51	2308	4–18
2043	9–43	2104	9–16	2192	9–42	2312	6–23
2049	9–43	2105	9–31	2193	9–43	2326	2–48
2050	9–43	2106	9–5	2194	5–5	2327	2–48
2052	9–43	2107	5–22	2195	5–32	2328	5–20
2053	4–49	2108	9–5	2196	5–33	2329	2–22
2054	11–13	2109	4–48	2197	5–33	2331	5–20
2055-1	9–45	2110	4–49	2198	9–44	2332	5–20
2056	9–44	2113-1	9–45	2199	8–33	2341	2–9
2059	9–44	2115	9–44	2201	9–13	2347	2–48
2060	5–5	2117	4–49	2202	5–26	2348	2–48
2061	4–8	2118	5–23	2203	4–33	2350	8–23
2061-1	4–8	2119	5–23	2204	9–44	2351	8–24
2062	5–35	2120	4–49	2205	11–8	2353	2–12

Question Number	Page Number	Question Number	Page Number	Question Number	Page Number	Question Number	Page Number
3787	9–36	3829-3	1–24	3875	2–31	3932	5–30
3787-1	9–37	3830	1–25	3876	2–31	3933	5–30
3788	9–37	3831	9–42	3877	2–31	3934	5–30
3790	11–7	3832	5–24	3878	2–31	3935	5–31
3791	11–7	3833	5–35	3879	2–31	3936	5–31
3792	11–12	3834	5–35	3880	2–31	3937	5–31
3792-1	11–12	3835	5–36	3881	2–32	3938	5–31
3793	11–13	3836	5–36	3882	2–32	3939	5–31
3794	11–13	3837	4–27	3883	2–32	3940	5–31
3795	11–13	3838	5–22	3884	2–32	3940-1	5–32
3796	11–13	3838-1	5–21	3885	2–37	3951	5–10
3797	11–14	3839	5–22	3886	2–37	3952	5–10
3798	11–13	3840	5–22	3887	8–21	3953	5–10
3799	9–37	3841	5–21	3888	8–21	3954	5–10
3800	11–16	3841-1	5–22	3889	8–21	3955	5–10
3800-1	11–16	3842	5–21	3890	8–22	3955-1	5–10
3801	11–15	3844	5–24	3891	8–29	3955-2	5–10
3802	11–16	3845	5–24	3892	8–29	3955-3	5–11
3802-1	11–16	3846	5–24	3893	8–22	3955-4	5–11
3803	11–15	3847	5–25	3894	8–22	3955-5	5–11
3804	11–11	3848	5–25	3895	2–37	3956	6–20
3805	5–13	3849	5–36	3896	2–38	3957	5–9
3806	5–13	3850	5–25	3897	2–38	3958	2–41
3807	5–4	3851	5–25	3898	2–38	3959	2–41
3808	5–4	3852	5–25	3899	2–38	3960	2–41
3809	5–5	3853	5–25	3900	2–38	3961	2–41
3810	5–5	3854	4–48	3901	2–38	3962	2–41
3811	11–8	3855	4–48	3902	2–39	3963	2–42
3812	11–8	3856	4–48	3903	2–39	3964	2–42
3813	4–34	3857	2–29	3904	2–39	3965	2–42
3814	10–8	3858	2–29	3905	2–39	3966	2–42
3815	8–5	3859	2–29	3906	2–39	3967	2–42
3816	9–17	3860	2–30	3907	2–39	3968	2–43
3817	9–17	3861	8–20	3908	2–39	3969	2–43
3818	4–38	3862	8–20	3909	2–40	3970	2–43
3819	11–17	3863	8–21	3910	2–40	3971	2–43
3819-1	11–17	3864	8–41	3911	2–40	3972	2–43
3820	11–17	3865	8–41	3912	2–40	3973	2–43
3821	11–18	3866	8–41	3913	2–40	3974	2–44
3822	11–18	3867	8–41	3914	2–40	3975	2–44
3824	1–24	3868	8–41	3915	2–40	3976	2–44
3825	1–24	3869	2–30	3916	5–38	3977	2–44
3826	1–24	3870	2–30	3916-1	5–38	3978	2–44
3827	1–24	3871	2–30	3931	5–30	3979	2–45
3828	1–25	3872	2–30	3931-1	5–30	3980	2–45
3829	1–25	3873	2–30	3931-2	5–30	3981	2–45
3829-2	1–24	3874	2–30	3931-3	5–30	3982	2–45

Cross-Reference B
Learning Statement Code and Question Number

The expression "learning statement," as used in FAA airman testing, refers to measurable statements about the knowledge a student should be able to demonstrate following a certain segment of training. When you take the applicable airman knowledge test required for an airman pilot certificate or rating, you will receive an Airman Knowledge Test Report. The test report will list the learning statement codes for questions you have answered incorrectly. Match the codes given on your test report to the ones in the FAA Learning Statement Codes (listed below in this cross-reference). Use Cross-Reference A in this book to find the page number for the question numbers listed below.

Your instructor is required to provide instruction on each of the areas of deficiency listed on your Airman Knowledge Test Report (as LSCs), and give you an endorsement for this instruction. The Airman Knowledge Test Report must be presented to the examiner conducting your practical test. During the oral portion of the practical test, the examiner is required to evaluate the noted areas of deficiency.

The FAA sample questions for the Private Pilot Airplane (PAR) and the Instrument Rating Airplane Airman Knowledge Tests now show two types of codes associated with each question:

- The Learning Statement Code(s) (LSCs) associated with the question topic area. The LSC codes currently appear on the Airman Knowledge Test Report for any missed knowledge test questions.
- The "Airman Certification Standards" (ACS) code for the question topic area. The FAA expects the ACS codes to replace the LSC codes on the PAR Airman Knowledge Test Report within the next 12–18 months.

ASA provides additional information on these new ACS codes on the *Private Pilot Test Prep* product web page: **www.asa2fly.com/reader/TPP**—visit this "Reader Resource" web page to learn more about the Airman Certification Standard.

If you received a code on your Airman Test Report that is not listed in this cross-reference, email ASA at **cfi@asa2fly.com**. We will provide the definition so you can review that subject area.

The FAA appreciates testing experience feedback. You can contact the branch responsible for the FAA Knowledge Exams directly at:

Federal Aviation Administration
AFS-630, Airman Testing Standards Branch
PO Box 25082
Oklahoma City, OK 73125
Email: AFS630comments@faa.gov

Learning Statement Code	FAA Reference	Subject Description (or Topic 〉 Content 〉 Specific classification) Question Numbers
PLT003	FAA-H-8083-25	Weight and Balance 〉 Center of Gravity 〉 Stability *3287, 3672, 3729*
PLT005	FAA-H-8083-25	Aircraft Performance 〉 Computations 〉 Density Altitude *2356, 3292, 3294*
PLT006	FAA-H-8083-13	Flight Operations 〉 Soaring Techniques 〉 Performance *3345, 3346, 3347*
PLT008	FAA-H-8083-25	Aircraft Performance 〉 Computations 〉 Landing Distance *3689, 3690, 3691, 3692, 3693, 3694, 3695, 3696, 3697, 3698, 3699, 3700, 3701*
PLT011	FAA-H-8083-25	Aircraft Performance 〉 Computations 〉 Takeoff Distance *2113-1, 3702, 3703, 3704, 3705, 3706, 3707, 3708, 3940-1*
PLT012	FAA-H-8083-25 SAC	Aircraft Performance 〉 Computations 〉 Cruise Navigation 〉 Pilotage 〉 Aeronautical Charts; Calculations Navigation 〉 Radio 〉 VOR *2001, 2099, 2101, 2105, 2222, 3348, 3349, 3529-1, 3529-3, 3529-4, 3537, 3538, 3539, 3545, 3546, 3547, 3550, 3550-1, 3551, 3556, 3558, 3564, 3564-1, 3564-2, 3565, 3568, 3569, 3571, 3572, 3573, 3574, 3575, 3576, 3634, 3678, 3679, 3680, 3681, 3816, 3817*
PLT013	FAA-H-8083-25	Aircraft Performance 〉 Computations 〉 Crosswind *3683, 3684, 3685, 3686, 3687, 3688*
PLT015	FAA-H-0883-25	Calculate flight performance/planning–range *2230*
PLT019	FAA-H-8083-25	Aircraft Performance 〉 Computations 〉 Density Altitude; Pressure Altitude *3293, 3295, 3297, 3298*
PLT021	FAA-H-8083-1 FAA-H-8083-21 FAA-H-8083-25	Weight and Balance 〉 Center of Gravity 〉 Computations *2350, 2351, 3662, 3663, 3663-1, 3664, 3666, 3667, 3674, 3675, 3676, 3677, 3720, 3721, 3722, 3723, 3724, 3725, 3726, 3727, 3728, 3730, 3731, 3815, 3861, 3863*
PLT022	AC 60-22	Define Aeronautical Decision Making (ADM) *2079, 2085*
PLT023	AC 00-6 FAA-H-8083-25	Aircraft Systems 〉 Flight Instruments 〉 Altimeter; Altitude Weather 〉 Meteorology 〉 Pressure *3256, 3257, 3258, 3259, 3260, 3388, 3392, 3393*
PLT025	FAA-H-8083-25	Define Bernoulli's Principle *3201-1*
PLT026	AC 00-45	Weather 〉 Aeronautical Weather Reports 〉 Aviation Routine Weather Reports (METAR) *3463*
PLT027	FAA-H-8083-21	Aerodynamics 〉 Principles of Flight 〉 Coning *3321*

Learning Statement Code	FAA Reference	Subject Description (or Topic) Content) Specific classification) Question Numbers
PLT039	AIM	Airport Operations) Marking/Signs) Segmented Circle *3805, 3807, 3808, 3809, 3810*
PLT040	AIM SAC	Airspace) Controlled) Class B Navigation) Pilotage) Airspace *2050, 2138-1, 3599, 3600, 3623*
PLT041	FAA-H-8083-25	Aircraft Systems) Flight Instruments) Altimeter *3250, 3251, 3252, 3253, 3253-1, 3254*
PLT044	AIM	Airport Operations) Tower Controlled) Ground Operations *2003, 2012, 3119, 3792-1, 3811*
PLT054	FAA-H-8083-13	Aerodynamics) Principles of Flight) Performance Flight Operations) X-C) Performance *3864, 3865, 3866, 3867, 3868*
PLT057	FAA-H-8083-11	Aircraft Performance) Computations) Altitude *3888, 3889, 3890, 3891, 3892, 3893, 3894*
PLT059	AC 00-45	Weather) Aeronautical Weather Reports) Aviation Routine Weather Reports (METAR) *3462, 3464, 3465, 3466, 3467*
PLT061	AIM AC 00-45	Weather) Aeronautical Weather Reports) Pilot Weather Reports *3472, 3473, 3474, 3475, 3476*
PLT064	AIM A/FD FAA-H-8083-25 SAC	Airport Operations) Uncontrolled) Radio Communications Airspace) Controlled) Class E Airspace) Other) Military Training Routes Airspace) Special Use) MOA Navigation) Pilotage) Aeronautical Charts; Airspace; Calculations Navigation) Radio) VOR Publications) Airport Facility Directory) Parachute Jumping *2014, 2055-1, 2059, 2115, 2179, 2198, 2204, 2367, 3068-2, 3520, 3530, 3531, 3535, 3536, 3543, 3553, 3567, 3601, 3603, 3606, 3607, 3608, 3609, 3610, 3611, 3612, 3619, 3620-1, 3620-2, 3621-2, 3621-3, 3627, 3628, 3629, 3630, 3631, 3632, 3633, 3635, 3636, 3637, 3638, 3639, 3640, 3644, 3645, 3646, 3647, 3831, 3841-1*
PLT072	AC 00-45	Weather) Aeronautical Weather Forecasts) Terminal Aerodrome Forecasts (TAF) *3479, 3480, 3481, 3482, 3483, 3484, 3485, 3486*
PLT074	FAA-H-8083-25	Aerodynamics) Load Factor) Steep Turns *2215, 2216, 2371*
PLT076	AC 00-45	Weather) Aeronautical Weather Forecasts) Winds/Temperatures Aloft Forecast *3500, 3501, 3502, 3503*
PLT077	AIM	Airport Operations) Marking/Signs) Airport Markings; Displaced Threshold; Tetrahedron, Traffic Pattern *3773, 3774, 3776, 3806*

Learning Statement Code	FAA Reference	Subject Description (or *Topic* ⟩ *Content* ⟩ *Specific* classification) Question Numbers
PLT078	A/FD	Navigation ⟩ Pilotage ⟩ Aircraft/Facility Directory *2107, 2119, 3513, 3838, 3838-1, 3839, 3840, 3841, 3842*
PLT088	FAA-H-8083-25	Aircraft Systems ⟩ Flight Instruments ⟩ Airspeed Indicator *3265, 3266, 3267, 3268, 3269, 3270, 3271, 3272, 3273*
PLT090	FAA-H-8083-25	Navigation ⟩ Radio ⟩ ADF/NDB; VOR *3533, 3560, 3561, 3570, 3577, 3578, 3579*
PLT092	FAA-H-8083-25	Weight and Balance ⟩ Center of Gravity ⟩ Computations *3663-2, 3669, 3670, 3671, 3673*
PLT097	FAA-H-8083-25	Human Factors ⟩ Aeromedical Factors ⟩ Carbon Monoxide Poisoning *3832, 3848*
PLT098	AIM	Human Factors ⟩ Aeromedical Factors ⟩ Fitness for Flight *2089, 2090, 2202*
PLT099	FAA-H-8083-25	Flight Operations ⟩ Night ⟩ Scan *2096, 3712, 3713, 3714*
PLT101	AIM FAA-H-8083-25 SAC	Navigation ⟩ Pilotage ⟩ Aeronautical Charts; Airspace; Calculations; Flight Plans Navigation ⟩ Radio ⟩ VOR Publications ⟩ Aeronautical Charts ⟩ Sectionals *3117, 3421, 3530-1, 3559, 3566, 3621-1, 3624, 3625, 3637-1, 3641, 3642, 3643*
PLT103	FAA-H-8083-25	Human Factors ⟩ ADM ⟩ Hazardous Attitudes *2074, 2176, 2195, 2196, 3931-1, 3931-2, 3932, 3933, 3934, 3935, 3936*
PLT104	FAA-H-8083-25	Human Factors ⟩ ADM, CRM ⟩ Operational Pitfalls *2082, 2083, 2197, 3931, 3938, 3940*
PLT112	FAA-H-8083-3	Airport Operations ⟩ Taxiing ⟩ Flight Controls *2015, 3305, 3306, 3307, 3308, 3327, 3336, 3337*
PLT114	FAA-H-8083-11	Aircraft Systems ⟩ Structures ⟩ Balloon *2347, 2348*
PLT115	FAA-H-8083-25	Aircraft Systems ⟩ Powerplant ⟩ Fueling; Ignition *3238, 3238-1, 3239*
PLT116	FAA-H-8083-25	Publications ⟩ Advisory Circulars ⟩ Acquisition; Subject Numbering *2004, 2052, 2062, 2066, 2106, 2108, 2109, 2110, 2117, 2138-2, 2226, 3709, 3854, 3855, 3856*
PLT118	FAA-H-8083-25	Aircraft Systems ⟩ Flight Instruments ⟩ Directional Gyro *3276*
PLT119	FAA-H-8083-3	Flight Operations ⟩ Collision Avoidance ⟩ Aircraft Position Lights *2020, 3162, 3715, 3716, 3717, 3916, 3916-1*
PLT120	AC 00-6	Weather ⟩ Meteorology ⟩ Thunderstorms *3449*

Learning Statement Code	FAA Reference	Subject Description (or *Topic* ⟩ *Content* ⟩ *Specific classification*) Question Numbers
PLT121	FAA-H-8083-25	Weight and Balance ⟩ Center of Gravity ⟩ Computations *3665, 3668*
PLT122	FAA-H-8083-25	Recall aircraft operations—checklist usage *2063, 2068*
PLT123	FAA-H-8083-3	Flight Operations ⟩ Climb ⟩ Speed *2326, 3011, 3012-1, 3364*
PLT124	FAA-H-8083-25	Aircraft Performance ⟩ Computations ⟩ Density Altitude; Landing Distance *3290, 3296, 3299, 3300, 3372*
PLT125	AIM	Flight Operations ⟩ Normal Procedures ⟩ Scan *2229, 3814, 3909*
PLT126	AC 91-13	Recall airport performance—cold weather operations *2353, 2354*
PLT127	FAA-H-8083-25	Aircraft Performance ⟩ Computations ⟩ Density Altitude *2067, 3291*
PLT128	AC 00-6	Weather ⟩ Meteorology ⟩ Icing *3431, 3432, 3956*
PLT129	FAA-H-8083-21	Flight Operations ⟩ Takeoff ⟩ Helicopter *2199*
PLT130	FAA-H-8083-25	Recall aircraft performance — fuel *3907*
PLT131	FAA-H-8083-25	Aircraft Performance ⟩ Atmospheric Effects ⟩ Ground Effect *2223-2, 3312, 3313, 3314, 3315, 3324*
PLT132	FAA-H-8083-25	Aircraft Systems ⟩ Flight Instruments ⟩ Attitude Indicator *2225-1, 3264, 3278, 3341, 3342*
PLT133	FAA-H-8083-3	Flight Operations ⟩ Climb ⟩ Speed *3914*
PLT134	FAA-H-8083-25	Aerodynamics ⟩ Principles of Flight ⟩ Frost *2234, 2283, 3206*
PLT136	FAA-H-8083-25	Aircraft Systems ⟩ Powerplant ⟩ Carburetor *3236*
PLT140	AIM	Airport Operations ⟩ LAHSO ⟩ Procedures & Responsibility *3951, 3953, 3954*
PLT141	14 CFR 91 AIM FAA-H-8083-3	Airport Operations ⟩ Lighting ⟩ Rotating Beacon; Taxiway Airport Operations ⟩ Marking/Signs ⟩ Direction Signs; Runway; Taxiway Regulations ⟩ 14 CFR Part 91 ⟩ Light Gun Signals *2024, 2025, 2026, 2028, 2029, 2030, 2031, 2206, 2218, 3111, 3112, 3113, 3114, 3115, 3116, 3656-1, 3718, 3769, 3770, 3771, 3772, 3777, 3778, 3778-1, 3778-2, 3778-3, 3778-4, 3778-5, 3955, 3955-1, 3955-2, 3955-3, 3955-4, 3955-5, 3957*

Learning Statement Code	FAA Reference	Subject Description (or Topic 〉 Content 〉 Specific classification) Question Numbers
PLT147	14 CFR 91 AIM	Airport Operations 〉 Lighting 〉 PAPI; VASI Regulations 〉 14 CFR Part 91 〉 Airport Operations *3121, 3760, 3762-1, 3764, 3765, 3766, 3767*
PLT149	FAA-H-8083-21	Recall airport preflight/taxi operations—procedures *2328, 2331*
PLT150	AIM	Airport Operations 〉 Tower Controlled 〉 Radio Communications *3123-1, 3789, 3804*
PLT153	FAA-H-8083-11	Aircraft Performance 〉 Limitations 〉 Airship Flight Operations 〉 Landing 〉 Descents Flight Operations 〉 Maneuvers 〉 Advanced; Basic Flight Operations 〉 Normal Procedures 〉 Buoyancy Weight and Balance 〉 Aircraft Loading 〉 Ballast *3368, 3369, 3370, 3371, 3373, 3374, 3375, 3376, 3377, 3378*
PLT158	FAA-H-8083-11	Recall airship — pressure height/manometers *3380*
PLT161	14 CFR 71 14 CFR 91 AIM A/FD SAC	Aircraft Systems 〉 Avionics 〉 Transponder Airspace 〉 Controlled 〉 Class C; Class D Airspace 〉 Uncontrolled 〉 Class G Publications 〉 Airport Facility Directory 〉 Airport Remarks Regulations 〉 14 CFR Part 71 〉 Airspace Regulations 〉 14 CFR Part 91 〉 Aircraft Speed; Airspace; Special VFR; Transponder Operations *2049, 3053, 3054, 3068, 3068-1, 3099, 3100, 3118, 3126, 3127, 3128, 3130, 3152, 3153, 3154, 3165, 3166, 3622, 3626, 3779, 3780, 3781, 3782, 3787, 3799, 3802-1, 3803, 3813*
PLT162	AIM	Airspace 〉 Controlled 〉 Class D *2043, 2056, 2192, 2193, 3787-1, 3788*
PLT163	14 CFR 91	Regulations 〉 14 CFR Part 91 〉 Airspace; Class D Operations *2040, 2061-1, 2137, 2138, 2186-1, 2203, 3056, 3057, 3069, 3134, 3135, 3136, 3137, 3142, 3143, 3144, 3145, 3146, 3147, 3148, 3149*
PLT165	AC 00-6 FAA-H-8083-25	Aircraft Systems 〉 Flight Instruments 〉 Altimeter Weather 〉 Meteorology 〉 Temperature *3255, 3382*
PLT166	FAA-H-8083-25	Aircraft Systems 〉 Flight Instruments 〉 Altimeter; Attitude Indicator *3261, 3277*
PLT167	AC 00-6 FAA-H-8083-25	Aircraft Systems 〉 Flight Instruments 〉 Altimeter Weather 〉 Meteorology 〉 Pressure *3387, 3390, 3391*
PLT168	FAA-H-8083-25	Aerodynamics 〉 Principles of Flight 〉 Angle of Attack Aerodynamics 〉 Stall/Spins 〉 Stalls *3203, 3204, 3204-1, 3311, 3317*

Learning Statement Code	FAA Reference	Subject Description (or Topic ⟩ Content ⟩ Specific classification) / Question Numbers
PLT169	FAA-H-8083-21	Flight Operations ⟩ Emergency Procedures ⟩ Approach/Landing / *3738*
PLT170	FAA-H-8083-11	Flight Operations ⟩ Approach ⟩ High-Wind Landing / *2002, 2017, 2234-1, 3120, 3122, 3308-1, 3339, 3744, 3745*
PLT172	AIM	Recall ATC — system/services / *2205, 3796*
PLT173	AC 00-6	Weather ⟩ Meteorology ⟩ Stability / *3403, 3404, 3405, 3411, 3758*
PLT175	FAA-H-8083-21	Flight Operations ⟩ Emergency Procedures ⟩ Autorotations / *3742*
PLT177	FAA-8083-1 / FAA-H-8083-11	Flight Operations ⟩ Cruise ⟩ Altitude / Flight Operations ⟩ Emergency Procedures ⟩ Balloon / Flight Operations ⟩ Landing ⟩ Touchdown / Weight and Balance ⟩ Aircraft Loading ⟩ Definitions / *3351, 3360, 3363, 3887, 3895, 3899*
PLT183	FAA-H-8083-11	Recall balloon flight operations — ascent/descent / *3367*
PLT184	FAA-H-8083-11	Flight Operations ⟩ Normal Procedures ⟩ Preflight / *3900, 3901*
PLT185	FAA-H-8083-13	Aerodynamics ⟩ Principles of Flight ⟩ Turns / *3343, 3344*
PLT187	FAA-H-8083-25	Aircraft Systems ⟩ Flight Instruments ⟩ Turn Coordinator / *3275*
PLT189	FAA-H-8083-25	Aircraft Systems ⟩ Powerplant ⟩ Carburetor Heat / *3232, 3234*
PLT190	FAA-H-8083-25	Aircraft Systems ⟩ Powerplant ⟩ Carburetor; Carburetor Heat / *2341, 3229, 3231, 3235, 3958, 3964, 3975*
PLT191	FAA-H-8083-25	Aircraft Systems ⟩ Powerplant ⟩ Carburetor / *3225*
PLT192	AC 00-6	Weather ⟩ Meteorology ⟩ Clouds; Stability; Thunderstorms / *3406, 3407, 3415, 3416, 3417, 3418, 3419, 3420, 3433*
PLT194	AIM / FAA-H-8083-25	Air Traffic Control Procedures ⟩ En Route ⟩ Radar / Airspace ⟩ Procedures ⟩ Scan / Human Factors ⟩ Aero-medical Factors ⟩ Fitness for Flight; Spatial Disorientation / *2054, 2064, 3710, 3710-1, 3792, 3793, 3794, 3795, 3834, 3835, 3836*
PLT196	AIM	Airport Operations ⟩ Tower Controlled ⟩ ATIS / *3605-2, 3791*

Learning Statement Code	FAA Reference	Subject Description (or Topic) Content) Specific classification) Question Numbers
PLT197	FAA-H-8083-21	Aerodynamics) Principles of Flight) Coriolis Effect *3322*
PLT198	FAA-H-8083-3	Flight Operations) Cruise) Ground Track *2103, 2104, 2177, 3529-2*
PLT199	FAA-H-8083-21	Aerodynamics) Principles of Flight) Flight Controls *3318*
PLT200	FAA-H-8083-25	Navigation) Pilotage) Calculations *2100*
PLT201	14 CFR 91	Regulations) 14 CFR Part 91) Airport Operations *3123*
PLT204	AIM	Instrument Procedures) Communications) Reports *2007-1, 2007-2, 3613, 3614, 3615, 3790, 3797*
PLT205	AIM	Recall effects of alcohol on the body *2087*
PLT206	AC 00-6	Weather) Meteorology) Pressure *3289, 3394*
PLT207	FAA-H-8083-25	Aircraft Systems) Electrical) Charging Systems *2238, 2364, 3969*
PLT208	FAA-H-8083-3	Flight Operations) Emergency Procedures) Engine Failure *3202-4, 3202-5, 3223-1, 3711, 3741, 3902, 3904, 3911, 3915*
PLT213	FAA-H-8083-25	Aerodynamics) Stability/Control) Longitudinal Stability; Stability *3210, 3211*
PLT214	FAA-H-8083-5	Aircraft Systems) Structures) Washout *3211-1, 3976, 3977, 3979, 3981, 3982*
PLT215	FAA-H-8083-25	Aircraft Systems) Flight Instruments) Compass *3279, 3279-2, 3280, 3281, 3282, 3283, 3283-1, 3284, 3285, 3286*
PLT217	FAA-H-8083-21	Recall flight maneuvers — quick stop *3743*
PLT219	FAA-H-8083-3	Flight Operations) Maneuvers) Basic *3202-1, 3202-2, 3202-3, 3880, 3897, 3898, 3910*
PLT221	FAA-H-8083-3	Aerodynamics) Principles of Flight) Landings *3379, 3719, 3748, 3749, 3877, 3878, 3879, 3883, 3884, 3912, 3913, 3994, 3995*
PLT222	FAA-H-8083-21	Flight Operations) Takeoff) Helicopter *3739, 3740, 3747, 3998*
PLT225	AIM	Navigation) Pilotage) Flight Plan *2175, 3818*

Learning Statement Code	FAA Reference	Subject Description (or Topic 〉 Content 〉 Specific classification) Question Numbers
PLT226	AC 00-6	Weather 〉 Meteorology 〉 Fog; Icing *3443, 3445, 3446, 3447*
PLT234	FAA-H-8083-25	Recall forces acting on aircraft — 3 axis intersect *3213*
PLT237	FAA-H-8083-11	Flight Operations 〉 Launch Procedures 〉 False Lift *3359, 3365, 3366*
PLT241	FAA-H-8083-13	Aerodynamics 〉 Principles of Flight 〉 Horizontal Lift *3205, 3340*
PLT242	FAA-H-8083-25	Aerodynamics 〉 Principles of Flight 〉 Forces Acting on Aircraft; Horizontal Lift *3201, 3202, 3301, 3319*
PLT243	FAA-H-8083-25	Aerodynamics 〉Principles of Flight 〉 Torque; Turning Tendency *3207, 3208, 3209*
PLT245	FAA-H-8083-3	Aerodynamics 〉 Stall/Spins 〉 Spins *3309, 3310, 3382*
PLT249	FAA-H-8083-25	Aircraft Systems 〉 Powerplant 〉 Carburetor; Carburetor Heat; Mixture Control *3226, 3228*
PLT250	FAA-H-8083-25	Aircraft Systems 〉 Powerplant 〉 Fuel Grade *3237, 3241, 3242, 3243, 3355, 3886*
PLT251	FAA-H-8083-11	Flight Operations 〉 Emergency Procedures 〉 Balloon *3356, 3362, 3906*
PLT253	FAA-H-8083-25	Aircraft Systems 〉 Powerplant 〉 Electric Fuel Pump; Mixture Control *3221-1, 3224, 3227, 3230, 3230-1, 3233, 3243-1, 3352, 3353, 3959, 3960, 3961, 3962, 3963, 3974*
PLT254	FAA-H-8083-11	Aircraft Systems 〉 Fuel/Oil 〉 Fueling; Tanks *3354, 3357, 3358, 3361, 3885*
PLT256	FAA-H-8083-13	Recall glider information — effect of loading *3862*
PLT257	FAA-H-8083-3	Recall glide performance — speed/distance/ballast/lift/drag *2239*
PLT259	FAA-H-8083-21	Recall ground resonance — conditions to occur *2329, 3332*
PLT260	FAA-H-8083-21	Recall gyroplane — aerodynamics/rotor systems *2327, 2332*
PLT263	AC 00-6	Weather 〉 Meteorology 〉 Thunderstorms; Turbulence *3425, 3442*
PLT264	FAA-H-8083-21	Recall helicopter approach/settling with power *3734*

Learning Statement Code	FAA Reference	Subject Description (or Topic ⟩ Content ⟩ Specific classification) Question Numbers
PLT265	FAA-H-8083-21	Flight Operations ⟩ Emergency Procedures ⟩ Ground Resonance *3338*
PLT268	FAA-H-8083-21	Aerodynamics ⟩ Principles of Flight ⟩ Helicopter Hovering Flight *3733*
PLT271	FAA-H-8083-25	Human Factors ⟩ ADM ⟩ Judgement; Risk Management *2073, 3931-3*
PLT274	AC 00-6	Weather ⟩ Meteorology ⟩ Icing *3429, 3430*
PLT278	FAA-H-8083-25	Aircraft Systems ⟩ Flight Instruments ⟩ Airspeed Indicator *3274, 3682*
PLT280	AIM	Recall inflight illusions—causes/sources *2240*
PLT281	FAA-H-8083-25	Publications ⟩ AFD ⟩ Revisions *2118, 3619-1*
PLT284	AC 00-45	Weather ⟩ Aeronautical Weather Forecasts ⟩ Winds/Temperatures Aloft Forecast *3505, 3506*
PLT285	FAA-H-8083-21	Flight Operations ⟩ Maneuvers ⟩ Basic *3335, 3732, 3735, 3736, 3737*
PLT290	AC 00-45 AIM	Weather ⟩ Aeronautical Weather Forecasts ⟩ AIRMETS/SIGMETS; SIGMETS Weather ⟩ Hazardous ⟩ Thunderstorms *3495, 3496, 3497, 3498, 3499*
PLT300	AIM	Recall instrument/navigation system checks/inspections—limits/tuning/identifying/logging *3598-1*
PLT301	AC 00-6	Weather ⟩ Meteorology ⟩ Moisture; Temperature *3383, 3384, 3385, 3402*
PLT303	AC 00-6	Recall L/D ratio *3350, 3650*
PLT304	FAA-H-8083-13	Flight Operations ⟩ Launch Procedures ⟩ Aerotow Takeoffs; Climbing Turns *3857, 3858, 3876, 3896*
PLT309	FAA-H-8083-25	Aerodynamics ⟩ Load Factor ⟩ Flight Maneuvers; Steep Turns *3214, 3215, 3216, 3218*
PLT311	FAA-H-8083-25	Aerodynamics ⟩ Load Factor ⟩ Airspeed *3217*
PLT312	FAA-H-8083-25	Aerodynamics ⟩ Load Factor ⟩ Stalling Speed *3316*
PLT313	FAA-H-8083-1	Recall loading—limitations/terminology *2174, 2182*

Learning Statement Code	FAA Reference	Subject Description (or Topic 〉 Content 〉 Specific classification) / Question Numbers
PLT316	FAA-H-8083-25	Weather 〉 Aeronautical Weather Reports 〉 Weather Briefings *3468, 3469, 3470*
PLT320	FAA-H-8083-25	Navigation 〉 Pilotage 〉 Aeronautical Charts *2102, 3279-1*
PLT323	AIM	Air Traffic Control Procedures 〉 Communications 〉 Flight Service Stations Navigation 〉 Pilotage 〉 NOTAMs Publications 〉 NOTAMs 〉 FDC NOTAMs *2120, 2121, 3999*
PLT324	FAA-H-8083-25	Aircraft Systems 〉 Powerplant 〉 Oil System *3245*
PLT328	FAA-H-8083-1 FAA-H-8083-25	Weight and Balance 〉 Aircraft Loading 〉 Limitations Weight and Balance 〉 Center of Gravity 〉 Computations *2183, 3288, 3661, 3859, 3860*
PLT330	AIM	Human Factors 〉 Aero-medical Factors 〉 Fitness for Flight *3844*
PLT332	AIM	Human Factors 〉 Aero-medical Factors 〉 Fitness for Flight *2091, 2092, 2093, 3845, 3846, 3847*
PLT333	AIM	Human Factors 〉 Aero-medical Factors 〉 Fitness for Flight *3833, 3849*
PLT334	FAA-H-8083-25	Human Factors 〉 Aero-medical Factors 〉 Spatial Disorientation *2097, 3850, 3851, 3852, 3853, 3939*
PLT335	FAA-H-8083-25	Navigation 〉 Radio 〉 VOR *2178, 2201, 3552*
PLT337	FAA-H-8083-25	Aircraft Systems 〉 Pitot/Static 〉 Airspeed Indicator; Blockage *3247, 3248, 3249, 3262*
PLT340	FAA-H-8083-3	Recall positive exchange of flight controls *2069*
PLT342	FAA-H-8083-25	Aircraft Systems 〉 Powerplant 〉 Mixture Control *3221, 3244, 3651, 3652, 3965, 3966*
PLT343	FAA-H-8083-3 FAA-H-8083-25	Aircraft Systems 〉 Powerplant 〉 Lubrication; Mixture Control *3222, 3653, 3656, 3967, 3968, 3971, 3972, 3973*
PLT345	AC 00-6 FAA-H-8083-25	Weather 〉 Meteorology 〉 Pressure *3386, 3389*
PLT346	FAA-H-8083-5	Aircraft Systems 〉 Flight Controls/Primary 〉 Keel Pocket *3978, 3980, 3983, 3984, 3985, 3986, 3987, 3988, 3989, 3990, 3991, 3992, 3993*
PLT349	FAA-H-8083-21	Recall procedures for confined areas *3746*

Learning Statement Code	FAA Reference	Subject Description (or Topic ⟩ Content ⟩ Specific classification) Question Numbers
PLT351	FAA-H-8083-25	Aerodynamics ⟩ Stability/Control ⟩ Downwash Aircraft Systems ⟩ Propeller ⟩ Adjustable-Pitch; Efficiency *3212, 3246, 3654, 3655*
PLT354	AIM	Recall radio — GPS/RNAV/RAIM *3598-2, 3598-3, 3598-4*
PLT366	49 CFR 830	Regulations ⟩ NTSB Part 830 ⟩ Immediate Notification to NTSB; Incident Reports; Preservation of Aircraft Wreckage *2189, 2211, 2212, 3194, 3195, 3196, 3197, 3198, 3199, 3200*
PLT369	14 CFR 91	Regulations ⟩ 14 CFR Part 91 ⟩ Aerobatic Flight *3173*
PLT370	AIM	Airspace ⟩ Controlled ⟩ Clearance; Services Provided *3798, 3837*
PLT371	14 CFR 1	Regulations ⟩ 14 CFR Part 1 ⟩ Certification of Aircraft; Certification of Airmen *3001, 3002, 3003, 3004*
PLT372	14 CFR 91	Regulations ⟩ 14 CFR Part 91 ⟩ Annual Inspection; Maintenance Inspections *3182, 3185, 3186, 3189, 3190*
PLT373	14 CFR 91	Regulations ⟩ 14 CFR Part 91 ⟩ Aircraft Operating Limitations *3075, 3178*
PLT374	14 CFR 91	Regulations ⟩ 14 CFR Part 91 ⟩ Aircraft Return to Service; Airworthiness; Airworthiness Certificate *3180-1, 3181-1, 3181-2, 3181-3, 3660*
PLT375	14 CFR 91	Regulations ⟩ 14 CFR Part 91 ⟩ Aircraft Return to Service *3013-2, 3013-3, 3183, 3184*
PLT376	14 CFR 91 AIM	Regulations ⟩ 14 CFR Part 91 ⟩ Special VFR Airspace ⟩ Other ⟩ Wild Life Refuges *2053, 3150, 3151, 3618*
PLT377	14 CFR 91	Regulations ⟩ 14 CFR Part 91 ⟩ Airworthiness Certificate *3180-2, 3187*
PLT378	14 CFR 39	Recall regulations — Airworthiness Directives *3012-3*
PLT381	14 CFR 91	Regulations ⟩ 14 CFR Part 91 ⟩ Altimeter Settings *3105, 3106, 3107*
PLT383	14 CFR 91	Regulations ⟩ 14 CFR Part 91 ⟩ Airworthiness Certificate; Minimum Safe Altitudes *3097, 3098, 3179*
PLT384	14 CFR 91	Regulations ⟩ Briefing of passengers *3085-1*

Learning Statement Code	FAA Reference	Subject Description (or Topic ⟩ Content ⟩ Specific classification) / Question Numbers
PLT387	14 CFR 61	Regulations ⟩ 14 CFR Part 61 ⟩ Change of Address *3035*
PLT389	FAA-H-8083-11	Flight Operations ⟩ Launch Procedures ⟩ Location and Obstacles *3908*
PLT393	14 CFR 91 AIM	Airspace ⟩ Special Use ⟩ MOA Regulations ⟩ 14 CFR Part 91 ⟩ Airspace *2122, 3125, 3602, 3783, 3783-1, 3784, 3785*
PLT395	14 CFR 1	Regulations ⟩ 14 CFR Part 1 ⟩ Night *2213, 3005, 3025*
PLT399	14 CFR 61	Regulations ⟩ 14 CFR Part 61 ⟩ Inspection of Certificate; Medical Certificates; Pilot Certificate *2129, 3016, 3017, 3018, 3019*
PLT400	14 CFR 91	Regulations ⟩ 14 CFR Part 91 ⟩ Aircraft Operating Limitations *3075-1, 3159*
PLT401	14 CFR 91	Regulations ⟩ 14 CFR Part 91 ⟩ PIC Responsibility/Authority *3059, 3076*
PLT402	14 CFR 91 AIM	Aircraft Systems ⟩ Avionics ⟩ Emergency Locator Transmitter (ELT) *3160, 3161, 3819, 3819-1, 3820, 3821, 3822*
PLT403	14 CFR 91	Regulations ⟩ 14 CFR Part 91 ⟩ ATC Clearances *3109*
PLT405	14 CFR 91	Recall regulations— equipment/instrument/certificate requirements *3172*
PLT407	14 CFR 61	Regulations ⟩ 14 CFR Part 61 ⟩ PIC Recent Flight Experience; Privileges and Limitations *3036, 3037, 3067-1*
PLT411	14 CFR 61	Regulations ⟩ 14 CFR Part 61 ⟩ Certification: Pilots, Flight Instructors, and Ground Instructors *3030, 3030-1*
PLT413	14 CFR 91	Regulations ⟩ 14 CFR Part 91 ⟩ Fuel Requirements *3131, 3132, 3133*
PLT414	14 CFR 91	Regulations ⟩ 14 CFR Part 91 ⟩ Right-of-Way *3089, 3090, 3091, 3092, 3093, 3094, 3095, 3096*
PLT416	49 CFR 830	Recall regulations—immediate notification *2214*
PLT425	14 CFR 91	Recall regulations— maintenance reports/records/entries *3193*
PLT426	14 CFR 91	Regulations ⟩ 14 CFR Part 91 ⟩ Aircraft Return to Service *3012-2, 3188, 3191*

Learning Statement Code	FAA Reference	Subject Description (or Topic ⟩ Content ⟩ Specific classification) Question Numbers
PLT427	14 CFR 61	Regulations ⟩ 14 CFR Part 61 ⟩ Medical Certificates *3063*
PLT430	14 CFR 91	Regulations ⟩ 14 CFR Part 91 ⟩ Minimum Safe Altitudes *3101, 3102, 3103, 3104*
PLT431	14 CFR 91	Regulations ⟩ 14 CFR Part 91 ⟩ Formation Flight *2133-1, 3088*
PLT434	14 CFR 91	Recall regulations / operational procedures for a controlled airport *3124*
PLT435	AIM	Airport Operations ⟩ Communications ⟩ Inbound *2006, 2007, 2034-1, 2060, 2194, 3604, 3605, 3605-1*
PLT438	14 CFR 91	Regulations ⟩ 14 CFR Part 91 ⟩ Oxygen Requirements *3163, 3164*
PLT440	14 CFR 91	Regulations ⟩ 14 CFR Part 91 ⟩ PIC Responsibility/Authority *3073, 3083*
PLT441	14 CFR 91	Recall regulations—pilot briefing *2232*
PLT442	14 CFR 61	Regulations ⟩ 14 CFR Part 61 ⟩ PIC Recent Flight Experience *3029, 3031, 3032, 3033, 3034, 3040, 3041*
PLT443	FAA-H-8083-25	Human Factors ⟩ ADM ⟩ Pilot Self-Assessment *2078, 3937*
PLT444	14 CFR 91 AIM	Airspace ⟩ Special Use ⟩ Alert Areas Regulations ⟩ 14 CFR Part 91 ⟩ PIC Responsibility/Authority; Preflight Actions *2033, 2308, 3070, 3071, 3072, 3074, 3082, 3108, 3108-1, 3110, 3658, 3786, 3952*
PLT445	14 CFR 91 AIM FAA-H-8083-25	Airport Operations ⟩ Preflight ⟩ Pilot Responsibility Regulations ⟩ 14 CFR Part 91 ⟩ Preflight Actions Weather ⟩ Aeronautical Weather Reports ⟩ Weather Briefings *3080, 3081, 3526, 3659*
PLT446	14 CFR 43	Regulations ⟩ 14 CFR Part 43 ⟩ Preventive Maintenance *3013-1, 3014*
PLT447	14 CFR 61	Regulations ⟩ 14 CFR Part 61 ⟩ Medical Certificates *3020, 3021, 3022, 3023, 3039, 3062*
PLT448	14 CFR 61	Regulations ⟩ 14 CFR Part 61 ⟩ Privileges and Limitations *2123, 2130, 3026, 3027, 3038, 3043, 3044, 3045, 3046, 3047, 3048, 3049, 3050, 3052, 3052-1, 3055, 3058, 3060, 3061, 3064, 3065, 3066, 3067*
PLT449	14 CFR 61	Regulations ⟩ 14 CFR Part 61 ⟩ Flight Review *3028*

Learning Statement Code	FAA Reference	Subject Description (or Topic 〉 Content 〉 Specific classification) Question Numbers
PLT451	14 CFR 61	Regulations 〉14 CFR Part 61 〉 Privileges and Limitations; Type Rating *3024*
PLT462	AIM	Airport Operations 〉Lighting 〉Runway Lighting *3768*
PLT463	14 CFR 61 14 CFR 91	Regulations 〉14 CFR Part 61 〉 Drugs/Alcohol Regulations 〉14 CFR Part 91 〉 Alcohol or Drugs *2126, 2127, 2128, 3077, 3078, 3079, 3079-1*
PLT464	14 CFR 91	Regulations 〉14 CFR Part 91 〉 PIC Responsibility/Authority *3084*
PLT465	14 CFR 91	Regulations 〉14 CFR Part 91 〉 Seat Belts *3085, 3086, 3087*
PLT467	14 CFR 91	Regulations 〉14 CFR Part 91 〉 Airspace; Flight Rules General; VFR Cruising Altitude/Flight Level *2061, 3051, 3138, 3155, 3156, 3157, 3158*
PLT468	14 CFR 91	Regulations 〉14 CFR Part 91 〉 Airspace *3139, 3140, 3141*
PLT470	FAA-H-8083-21	Aerodynamics 〉Principles of Flight 〉Coriolis Effect; Retreating Blade Stall Aircraft Systems 〉Flight Controls/Primary 〉Tail Rotor *3320, 3323, 3325, 3326, 3328, 3329, 3330, 3331, 3334*
PLT472	FAA-H-8083-21	Flight Operations 〉Emergency Operations 〉Main Rotor *3333*
PLT473	FAA-H-8083-25	Aircraft Systems 〉Flight Controls/Secondary 〉Flaps *3219, 3220, 3905*
PLT477	FAA-H-8083-25	Aerodynamics 〉Stall/Spins 〉Stalls *2225, 2233, 3263*
PLT478	FAA-H-8083-25	Aircraft Systems 〉Powerplant 〉Ignition; Magnetos *2242, 3223, 3223-2, 3240, 3970*
PLT479	FAA-H-8083-3	Aircraft Systems 〉Powerplant 〉Engine Starting *3657*
PLT486	FAA-H-8083-3	Airport Operations 〉Taxiing 〉Flight Controls *2016, 3302, 3303, 3304, 3903*
PLT492	AC 00-6	Weather 〉Meteorology 〉Stability *3408*
PLT493	AC 00-6	Weather 〉Meteorology 〉Moisture *3401*
PLT494	AC 00-6	Weather 〉Meteorology 〉Thermals *3448, 3471, 3471-1, 3751, 3752, 3753, 3754, 3755, 3756, 3757, 3881*

Learning Statement Code	FAA Reference	Subject Description (or Topic 〉 Content 〉 Specific classification) Question Numbers
PLT495	AC 00-6	Weather 〉 Meteorology 〉 Thunderstorms 3434, 3435, 3436, 3437, 3438, 3439, 3440, 3441, 3452, 3521
PLT496	FAA-H-8083-13	Recall towrope — strength/safety links/positioning 3174, 3175, 3176, 3177
PLT497	AIM	Aircraft Systems 〉 Avionics 〉 Transponder 2005, 3129, 3800, 3800-1, 3801, 3802, 3996
PLT501	AC 00-6	Recall turbulence—types/characteristics/reporting/corrective actions 2159, 2236
PLT502	14 CFR 91	Regulations 〉 14 CFR Part 91 〉 Light Gun Signals 3812, 3869, 3870, 3871, 3872, 3873, 3874, 3875
PLT506	14 CFR 1	Regulations 〉 14 CFR Part 1 〉 V-speeds 3006, 3007, 3008, 3009, 3010
PLT508	14 CFR 91	Recall VOR/altimeter/transponder checks — identification/tuning/identifying/logging 3192
PLT509	AIM	Airport Operations 〉 Wake Turbulence 〉 Strength; Vortex Avoidance Flight Operations 〉 Wake Turbulence 〉 Vortex Avoidance; Vortex Behavior 2039, 3824, 3825, 3826, 3827, 3828, 3829, 3829-2, 3829-3, 3830
PLT511	AC 00-6 FAA-H-8083-25	Weather 〉 Meteorology 〉 Fronts; Stability 2312, 3412, 3413, 3414, 3422, 3423, 3424
PLT512	AC 00-6	Weather 〉 Meteorology 〉 Fog; Moisture; Stability; Temperature 2369, 3381, 3397, 3398, 3399, 3400, 3409, 3410, 3444
PLT514	AC 00-45 FAA-H-8083-25	Weather 〉 Aeronautical Weather Forecasts 〉 Aviation Area Forecasts (FA) Weather 〉 Aeronautical Weather Reports 〉 Aviation Routine Weather Reports (METAR); Weather Briefings 3455, 3456, 3457, 3458, 3459, 3460, 3461, 3487, 3525, 3527, 3528, 3528-1
PLT515	AIM	Navigation 〉 Pilotage 〉 Radio Communications Weather 〉 Aeronautical Weather Reports 〉 En Route Flight Advisory Service (EFAS) 3477
PLT516	AC 00-6 FAA-H-8083-3	Airport Operations 〉 Taxiing 〉 Flight Controls Weather 〉 Meteorology 〉 Wind 3395, 3396, 3450, 3451, 3750
PLT517	AC 00-6	Recall winds associated with high/low-pressure systems 2170
PLT518	AC 00-6 FAA-H-8083-25	Weather 〉 Meteorology 〉 Windshear 2163, 3426, 3427, 3428